THE WEST
IN THE
WIDER WORLD

SOURCES AND PERSPECTIVES

VOLUME 2
FROM EARLY MODERNITY TO THE PRESENT

RICHARD LIM
Smith College

DAVID KAMMERLING SMITH
Eastern Illinois University

BEDFORD/ST. MARTIN'S   Boston ◆ New York

For Bedford/St. Martin's

Publisher for History: Patricia A. Rossi
Developmental Editors: Louise Townsend, Jan Fitter
Executive Editor for History: Elizabeth M. Welch
Production Editor: Ara Salibian
Senior Production Supervisor: Maria Gonzalez
Marketing Manager: Jenna Bookin Barry
Editorial Assistant: Brianna Germain
Production Assistant: Kendra LeFleur
Copyeditor: Rosemary Winfield
Text Design: DeNee Reiton Skipper
Cover Design: Billy Boardman
Cover Art: Image A: *British and other foreign vessels off Yokohama.* C. D. Wertheim
Collection/Werner Forman Archive/Art Resource, NY. Image B: *Map of the World.*
© Michael Maslan Historic Photographs/CORBIS
Composition: the dotted i
Printing and Binding: R. R. Donnelley & Sons Company

President: Joan E. Feinberg
Editorial Director: Denise B. Wydra
Director of Development for History: Jane Knetzger
Director of Marketing: Karen Melton
Director of Editing, Design, and Production: Marcia Cohen
Managing Editor: Elizabeth M. Schaaf

Library of Congress Control Number: 2002108120

Manufactured in the United States of America.
8 7 6 5 4 3
f e d c b a

For information, write: Bedford/St. Martin's, 75 Arlington Street, Boston, MA 02116
(617-399-4000)

ISBN: 0-312-20459-0

Acknowledgments

PREFACE

How did the West become the West? *The West in the Wider World: Sources and Perspectives* is a two-volume collection of primary documents, images, and interpretations that focuses on this central historical question. To study the development of Western civilization is to examine a complex and diverse set of historical encounters that span a period of four millennia. As a notion whose origins first significantly appeared during conflicts between the ancient Greeks and Persians in the fifth century B.C., the West has since been continually redefined and embraced by groups who used the idea to make sense of their own place in the world. But if these groups claimed the Western identity created in the course of cultural, economic, political, and military contacts with their neighbors, others resisted it—often with profound consequences, as contemporary events in the international arena most recently reveal.

In today's world of increased contact and conflict among peoples from all parts of the globe, understanding the evolution of the Western tradition becomes essential. A major concern of our reader, as reflected in the choice of chapter topics and sources, is to underscore the centrality of encounters between civilizations to the historical development and identity of the West, and indeed, of all cultures and traditions. We stress the need to understand that no society develops in isolation from its neighbors and that interactions with and reactions to others greatly influence any given society's internal development. Using the basic chronological framework of survey textbooks for the Western civilization course, *The West in the Wider World* examines a series of cross-cultural encounters fundamental to the development of the West—and offers its readers the opportunity to explore the perspectives of the historical figures and the nature and consequences of their interactions with others.

CONTENT AND ORGANIZATION

Both volumes of *The West in the Wider World* are organized into fourteen chapters that parallel and support major issues and topics in the Western civilization course syllabus. Each chapter focuses on a specific event, theme, or context that brings to light important ways in which the West created its own identity through interactions with other cultures and civilizations. The sources in each chapter—eight on average, for a total of over 120 selections per volume—address the same cross-cultural interaction from different perspectives, thus encouraging students to evaluate and compare viewpoints, arguments, and methods; in short, to think historically. In the persistent battle that instructors fight in survey courses between breadth of coverage and depth of analysis, we believe that collections of sources focused around a specific theme lead students to develop skills of historical interpretation and synthesis more effectively than do collections of thematically unrelated documents. Further, the comparison among sources permits students to identify changing definitions of the West and to analyze how and why these rein-terpretations took place.

Historical documents claim a privileged role in *The West in the Wider World*, for eyewitness accounts offer the most direct evidence of contemporaries' experi-ence. Most chapters include visual primary sources and secondary sources as well, however. The visual sources encourage students to interpret images by their con-tent and by the historical context in which they appeared. Further, images often are clustered so that two or three visual sources on a single issue appear together. The use of multiple images permits students unaccustomed to interpreting visual sources to compare images and hence to consider how and why images with a sim-ilar theme often convey different messages. Additionally, the ideas drawn from the visual sources connect with the ideas contained in the chapter's written sources. The secondary sources by noted scholars provide a broader framework for under-standing the primary sources within a chapter. Such secondary sources also extend the student's understanding of an issue while providing guideposts to shifting def-initions of the West.

In addition to Western perspectives, chapters offer sources by authors from outside the Western tradition. These selections enrich the book by adding diverse voices and by suggesting how cross-cultural interactions—sometimes peaceful, often aggressive—influenced other societies while profoundly shaping the devel-opment of the West. Further, these sources illustrate how interactions with other societies significantly affected the West's understanding and definition of these cul-tures as well as of itself.

LEARNING AIDS

Recognizing the difficulties many students face in grappling with primary and sec-ondary source material, we have provided a variety of learning aids to guide their reading and to suggest important issues for analysis and class discussion. Each vol-ume opens with **two volume introductions,** one that discusses the book's central theme of the impact of cross-cultural exchange on the origins and development of the West and one that explains how to read and interpret primary documents, vi-sual sources, and secondary sources. **Chapter introductions** provide historical context for the issues raised in the chapter and connect these issues to those of pre-vious chapters. In addition, most chapters are divided into two or three sections, with **section introductions** that develop further context for the sources and help students interpret the selections effectively. The selections themselves open with **source headnotes** that introduce the author and the historical context of the source's creation; **gloss notes** appear wherever useful to ensure students' under-standing of the text. Following each source, **Questions for Analysis** help students to identify central issues within the source as well as to draw comparisons among selections within a given chapter. Each chapter concludes with **Chapter Questions** intended to draw out broader issues of interpretation both from within a single chap-ter and across chapters, asking students to chart changing assumptions and defini-tions with regard to Western identity.

We are proud as well of our source collection's distinctive **map program.** Some of the maps serve as visual sources for students to interpret, while others display information related to the theme of the chapter and to geographic references in the sources. Examining the maps, students can see for themselves the shifting contours of the West through time.

ACKNOWLEDGMENTS

A reader seeking to cover several thousand years of human history cannot be assembled without the help and assistance of many individuals. Developing materials on such a broad array of topics, we have felt deep thanks for the many historians who have shared their expertise with us. It is a pleasure to express here our gratitude to Ernest Benz, Smith College; Palmira Brumett, University of Tennessee; Michael Dettelbach, Boston University; Kevin M. Doak, University of Illinois; Lynn Hunt, University of California at Los Angeles; Margaret Jacobs, University of California at Los Angeles; Joy Kammerling, Eastern Illinois University; Keith Lewinstein, Center for Near Eastern Studies, Harvard University; Daniel McMillan, independent scholar; Walter Ötsch, Johannes Kepler University; David Schalk, Vassar College; Anita Shelton, Eastern Illinois University; Victoria Thompson, Arizona State University; Ruth Wodak, University of Vienna; and Andrew Zimmerman, George Washington University. We thank as well other individuals who have shared their expertise with us in many ways: Eleanor Cartelli, Christiane Eydt-Beebe, Erin Flood, Barry Hudek, Minky Hyun, Laura Kent, Jill Laureman, and Corinne Russell.

From our first to final draft, we benefited also from the thoughtful evaluations of the many teachers who read and critiqued the manuscript throughout its development. Their comments and suggestions helped us greatly to focus our efforts and to achieve our goals: Kathryn Abbott, Western Kentucky University; F. E. Beemon, Middle Tennessee State University; Robert F. Bromber, United States Air Force Academy; David Cherry, Montana State University at Bozeman; Carolyn Conley, University of Arizona at Birmingham; Michael Doyle, Princeton University; Katherine Haldane Grenier, The Citadel; Maura O'Connor, University of Cincinnati; Patricia O. O'Neill, Central Oregon Community College; John L. Pesda, Camden County College; Carole Putko, San Diego State University; Paul G. Randolph, Pepperdine University; Michael Richards, Sweet Briar College; Harold Strangeman, Lake Land College; and Larissa J. Taylor, Colby College.

We wish as well to thank and acknowledge the fine editorial staff of Bedford/St. Martin's. President Joan E. Feinberg and her predecessor Charles H. Christensen offered enthusiastic support throughout the project. Our original sponsoring editor, Katherine E. Kurzman, got the project safely off the ground, and Patricia A. Rossi, publisher for history, organized a team to see it through to completion. Elizabeth M. Welch, executive editor for history, provided a firm and guiding hand as the manuscript developed, helping us to balance the many considerations that go into such an endeavor. Developmental editors Louise Townsend and Jan Fitter supplied us with superb advice that marks every page of the book. Special thanks must go to Jan for her diligent reading and rereading of drafts as the manuscript neared completion. Rosemary Winfield copyedited the manuscript with a hawklike eye to clarity and style, while our project editor, Ara Salibian, expertly managed production of the book. To DeNee Skipper and Billy Boardman, designers of the text interior and covers, respectively, we extend our gratitude for two handsome volumes. And to Joan Scafarello and Sandy Schechter, our tireless permissions editors, we offer sincere thanks for the often thankless task of obtaining permission to reproduce sources that span time and space.

Finally, David Kammerling Smith offers his thanks to his wife, Joy Kammerling, who makes the wider world come alive for him. He dedicates this book to the woman of his youth, his mother Dorothy Louise Smith, and to the delights of his adulthood, his daughters Meret Eugenie Kammerling and Thea Grace Kammerling.

R. L.
D. K. S.

CONTENTS

Preface   iii

Approaching the West: An Introduction   xvii

Guide to Interpreting Sources   xxi

Maps   xxxii

About the Editors   xxxiii

1 TWO WORLDS COLLIDE: RENAISSANCE EUROPE AND THE AMERICAS   1

The encounter between the peoples of the Americas and the peoples of Europe led to mutual misunderstandings and confusion as both sides sought to define who and what these "new" peoples were. As the Europeans sought to establish political, military, and economic dominance over the Amerindians, debate emerged among European leaders, who recognized that these definitions had implications for colonial practices. Sources focus on (1) the efforts by Europeans and Amerindians to describe and define each other; and (2) the efforts by Europeans to situate Americans within European religious, political, and ethnographic categories and to account for the effects of the Americas on European daily life.

The European Arrival   3

1. Christopher Columbus, *Log of the First Voyage* (1492)   3
2. *Codex Florentino* (1555)   6
3. Hernando Cortés, *Second Dispatch to Charles V* (1520)   9
4. Bernal Díaz, *Chronicles* (c. 1560)   12
5. *Images of the Encounter: German Woodcut of 1505 and Spanish Incan Woodcut* (c. 1600)   15

The Americas in Europe   17

6. Roger Schlesinger, *In the Wake of Columbus* (1996)   18
7. Juan Ginés de Sepúlveda, *Democrates Secundus* (1544)   21
8. Bartolomé de Las Casas, *In Defense of the Indians* (1551)   24
9. Michel de Montaigne, *Of Cannibals* (1580s)   27

2 CHALLENGES TO CHRISTENDOM IN REFORMATION EUROPE   30

Western Christendom believed itself under siege in the sixteenth and seventeenth centuries, from religious revolutionaries and intellectual innovators within and from infidels without. As debates occurred between defenders of traditional Catholic doctrine and religious and intellectual dissidents, various factions sought to define themselves and their opponents in relation both to the Christian faith and to the threats, real and imagined, posed to Western Christendom by non-Christians. Sources focus on (1) the challenge to traditional Catholic religious authority posed by the Protestant reform movement and the use within Reformation debates of the real and perceived threats posed to Christianity by Ottoman Turks and European Jews; and (2) the challenge to Catholic religious authority posed by the new science.

Christendom and Reformation   *32*

1. Ogier Ghiselin de Busbecq, *Travels into Turkey* (c. 1561)   32
2. Martin Luther, *On Christian Liberty* and *Address to the Christian Nobility of the German Nation* (1520)   34
3. Thomas More, *A Dialogue Concerning Heresies* (1529)   38
4. Johannes Brenz, *Booklet on the Turk* (1531)   40
5. Andreas Osiander, *Whether It Is True and Believable that Jews Secretly Kill Christian Children and Use Their Blood* (c. 1529)   43
6. *Two Woodcuts: Turks and Jews* (1530 and c. 1475)   45

Religion and the Natural World   *47*

7. Heinrich Kramer and Jakob Sprenger, *The Hammer of Witches* (1486)   48
8. Nicolaus Copernicus, *On the Revolutions of the Heavenly Orbs* (1543)   51
9. Galileo Galilei, *Letter to the Grand Duchess Christina* (1615)   54

3   THE CHRISTIANIZING MISSION: JESUITS IN AMERICA AND CHINA   57

As Europeans circled the globe, they dreamed not only of colonizing lands and expanding trade but also of carrying the message of Christianity to new peoples. The Christianizing mission was taken up most vigorously by the newly created Roman Catholic order of the Jesuits, who established mission outposts among peoples as diverse as the Chinese and the Huron peoples of the Great Lakes region. In both contexts, the Jesuits considered how to adapt Christianity and their missionary activities to local religious and political contexts. The reports that Jesuits sent back to Europe describing their missionary efforts and the non-European peoples they encountered were published and circulated widely, becoming important sources of information on the societies described. Sources in this chapter focus on the images of Chinese and Amerindian society that Jesuit missionaries presented in their texts and on the responses of the Chinese and Huron to the Europeans.

1. Jean de Brébeuf, *Jesuit Relations of 1636* 59

2. Venerable Marie de l'Incarnation, *Relation of 1654* 63

3. A Micmac Leader, reported by Chrestien LeClerq, *New Relation of Gaspesia* (1691) 66

4. Matteo Ricci, *Journals* (1615) 68

5. *History of the Ming* (18th century) 73

4 EUROPEAN COLONIZATION AND THE EARLY MODERN STATE: FRANCE AND RUSSIA IN COMPARATIVE PERSPECTIVE 77

As seventeenth-century Europeans extended their presence across the globe, the European states sought to organize colonization (and its presumed economic benefits) to enhance their own power. The European states developed a set of economic policies, collectively called *mercantilism,* to define their relationships with non-European civilizations. At the same time, European monarchs and their central states sought to redefine and enhance their authority at home against various domestic rivals, especially the nobility. These two processes—colonization and centralization—shared many common features and goals. Sources focus on (1) the seventeenth-century colonization by France in the Western Hemisphere and by Russia in Siberia; and (2) the political and economic centralization in France under the Bourbon monarchs and in Russia under Peter the Great.

Colonizing Abroad 78

1. *The Tsars' Correspondence in the Conquest of Siberia* (17th century) 79

2. *French Administrative Correspondence with Its American Colonies* (17th century) 83

3. Otreouti, *Speech to the Governor of New France* (1684) 87

4. Anthony Pagden, *Lords of All the World* (1995) 88

Colonizing at Home 90

5. Cardinal Richelieu, *Political Testament* (c. 1630s) 91

6. *Administrative Correspondence within France* (17th century) 93

7. *Decrees of Peter the Great* (early 18th century) 98

5 RETHINKING THE WORLD: THE ENLIGHTENMENT 104

As Europeans traversed the globe in the seventeenth and eighteenth centuries, information, commodities, and people from across the globe came into Europe. European thinkers sought to organize this information about the wider world, creating knowledge useful to the Europeans. This "rethinking of the world" occurred as part of the Enlightenment, a broad movement in which European authors and artists applied a critical spirit to judge whether European institutions and traditions aided or hindered the advancement of humankind. Progress, they believed, could be achieved through a systematic reform (or elimination) of institutions and practices that defended ignorance and superstition at the expense of reason. Sources focus on European authors' effort to understand the nature of progress as they organized knowledge about the world outside of Europe.

1. Baron de Montesquieu, *The Spirit of the Laws* (1748)   105
2. Voltaire, *Essay on the Customs and Spirit of Nations* (1756)   107
3. Cornelius de Pauw, *Philosophical Inquiry into the Americas* (1768–1769)   110
4. Jean-Jacques Rousseau, *Discourse on the Origins of Inequality* (1755)   112
5. Mungo Park, *Travels in the Interior Districts of Africa* (1797)   115
6. Beth Fowkes Tobin, *Picturing Imperial Power* (1999)   118
7. Immanuel Kant, *Observations on the Feeling of the Beautiful and the Sublime* (1764)   122
8. Johann Gottfried von Herder, *Outlines of a Philosophy of the History of Man* (1784)   126

6   SLAVERY, ABOLITIONISM, AND REVOLUTION   130

Beginning in the sixteenth century, Europeans transported to the Americas millions of black Africans to serve as chattel slaves. As the slave trade reached its peak during the late eighteenth century, an abolitionist movement grew in strength and in number. This movement, however, faced severe opposition from the merchant and colonial interests who made vast profits from slavery and the slave trade. The abolitionists found their first major success when the French government abolished slavery in its highly profitable Caribbean sugar colonies in the midst of the French Revolution. Sources focus on (1) the diversity of abolitionist arguments drawing on religious and Enlightenment ideals; and (2) the French debates over slavery and the slave trade during the French Revolution and the responses in France's most profitable slave colony, Saint Domingue.

The Rise of the Abolitionist Movement   130

1. Adam Smith, *The Wealth of Nations* (1776)   132
2. Olaudah Equiano, *The Interesting Narrative of the Life of Olaudah Equiano* (1789)   134
3. Plymouth Committee of the Society for the Abolition of the Slave Trade, *Plan of an African Ship's Lower Deck* (1788)   137

4. Abbé Raynal, *History of the East and West Indies* (1770, rev. 1780)   139

Slavery and Revolution   142

5. *Declaration of the Rights of Man and Citizen* (1789)   143
6. Society of the Friends of Blacks, *Address to the National Assembly in Favor of the Abolition of the Slave Trade* (1790)   145
7. Antoine Barnave, *Speech to the National Assembly* (1790)   147
8. *My Odyssey* (1793)   150
9. François Toussaint-L'Ouverture, *Letters* (1797 and 1799)   153

7 NAPOLEON IN EGYPT   157

In 1798, Napoleon Bonaparte invaded Egypt, intending to disrupt British trade, establish a French colony, and perhaps strike at British India. Along with his troops, Napoleon brought 150 French scholar-scientists equipped with libraries and scientific instruments. These scholars of the Enlightenment explored Egypt, investigated its history and arts, measured and catalogued its monuments, and recorded its geographic features. On return to France, these scholars produced the twenty-three-volume *Description of Egypt,* in which they sought to describe the entirety of Egyptian natural and human history. Sources focus on the anticipations of the campaign, the activities of the French scholars, and the expedition's crystallization of an Orientalist tradition in Western thought in the *Description of Egypt.*

1. Louis Antoine Fauvelet de Bourrienne, *Memoirs of Napoleon Bonaparte* (1829)   158
2. Napoleon Bonaparte, *Statements and Proclamation on the Egyptian Campaign* (1798–1804)   161
3. Abd al-Rahman al-Jabarti, *Chronicle* (early 19th century)   163
4. Vivant Denon, *Travels in Upper and Lower Egypt* (1802)   165
5. *Description of Egypt* (1809–1828)   168
6. *Images of Egypt* (early 19th century)   172
7. Edward Said, *Orientalism* (1978)   175

8 THE GREAT TRANSFORMATION: RESPONSES TO INDUSTRIALIZATION AT HOME AND AWAY   179

In the decades following the French Revolution, a new industrial society was emerging that transformed deeply rooted political, social, and cultural structures in the most economically advanced regions of Europe and North America. Contending forces within these societies struggled to define the West's new industrial society along conservative, liberal, or socialist lines. The West's growing power forced its neighbors to respond to both the industrializing nations' political and economic power and to the idea of industrialization itself. Sources focus on (1) the contending redefinition of Western society, especially along liberal and socialist lines; and (2) reactions to and interpretations of industrialization by individuals in Russia and the Ottoman empire.

Defining the Industrial Era   *180*

1. John Stuart Mill, *Considerations on Representative Government* (1861)   181
2. Andrew Ure, *Philosophy of Manufactures* (1835)   184
3. *Testimony for the Factory Act of 1833*   186
4. Karl Marx and Friedrich Engels, *The Communist Manifesto* (1848)   189
5. Flora Tristan, *Workers' Union* (1843)   192

The Border Lands   *194*

6. Vissarion Belinsky, *Letter to N. V. Gogol, July 3, 1847*   196
7. Nikolai Danilevsky, *Russia and Europe* (1869)   198
8. Khayr al-Din al-Tunisi, *The Surest Path* (1869)   201
9. *Ottoman Cartoons* (1909 and 1911)   204

9 THE FIRST OPIUM WAR   207

In the early eighteenth century, the Chinese government placed strong restrictions on trade with the "barbarian foreigners" from Europe. By the nineteenth century, Britain was frustrated with Chinese policies as Britain sought to expand and integrate its Asian markets. The opium poppy, grown in abundance in regions of northern India that Britain either controlled or influenced, became the product that British merchants promoted in anticipation that a growing demand in China for opium would force the Chinese market to open to greater trade. In 1839, the First Opium War broke out between China and Britain as Chinese officials sought to destroy the large, illegal trade in opium. Sources focus on (1) the public debates over British economic and war policies; and (2) the responses to the Opium Wars in Britain and China.

The Opium Crisis   *208*

1. Lin Zexu, *Letter to Queen Victoria* (1839)   209
2. Algernon Thelwell, *The Iniquities of the Opium Trade with China* (1839)   212
3. Samuel Warren, *The Opium Question* (1840)   214
4. Bombay Times, *Editorial of May 23, 1839*   217
5. Leeds Mercury, *Editorial of September 7, 1839*   220
6. Punch, *Important News from China* (1841)   222

Responses to the Opium Wars   223

7. Arthur Cunynghame, *The Opium War: Being Recollections of Service in China* (1845)   224

8. Michael Adas, *Machines as the Measure of Men* (1989)   226

9. Feng Guifen, *Theory of Self-Strengthening* (1860)   230

10   THE IMPERIALIST IMPULSE ABROAD AND AT HOME   234

The late nineteenth century marked the zenith of European imperialism. The imperialist impulse appeared most obviously in the "scramble for Africa" in the 1870s and 1880s. As Europeans grabbed colonial lands, they also felt a need to justify their expanding power. As a result, imperialist ideology flourished but so too did criticism of imperialist ideology and practices. Imperialism also resonated within European society and culture and entered into political debates. Sources focus on (1) European debates over the purpose and justification of imperialist activities; and (2) the influence of imperial culture in European society.

Imperialism Away   234

1. *Maps of Africa*   235

2. Charles Darwin, *The Descent of Man* (1871)   239

3. Karl Pearson, *National Life from the Standpoint of Science* (1901)   241

4. Friedrich Fabri, *Does Germany Need Colonies?* (1879)   244

5. Joseph Chamberlain, *The True Conception of Empire* (1897)   246

6. Edmund D. Morel, *King Leopold's Rule in Africa* (1904)   249

7. Vladimir Lenin, *Imperialism: The Highest Stage of Capitalism* (1917)   251

Imperialism at Home   254

8. Andrew Zimmerman, *Anthropology and Antihumanism in Imperial Germany* (2001)   254

9. *British Imperial Advertisements* (1885 and 1891)   257

10. William Booth, *In Darkest England* (1890)   260

11. Antoinette M. Burton, *The White Woman's Burden* (1992)   262

11   EUROPE SHAKEN   266

Between 1890 and 1930, a series of developments shook European society. The First World War devastated the peoples and the landscape of Europe, raising questions as to the presumed "superiority" of Western civilization. Further, the establishment of the Soviet Union challenged the traditions of Western political and economic liberalism. As the imperial nations of Europe struggled, challenges arose from within their empires as colonial lands demanded greater independence and from non-Western industrializing societies, especially Japan. Sources focus on (1) the challenges to Western confidence presented by the First World War and the establishment of the Soviet Union; and (2) the challenges to Western imperial power presented by the colonial independence movement and by the rise of Japan.

Challenges in Europe   266

1. Ernst Jünger, *The Storm of Steel* (1921)   267
2. Anna Eisenmenger, *Blockade* (1918)   269
3. Vladimir Lenin and Georgy Chicherin, *Are You a Trade Unionist? An Appeal to British Workers* (1920)   272
4. Winston Churchill, *The World Crisis* (1929)   275

Imperialism Challenged   277

5. Mohandas Gandhi, *Indian Home Rule* (1909)   278
6. Gilbert Elliot-Murray-Kynynmound, the Earl of Minto, *Despatch to John Morley, March 21, 1907*   280
7. Baron Albert d'Anethan, *Dispatches from Japan* (1894 and 1904)   282
8. Punch, *Three Cartoons* (1904 and 1905)   285
9. Kita Ikki, *Plan for the Reorganization of Japan* (1919)   289
10. William Inge, *The White Man and His Rivals* (1922)   291

12   ETHNICITY AND NATIONALISM IN STALIN'S SOVIET UNION AND HITLER'S THIRD REICH   295

After World War I, newly established authoritarian states redefined the requirements for membership in their civil societies. In both Nazi Germany and the Soviet Union, ethnicity served an important role in defining and implementing those requirements. Sources focus on (1) the ideological frameworks and ethnic and national policies used by the Soviet Union in the Ukraine in the 1920s and 1930s that resulted in the Ukrainian famine; and (2) the ideological frameworks and ethnic and national policies used by the Nazis in Germany in the 1930s and 1940s that resulted in the Holocaust.

Nationality and Agriculture in the Soviet Ukraine   295

1. Joseph Stalin, *Problems of Agrarian Policy in the USSR* (1929)   297
2. James E. Mace, *Communism and the Dilemmas of National Liberation* (1983)   299
3. Antonina Solovieva, *Sent by the Komsomol* (1964)   302
4. Miron Dolot, *Execution by Hunger* (1985)   305

Ethnicity and Citizenship in Nazi Germany   307

   5. Adolf Hitler, *Mein Kampf* (1925)   308

   6. *Nazi Jewish Policies* (1935, 1939, 1942)   311

   7. *Nazi Art* (1930s)   315

   8. Melita Maschmann, *Account Rendered* (1963)   317

   9. Primo Levi, *Survival in Auschwitz* (1947)   319

13 THE CALL FOR LIBERATION IN THE ERA OF THE COLD WAR   325

Following the Second World War, the colonial liberation movement expanded as colonies across the globe sought to declare independence. The cold war conflict, however, both complicated and structured the relationships forming among the colonial liberation movements, the colonizing powers, the newly independent states, and the new superpowers of the United States and the Soviet Union. Further, these decolonizing movements affected politics within Europe as European populations responded to the decolonization movement. Also, during the postwar era, groups disadvantaged in European society called for liberation from their political, economic, and social disenfranchisement. Sources focus on (1) decolonization in the Congo and the context of the cold war; (2) French debates over the Algerian independence movement; and (3) the rise of the women's and gay liberation movements in Europe.

Independence in the Congo: 1960   327

   1. *Proclamation of Independence of Katanga* (1960)   328

   2. United Nations Security Council Official Record, *Statements of Ambassadors from the Soviet Union and the United States* (July 20, 1960)   330

   3. Patrice Lumumba, *Radio Address* (1960)   335

Algerian Independence in France: 1957 to 1959   337

   4. Jean-Paul Sartre, *You Are Super* (1957)   338

   5. Jacques Soustelle, *The Algerian Drama and French Decadence* (1957)   341

   6. Paul Ricoeur, *The Etienne Mathiot Case* (1958)   344

   7. Albert Camus, *Algeria (1958)*   346

   8. Ahmed Taleb-Ibrahimi, *Letter to Albert Camus* (1959)   348

Liberation at Home   351

   9. Simone de Beauvoir, *The Second Sex* (1949)   351

   10. Daniel Guérin, *Shakespeare and Gide in Prison* (1959)   354

14 THE NEW EUROPE? 357

In the decades following the Second World War, the global political and economic power of western and central Europe waned. European leaders sought to strengthen Europe—while also preventing a recurrence of the warfare that already had devastated Europe twice in the twentieth century—by creating a more unified structure for European economic and political life. Movements toward European unification began in the 1950s but gained rapid momentum in the 1980s. The 1980s also saw a rise in antiforeigner violence in western and central Europe aimed at recent immigrants. Both European unification and immigration directly raise the question, "What is Europe?" Sources focus on (1) the movement of non-European peoples into Europe and the rise of antiforeigner sentiment and violence; and (2) debates over European unification.

The New Europeans *358*

1. *Measuring the New Europe* (1950–1997) 358
2. Skrewdriver, *Song Lyrics* (1982–1984) 361
3. Austrian Freedom Party, "*Austria First*" *Petition* (1992) 364
4. *The Affair of the Headscarf* (1989) 366

The European Experiment *371*

5. Margaret Thatcher, *Speech at the College of Europe* (1988) 371
6. François Mitterand, *Speech to the European Parliament* (1995) 374
7. The National Front, *The Patriot's Talking-Points* (2001) 377
8. Philippe de Schoutheete, *The Case for Europe* (2000) 380

CONCLUSION: WHITHER THE WEST? 384

What are the challenges to the idea of the West in today's wider world?

Approaching the West: An Introduction

HISTORY AND THE PAST

Equating *history* with "the events of the past" is a common mistake. Many people assume that history is a fixed body of knowledge that is best learned through the memorization of facts about dates, people, and events. Rather than history, such an understanding of the past is better called *chronology*—dates of wars and battles, lists of monarchs and their reigns, and similar facts and figures. This information is necessary to history, but it marks only the beginning of understanding the past.

History is not the events of the past but rather our attempt to make sense of the past. This effort includes not only discovering what happened but interpreting how and why the events occurred. The ancient Greek writer Herodotus, known as the "Father of History," used the Greek word *historia* to designate the research and mental activities that people need to investigate human actions in the past. But notice how that idea emphasizes both people living in the past and in the present. History is not just about "them"—those people who lived in the past—but about us as well. As we change throughout our lives and from generation to generation—as we are different from our parents and grandparents and as our children and grandchildren will be different from us—so history changes. Each generation raises and considers issues that seem relevant and compelling to it. New generations may even add new facts to our understanding of an event as they identify new issues that previous generations did not consider. In this way, we create new questions and answers about the past, often using the same, or slightly expanded, sets of historical data that others have used before. History is not a fixed idea. The facts about what happened may not change, but how we interpret those facts changes and will develop as people and their cultures continue to change over time.

THE IMPORTANCE OF THE WEST

Increased contact and conflict between peoples from all parts of the globe have made the understanding of cross-cultural encounters a central historical question today. For much of the twentieth century, the rivalry and tensions between the great ideological systems of the day—such as fascism, communism, democracy, and free-market capitalism—dominated the world historical scene and greatly affected the character of encounters among peoples. With the end of the cold war and the apparent, though perhaps temporary, triumph of the ideas of democracy and capitalism in the West, the cultural contacts and conflicts among peoples assumed an even more central place in the world's agenda. Recent events that have pitted the United States against militant groups claiming legitimacy from the teachings of Islam represent only one such example.

Such conflicts are often regarded in the media as wars between different and incompatible cultures in general and between the West and the non-West in particular. Late twentieth- and early twenty-first-century writers, especially those from North America, have called attention to what they call the "triumph of the West," whose values of human rights, liberal democracy, religious pluralism, and free-market appear to have conquered and made obsolete all other competing ideas. These admiring writers are building on a venerable European intellectual tradition that emphasizes the continuing progress of Western civilization as it transforms the entire world, molding it into its own image. At the same time, the West has its fair share of critics who point to the often thoughtless, brutal, and even murderous acts committed in the name of the Western civilization and its values. These critics are answered by champions of the West, who call attention to atrocities that were and continue to be committed in places where the values of the West have yet to take root, arguing that progress can be achieved only through the wholesale introduction of Western values in those countries. For them, Western civilization represents the new global or universal culture that others ought to emulate.

At the same time, the growing immigration of people from the non-West into the West has provoked many internal debates regarding the nature of the identity of the West and notions of nationhood based on Western values. The West is now increasingly identified with economic prosperity and political stability, which many claim are derived from its core Western values—individualism, free-market capitalism, and democratic institutions. The influx of people from the non-West threatens to alter Western nations not only demographically but culturally as well. While some greet this development as an opportunity to develop a multicultural sense of national identity, many are troubled by what they regard as a challenge to their own ethnic or cultural identity as a people or nation.

Statements made about the West therefore speak to today's issues and concerns. Ideas often asserted as Western values—such as human rights, liberal democracy, religious pluralism, and free-market capitalism—are invoked in contemporary debates over political, social, and economic priorities and agendas, in the West and elsewhere. Within this fraught political climate, historians have turned to the question of the West, seeking to understand the West not as a geographic space but as an idea—as a construction of the human imagination. In a world in which the West is called on to justify or defend political, economic, and social values and practices, understanding the history of the idea of the West becomes essential.

IN SEARCH OF THE WEST

What is the West? Where is the West located, and when does its history begin? Every book that considers the breadth of Western civilization must establish a starting point from which a distinctive history of the West is presumed to have begun and must mark out the territories in which that history developed. This task is not an easy one, for there is neither a precise date nor a single event that signals the birth of the West. Nor can the West or even Europe be defined in unambiguous geographic terms. Where indeed does Europe end and Asia begin, for in terms of physical geography Europe should be seen as an appendage—the western extreme—of the Asian continent. This ambiguity is significant today, as Turks and Russians debate whether their country should be seen as part of the West while the nations of western and central Europe debate whether Turkey should be invited into the European Union. Also, consider most Western civilization textbooks and how they define the origins of the West in geographical terms. These books typically treat the ancient civilizations of the Middle East (Mesopotamia, Syria, and Palestine) and North Africa (Egypt) before they arrive at the chapters on the ancient Greeks and Romans. Yet all of the former existed on territories that now are considered non-European and largely non-Western.

This reader regards the identity of the West as its central historical question. By entitling it *The West in the Wider World,* we do not suggest that there is a distinctly identifiable West that has interacted with other, non-Western societies over time. Instead, our theme is the very ambiguity of the term *the West*—a West that is an idea even more than a distinct place. We propose that both West and non-West have evolved as ideas or cultural labels as a result of historical encounters between different groups of people. No group achieves an identity or defines itself in complete isolation from other groups, and to be meaningful, such a self-definition must, explicitly or implicitly, refer to others. Most historical societies have developed in reference to the contacts—political, economic, and cultural—they make with their neighbors. Ancient Greeks and Romans encountered peoples throughout the Mediterranean basin; medieval Christians, Muslims, and Jews interacted with each other and with men and women from as far away as East Asia and Sub-Saharan Africa; Europeans in the age of the Renaissance "discovered new worlds" with which to interact; and so the story goes.

As these societies made contact with other cultures, they defined, characterized, and stereotyped both themselves and those they encountered. In short, they created identities for themselves and for others, identities that influenced and that were influenced by the new political and social relationships they established. Many aspects of these identities, both idealistic and horrific in their implications, remain part of our culture today, shaping our images of and relationships with other cultures as well as our understanding of who we are ourselves.

Studying the varied and complicated nature of these cultural encounters requires more than reading a smooth historical narrative that gives the chronology of major events. We must also study the outlooks and interpretations of those who experienced the past—individuals who expressed their viewpoints in their own time. In each chapter of this book, we present thematically organized sources, most written or created by people in the past, that look at historical events from a variety of perspectives. As much as the surviving evidence allows, we provide sources that reveal the viewpoints of the various protagonists. By studying these sources, first individually and later in combination, we can begin to appreciate the interactions from all sides. However, such knowledge is often far from complete, especially when we have only the stories told by the historical "winners," whose victories have allowed them to impose their interpretations of the past on posterity—on us. We need to develop the skills to read between the lines, to be alert to the stories of other players based on the evidence we have collected. Thereby we may understand these cross-cultural encounters and, therefore, ourselves.

GUIDE TO INTERPRETING SOURCES

PRIMARY AND SECONDARY SOURCES: WHY READ THEM?

The West in the Wider World: Sources and Perspectives is a collection of primary and secondary historical sources that help you understand the creation of the West as it developed in relation to the wider world. *Primary sources* are those sources that have come down to us from an earlier period, often created by participants in or observers of the events they describe or for which they provide evidence. For example, a diary, a law, or a newspaper article speaks to the outlook of its author as well as to the historical context in which it was produced. A primary source also might come from a period after the events it describes and may draw on or excerpt earlier sources that may or may not still exist. Even though documentary—that is, written—sources are important as primary sources, everything is grist for the historian's mill. Tools, furniture, weapons, artwork, costumes, and architecture represent nonwritten sources that can be as important as the written word for our understanding of human society in the past.

Sometimes a historian picks and chooses among a wealth of primary sources, focusing on those that seem to relate best to the questions being asked. At other times a historian, especially a scholar of a remote past from which limited sources survive, has to draw on everything that comes to hand. In either case, the historian pieces together a picture from partial and disjointed evidence. The analogy of putting a jigsaw puzzle together is not too far off the mark, but the historian most likely does not have all the pieces needed to create a "whole picture." Knowing how to fill in the gaps is where historical judgment and insight come into play.

Once a historian builds a historical interpretation based on primary sources, his or her resulting work becomes a *secondary source*. Secondary sources tell us what sources historians have used and how they have used those sources to interpret the past. They highlight particular issues or debates and help us look at primary sources in new and interesting ways. For this reason, some secondary sources are included in this collection.

Primary and secondary sources allow you to interpret the past for yourself. In this book, primary sources claim a privileged role because they are direct evidence of their time. By studying primary sources, you can sharpen your own thinking and reach historical conclusions with confidence. Such interpretation involves asking and answering questions, as discussed on the next page. Mastering the questions to ask of the sources will give you the intellectual training you need to become a good historian. These skills will serve you well both in school and throughout your life. Today we live in a world pervaded by the mass media and have easy access, through the Internet and other means, to more information than we can readily process and evaluate. Learning how to read historical sources will help you become a discriminating consumer of information.

PRIMARY SOURCES: HOW TO READ THEM

Each chapter of this book presents several primary sources that are organized thematically around a certain moment or topic in Western history. Each chapter begins with an introduction, and most chapters also have two or three section introductions. These introductions set out the larger themes and contexts that surround the sources in the chapter and make them meaningful. Each individual source has been introduced with a headnote that conveys the essential information that you need to understand and interpret the source accurately. The "Questions for Analysis" that follow each source showcase some important questions that a reader might ask of a source as part of his or her historical interpretation.

A few questions should guide your interpretation of almost any source. Here we rehearse some of these guidelines and then interpret a sample primary source to illustrate how you might follow them. When you first come to a primary source, after having read the introductory material, you should ask yourself the following questions.

Author   Who was the author, and when did he or she write? Several issues might be significant to the author's purpose and prejudices. Was the author male or female? What was his or her economic or social status? Did the author have a professional or employment status that might be significant? For example, if the author was a male government minister, would his official and political position have significantly affected his public comments about the conduct of an ongoing war? What else might have affected the author's understanding or ability to observe the issues or events described?

Nature of the Source   If you are examining a written source, what is the type of writing, and how does the specific genre affect the presentation? Is it part of a history, a chronicle, or some other self-consciously historical work? Is it a letter or part of a diary? Is it part of an official document?

(Intended) Audience   What can we know about the author's intended audience? The form or genre of the source often reveals who the intended audience was. For example, a political treatise written in Latin was intended for an educated male audience, while popular songs in the vernacular were calculated to reach people from all levels of income and literacy. Sometimes the author even names the intended audience or makes comments that only a certain audience could be counted on to understand. The intended audience often affects the author's style and his or her specific arguments. For example, an author arguing in favor of establishing colonies might shape his argument differently if preparing his text for merchants than he would if preparing his text for government administrators.

Main Points   What are the major points that the author is trying to convey? These points include both specific arguments and the justifications for those arguments. The justifications for the argument might be as important as the author's ultimate conclusions. For example, many authors might argue that foreigners should not be admitted into a nation, but their stated justifications might invoke reasons based on economic, cultural, and ethnic or racial factors.

(Narrow) Interpretation   What can answers to these questions tell us about the author's point of view, approach, attitude, and biases? Is the author trying to promote a certain idea or image? What can the source not tell us and why?

(Broad) Interpretation   What is the historical value of the source, and how does it contribute to our understanding of the particular author, society, and period in question? How might you compare this source with other sources? Does it challenge or reinforce the perspectives offered by those other sources? What can comparing the sources tell us about the historical issue or society in question?

Having considered the principles of interpretation, let us turn to a concrete example of a primary historical document. A discussion of how such a document might be interpreted follows.

Sample Source

1

"... THE WHOLE PLACE STANK."

Bernal Díaz
Chronicles   (c. 1560)

Bernal Díaz del Castillo (c. 1492–c. 1581) was a soldier in Hernando Cortés's army during the Spanish conquest of the Aztec empire in Mexico, which took place in the 1520s. In his old age, Díaz wrote his memoirs of the conquest from the perspective of the common soldier, challenging academic works that he believed too harshly criticized the process of the conquest. Further, Díaz sought to counter works that he believed overemphasized Cortés's role in the conquest at the expense of Cortés's subordinate officers and troops. And he also hoped to make money publishing his memoirs. In the excerpt below, Díaz describes his reaction to Tenochtitlán and to the Aztec religion on his first arrival in the Aztec capital city.

See page 12 for the text of the document.

QUESTIONS FOR ANALYSIS

1. According to Díaz, how does Montezuma seek to impress the Spaniards? What impresses Díaz?

2. How does Díaz's description of the Aztec temple refer to religious objects that would be familiar to Díaz, a Catholic Christian?

3. How does Díaz's description of the Aztec temple associate the temple with Christian images of evil?

4. How would Díaz's description of the Aztec temple serve as a response to the academic critics of the cruelty of the Spanish invaders?

INTERPRETING DÍAZ'S ACCOUNT

Let us first determine who Díaz was, what he wrote, and for whom his work was intended. Then we can evaluate the historical value of his account.

To answer these questions, we need to make use of the information provided in the headnote in addition to the internal evidence from the excerpt of the primary source itself. Díaz was a Spanish conquistador, an explorer and conqueror from the sixteenth century who participated in the campaigns that turned Aztec Mexico into one of Spain's richest new colonial possessions. The selected passages, drawn from the memoirs he wrote, describe events in which he often was an eyewitness and a participant.

This information allows us to begin assessing Díaz's writings as a historical source. Can we trust his description of the interactions between the Spaniards and the Aztecs as straightforward, reliable descriptions? After all, he witnessed the events. But although Díaz was there, the *Chronicles* actually was written years later. Was it an imperfect recollection, or was it based on other records? We may, for instance, try to determine from the source whether any hints there suggest that Díaz wrote a daily journal that he later drew on to compose the *Chronicles*. Also, we may want to determine from the source how important Díaz himself was in the Spanish expedition and what access he might have had to the decision-making meetings of Cortés and his immediate subordinates. How informed an observer could he have been?

The headnote tells us that Díaz was responding to two different sets of opinions. First, he was attempting to refute academic critiques who claimed that the expedition was too rushed and brutal. His portrayal of the Aztecs as evil, pagan, and rich serves just this purpose (p. 12). Second, he wished to represent the expedition more "in the round" by placing Cortés's leadership role within the proper context and by making known the efforts of the other Spaniards in the expedition (p. 12). From these two goals we can conclude that firsthand narratives may not always be the best primary historical evidence and that even eyewitness accounts should be viewed critically. An author could have been too personally involved in an event to make a fully dispassionate analysis of it. By the same token, it is not the case that older sources are more reliable than newer sources. An author who participated in an event may wish to present a particular version of history and might do so by knowingly distorting factual information.

Determining an author's reliability is not an easy task. An author's bias or perspective can creep into an account in subtle as well as not-so-subtle ways. Sometimes an author does this for literary effect, to elicit a desired reaction from his or her intended audience. Most sources and authors are both reliable and unreliable, and we as historians must learn to grasp what a source can say and what its limitations are. For instance, while the false testimony of a sworn legal witness is not reliable information for reconstructing the facts of the case, it can tell the judge and the jury much about the perspectives and positions of the person who is telling the lies.

Díaz clearly wanted to spin a good yarn and picked his material carefully for that purpose. He also limited its point of view to appeal to a particular audience. It does not appear that Díaz asked for or heard the Aztec's version of the encounter.

Having considered the author, the nature of the source, and its reliability, it is time to turn to the historical value and significance of the work. What historical understanding can we derive from this account? What does it say about the nature of encounters across civilizations and of social identities in the sixteenth century? To answer these questions we first have to imagine the experience and reaction of the typical reader of this account in early modern Spain. A textbook will tell you that most of these sixteenth-century readers would not have visited Mexico; presumably most never left Spain at all. Spain was then embarked on a vast colonial enterprise, bringing in unheard of riches and creating exciting opportunities for those who dared venture overseas. Those who stayed at home might or might not become rich from this empire, but they could certainly feel proud about what their society was able to accomplish.

Studying the source tells us that Díaz communicated to his audience an image of Aztec civilization that contrasted starkly to the civilization of his native Castile (a region of Spain). The story he presents therefore is not just about how the Aztecs lived; it is implicitly and sometimes even explicitly about how "they" are different from "us." Notice the words and phrases that Díaz uses to describe aspects of Aztec society—references to "cursed idols," "evil temples," and gory details of human sacrifice. Díaz's language conveys moral judgment and reflects the perspective that he and his readers shared. The Christian identity of author and audience comes into play; so too do their common assumptions about what constitute good and bad deeds. Díaz therefore could expect that his assessment of the Aztecs as heathens, whose barbarism was amplified by their ignorance of Christianity, would strike a deep chord with his audience. He tried to make his readers, who had not seen sights of human sacrifice in Mexico, join in the experience by offering a familiar comparison: "the floor was so bathed in it [blood] that in the slaughterhouses of Castille there was no such stink."

On the other side of the balance, you should also notice that Díaz expresses wonder at many of the things that the Aztecs created. The size and busyness of the port excited great amazement even among the most seasoned travelers in his party who had visited the greatest cities of the "Old World," Europe. While the Aztecs were presented as inferior and barbaric, their civilization was nonetheless not entirely without merit. Their great wealth and the splendor of their civilization, as manifested in its physical monuments and amenities, marked them out as special. But Díaz was not trying to make his readers at home admire the Aztecs. He was trying to create an alluring image of Mexico that would add to the appeal of his story and also prompt some Spaniards to seek fame, fortune, and adventure in Mexico. The combination of the Aztec moral decadence and their great wealth made them suitable objects for two mutually reinforcing operations—conversion and colonization. The bejeweled idols mentioned in the story perfectly embody this dual message—that the pagan and barbaric Aztecs were in need of Christian salvation and Christian rule and that wondrous riches awaited those who would come to Mexico to help bring this about. Such a portrayal also was calculated to defuse the criticisms made by those Spaniards who claimed that the expedition had been too harsh on the natives, one of Díaz's fundamental goals.

Accounts such as this one, together with travelers' tales from sailors, merchants, soldiers, and missionaries, created for those in Spain a compelling image of what the outside, non-Western world had to offer. The value of this story goes beyond what it says about the diplomatic negotiations between the Aztecs and the Spaniards and how Aztec religion and society functioned. It allows us to understand how the Spaniards imagined the Aztecs, creating a distinct image that served their own purposes. This image enabled Spaniards to accept a wholesale transformation—virtually the destruction—of the traditional Aztec civilization. It enabled them to justify their new conquest in Mexico as a venture that was good for both the pocketbook and the soul.

INTERPRETING A VISUAL SOURCE

A good historian tries to make use of every source of information at his or her disposal. While written primary sources form an important part of historical evidence, a variety of nonwritten sources provide invaluable information and perspectives. Nonwritten sources come in a variety of forms, including pictorial representations, material objects, and archaeological evidence.

In this reader you will find a number of pictorial representations that serve as primary sources to help you understand a particular historical interaction. Like the written sources, these visual sources are introduced with headnotes giving information that will help you interpret them accurately and meaningfully. The Questions for Analysis that follow each source direct your attention to specific aspects of the visual source and invite you to relate it to other materials in the same chapter.

The proper evaluation of a nonwritten source follows some of the basic guidelines that apply when you read a written source document. For a visual source, you should ask yourself the following questions.

Artist/Patron   Who was the artist or creator of the image? If this is not known, what can we know about the person who commissioned the image to be made or about the context in which the image appeared? For example, did the commissioner of a woodcut print stand to gain financially or politically from the widespread circulation of the image and its underlying message?

Nature of the Image   What is the type of image, and how does the specific artistic form affect the presentation? For example, a formal portrait, designed to appear in a structured environment that allows careful viewing, permits artistic detail and nuance, whereas a wall poster, designed to appear in any context and likely to be viewed fleetingly, requires blunt images and messages.

(Intended) Viewers   Was the source meant originally for private viewing or for public consumption? What was the nature of its intended audience? Did it circulate beyond its intended audience, and what can we know about how it was appreciated or used? For example, we might distinguish between a political message conveyed in an unpublished private letter and one that was articulated in the columns of a printed newspaper.

Message of the Image   What are the major points that the artist/patron is trying to convey by means of this particular representation? These often may be understood by comparing the internal components of the painting or by comparing the components of the painting with general social norms and values of the time.

(Narrow) Interpretation   What can answers to the above questions tell us about the point of view, approach, biases, and attitude of the creator of the image?

(Broad) Interpretation   What is the historical value of the source, and how does it contribute to our understanding of a particular individual, group, or society? What does comparison with other sources tell us about the historical theme in question?

Sample Source

2

"THEY ALSO EAT ONE ANOTHER. . . ."

Image of the Encounter: German Woodcut of 1505

As stories of the early explorers' adventures in the Americas circulated in Europe, European artists drew images of the indigenous people, often to accompany printed texts. As with the printed texts, artists took up one of the most popular and lurid themes in exploration literature—cannibalism. Christian intellectual traditions clearly condemned cannibalism as a savage and barbaric practice. The visual source below was produced in Germany, most likely in Augsburg, in 1505 and marks the first significant depiction in Europe of the peoples of the Americas. The caption underneath the image reads, in part, "They also eat one another, even those who are slain, and singe their flesh in the smoke."

See page 15 for the image.

QUESTIONS FOR ANALYSIS

1. What does the woodcut show the indigenous Americans doing?
2. What is significant about the image's mixture of familiar with unfamiliar activities? What is significant about food as a symbol in the woodcut?

3. What might a sixteenth-century viewer conclude about the peoples of the Americas and about the practice of cannibalism from viewing the woodcut?

4. How does the image of Amerindians conveyed by the woodcut compare with the image conveyed in Bernal Díaz's text (Sample Source 1)? How do the two sources convey similar or different messages about the native peoples of the Americas?

INTERPRETING THE WOODCUT

What do we know about the creator of this image? The headnote does not identify the artist who created this woodcut. But knowing the identity of the author or artist, something that is not always possible, is sometimes less important than understanding the historical setting in which the text or image was created. In this case, the woodcut was produced just thirteen years after Columbus's first voyage across the Atlantic Ocean. It was therefore one of the very first images of the so-called New World that people in Europe would have had seen, a point emphasized by the headnote. At that time, all but a relative handful of Europeans would have had to rely exclusively on travelers' tales and images such as this one for information about the peoples who inhabited the Americas.

What can we learn about the audience? While there is no explicit information either in the headnote or on the image about the audience, the nature of the artistic medium gives us certain clues about who would have viewed it. Of course, a woodcut would be printed, allowing for the relatively cheap production of words and images on paper. The ability to mass produce such prints made the images accessible to a wide spectrum of the population.

How do we "read" this image? First, we need to note the main features of the picture. The woodcut uses simple lines to represent visual reality. In the foreground, a tribe of partially clothed men, women, and children is portrayed in a charming domestic setting to which a European audience could readily relate. But on closer examination, it is revealed that the Amerindians' domestic activities involve feasting on the severed limbs of certain unidentified individuals: they could be Europeans, natives who belonged to the tribe, or other natives. The adults wear headdresses made of vegetation, and all are clothed in loincloths made from leaves. Some of the standing men hold weapons for war or hunting, such as bows and spears. As with the costumes, the setting is a rustic one: some tree trunks are formed into a pavilion of sorts, and flat rocks provide seats. Finally, the entire scene takes place by the sea. In the background is the (Atlantic) ocean, on which floats a European-style ship with the closer one showing two Christian crosses prominently emblazoned on its sails.

How would you interpret this image? It makes a strong statement about the nature of the inhabitants of the Americas encountered by the Europeans. The image tells its viewers that the Amerindians lived simple and rather savage lives that involved the practice of eating human flesh—cannibalism, a practice that most Europeans at the time regarded as taboo. The caption—"They also eat one another, even those who are slain, and singe their flesh in the smoke"—suggests that the cannibals eat the flesh of enemies or strangers as well as that of members of their own tribe. All this serves to attribute to the inhabitants of the Americas an outrageous level of barbarity that no European audience would find either understandable or acceptable. The picture thus presents a fascinating yet fearsome image of what the "New World" has in store for visiting Europeans. At the same time, the domestic aspects of the cannibals in the picture suggest social relationships that make the Amerindians "human," an interesting opinion given that their "humanity" was still being debated among Europeans in 1505. By presenting the domestic side of the Amerindians, the image might help to alleviate anxieties over the hazard of approaching these people and to reinforce the idea that they needed to be reformed through conversion to Christianity.

A sense of the broader historical significance of such an image can be gained by making certain comparisons. The Aztec society described in the Bernal Díaz text (see Sample Source 1), one that Europeans would conquer with relative ease, promised great material rewards. The cannibal tribe in the German woodcut comes across as a much more formidable enemy, and the image does not even suggest that treasures await those who decided to brave the risk.

READING A SECONDARY SOURCE

History is a collective enterprise. Historians rely on the work of other historians to learn what events happened and also what questions to ask when approaching the past. Sometimes this process involves engaging in a debate—typically through secondary sources such as books and articles—over what constitutes the best interpretation of the available primary sources.

The secondary sources included in this reader serve several purposes. Some expand on important themes hinted at in the primary sources. Others provide interesting theories about specific interactions, which can then be critiqued through a firsthand examination of the primary sources themselves.

The proper evaluation of a secondary source follows some of the basic guidelines for other types of sources. Like the primary sources in each chapter, secondary sources are accompanied by headnotes and Questions for Analysis. In reading a secondary source, you should ask yourself the following questions.

Author Who was the author of the article or book chapter? Can you tell in what ways his or her training or background contributed to how the argument is presented? For example, how might a historian of ancient Greece explain the rise of Western civilization differently from a historical sociologist or political scientist?

Use of Primary Sources How does the scholar integrate the use of primary sources in his or her argument? Is this a good model for you to follow?

The Point or Argument What are the major points that the scholar is trying to convey?

(Narrow) Interpretation What does investigating the above questions tell us about the specific argument made by the scholar?

(Broad) Interpretation What is the historical relevance of the argument, and how does it contribute to our understanding of the broader themes of the chapter?

Sample Source

3

". . . THE INDIAN DISEASE . . ."

Roger Schlesinger
In the Wake of Columbus (1996)

The historian Roger Schlesinger has written extensively on the interactions between cultures and civilizations during the Renaissance. In the excerpt below, he considers the impact of the Americas on European daily life.

See page 18 for the text of the document.

QUESTIONS FOR ANALYSIS

1. According to Schlesinger, what positive benefits accrued to Europeans as a result of their interactions with the Americas? What negative consequences?
2. According to Schlesinger, what role did sexuality play in the European conception of Amerindian society? How does Schlesinger's discussion of the European understanding of the tomato reinforce this issue?
3. How did Amerindians provide Europeans with an "explanation" of the outbreak of syphilis? What evidence supports competing interpretations?

INTERPRETING SCHLESINGER'S ACCOUNT

This excerpt comes from Roger Schlesinger's study, published in 1996, on the interactions between the Americas and Europe in the sixteenth and seventeenth centuries. This topic is central to our broader theme of the West in the wider world. It speaks to how the discovery of a part of the world hitherto unknown to Europeans affected the Europeans.

What are Schlesinger's main points in this excerpt? The account explains the nature and impact of a number of European imports from the Americas. The first imports discussed are the food crops that were introduced into Europe from the Americas. Many of the ingredients that we now associate with European or Western cuisine, a central aspect of European cultural identity today, were unknown to the people of Europe before the sixteenth century.

Another import may or may not be an import from the Americas. While some modern historians propose that the sexually transmitted disease syphilis was an import from the Americas, Schlesinger stresses that this point is still unresolved. He then lays out how the varied and conflicting understandings of the origins of syphilis can be used by historians to clarify the cultural horizons and worldview of the people who held them. In particular, by associating syphilis with the Americas, the Europeans could comfortably brand the disease a "foreign" element coming to them from an alien country where the inhabitants lived what Europeans believed was an immoral way of life. This point illustrates a recurring aspect of cultural encounters: one group employs its own stereotypes of another group to explain to themselves why the others are different and often inferior.

You can sharpen your understanding of this secondary source by placing it beside the two preceding sample sources. For instance, how do Díaz's condemnations of Amerindians' religious practices and the German woodcut's depiction of cannibalism echo points raised in Schlesinger's discussion of syphilis?

Note how Schlesinger has gathered a wide variety of factual information and deployed it to illustrate a number of important points that have a direct bearing on the theme of Europe's interaction with the Americas. How is his presentation different from that found in a primary written or visual source? In other words, how can reading a work of secondary scholarship complement the interpretation of primary sources? We may find, as one example, that the points and questions raised by a secondary interpreter are informed by contemporary concerns about cultural encounters. We also may find that the author tries to examine different perspectives and place them in an interpretive historical context in a way that primary sources do not always do. This is a particularly important contribution that secondary sources can make.

Reading a good secondary source and seeing how a well-trained, thoughtful historian practices his or her craft can serve as an excellent lesson in how to think critically about primary sources and the past. This reader offers you the raw material for developing the skills and confidence you need to become a master of this craft.

MAPS

1.1 EUROPEAN VOYAGES TO THE AMERICAS 2

2.1 REFORMATION EUROPE, C. 1550 31

3.1 NATIVE NATIONS AND EUROPEAN SETTLEMENTS IN THE GREAT LAKES REGION 58

4.1 RUSSIAN CONQUEST OF SIBERIA 79

6.1 THE ATLANTIC SLAVE TRADE 131

8.1 DECLINE OF THE OTTOMAN EMPIRE TO 1923 195

9.1 THE OPIUM TRADE IN CHINA 208

10.1 POLITICAL DIVISIONS IN AFRICA, 1914 236

10.2 ETHNIC GROUPS IN AFRICA 237

10.3 ENVIRONMENTAL ZONES AND TRADE ROUTES IN AFRICA 238

13.1 THE DECOLONIZATION OF AFRICA, 1951 TO 1990 326

14.1 EUROPEAN MIGRATION FLOWS, C. 1970 359

14.2 STATISTICS ON SELECTED EUROPEAN NATIONS, C. 1993 360

ABOUT THE EDITORS

Richard Lim, Associate Professor of History at Smith College, earned his A.B. at the University of California at Berkeley and his Ph.D. at Princeton University. His publications include *Public Disputations, Power, and Social Order in Late Antiquity* (1995) and articles on the history and culture of late antiquity. A recipient of the Rome Prize Fellowship at the American Academy in Rome and the National Endowment of the Humanities Fellowship, he is currently working on a book on public spectacles and civic transformation in five cities within the later Roman Empire.

David Kammerling Smith, Associate Professor of History at Eastern Illinois University, received his M.S. Ed. (1986) from Indiana University and both a M.A. (1990) and a Ph.D. (1995) in European history from the University of Pennsylvania. A specialist in French history, he has published articles on political, economic, and cultural history in the *Journal of Modern History* and *French Historical Studies,* among other journals, and contributed to major reference works, such as *The Encyclopedia of the Enlightenment.* A recipient of numerous grants, including a Bourse Chateaubriand and a Mellon Foundation Fellowship, he is currently working on a book on the structure and language of economic policy making in early eighteenth-century France. At Eastern Illinois University, he has taught both Western civilization and world history and has developed specialized courses that integrate national historical narratives into the framework of world history.

Chapter 1

Two Worlds Collide: Renaissance Europe and the Americas

Christopher Columbus departed Palos, Spain, on August 3, 1492, seeking to establish a new route to East Asia by sailing westward across the Atlantic Ocean. It was an act of tremendous courage and arrogant pride. In the fifteenth century, long-standing trade networks between Europe and Asia had been disrupted by the rising empire of the Ottoman Turks. A direct route to East Asia would bypass "the Turkish menace" and, more important, Venetian and Greek middlemen offered rich financial rewards. Columbus wanted those earthly benefits, but inspired by Renaissance humanists who valued the active, heroic, creative human male, Columbus also sought immortal fame and intellectual redemption.

For a decade, Columbus had sought support for his venture from the courts of Europe. His plans persistently were rejected, in large measure because nearly all European astronomers agreed on the size of the earth and the impossibility of traveling from Europe to East Asia across such a vast expanse of ocean. Columbus, however, basing his arguments on controversial sources of knowledge, including the writings of the earlier Venetian explorer Marco Polo and maps originating in Islamic civilization, asserted that the experts were incorrect, that the earth was considerably smaller than thought, and that a well-equipped and disciplined crew could make the voyage to the Indies. Further, Europeans had integrated several nautical inventions developed across the globe, such as the compass and the stern-post rudder by the Chinese, the astrolabe and lateen sails by Arabians, and improved rigging by the Europeans themselves, which made Columbus's voyage conceivable.

Columbus's persistence paid off when Ferdinand of Aragon and Isabella of Castile, having just captured the last Muslim stronghold on the Iberian peninsula, sponsored his voyage (Map 1.1). Inspired by religious zeal, the Spanish monarchs also feared the success of Spain's Portuguese rivals, who were seeking a water route to Asia by traveling down the coast of Africa and rounding the Cape of Good Hope (a feat accomplished by Vasco da Gama in 1498). Thus, hoping to arrive in Asia before the Portuguese, Isabella supplied Columbus with three ships and ninety men to search not for a "new world" but for a new route to Asia. Columbus's luck had turned, but even he was not aware how much. The scholars had been correct regarding the size of the earth, but Columbus and his crew stumbled on the Americas at precisely the location that he expected to find Asia. Even after four voyages to the Caribbean islands, Columbus died believing that his theories had been verified and that he had discovered islands just off the coast of China.

What Columbus discovered was not the "new world" he claimed, for the Americas were well populated, but "a world unknown" to Europeans. The vastness

1

MAP 1.1 EUROPEAN VOYAGES TO THE AMERICAS

and diversity of this unknown world provided ample opportunity for Europeans to see many different Americas and Americans, from the preliterate and pretechnological Arawak peoples first encountered by Columbus to the politically and economically sophisticated Aztec and Inca empires, whose architecture, technology, and science amazed and rivaled the Europeans. As Europeans and Amerindians confronted each other, each sought to make sense of the other through (and to mold each other to fit) the preconceptions drawn from the stories, myths, and legends found within each culture—stories of godly visitors, strange invaders, cannibalistic savages, and vast wealth.

The European explorers confronted new customs and rituals among the indigenous peoples they encountered. The first generation of explorers described their experiences with these "strange practices" and thereby crafted identities for the Amerindians. These identities, the process of their formation, and their implications as Europeans established military, political, and economic predominance in the Americas provide many glimpses into the world of the Renaissance. As colonization progressed, Europeans sought to understand the place of the Amerindians within the civilized world. Drawing on the traditions of ancient Greece and Rome and responding to the activities of colonial regimes, writers defined the level of civilization found among the Amerindians by identifying those things that characterize civilized society. Thus, Renaissance writers defined their own societies as well as those encountered in the Americas. Further, the Americas may not have been a new world, but this unknown world unleashed the Renaissance imagination and inspired writers to speculate about what a new or at least different world could be like.

THE EUROPEAN ARRIVAL

The first generation of Europeans to arrive in the Americas lacked the most basic information about these unknown lands. It took nearly two decades after Columbus's first landing in 1492 to determine definitively that the Americas were distinct and distant from Asia. Instead, Europeans arrived with a different type of knowledge. They knew the political, economic, and social practices that shaped European society. They knew biblical stories of good and evil. They knew the myths and legends, heroes and villains of Europe and of ancient Greece and Rome. They read about bizarre and exotic creatures that ancient authors claimed lived in distant lands. These political, economic, social, biblical, and literary systems that helped Europeans understand their own world also provided the framework for helping them understand the Americas. Further, Amerindian reactions to the Europeans— as murderers, gods, trading partners, and colonizers—affected the explorers' understanding of these indigenous peoples and, thus, of themselves.

1

". . . THE LAND APPEARED. . . ."

Christopher Columbus
Log of the First Voyage (1492)

As Christopher Columbus (1451–1506) traveled to and from the Americas, he kept a log that recorded technical information about the voyage, descriptions of his official actions, and reactions to the things and people he saw. On his return to Spain, Columbus presented the log—the official record of "his glorious achievement" and of the glory and wealth he was bringing to the Spanish crown—to Ferdinand and

---

Oliver Dunn and James E. Kelley, Jr., eds. and trans., *The "Diario" of Christopher Columbus's First Voyage to America: Abstracted by Fray Bartolomé de las Casas* (Norman: University of Oklahoma Press, 1989), 63, 65, 67, 69, 71, 89, 99, 101.

Isabella. Sadly, this log has been lost, as has Columbus's private copy of the log. In the 1530s, however, Bartolomé de Las Casas prepared a partly summarized, partly quoted version of Columbus's private copy. Las Casas, a Spanish merchant who later in life took religious orders, was a friend and admirer of Columbus. This selection from the Las Casas summary recounts some of Columbus's experiences during his first days in the Americas as he reacted to the Arawak people and the Caribbean Islands he encountered.

Friday, 12 October [1492]

At two hours after midnight the land appeared, from which they were about two leagues[1] distant. They hauled down all the sails . . . , passing time until daylight Friday, when they reached an islet of the Lucayas, which was called Guanahani[2] in the language of the Indians. Soon they saw naked people; and the Admiral went ashore in the armed launch. . . .

Soon many people of the island gathered there. What follows are the very words of the Admiral in his book about his first voyage to, and discovery of, these Indies. I, he says, in order that they would be friendly to us—because I recognized that they were people who would be better freed [from error] and converted to our Holy Faith by love than by force—to some of them I gave red caps, and glass beads which they put on their chests, and many other things of small value, in which they took so much pleasure and became so much our friends that it was a marvel. Later they came swimming to the ships' launches where we were and brought us parrots and cotton thread in balls and javelins and many other things, and they traded them to us for other things which we gave them, such as small glass beads and bells. In sum, they took everything and gave of what they had very willingly. But it seemed to me that they were a people very poor in everything. All of them go around as naked as their mothers bore them; and the women also, although I did not see more than one quite young girl. And all those that I saw were young people, for none did I see of more than 30 years of age. They are very well formed, with handsome bodies and good faces. Their hair [is] coarse—almost like the tail of a horse—and short. They wear their hair down over their eyebrows except for a little in the back which they wear long and never cut. Some of them paint themselves with black, and they are of the color of the [Canary Islanders], neither black nor white, and some of them paint themselves with white, and some of them with red, and some of them with whatever they find. And some of them paint their faces, and some of them the whole body, and some of them only the eyes, and some of them only the nose. They do not carry arms nor are they acquainted with them, because I showed them swords and they took them by the edge and through ignorance cut themselves. They have no iron. Their javelins are shafts without iron and some of them have at the end a fish tooth and others of other things. All of them alike are of good-sized stature and carry themselves well. I saw some who had marks of wounds on their bodies and I made signs to them asking what they were; and they showed me how people from other islands nearby came there and tried to

---

[1] About 6.4 nautical miles.
[2] San Salvador, also known as Watlings Island.

take them, and how they defended themselves. . . . They should be good and intelligent servants, for I see that they say very quickly everything that is said to them; and I believe that they would become Christians very easily, for it seemed to me that they had no religion. Our Lord pleasing, at the time of my departure I will take six of them from here to Your Highnesses in order that they may learn to speak. . . .

Saturday, 13 October . . .

I was attentive and labored to find out if there was any gold; and I saw that some of them wore a little piece hung in a hole that they have in their noses. And by signs I was able to understand that, going to the south or rounding the island to the south, there was there a king who had large vessels of it and had very much gold. . . . And so I will go to the southwest to seek gold and precious stones.

Tuesday, 16 October . . .

[*After four days sailing, Columbus arrives at Long Island, where he has been told he will find gold.*]

These people are like those of the said islands in speech and customs except that these now appear somewhat more civilized and given to commerce and more astute. Because I see that they have brought cotton here to the ship and other little things for which they know better how to bargain payment than the others did. And in this island I even saw cotton cloths made like small cloaks, and the people are more intelligent, and the women wear in front of their bodies a little thing of cotton that scarcely covers their genitals. . . . I do not detect in them any religion and I believe that they would become Christians very quickly because they are of very good understanding. . . .

Friday, 19 October . . .

[*Columbus sails to Crooked Island.*]

All of this coast and the part of the island that I saw is almost all beach, and the island the most beautiful thing that I have seen. For if the others are very beautiful this one is more so. It is an island of many very green and very large trees. And this land is higher than the other islands found, and there are on it some small heights; not that they can be called mountains, but they are things that beautify the rest; and it seems to have much water. There in the middle of the island, from this part northeast, it forms a great bight[3] and there are many wooded places, very thick and of very large extent. I tried to go there to anchor in it so as to go ashore and see so much beauty; but the bottom was shoal and I could not anchor except far from land and the wind was very good for going to this cape where I am anchored now, to which I gave the name Cabo Hermoso,[4] because such it is. And so I did not anchor

---

[3] Cove.
[4] Beautiful Cape.

in that bight and also because I saw this cape from there, so green and so beautiful; and likewise are all the other things and lands of these islands, so that I do not know where to go first; nor do my eyes grow tired of seeing such beautiful verdure and so different from ours. And I even believe that there are among them many plants and many trees which in Spain are valued for dyes and for medicinal spices; but I am not acquainted with them, which gives me much sorrow. And when I arrived here at this cape the smell of the flowers or trees that came from land was so good and soft that it was the sweetest thing in the world.

QUESTIONS FOR ANALYSIS

1. As Columbus encounters the land and the Arawak people, what characteristics does he notice about them? What do his comments suggest about his goals and expectations for his voyage?
2. How does Columbus begin to distinguish among the Arawak people on different islands and to think about them and their potential? What is significant about his references to Arawak women?
3. How does Columbus indicate that he considers himself and his men superior to the Arawak? What role does Christianity seem to play in Columbus's mission?
4. How might Columbus's log entries be influenced by his reasons for preparing the log?

2

". . . MONTEZUMA COULD NEITHER SLEEP NOR EAT. . . ."

Mexican Accounts of the Conquest of Mexico
Codex Florentino   (1555)

The arrival of Hernando Cortés into the valley of central Mexico in 1519 brought dramatic changes to the indigenous peoples who lived there and especially to the largest and most powerful of the Mexican clans, the Aztecs. Most reports of these changes come from Europeans. In the 1530s and 1540s, however, Spanish missionaries collected accounts of these dramatic events from Mexicans, primarily those who had converted to Catholicism. In compiling the Codex Florentino, *published in 1555, the missionary Bernardino de Sahagún used Mexican scholars of the Nahuatl language and over a dozen Aztec elders who had experienced Cortés's arrival to interpret and edit the Mexican oral traditions that missionaries had collected. These texts demonstrate how the Mexicans sought to understand the actions of the Aztec king, Montezuma, and how Montezuma sought to understand Cortés's arrival.*

Miguel Leon-Portilla, ed., *The Broken Spears: The Aztec Account of the Conquest of Mexico* (Boston: Beacon Press, 1962, 1990), 22–23, 29–31, 63–66, 68.

[*"Small Floating Mountains" Carrying Men Have Appeared off the Coast*]

The year 13-Rabbit[1] now approached its end. And when it was about to end, they [the Spanish] appeared, they were seen again. The report of their coming was brought to Montezuma, who immediately sent out messengers. It was as if he thought the new arrival was our prince Quetzalcoatl.[2]

This is what he felt in his heart: *He has appeared! He has come back! He will come here, to the place of his throne and canopy, for that is what he promised when he departed!* . . .

[*As the Spanish approach Tenochtitlán, the Aztec capital, Montezuma sends messengers to greet them with gifts.*]

While the messengers were away, Montezuma could neither sleep nor eat, and no one could speak with him. He thought that everything he did was in vain, and he sighed almost every moment. He was lost in despair, in the deepest gloom and sorrow. Nothing could comfort him, nothing could calm him, nothing could give him any pleasure.

He said: "What will happen to us? Who will outlive it? Ah, in other times I was contented, but now I have death in my heart! My heart burns and suffers, as if it were drowned in spices . . . ! But will our lord come here?" . . .

[*The messengers return and report to Montezuma.*]

He was . . . terrified to learn how the cannon roared, how its noise resounded, how it caused one to faint and grow deaf. The messengers told him: "A thing like a ball of stone comes out of its entrails: it comes out shooting sparks and raining fire. The smoke that comes out with it has a pestilent odor, like that of rotten mud. This odor penetrates even to the brain and causes the greatest discomfort. If the cannon is aimed against a mountain, the mountain splits and cracks open. If it is aimed against a tree, it shatters the tree into splinters. This is a most unnatural sight, as if the tree had exploded from within."

The messengers also said: "Their trappings and arms are all made of iron. They dress in iron and wear iron casques on their heads. Their swords are iron; their bows are iron; their shields are iron; their spears are iron. Their deer[3] carry them on their backs wherever they wish to go. These deer, our lord, are as tall as the roof of a house.

"The strangers' bodies are completely covered, so that only their faces can be seen. Their skin is white, as if it were made of lime. They have yellow hair, though some of them have black. Their beards are long and yellow, and their moustaches are also yellow. Their hair is curly, with very fine strands. . . .

"Their dogs are enormous, with flat ears and long, dangling tongues. The color of their eyes is a burning yellow; their eyes flash fire and shoot off sparks. Their bellies are hollow, their flanks long and narrow. They are tireless and very powerful. They bound here and there, panting, with their tongues hanging out. And they are spotted like an ocelot."

---

[1] Referring to the Aztec calendar system.
[2] Powerful Aztec god who was expected to return from the sea to reclaim the Aztec throne.
[3] Horses.

When Montezuma heard this report, he was filled with terror. It was as if his heart had fainted, as if it had shriveled. It was as if he were conquered by despair. . . .

[*Cortés Approaches Tenochtitlán.*]

Thus Montezuma went out to meet them, there in Huitzillan.[4] He presented many gifts to the Captain and his commanders, those who had come to make war. He showered gifts upon them and hung flowers around their necks; he gave them necklaces of flowers and bands of flowers to adorn their breasts; he set garlands of flowers upon their heads. Then he hung the gold necklaces around their necks and gave them presents of every sort as gifts of welcome.

When Montezuma had given necklaces to each one, Cortés asked him: "Are you Montezuma? Are you the king? Is it true that you are the king Montezuma?"

And the king said: "Yes, I am Montezuma." Then he stood up to welcome Cortés; he came forward, bowed his head low and addressed him in these words: "Our lord, you are weary. The journey has tired you, but now you have arrived on the earth. You have come to your city, Mexico. You have come here to sit on your throne, to sit under its canopy.

"The kings who have gone before, your representatives, guarded it and preserved it for your coming. . . . The people were protected by their swords and sheltered by their shields.

"Do the kings know the destiny of those they left behind, their posterity? If only they are watching! If only they can see what I see!

"No, it is not a dream. I am not walking in my sleep. I am not seeing you in my dreams. . . . I have seen you at last! I have met you face to face! I was in agony for five days, for ten days, with my eyes fixed on the Region of the Mystery. And now you have come out of the clouds and mists to sit on your throne again.

"This was foretold by the kings who governed your city, and now it has taken place. You have come back to us; you have come down from the sky. Rest now, and take possession of your royal houses. Welcome to your land, my lords!"

When Montezuma had finished, La Malinche[5] translated his address into Spanish so that the Captain could understand it. Cortés replied in his strange and savage tongue, speaking first to La Malinche: "Tell Montezuma that we are his friends. There is nothing to fear. We have wanted to see him for a long time, and now we have seen his face and heard his words. Tell him that we love him well and that our hearts are contented." . . .

When the Spaniards were installed in the palace, they asked Montezuma about the city's resources and reserves and about the warriors' ensigns and shields. They questioned him closely and then demanded gold.

Montezuma guided them to it. They surrounded him and crowded close with their weapons. He walked in the center, while they formed a circle around him.

When they arrived at the treasure house called Teucalco, the riches of gold and feathers were brought out to them: ornaments made of quetzal feathers, richly

---

[4] The community of Tenochtitlán immediately in front of the palace of Montezuma.

[5] Cortés's translator (see Source 4, note 4 for further information).

worked shields, disks of gold, and necklaces of the idols, gold nose plugs, gold greaves and bracelets and crowns.

The Spaniards immediately stripped the feathers from the gold shields and ensigns. They gathered all the gold into a great mound and set fire to everything else, regardless of its value. Then they melted down the gold into ingots.[6] As for the precious green stones, they took only the best of them; the rest were snatched up by the Tlaxcaltecas.[7] The Spaniards searched through the whole treasure house, questioning and quarreling, and seized every object they thought was beautiful.

---

[6] Bars convenient for storage and transport.
[7] A confederation of four Mexican clans severely oppressed by the Aztecs who became Cortés's most loyal Mexican allies.

QUESTIONS FOR ANALYSIS

1. How did Montezuma react to and interpret the news of the strangers' arrival? How did mythology influence interactions between the Aztecs and the Spaniards?

2. What image of Montezuma as a leader emerges from these texts?

3. Whose perspective is presented in the *Codex Florentino*? How does the composition of this text affect our interpretation of it?

4. How did the Aztecs' accounts of their reactions to the arrival of the Spanish compare with Columbus's account of the Arawaks' reactions to his arrival (Source 1)? What might account for these different descriptions?

3

". . . I ORDERED HIM TO BE PUT IN CHAINS. . . ."

Hernando Cortés
Second Dispatch to Charles V (1520)

Hernando Cortés (1485–1547), born of poor noble parents, rose to prominence in the Spanish West Indies and in 1519 led an expedition to the recently discovered Yucatan peninsula. In Mexico, Cortés sought to gain authority over the Aztec empire by establishing control over the Aztec king, Montezuma, and by working through the Aztec ruling class—a goal that required him to understand the nature of Aztec rule. The Aztecs, however, soon drove the Spanish out of their capital, Tenochtitlán. As Cortés prepared to retake Tenochtitlán in 1520, he wrote the following report of his activities and sent it to Charles V, king of Spain and Holy Roman Emperor. Confident of victory, the report describes the marvelous Aztec capital—its marketplace, religion, and political

---

Harry M. Rosen, ed., *Conquest: Dispatches of Cortés from the New World* (New York: Grosset and Dunlap, 1962), 45–47, 51–52.

structure—as Cortés sought to impress Charles V with the kingdom that Cortés would soon deliver to him.

After I had been in the city of Tenochtitlán six days, it seemed to me, even from what little I had seen, that it would be in the best interests of Your Royal Highness and our security that Montezuma should be in my power, and not entirely at liberty, so that he might not relax in his disposition to serve Your Highness. We Spaniards are somewhat touchy and importunate, and, if by some chance we should provoke him and he should become angry, he could do us such injury with his great power, that there would remain no recollection of us. Besides, having him in my power, all the other countries who were subject to him would come to know Your Majesty and accept your royal service, which is what afterwards happened.

I decided to seize him and confine him in my quarters, which are very strong. As I was considering all the ways in which I could accomplish this without provoking any commotion upon his arrest, I remembered what my captain at Vera Cruz had written about the occurrence in Almeria.[1] I stationed sufficient guards in the cross streets, and went to the palace of Montezuma, as I had at other times. We conversed lightly on pleasant subjects, and he gave me some valuables in gold and one of his daughters, and also gave some daughters of other lords to some of my companions. Then I told him that I had learned what had happened in Almeria, and about the Spaniards who had been killed there, and that Quauhpopoca gave as his excuse that he had acted on Montezuma's orders, and as his vassal, could not have done otherwise. I said that I did not believe Quauhpopoca's excuse, and it seemed to me that Montezuma ought to send for him and the other chiefs who had helped him so that the truth could be established and the guilty punished. Then Your Majesty could clearly see his good intentions. Otherwise the reports about those wicked men might provoke Your Highness to anger against him, so that instead of the favors Your Highness would grant him, only evil would result. Montezuma immediately sent for some of his people, and gave them a small stone figure, like a seal, which he wore tied to his arm. He ordered them to go to Almeria. . . .

[Montezuma is kept under house arrest.]

Some fifteen or twenty days after Montezuma's imprisonment, the Indians who had been sent for Quauhpopoca and the others returned, bringing Quauhpopoca and one of his sons, and fifteen other persons who they said had taken part in the murders. Quauhpopoca was carried in a litter, very much in the style of the lord that he was. They were delivered to me, and I kept them under guard in prison. Later when they confessed that they had killed the Spaniards, I had them interrogated as to whether they were vassals of Montezuma. Quauhpopoca answered by asking if there existed any other lord of whom he might be vassal, as much as to say that there was no other. I also asked them if what had been done there was by Montezuma's order, and they answered "No." They were condemned to be burned, but as the sentence was being carried out, all of them with one voice declared that Montezuma had

---

[1] Quauhpopoca, leader of Almeria, had killed two Spanish soldiers after luring them to Almeria with a false pledge of obedience to Spain. Almeria was located near Vera Cruz, Cortés's base camp on the coast of the Gulf of Mexico.

ordered them to do it, and that they had only obeyed his command. So they were burned publicly, in one of the squares, without occasioning any tumult. As soon as they confessed that Montezuma commanded them to kill the Spaniards, I ordered him to be put in chains, which frightened him a good deal.

That day, after I had spoken to him, I removed the irons. . . .[2]

After the imprisonment of Montezuma, the lord of . . . Aculuacan, Cacamazin, rebelled against Montezuma and against Your Majesty's service, to which he had offered himself. Although he was called upon many times to obey your royal mandates, he never complied. When Montezuma sent to summon him, he answered that anyone who wanted anything of him should come to his country, and there he would show what he was worth and what service he was obliged to render. I also learned that he had gathered a great number of warriors, well prepared for action. The rebellion could not go unpunished, and I asked Montezuma what he thought we should do. Montezuma explained that to seize him by force would be dangerous, for Cacamazin had many forces and could not be taken without great risk of many people perishing. However, there were many chiefs from Aculuacan who lived with Montezuma and whom he paid. He would speak with them to win over some of Cacamazin's people. Then, when we were sure that they would favor our ventures, we could take him with safety.

Montezuma came to an understanding with those persons, who induced Cacamazin to meet them in the city of Tezcuco to deliberate on certain matters of state. There they assembled in a very beautiful palace on the borders of the lake, so constructed that canoes can pass under it. They had secretly prepared canoes, with forces in readiness in case Cacamazin should resist imprisonment. In the midst of the conference the chiefs seized him, before his people suspected anything, and brought him across the lake to Tenochtitlán. When they arrived they placed him in a litter, as was customary and required by his rank, and brought him to me. I ordered chains put on him, and held him in safe keeping.

Acting on the advice of Montezuma, in the name of Your Majesty, I placed his son, whose name is Cucuzcacin, in command there, and I ordered all the tribes and lords of that province to obey him as ruler until Your Highness should order otherwise, which they did.

QUESTIONS FOR ANALYSIS

1. How does Cortés describe the Quauhpopoca and Cacamazin rebellions in the language of European political practices that would be familiar to Charles V? Why would he do this?

2. Why does Cortés place Montezuma under house arrest? How does Cortés use the killing of the Spaniards in Almeria to his advantage?

3. How does the depiction of Montezuma in Cortés's account compare to that in the Mexican account (Source 2)? What might account for the similarities or differences?

4. How does Cortés seek to impress Charles V with the Aztec empire?

---

[2] Cortés's goal had been to scare the Aztec king into obedience.

4

". . . THE WHOLE PLACE STANK."

Bernal Díaz
Chronicles (c. 1560)

Bernal Díaz del Castillo (c. 1492–c. 1581) was a soldier in Cortés's army during his conquest of the Aztec empire in the 1520s. In his old age, Díaz wrote his memoirs of the conquest from the perspective of the common soldier, challenging academic works that he believed too harshly criticized the process of the conquest. Further, Díaz sought to counter works that he believed overemphasized Cortés's role in the conquest at the expense of Cortés's subordinate officers and troops. He also hoped to make money publishing his memoirs. In the excerpt below, Díaz describes his reactions to Tenochtitlán and to the Aztec religion on his first arrival in the Aztec capital city.

Montezuma, accompanied by two priests, came out from an oratory[1] dedicated to the worship of his cursed idols at the top of the *cu*.[2] . . .

Montezuma took him [Cortés] by the hand and bade him look at his great city and at all the other cities rising from the water, and the many towns around the lake; and if he had not seen the market place well, he said, he could see it from here much better.

There we stood looking, for that large and evil temple was so high that it towered over everything. From there we could see all three of the causeways that led into Mexico.[3] . . .

We saw the fresh water that came from Chapultepec, which supplied the city, and the bridges on the three causeways, built at certain intervals so the water could go from one part of the lake to another, and a multitude of canoes, some arriving with provisions and others leaving with merchandise. We saw that every house in this great city and in the others built on the water could be reached only by wooden drawbridges or by canoe. We saw temples built like towers and fortresses in these cities, all whitewashed; it was a sight to see. . . .

After taking a good look and considering all that we had seen, we looked again at the great square and the throngs of people, some buying and others selling. The buzzing of their voices could be heard more than a league away. There were soldiers among us who had been in many parts of the world, in Constantinople and Rome

---

[1] Private chapel or place for prayer.
[2] Large temple structure.
[3] Meaning the Aztec capital city Tenochtitlán.

Albert Idell, ed. and trans., *The Bernal Díaz Chronicles: The True Story of the Conquest of Mexico* (Garden City, N.Y.: Doubleday, 1957), 158–61.

and all over Italy, who said that they had never before seen a market place so large and so well laid out, and so filled with people.

To get back to our captain [Cortés], he said to Fray Bartolomé de Olmedo, who happened to be close by, "It seems to me, Father, that it might be a good idea to sound out Montezuma on the idea of letting us build our church here." The Father replied that it might be, if it was successful, but it didn't seem to him to be a good time to bring it up, for Montezuma did not seem to be in the mood to agree to anything like that.

Then Cortés said to Montezuma, through Doña Marina,[4] "Your Highness is indeed a great prince, and it has delighted us to see your cities. Now that we are here in your temple, will you show us your gods?"

Montezuma replied that he would first have to consult with his priests. After he had spoken with them, he bade us enter a small tower room, a kind of hall where there were two altars with very richly painted planks on the ceiling. On each altar there were two giant figures, their bodies very tall and stout. The first one, to the right, they said was Uichilobos, their god of war. It had a very broad face with monstrous, horrible eyes, and the whole body was covered with precious stones, gold, and pearls that were stuck on with a paste they make in this country out of roots. The body was circled with great snakes made of gold and precious stones, and in one hand he held a bow and in the other some arrows. A small idol standing by him they said was his page; he held a short lance and a shield rich with gold and precious stones. Around the neck of Uichilobos were silver Indian faces and things that we took to be the hearts of these Indians, made of gold and decorated with many precious blue stones. There were braziers with copal incense, and they were burning in them the hearts of three Indians they had sacrificed that day. All the walls and floor were black with crusted blood, and the whole place stank.

To the left stood another great figure, the height of Uichilobos, with the face of a bear and glittering eyes made of their mirrors, which they call *tezcal*. It was decorated with precious stones the same as Uichilobos, for they said that the two were brothers. This Tezcatepuca was the god of hell and had charge of the souls of the Mexicans. His body was girded with figures like little devils, with snakelike tails. The walls were so crusted with blood and the floor was so bathed in it that in the slaughterhouses of Castile there was no such stink. They had offered to this idol five hearts from the day's sacrifices. . . .

---

[4] Also called La Malinche, she served as Cortés's interpreter, secretary, confidant, and mistress during the conquest of the Aztec empire. Born into a noble Aztec family (and thus a native speaker of Nahuatl, the language of the Aztecs), La Malinche had been sold into slavery to Mayan-speaking people. Cortés's first landfall had been in Mayan-speaking areas, where he ransomed Jeronimo de Aguilar, a Catholic priest who had been shipwrecked years previously and held as a slave, during which time he learned Mayan. Shortly afterward, La Malinche was among twenty young female slaves presented to Cortés (who had them converted to Christianity and baptized, at which time La Malinche received the name Doña Marina). When Cortés arrived in the Aztec empire and encountered Nahuatl-speaking people, he learned of La Malinche's ability to speak the language. Thus, Jeronimo de Aguilar translated Cortés's Spanish into Mayan, and La Malinche translated the Mayan into Nahuatl so that Cortés could communicate with the Aztec emperor.

There was a tremendous drum there, and when they beat it the sound was as dismal as an instrument from hell and could be heard more than two leagues away. They said that it was covered with the skins of very large snakes. In that small place there were many diabolical things to see, horns, trumpets, knives, hearts that had been burned in incense before their idols, and all crusted with blood. I cursed the whole of it. It stank like a slaughterhouse, and we hurried to get away from such a bad smell and worse sight.

Our captain said to Montezuma, half laughingly, "Lord Montezuma, I do not understand how such a great prince and wise man as yourself can have failed to come to the conclusion that these idols of yours are not gods, but evil things— devils is the term for them. So that you and your priests may see it clearly, do me a favor: Let us put a cross on top of this tower, and in one part of these oratories, where your Uichilobos and Tezcatepuca are, we will set up an image of Our Lady [an image that Montezuma had already seen], and you will see how afraid of it these idols that have deceived you are."

The two priests with Montezuma looked hostile, and Montezuma replied with annoyance, "Señor Malinche [Cortés], if I had thought that you would so insult my gods, I would not have shown them to you. We think they are very good, for they give us health, water, good seed-times and weather, and all the victories we desire. We must worship and make sacrifices to them. Please do not say another word to their dishonor."

When our captain heard this and saw how changed Montezuma was, he didn't argue with him any more, but smiled and said, "It is time for Your Highness and ourselves to go."

Montezuma agreed, but he said that before he left he had to pray and make certain offerings to atone for the great sin he had committed in permitting us to climb the great *cu* and see his gods, and for being the cause of the dishonor that we had done them by speaking ill of them.

Cortés said, "If it is really like that, forgive me, sir."

QUESTIONS FOR ANALYSIS

1. According to Díaz, how does Montezuma seek to impress the Spaniards? What impresses Díaz?

2. How does Díaz's description of Tenochtitlán compare to Columbus's description of the Arawak people (Source 1)? Combining Cortés's description of the Aztec political system (Source 3) with Díaz's description of Tenochtitlán, what image is created of Aztec civilization?

3. Which Aztec religious objects would have been familiar to Díaz as a Catholic? How does Díaz use Christian images of evil to describe the Aztec temple?

4. How can Díaz's description of the Aztec be seen as a response to those who criticized the severity of the conquest?

5

Images of the Encounter: German Woodcut of 1505 and Spanish Incan Woodcut (c. 1600)

After the European arrival in the Americas, both Europeans and Amerindians used traditional visual forms to represent aspects, or imagined aspects, of their encounters. As stories of the explorers' adventures circulated in Europe, European artists drew images of the indigenous people, often to accompany printed texts. One of the most popular and lurid themes in exploration literature was cannibalism, which was condemned as a savage and barbaric practice by Christian Renaissance intellectuals. The German woodcut of 1505 marks the first significant depiction in Europe of the peoples of the

GERMAN WOODCUT OF 1505

**WOODCUT FROM THE FIRST NEW CHRONICLE
AND GOOD GOVERNMENT**
*The Amerindian asks what Spaniards eat.
The Spaniard replies, "Gold and Silver."*

Americas and their lives. The caption accompanying the image (not shown) reads, in part, "They also eat one another, even those who are slain, and singe their flesh in the smoke."

The woodcut from The First New Chronicle and Good Government *was drawn by Felipe Guaman Poma de Ayala (c. 1530s–c. 1620), who was born of a Spanish father and a Peruvian mother descended from the Inca nobility. About the time of Guaman Poma's birth, the Spaniard Francisco Pizarro conquered the Inca empire that dominated the central Andean region (see Map 1.1). Raised in Inca society but working frequently for Spanish and Catholic officials, Guaman Poma saw terrible abuses inflicted by the Spanish colonial regime. Beginning in the 1580s and drawing on stories he had heard of the Inca past and of its conquest, Guaman Poma wrote* The First

New Chronicle and Good Government, *a rambling text of 800 pages and 400 full-page illustrations that freely mixed Spanish and Quecha, the language of the Andean people. The text, written to the king of Spain, presents an idealized Andean past over-thrown by a brutal and unjust colonial regime that fails to implement the ideals of its Christian beliefs. In the image, Guaman Poma comments directly on the initial arrival of the Spanish.*

QUESTIONS FOR ANALYSIS

1. How does the German woodcut's depiction of the Amerindian men and women compare to the European descriptions in Sources 1, 3, and 4? In what activities are the people engaged? What does the artist accomplish by mixing familiar with unfamiliar activities?

2. What could a sixteenth-century viewer of the German woodcut conclude about the peoples of the Americas and about the practice of cannibalism?

3. How does Guaman Poma's depiction of the initial encounter between the Inca and Spanish suggest the possibility of peace? How does it suggest a different future?

4. How do both images use food as a significant symbol?

THE AMERICAS IN EUROPE

As Europeans intruded into the Americas, the Americas also intruded into Europe. Europeans returned to their homelands with the products of the Americas—its plants, animals, and other commodities of value—as well as ideas about the Americans. Europeans across the social spectrum found their lives—the foods they ate, the economies in which they worked, and the wars in which they fought—affected by the Americas. European states quickly had to craft policies to oversee their growing empires. Political rivalries in Europe and conflicting religious and economic interests in the Americas, however, created difficulties as European statesmen sought to set the process of colonization within European political, legal, and ethical traditions. A central issue in these debates was the status of the indigenous peoples of the Americas. A papal bull of 1537 by Pope Paul III definitively declared the Amerindians to be human; however, whether they were civilized, a status that carried political and legal implications, and whether they could be enslaved became matters of significant debate. According to Roman law, all people were free in a state of nature, but human conventions, historical accidents, and environment had rendered some free, some slaves, and some slaves by nature. These terms of Roman law, European Renaissance conceptions of civilization (which drew heavily from Roman and Greek sources), and Christian concerns with salvation framed much of the debate over the Amerindians.

Renaissance authors and philosophers also saw an opportunity to write their own ideas and thoughts on this "unknown page." At first, authors such as Peter Martyr d'Anghera (1457–1526) collected stories from those returning from the Americas and published them in sensational works. In *Decades of the New World*, Martyr duly recounted stories of savagery and cruelty by the Amerindians but generally presented the indigenous people as enjoying a blissful paradise. Soon, more sophisticated authors took up the Americas as a literary motif and crafted imaginative accounts of this unknown world and its meaning for Europe.

6

"... THE INDIAN DISEASE ..."

Roger Schlesinger
In the Wake of Columbus   (1996)

The historian Roger Schlesinger has written extensively on the interactions between cultures and civilizations in the Renaissance. In the excerpt below, he considers the impact of the Americas on European daily life.

For millions of ordinary Europeans, the exploration and conquest of America meant a more varied and nutritious diet and new medicines, but also a new and terrifying disease. The ways in which Europeans responded to these positive and negative elements in their lives provide valuable insights about European attitudes towards America and help define more precisely the nature of the American impact on all levels of European society. . . .

The basic diet of Europeans before 1492 had remained rather constant for a very long time. Indeed, it had been established in the period following the Neolithic era (approximately 20,000 B.C. to 10,000 B.C.) and consisted primarily of wheat, barley, oats, and rye. In the wake of Columbus's voyages all of this changed. The European diet became rich and varied. Just consider this list of products that originated in America and found their way, eventually, into Europeans' lives: maize (corn), various kinds of beans (especially "French" beans and lima beans), peanuts, potatoes, sweet potatoes, manioc (cassava and tapioca), squashes, pumpkins, papaya, guava, avocado, pineapple, tomatoes, red and green chile peppers, chocolate, turkey, vanilla, and, unfortunately, tobacco. Most of these items came from Central and South America. In the early sixteenth century, North America also provided a great abundance and new varieties of fish (as well as animal furs and timber). Collectively, these products made the single most valuable addition to Europe's ability to produce food since the very beginnings of agriculture. As far as dietary habits are concerned, no other series of events in all world history brought as much significant change as did European overseas expansion. . . .

Roger Schlesinger, *In the Wake of Columbus: The Impact of the New World on Europe, 1492–1650* (Wheeling, Ill.: Harlan Davidson, 1996), 81–82, 85–86, 100–102.

Perhaps no American food is a better illustration of some of the strange notions that Europeans had about American foods than the tomato. The first written mention of the tomato appeared in a commentary on the ancient Greek botanist Dioscorides[1] by Petrus Matthiolus[2] in 1544. He considered the tomato a species of mandrake recently brought to Italy and prepared like eggplant. . . .

By the 1570s, tomatoes had acquired an excellent reputation for medicinal properties. The Italian Melchior Guilandini[3] declared that they were useful as treatments for rheumatism and similar ailments, and German medical authorities agreed. In 1588, for example, Joachim Camerarius[4] said that it was effective against scabies (a highly contagious skin disease). For his part, J. T. Tabernaemontanus[5] thought that tomato juice was an effective remedy for St. Anthony's fire[6] and other "fluxes."[7] Other experts, no doubt influenced by the plant's erroneous Latin name (*pomum amoris*), concluded that it must be an aphrodisiac, or at least so beautiful as to "command love." How else could it have acquired the name love apple?

Sixteenth-century Europeans had little interest in the food value of tomatoes. Generally, they considered them nothing more than a curiosity with some ornamental value. . . .

Questions of how and why syphilis suddenly appeared in Europe at the end of the fifteenth century are among the most controversial problems in the history of medicine. In general, there are two competing theories about its origins. Some scholars contend that Columbus brought syphilis back to Europe from America in 1493, but others believe that the strain of venereal syphilis which struck Renaissance Europe had existed there long before the voyages of exploration. Neither of these interpretations has completely conquered its rival, however, so the debate continues even today. For sixteenth-century Europeans, on the other hand, these issues did not appear to be nearly so difficult to solve. From the 1490s, they believed that a new disease had swept across Europe, and they named it according to the supposed place of origin. For example, the French called it the Neapolitan[8] disease; the Italians and Germans called it the French disease; and the English called it the French or the Spanish disease. Everybody blamed the appearance of the disease on an alien group—they just could not agree on which one.

Among these terms for syphilis, "Spanish disease" is the most fascinating because it indicates what Europeans came to believe about the ultimate origin of the affliction. In 1518, a quarter of a century after the fact, a book published in Venice

---

[1] Pedanius Dioscorides (40–c. 90), Greek physician and botanist.
[2] Pier Andrea Mattioli (1501–1577), Italian physician and botanist.
[3] Melchior Wieland [Guilandini/Guilandinus] (1520–1589), German botanist who spent most of his adult life in Italy.
[4] Joachim Camerarius (1534–1598), German physician and botanist.
[5] Jacob Theodorus Tabernaemontanus (c. 1522–1590), German physician and botanist.
[6] Illness common in the era caused by a fungus that grows on rye bread. Victims had the sensation of being burned at the stake, before their fingers, toes, hands, and feet dropped off and madness ensued.
[7] General term for ailments that caused fluids to flow from the body.
[8] Naples, Italy.

first mentioned the theory that a "Spanish disease" had been imported from America (or the West Indies) by sailors who accompanied Columbus on his first voyage in 1492–93. Indeed, two of the most important historians of the early Spanish empire in America, Bartolomé de Las Casas[9] and Gonzalo Fernández de Oviedo,[10] both asserted that members of Columbus's crew had brought syphilis to Europe from America. Oviedo, himself, made several voyages to the West Indies and reported that he had found evidence of the new disease among Native Americans, and Las Casas claimed that the natives had told him that they had known the disease before the arrival of the Europeans. Both historians noted that the sickness appeared to be much less dangerous for the infected natives than for the Spaniards, a contrast one might expect if one group had long contact and exposure to it and the other none at all. . . .

By placing the origins of this disease in America, Europeans tried to incorporate it into their society with as little trauma as possible. They found some comfort in believing that syphilis, as an evil, came from a foreign place—at first a nearby country (hence, the French, Spanish, English disease), and then better yet, from a distant and alien territory (America), inhabited by an "enemy." By attributing the origin of syphilis to Native Americans, then, Europeans were undoubtedly suggesting that the origins of the sickness (or evil), which was tied to sexual excess, was located as far from European civilization as possible—in the totally alien, and for them, heathen civilization of Native Americans. Moreover, the fact that the disease attacked its victims' sexual organs fit nicely with the Europeans' tendency to stereotype Native Americans as extremely lustful people. For example, Amerigo Vespucci,[11] who provided Europeans with many of their earliest images of Native American life, wrote that Native Americans had as many wives as they desired and lived in promiscuity without regard to blood relations. Mothers lie with sons, he wrote, and brothers with sisters. Oviedo gave a similar account that frequently emphasized the libidinous habits of the women in the Americas. He certainly had no doubts about the origin of syphilis and thought it should be called the "Indian disease."

QUESTIONS FOR ANALYSIS

1. According to Schlesinger, what positive benefits accrued to Europeans as a result of their interaction with the Americas? What negative consequences?

2. How does Schlesinger's description of the European adoption of American plant and animal products compare to Columbus's reaction to the American environment (Source 1)?

3. According to Schlesinger, what role did sexuality play in the European conception of Amerindian society? How did Europeans' understanding of the tomato reinforce this issue?

---

[9] Bartolomé de Las Casas (1474–1566), Spanish cleric who helped to preserve Columbus's record of his voyages.
[10] Gonzalo Fernández de Oviedo y Valdés (1478–1557), Spanish chronicler of the early voyages to the Americas.
[11] Amerigo Vespucci (1454–1512), Italian merchant and explorer of the Americas.

4. How did Amerindians provide Europeans with an "explanation" of the outbreak of syphilis?

7

". . . AS MEN FROM BEASTS."

Juan Ginés de Sepúlveda
Democrates Secundus   (1544)

The public debate over the status of the Amerindians reached its peak in 1550, when Charles V, king of Spain and Holy Roman Emperor, ordered two of the leading contestants, Juan Ginés de Sepúlveda and Bartolomé de Las Casas (Source 8), to debate the issue at the University of Valladolid before a panel of lawyers and theologians. Sepúlveda (1490–1573), a scholar and theologian born into the Spanish aristocracy, argued that the Spanish, as a superior people, had the right to enslave the inferior Amerindians. The selection below from Sepúlveda's work Democrates Secundus or the Treatise on the Just Causes of War against the Indians *demonstrates how Sepúlveda defined the Spanish and Amerindian civilizations in relationship to one another to make his case.*

It is established then, in accordance with the authority of the most eminent thinkers, that the dominion of prudent, good, and humane men over those of contrary disposition is just and natural. Nothing else justified the legitimate empire of the Romans over other peoples, according to the testimony of St. Thomas[1] in his work on the rule of the Prince. St. Thomas here followed St. Augustine.[2] . . . God gave the Romans their empire so that, with the good legislation that they instituted and the virtue in which they excelled, they might change the customs and suppress and correct the vices of many barbarian peoples. . . .

[Therefore,] you can easily understand . . . if you are familiar with the character and moral code of the two peoples, that it is with perfect right that the Spaniards exercise their dominion over those barbarians of the New World and its adjacent islands. For in prudence, talent, and every kind of virtue and human sentiment they are as inferior to the Spaniards as children are to adults, or women to men, or the cruel and inhumane to the very gentle, or the excessively intemperate to the continent and moderate.

---

[1] Thomas Aquinas (c. 1225–1274), major Italian Christian theologian.
[2] Augustine (354–430), Christian bishop in Roman North Africa and major theologian.

Charles Gibson, ed., *The Spanish Tradition in America* (New York: Harper and Row, 1968), 115–20.

But I do not think that you expect me to speak of the prudence and talent of the Spaniards, for you have, I think, read Lucan, Silius Italicus, the two Senecas, and among later figures St. Isidore, who is inferior to none in theology, and Averroes and Avempace, who are excellent in philosophy, and in astronomy King Alfonso, not to mention others whom it would take too long to enumerate.[3] And who is ignorant of the Spaniards' other virtues: courage, humanity, justice, and religion? I refer simply to the princes and to those whose aid and skill they utilize to govern the state, to those, in short, who have received a liberal education. . . .

As for the Christian religion, I have witnessed many clear proofs of the firm roots it has in the hearts of Spaniards, even those dedicated to the military. . . . What shall I say of the Spanish soldiers' gentleness and humanitarian sentiments? Their only and greatest solicitude and care in the battles, after the winning of the victory, is to save the greatest possible number of vanquished and free them from the cruelty of their allies. Now compare these qualities of prudence, skill, magnanimity, moderation, humanity, and religion with those of those little men [of America] in whom one can scarcely find any remnants of humanity. They not only lack culture but do not even use or know about writing or preserve records of their history—save for some obscure memory of certain deeds contained in painting. They lack written laws and their institutions and customs are barbaric. And as for their virtues, if you wish to be informed of their moderation and mildness, what can be expected of men committed to all kinds of passion and nefarious lewdness and of whom not a few are given to the eating of human flesh. Do not believe that their life before the coming of the Spaniards was one of Saturnine[4] peace, of the kind that poets sang about. On the contrary, they made war with each other almost continuously, and with such fury that they considered a victory to be empty if they could not satisfy their prodigious hunger with the flesh of their enemies. This form of cruelty is especially prodigious among these people, remote as they are from the invincible ferocity of the Scythians,[5] who also ate human bodies. But in other respects they are so cowardly and timid that they can scarcely offer any resistance to the hostile presence of our side, and many times thousands and thousands of them have been dispersed and have fled like women, on being defeated by a small Spanish force scarcely amounting to one hundred.

So as not to detain you longer in this matter, consider the nature of those people in one single instance and example, that of the Mexicans, who are regarded as the most prudent and courageous. Their king was Montezuma, whose empire extended the length and breadth of those regions and who inhabited the city of Mexico. . . . Informed of the arrival of Cortés and of his victories and his intention to go to Mexico under pretext of a conference, Montezuma sought all possible means to divert him from his plan. Failing in this, terrorized and filled with fear, he received him in the city with about three hundred Spaniards. Cortés for his part,

---

[3] All scholars of Spanish origin, although the birthplace of Silius Italicus is debated.
[4] Steady, slow to act or change.
[5] Ancient, nomadic Indo-European people originally from central Asia who moved into southern Russia in the eighth and ninth centuries B.C.

after taking possession of the city, held the people's cowardliness, ineptitude, and rudeness in such contempt that he not only compelled the king and his principal subjects, through terror, to receive the yoke and rule of the king of Spain, but also imprisoned King Montezuma himself. . . . Could there be a better or clearer testimony of the superiority that some men have over others in talent, skill, strength of spirit, and virtue? Is it not proof that they are slaves by nature? For the fact that some of them appear to have a talent for certain manual tasks is not argument for their greater human prudence. We see that certain insects, such as the bees and the spiders, produce works that no human skill can imitate. . . .

I have made reference to the customs and character of the barbarians. What shall I say now of the impious religion and wicked sacrifices of such people, who, in venerating the devil as if he were God, believed that the best sacrifice that they could placate him with was to offer him human hearts? . . . Opening up the human breasts they pulled out the hearts and offered them on their heinous altars. And believing that they had made a ritual sacrifice with which to placate their gods, they themselves ate the flesh of the victims. These are crimes that are considered by the philosophers to be among the most ferocious and abominable perversions, exceeding all human iniquity. And as for the fact that some nations, according to report, completely lack religion and knowledge of God, what else is this than to deny the existence of God and to live like beasts? In my judgment this crime is the most serious, infamous, and unnatural. . . . How can we doubt that these people—so uncivilized, so barbaric, contaminated with so many impieties and obscenities—have been justly conquered by such an excellent, pious, and just king, as Ferdinand was and as the Emperor Charles is now, and by a nation excellent in every kind of virtue, with the best law and best benefit for the barbarians? Prior to the arrival of the Christians they had the nature, customs, religion, and practice of evil sacrifice as we have explained. Now, on receiving with our rule our writing, laws, and morality, imbued with the Christian religion, having shown themselves to be docile to the missionaries that we have sent them, as many have done, they are as different from their primitive condition as civilized people are from barbarians, or as those with sight from the blind, as the inhuman from the meek, as the pious from the impious, or to put it in a single phrase, in effect, as men from beasts.

QUESTIONS FOR ANALYSIS

1. What are the basic premises of Sepúlveda's argument that superior peoples may enslave inferior peoples? What does he mean by calling the Amerindians "slaves by nature"?

2. What does Sepúlveda identify as the virtues of the Spaniards and the deficiencies of the Amerindians? What proof does he offer for his assertions?

3. For Sepúlveda, what characteristics or practices identify an advanced people?

4. How do Sepúlveda's characterization of the Aztec people compare to the characterizations by Díaz (Source 4) and Cortés (Source 3)?

8

"THE INDIAN RACE IS NOT THAT BARBARIC. . . ."

Bartolomé de Las Casas
In Defense of the Indians   (1551)

Opposing Sepúlveda in the debate at the University of Valladolid (Source 7) was Bartolomé de Las Casas (1474–1566). Born to a family of small merchants, Las Casas spent thirteen years in the Spanish colony of Hispaniola. In 1514, however, he renounced all his property rights in America and returned to Spain, where he eventually took religious orders and passionately lobbied the Spanish government to provide greater protections to the Amerindians. The selection that follows is part of Las Casas's response to Sepúlveda at the Valladolid debate, in which Las Casas, working within a European framework of thought, challenges both Sepúlveda's knowledge of the Amerindians and his philosophical principals.

[T]he distinction the Philosopher[1] makes between the two . . . kinds of barbarian is evident. For those he deals with in the first book of the *Politics* . . . are barbarians without qualification, in the proper and strict sense of the word, that is, dull witted and lacking in the reasoning powers necessary for self-government. They are without laws, without king, etc. For this reason they are by nature unfitted for rule.

However, he admits, and proves, that the barbarians he deals with in the third book of the same work have a lawful, just, and natural government. Even though they lack the art and use of writing, they are not wanting in the capacity and skill to rule and govern themselves, both publicly and privately. Thus they have kingdoms, communities, and cities that they govern wisely according to their laws and customs. . . . This is made clear by the Philosopher and Augustine.[2] . . .

Now if we shall have shown that among our Indians of the western and southern shores[3] (granting that we call them barbarians and that they are barbarians) there are important kingdoms, large numbers of people who live settled lives in a society, great cities, kings, judges and laws, persons who engage in commerce, buying, selling, lending, and the other contracts of the law of nations, will it not stand proved that the Reverend Doctor Sepúlveda has spoken wrongly and viciously against peoples like these, either out of malice or ignorance of Aristotle's teaching, and, therefore, has falsely and perhaps irreparably slandered them before the entire world? From the fact that the Indians are barbarians it does not necessarily follow

---

[1] Aristotle (384–322 B.C.), Greek philosopher.
[2] Augustine (354–430), Christian bishop in Roman North Africa and major theologian.
[3] Central and South America.

Bartolomé de Las Casas, *In Defense of the Indians,* ed. and trans. Stafford Poole (De Kalb: Northern Illinois University Press, 1974), 41–46.

that they are incapable of government and have to be ruled by others, except to be taught about the Catholic faith and to be admitted to the holy sacraments. They are not ignorant, inhuman, or bestial. Rather, long before they had heard the word Spaniard they had properly organized states, wisely ordered by excellent laws, religion, and custom. They cultivated friendship and, bound together in common fellowship, lived in populous cities in which they wisely administered the affairs of both peace and war justly and equitably, truly governed by laws that at very many points surpass ours, and could have won the admiration of the sages of Athens. . . .

I would like to hear Sepúlveda, in his cleverness, answer this question: Does he think that the war of the Romans against the Spanish[4] was justified in order to free them from barbarism? And this question also: Did the Spanish wage an unjust war when they vigorously defended themselves against them?

Next, I call the Spaniards who plunder that unhappy people torturers. Do you think that the Romans, once they had subjugated the wild and barbaric peoples of Spain, could with secure right divide all of you among themselves, handing over so many head of both males and females as allotments to individuals? And do you then conclude that the Romans could have stripped your rulers of their authority and consigned all of you, after you had been deprived of your liberty, to wretched labors, especially in searching for gold and silver lodes and mining and refining the metals? And if the Romans finally did that, as is evident from Diodorus,[5] [would you not judge] that you also have the right to defend your freedom, indeed your very life, by war? Sepúlveda, would you have permitted Saint James to evangelize your own people of Córdoba in that way? For God's sake and man's faith in him, is this the way to impose the yoke of Christ on Christian men? Is this the way to remove wild barbarism from the minds of barbarians? Is it not, rather, to act like thieves, cut-throats, and cruel plunderers and to drive the gentlest of people headlong into despair? The Indian race is not that barbaric, nor are they dull witted or stupid, but they are easy to teach and very talented in learning all the liberal arts, and very ready to accept, honor, and observe the Christian religion and correct their sins (as experience has taught) once priests have introduced them to the sacred mysteries and taught them the word of God. They have been endowed with excellent conduct, and before the coming of the Spaniards, as we have said, they had political states that were well founded on beneficial laws.

Furthermore, they are so skilled in every mechanical art that with every right they should be set ahead of all the nations of the known world on this score, so very beautiful in their skill and artistry are the things this people produces in the grace of its architecture, its painting, and its needlework. But Sepúlveda despises these mechanical arts, as if these things do not reflect inventiveness, ingenuity, industry, and right reason. For a mechanical art is an operative habit of the intellect that is usually defined as "the right way to make things, directing the acts of the reason, through which the artisan proceeds in orderly fashion, easily, and unerringly in the very act of reason." So these men are not stupid, Reverend Doctor. Their skillfully

---

[4] Ancient Rome's conquest of the Iberian Peninsula.
[5] Diodorus Siculus (1st century B.C.), Greek historian who wrote a history of the world.

fashioned works of superior refinement awaken the admiration of all nations, because works proclaim a man's talent....

In the liberal arts that they have been taught up to now, such as grammar and logic, they are remarkably adept. With every kind of music they charm the ears of their audience with wonderful sweetness. They write skillfully and quite elegantly, so that most often we are at a loss to know whether the characters are handwritten or printed.... I have seen [this] with my eyes, felt with my hands, and heard with my own ears while living a great many years among those peoples.

Now if Sepúlveda had wanted, as a serious man should, to know the full truth before he sat down to write with his mind corrupted by the lies of tyrants, he should have consulted the honest religious who have lived among those peoples for many years and know their endowments of character and industry, as well as the progress they have made in religion and morality....

As to the terrible crime of human sacrifice, which you exaggerate, see what Giovio[6] adds.... "The rulers of the Mexicans have a right to sacrifice living men to their gods, provided they have been condemned for a crime."...

From this it is clear that the basis for Sepúlveda's teaching that these people are uncivilized and ignorant is worse than false. Yet even if we were to grant that this race has no keenness of mind or artistic ability, certainly they are not, in consequence, obliged to submit themselves to those who are more intelligent and to adopt their ways, so that, if they refuse, they may be subdued by having war waged against them and be enslaved, as happens today. For men are obliged by the natural law to do many things they cannot be forced to do against their will. We are bound by the natural law to embrace virtue and imitate the uprightness of good men. No one, however, is punished for being bad unless he is guilty of rebellion. Where the Catholic faith has been preached in a Christian manner and as it ought to be, all men are bound by the natural law to accept it, yet no one is forced to accept the faith of Christ. No one is punished because he is sunk in vice, unless he is rebellious or harms the property and persons of others....

Therefore, not even a truly wise man may force an ignorant barbarian to submit to him, especially by yielding his liberty, without doing him an injustice. This the poor Indians suffer, with extreme injustice, against all the laws of God and of men and against the law of nature itself.

QUESTIONS FOR ANALYSIS

1. What is the basic premise of Las Casas's argument? How does Las Casas directly attack Sepúlveda's basic premise?

2. What does Las Casas assert are the positive qualities held by the Amerindians? What claims does he make about his sources of evidence?

3. For Las Casas, what marks a civilized people, and how do his criteria compare with Sepúlveda's?

4. The judges of the debate between Sepúlveda and Las Casas could not declare a winner. What aspects of Sepúlveda's and Las Casas's arguments would appeal

---

[6] Paolo Giovio (1486–1552), bishop of Nocera (southern Italy) and historian.

to them? Why does Las Casas raise the example of Rome's conquest of Spain under Caesar Augustus?

9

"THE LAWS OF NATURE GOVERN THEM STILL. . . ."

Michel de Montaigne
Of Cannibals   (1580s)

Between 1562 and 1598, France fell into a long and bloody civil war. Fought for both political and religious reasons, the Wars of Religion weakened France politically and left many French nobles searching for political stability. One such group of Frenchmen, called the politiques, *argued in favor of religious toleration and submission to a strong monarch as the best remedy for France's political ailments. One of the most influential* politiques *was Michel de Montaigne (1533–1592), a French nobleman, jurist, and government official whose greatest legacy was his writing. His most famous work,* Essays, *remains one of the most innovative and influential works in European literature. In one of his best-known essays, "Of Cannibals," Montaigne used the peoples of the Americas to make a stinging critique of the troubles of his own age in France.*

I had with me for a long time a man that had lived ten or twelve years in that other world which has been discovered in our century, in the place where Villegaignon landed, which he called Antarctic France.[1] This discovery of so vast a country seems worthy of consideration. I do not know if I can be sure that in the future there may not be another such discovery made, so many greater men than we having been deceived in this. I am afraid our eyes are bigger than our bellies and that we have more curiosity than capacity. We grasp at all, but catch nothing but wind. . . .

This man that I had was a plain ignorant fellow, which is a condition fit to bear true witness; for your sharp sort of men are much more curious in their observations and notice a great deal more, but they gloss them; and to give the greater weight to their interpretation and make it convincing, they cannot forbear to alter the story a little. . . . We should have a man either of irreproachable veracity, or so simple that he has not wherewithal to contrive and to give a color of truth to false tales, and who has not espoused any cause. Mine was such a one; and, besides that, he has divers times brought me several seamen and merchants whom he had known on that voyage. I do, therefore, content myself with his information without inquiring what the cosmographers say about it. . . .

---

[1] Nicholas Villegaignon (1510–1572) landed in Brazil in 1557.

Michel de Montaigne, *Montaigne: Selected Essays,* ed. Blanchard Bates (New York: Modern Library [Random House], 1949), 74, 77–79, 82–84.

I find that there is nothing barbarous and savage in this nation according to what I have been told, except that everyone gives the title of barbarism to everything that is not according to his usage; as, indeed, we have no other criterion of truth and reason than the example and pattern of the opinions and customs of the country wherein we live. There is always the perfect religion, there the perfect government, there the perfect and accomplished usage in all things. They are savages in the same way that we say fruits are wild, which nature produces of herself and by her ordinary course; whereas, in truth, we ought rather to call those wild whose natures we have changed by our artifice and diverted from the common order. In the former, the genuine, most useful, and natural virtues and properties are vigorous and active, which we have degenerated in the latter, and we have only adapted them to the pleasure of our corrupted palate. And yet, for all this, the flavor and delicacy found in various uncultivated fruits of those countries are excellent to our taste, worthy rivals of ours. . . .

These nations then seem to me to be barbarous so far as having received very little fashioning from the human mind and as being still very close to their original simplicity. The laws of Nature govern them still, very little vitiated by ours. . . . [I]t is a nation wherein there is no manner of traffic, no knowledge of letters, no science of numbers, no name of magistrate or of political superiority; no use of servitude, riches or poverty; no contracts, no successions, no dividing of properties, no employments, except those of leisure; no respect of kindred, except for the common bond; no clothing, no agriculture, no metal, no use of wheat or wine. The very words that signify lying, treachery, dissimulation, avarice, envy, detraction, and pardon were never heard of.[2] . . .

They have wars with the nations that live farther inland beyond their mountains, to which they go quite naked and without other arms than their bows and wooden swords pointed at one end like the points of our spears. The obstinacy of their battles is wonderful; they never end without slaughter and bloodshed; for as to running away and fear, they know not what it is. Everyone for a trophy brings home the head of an enemy he has killed and fixes it over the door of his house. After having a long time treated their prisoners well and with all the luxuries they can think of, he to whom the prisoner belongs forms a great assembly of his acquaintances. He ties a rope to one of the arms of the prisoner, by the end of which he holds him some paces away for fear of being struck, and gives to the friend he loves best the other arm to hold in the same manner; and they two, in the presence of all the assembly, dispatch him with their swords. After that they roast him and eat him among them and send some pieces to their absent friends. They do not do this, as some think, for nourishment, as the Scythians[3] anciently did, but as a representation of an extreme revenge. And its proof is that having observed that the Portuguese, who were in league with their enemies, inflicted another sort of death on them when they captured them, which was to bury them up to the waist, shoot the rest of the body full of arrows, and then hang them; they thought that these people from the other world (as men who had sown the knowledge of a great many

---

[2] A 1603 translation of this passage into English is quoted almost word for word in William Shakespeare's *The Tempest* (act 2, scene 1).
[3] Ancient, nomadic people originally from central Asia who moved into southern Russia in the eighth and ninth centuries B.C.

vices among their neighbors and were much greater masters in all kind of wickedness than they) did not exercise this sort of revenge without reason, and that it must needs be more painful than theirs, and they began to leave their old way and to follow this. I am not sorry that we should take notice of the barbarous horror of such acts, but I am sorry that, seeing so clearly into their faults, we should be so blind to our own. I conceive there is more barbarity in eating a man alive than in eating him dead, in tearing by tortures and the rack a body that is still full of feeling, in roasting him by degrees, causing him to be bitten and torn by dogs and swine (as we have not only read, but lately seen, not among inveterate enemies, but among neighbors and fellow-citizens, and what is worse, under color of piety and religion), than in roasting and eating him after he is dead. . . .

We may, then, well call these people barbarians in respect to the rules of reason, but not in respect to ourselves, who, in all sorts of barbarity, exceed them. Their warfare is in every way noble and generous and has as much excuse and beauty as this human malady is capable of; it has with them no other foundation than the sole jealousy of valor. Their disputes are not for the conquests of new lands, for they still enjoy that natural abundance that supplies them without labor and trouble with all things necessary in such abundance that they have no need to enlarge their borders. And they are still in that happy stage of desiring only as much as their natural necessities demand; all beyond that is superfluous to them.

QUESTIONS FOR ANALYSIS

1. How does Montaigne establish his humility? What does he say are the characteristics of a barbarian?
2. How do Montaigne's claims about the source of his knowledge compare to Las Casas's claims of knowledge about the Amerindians (Source 8)? How do these claims indicate sources of knowledge that could challenge the Roman Catholic church's traditional control of knowledge and learning?
3. According to Montaigne, how do Europeans act more savagely than Amerindians? What marks Amerindians as virtuous and Europeans as unvirtuous?
4. Do the real indigenous peoples of the Americas matter to Montaigne? What are the implications of this?

CHAPTER QUESTIONS

1. In the preceding sources, what were the most common European reactions to Amerindian civilizations? What was the range of reactions?
2. When encountering this unknown world, how did European cultural and intellectual traditions, economic desires, and political experiences shape Europeans' efforts to understand and define Amerindians? How did Amerindians influence Europeans' conceptions of them?
3. What fictions did Europeans create about the Americas? How did these colonial fictions justify European supremacy over Amerindians?

Chapter 2

CHALLENGES TO CHRISTENDOM IN REFORMATION EUROPE

Western Christendom—the lands that officially practiced Christianity and shared a common Latin clerical culture, intellectual tradition, and, until the Reformation, recognition of Roman papal authority over spiritual affairs—believed itself under siege in the sixteenth and seventeenth centuries. The Muslim Ottoman Turks had expanded power rapidly in the fifteenth century, and in the 1520s, Sultan Suleiman the Magnificent led Ottoman armies to the gates of Vienna and seized land throughout southeastern Europe. Europeans were not only terrified by the armies of Suleiman, whom they called the "scourge of God," but scandalized that some European princes and monarchs allied with the Muslim Turks against their princely Christian rivals in Europe. Christendom, it seemed, would no longer unify in opposition to the "infidel Muslims."

Challenges to Christendom not only arrived from outside "the Faith" but also sprang from among the Christian faithful. During the fifteenth and sixteenth centuries, many church officials, scholars, and secular leaders called for reforms of the spiritual and financial corruption that had become widespread in the Roman Catholic church. Out of this reformist tradition emerged a religious revolution called the Reformation, initiated in 1517 by the Catholic monk Martin Luther. Luther, as others before him, called for serious religious reforms; however, his fierce "protests" against what he believed to be abuses of papal authority—and the pope's unequivocal rejection of such calls for reform—led to a rupture in Christendom. Various "protestant" denominations formed that severed allegiance to the papacy and altered, to varying degrees, clerical culture and intellectual traditions. With the aid of the newly invented printing press, the ideas and arguments of Protestants and Catholics circulated far beyond traditional clerical circles. Protestants and Catholics crafted arguments to appeal to the urban, literate audiences who followed Reformation debates and influenced local religious policies. In their debates, pastors and priests drew on traditional prejudices and assumptions, including the commonly perceived threat to Christendom posed by Europe's Jewish population. Both Catholics and Protestants sought to discredit one another with accusations of "Jewish tendencies" or sympathies. Further, they linked the religious threat of either Catholicism or Protestantism with the military threat of the Ottoman Turks, suggesting a Christendom under siege from both within and without (Map 2.1).

Christendom also faced challenges in a different quarter—its traditional control over learning and knowledge. The medieval church had allowed scholars—nearly all of whom where clerics—considerable latitude to discuss and debate ideas as long as those ideas remained within the framework of Christian thought and the church remained the final arbiter of knowledge. Scholars were expected to

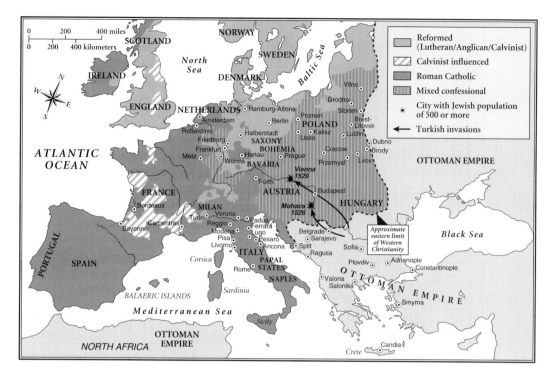

MAP 2.1 REFORMATION EUROPE, C. 1550

By the mid-sixteenth century, Western Christendom had fractured into conflicting religious confessions and was responding to growing Ottoman Muslim power. The Ottoman leader Sultan Suleiman the Magnificent effectively played on political and religious conflicts among Europeans in expanding Ottoman power.

define their ideas by using Christian scriptures and recognized religious authorities and to situate their ideas within the structures of Christian theology. In the sixteenth and seventeenth centuries, however, the church's control over scholarship came under significant challenge, led by the natural philosophers—scholars who studied the workings of nature. As European "scientists" reconsidered nature, they began to challenge the medieval church's "truth" about how the universe functioned. Because European natural philosophers recognized that research into nature that contradicted religious doctrine would meet with a hostile reception, most supported the Christian faith and sought to establish their scientific labors as part of a Christian investigation of the natural world that reaffirmed and supported rather than undermined the Christian faith. Western society thereafter would still be identified as "Christian" but also increasingly as "scientific." Between the challenges of the Protestant movement and the challenges of the scientific revolution, the idea of Christendom—a Christian Europe unified by faith and obedience to a single religious authority—weakened but certainly did not vanish as a central component to Western civilization.

CHRISTENDOM AND REFORMATION

The Protestant Reformation occurred at the same time that the empire of the Muslim Ottoman Turks was offering its greatest threat to Christendom. As Suleiman the Magnificent led his troops to the gates of Vienna, the direction of the Crusades seemed to have been reversed. Rather than capturing the Holy Lands, Europeans now struggled to repel the "infidel" invader. Yet at the same time, Europe was also in a fierce international struggle. The Habsburg monarch Charles V had established the largest European empire since Charlemagne eight hundred years earlier, holding the crowns of both Spain and the Holy Roman Empire. The French Valois dynasty suddenly found itself encircled and seeking allies, including the "infidel Turks," to resist its traditional Habsburg rivals. These political conflicts bore heavily on the Reformation as Protestants and Catholics interpreted Turkish threats and successes through their own theological lenses. Certainly, all parties argued, the Turkish victories must indicate some failing on the part of Christendom. Partisans of both sides offered conflicting opinions through everything from scholarly treatises to comical woodcuts and cartoons, the latter especially important as the Reformation debates reached downward in the social hierarchy. Both Protestants and Catholics indulged in fiery, outlandish language to build support for their causes and drew on popular prejudices, resentments, and fears toward the Turks and toward Europe's persecuted religious minority—the Jews.

1

"THE CLUB THEY ARE BEATEN WITH, THEY COUNT SACRED."

Ogier Ghiselin de Busbecq
Travels into Turkey (c. 1561)

Ogier Ghiselin de Busbecq (1522–1590), a Flemish nobleman, served as a diplomat for the Holy Roman Emperors Charles V and Ferdinand I and in 1555 was assigned to Constantinople, the capital of the Muslim Ottoman empire. During Busbecq's seven years in Turkey, the Ottoman empire was ruled by Suleiman the Magnificent (c. 1496–1566), an active military leader who expanded his empire into southeastern Europe. During his years in Turkey, Busbecq wrote four long letters to a friend and fellow diplomat, seeking to impress his friend by contrasting the victorious military of the Ottoman state with the disorganized, undisciplined mercenary armies on which European princes relied. Although these letters were written after the Reformation had begun, they identify the Turkish menace to Christendom that had pervaded throughout the preceding decades.

Ogier Busbecq, *Travels into Turkey*, 3rd ed. (Glasgow, 1761), 179–80, 183–84.

I lived [in a Turkish military camp] three months, and had an opportunity to view the camp of the Turks, which was extended all over the neighboring fields, and to discover some parts of their discipline. . . . I clothed myself as Christians do in that country, and with one or two attendants walked up and down their camp *incognito.* The first thing I saw, was, the soldiers of each unit quartered with great order in their several ranks, and that with a great deal of silence, (it is far otherwise in Christian camps) all hush; not a quarrel, nor the least disorder or noise amongst them in their jollities. Besides they are wonderfully cleanly; no dunghill or noisome smell to offend the eye or ear; all their ordure they bury under ground, or throw it far enough off. When they have occasion to ease nature, they dig a pit with a spade, and there bury their excrements; so that there is no ill smell at all. Besides, there are no drinking matches amongst them, no playing with cards or dice (the bane of the Christian army!). . . . The Turks are of opinion, that no souls go more directly to heaven, than those of valiant men, who lost their lives in the field; and that virgins do pour out daily prayers to God for their safety. . . .

They use wine at no time of the year, they count it profane and irreligious so to do; especially, they abhor it on their fasts;[1] then no man is so much as to smell it, much less to taste it. . . . For this reason all was quiet in the camp, and the greatest composure imaginable, especially at the feast-time: so much did camp-discipline, and a strictness, received from their ancestors, prevail upon them!

The Turks punish all vice and wickedness very severely; their punishments are, loss of their places, sale of their goods, thrashing with clubs, death: but club-thrashing is most common, from which the Janissaries[2] themselves are not free; though they may not, as such, be put to death. Their lighter offences are chastised by the club; their more heinous by cashiering or degrading,[3] which they count worse than death, because commonly they are put to death afterwards; for being stripped of the ensigns of Janissaries, they are banished to the farthest garrison of the empire, where they live contemptible and inglorious, till, upon any light occasion, they are put to death; yet not as Janissaries, but as common soldiers only.

And here let me acquaint you with the patience of the Turks in receiving that punishment; they will receive sometimes an hundred blows on their legs, their feet and buttocks, with wonderful patience; so that diverse clubs are broke, and the executioner cries out, "Give me another!" Yea, sometimes the chastisement is so severe, that several pieces of torn flesh must be cut off from the wounded parts before any thing can be applied to cure them. Yet for all this, they must go to their officer, who commanded them to be punished; they must kiss his hand, and give him thanks; nay, they must also give the executioner a reward for beating them. The club they are beaten with, they count sacred.

---

[1] Muslims fast from dawn to sunset during the month of Ramadan.
[2] Janissaries comprised an enslaved elite in the Ottoman empire. Taken captive as boys, largely from Greek Orthodox Christian families, they were forced to convert to Islam and were trained and educated rigorously to fight for Islam and to administer the Ottoman empire.
[3] Either dismissal from the army or a reduction in military rank.

QUESTIONS FOR ANALYSIS

1. What characteristics of the Turks' military camp draw Busbecq's attention?
2. What does Busbecq identify as the reasons for Ottoman military superiority over the Christian army?
3. How does Busbecq's letter indicate the importance of religion to secular governments?
4. How is the image of "the Turkish menace" reinforced by Busbecq's comments?

2

"ONE THING, AND ONLY ONE THING, IS NECESSARY FOR CHRISTIAN LIFE. . . ."

Martin Luther
On Christian Liberty and *Address to the Christian Nobility of the German Nation*   (1520)

In 1517, Martin Luther (1483–1546) launched a reform movement within the Catholic church, attacking what he saw as abuses of papal authority. In 1520, Luther published two important works, On Christian Liberty *and* Address to the Christian Nobility of the German Nation. *In these works he challenged the doctrines and institutions of Roman Catholicism and sought support for his reform movement among the educated clergy and political leaders. In the first work, he addressed the most fundamental Christian doctrine—that of salvation—and distinguished his views from those of the Catholic church. Within Catholic theology, salvation occurred through the believer's faith in Christ and the performance of good works, especially the Sacraments—rituals such as baptism, confession, and penance that required the participation of an ordained priest. Thus Catholic officials controlled access to salvation, a position Luther thoroughly rejected. In the second work, he called on the German nobility to reform the church since the church hierarchy, Luther claimed, refused to reform itself. Through these works, Luther called into question the Roman Catholic identity of western Europe.*

On Christian Liberty

[L]et us consider the inner man to see how a righteous, free, and pious Christian, that is, a spiritual, new, and inner man, becomes what he is. It is evident that no external

---

Martin Luther, "The Freedom of a Christian," trans. W. A. Lambert, rev. Harold Grimm, in *Luther's Works.* Vol. 31, *Career of the Reformer: I,* ed. Harold Grimm (Philadelphia: Fortress Press, 1957), 344–47; Martin Luther, "To the Christian Nobility of the German Nation . . . ," trans. Charles M. Jacobs, rev. James Atkinson, in *Luther's Works.* Vol. 44, *The Christian in Society: I* (Philadelphia: Fortress Press, 1966), 124, 126–27, 129–31, 133–34, 136–39, 141, 143–44.

thing has any influence in producing Christian righteousness or freedom, or in producing unrighteousness or servitude. . . . It does not help the soul if the body is adorned with the sacred robes of priests or dwells in sacred places or is occupied with sacred duties or prays, fasts, abstains from certain kinds of food, or does any work that can be done by the body and in the body. The righteousness and the freedom of the soul require something far different since the things which have been mentioned could be done by any wicked person. Such works produce nothing but hypocrites. . . .

One thing, and only one thing, is necessary for Christian life, righteousness, and freedom. That one thing is the most holy Word of God, the gospel of Christ. . . .

You may ask, "What then is the Word of God . . . ?" I answer: The Apostle [Paul] explains this in Romans 1. The Word is the gospel of God concerning his Son, who was made flesh, suffered, rose from the dead, and was glorified through the Spirit who sanctifies. To preach Christ means to feed the soul, make it righteous, set it free, and save it, provided it believes the preaching. Faith alone is the saving and efficacious use of the Word of God, according to Rom. 10 [:9]: "If you confess with your lips that Jesus is Lord and believe in your heart that God raised him from the dead, you will be saved." . . . Therefore it is clear that, as the soul needs only the Word of God for its life and righteousness, so it is justified by faith alone and not any works; for if it could be justified by anything else, it would not need the Word, and consequently it would not need faith. . . .

Since, therefore, this faith can rule only in the inner man, as Rom. 10 [:10] says, "For man believes with his heart and so is justified," and since faith alone justifies, it is clear that the inner man cannot be justified, freed, or saved by any outer work or action at all, and that these works, whatever their character, have nothing to do with this inner man.

Address to the Christian Nobility of the German Nation

It is not from sheer impertinence or rashness that I, one poor man, have taken it upon myself to address your worships.[1] All the estates of Christendom, particularly in Germany, are now oppressed by distress and affliction, and this has stirred not only me but everybody else to cry out time and time again and to pray for help. . . .

The Romanists[2] have very cleverly built three walls around themselves. Hitherto they have protected themselves by these walls in such a way that no one has been able to reform them. As a result, the whole of Christendom has fallen abominably.

In the first place, when pressed by the temporal power[3] they have made decrees and declared that the temporal power had no jurisdiction over them, but that, on the contrary, the spiritual power is above the temporal. In the second place, when the attempt is made to reprove them with the Scriptures, they raise the objection that only the pope may interpret the Scriptures. In the third place, if threatened with a council, their story is that no one may summon a council but the pope. . . .

---

[1] The German nobility.
[2] Advocates of papal supremacy over secular authority.
[3] Those having authority over the affairs of the world, such as monarchs and nobles.

Let us begin by attacking the first wall. . . . Paul says in I Corinthians 12 [:12–13] that we are all one body, yet every member has its own work by which it serves the others. This is because we all have one baptism, one gospel, one faith, and are all Christians alike; for baptism, gospel, and faith alone make us spiritual and a Christian people. . . .

It follows from this argument that there is no true, basic difference between laymen and priests, princes and bishops, between religious and secular, except for the sake of office and work, but not for the sake of status. They are all of the spiritual estate, all are truly priests, bishops, and popes. . . .

Therefore, just as those who are now called "spiritual," that is, priests, bishops, or popes, are neither different from other Christians nor superior to them, except that they are charged with the administration of the word of God and the sacraments, which is their work and office, so it is with the temporal authorities. They bear the sword and rod in their hand to punish the wicked and protect the good. . . .

Consider for a moment how Christian is the decree which says that the temporal power is not above the "spiritual estate" and has no right to punish it. That is as much as to say that the hand shall not help the eye when it suffers pain. Is it not unnatural, not to mention un-Christian, that one member does not help another and prevent its destruction? In fact, the more honorable the member, the more the others ought to help. I say therefore that since the temporal power is ordained of God to punish the wicked and protect the good, it should be left free to perform its office in the whole body of Christendom without restriction and without respect to persons, whether it affects pope, bishops, priests, monks, nuns, or anyone else. . . .

For these reasons the temporal Christian authority ought to exercise its office without hindrance, regardless of whether it is pope, bishop, or priest whom it affects. Whoever is guilty, let him suffer. . . .

The second wall is still more loosely built and less substantial. The Romanists want to be the only masters of Holy Scripture, although they never learn a thing from the Bible all their life long. They assume the sole authority for themselves, and, quite unashamed, they play about with words before our very eyes, trying to persuade us that the pope cannot err in matters of faith,[4] regardless of whether he is righteous or wicked. . . . [I]f what they claim were true, why have Holy Scripture at all? Of what use is Scripture? Let us burn the Scripture and be satisfied with the unlearned gentlemen at Rome who possess the Holy Spirit! . . .

The third wall falls of itself when the first two are down. When the pope acts contrary to the Scriptures, it is our duty to stand by the Scriptures, to reprove him and to constrain him, according to the word of Christ. . . .

Therefore, when necessity demands it, and the pope is an offense to Christendom, the first man who is able should, as a true member of the whole body, do what he can to bring about a truly free council.[5] No one can do this so well as the temporal authorities, especially since they are also fellow-Christians, fellow-priests, fellow-members of the spiritual estate, fellow-lords over all things. . . .

---

[4] The Catholic church did not confirm the doctrine of papal infallibility until the nineteenth century; however, the claim had been made repeatedly since the Middles Ages.

[5] A church council free of papal control.

With this I hope that all this wicked and lying terror with which the Romanists have long intimidated and dulled our conscience has been overcome, and that they, just like all of us, shall be made subject to the sword.[6] . . .

Of what use to Christendom are those people called cardinals?[7] I shall tell you. Italy and Germany have many rich monasteries, foundations, benefices, and livings.[8] No better way has been discovered of bringing all these to Rome than by creating cardinals and giving them bishoprics, monasteries, and prelacies[9] for their own use and so overthrowing the worship of God. You can see that Italy is now almost a wilderness: monasteries in ruins, bishoprics despoiled, the prelacies and the revenues of all the churches drawn to Rome, cities decayed, land and people ruined because services are no longer held and the word of God is not preached. And why? Because the cardinals must have the income! No Turk could have devastated Italy and suppressed the worship of God so effectively!

Now that Italy is sucked dry, the Romanists are coming into Germany. They have made a gentle beginning. But let us keep our eyes open! Germany shall soon be like Italy. We have a few cardinals already. The "drunken Germans" are not supposed to understand what the Romanists are up to until there is not a bishopric, a monastery, a living, a benefice, not a red cent left. . . .

In former times German emperors and princes permitted the pope to receive annates[10] from all the benefices of the German nation. . . . This permission was given, however, so that by means of these large sums of money the pope might raise funds to fight against the Turks and infidels in defense of Christendom. . . . The popes have so far used the splendid and simple devotion of the German people—they have received this money for more than a hundred years and have now made it an obligatory tax and tribute, but they have not only accumulated no money, they have used it to endow many posts and positions at Rome and to provide salaries for these posts. . . .

When they pretend that they are about to fight the Turks, they send out emissaries to raise money. They often issue an indulgence[11] on the same pretext of fighting the Turks. They think that those half-witted Germans will always be gullible, stupid fools, and will just keep handing over money to them to satisfy their unspeakable greed. And they think this in spite of the fact that everybody knows that not a cent of the annates, or of the indulgence money, or of all the rest, is spent to fight the Turk. It all goes into their bottomless bag. They lie and deceive. They make laws and they make agreements with us, but they do not intend to keep a single letter of them. Yet all this is done in the holy names of Christ and St. Peter.

QUESTIONS FOR ANALYSIS

1. What Catholic religious beliefs and practices does Luther criticize? How does he criticize them?

---

[6] Subject to the authority of monarchs and nobles.

[7] Catholic official who serves as a member of the pope's council.

[8] Forms of church revenues or revenue-producing institutions.

[9] Church offices tied to control over certain church lands.

[10] Income from vacant benefices.

[11] A remittance of punishment in purgatory for one's sins. The sale of such remittances sparked Luther's initial efforts at church reform.

2. What different strategies does Luther use to build support for his arguments and his movement? What tone does Luther use in each of the two texts? Why might he have changed his tone for each audience?

3. What roles do ethnic identity and religious identity play in the texts? How does Luther's use of the Ottoman Turks to express fears similar to Busbecq's (Source 1)?

4. How do Luther's arguments challenge the idea of Christendom? What new kind of organizational structure for Christendom does Luther's argument suggest?

3

". . . DEFENDING CHRISTENDOM BY THE SWORD."

Thomas More
A Dialogue Concerning Heresies   (1529)

The English Renaissance humanist and statesman Thomas More (1477–1535) gained fame in his own age as an author of religious, historical, and fictional works and as an effective diplomat and political advisor for King Henry VIII of England. More and his friend the Dutch humanist Desiderius Erasmus (1469–1536) became the leading spokesmen for the many educated scholars and officials who supported the call for reforms within the Roman Catholic church but who rejected the Protestant movement's denouncement of papal authority and division of Western Christendom into contending religious confessions. In 1529, More published A Dialogue Concerning Heresies *at the request of the bishop of London to refute for the "unlearned" the Protestant heresy. In the excerpt below, More considers how the Lutheran movement threatened the defense of Christendom from the Muslim Turks. Unfortunately for More, Henry VIII's efforts to annul his marriage would lead Henry to remove the Church of England from papal authority, an act that More rejected, prompting Henry to arrest More and have him tried and executed for treason in 1535.*

[T]here are some . . . that either through high-pretended piety or a feigned observance of the counsels of Christ, would that no man should punish any heretic or infidel, even though they invade us and did us all the harm they possibly could. And in this opinion is Luther and his followers, who, among their other heresies, hold for a plain conclusion that it is not permissible to any Christian man to fight against the Turk or to make any resistance against him though he come into Christendom with a great army and labor to destroy all. For they [Lutherans] say that all

Thomas More, *A Dialogue Concerning Heresies*, in *The Complete Works of St. Thomas More*, Vol. 6, pt. 1, ed. Thomas M. C. Lawler, Germain Marc'hadour, and Richard C. Marius (New Haven: Yale University Press, 1981), 411–15. (Orthography modernized and language clarified by David Kammerling Smith.)

Christian men are bound to the counsel of Christ by which they say that we are forbidden to defend ourselves and that Saint Peter was, as you state, reproved by our Savior when he struck off Malchus' ear although he did it in the defense of his own master [Christ], the most innocent man there ever was.[1] And to this they add . . . that since the time that Christian men first fell to fighting, it [Christendom] has never increased but always diminished and decayed. So that today the Turk has restricted us within very narrow limits, and they [Lutherans] say that they [Turks] will restrict us even more as long as we go about defending Christendom by the sword. They [Lutherans] say that it [Christendom] should be as it was in the beginning—increased so to be continued and preserved only by patience and martyrdom. Thus holily speak these Godly fathers of Luther's sect, laboring to obtain that no man should withstand the Turk but let him win all. And when it should come to that, then would they [Lutherans] . . . win all again by their patience, high virtues, and martyrdom—even though these do not now permit them [Lutherans] to resist their beastly voluptuousness, but [they] break their vows and take harlots under the name of wives. And though they may not fight against the Turk, [they] arise up in great numbers to fight against their own Christians. It is, I trust, no great mystery to perceive whom they [Lutherans] labor to please that have that opinion. And if the Turks happen to come in, there is little doubt whose part they [Lutherans] will take and that Christian people likely will find no Turks as cruel as them [Lutherans]. It is a gentle holiness to abstain, due to devotion, from resisting the Turk and in the meanwhile to rise up as a mob and fight against Christian men and destroy, as that sect [Lutherans] has done to many a good religious house; spoiled, maimed, and slain many a good virtuous man; [and] robbed, polluted, and pulled down many a goodly church of Christ. . . .

[T]hese holy Lutherans, who sow schisms and seditions among Christian people, lay the loss [of Christians] to opposing the Turk's invasion and resisting his malice where they should rather, if they had any reason in their heads, lay it to the contrary. For when Christian princes have done their duty against miscreants and infidels, there are plenty of stories and monuments that witness the manifest aid and help of God in great victories given to good Christian princes by his almighty hand. But on the other side, the ambition of Christian rulers, desiring each other's dominion, has set them at war and deadly destruction among themselves. While each has aspired to enhance his own [dominion], they have been little concerned with what came of the common body of Christendom. God, revenging of their inordinate appetites, has withdrawn his help and shown that while each of them labor to eat up the other, he regards as insignificant tolerating the Turk to prosper, even to the extent that if their [Christian princes'] blind affections do not soon look to Christendom, he [the Turk] shall not fail (which our Lord forbids) within short process to swallow them all. . . .

Christ and his holy apostles exhort every man to patience and sufferance without requiting evil deeds or making any defense but using further sufferance and doing also good for evil. Yet this counsel does not bind a man so that he shall of necessity, against common nature, suffer another man to kill him without cause nor prevent

---

[1]According to Christian scriptures, when Jesus was arrested, his disciple Peter sought to protect Jesus by drawing a dagger and cutting off the ear of an arresting soldier. Jesus told Peter to put away the dagger and then healed the soldier's ear (John 18:1–11; Luke 22:47–52).

any man from defending another whom he sees innocent and invaded and oppressed by malice. In which case nature, reason, and God's command binds . . . the prince to the safeguard of his people by placing himself in peril. . . .

And by this reason is not only excusable but commendable the coming war which every people take in the defense of their country against enemies that would invade it, since every man fights not for the defense of himself on account of a private affection to himself, but on account of a Christian charity for the safeguard and preservation of all others. Such reason has its place in all battles of defense, so has it most especially in the battle by which we defend the Christian countries against the Turks, in that we defend each other from far more peril and loss: of worldly substance, bodily hurt, and the perdition of men's souls.

QUESTIONS FOR ANALYSIS

1. According to More, how does a divided Christianity threaten Christendom? In what different ways has the Lutheran movement damaged Christendom?

2. How does More's explanation for the success of the Turks compare to Luther's suggestion for the Turks' success (Source 2)? How does the "Turkish menace" become a rhetorical tool in the Reformation debates?

3. What tensions are created between More's defense of Christendom and his emphasis on the role played by secular princes in preserving Christendom? How do both More and Luther emphasize the role played by secular leaders in the preservation of Christendom?

4. How does More seek to use the idea of Christendom to undermine support for the Lutheran movement? How does More set the Lutherans as outside the community of "Christians"?

"... COMBAT THE MURDEROUS TURK."

Johannes Brenz
Booklet on the Turk (1531)

In the 1520s, the Muslim Ottoman army invaded central Europe, laying siege to Vienna in 1529 and threatening a second assault in 1532. In response to the "Turkish menace," many priests and pastors wrote popular tracts to explain the Turkish threat to the German-speaking peoples. In 1531, the Lutheran theologian Johannes Brenz wrote

Johannes Brenz, *Booklet on the Turk,* trans. John W. Bohnstedt, in *The Infidel Scourge of God: The Turkish Menace as Seen by German Pamphleteers of the Reformation Era,* in *Transactions of the American Philosophical Society,* Vol. 58, pt. 9 (Philadelphia: American Philosophical Society, 1968), 46–48.

Booklet on the Turk, *in which he offered a religious interpretation of the Muslim Turkish assaults on Christian Europe and explained how Christians should respond.*

Now that there is a general outcry about the Turk's being on the march, with the intention of overrunning all Germany—what are the preachers and other God-fearing people to do? . . .

Answer: Germany is full of wickedness; every kind of roguery prevails among both rulers and subjects. At the same time, the Gospel has been revealed to Germany, but it is being reviled and vilified as "heresy."[1] Therefore, if God is to follow His wont, a very severe punishment is in store for Germany. For it has always been God's wont, when a land was filled with wickedness, to have the Gospel preached there [as a warning and corrective]; then, if the Gospel accomplished nothing and was rejected, He inflicted His punishment. Thus before the Flood, when the world was wicked, He sent Noah, who was treated with contempt along with his Gospel. . . .

Well, my dearly beloved, pious Christians, now that sin and vice, enormous evil and wrongdoing are no longer considered to be a disgrace in Germany, and the Gospel has been revealed for the benefit of the God-fearing, it behooves an upright preacher to admonish his people to amend their lives and turn from their horrible sins. All the signs indicate, that a divine punishment is at hand but can still be turned from us through amendment of life. . . .

The preachers are also obligated earnestly to exhort the Emperor and princes [of Germany] to perform their appointed task—to resist the Turk with the sword. The rulers should not worry about the possibility that the Turk's might may be greater than their own; instead, they should obey God's command and precept, confidently believing that He will help them to combat the murderous Turk. And the subjects are duty-bound to assist their lords, thus safeguarding themselves, their wives, and their children. Such obedience is a good, holy work; if anyone perish while performing it, he should not doubt that he dies in obedience to God; and if otherwise he truly believes in Christ, he will certainly attain eternal bliss. . . .

Every civil authority owes it to God to maintain law and order, to protect the land and the people from wrongful violence and murder, as St. Paul teaches in Romans 13 [3–4]. Now, the Turk is attacking Germany even though he has no right or provocation to do so; his assault is like that of a murderer. Just as the government is obligated to punish thieves and murderers, or to take preventive action as soon as the aggressive intentions of such persons become known, so the government is obligated to resist the Turk, an undisguised brigand and murderer. . . .

That they are nothing but undisguised criminals the Turk themselves prove, not only by their deeds but by their law, for their Muhammad commanded them to commit perpetual aggression, to conquer lands and peoples. . . .

When the Turks win a victory they conduct themselves not as honorable warriors but as the worst miscreants on earth. After their conquest of Constantinople

---

[1] Brenz refers to Lutheranism.

the Turkish tyrant [Mehmed II] had the wives and children of the [Byzantine] Emperor and princes brought to a banquet, where he violated them and then had them chopped to pieces while the banquet was still in progress. Such doings, far from being rare among the Turks, are their customary way of celebrating a military triumph....

It is for this reason, true and constant in the eyes of God, that every Christian may be certain of doing a good work when fighting against the Turk—the rulers as leaders, the people as subjects required by God to obey the government....

God indicates what He thinks of this [Turkish] empire, namely, that the Muslim religion and regime are unadulterated blasphemy and criminality. [Islam] is blasphemy because it rejects Christ and the Gospel. [The regime] is criminal not only in its war practices, but also in its other aspects, for it keeps no moral discipline and fails to punish the most horrible vices and unchastity. A participant in such terrible sins is anyone who willingly submits to the Turk and does not act in such a way as to show his heartfelt disapproval. Since we are duty-bound to show our unwillingness to accept the Turkish Empire, everyone should understand that he does a very good and Christian deed in resisting any Turkish attempt to conquer Germany....

The praiseworthy deeds and examples of the emperors and kings of old, and of the many princes who participated in the campaigns,[2] should inspire and move the present Emperor, kings, princes, and subjects to preserve and protect the land and the people, as their ancestors did before them. . . . [Such a vigorous effort has heretofore been lacking], and the reason for this lack is well known: unfortunately there are many who incite the kings and princes to shed innocent [Protestant] blood in Germany [instead of concentrating upon the Turkish foe], and publicly advocate such a course in their writings. May God protect us from such men and thwart their Cain's[3] counsels!

QUESTIONS FOR ANALYSIS

1. How does Brenz interpret the Turkish advance, and how does his interpretation compare to More's explanation (Source 3)? How might both of these interpretations be comforting to sixteenth-century German Christians?

2. According to Brenz, in what different ways should Christian rulers and Christian commoners respond to the Turkish advances? In what terms does Brenz justify warfare against the Turks?

3. What differences does Brenz identify between Islam and Christianity?

4. How does Brenz define the Lutheran tradition as the rightful heir of the Judeo-Christian tradition? How does Brenz use the Turkish menace to justify a new Christian identity for Europe based on the Lutheran tradition?

---

[2] The Crusades by Europeans to conquer the Holy Lands from Muslims in the eleventh through fourteenth centuries.

[3] According to Jewish scriptures, Cain, a son of Adam and Eve, killed his brother Abel.

5

Andreas Osiander

Whether It Is True and Believable that Jews Secretly Kill Christian Children and Use Their Blood (c. 1529)

The religious passions unleashed by the Reformation also struck at Europe's most prominent non-Christian religious minority—the Jews. Both Protestant and Catholic authors alleged that the religious doctrine of the opposing tradition was inspired by Jewish religious traditions. Europe's Jews had long suffered legal discrimination, attacks on their persons and property, and even accusations of "Blood Libel" or "Ritual Murder"—that they secretly stole Christian children and drained their blood for medical and religious purposes. In 1529 or 1530, the Nuremberg pastor Andreas Osiander (1498–1552) wrote a privately circulated defense of the Jews against the "Blood Libel" charge. An outspoken and controversial supporter of the Protestant reform movement, Osiander was a skilled linguist—one of the few Christians of his age to master the Hebrew language in which the Jewish scriptures had been written. He also was acquainted with the Jewish community that lived just outside Nuremberg's city walls and with Jewish scholars who lived throughout the German lands. In 1540, two Jews published Osiander's text as they defended a Jew accused of ritual murder. Osiander's defense of the Jews sparked fierce reactions among both Catholics and Protestants, who sought to identify themselves unequivocally as enemies of the Jewish "Christ-killers."

I am said to have had a good, long relationship with the Jews and know their language, law, and customs. I do not wish to conceal any truth, but rather with great diligence disprove the stories that I hear and what people would like to believe— that the Jews must have innocent Christian blood, for without it they cannot live. It is said that for this reason, in some places, they have lured away Christian children, secretly murdered them, and taken their blood. . . . I have thought long and earnestly about these things . . . and I have found nothing, nor discovered or heard of anything which persuades me to believe such suspicion and accusation. . . .

It is against [the Jews'] own Law, which they did not fabricate, but rather received it from the almighty God, adopted [it] and consented to observe it. As it is written in the first book of Moses "whoever sheds the blood of man, by man shall his blood be shed."[1] . . . Moreover the whole law and all scripture are full of examples

---

[1] Genesis 9:6.

Andreas Osiander, *Gesamtausgabe.* Vol. 7, *Schriften und Briefe 1539 bis März 1543*, ed. Gerhard Müller and Gottfried Seebass (Gutersloh: Gutershloher Verlagshaus Mohn, 1988), 223, 225–27, 230–31, 233, 246–47. (Translated by Joy M. Kammerling.)

that bloodshed is always punished harshly and that all of the prophets threaten and declare that future punishment and misfortune more often than not results from the shedding of blood. . . . Doubtless the Jews know this, for they read it [the Jewish Law] all day and study and practice their Law with great diligence. . . .

The law was given not only to the Jews in Scripture but by nature is also planted in the hearts of all people, that the shedding of blood is unjust and forbidden; furthermore one finds no people on earth so blind, who would praise or tolerate such killing. Although it is true that people in some lands eat human flesh, they only do so if [those eaten] are old and give their consent. . . . [The Jews] would not disdain or forget the Law against the shedding of blood, for it is written in their hearts . . . and it is not believable that they would go against their own hearts and consciences. . . .

[S]ome say . . . that the Jews must have the blood of children or they will die. . . . [S]ome say that the Jews hemorrhage, which they cannot stop without the blood of innocent Christian children. How could they conceal it when they have been imprisoned for days and years and one does not find blood on their clothing? . . . [T]his is against nature and human reason, for when God wants to punish people with a special illness, he punishes them with illnesses they cannot heal. . . . Why should the blood of Christian children be so valuable? Because they are children? Then the blood of Turkish children could also be used, for they are children, too. However, when has it ever been said that the Jews have killed Turkish children? Yet if it [the blood] is valuable because they are Christians, then the blood of older Christians would also be valuable. . . .

Why would [the Jews] sin so horribly against God, against their Law, against their consciences, against the authorities, against all of Christendom, against their very lives? . . . If they need blood, they could simply drain some blood from a child without harming him. . . . Who could believe such devilish fantasy, since it is against God's Word, nature, and all reason.

Since the birth of Christ, at no time has there been mention of this charge of child murder in any place. However, it all began in the last two or three hundred years, when the monks and priests caused all sorts of roguery and deceit, with pilgrimages and other false miracles, openly fooling and blinding Christians. . . . They saw that the Jews better understand the Scriptures than they [the Catholic clergy] do; thus, [the Catholic clergy] have treated them [the Jews] disparagingly with hatred and persecution, going so far as to call for the burning of their books. But God would not allow this for the good of Christianity, so that through the Hebrew language Christians might return to a correct understanding of their faith. Thus it is to be feared that these enemies of the Jews have fabricated and spread these falsehoods about the Jews, since they also treat Christians, whom they call Lutherans, in the same manner. . . .

Because of my simplicity and ignorance, I cannot really suspect anyone [of killing children], but would rather excuse everyone, particularly the authorities. I do not hold [them] accountable . . . except for believing too easily the enemies of the Jews, and for putting too much trust in false counsel. . . . [M]oreover I want to show that if people want to find the guilty party, they should look namely at . . . first, whether the lord is a poor, miserly tyrant or a drunken, gambling, womanizing spend-thrift. . . . Second, if the lord is a pious, honest, and god-fearing man, judge that his councilors and advisors, clerks, servants, judges and jurors are wicked. Third, whether priests or monks do not want to whip up great miracles and create new pilgrimages in order to gain the appearance of greater sanctity. Or perhaps they want simply to exterminate the Jews. Fourth, one should discover whether several subjects [of the region], through usury, are heavily indebted to the Jews and would thus save their household and honor if the Jews were ruined. . . . Sixth, whether or not some children are killed in accidents. . . . For example, a coach-builder or his servant could have lost his grip on an axe, or [the blade] could have flown off the handle and hit a child, and out of fear they did not reveal it, but made it appear so that the Jews would be blamed. Seventh, . . . whether or not the father and mother are negligent and lazy people, who due to their own neglect [have allowed] the children to stab themselves, fall to death, or be drowned, and . . . fearing shame and ill-repute, made it appear so that the Jews would be blamed.

If any of these . . . possibilities above fails to lead to the guilty perpetrator, then I truly would not know where to look any further, but perhaps would have to reconsider and finally also believe that the Jews are guilty.

QUESTIONS FOR ANALYSIS

1. Whom does Osiander criticize? Whom does he praise or exonerate? Why might he make these choices?
2. What authorities and arguments does Osiander use to defend the Jews?
3. In what ways does Osiander express respect for the Jews? In what ways is he ambiguous toward them?
4. How does Osiander's attitudes toward and use of the Jews compare to Brenz's attitude toward and use of the Turks (Source 4)?

6

". . . THE RAGING TURKISH TYRANT . . ."

Two Woodcuts: Turks and Jews   (1530 and c. 1475)

In the sixteenth century, woodcuts provided an effective means to reach a broad audience, often by relying on grotesque or humorous imagery. Woodcuts commonly accompanied written texts but also developed their own traditions and motifs. The following two woodcuts address different topics and are instructive in both their similarities and differences. The first woodcut, by Erhard Schön, appeared in Vienna in 1530 and depicts Turkish atrocities during the siege of Vienna the previous year. The second woodcut, probably from Florence around 1475, appeared in a book entitled The Martyrdom of Simon of Trent. *When a child named Simon disappeared on Easter Day 1475, his parents accused Jews of kidnapping and murdering the boy. The accusation of "Ritual Murder"—that Jews secretly stole Christian children and drained their blood for medical and religious purposes—led to prolonged tortures for members of the local Jewish community, and the confessions and trial that ensued became sensational news throughout northern Italy and southern Germany.*

Ich Herre Gott in dem höchsten thron
Schaw disen grossen jamer an
So der Thürckisch wütend Thyran
Im Wiener walde hat gethan
Ellendt ermort junckfraw vnd frawen
Die kindt mitten entzwey gehawen
Zertretten vnd entzwey gerissen
An spitzig pfäl thet er sie spissen
O vnser hyrte Jhesu Ch:ist
Der du gnedig Barmhertzig bist
Deyn zorn von dem volck ab wende
Errett es auß des Thürcken hende.

¶ Hanns Guldenmundt
zu Nürmberg.

THE OTTOMAN SIEGE OF VIENNA

Accompanying text:

God on the highest throne
Look at this great misery
That the raging Turkish tyrant
Has caused in the Vienna forest.
Maliciously he murders virgins and women.
The children, hacked apart in the middle,
Crushed and torn apart.
He has impaled them on sharpened poles.
Oh, our shepherd Jesus Christ,
You who are so merciful,
Turn away your wrath from the people.
Save the people from the hand of the Turk.

QUESTIONS FOR ANALYSIS

1. What images does each woodcut use to identify the figures as Muslims or Jews? How do these images compare to the texts in this chapter focused on Muslims (Sources 1, 3, and 4) and Jews (Source 5)?

2. What themes or images appear in both woodcuts? What is the significance of these images for their audience?

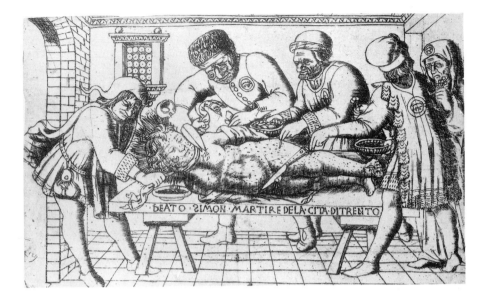

THE RITUAL MURDER OF SIMON OF TRENT

Accompanying text:

Let every believer weep over the just blood of Blessed Simon, spilt in Trent, tortured by the Jews, as you see here. His mother, Maria, says she still mourns [for him]. On this 21st day of March, 1475, may his soul pray Jesus for us in town and in the countryside. His body does not refuse to work miracles.

3. How do the images suggest different attitudes and fears toward Muslims and Jews? How do the woodcuts portray Muslims as a threat from outside of European Christian society and Jews as a threat from the inside?

4. What responses do these woodcuts seek to elicit? What role does sexual imagery play in these woodcuts?

RELIGION AND THE NATURAL WORLD

During the high Middle Ages, Christian theologians synthesized Christian theology and recently translated texts of ancient Greek scientists and philosophers, especially the writings of Aristotle, into an official, orthodox interpretation of the cosmos and its workings. The medieval Christian cosmos was a place of logic and of magic in which all of nature functioned according to God's purposeful design of the universe; thus, nature's actions followed from its spiritual origins. In the fifteenth century, however, another wave of Greek and Roman sources arrived in Europe, carried by Byzantine scholars who fled to northern Italy when Constantinople fell to the Ottoman Turks in 1453. These ancient texts, which had been unknown to Europeans and had been preserved and substantially advanced in the medieval Islamic world, sparked renewed investigations into the workings of nature. They introduced Europeans to ancient philosophical and scientific traditions that emphasized more mystical understandings of the universe, especially a mysticism that could be deciphered in the language of mathematics. These new texts excited scholars, who soon posited new theories and observations of the natural world that contradicted orthodox Catholic and Protestant interpretations of the cosmos. Recognizing the danger in challenging religious authority and in exploring ideas that had been inspired by Islamic scholarship and translated by Jewish scholars, European scholars sought to establish their scientific labors as an unequivocally Christian endeavor. Further, they began to carve out a space for scientific inquiry distinct from religious scholarship that would be carried out in the presumed detached, objective language of nature itself—mathematics.

7

". . . SHE ALWAYS DECEIVES."

Heinrich Kramer and Jakob Sprenger
The Hammer of Witches (1486)

In 1486 Heinrich Kramer (d. 1505) and Jakob Sprenger (c. 1436–1495), Inquisitors authorized by the pope to interrogate suspected witches and heretics, published The Hammer of Witches *to serve as an instruction manual for witchcraft investigations throughout Europe. The text consolidated Christian beliefs about witchcraft, provided definitions of witchcraft, and outlined the legal procedures for witchcraft prosecutions. While not itself a text of "natural philosophy," as science was called,* The Hammer of Witches *demonstrates that actions of nature were interpreted through a religious framework that gave priority to understanding the spiritual significance of natural occurrences. The text also demonstrates how medieval Christianity's gendered religiosity merged with its interpretation of nature. Beginning in the 1540s, Protestant and Catholic religious and secular authorities undertook investigations of witchcraft, using* The Hammer of Witches *as their investigative guide, and ordered at least 100,000 executions, with the majority of the victims being women.*

Why Superstition Is Chiefly Found in Women

As for the first question, why a greater number of witches is found in the fragile feminine sex than among men; it is indeed a fact that it were idle to contradict, since it is accredited by actual experience, apart from the verbal testimony of credible witnesses. . . .

Heinrich Kramer and James Sprenger, *The Malleus Maleficarum of Heinrich Kramer and James Sprenger,* trans. Montague Summers (London: Lohn Rodker, 1928) (Reprinted New York: Dover, 1971), 41–44, 66, 118–19, 144–47.

Now the wickedness of women is spoken of in Ecclesiasticus xxv:[1] There is no head above the head of a serpent: and there is no wrath above the wrath of a woman. I had rather dwell with a lion and a dragon than to keep house with a wicked woman. And among much which in that place precedes and follows about a wicked woman, he concludes: All wickedness is but little to the wickedness of a woman. Wherefore S. John Chrysostom says on the text, It is not good to marry (S. Matthew xix):[2] What else is woman but a foe to friendship, an unescapable punishment, a necessary evil, a natural temptation, a desirable calamity, a domestic danger, a delectable detriment, an evil of nature, painted with fair colours! Therefore if it be a sin to divorce her when she ought to be kept, it is indeed a necessary torture; for either we commit adultery by divorcing her, or we must endure daily strife. . . .

Wherefore in many vituperations that we read against women, the word woman is used to mean the lust of the flesh. As it is said: I have found a woman more bitter than death, and a good woman subject to carnal lust.

Others again have propounded other reasons why there are more superstitious women found than men. And the first is, that they are more credulous; and since the chief aim of the devil is to corrupt faith, therefore he rather attacks them. . . . The second reason is, that women are naturally more impressionable, and more ready to receive the influence of a disembodied spirit; and that when they use this quality well they are very good, but when they use it ill they are very evil.

The third reason is that they have slippery tongues, and are unable to conceal from their fellow-women those things which by evil arts they know; and, since they are weak, they find an easy and secret manner of vindicating themselves by witchcraft. . . .

[A]s regards intellect, or the understanding of spiritual things, they seem to be of a different nature from men; a fact which is vouched for by the logic of the authorities, backed by various examples from the Scriptures. Terence says: Women are intellectually like children.[3] . . .

But the natural reason is that she is more carnal[4] than a man, as is clear from her many carnal abominations. And it should be noted that there was a defect in the formation of the first woman, since she was formed from a bent rib, that is, a rib of the breast, which is bent as it were in a contrary direction to a man. And since through this defect she is an imperfect animal, she always deceives. . . .

That Witches Who Are Midwives in Various Ways Kill the Child Conceived in the Womb

[C]ertain witches, against the instinct of human nature, and indeed against the nature of all beasts, with the possible exception of wolves, are in the habit of devouring

---

[1] Ecclesiasticus, written by the Jewish religious thinker Ben Sira between 180 and 175 B.C., is accepted within Roman Catholic scriptures but not within Jewish or Protestant scriptures.
[2] St. John Chrysostom (347–407), born in Antioch in present-day west central Turkey, composed ninety homilies on the book of Matthew.
[3] Publius Terentius (c. 195–c. 159 B.C.), North African Roman comic dramatist.
[4] Fleshly, sexual.

and eating infant children. And concerning this, the Inquisitor of Como,[5] who has been mentioned before, has told us the following: that he was summoned by the inhabitants of the County of Barby[6] to hold an inquisition, because a certain man had missed his child from its cradle, and finding a congress of women in the nighttime, swore that he saw them kill his child and drink its blood and devour it. . . .

How, as It Were, They Deprive Man of His Virile Member

[T]hey [witches] can take away the male organ, not indeed by actually despoiling the human body of it, but by concealing it with some glamour.[7] . . .

[An] experience is narrated by a certain venerable Father from the Dominican House of Spires,[8] well known in the Order for the honesty of his life and for his learning. "One day," he says, "while I was hearing confessions, a young man came to me and, in the course of his confession, woefully said that he had lost his member. Being astonished at this, and not being willing to give it easy credence, since in the opinion of the wise it is a mark of light-heartedness to believe too easily, I obtained proof of it when I saw nothing on the young man's removing his clothes and showing the place. Then, using the wisest counsel I could, I asked whether he suspected anyone of having so bewitched him. And the young man said that he did suspect someone, but that she was absent and living in Worms.[9] Then I said: 'I advise you to go to her as soon as possible and try your utmost to soften her with gentle words and promises'; and he did so. For he came back after a few days and thanked me, saying that he was whole and had recovered everything. And I believed his words, but again proved them by the evidence of my eyes." . . .

Here Followeth How Witches Injure Cattle in Various Ways

[T]hey can cause this in various ways by witchcraft. For on the more holy nights according to the instructions of the devil and for the greater offence to the Divine Majesty of God, a witch will sit down in a corner of her house with a pail between her legs, stick a knife or some instrument in the wall or a post, and make as if to milk it with her hands. Then she summons her familiar who always works with her in everything, and tells him that she wishes to milk a certain cow from a certain house, which is healthy and abounding in milk. And suddenly the devil takes the milk from the udder of that cow, and brings it to where the witch is sitting, as if it were flowing from the knife. . . .

[S]hepherds have often seen animals in the fields give three or four jumps into the air, and then suddenly fall to the ground and die; and this is caused by the power of witches at the instance of the devil. . . .

_____
[5] City in northern Italy.
[6] Region in southeastern France.
[7] Magic.
[8] Speyer, city in west central Germany.
[9] City in west central Germany a day's walk from Speyer.

How They Raise and Stir Up Hailstorms and Tempests, and Cause Lightning to Blast Both Men and Beasts

That devils and their disciples can by witchcraft cause lightnings and hailstorms and tempests, and that the devils have power from God to do this. . . .

S. Thomas[10] in his commentary on Job says as follows: It must be confessed that, with God's permission, the devils can disturb the air, raise up winds, and make the fire fall from heaven. . . . [W]inds and rain and other similar disturbances of the air can be caused by the mere movement of vapours released from the earth or the water; therefore the natural power of devils is sufficient to cause such things. So says S. Thomas.

For God in His justice using the devils as his agents of punishment inflicts the evils which come to us who live in this world.

---

[10] Thomas Aquinas (c. 1225–1274), major Italian Catholic theologian.

QUESTIONS FOR ANALYSIS

1. What are the authors' explanations for women's susceptibility to witchcraft? How do the authors base their arguments within both religion and nature?

2. What evidence do the authors use to justify their arguments? What attitudes toward the natural world are revealed in the text?

3. How do the authors define Christianity as fundamentally male? What implications does this definition have for the status of women in society?

4. For fifteenth-century Christians, how might the authors' theories of witchcraft make the natural world seem less intimidating?

8

". . . A WORK WHICH I HAD KEPT HIDDEN . . ."

Nicolaus Copernicus
On the Revolutions of the Heavenly Orbs   (1543)

Nicolaus Copernicus (1473–1543), a Catholic priest, participated as a young man in a papal conference on reforms needed in the liturgical calendar that prescribed the dates for the Catholic church's religious ceremonies and festivals. Although the calendar conference produced no reforms, Copernicus spent decades privately working to resolve technical difficulties in the astronomy of sixteenth-century Europe. As his ideas developed, Copernicus became convinced that a heliocentric (sun-centered) model for

---

Nicolaus Copernicus, *On the Revolutions of the Heavenly Orbs* (Chicago: University of Chicago Great Books Collection, 1952), 506–9.

the universe made greater mathematical sense than the geocentric (earth-centered) model of the universe that had become part of Roman Catholic religious doctrine. Aware that his ideas challenged religious orthodoxy, Copernicus delayed publishing his ideas until old age in a work written primarily for astronomers and mathematicians, On the Revolutions of the Heavenly Orbs. *The excerpt below from that work is Copernicus's "Preface and Dedication to Pope Paul III."*

I can reckon easily enough, Most Holy Father, that as soon as certain people learn that in these books of mine which I have written about the revolutions of the spheres of the world I attribute certain motions to the terrestrial globe, they will immediately shout to have me and my opinion hooted off the stage. For my own works do not please me so much that I do not weigh what judgments others will pronounce concerning them. And although I realize that the conceptions of a philosopher are placed beyond the judgment of the crowd, because it is his loving duty to seek the truth in all things, in so far as God has granted that to human reason; nevertheless I think we should avoid opinions utterly foreign to rightness. And when I considered how absurd this "lecture" would be held by those who know that the opinion that the Earth rests immovable in the middle of the heavens as if their centre had been confirmed by the judgments of many ages—if I were to assert to the contrary that the Earth moves; for a long time I was in great difficulty as to whether I should bring to light my commentaries written to demonstrate the Earth's movement. . . .

But my friends made me change my course in spite of my long-continued hesitation and even resistance. First among them was Nicholas Schonberg, Cardinal of Capua,[1] a man distinguished in all branches of learning; next to him was my devoted friend Tiedeman Giese, Bishop of Culm,[2] a man filled with the greatest zeal for the divine and liberal arts: for he in particular urged me frequently and even spurred me on by added reproaches into publishing this book and letting come to light a work which I had kept hidden among my things for not merely nine years, but for almost four times nine years. . . .

[N]othing except my knowledge that mathematicians have not agreed with one another in their researches moved me to think out a different scheme of drawing up the movements of the spheres of the world. For in the first place mathematicians are so uncertain about the movements of the sun and moon that they can neither demonstrate nor observe the unchanging magnitude of the revolving year. . . .

[W]hen I had meditated upon this lack of certitude in the traditional mathematics concerning the composition of movements of the spheres of the world, I began to be annoyed that the philosophers, who in other respects had made a very

---

[1] Nicholas Schonberg (1472–1537), Roman Catholic cardinal who had learned of Copernicus's general ideas in 1536.
[2] Tiedeman Giese (1480–1550), Roman Catholic bishop and long, close friend of Copernicus.

careful scrutiny of the least details of the world, had discovered no sure scheme for the movements of the machinery of the world, which has been built for us by the Best and Most Orderly Workman of all. Wherefore I took the trouble to reread all the books by philosophers which I could get hold of, to see if any of them even supposed that the movements of the spheres of the world were different from those laid down by those who taught mathematics in the schools. And as a matter of fact, I found first in Cicero[3] that Nicetas[4] thought that the Earth moved. And afterwards I found in Plutarch[5] that there were some others of the same opinion. . . .

Therefore I also, having found occasion, began to meditate upon the mobility of the Earth. And although the opinion seemed absurd, nevertheless because I knew that others before me had been granted the liberty of constructing whatever circles they pleased in order to demonstrate astral phenomena, I thought that I too would be readily permitted to test whether or not, by the laying down that the Earth had some movement, demonstrations less shaky than those of my predecessors could be found for the revolutions of the celestial spheres. . . .

I have no doubt that talented and learned mathematicians will agree with me, if—as philosophy demands in the first place—they are willing to give not superficial but profound thought and effort to what I bring forward in this work in demonstrating these things. And in order that the unlearned as well as the learned might see that I was not seeking to flee from the judgment of any man, I preferred to dedicate these results of my nocturnal study to Your Holiness rather than to anyone else; because, even in this remote corner of the earth where I live, you are held to be most eminent both in the dignity of your order and in your love of letters and even of mathematics; hence, by the authority of your judgment you can easily provide a guard against the bites of slanderers. . . .

QUESTIONS FOR ANALYSIS

1. How does Copernicus express intellectual humility in the text? Why might he do this?
2. To what different types of authority does Copernicus appeal to justify his publication of his book? How does he use various authorities differently?
3. Through his appeals to authority, what terms does Copernicus use to define his ideas and their validity? How does Copernicus's understanding of appropriate proof and evidence in study of the natural world compare to *The Hammer of Witches'* use of proof and evidence?
4. How does Copernicus's discussion of mathematics and mathematicians challenge the church's control over learning and knowledge?

---

[3] Marcus Tullius Cicero (106–43 B.C.), Roman orator, statesman, and author.
[4] Nicetas (or Hicetas) (5th century B.C.), Greek astronomer.
[5] Plutarch (c. 46–c. 120), Greek biographer and moralist.

9

"For the Bible is not chained . . ."

Galileo Galilei
Letter to the Grand Duchess Christina   (1615)

Both Catholic and Protestant authorities condemned Copernicus's theory that the earth rotated around the sun (Source 8), and few astronomers adopted his theories. By the 1590s, however, interest in Copernicus's theories began to revive. Galileo Galilei (1564–1642), an Italian physicist turned astronomer, added weight to the Copernican theory in 1609 when he made a series of important celestial observations and discoveries with a telescope he designed. Galileo recognized the threat that the "new science" and religious authority posed to one another. He sought to address that threat and to define a new relationship between religious truth and truth about the natural world in his "Letter to the Grand Duchess Christina," which he published to build support for the "new science" among northern Italy's educated clergy, the politically influential princely families, and the economically important merchant community.

Some years ago, as Your Serene Highness well knows, I discovered in the heavens many things that had not been seen before our own age.[1] The novelty of these things, as well as some consequences which followed from them in contradiction to the physical notions commonly held among academic philosophers, stirred up against me no small number of professors—as if I had placed these things in the sky with my own hands in order to upset nature and overturn the sciences. . . .

Showing a greater fondness for their own opinions than for truth, they sought to deny and disprove the new things which, if they had cared to look for themselves, their own senses would have demonstrated to them. To this end they hurled various charges and published numerous writings filled with vain arguments, and they made the grave mistake of sprinkling these with passages taken from places in the Bible which they had failed to understand properly, and which were ill suited to their purposes. . . .

Contrary to the sense of the Bible and the intention of the holy Fathers, if I am not mistaken, they would extend such authorities until even in purely physical matters—where faith is not involved—they would have us altogether abandon reason and the evidence of our senses in favor of some biblical passage, though under the surface meaning of its words this passage may contain a different sense. . . .

---

[1] In 1609, Galileo crafted a telescope through which he observed mountains and craters on the moon's surface, the moons of Jupiter, and dark spots on the sun, among other discoveries.

Stillman Drake, trans., *Discoveries and Opinion of Galileo* (Garden City, N.Y.: Doubleday Anchor Books, 1957), 177, 179, 181–83, 185–87.

54

The reason produced for condemning the opinion that the earth moves and the sun stands still is that in many places in the Bible one may read that the sun moves and the earth stands still. Since the Bible cannot err, it follows as a necessary consequence that anyone takes an erroneous and heretical position who maintains that the sun is inherently motionless and the earth movable.

With regard to this argument, I think in the first place that it is very pious to say and prudent to affirm that the holy Bible can never speak untruth—whenever its true meaning is understood. But I believe nobody will deny that it is often very abstruse, and may say things which are quite different from what its bare words signify. Hence in expounding the Bible if one were always to confine oneself to the unadorned grammatical meaning, one might fall into error. Not only contradictions and propositions far from true might thus be made to appear in the Bible, but even grave heresies and follies. Thus it would be necessary to assign to God feet, hands, and eyes, as well as corporeal and human affections, such as anger, repentance, hatred, and sometimes even the forgetting of things past and ignorance of those to come. These propositions uttered by the Holy Ghost were set down in that manner by the sacred scribes in order to accommodate them to the capacities of the common people, who are rude and unlearned. For the sake of those who deserve to be separated from the herd, it is necessary that wise expositors should produce the true senses of such passages, together with the special reasons for which they were set down in these words. This doctrine is so widespread and so definite with all theologians that it would be superfluous to adduce evidence for it. . . .

This being granted, I think that in discussions of physical problems we ought to begin not from the authority of scriptural passages, but from sense-experiences and necessary demonstrations; for the holy Bible and the phenomena of nature proceed alike from the divine Word. . . . It is necessary for the Bible, in order to be accommodated to the understanding of every man, to speak many things which appear to differ from the absolute truth so far as the bare meaning of the words is concerned. But Nature, on the other hand, is inexorable and immutable; she never transgresses the laws imposed upon her, or cares a whit whether her abstruse reasons and methods of operation are understandable to men. For that reason it appears that nothing physical which sense-experience sets before our eyes, or which necessary demonstrations prove to us, ought to be called in question (much less condemned) upon the testimony of biblical passages which may have some different meaning beneath their words. For the Bible is not chained in every expression to conditions as strict as those which govern all physical effects; nor is God any less excellently revealed in Nature's actions than in the sacred statements of the Bible. . . .

I do not feel obliged to believe that that same God who has endowed us with senses, reason, and intellect has intended to forgo their use and by some other means to give us knowledge which we can attain by them. . . .

[T]he Holy Ghost did not intend to teach us whether heaven moves or stands still. . . . I would say here something that was heard from an ecclesiastic of the most eminent degree: "That the intention of the Holy Ghost is to teach us how one goes to heaven, not how heaven goes." . . .

[I]t being true that two truths cannot contradict one another, it is the function of wise expositors to seek out the true senses of scriptural texts. These will unquestionably accord with the physical conclusions which manifest sense and necessary demonstrations have previously made certain to us. Now the Bible, as has been remarked, admits in many places expositions that are remote from the signification of the words for reasons we have already given. Moreover, we are unable to affirm that all interpreters of the Bible speak by divine inspiration, for if that were so there would exist no differences between them about the sense of a given passage. Hence I should think it would be the part of prudence not to permit anyone to usurp scriptural texts and force them in some way to maintain any physical conclusion to be true, when at some future time the senses and demonstrative or necessary reasons may show the contrary.

QUESTIONS FOR ANALYSIS

1. How does Galileo characterize his opponents? How does this characterization compare with Copernicus's fears of those who would ridicule him (Source 8)?
2. According to Galileo, how is knowledge about the natural world different from knowledge about the spiritual world? How does each world operate as a source of truth?
3. How does Galileo's argument enhance the status of scientific knowledge? How does Galileo define science as a Christian enterprise?
4. How could religious officials see Galileo's ideas as a threat to their authority?

CHAPTER QUESTIONS

1. In what ways is a singular idea of Christendom being challenged throughout the texts in this chapter?
2. How do the Reformation's challenges to Christendom compare to Europeans' emphasis on Christianity as a defining component of the relationship between Europe and the Americas (Chapter 1)?
3. Within the Reformation debates, how do writers use Muslims and Jews to help sustain an ideal of a singular Christianity? How do the scientific texts seek to expand the framework for the Christian identity of the West?

Chapter 3

THE CHRISTIANIZING MISSION: JESUITS IN AMERICA AND CHINA

In the wake of the Protestant Reformation, the Roman Catholic church recognized a need to reaffirm and clarify Catholic doctrines and to root out many of the abuses in the church's organization. These efforts, which occurred most noticeably in the mid- and late sixteenth century, are often identified as the Counter Reformation. One of the principle agents of the Counter Reformation was a new religious order, the Jesuits (or Society of Jesus), founded in 1540 by the Spanish soldier and nobleman Ignatius of Loyola. Ignatius organized the Jesuits on highly centralized, military principles, stressing unflinching obedience. The Jesuits vigorously defended the papacy against any threat to its authority, including efforts by monarchs to seize greater control over church affairs. The Jesuit order grew rapidly, focusing its efforts on education and scholarship and on missionary work.

Jesuit missionaries soon began to work in Asia, Africa, and the Americas. Well-educated and willing to endure significant hardships, Jesuit missionaries demonstrated considerable flexibility as they adjusted personally to diverse cultures and as they sought to convert local peoples to Christianity. To attract individuals to Christianity, the Jesuits often sought "accommodation" between local religious beliefs and practices and Catholic doctrine and rituals. While defending the Christian faith, Jesuits identified similarities between Christian and non-Christian beliefs and practices that could be used to lead the "pagans" to embrace Christianity. Accommodating non-Christian spirituality within a Christian framework raised difficult issues about where accommodation ended and heresy began. For the Jesuits, accommodation remained subordinated to the central goal of conversions to Christianity. Nevertheless, the Jesuits' critics in Europe, especially their rivals within the Catholic church, exploited the Jesuits' accommodationism to accuse the Jesuits of tolerating, even condoning, pagan religious practices.

The Jesuits' efforts at religious accommodation indicate an important issue. Their missionary activities were shaped not only by the Jesuits' assumptions and goals but also by the civilizations that they encountered. This chapter focuses on the Jesuits' work among two vastly different peoples—the Huron people of North America and the Chinese. The Huron, a confederacy of four tribes based in the Great Lakes region, were a settled, preliterate people with a largely decentralized political organization. The Jesuits arrived in the area as part of a modest French presence. French traders and administrators who came to New France lived largely in several fortress towns along the St. Lawrence River (Map 3.1). Rather than an empire of military conquest in the spirit of Cortés, the French established political alliances with factions of the Indian nations, and numerous commercial ties

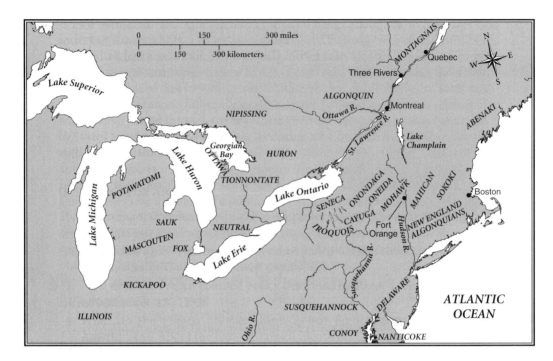

MAP 3.1 NATIVE NATIONS AND EUROPEAN SETTLEMENTS IN THE GREAT LAKES REGION

French settlers tended to remain in French settlements, whereas Jesuit missionaries often lived in Huron villages and with other Amerindian peoples to better learn their culture and beliefs.

focused on the trade in furs (discussed in Chapter 4). Wars and battles certainly occurred, but unlike the Amerindians under Spanish domination in Central and South America, the Amerindians of New France retained much autonomy while also becoming enmeshed in French political and economic alliances. In contrast, in China the Jesuits confronted a political structure more centralized and bureaucratized than any in Europe. The Chinese literary and philosophical traditions dated to before the writings of the ancient Greeks and contained a large and sophisticated corpus of scholarship. While impressed with European astronomy and clock making, Chinese political leaders remained deeply suspicious of the Europeans, highly regulated their trade with China, and limited their ability to travel throughout the Chinese Empire.

1

Jean de Brébeuf
Jesuit Relations of 1636

In the 1630s and 1640s, the Jesuits focused their missionary efforts in New France on the Huron, a settled, Iroquoian people who lived around Lake Huron. In 1625, the Jesuit missionary Jean de Brébeuf (1593–1649) arrived in New France and spent most of his adulthood living among the Huron, observing their culture and learning about their beliefs through discussions with Huron friends. Brébeuf and other missionaries prepared letters and reports of their activities and their observations, which were sent to their superior at Quebec. The superior compiled and edited these reports, which were then sent to Paris and underwent a further editorial process. About one year after originally drafted, the compiled reports were published annually under the title Jesuit Relations *for the benefit of the pious and potential donors in France. The* Jesuit Relations *provided some of the most detailed ethnographic descriptions of Amerindian culture available to Europeans in the seventeenth and eighteenth centuries. In the following selection from Brébeuf's report of 1636, Brébeuf outlines the Huron religious and political systems. Brébeuf himself was tortured and killed by the Huron's bitter enemies, the Iroquois, in 1649 and canonized as a saint of the Roman Catholic church in 1930.*

That the Hurons Recognize Some Divinity;
Of Their Superstitions and of Their Faith in Dreams

As these poor Indians are men, they have not been able to deny the existence of God altogether. Because they are given to vice, however, they are only able to form conceptions of him that are unworthy of his greatness. They have neither sought nor recognized him except on the surface of created things, in which they have hoped to find fortune or dreaded misfortune. They address themselves to the earth, the rivers, the lakes, the dangerous rocks, and, above all, to the sky, in the belief that these things are animate and that some powerful spirit or demon resides there.

They are not contented simply to make wishes; rather, they often accompany these with a sort of sacrifice. I have noticed two kinds of these. One type is to render them [the spirits] propitious and favorable, and the other is to appease them when they have received what they imagine to be some disgrace from them or believe they have incurred their anger or indignation. Here are the ceremonies they employ in these sacrifices. They throw some tobacco into the fire, and if it is, for example, to the sky that they address themselves, they say, *Aronhiaté onné aonstaniwas taitenr,* "O sky, here is what I offer thee in sacrifice. Have pity on me, assist me." If

---

Allan Greer, ed., *The Jesuit Relations: Natives and Missionaries in Seventeenth-Century North America* (Boston: Bedford/St. Martin's, 2000), 46–48, 51–52, 55, 57–58.

59

it is to implore health, *Taenguiaens,* "Heal me." They have recourse to the sky for al-most all their needs, and respect the great bodies in it above all creatures, and remark in it in particular something divine. Indeed, it is, after man, the most vivid image we have of divinity. There is nothing which represents divinity to us so clearly. We perceive its omnipotence in all the prodigious effects the heavens cause here on earth, its immensity in the sky's vast extent, its wisdom in the orderly move-ment of the heavenly bodies, its goodness in the benign influences it sheds contin-ually over all creatures, and its beauty in the sun and in the aspect of the stars. I say this to show how easy it will be, with time and divine aid, to lead these peoples to a knowledge of their Creator, since they already give special honor to a part of His creation which is such a perfect image of Him. And, furthermore, I may say it is really God whom they honor, though blindly, for they imagine in the heavens an *oki,* that is to say, a demon or power which rules the seasons of the year, which holds in check the winds and the waves of the sea, which can render favorable the course of their voyages and assist them in every time of need. They even fear his anger and invoke him as a witness in order to render their faith inviolable when they make some promise of importance, or agree to some bargain or treaty of peace with an enemy. Here are the terms they use: *Hakrihoté ekaronhiaté tout Icwakhier ekentaté,* "The sky knows what we are doing today." And they think that if, after this, they should violate their word or break their alliance, the sky would certainly chastise them. . . .

The Hurons hold that fish are possessed of reason, as are the deer and moose as well, and that is why they do not throw to the dogs either the bones of the latter when they are hunting or the refuse of the former when fishing; otherwise, the oth-ers would be warned and would hide themselves and not let themselves be caught. Every year they marry their nets, or seines, to two little girls, who must be only six or seven years of age, to ensure that they still retain their virginity, a very rare quality among them. The celebration of these nuptials takes place at a fine feast, where a net is placed between the two virgins. This is to make it happy to catch fish. Still, I am very glad that virginity receives among them this kind of honor, as it will help us some-day to make them understand the value of it. Fish, they say, do not like the dead, and hence they abstain from going fishing when someone related to them dies. . . .

They have a faith in dreams which surpasses all belief. If Christians were to put into execution all their divine inspirations with as much care as our Indians carry out their dreams, no doubt they would very soon become great saints. They look upon their dreams as ordinances and irrevocable decrees; to delay the execution of them would be a crime. An Indian of our village dreamed this winter, shortly after he had fallen asleep, that he ought straightaway to make a feast. Though it was the middle of the night, he immediately arose and came and woke us to borrow one of our kettles.

The dream is the oracle that all these poor peoples consult and listen to, the prophet which predicts future events, the Cassandra[1] which warns of misfortunes threatening them, the physician who treats them in their sicknesses, the Aescu-lapius[2] and Galen[3] of the whole country: It is their most absolute master. . . .

---

[1] Prophetess of Greek mythology who persistently foretold of disaster and misfortune.
[2] Ancient Roman god of medicine and healing.
[3] Galen (c. 130–c. 200), Greek physician whose writings were the basis of Western medicine into the seventeenth century.

Of the Polity of the Hurons and of Their Government

I do not claim here to put our Indians on the same level as the Chinese, Japanese, and other perfectly civilized nations, but only to distinguish them from the condition of beasts (to which the opinion of some has reduced them) and to rank them among men, and to show that among them there is even some sort of political and civic life. It is quite important, in my opinion, to note that they live assembled in villages, with sometimes as many as fifty, sixty, or a hundred cabins (that is to say, three hundred to four hundred households); that they cultivate the fields, from which they obtain sufficient food to maintain themselves year-round; and that they live together in peace and friendship. I certainly believe that there is not, perhaps, under heaven a nation more praiseworthy in this respect than the Nation of the Bear.[4] Setting aside a few evil-minded persons, such as one meets almost everywhere, they have a gentleness and affability almost incredible for savages. They are not easily annoyed, and, moreover, if they have received wrong from anyone, they often conceal the resentment they feel; at least one finds here very few who allow themselves any display of anger or vengeance.

They maintain such perfect harmony by visiting one another frequently, by helping one another in time of sickness, and by their feasts and their marriage alliances. When they are not busy with their fields, hunting, fishing, or trading, they spend less time in their own cabins than in those of their friends. If they fall sick or desire anything for their health, there is a rivalry as to who will show himself most obliging. If they have any unusually good delicacy, as I have already said, they offer a feast for their friends and hardly ever eat it alone. In their marriages there is this remarkable custom: They never marry anyone related to them in any way, either directly or collaterally; instead, they always make new marital alliances, which is very helpful in maintaining goodwill. Moreover, by this habit of visiting one another—given that they possess, for the most part, rather good minds—they arouse and influence one another wonderfully.

Consequently, almost none of them are incapable of conversing or of reasoning very well, and in good terms, on matters within their knowledge. The councils, too, held almost every day in the villages on almost all matters, improve their capacity for speaking. Anyone who wishes may be present and may express his opinion, though it is the elders who are in the ascendant and it is their judgment that decides issues. Let it be added also that propriety, courtesy, and civility, which are, as it were, the flower and charm of ordinary human conversation, are not lacking among these people. They call a polite person *Aiendawasti*. To be sure, you do not observe among them any of those hand kissings, compliments, and vain offers of service which do not pass beyond the lips. Yet they do render certain civilities to one another and preserve, through a sense of propriety, various ceremonies in their visits, dances, and feasts. Neglect of such courtesy and propriety would lead to immediate censure, and if anyone made such blunders repeatedly, he would soon become a byword in the village and would lose all his influence. . . .

Furthermore, if laws are like the governing wheel regulating a community—or, to be more exact, are the soul of a commonwealth—it seems to me that, in view

---

[4] The Attignaouantans, one of the four tribes that comprised the Huron confederacy.

of the perfect understanding that reigns among them, I am right in maintaining that they are not without laws. They punish murderers, thieves, traitors, and witches, and although they are not as severe with murderers as their ancestors were, still there is little disorder in this connection. . . .

Besides having some sort of laws maintained among themselves, there is also a certain order established as regards foreign nations. Firstly, concerning commerce, several families have their own private trade, and the first man who discovers it is considered master of a trade route. The children share the rights of their parents in this respect, as do those who bear the same name. No one else goes into it without permission, and this is given only in consideration of presents. The master allows only as many or as few as he wishes to share in the trade. If he has a good supply of merchandise, it is to his advantage to go trading with only a few companions, for thus he secures all that he desires in the country [where he goes to trade]. It is this [ownership of trade routes] which constitutes their most prized possession, and, if anyone should be bold enough to pursue trade without permission of the owner, doing his best to transact business in secret, and if he is surprised en route, he will be treated as no better than a thief. . . .

As regards the authority of commanding, here is what I have observed. All the affairs of the Hurons come under one of two headings: The first are essentially affairs of state—whether they concern either citizens or foreigners, the public or the individuals of a village—such as feasts, dances, games, lacrosse matches, and funeral ceremonies. The second are affairs of war. There are different captains for each of these affairs. In the large villages there will be sometimes several captains, for both civil administration and for war, and they divide among themselves the families of the village into so many captaincies. One even finds captains to whom all these governments report, because their intelligence, popularity, wealth, or other qualities have made them particularly influential in the country. There are none, however, chosen to be greater than the others. The first rank is held by those who have acquired it by their intelligence, eloquence, magnificence, courage, and wise conduct. Consequently, the affairs of the village are referred principally to whichever of the captains possesses these qualifications. The same is true with regard to the affairs of the whole country, in which the men of greatest intelligence are the leading captains. Usually there is one only who bears the burden of all, and it is in his name treaties of peace are made with foreign peoples. . . .

They reach this degree of honor partly through succession and partly through election. Their children do not usually succeed them, but rather their nephews and grandsons. The latter do not inherit these petty royalties, like the dauphins of France[5] or children inheriting from their fathers. Instead, they are accepted by the whole country only if they possess the proper personal qualifications and agree to accept the position. There are some men who refuse these honors, either because they lack aptitude in speaking or sufficient discretion or patience, or because they like a quiet life, for these positions entail service more than anything else. . . . These captains do not govern their subjects by means of command and absolute power, as they have no force at hand to compel them to their duty. Their government is only civil, and they merely represent what is to be done for the good of the village

---

[5] Title of eldest son and heir of the king of France.

or of the whole country. Beyond that, everyone does as they please. . . . I should like here to ask those who have a low opinion of our Indians, what they think of this method of conducting affairs.

QUESTIONS FOR ANALYSIS

1. How do Brébeuf's Christian beliefs establish the foundation of his understanding of Huron religious beliefs and practices? What links, or potential links, does he see between Christian and Huron beliefs?
2. What practices does Brébeuf describe as evidence that the Huron have a political and civic life? What European practices are comparable to these Huron practices?
3. In praising some Huron political and social practices, how does Brébeuf implicitly criticize European practices?
4. How might the context in which the missionary reports were written—individual missionaries living among the Huron, often isolated from other Europeans—have affected the missionaries' descriptions of the Huron people? How might the editorial process have affected the final version of the *Jesuit Relations* published in France?

$$2$$

"... INFLAMED WITH ZEAL FOR THE SALVATION OF SOULS!"

Venerable Marie de l'Incarnation
Relation of 1654

The missionary impulse derived from many sources. In addition to the Jesuits' vigorous obedience and scholarly curiosity, less structured but no less meaningful impulses led individuals to missionary work. In the seventeenth century, a revival of Christian mysticism, especially among educated women from prominent families, led a few women to leave families or convents to seek union with the divine by working among the "pagans." One such prominent woman was Marie de l'Incarnation (1599–1672). Born Marie Guyard in Tours, France, Marie joined the Ursulines, a Roman Catholic religious order for women that focused on providing instruction in religious doctrine. At the age of thirty-four, Marie experienced a mystical vision that led her to organize a small missionary effort to New France. In 1639, Marie and a few Ursuline sisters arrived in Quebec and established the first congregation of women in North America, where for the next thirty-two years Marie worked diligently for the instruction and conversion of the Iroquois people. In 1654, Marie wrote the Relation, *excerpted on the following page, in which she narrated her life as mystic and missionary—two issues intimately connected for Marie.*

John J. Sullivan, trans., *The Autobiography of Venerable Marie of the Incarnation, O.S.U. Mystic and Missionary* (Chicago: Loyola University Press, 1964), 95, 126–29.

[A]t the age of thirty-four or thirty-five, I entered upon the state which had been intimated to me and which I was awaiting. This was a communication of the apostolic spirit, which was none other than the Spirit of Jesus Christ, which took possession of my spirit in order that I might no longer live except in and through Him and be wholly devoted to the interests of this divine and most adorable Master through zeal for His glory, so that He might be known, loved, and adored by all the nations which He had redeemed by His precious blood. My body remained within the confines of our monastery, but my spirit could not be confined for it was bound to the Spirit of Jesus. This Spirit transported me in spirit to the Indies, to Japan, to America, to the East, to the West, to parts of Canada among the Hurons, and to all the habitable parts of the earth where there were souls, all of whom I saw as belonging to Jesus Christ. With an interior certainty I beheld the demons triumph over those poor souls whom they snatched from the domain of Jesus Christ, our divine Master and sovereign Lord, who had redeemed them by His precious blood. At the sight of all this I was consumed with zeal for them; I could bear it no longer. I embraced all these poor souls, I took them to my heart and offered them to the eternal Father, saying to Him that it was time that He saw that justice was done in favor of my Spouse; that He well knew that He had promised His Son all nations for His heritage. . . .

[*Marie and her party arrive in New France.*]

On the following day Fathers Vimont[1] and Le Jeune[2] and the other fathers of the mission took us to the village of the savages, our very dear brethren. There we were very consoled on hearing them chant the praises of God. We were filled with joy to find ourselves among our good neophytes,[3] and they, on their part, were so happy to see us. The "first Christian" gave us his daughter, and in a few days more were given to us, together with the French girls who were old enough for instruction.

We were given a small house to serve as our lodging until a suitable place would be chosen for building our monastery. There were only two small rooms, but we considered ourselves better off with them, since we had with us the treasure we had come to seek—that is, our dear neophytes—than if we possessed a kingdom. This little house was soon serving as a hospital because of an outbreak of smallpox among the savages. Since we didn't have any furniture as yet, all the beds were on the floor, and indeed there were so many of them that we had to walk over the beds of the sick. Three or four of the savage girls died. His Divine Majesty gave to my sisters so great a fervor and courage that not one of them experienced any aversion to the ills and the filth of the savages. Madame de la Peltrie[4] wanted to have the first place in serving the sick. Although hers was a very delicate constitution, she busied herself in the most humble offices. How precious are the firstfruits of the spirit when it has been inflamed with zeal for the salvation of souls! . . .

---

[1] Barthelemy Vimont (1594–1667), Jesuit priest and General Superior of the Missions of New France from 1639 to 1648.
[2] Paul Le Jeune (1591–1664), Jesuit missionary.
[3] The newly converted Iroquois.
[4] Madeleine de la Peltrie (1603–1671), temporal foundress of the Ursuline mission in New France who worked closely with Marie de l'Incarnation.

By this time there was a large number of savages of both sexes who came to us. We instructed them and conversed with them, and this was a very great consolation for myself. For four or five successive years we exercised continual charity on behalf of these poor savages who came to us from the different nations. We had many resident and transient students, who were committed to us to prepare them for baptism and other sacraments. The savages are very dirty, and their practice of smoke-drying their food gives them a bad odor, to say nothing of the fact that they do not use linen. But these things did not beget any aversion in us; on the contrary, we vied with one another as to who would scour the dear girls when they were brought to us for instruction. . . .

Now that I have seen this country I recognize it as the one which our Lord showed me in a dream six years ago. These great mountains, the vast areas, the site and the configuration, which were still engraved on my mind as at the time of the dream—all this was exactly as I had seen it, except that I don't see as much fog now as I did then. This greatly renewed the fervor of my vocation as well as my attraction, through a complete abandonment of myself, to suffer and to do whatever our Lord would wish of me in this new abode and manner of life which would now be mine. It was a manner of life so entirely different from that of our monasteries in France as far as poverty and frugality were concerned, but not any different from the standpoint of regularity and religious observance.

In the beginning we used high cedar posts, in place of a high fence for a cloister wall, and we were allowed to grant entrance to savage girls and ladies, resident and extern, and to the French girls, all for the purpose of instruction. Our quarters were so small that a room about sixteen feet square served as our choir, parlor, dormitory, refectory, while another room served as a classroom for the French and savage girls and for our kitchen. We had to make a lean-to for an exterior chapel and sacristy.

The filthiness of the savage girls, who were not yet used to the cleanliness of the French, sometimes caused us to find a shoe in our soup pot, while daily we would find hair and charcoal in it; but this didn't cause us any disgust. The persons who visited us, and to whom by way of recreation we would recount this, couldn't understand how we could get used to that sort of thing, nor how we could caress and take on our knees the little savage orphans who were given to us, for they were greasy from a little grease-stiffened rag which covered a small part of their bodies and gave off a very bad odor. And yet all of this was actually a source of delight for us much greater than one would even begin to suspect. When they were somewhat prepared for it, we removed the grease from them over a period of many days, for this grease along with the filth stuck to their skin like glue. Then we clothed them in linen and a little tunic so as to protect them from vermin, with which they were covered when brought to us.

Thanks to the goodness and mercy of God, the vocation and the love He has given me for the savages is always the same. I nourish in my heart a tender affection for them all, trying by my poor prayers to gain them for heaven, and I feel constantly disposed to give my life for their salvation, if I were worthy to do so, by offering myself as a continual holocaust[5] to His Divine Majesty for the salvation of these poor souls.

---

[5] A complete sacrifice.

QUESTIONS FOR ANALYSIS

1. What about the Amerindians attracts Marie's attention? How does she use cleanliness as a metaphor for spirituality in the text?
2. How does her religiosity facilitate her missionary efforts?
3. How does her religiosity shape her understanding of her relationship with the Amerindians?
4. How does Marie's description of the Amerindians compare with Brébeuf's report (Source 1)? What do their reports indicate about the structuring of gender roles in the colonial setting?

3

"WHICH OF THESE TWO IS WISEST AND HAPPIEST. . . ."

A Micmac Leader, reported by Chrestien LeClerq
New Relation of Gaspesia   (1691)

Chrestien LeClerq (1641–c. 1695) was a Catholic missionary in New France between 1675 and 1687. A priest of the Recollet order, he worked with the Micmac and Etchemin peoples of the Gaspé peninsula (the southern side of the mouth to the St. Lawrence River). Catholic missionaries had considerable success working in this area, and some Micmac adopted European practices and religious beliefs. In his work New Relation of Gaspesia, *published on his return to France, LeClerq described this process and supported the Recollet missionary efforts, which were then struggling in New France. In 1680, LeClerq was asked to serve as interpreter for a group of French colonists who wanted to convince the local Micmac population to establish a permanent Micmac residence. In the excerpt below, LeClerq recalls the response of the Micmac leader to this proposition.*

I am greatly astonished that the French have so little cleverness, as they seem to exhibit in the matter of which thou hast just told me on their behalf, in the effort to persuade us to convert our poles, our barks, and our wigwams into those houses of stone and of wood which are tall and lofty, according to their account, as these trees. Very well! But why now . . . do men of five to six feet in height need houses which are sixty to eighty? For, in fact, as thou knowest very well thyself, Patriarch—do we not find in our own all the conveniences and the advantages that you have with yours, such as reposing, drinking, sleeping, eating, and amusing ourselves with our

Chrestien LeClerq, *New Relation of Gaspesia: With the Customs and Religion of the Gaspesian Indians,* trans. William F. Ganong (Toronto: Champlain Society, 1910) (Reprinted New York: Greenwood Press, 1968), 103–6.

friends when we wish? This is not all. . . . [H]ast thou as much ingenuity and cleverness as the Indians, who carry their houses and their wigwams with them so that they may lodge wheresoever they please, independently of any seignior whatsoever? Thou art not as bold nor as stout as we, because when thou goest on a voyage thou canst not carry upon thy shoulders thy buildings and thy edifices. Therefore it is necessary that thou preparest as many lodgings as thou makest changes of residence, or else thou lodgest in a hired house which does not belong to thee. As for us, we find ourselves secure from all these inconveniences, and we can always say, more truly than thou, that we are at home everywhere, because we set up our wigwams with ease wheresoever we go, and without asking permission of anybody. Thou reproachest us, very inappropriately, that our country is a little hell in contrast with France, which thou comparest to a terrestrial paradise, inasmuch as it yields thee, so thou sayest, every kind of provision in abundance. Thou sayest of us also that we are the most miserable and most unhappy of all men, living without religion, without manners, without honour, without social order, and, in a word, without any rules, like the beasts in our woods and our forests, lacking bread, wine, and a thousand other comforts which thou hast in superfluity in Europe. Well, my brother, if thou dost not yet know the real feelings which our Indians have towards thy country and towards all thy nation, it is proper that I inform thee at once. I beg thee now to believe that, all miserable as we seem in thine eyes, we consider ourselves nevertheless much happier than thou in this, that we are very content with the little that we have; and believe also once for all, I pray, that thou deceivest thyself greatly if thou thinkest to persuade us that thy country is better than ours. For if France, as thou sayest, is a little terrestrial paradise, art thou sensible to leave it? And why abandon wives, children, relatives, and friends? Why risk thy life and thy property every year, and why venture thyself with such risk, in any season whatsoever, to the storms and tempests of the sea in order to come to a strange and barbarous country which thou considerest the poorest and least fortunate of the world? Besides, since we are wholly convinced of the contrary, we scarcely take the trouble to go to France, because we fear, with good reason, lest we find little satisfaction there, seeing, in our own experience, that those who are natives thereof leave it every year in order to enrich themselves on our shores. We believe, further, that you are also incomparably poorer than we, and that you are only simple journeymen, valets, servants, and slaves, all masters and grand captains though you may appear, seeing that you glory in our old rags and in our miserable suits of beaver which can no longer be of use to us, and that you find among us, in the fishery for cod which you make in these parts, the wherewithal to comfort your misery and the poverty which oppresses you. As to us, we find all our riches and all our conveniences among ourselves, without trouble and without exposing our lives to the dangers in which you find yourselves constantly through your long voyages. And, whilst feeling compassion for you in the sweetness of our repose, we wonder at the anxieties and cares which you give yourselves night and day in order to load your ship. We see also that all your people live, as a rule, only upon cod which you catch among us. It is everlastingly nothing but cod—cod in the morning, cod at midday, cod at evening, and always cod, until things come to such a pass that if you wish some good morsels, it is at our expense; and you are obliged to have recourse to the Indians, whom you despise so much, and to beg them to go a-hunting that you may be regaled. Now tell me this one little thing, if thou hast any sense: Which of these two is the wisest and happiest—he who labours without ceasing and only obtains, and that with great trouble, enough to live on, or he who rests in comfort and finds all that he needs in the pleasure of hunting and fishing? It is true . . . that we have not always had the use of bread and of wine which your France produces; but, in fact, before the arrival of the French in these parts, did not the Gaspesians live much longer than now? And if we have not any longer among us any of those old men of a hundred and thirty to forty years, it is only because we are gradually adopting your manner of living, for experience is making it very plain that those of us live longest who, despising your bread, your wine, and your brandy, are content with their natural food of beaver, of moose, of waterfowl, and fish, in accord with the custom of our ancestors and of all the Gaspesian nation. Learn now, my brother, once for all, because I must open to thee my heart: there is no Indian who does not consider himself infinitely more happy and more powerful than the French.

QUESTIONS FOR ANALYSIS

1. On what issues does the Micmac leader judge the French? How does he judge the wealth of the French?

2. What is the basis for the Micmac leader's criticism of the French? In what terms does he define the French?

3. How might the French audience reading this account respond to the Micmac leader's statements?

4. Why might LeClerq, writing his *Relation* to build support for missionary efforts, include the Micmac account in his book?

4

". . . FAR FROM BEING CONTRARY TO CHRISTIAN PRINCIPLES . . ."

Matteo Ricci

Journals (1615)

Born in central Italy, the Jesuit missionary Matteo Ricci (1552–1610) arrived in China in 1582 as the Jesuits were reformulating their missionary strategy for China. After several decades with little success, the Jesuits had begun to stress the importance of learning and adapting to the Chinese language and culture. Ricci and other Jesuits developed their knowledge of Chinese philosophy, literature, and science by learning from

Louis J. Gallagher, trans., *China in the Sixteenth Century: The Journals of Matthew Ricci: 1583–1610* (New York: Random House, 1942), 93, 95–98, 44–46, 49, 54–56.

Chinese intellectuals and even adopted the traditional dress of Chinese scholars. These scholars held influential political positions in China, for entrance into the Chinese bureaucracy required young men to pass a demanding series of examinations centered on the Confucian tradition in philosophy, literature, poetry, and the fine arts. The Jesuits, themselves well-trained scholars, built relationships with the Chinese scholar-bureaucrats by showing their respect for Chinese traditions while also demonstrating areas in which European scholarship could improve Chinese knowledge—for example, in astronomy and map making. While most scholar-bureaucrats remained suspicious of the Jesuits, Ricci had considerable success and, given the Chinese name Li Madou, was permitted to settle in the Chinese capital of Beijing in 1601. Here he spent the next nine years teaching European science to the Chinese and preaching the Christian gospel. In the last years of his life, Ricci began to write a history of Christianity in China, and in doing so he emphasized the mission's accommodationist policies that had sought to create a Christian-Chinese synthesis. The work was published in Europe five years after his death. In the excerpt below, Ricci outlines the Chinese religious and political traditions.

Of all the pagan sects known to Europe, I know of no people who fell into fewer errors in the early ages of their antiquity than did the Chinese. From the very beginning of their history it is recorded in their writings that they recognized and worshipped one supreme being whom they called the King of Heaven, or designated by some other name indicating his rule over heaven and earth. It would appear that the ancient Chinese considered heaven and earth to be animated things and that their common soul was worshipped as a supreme deity. As subject to this spirit, they also worshipped the different spirits of the mountains and rivers, and of the four corners of the earth. They also taught that the light of reason came from heaven and that the dictates of reason should be hearkened to in every human action. Nowhere do we read that the Chinese created monsters of vice out of this supreme being or from his ministering deities, such as the Romans, the Greeks, and the Egyptians evolved into gods or patrons of the vices.

One can confidently hope that in the mercy of God, many of the ancient Chinese found salvation in the natural law,[1] assisted as they must have been by that special help which, as the theologians teach, is denied to no one who does what he can toward salvation, according to the light of his conscience. That they endeavored to do this is readily determined from their history of more than four thousand years, which really is a record of good deeds done on behalf of their country and for the common good. The same conclusion might also be drawn from the books of rare wisdom of their ancient philosophers. These books are still extant and are filled with most salutary advice on training men to be virtuous. In this particular respect, they seem to be quite the equals of our own most distinguished philosophers. . . .

---

[1]Ricci draws on the idea of natural law as developed by Thomas Aquinas, which emphasized that the part of the eternal law of divine reason that is embedded in nature itself is knowable to all humanity through the application of human reason.

Although the Literati,[2] as they are called, do recognize one supreme deity, they erect no temples in his honor. No special places are assigned for his worship, consequently no priests or ministers are designated to direct that worship. We do not find any special rites to be observed by all, or precepts to be followed, nor any supreme authority to explain or promulgate laws or to punish violations of laws pertaining to a supreme being. Neither are there any public or private prayers or hymns to be said or sung in honor of a supreme deity. The duty of sacrifice and the rites of worship for this supreme being belong to the imperial majesty alone. . . .

The most common ceremony practiced by all the Literati, from the King down to the very lowest of them, is that of the annual funeral rites. . . . [T]hey consider this ceremony as an honor bestowed upon their departed ancestors, just as they might honor them if they were living. They do not really believe that the dead actually need the victuals which are placed upon their graves, but they say that they observe the custom of placing them there because it seems to be the best way of testifying their love for their dear departed. Indeed, it is asserted by many that this particular rite was first instituted for the benefit of the living rather than for that of the dead. In this way it was hoped that children, and unlearned adults as well, might learn how to respect and to support their parents who were living, when they saw that parents departed were so highly honored by those who were educated and prominent. This practice of placing food upon the graves of the dead seems to be beyond any charge of sacrilege and perhaps also free from any taint of superstition, because they do not in any respect consider their ancestors to be gods, nor do they petition them for anything or hope for anything from them. However, for those who have accepted the teachings of Christianity, it would seem much better to replace this custom with alms for the poor and for the salvation of souls. . . .

The ultimate purpose and the general intention of this sect, the Literati, is public peace and order in the kingdom. They likewise look toward the economic security of the family and the virtuous training of the individual. The precepts they formulate are certainly directive to such ends and quite in conformity with the light of conscience and with Christian truth. They make capital of five different combinations, making up the entire gamut of human relations; namely, the relations of father and son, husband and wife, master and servants, older and younger brothers, and finally, of companions and equals. According to their belief, they alone know how to respect these relationships, which are supposed to be wholly unknown to foreigners, or if known, wholly neglected. Celibacy is not approved of and polygamy is permitted. Their writings explain at length the second precept of charity: "Do not do unto others what you would not wish others to do unto you." It really is remarkable how highly they esteem the respect and obedience of children toward parents, the fidelity of servants to a master, and devotion of the young to their elders. . . .

The Literati deny that they belong to a sect and claim that their class or society is rather an academy instituted for the proper government and general good of the kingdom. One might say in truth that the teachings of this academy, save in some few instances, are so far from being contrary to Christian principles, that such an

---

[2] Those trained in traditional Confucian philosophy and Chinese arts and literature.

institution could derive great benefit from Christianity and might be developed and perfected by it. . . .

Only such as have earned a doctor's degree or that of licentiate[3] are admitted to take part in the government of the kingdom, and due to the interest of the magistrates and of the King himself there is no lack of such candidates. Every public office is therefore fortified with and dependent upon the attested science, prudence, and diplomacy of the person assigned to it, whether he be taking office for the first time or is already experienced in the conduct of civil life. . . .

Tax returns, impost, and other tribute, which undoubtedly exceed a hundred and fifty million[4] a year, as is commonly said, do not go into the Imperial Exchequer, nor can the King dispose of this income as he pleases. The silver, which is the common currency, is placed in the public treasury, and the returns paid in rice are placed in the warehouses belonging to the government. The generous allowance made for the support of the royal family and their relatives, for the palace eunuchs and the royal household, is drawn from this national treasury. In keeping with the regal splendor and dignity of the crown, these annuities are large, but each individual account is determined and regulated by law. Civil and military accounts and the expenses of all government departments are paid out of this national treasury, and the size of the national budget is far in excess of what Europeans might imagine. Public buildings, the palaces of the King and of his relations, the upkeep of city prisons and fortresses, and the renewal of all kinds of war supplies must be met by the national treasury. . . .

[*Ricci describes the many government bureaus and officials.*]

Besides the classes or orders of the magistrates already described and many others which we shall pass over because they differ but little from our own, there are two special orders never heard of among our people. These are the Choli and the Zauli, each consisting of sixty or more chosen philosophers, all prudent men and tried, who have already given exceptional proof of their fidelity to the King and to the realm. These two orders are reserved by the King for business of greater moment pertaining to the royal court or to the provinces, and by him they are entrusted with great responsibility, carrying with it both respect and authority. They correspond in some manner to what we would call keepers of the public conscience, inasmuch as they inform the King as often as they see fit, of any infraction of the law in any part of the entire kingdom. No one is spared from their scrutiny, even the highest magistrates, as they do not hesitate to speak, even though it concerns the King himself or his household. If they had the power of doing something more than talking, or rather of writing, and if they were not wholly dependent upon the King whom they admonish, their particular office would correspond to that of the Lacedemonian Ephors.[5] And yet they do their duty so thoroughly that they are a source of wonder to outsiders and a good example for imitation. Neither King nor magistrates can escape their courage and frankness, and even when they

---

[3] Those who passed certain stages of the examination system.
[4] The unit of currency is not mentioned.
[5] High magistrate in ancient Greece.

arouse the royal wrath to such an extent that the King becomes severely angry with them, they will never desist from their admonitions and criticism until some remedy has been applied to the public evil against which they are inveighing. In fact, when the grievance is particularly acute, they are sure to put a sting into their complaints and to show no partiality where the crown or the courts are concerned. This same privilege of offering written criticism is also granted by law to any magistrate and even to a private citizen, but for the most part it is exercised only by those to whose particular office it pertains. Numerous copies are made of all such written documents submitted to the crown and of the answers made to them. In this way, what goes on in the royal headquarters is quickly communicated to every corner of the country. . . .

Before closing this chapter on Chinese public administration, it would seem to be quite worthwhile recording a few more things in which this people differ from Europeans. To begin with, it seems to be quite remarkable when we stop to consider it, that in a kingdom of almost limitless expanse and innumerable population, and abounding in copious supplies of every description, though they have a well-equipped army and navy that could easily conquer the neighboring nations, neither the King nor his people ever think of waging a war of aggression. They are quite content with what they have and are not ambitious of conquest. In this respect they are much different from the people of Europe, who are frequently discontent with their own governments and covetous of what others enjoy. While the nations of the West seem to be entirely consumed with the idea of supreme domination, they cannot even preserve what their ancestors have bequeathed them, as the Chinese have done through a period of some thousands of years. . . .

Another remarkable fact and quite worthy of note as marking a difference from the West, is that the entire kingdom is administered by the Order of the Learned, commonly known as The Philosophers. The responsibility for orderly management of the entire realm is wholly and completely committed to their charge and care. The army, both officers and soldiers, hold them in high respect and show them the promptest obedience and deference, and not infrequently the military are disciplined by them as a schoolboy might be punished by his master. Policies of war are formulated and military questions are decided by the Philosophers only, and their advice and counsel has more weight with the King than that of the military leaders. In fact very few of these, and only on rare occasions, are admitted to war consultations. Hence it follows that those who aspire to be cultured frown upon war and would prefer the lowest rank in the philosophical order to the highest in the military, realizing that the Philosophers far excel military leaders in the good will and the respect of the people and in opportunities of acquiring wealth. What is still more surprising to strangers is that these same Philosophers, as they are called, with respect to nobility of sentiment and in contempt of danger and death, where fidelity to King and country is concerned, surpass even those whose particular profession is the defense of the fatherland. Perhaps this sentiment has its origin in the fact that the mind of man is ennobled by the study of letters. Or again, it may have developed from the fact that from the beginning and foundation of this empire the study of letters was always more acceptable to the people than the profession of arms, as being more suitable to people who had little or no interest in the extension of the empire.

QUESTIONS FOR ANALYSIS

1. What similarities does Ricci emphasize between Christianity and Chinese religion? How is his description of Chinese religion accommodationist?

2. How does Ricci account for Chinese religious rituals focused on ancestors? How might the context of Ricci's missionary work encourage his accommodationist policies?

3. What images of the Chinese state does Ricci create? How do these images reinforce his accommodationist policies in religion?

4. In praising Chinese political practices, how does Ricci implicitly criticize European practices? How does his criticism of European practices compare to Brébeuf's discussion of Huron political practices (Source 1)?

5

"HE IS, IN FACT, A PUZZLE TO US."

History of the Ming   (18th century)

In 1644, the Ming dynasty in China collapsed, and the imperial throne was seized by well-organized clans of Jurchen tribesmen from Manchuria who adopted the name Manchu and ruled as the Qing dynasty. In order to gain control over China and rule effectively, the Qing emperors needed the political expertise of the traditional scholar-bureaucrats who managed China's sprawling population and resources. Many scholar-bureaucrats, who had been trained in a Confucian tradition that valued loyalty to the emperor, refused to transfer their loyalty from the Ming to the new Qing dynasty—an attitude reinforced by the fact that the Manchu were neither ethnically nor culturally Han Chinese. Some scholars went so far as to kill or maim themselves to preclude serving the Qing. In the 1680s, as part of an effort to win over older scholar-bureaucrats and recruit new ones, the Qing emperor Kangxi sponsored a collaborative project to write the history of the Ming dynasty. The project, which continued long into the eighteenth century, permitted the Qing to honor the idea of loyalty while leaving scholars dependant on the state for support. Further, the Qing could oversee the content of this history to preclude anti-Qing attitudes. The excerpt below from History of the Ming *discusses the Jesuits' activities in China in the early sixteenth century.*

All these people came from European countries and believed in a religion called Roman Catholicism. Jesus, the man whom they worshipped, was born . . . during the reign of Han Aidi [6–1 B.C.] in a country called Judea. Fifteen hundred eighty-

Dun J. Li, ed., *China in Transition: 1517–1911* (New York: Van Nostrand Reinhold, 1969), 14–17.

one years later, in the ninth year of Wanli [1581], Li Madou [Ricci] sailed 90,000 li[1] across the ocean and arrived at Macao off Guangzhou. With his arrival in China came his religion.

In the twenty-ninth year of Wanli [1601] Li Madou arrived at Beijing. He called himself a man of the Great Western Ocean, and, through the intermediation of a eunuch named Ma Tang, presented his native products to the emperor as tribute. Responding to his presence, the Ministry of Rites[2] memorialized the emperor as follows: "In the *Institutions*[3] only a country called Suoli of the Western Ocean is listed. Since there is no mention of the so-called Great Western Ocean, we do not know whether this man has stated the truth. Moreover, he stayed in China for twenty years before he paid his tribute. This procedure is totally different from that normally followed by other foreigners who, admiring China and her moral superiority, come here to present their treasures. The tribute this man has presented consists of the images of a Heavenly Lord and His Mother,[4] a tribute that is highly irregular. He has also brought with him 'bones of the immortals.'[5] The term 'bones of the immortals' is self-contradictory since a true immortal can fly by himself without any bones. These things, to quote Han Yu,[6] are 'unclean, inauspicious items that should not be allowed to enter the imperial palace.' . . . Having been ordered by Your Majesty to report to this ministry, this man Li Madou, instead of proceeding to the ministry's foreign quarters as he was supposed to do, chose to live in a Buddhist temple without being authorized to do so. He is, in fact, a puzzle to us. However, according to the precedents governing tribute-bearing envoys, a foreigner who pays tribute to China should be given gifts and granted dinners in return. It is hereby suggested that this Li Madou be granted hats and belts and be sent back to his own country. He should not be allowed to live in the two capitals [Beijing and Nanjing] or to associate with Chinese. Only in this way can unpleasant incidents be prevented." The emperor did not reply. . . .

Later the emperor, pleased that this man [Ricci] had come such a long way to visit China, granted him living quarters and a food allowance, plus numerous gifts. All the ministers at court thought highly of the man and associated with him. Li Madou was so happy with his new home that he decided to stay until the end of his life. He died in the fourth month of the thirty-eighth year of Wanli [1610] and was buried in the western suburb of Beijing.

On the first day of the eleventh month of the same year [1610] there was an eclipse of the sun. The court astronomers had made so many errors in forecasting heavenly phenomena that suggestions were made that the old calendar be examined and corrected. In the following year [1611] an official named Zhou Ziyu remarked that many Sinicized Westerners such as Pang Dio [Didacus de Pantoya] and Xiong Sanba [Sebastianus de Ursis] were versed in the making of calendars and

---

[1] Three li equal roughly one mile.
[2] The powerful bureau that oversaw court ritual and etiquette and directed the examination system.
[3] An official text of the Ming dynasty published in 1502.
[4] Jesus and Mary.
[5] Relics, such as the bones of saints.
[6] Han Yu (768–824), famous essayist and poet.

that their calendar books were superior to those in China. These Westerners, he continued, should be ordered to translate these books into Chinese and present them to the government for reference purposes. Meanwhile Weng Zhengchun, vice-president of the Ministry of Rites, petitioned the emperor to follow the precedent of adopting the Muslim calendar early in the Hongwu period [1368–1398] by inviting Dio and others to help prepare a new calendar. The emperor agreed.

After Li Madou reached China, many others followed. One of them, Wang Fengsu,[7] took up residence in Nanjing and used his Roman Catholicism to confuse and deceive the masses. He enticed and led astray many intellectuals as well as ordinary citizens. His activities aroused the resentment of Xu Ruke, a secretary in the Ministry of Rites. Xu was particularly resentful when foreigners boasted of the achievements of their respective countries, which, they said, were far superior to those of China. Xu gave two of them paper and pen and asked them to write down what they could remember about their home countries. When their writings were compared, it was found that the contents were not only erroneous but also contradicted each other. It was then that he decided to advocate their expulsion. . . .

Yu Mozi, another [Chinese] official, also memorialized the emperor with the same recommendation. "Since Li Madou's arrival in the east," said Yu, "China again has a religion called Roman Catholicism.[8] Foreigners like Wang Fengsu and Yang Manuo [Emmanuel Diaz] take advantage of their residence in the capital to spread deceptive ideas, and those who have fallen under their unhealthy influence number no fewer than ten thousand. On the first and fifteenth days of each month, frequently more than a thousand persons are assembled for worship. Our country has specific orders to prohibit the spread of foreign and heretical doctrines. Yet these people openly gather in the evening and choose not to disperse until early in the morning, just as the White Lotus Society and other Daoist sects[9] used to do. . . ."

The emperor assented to Yu's request and, in the twelfth month of the same year [1616], ordered Wang Fengsu, Dio, and others to proceed to Guangdong[10] and from there sail for home. . . . Later Wang Fengsu changed his name and reappeared in Nanjing, preaching and proselytizing as usual. The officials in the capital did not know anything about his activities.

The country that these foreigners came from was skilled in making cannons. The cannons it made were even larger than those of the "Western Ocean." Some of these cannons wound up in China, but the Chinese were unable to operate them. During the Tianqi and Zhongzhen periods [1621–1644] the government was waging war in the Northeast, and foreigners at Macao[11] were often invited to the capital to teach the soldiers how to use foreign cannons. These foreigners were generally very enthusiastic with their assistance.

During the Zhongzhen period [1628–1644] the calendar then in use became even more inaccurate. Xu Guangqi, President of the Ministry of Rites, requested

---

[7] His Western name cannot be clearly identified.
[8] Roman Catholic missionaries came to China as early as the thirteenth century.
[9] A popular religion in China, Daoism occasionally fostered fanatical sects that the state authorities saw as threatening.
[10] Province in southern China that was the center for foreign trade.
[11] Portuguese trade port in southern China.

the emperor's approval to establish an institute to revise the old calendar and to order such men as Le Yahu [Jacobus Rho] and Tang Rouwang [Johannes Adam Schall von Bell] to use their country's calendar as reference for the proposed revision. The emperor granted this request, but it took a long time for the new calendar to be completed. The new calendar was called the Zhongzhen Calendar, after the emperor's reigning title. It was much more accurate than the Datong Calendar and was praised highly by those who were in a position to know.

The people who came from the Great Western Ocean were mostly intelligent and highly knowledgeable. They were only interested in spreading their religion and did not care for fame or wealth. The books they wrote dealt with topics which the Chinese rarely mentioned, and those who loved different and strange things were anxious to learn from them. Chinese intellectuals like Xu Guangqi and Li Zhizao[12] were the first to show such interest and helped them to publish their Chinese writings. As a result, this religion, called Roman Catholicism, suddenly flourished in China.

QUESTIONS FOR ANALYSIS

1. What Jesuit activities or behaviors raised suspicions among the Chinese scholar-bureaucrats? How do these suspicions compare with the criticisms made by the Micmac leader about the French (Source 3)?

2. What did the Jesuits do to ingratiate themselves to the Chinese leadership?

3. How does the text express ambiguity toward the Jesuits? In what terms do the Chinese scholar-bureaucrats define the Jesuits?

4. What does the presence of the Jesuits seem to signify to the Chinese scholar-bureaucrats? How might this interpretation have been shaped by Ming loyalists long after the collapse of the Ming dynasty?

CHAPTER QUESTIONS

1. How do the attitudes of Brébeuf and Ricci toward the peoples they seek to convert compare to the attitudes of Sepúlveda and Las Casas (Chapter 1, Sources 7 and 8) toward the Amerindians?

2. How does the religious background of Brébeuf, Ricci, and Marie de l'Incarnation shape their efforts to understand and to respond to these civilizations? How does the missionaries' Christian self-identity affect their understanding of these other civilizations and of the relationship of European Christians to them?

3. What similarities and differences exist between the responses of the Micmac leader and the Chinese scholar-bureaucrats to Europeans and the responses of the Aztecs (Chapter 1, Source 2)? What might account for these differences?

---

[12] Both converted to Roman Catholicism.

Chapter 4

EUROPEAN COLONIZATION AND THE EARLY MODERN STATE: FRANCE AND RUSSIA IN COMPARATIVE PERSPECTIVE

The seventeenth century marked a tumultuous and confusing era in Europe as war, rebellion, and economic depression affected nearly every nation. Monarchs across Europe sought to increase their authority by building new, centralized governments that would augment their international power and diminish the political authority of their domestic political competitors, such as great and local nobles, representative assemblies, independent law courts, and local and regional governments. The monarchs' challenge to established political structures and to people's political, social, and religious identities provoked resistance, however, resulting in international and civil wars and popular rebellions. Theoretically, society was divided into orders or estates so that a person's relationship to the government occurred through his or her order or estate rather than individually. Nobles thus marked their status within the noble order by the political, economic, and social privileges they held. Yet the idea of a society of orders faced challenges in practice. A growing class of wealthy financiers and merchants sought recognition of their importance to society and to the governments that were chronically in need of financing. And local officials and populations often identified themselves through their localities: they thought of themselves as Franconian, Catalane, Nîmois, or Venetian far more than German, Spanish, French, or Italian. Monarchs found these contending sources of identity at times frustrating barriers to establishing more unified realms yet also at times useful political tools as they sought to enhance royal authority.

As monarchs and centralizing state officials sought to expand their control of political affairs and their coordination of economic, legal, religious, and social policies across the patchwork of provinces and localities that made up their realms, they challenged the multitude of rights and practices—such as tax exemptions, trading privileges, religious liberties, and traditions of inheritance—that individuals and communities used to define their place in the political and social world. The citizens of Nîmes, for instance, defined themselves as holding a traditional right of free manufacturing so that anyone could manufacture any product. When the French king attempted to introduce guilds into Nîmes to better direct manufacturing, he challenged not only economic practices but the sense of what it meant to be Nîmois—to be someone who lived in a town of free manufacturing.

As monarchs worked to strengthen and unify their realms, they needed new resources to support them both in warfare and in peacetime. In addition to encouraging economic development within their own states, many monarchs followed

Spain's example and sought wealth by establishing colonial empires abroad. A set of economic practices often collectively called *mercantilism* emerged to produce these resources in both domestic economies and colonial empires. Mercantilism never constituted an economic theory but is best understood as a series of economic policies, undergirded by a few economic assumptions, that aimed to increase the wealth and power of a central state. Mercantilist policies assumed a finite quantity of wealth in the world, often measured by gold and silver bullion, so that one country's gain implied a competitor's loss. To strengthen itself economically, the state should encourage a large population and direct its resources to create a favorable balance of trade by exporting more goods than it imports. As a result, competitors would pay for the excess in exported goods with gold and silver bullion that then could be taxed.

The specific policies enacted in the pursuit of these mercantilist goals varied substantially, but they led to certain political consequences. Kings and their ministers found that enforcing mercantilist plans for economic resources also supported their efforts to centralize political authority at home. Further, mercantilist policies justified royal supervision of the colonizing effort, further enhancing the state's treasury and expanding its political authority. In short, state building and colonization were linked phenomena that sought to increase the power of central governments against foes at home and away. And in pursuing these policies, monarchs challenged the traditional political forms and institutions by which most individuals in Europe and in European colonies identified themselves. This chapter compares the experiences of France and Russia in state building and colonization as monarchs in both realms sought to establish new, centralized political systems and to establish and consolidate colonial empires. Both cases highlight the political and economic issues that undergirded much of European colonial expansion.

COLONIZING ABROAD

During the seventeenth century, France joined the colonization of the Americas, establishing colonies in the northern Americas and in the Caribbean islands. As France moved westward, Russia expanded its authority eastward into the northern Asian landmass of Siberia (Map 4.1). The French monarchs and Russian tsars who sponsored colonial expansion sought economic gain from their ventures. In securing economic benefits, both monarchies also had to establish political authority over diverse cultures and peoples. Two sharp differences marked the two colonizing efforts. First, the Russians had few competitors in their drive across Siberia and no formidable Siberian opposition. The French, in contrast, faced significant internal opposition in some of their American lands and sustained competition and warfare from European rivals. In short, French colonization had a more precarious existence. Second, the Russians, who moved eastward across an uninterrupted landmass, encountered cultures less dramatically different from themselves than did the French, who traveled across an ocean. Nevertheless, in both the French and Russian examples, colonization was about economic and political power. Monarchs wanted their colonies to establish authority in distant lands and to do so in ways that would bring honor, glory, and economic benefits back to Europe and that would strengthen monarchial rule against political rivals in Europe.

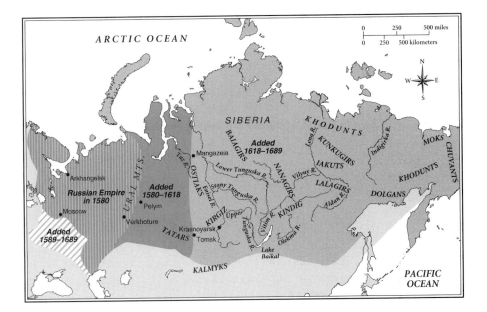

MAP 4.1 RUSSIAN CONQUEST OF SIBERIA
Many of the cities, rivers, and Siberian ethnic groups listed in Source 1 are identified on this map.

1

". . . OUR MIGHTY TSARIST HAND . . ."

The Tsars' Correspondence in the Conquest of Siberia   (17th century)

In the sixteenth century, attracted by the hope of better access to Asian commodities and new revenues to support the tsars' government, Russia began expanding eastward across northern Asia, claiming authority over large territories in which lived bands of loosely organized Siberian peoples. The tsarist state worked to establish political and economic control over the indigenous peoples of Siberia so that Russian merchants would prosper and deliver needed tax revenues into state coffers. The state established a network of officials to direct political and economic affairs—particularly to oversee the collection of iasak, *the basic fur tribute paid by subject peoples. Russian officials in Siberia negotiated between demands from Moscow and local political and economic circumstances. Although the Siberian peoples could not consistently withstand Russian*

Basil Dmytryshyn, E.AP. Crownhat-Vaughn, and Thomas Vaughn, eds. and trans., *Russia's Conquest of Siberia, 1558–1700: To Siberia and Russian America, Three Centuries of Russian Eastward Expansion. A Documentary Record* (Portland: Western Imprints, the Press of the Oregon Historical Society, 1985), 1:69–70, 75–77, 152–55, 340–41.

encroachment, they could affect the practices and policies of the Russian colonizers by harassing Russian officials. In addition, state officials had to support the activities of Russian merchants while restraining their abuses of Siberian peoples. The documents below—letters to and from the tsars—suggest some of the goals, problems, and practices that marked Russia's drive eastward to the Pacific Ocean and beyond.

Letter from Tsar Vasily (r. 1606–1610) to the Tsar's Governor in Pelym,[1] August 6, 1609

On October 8, 1608, you reported to us that in accordance with our decree you were to order that between 50 and 100 agricultural workers be brought into the Pelym district, to Tabarinsk volost.[2] These were to include fathers, sons, uncles, nephews, brothers and neighboring people who did not have any tax obligations. You were authorized to draw funds from our Treasury to pay them to help with the horses, do field work, and construct outbuildings. You reported that there were no volunteers in the nomadic camps who could be taken to do agricultural work in Pelym, but that you could find them in Perm and Sol Kamskaia;[3] but that unless we issued a decree they would not agree to this kind of labor. There was no money in the Treasury to pay them to help construct the outbuildings. Consequently you are requesting that we issue a decree concerning this.

When you receive this our letter, you are to send a reliable *syn boiarskii*[4] with as many soldiers as possible to go from Pelym to Great Perm and Sol Kamskaia. Instruct him that when he reaches Verkhotur'e[5] he is to obtain 150 rubles . . . to be used to encourage agricultural workers to enlist in Perm and in Sol Kamskaia. . . .

The town crier is to announce this in Perm and in Sol Kamskaia, and in the districts and in the market places and at small trade fairs, day after day. The crier is to call out, "Anyone who wishes to go as a peasant to Tabarinsk may settle there by our decree, cultivate the land as agreed, on any plot of land he chooses!"

Funds for the land and all necessities, as well as financial assistance for buying horses and constructing outbuildings has been authorized from our Treasury. . . .

Once an agreement with them is reached about privileges and assistance, they are to be given seeds and sets for our fields. They are to sign the agreements and receive money, and then their names and the contracts are to be brought to Pelym. These peasants are to receive one or two rubles per man or per family, either in Perm or in Sol Kamskaia, to enable them to move to Pelym.

Letter from Tsar Michael (r. 1613–1645) to the Tsar's Governor in Mangazeia,[6] March 20, 1616

[*The tsar had received a report on the travels of a merchant named Kurkin in the Enisei River region of central Siberia.*]

---

[1] City in the eastern Ural Mountains.
[2] An administrative unit near Pelym.
[3] Two cities in the western Ural Mountains.
[4] Impoverished nobles who served as middle-ranking military and civil officials.
[5] Trading center in the eastern Ural Mountains.
[6] Fur-trading city in northwest Siberia.

A foreigner named Sava Frianchuzhenin told them that seven years before some Dutchmen had come by sea to Mangazeia and tried to enter the Enisei. They returned in summer and reported the summer had been so cold they could not get through the ice into the Enisei. However they continued to wait, and when the wind changed to the south they were at last able to enter the Enisei.

Kondratii Kurochkin and a Tobolsk soldier named Kondratii Korel had told them about the Enisei route, and had said that every year many merchants and promyshlenniks[7] go from Arkhangelsk[8] to Mangazeia with all kinds of European goods and provisions. . . .

Stepan Zabelin told the boiar Prince Ivan Semenovich that he had heard from promyshlenniks in Mangazeia that Europeans were hiring guides in Arkhangelsk to take them to Mangazeia, but that the guides did not dare take them there without a decree from us. . . .

Merchants and promyshlenniks are to be given strict orders not to reveal the route to Mangazeia to foreigners, and not to guide them there. If foreigners come to the Enisei or to Mangazeia to trade, they are not to be allowed to carry on trade. If it is possible to bring them into the town in some way, you are to order that they be detained in Mangazeia until we have issued a decree.

When you receive this our letter, you are immediately to send as many of our military officials and promyshlenniks as possible to the mouth of the Enisei. Order them to survey the mouth of the Enisei to determine whether there is some place near the mouth which is suitable for building a fort. . . . They are also to find out what people inhabit the area, and how near the mouth of the Enisei they live. . . .

Order them to take a census of all the natives who live the following distances in versts from the proposed site: 2, 3, 5, 6, 10, 15, 20, 30, 40, 50, 100, and farther. Note their names and patronymics, their occupations, the town to which they pay tribute, what kind of tribute they pay, or whether they do not pay any tribute. Order them to write down all these details in their books. They are also to inquire of these people whether the Europeans who have previously come to the Enisei by sea to trade have come in sailing vessels or in river boats. What manner of trade goods did they bring? How many came?

Letter from Tsar Michael to the Tsar's Governor in Tomsk,[9] May 3, 1636

In the year 1635 traitorous and disobedient Kirgiz people[10] came to Krasnoiarsk[11] fort, together with many other natives, and killed many of the officials and agricultural peasants, and drove off their horses. This Kirgiz attack caused great losses. . . .

On September 14, 1635, the same Kirgiz people, having joined forces with natives disloyal and disobedient to us, . . . attacked Krasnoiarsk fort and drove off all

---

[7] Footloose Russian hunters, traders, or trappers who worked for themselves, in groups of other promyshlenniks, or for wealthy merchants or government officials on such assignments as exploration, conquest, and pacification of the natives.

[8] Major port on the White Sea.

[9] Port on the Tom River.

[10] Pastoral, Turkic people from central Siberia.

[11] Krasnoyarsk, city in western Siberia.

the horses belonging to the officials and the agricultural peasants. They killed many peasants in the fields and burned all our grain in the fields. . . .

[Y]ou are to order that this problem in Krasnoiarsk fort be investigated carefully. In the future our officials are to remain in Krasnoiarsk fort and protect the fort, the agricultural peasants and the tribute-paying people from hostile and traitorous natives. . . .

You are to order them . . . to invoke God's mercy and fight these hostile people. Pursue them, as far as merciful God will help you, so that these hostile lands and their war-like and traitorous inhabitants will be pacified through battle and turned from their evil ways. You are to protect yourself and Krasnoiarsk fort and our agricultural peasants and the tribute-paying people from them. Do not permit any interference in the collection of the tribute, as has been the case in the past. Try, insofar as you are able, to gain the most profit. . . .

You are to strengthen your position by ordering that hostages be taken. These are to be leaders or their children and brothers and relatives. They are to be held in Krasnoiarsk fort, with great care. You are to issue orders to these people, and assure them of our favor, so that they will live in their encampments and pay our tribute, as much as possible, without interruption, as their brothers did previously. They may hunt without interference, and are not to commit any treason. As soon as they come under our mighty Tsarist hand and pay tribute to us and give hostages, we will reward them by not sending our officials into battle against them. . . .

[Y]ou are to write to Fedor [Miakirin, administrator in Krasnoiarsk] in the strongest possible terms warning him of our disfavor if he and his men inflict any unnecessary hardships or impose burdens on our former tribute-paying people who come back under our mighty Tsarist hand, and thereby drive them away from us. They are to be assured of our favor, so that with this in mind they will persuade their relatives to pay us tribute, and to bring other persons from hostile lands to come under our Tsarist mighty hand and pay as much tribute as possible, as much as their relatives used to pay.

Petition from Three Native Princes of the Kolyma Iakutsk People,[12] to Tsar Alexis, 1657–1658

Sovereign, our petition concerns the official Grigorii Ivanov Tatarinov. . . . [He] beat us many times and ordered us your orphans to bring swans, geese and berries, in addition to our tribute, to the tribute collector at the winter quarters. Sovereign, in the fall of 1658 in addition to your Sovereign's tribute collection, Grigorii and his men took six sables with bellies and tails from me, prince Cherm, because we had failed to go to the tribute winter quarters with the swans, geese and berries.

After I, your orphan, prince Kiltig, brought in your Sovereign's tribute collection, he put me into prison and tortured me in order to obtain two sables. He ordered my brothers to ransom me with sables, and he beat me mercilessly. . . .

Grigorii hit the tribute collector Ivan Dorofeev in the face and sent him away from your tribute collection; then with the tribute collector gone, he set aside the best

---

[12] Indigenous people from east central Siberia.

sables we your orphans had brought and kept them for himself. They pay us one arrow per sable . . . , but they do not give us anything for others, and they make us accept inferior goods such as axes and arrows and steel for making fires, and saws and knives and poor dogs. They take sables from us for these things while they are collecting your Sovereign tribute. They select the best sables and set aside what they call damaged and spoiled and torn pelts, so this creates a shortage in our tribute. We have to make up this shortage by hunting in the winter without food and with great hardship. . . .

They order us to come to the winter quarters every week to bring sables, and if we do not bring any in some week, they beat us and lock us up and torture us to get sables. They also take our children for our debts. They take our young girls for sables, for a very small price, and then sell them to Russian men. Because of all the travel we cannot procure enough food, and so we have often suffered great famine.

QUESTIONS FOR ANALYSIS

1. What economic policies do the tsars pursue, and how do these policies compare to the ideas of mercantilism (see the chapter introduction)? How do the tsars' economic policies support the political goals of colonization?

2. Over whom do the tsars seek to establish political authority and control, and how do they intend to do so? What might their methods suggest about the problems of colonization?

3. What are the Russians' attitudes toward the Siberian peoples? How do they distinguish among various indigenous peoples, and what does this indicate about the goals of colonization?

4. What information do the tsars want Russian officials to collect, and why might they want such information?

2

"... ATTRACT THE SAVAGES ..."

French Administrative Correspondence with Its American Colonies (17th century)

In the seventeenth century, France established colonies in the Caribbean islands and in northern parts of the Americas. In the latter half of the seventeenth century, French administrators, led by Louis XIV's principal minister of finance and commerce, Jean-Baptiste Colbert, sought to organize and regulate French colonial affairs under

Pierre Clément, ed., *Lettres Instructions et Mémoires de Colbert.* Vol. 3, pt. 2, *Instructions au Marquis de Seignlay: Colonies* (Paris, 1865), 398, 400–401, 402–5, 657. (Translated by David Kammerling Smith.)

stronger royal direction. The following documents—two letters from Colbert and a royal ordinance—indicate some of the goals, problems, and practices that marked the French state's endeavor to benefit from its colonizing efforts.

Instructions from Colbert to M. de la Rabesnières de Treillebois, Ship's Captain, October 1, 1667

The King, having resolved to send a squadron of his ships to America in the Antilles Islands, commanded by Mr. de la Rabesnières de Treillebois, His Majesty wanted to inform [Treillebois] of the plans [the King] has proposed for this voyage, to guide his voyage so that it gains the advantages expected from his zeal, capacity, and experience in naval matters.

Thus, he will be informed that the plan of His Majesty is:

1. To assure the peace and tranquility of his subjects inhabiting these islands.

2. To assure the possession of the islands to the West India Company[1] that His Majesty has created, to fortify its commerce, in excluding foreigners, and to oblige the inhabitants to submit themselves willingly to the regulations and ordinances of the Company.

3. To show to the English on the island of Barbados that His Majesty wants to protect [the Antilles] more strongly than ever before, in order to invite them to live in peace and execute in good faith the treaties between His Majesty and the King of England. . . .

5. To exclude from the commerce of the [Antilles] all foreigners. . . . His Majesty desires that in the visits that [Treillebois] will make on all the islands, if he encounters some foreign vessels, he will require them to justify whether or not they have permission from the West India Company. If they do, he will make them execute [the terms of this permission] punctually. But if they do not, His Majesty desires that [Treillebois] prevents them from loading or unloading anything in the islands, that he gives them 24 hours to raise their sails and leave, and if this time passes, he seizes or sinks them, His Majesty previously having forbidden all foreigners from trafficking in the islands. His Majesty also wants him to visit all foreign ships and to reclaim the Frenchmen whom he finds in their crews.

Instructions from Colbert to M. de Bouteroue, Departing as Intendant[2] for Justice, Police, and Finances in Canada, April 5, 1668

Principal Issues to Which the Intendant Sent by the King to Canada Should Apply Himself

Immediately after his arrival, he [Bouteroue] must make a general census of all the inhabitants of the country, noting their age, sex, and estate, marital status, and number of children.

---

[1] The West India Company was a privately owned company that was granted a royal charter and monopolistic privileges to trade in the West Indies.
[2] An official appointed by the king to represent royal authority in a French province or colony. Intendants served a crucial role in extending royal authority throughout the realm.

Inform himself, every three months, of the number of deaths, births, and marriages.

Renew the census every year to know if the colony has grown.

The growth of the colony must be the guiding principle and goal of all the intendant's conduct, so that he is never satisfied on this point, and must apply himself incessantly to find all the expedients imaginable to preserve the inhabitants, to multiply them by marriages, and to attract new people. . . .

Excite, by all methods possible, the people to work to clear land for good agriculture, to establish manufacturing, and to develop some maritime trade. . . .

Investigate with great care the mines within the country, such as those of coal, iron, and lead, and establish work there. . . .

With regard to spiritual matters, the opinion of [those in the colony] is that the bishop of Pétrée[3] and the Jesuits establish their authority too strongly by the fear of excommunications and by the too strict of life that they want to maintain.

The intendant must observe all which occurs on this issue without taking part in blaming their [the Jesuits'] conduct, but only in regarding and esteeming them as men of an exemplary piety who have contributed a lot to the discovery and preservation of this country, intervening occasionally to bring them to soften this excessive strictness. It is very important that the bishop and the Jesuits never become aware that he would want to censure their conduct because he would render himself nearly useless to the service of the King. . . .

Up to now, it seems that the maxim of the Jesuits has been to not call the natural inhabitants of this country into common life with the French, either by giving them common lands and housing, by the education of their children, or by marriages. Their [the Jesuits'] reason was that they believe they will conserve the principles and holiness of our religion more purely in keeping the converted savages in their ordinary form of life rather than in bringing them among the French. As it is very easy to see how this maxim is far removed from all good management, as much for religion as for the State, it is necessary to act gently to make them change it and employ all temporal authority to attract the savages [to live] among the French, this which can be done by marriages and by the education of their children.

The commerce of wine and liquor with the savages . . . was a subject of perpetual conflict between the bishop of Pétrée and the Jesuits, on one hand, and the principal inhabitants and those who trade in this country, on the other. The Bishop and the Jesuits have claimed that these liquors intoxicate the savages, that the savages are not able to take them in moderation, and that drunkenness makes them lazy in hunting and gives them all sorts of bad habits, as much for religion as for the State. The principal inhabitants and the traders, to the contrary, claim that the desire to have liquor, which is traded by everyone, obliges the savages to go hunt with more diligence. It is necessary to examine these two sentiments, and the intendant give his reasoned opinion to the King.

---

[3] François Xavier de Laval-Montmorency (1621–1708), appointed bishop of Pétrée (or Petraea) and vicar-apostolic of Canada in 1658.

Royal Ordinance, April 5, 1669

The king . . . [having reviewed documents on] the number of Frenchmen that the King has sent [to Canada] the previous four or five years, the number of families established there, the lands that have been cleared and cultivated, and everything that concerns the situation in that land, and having recognized the considerable growth that this colony has received by the care taken with it, it is hoped that in continuing these same cares, [the colony] will be able to support itself in a few years. And desiring that the inhabitants of this land participate in the favors that His Majesty has made to his people in consideration of the multiplicity of infants and to induce them to marriage, His Majesty has ordered and orders that in the future all the inhabitants of [the colony] who have as many as 10 living children, born in legitimate marriages, and being neither priests, monks, nor nuns, will be paid a pension of 300 livres[4] annually, the money being remitted in the colony. And those who have a dozen children, 400 livres.

His Majesty desires further that it be paid by the orders of the intendant to all boys who marry at 20 years of age and younger and girls at 16 and younger,[5] 20 livres each on the day of their marriages, which will be called "the gift of the king." . . .

[Ordered that] there be made a general division of all the inhabitants by parishes and villages; that some honors be created for the principal inhabitants who take care of the affairs of each town . . . ; that those who have the greatest number of children always be given preference over others, unless some reason prevents it; that there be established some pecuniary penalty payable to the local hospitals against the fathers who do not marry off their children at the age of 20 for boys and 16 for girls.

QUESTIONS FOR ANALYSIS

1. What colonial policies does Colbert pursue, and how do these policies compare to ideas of mercantilism (see the chapter introduction)? How do they compare to the policies set out in the Russian administrative documents (Source 1)?

2. What various European parties participated in colonization, and how do the documents indicate their diverse interests? What do these interests suggest about the problems of colonization?

3. What different goals do the Jesuits and the French administrators have for the Amerindian populations? How does each define the relationship between the Amerindians populations and Western society? How does this conflict reflect differences in how they each define Western culture?

4. What information does the French state want to collect about its colonies, and how might they use such information? How do French economic policies support political goals?

---

[4] French money of account.
[5] In seventeenth-century France, the average age of first marriage for men and women was mid- to late twenties.

3

"... DO NOT CHOAK THE TREE OF PEACE. ..."

Otreouti
Speech to the Governor of New France   (1684)

Otreouti was an orator for the Onondaga, one of the Five Nations of the Iroquois. In 1684, Joseph de La Barre, governor of New France, led an expedition into New York to punish the Iroquois for hunting in Canada and trading with the English. Hunger and disease weakened La Barre's troops, and he arranged a conference with Otreouti (also known as Garangula) to bluff the Iroquois into making concessions. Below is an excerpt from the French report on Otreouti's response.

Hear Yonnondio,[1] I do not Sleep, I have my eyes Open, and the Sun which enlightens me discovers to me a great Captain[2] at the head of a Company of Soldiers, who speaks as if he were Dreaming. He says that he only came to the Lake to smoke on the great Calumet[3] with the Onondagas. But Garangula says, that he sees the Contrary, that it was to knock them on the head, if Sickness had not weakened the Arms of the French.

I see Yonnondio Raving in a Camp of sick men, whose Lives the great Spirit has saved, by Inflicting this Sickness on them. Hear Yonnondio, Our Women had taken their Clubs, our Children and Old Men had carried their Bows and Arrows into the heart of your Camp, if our Warriors had not disarmed them....

Hear Yonnondio, we plundered none of the French, but those that carried Guns, Powder and Ball to the Twihtwies and Chictaghicks,[4] because those Arms might have cost us our Lives. Herein we follow the examples of the Jesuits, who stave all the Barrels of Rum brought to our Castle, lest the Drunken Indians should knock them on the Head. Our Warriors have not Beavers enough to pay for all these Arms that they have taken, and our Old Men are not afraid of the War. *This Belt preserves my Words.*

We carried the English into our Lakes, to traffick there with the Utawawas and Quatoghies, as the Adirondacks[5] brought the French to our Castles, to carry on a Trade which the English say is theirs. We are born free, We neither depend upon Yonnondio nor Corlaer.[6]

---

[1] Iroquois title for the French governor of Canada.
[2] La Barre.
[3] Ceremonial pipe.
[4] The Miami and Illinois indians.
[5] The Ottawa, Huron, and Algonquin indians.
[6] Iroquois title for the English governor of New York.

Cadwallader Colden, *The History of the Five Indian Nations: Depending on the Province of New-York in America* (1727) (Reprinted Ithaca, N.Y.: Cornell University Press, 1958), 54–56.

We may go where we please, and carry with us whom we please, and buy and sell what we please. If your Allies be your Slaves, use them as such, Command them to receive no other but your People. *This Belt preserves my Words.*

We knockt the Twihtwies and Chictaghiks on the head, because they had cut down the Trees of Peace,[7] which were the Limits of our Country. They have hunted Beavers on our Lands: They have acted contrary to the Custom of all Indians; for they left none of the Beavers alive, they kill'd both Male and Female. . . .

Hear Yonondio, What I say is the Voice of all the Five Nations. Hear what they Answer, Open your Ears to what they Speak. . . . [W]hen they [the Five Nations] buried the Hatchet at Cadarackui[8] (in the presence of your Predecessor) in the middle of the Fort, they planted the Tree of Peace, in the same place, to be there carefully preserved, that, in place of a Retreat for Soldiers, that Fort might be a Rendevouze of Merchants; that in place of Arms and Munitions of War, Beavers and Merchandise should only enter there.

Hear, Yonondio, Take care for the future, that so great a Number of Soldiers as appear here do not choak the Tree of Peace planted in so small a Fort. It will be a great Loss, if after it had so easily taken root, you should stop its growth, and prevent its covering your Country and ours with its Branches.

---

[7] Metaphor for bringing war into Iroquois lands.
[8] Fort Frontenac on Lake Ontario, present-day Kingston, Ontario.

QUESTIONS FOR ANALYSIS

1. Does Otreouti fall for La Barre's bluff? How does Otreouti use gendered language in responding to La Barre?
2. What political and economic values does Otreouti assert during his speech? How do these compare to French political and economic values as expressed in the French administrative documents (Source 2)?
3. How would you characterize Otreouti's attitudes toward the French? How do his attitudes compare to the French attitudes toward the indigenous Americans (Source 2)?

"... SAVAGISED THE FRENCH ..."

Anthony Pagden
Lords of All the World   (1995)

The historian Anthony Pagden has written extensively on the ideology and culture of colonization. In the following excerpt, Pagden suggests that the French viewed their relationships with the Amerindians differently than either the Spanish or English.

Anthony Pagden, *Lords of All the World* (New Haven: Yale University Press, 1995), 149–51.

[T]he French had established their first colonies with the explicit, if loosely understood, intention of creating a single cultural, as well as legal, and—uniquely in the French case—racial, community. Under the terms of the creation of the Company of 100 Associates,[1] both the French settlers, their descendants and those Native Americans

> who have come to an understanding of the faith and have made a profession thereof, should be supposed and held to be French nationals, and as such might come to live in France whenever they wished.

After 1663, when the West India Company took over responsibility for the settlements in Canada . . . and the West Indies, the French settlers were encouraged to intermarry with the Native Americans. Although Colbert described the Iroquois as "true savages having nothing that is human about them except the appearance of men," he could also, with no apparent sense of contradiction and in the same document, speak of the pressing need to "oblige the savages to settle among us, and to [learn] our customs and our language." The act of foundation of the West India Company, for which Colbert was responsible, granted to all immigrants to America, "the same liberties and franchises which they had while living in this kingdom." More strikingly still, it extended the terms made in the Act Founding the Company of 100 Associates to

> those who are born of [the colonists] and the savages who have converted to the Catholic Apostolic and Roman Faith, to be registered and counted as denizens and French natives, and as such entitled for all rights of succession, good laws and other dispositions, without being obliged to obtain any letter of naturalization. . . .

Colbert's "Frenchification" scheme had been launched partly because he believed that a massive increase in the population of the American colonies was necessary if they were to survive in the face of English hostility, and also because he believed that this objective could be more easily achieved by this means than by mass migration. It had also, however, been his intention to extend to Canada and the Caribbean Louis XIV's project for a "unified state," united in speech, customs, religion, king, and in this case blood. . . .

The Spaniards, whose native populations had entered the historiography of the empire as noble, if primitive, warriors, were seen, at least at first, as potential marriage partners, although the crown did nothing to encourage such unions. Some members of the *conquistador* class even attempted liaisons with what they identified as a native aristocracy. . . . [However, r]acial integration in Spanish America, although it was to result in wholly new groups of peoples with distinctive cultures, and ultimately distinctive political aspirations of their own, played no part in the crown's conception of the empire as a single cultural and political unit.

The English . . . found the prospect of intermarriage with Native Americans abhorrent. As Sir Josiah Child remarked in 1665, the Spaniards had benefited from having settled in areas where cities and plantations already existed and which had indigenous populations with whom they could interbreed, whereas the British had only "wild Heathens, with whom they could not, nor ever have been known to mix." . . .

---

[1] French trading company created under royal charter to control trade in New France.

Of all the European powers only the French had attempted to replicate their society in America with a mixed population. . . . The long-term effect of Colbert's scheme had been, as Mirabeau[2] caustically noted in 1758, that "instead of French-ifying (*franciser*) the savages, these had savagised the French," making them, in his view, "incapable of that subordination which is the soul of all colonies." Little wonder that when François Volney,[3] one of the most perceptive observers of the colonial process, passed through the region in 1797 he found it to be largely inhabited by "Frenchmen of the age of Louis XIV who have become half Indian" together with "Englishmen of the last century."

QUESTIONS FOR ANALYSIS

1. According to Pagden, how did French policy toward the Amerindians differ from Spanish and English policies?
2. How does Pagden's description of French policy compare to descriptions in the French administrative documents (Source 2)?
3. How does the French colonial policy described by Pagden reinforce the goals of mercantilism?
4. What do the French policies imply about French attitudes toward the Amerindians? About the basis of French identity?

COLONIZING AT HOME

During the seventeenth century, the Bourbon dynasty that ruled France set out to establish political stability centered on a powerful monarchy. The Bourbon kings and their royal ministers enhanced the monarchy's political authority, successfully eliminating the nobility as a serious threat to royal authority and slowly bending local and regional officials to the royal will. The monarchy created a bureaucratic system with representatives of the king called *intendants* placed in each French province and other royal officials established in towns and municipalities. These officials extended the "royal gaze" by gathering political information for the crown and implementing mercantilist policies aimed at expanding the French economy. Both a wealthier France and profitable French colonies, it was hoped, would produce greater tax revenues that could support royal ambitions at home and in Europe. A persistent impediment to creating a fully centralized political system remained the vast array of political and economic privileges held by individuals, regions, and municipalities. Because these privileges also served as aspects of the local traditions and practices by which individuals and groups defined their place within the political world, royal efforts to alter them were resisted—sometimes violently and sometimes by careful political maneuvering. The intendants and other provincial officials were left to balance the desires of the monarch with the demands and threats of local officials and populations.

[2] Victor Riquetti, Marquis de Mirabeau (1715–1789), French political economist, in *The Friend of Humanity*.

[3] Constantin-François de Chasseboeuf, Comte de Volney (1757–1820), French philosopher, historian, and traveler.

In Russia, Peter the Great took inspiration from monarchs such as Louis XIV to launch a radical transformation of the Russian government and the Russian nobility. Peter saw in the western European states the model of technologically and administratively advanced societies, and he endeavored to remake Russia, and the conservative Russian nobility, in that image.

5

"... HONOR SHOULD BE MORE DEAR TO THEM THAN LIFE ITSELF...."

Cardinal Richelieu
Political Testament   (c. 1630s)

Cardinal Richelieu (1585–1642) came to prominence in France in the political turmoil that followed Henry IV's death in 1610. In 1624, the young King Louis XIII appointed Richelieu to direct the French state. Louis XIII both feared and respected Richelieu's abilities. Richelieu, for his part, established a dual goal — to make Louis XIII unchallenged in France and France unchallenged in Europe. In the excerpt below from Richelieu's "Political Testament," the cardinal outlines the "royal program" he pursued.

General Statement of the Royal Program

When Your Majesty resolved to admit me both to your council and to an important place in your confidence for the direction of your affairs, I may say that the Huguenots[1] shared the state with you; that the nobles conducted themselves as if they were not your subjects, and the most powerful governors of the provinces as if they were sovereign in their offices.

I may say that the bad example of all of these was so prejudicial to the welfare of this realm that even the best courts were affected by it, and endeavored, in certain cases, to diminish your legitimate authority as far as it was possible in order to carry their own powers beyond the limits of reason.

I may say that everyone measured his own merit by his audacity; that in place of esteeming the benefits which they received from Your Majesty at their proper worth, they all valued them only as they satisfied the demands of their imaginations; that the most scheming were held to be the wisest, and often found themselves the most prosperous.

I may further say that foreign alliances were scorned, private interests being preferred to those of the public, and in a word, the dignity of the royal majesty was

---

[1] French Calvinist Protestants.

Henry Bertram Hill, ed. and trans., *The Political Testament of Cardinal Richelieu* (Madison: University of Wisconsin Press, 1961), 9–11, 20–21, 31–32.

so disparaged, and so different from what it should be, because of the misdeeds of those who conducted your affairs, that it was almost impossible to recognize it. . . .

Notwithstanding these difficulties which I explained to Your Majesty, knowing how much kings may do when they make good use of their power, I dared to promise you, with assurance, that you would soon find remedies for the disorders in your state, and that your prudence, your courage, and the benediction of God would give a new aspect to this realm. I promised Your Majesty to employ all my industry and all the authority which it should please you to give to me to ruin the Huguenot party, to abase the pride of the nobles, to bring all your subjects back to their duty, and to restore your reputation among foreign nations to the station it ought to occupy. . . .

Reformation of the Nobility

[I]t is necessary to realize that the nobility is one of the principal organs of the state, capable of contributing much to its preservation and stability. . . .

While it is necessary so to support the nobles against those who would oppress them, it is also necessary to see that they in turn do not exploit those beneath them. It is a common enough fault of those born to this order to use violence in dealing with the common people whom God seems to have endowed with arms designed more for gaining a livelihood than for providing self-defense. It is most essential to stop any disorders of such a nature with inflexible severity so that even the weakest of your subjects, although unarmed, find as much security in the protection of your laws as those who are fully armed. . . .

While the nobility merits to be generously treated if it does well, it is necessary at the same time to be severe with it if it ever fails in what its status demands of it. I do not hesitate to say that those nobles who, degenerating from the virtuous conduct of their forebears, fail to serve the crown constantly and courageously with both their swords and their lives, as the laws of the state require, deserve the loss of the privileges of their birth and should be reduced to sharing the burdens of the common people. Since honor should be more dear to them than life itself, it would be much more of a punishment to them to be deprived of the former than the latter. . . .

The People

All students of politics agree that when the common people are too well off it is impossible to keep them peaceable. The explanation for this is that they are less well informed than the members of the other orders in the state, who are much more cultivated and enlightened, and so if not preoccupied with the search for the necessities of existence, find it difficult to remain within the limits imposed by both common sense and the law.

It would not be sound to relieve them of all taxation and similar charges, since in such a case they would lose the mark of their subjection and consequently the awareness of their station. Thus being free from paying tribute, they would consider themselves exempted from obedience. One should compare them with mules, which being accustomed to work, suffer more when long idle than when kept busy. But just as this work should be reasonable, with the burdens placed upon these animals proportionate to their strength, so it is likewise with the burdens placed upon the people. If they are not moderate, even when put to good public use, they are certainly unjust.

QUESTIONS FOR ANALYSIS

1. What does Richelieu identify as the central goals of the "royal program"?
2. How does Richelieu's description of the nobility and their role in society compare to his description of the people? How does his attitude toward the subjects of the French king compare to the attitudes toward the Amerindians in the French administrative correspondence (Source 2)?
3. How do Richelieu's descriptions of the nobility and the people reinforce the "royal program"?
4. How does Richelieu create a singular identity for France and yet also identify a France of social divisions?

"HIS MAJESTY DESIRES . . ."

Administrative Correspondence within France   (17th century)

As Louis XIV and his ministers expanded the royal government's influence and power throughout France, they confronted the myriad provincial and regional officials who resented royal encroachments on their local political and economic privileges—privileges that kept France politically and economically divided. Through both threats and new grants of privileges, Louis XIV and his ministers worked to "centralize" political authority by integrating national networks of powerful individuals and families centered in Paris with regional and municipal networks of influential local officials. The resultant arrangements, sometimes referred to as Absolutism, *enhanced the ability of the monarchy to make its will felt throughout France; however, the system operated more by compromise and negotiation through the various national and local political networks than by royal fiat. Louis XIV's minister chiefly responsible for economic affairs, Jean-Baptiste Colbert, gave particular emphasis to economic unification and economic growth, both of which he believed strengthened the power of the French monarchy. The following letters suggest the practices by which Louis XIV and his minister sought to fulfill that goal and the difficulties that they encountered.*

Pierre Clément, *Histoire du Système Protecteur en France* (Paris, 1854) (Reprinted New York: Burt Franklin, 1968), 262–63 (translated by David Kammerling Smith); Pierre Clément, ed., *Lettres Instructions et Mémoires de Colbert.* Vol. 2, pt. 2, *Industrie, Commerce* (Paris, 1863), 426–27 (translated by David Kammerling Smith); William Beik, *Louis XIV and Absolutism: A Brief Study with Documents* (Boston: Bedford/St. Martin's, 2000), 127–28, 136–37, 163–64.

Circular from Colbert to the Appointed Commissaires and Intendants, June 1, 1680

His Majesty desires that equality and justice in taxation and the suppression of all types of abuses and of expenses [in the collection of taxes] serves as a second relief to his people, in addition to those that he gives them by the reductions of taxes.

His Majesty desires, thus, that as soon as you have received this letter, you will begin to visit each district of your territory; that during this visit, you will examine with great care the state of agriculture products, the nature of the livestock, manufacturing, and all which contributes in each district to the attraction of bullion; that you examine with the same care everything that may contribute to the augmentation and nourishment of livestock and manufacturing, even establishing new ones of these.

Listen to all the complaints made to you because of the inequality of taxes on the rolls of the *taille*[1] and do all that you deem proper to suppress these abuses and establish the most equitable possible taxes.

His Majesty desires especially that you give him an account every three months, without exception, of the number of prisoners which have been arrested, whether due to the *taille* or due to the taxes on his farms.

He also desires that you prevent, as much as you are able, the General Receivers[2] of his finances and the receivers and collectors of the *taille* from seizing livestock because on their multiplication depends a large part of the wealth of the realm and the facility of the people to subsist and pay their taxes.

You also must hold your hand to the punctual execution of the declarations that prohibit seizing livestock for all types of debts.

Letter from Louis XIV to the Aldermen and Residents of Marseilles, August 26, 1664

Very-dear and well-loved: having considered how it would be useful to this realm to reestablish both internal and foreign commerce . . . we have resolved to hold, to this end, every two weeks in our presence a council of commerce in which all the interests of merchants and the methods to achieve this reestablishment will be examined and resolved, in addition to all that concerns manufacturing. We also tell you that we assign, in the expenses of our state, a million livres[3] each year for the reestablishment of manufacturing and the augmentation of navigation, without counting in this the other larger sums that we set aside for the West and East India Companies.[4]

That we work incessantly to abolish all the tolls which are raised on the navigable rivers.

---

[1] Important form of taxation for the French state.
[2] Private company that leased from the French state the right to collect certain taxes. The company kept as profit any taxes collected in excess of the leasing fee.
[3] French money of account.
[4] Private trading companies granted commercial privileges by the king.

That already there has been spent more than a million livres for the repairs of public roads, on which we will continue working incessantly.

That from the money of our treasury we will assist all those who want to undertake the reestablishment of old manufactories or who propose new ones. . . .

That we will lodge comfortably, at our court, each and every merchant who has affairs there, during all the time that they will be obliged to stay there, having ordered to the Grand Marshall of Housing of our House to identify a lodging proper for this affect that will be called "The House of Commerce."

That if the merchants want to deputize one of their number to our court to take care of their affairs, we will loge him in [the House of Commerce] and give him audiences on all occasions.

Letter from the Prince of Condé, Governor of Burgundy,[5] to Colbert, June 18, 1662

[*With regard to the meeting of the Estates of Burgundy[6] and its discussion of its "free gift" of tax revenues to the king: by granting the king the "free gift" of tax money, the Estates gained the right to control some tax collection in the province to reimburse the cost of the "free gift."*]

The next day they began to discuss the free gift. The matter was placed on the floor, and before it was voted, these gentleman sent a delegation to me to ask whether the sum the king was demanding included everything and whether the gift they gave the king would free them from all taxes, especially the "subsistence" and "winter quarters" [for the troops],[7] since, with peace restored, they hoped the king would free them from this expense. . . .

Since then the Estates have deliberated every day, persuaded that the extreme misery in this province—caused by the great levies it has suffered, the sterility [of the land] in recent years, and the disorders that have recently occurred—would induce the king to give them some relief. That is why they offered only 500,000 livres for the free gift. Then, after I had protested this in the appropriate manner, they raised it to 600,000, then 800,000, and finally 900,000 livres. Until then I had stood firm at 1.5 million, but when I saw that they were on the verge of deciding not to give any more . . . and seeing that it was only fear of impotence that was restraining them from making a larger effort, I finally came down to the 1.2 million livres contained in my instructions and invited them to deliberate again, declaring that I could not agree to present any other proposition to the king and that I believed that

---

[5] Louis II de Bourbon, prince of Condé (1621–1686), governor of Burgundy, a large territory in east-central France.

[6] Estates were assemblies in several French provinces that claimed authority over many aspects of politics in a province, especially taxation and finance. The Estates were composed of three chambers—the clergy, the nobility, and the third estate (which theoretically represented all nonclergy and nonnobles).

[7] Taxes levied to pay for troops passing through or temporarily lodged in private homes in the province.

there was no better way to serve their interests than to obey the king blindly. They agreed with good grace and came this morning to offer me a million. They begged me to leave it at that and not to demand more from them for the free gift; and since I told them they would have to do a little better to satisfy the king completely on this occasion, they again exaggerated their poverty and begged me to inform the king of it, but said that, rather than not please him, they preferred to make a new effort, and they would leave it up to me to declare what they had to do. I told them that I believed His Majesty would have the goodness to be satisfied with 1.05 million livres for the free gift, and they agreed, while pressing me to make the king aware of the extreme need they found themselves in, which I promised to do. So, Monsieur, there is the deed done. . . .

When I return, I will bring a list of those [members of the Estates] who acted best; His Majesty will decide if he considers them worthy of some sort of reward, as has always been the practice, and he will act as he sees fit.

Letter from Claude Bouchu, Intendant of Burgundy, to Colbert, December 10, 1664

[*With regard to a conflict about the jurisdiction over a murder case: Bouchu's claim for jurisdiction rested on reforms in the management of France's forests that the king had issued.*]

I wrote you by the last courier about the Parlement[8] of Dijon's attempt to block the implementation of a legal verdict I issued in collaboration with the requisite number of judges and in accordance with all proper procedures stipulated in the forest reform. Their attempt is contrary to the authority of the king. They know perfectly well that for two years I have had the authority to implement [the forest reform] in this city. They tolerated the trial for more than three weeks knowing full well that it concerned the murder by ambush of a forest guard, that [these guards] are indispensable agents for the preservation of our forests, and that [the murder concerned] an officer acting in the line of duty. If this act were to remain unpunished, it would become impossible to find any [guards] and the forests would be abandoned to the whims of anyone.

I thought I should inform you that the audacity of the officers of the Parlement increases day by day, and that while they are triumphing in their latest effort, they are announcing loudly that in the future they will impede the execution of all the king's orders. In effect they intimidate everyone who tries to function here and discourage everyone who has been issued a legal summons—whether for the forest reforms, the auditing of debts, the investigation of titles of nobility, or other things—from cooperating. If this continues, not only will I be obliged to stop where I am, but everything I've done up to this point, which is more than half of the job, will be overturned without hope of recovery.

---

[8] The parlements were the highest law courts in France and became centers of resistance to royal authority.

Letter from the Bishop of Saint Malo to Colbert, July 23, 1675

[*Peasants in Brittany reacted to new taxes imposed to help finance a war against Holland.*]

[The duchess of Rohan] was warned that on the preceding days the peasants of certain parishes near Pontivy were threatening to burn and pillage the house of one of the local [tax agents], named Lapierre, and several others yesterday and Sunday because the rabble were calling them extortionists. And they stood by their word, for on Sunday at midday an angry mass of them stormed into Pontivy, two thousand strong, threw themselves at Lapierre's house, broke in the door, pillaged all the furniture, took all the wine from the cellars . . . , rolled the barrels out into the streets, tapped them, and drank them all, except for a few that they transported out of town to divide among themselves. After they were quite drunk, they returned to the house, smashed all the furnishings, and demolished part of the building. The poor bourgeois of the city (which has no walls) didn't dare to repulse them or oppose their violence, so each bourgeois collected whatever he could in the way of furniture and papers and carted them away, fearing more pillage. . . .

[T]hey [the peasants] are loudly threatening to set fire to this abbey because they claim I am also an extortionist and they have been led to believe that I endorsed the gabelle.[9] . . .

I think you know, Monsieur, that this gabelle is their great monster, along with the stamped paper.[10] The [tax] agents in all the little towns around here no longer dare use [stamped paper], and most of them have abandoned their houses or been expelled by the owners for fear that they will be burned down. Almost all the nobles of lower Brittany and the surrounding districts are leaving their country houses and taking refuge in the principal cities, and bringing along what they can of their most precious furnishings and all their papers to keep them from being pillaged or burned. . . .

QUESTIONS FOR ANALYSIS

1. In economic terms, how do these documents demonstrate mercantilist principles (see the chapter introduction)?

2. In political terms, how do these documents demonstrate an effort to centralize political power in France? How do the instructions given in these letters seek to extend the "royal gaze" (see the section introduction)?

3. How do the documents show that a process of negotiation and compromise took place throughout the French centralizing effort? How do the economic and political goals evident in these documents both support one another and indicate limits to political centralization?

4. How do Colbert's economic and political goals and practices within France compare to his economic and political goals and practices in the French colonies (Source 2)? How would colonization and centralization reinforce each other?

---

[9] Salt tax.

[10] Stamp tax required on all official documents.

7

". . . A USEFUL SERVICE TO US OR TO THE STATE."

Decrees of Peter the Great   (early 18th century)

Peter the Great (1672–1725) set out to transform Russia. Peter had learned of the tech-nological and economic developments in western Europe from his evenings spent in Moscow's German quarter, where European visitors resided, and during his two jour-neys to central and western Europe. Peter compared the Russia of his day unfavorably with what he had seen in Europe—an impression solidified by Russia's military losses early in Peter's reign. In the wake of these military disappointments, Peter launched a reform movement to bring western European ideas and practices to Russia. Recog-nizing that his reforms required a class of state servants subject to his will, Peter set out to diminish the power of the deeply conservative Russian nobility and build an educated elite who would develop and use its talents for the benefit of the state. Further, Peter promoted economic development in Russia, especially when it served the tsar's inter-ests. The documents excerpted below suggest the range and goals of Peter's reforms—reforms that provoked considerable resistance among many Russian traditionalists.

Decree on Compulsory Education of the Russian Nobility, February 28, 1714

Send to every district some persons from mathematical schools to teach the chil-dren of the nobility—except those of freeholders and government clerks—math-ematics and geometry; as a penalty [for evasion] establish a rule that no one will be allowed to marry unless he learns these [subjects]. Inform all prelates to issue no marriage certificates to those who are ordered to go to schools.

Decrees on Western Dress and Shaving, 1701 and 1705

Western dress shall be worn by all the great nobles, high nobles, members of our councils and of our court, . . . gentry of Moscow, secretaries, . . . provincial gentry, middle nobles, established merchants, government officials, the tsar's bodyguard, members of the guilds purveying for our household, citizens of Moscow of all

Basil Dmytryshyn, ed., *Imperial Russia: A Source Book, 1700–1917* (New York: Holt, Rinehart, and Winston, 1967), 16; George Vernadsky, ed., *A Source Book for Russian History from Early Times to 1917.* Vol. 2, *Peter the Great to Nicholas I* (New Haven: Yale University Press, 1972), 347; Dmytryshyn 20–21, 18–19; Eugene Schuyler, *Peter the Great, Emperor of Russia* (New York: Scribner's, 1884), 44–45; James Cracraft, *Major Problems in the History of Imperial Russia* (Lexington, Mass.: Heath, 1994), 116; Vernadsky 349.

ranks, and residents of provincial cities . . . excepting the clergy (priests, deacons, and church attendants) and peasant tillers of the soil. The upper dress shall be of French or Saxon cut, and the lower dress and underwear—[including] waistcoat, trousers, boots, shoes, and hats—shall be of the German type. . . . [Likewise] the womenfolk of all ranks, including the priests', deacons', and church attendants' wives, the wives of the dragoons, the soldiers, and the tsar's bodyguard, and their children, shall wear Western dresses, hats, jackets, and underwear—undervests and petticoats—and shoes. From now on no one [of the above-mentioned] is to wear Russian dress or Circassian[1] coats, sheepskin coats, or Russian peasant coats, trousers, boots, and shoes.

Henceforth, in accordance with this, His Majesty's decree, all court attendants . . . provincial service men, government officials of all ranks, military men, all the established merchants, members of the wholesale merchants' guild, and members of the guilds purveying for our household must shave their beards and moustaches. But, if it happens that some of them do not wish to shave their beards and moustaches, let a yearly tax be collected from such persons: from court attendants . . . provincial service men, military men, and government officials of all ranks—60 rubles per person; from the established merchants and members of the wholesale merchants' guild of the first class—100 rubles per person. . . . As for the peasants, let a toll of two half-copecks per beard be collected at the town gates each time they enter or leave a town; and do not let the peasants pass the town gates, into or out of town, without paying this toll.

Table of Ranks

[Peter instituted the Table of Ranks to force nobles to enter into government service in the bureaucracy, army, and navy. The table created a ranking system for the service nobility.]

1. Those princes who are related to Us[2] by blood or those who are married to Our princesses always take precedence and rank over all other princes and high servants of the Russian state. . . .

3. Whoever shall demand respect higher than is due his rank, or shall illegally assume a higher rank, shall lose two months of his salary; if he serves without salary then he shall pay a fine equal to the salary of his rank; one third of that fine shall be given to the individual who reported on him, and the remainder will be given to a hospital fund. The observance of this rank procedure does not apply on such occasions as meetings among friends or neighbors or at social gatherings. . . .

8. Although We allow free entry to public assemblies, wherever the Court is present, to the sons of princes, counts, barons, distinguished nobles, and high servants of the Russian state, either because of their births or because of the positions

---

[1] Originating from Circassia, the northwest region of the Caucasus Mountains between the Black and Azov Seas.

[2] Peter, using the royal *we*.

of their fathers, and although We wish to see that they are distinguished in every way from other [people], We nevertheless do not grant any rank to anyone until he performs a useful service to Us or to the state.

Decree on Right of Factories to Buy Villages, January 18, 1721

Previous decrees have denied merchants the right to obtain villages. This prohibition was instituted because those people, outside their business, did not have any establishments that could be of any use to the state. Nowadays, thanks to Our decrees, as every one can see, many merchants have companies and many have succeeded in establishing new enterprises for the benefit of the state; namely: silver, copper, iron, coal and the like, as well as silk, linen, and woolen industries, many of which have begun operations. As a result, by this Our decree aimed at the increase of factories, We permit the nobility as well as merchants to freely purchase villages for these factories, with the sanction of the Mining and Manufacturing College, under one condition: that these villages be always integral parts of these factories. Consequently, neither the nobility nor merchants may sell or mortgage these villages without the factories . . . and should someone decide to sell these villages with the factories because of pressing needs, it must be done with the permission of the Mining and Manufacturing College. And whoever violates this procedure will have his possessions confiscated.

Decree on the Invitation to Foreigners, April 27, 1702

It is sufficiently known in all the lands which the Almighty has placed under our rule, that since our accession to the throne all our efforts and intentions have tended to govern this realm in such a way that all of our subjects should, through our care for the general good, become more and more prosperous. For this end we have always tried to maintain internal order, to defend the State against invasion, and in every possible way to improve and to extend trade. With this purpose we have been compelled to make some necessary and salutary changes in the administration, in order that our subjects might more easily gain a knowledge of matters of which they were before ignorant, and become more skillful in their commercial relations. We have therefore given orders, made dispositions, and founded institutions indispensable for increasing our trade with foreigners, and shall do the same in future. Nevertheless we fear that matters are not in such a good condition as we desire, and that our subjects cannot in perfect quietness enjoy the fruits of our labours, and we have therefore considered still other means to protect our frontier from the invasion of the enemy, and to preserve the rights and privileges of our State, and the general peace of all Christians, as is incumbent on a Christian monarch to do. To attain these worthy aims, we have endeavoured to improve our military forces, which are the protection of our State, so that our troops may consist of well-drilled men, maintained in perfect order and discipline. In order to obtain greater improvement in this respect, and to encourage foreigners, who are able to assist us in this way, as well as artists and artisans profitable to the State, to come in numbers to our country, we have issued this manifesto, and have ordered printed copies of it to be sent throughout Europe. And as in our residence of Moscow, the free exercise of religion of all other sects, although not agreeing with our church, is already allowed, so shall this be hereby confirmed anew in such wise that we, by the power granted to us by the Almighty, shall exercise no compulsion over the consciences of men, and shall gladly allow every Christian to care for his own salvation at his own risk.

Statute of the College of Manufacturing, December 3, 1723

His Imperial Majesty most mercifully ordains this Regulation of the College of Manufactures, in accordance with which it shall administer its affairs.

Whereas His Imperial Majesty, for the creation and increase of manufactures and factories, has been pleased to establish this special College.... He has therefore been pleased to grant it guidance according to the following points....

1. The College of Manufactures has supreme direction over all manufactures and factories and other matters relating to its administration throughout the Russian Empire, and must act in loyalty and zeal as it is here laid down....

6. Whereas His Imperial Majesty has sought diligently to establish and disseminate in the Russian Empire, for the common good and profit of His subjects, various manufactures and factories such as are found in other states, the College is hereby ordered diligently to seek ways in which to introduce these and other curious arts into the Russian Empire, especially those for which materials can be found within the Empire; and to introduce the appropriate privileges for those people who want to create places of manufacture.

7. His Imperial Majesty permits everybody, of whatever rank and quality, in any and all positions, to found manufactories wherever they find it right. This [invitation] is to be published everywhere....

8. The College must be careful, when granting privileges to somebody to found a factory, that others who might later want to found such are not excluded; for from the zeal [competition] between manufactures can come not only growth, but quality, and the manufactured goods will be sold at a moderate price, which would benefit His Majesty's subjects. Nevertheless, the College is to see that where [existing] factories are sufficient, the creation of other such factories does not corrupt manufacturing, especially by the making of [goods of] poor quality, even though they be sold cheaply.

9. The College must diligently inspect manufactories that are formed into [joint stock] companies, that they be maintained in good condition....

10. Factories founded or henceforth to be founded at His Majesty's expense, having been brought to a good condition, are to be made over to private persons; the College is to be diligent in this endeavor.

Letter from the Astrakhan Rebels to the Don Cossaks, July 31, 1705

[In 1705, a group of disgruntled Russians, led by military guards and Russian orthodox priests who believed Peter was destroying traditional Russia, launched a revolt against

Peter from the town of Astrakhan. Seeking support for their revolt, they wrote to the leaders of the Don cossacks, a free, self-governing military community located in south central Russia along the Don River and composed largely of peasants who had fled serfdom.]

We wish to inform you of what has happened in Astrakhan on account of our Christian faith, because of beard-shaving, German dress, and tobacco; how we, our wives, and our children were not admitted into churches in our old Russian dress; how men and women who entered the holy church had their clothes shorn and were expelled and thrown out; how all kinds of insults were heaped upon us, our wives, and our children; and how we were ordered to worship idolatrous manikins.[3] We have thrown these manikin idols out of the houses of the men in authority. Moreover, in the last year, 1704, they imposed on us, and collected, a [new] tax: one ruble "bath money" apiece; and they also ordered us to pay a [tax on] cellar space. The governor Timothy Rzhevskii, together with other men in authority, colonels and captains, took away all our firearms and wanted to kill us: of this plan we were informed by soldiers doing guard duty. They also took away from us, without orders, our bread allowance and forbade that it be issued to us. We endured all this for a long time. [At last,] after taking counsel among ourselves, in order not to forsake our Christian faith, not to worship idolatrously the manikin gods, not to have our souls and those of our wives and children destroyed in vain, and also moved by our great distress—for we could endure it no more to be in danger of losing our Christian faith—we resisted: we killed some of them and have put some others in prison. You, the Cossack leaders, and all the Host of the Don, please deliberate among yourselves, and stand up together with us to defend the Christian faith, and send a message [about your decision] to us at Astrakhan.

QUESTIONS FOR ANALYSIS

1. How do Peter's reforms aimed at Russians compare to his attitudes toward non-Russians? What is similar or different in how Peter dealt with these two groups?

2. What is the central goal of all of Peter's decrees? How did Russia's drive to establish political authority in Siberia (Source 1) compare to Peter's effort at political centralization?

3. Based on these texts, what are the ideas and values that Peter the Great identified as Western? What issues did the Astrakhan rebels focus on, and what was the basis of their rejection of Peter's reforms?

4. How do Peter's efforts to transform Russia compare to Louis XIV's efforts within France (Source 6)? What are the similarities and differences, and what might account for this?

---

[3] The Russian Orthodox church does not permit three-dimensional religious statues. The idols mentioned here were wig blocks.

CHAPTER QUESTIONS

1. What similarities and differences existed in how the colonizing French and Russians defined their relationship to non-European peoples? How did the practices of colonial control differ from the European ideals of the colonial relationship?

2. How did French colonization and centralization demonstrate similar goals and practices and reinforce each other? How did Russian colonization and centralization demonstrate similar goals and practices and reinforce each other? What similarities and differences existed between the responses of non-Europeans to colonization and of Europeans to centralization?

3. How do the goals and attitudes toward colonization in France and Russia in the seventeenth century compare to the goals and attitudes toward colonization by Spain in the late fifteenth and sixteenth centuries (Chapter 1)? What might account for the similarities and differences?

4. How do the activities of the French administrators and the French Jesuits (Chapter 3) in North America indicate a competition between them for influence over the Amerindians? What were their competing definitions for the future of the Amerindians? What do these competing definitions indicate about their competing goals for Europe's future?

Chapter 5

RETHINKING THE WORLD: THE ENLIGHTENMENT

By the beginning of the eighteenth century, the European age of exploration had come to a close. Europeans had made contact with most inhabited regions of the globe, with the notable exception of the interior of the African continent, and European statesmen and merchants now sought to organize and secure their relationships with colonies and trade networks in terms favorable to European power and wealth. These relationships, however, worked in both directions. As Europeans moved outward from their European base, information, ideas, commodities, and people from the wider world came into Europe—as missionary reports, travel memoirs by merchants and seamen, and correspondence from colonial administrators; as commodities such as coffee, tea, chocolate, tobacco, sugar, spices, dyes, colorful Indian fabrics, and Chinese porcelains and silks; and as people of non-European origin immigrated to major European cities. The black population of late eighteenth-century London, for example, may have exceeded 25,000. As the size of the "foreign presence" in Europe grew—in literary, material, and human form—European thinkers sought to organize this information, creating knowledge that was useful and meaningful to Europeans of the eighteenth century.

This process of "rethinking the world" occurred as part of a broader European intellectual and cultural movement known as the Enlightenment. Beginning in the late seventeenth century and coming to fruition in the eighteenth century, European authors and artists undertook a reevaluation of European beliefs and practices, applying a critical spirit to judge whether European institutions and traditions aided or hindered the advancement of humankind. This critical spirit emerged from numerous sources—reactions against efforts by states to enforce religious uniformity; travel literature that praised "savages" and non-Christian peoples; and, most important, the extension of the spirit of Newtonian science to an investigation of human social, political, economic, and cultural interactions. The Newtonian image of a universe that functioned according to knowable and immutable laws of nature influenced many Enlightenment authors to look for similar natural laws that they believed must govern the social affairs of humanity. These authors examined traditional European beliefs and practices in politics, economics, society, and culture, adopting a secular spirit that used critical reason rather than revealed religious doctrine to uncover the natural laws of human interactions. Further, the advancements made in science and technology during the eighteenth century provided proof that the human condition could be improved. The progress of humanity, Enlightenment authors believed, could be achieved as their systematic inquiry into human society led to the discovery of natural laws, which then would provide the basis for the reform (or elimination) of institutions and practices that perpetuated ignorance, intolerance, and superstition at the expense of reason.

As Enlightenment writers looked around the globe and organized their knowledge about the wider world, this concern with progress undergirded their analysis. In looking outside of Europe, they sought to understand why other civilizations had or had not progressed and thereby to understand the nature of progress itself. This remained a deeply Eurocentric approach, for Enlightenment characterizations of advanced societies or of progress derived from European experiences—principally the experiences of educated and privileged European men—and reinforced their own claims of power and authority. Further, these discussions of progress and of China, the Americas, Africa, and the rest of the world served principally to comment on, understand, define, and create a new identity for Europeans themselves.

1

"... CHINA IS A DESPOTIC STATE. ..."

Baron de Montesquieu
The Spirit of the Laws (1748)

Charles-Louis de Secondat, Baron de Montesquieu (1689–1755), was a French jurist and author who traveled across much of Europe and read broadly in law, political theory, and the sciences. In 1748, he published one of the most influential works of the Enlightenment, The Spirit of the Laws, *in which he abandoned the classical division of governments into monarchies, aristocracies, and democracies. Instead, Montesquieu emphasized a more historical approach that classified governments by their manner of directing policies: republican governments were based on virtue, monarchical governments on honor, and despotic governments on fear. Further, Montesquieu emphasized the effect of climate on a society. Finally, Montesquieu argued that the separation of political powers among various branches of government most effectively produces liberty. In the excerpt below, Montesquieu analyzes the Chinese government that had been praised by the Jesuit missionaries of the seventeenth century (Chapter 3, Source 4).*

A large empire presupposes a despotic authority in the one who governs. Promptness of resolutions must make up for the distance of the places to which they are sent; fear must prevent negligence in the distant governor or magistrate; the law must be in a single person; and it must change constantly, like accidents, which always increase in proportion to the size of the state.

If the natural property of small states is to be governed as republics, that of medium-sized ones, to be subject to a monarch, and that of large empires to be

Charles de Montesquieu, *The Spirit of the Laws*, ed. and trans. Anne M. Cohler, Basia Carolyn Miller, and Harold Samuel Stone (Cambridge: Cambridge University Press, 1989), 126–28.

dominated by a despot, it follows that, in order to preserve the principles of the established government, the state must be maintained at the size it already has and that it will change its spirit to the degree to which its boundaries are narrowed or extended.

Before completing this book, I shall answer an objection that may be raised about all I have said to this point.

Our missionaries speak of the vast empire of China as of an admirable government, in whose principle intermingle fear, honor, and virtue. I would therefore have made an empty distinction in establishing the principles of the three governments.

I do not know how one can speak of honor among peoples who can be made to do nothing without beatings.[1]

Moreover, our men of commerce, far from giving us an idea of the same kind of virtue of which our missionaries speak, can rather be consulted about the banditry of the mandarins. I also call to witness the great man, Lord Anson.[2] ...

Could it not be that the missionaries were deceived by an appearance of order, that they were struck by that continuous exercise of the will of one alone by which they themselves are governed and which they so like to find in the courts of the kings of India? For, as they go there only to make great changes, it is easier for them to convince princes that they can do everything than to persuade the peoples that they can suffer everything.

Finally, there is often something true even in errors. Particular and perhaps unique circumstances may make it so that the Chinese government is not as corrupt as it should be. In this country causes drawn mostly from the physical aspect, climate, have been able to force the moral causes and, in a way, to perform prodigies.

The climate of China is such that it prodigiously favors the reproduction of mankind. Women there have such great fertility that nothing like it is seen elsewhere on earth. The cruellest tyranny cannot check the progress of propagation. The prince cannot say, with the Pharaoh, *Let us oppress them wisely.* He would be reduced, rather, to formulating Nero's[3] wish that mankind should have only one head. Despite tyranny, China, because of its climate, will always populate itself and will triumph over tyranny.

China, like all countries where rice is grown, is subject to frequent famines. When the people are starving, they scatter to seek something to eat. Everywhere bands of three, four, or five robbers form: most are immediately wiped out; others grow and are also wiped out. But, in such a great number of distant provinces, a group may meet with success. It maintains itself, grows stronger, forms itself into an army, goes straight to the capital, and its leader comes to the throne.

The nature of the thing is such that bad government there is immediately punished. Disorder is born suddenly when this prodigious number of people lacks subsistence. What makes it so hard to recover from abuses in other countries is that the effects are not felt; the prince is not alerted as promptly and strikingly as in China.

---

[1] Montesquieu cites the French Jesuit Jean Baptiste du Halde (1674–1743), who had published a scholarly four-volume history of China in 1735.
[2] George Anson (1697–1762), British admiral who visited China in 1743 and in 1748, published a popular account of his voyage that harshly criticized Chinese culture and society.
[3] Nero Claudius Caesar Augustus Germanicus (37–68), Roman emperor.

He will not feel, as our princes do, that if he governs badly, he will be less happy in the next life, less powerful and less rich in this one; he will know that, if his government is not good, he will lose his empire and his life.

As the Chinese people become ever more numerous despite exposing their children,[4] they must work tirelessly to make the lands produce enough to feed themselves; this demands great attention on the part of the government. It is in its interest for everyone at every moment to be able to work without fear of being frustrated for his pains. This should be less a civil government than a domestic government.

This is what has produced the rules that are so much discussed. Some have wanted to have laws reign along with despotism, but whatever is joined to despotism no longer has force. This despotism, beset by its misfortunes, has wanted in vain to curb itself; it arms itself with its chains and becomes yet more terrible.

Therefore, China is a despotic state whose principle is fear. In the first dynasties, when the empire was not so extensive, perhaps the government deviated a little from that spirit. But that is not so today.

---

[4] The practice of infanticide.

QUESTIONS FOR ANALYSIS

1. Why must a large empire be despotic, according to Montesquieu? How does Montesquieu use his discussion of China to justify this assertion?

2. Why did Montesquieu need to clarify the status of China as a despotic state? How does his argument mark China as inferior to the western European states?

3. According to Montesquieu, how does nature affect the political status of China as a despotic state? What are the limitations of fear as a foundation of government?

4. How does Montesquieu see Chinese progress and despotism locked in a desperate struggle?

2

"WHY HAVE THE CHINESE ALWAYS REMAINED IN THAT STATE . . ."

Voltaire
Essay on the Customs and Spirit of Nations   (1756)

One of France's greatest writers, François-Marie Arouet (1694–1778), who wrote under the name Voltaire, published works of poetry, theater, history, philosophy, fiction, and prose essay. With wit and satire he critically exposed social and political tyranny, bigotry, and cruelty. A reformer rather than a revolutionary, Voltaire believed that

---

Voltaire, *Essai sur les moeurs et l'esprit des nations* (Paris: Editions Garnier Freres, 1963), 211, 213–16. (Translated by David Kammerling Smith.)

humanity would achieve lasting progress by critiquing the social and cultural beliefs and the institutions that supported intolerance and fanaticism. In 1756, Voltaire published a broadly historical work entitled Essay on the Customs and Spirit of Nations. *In the excerpt below from the first chapter of that work, Voltaire critiques the progress of Chinese civilization.*

Chinese towns have never had any fortifications other than those inspired by good sense to all nations before the use of artillery: a ditch, a rampart, a strong wall, and towers. Ever since the Chinese began to use cannons, they have not followed the model of our places of war. Whereas other countries fortify their localities, the Chinese fortified their empire. The Great Wall which separated and defended China from the Tartars,[1] built 137 years before our common era, still remains in a line of 500 leagues, rising on mountains, descending down precipices, having nearly around twenty of our feet in width and more than thirty in height: a monument superior to the pyramids of Egypt by its usefulness and by its immensity.

This rampart did not prevent the Tartars from profiting, in the course of time, from divisions in China and subjugating it. But the constitution of the State was neither weakened nor changed. The country of the conquerors has become part of the conquered State. And the Manchus,[2] masters of China, have done nothing but, arms in hand, submitted themselves to the laws of the country in which they have occupied the throne. . . .

This country, favored by nature, possesses nearly all the fruits transplanted to our Europe and many others that we lack. Wheat, rice, vines, vegetables, trees of all types cover the earth there. But the people have only made wine in recent times, satisfied by a sufficiently strong liquor that they know how to produce from rice.

The precious insect which produces silk is originally from China. . . . Thin, blazing white paper was made in China from earliest times. . . . The first epoch of porcelain was unknown [to Europe] as well as this beautiful glazing that Europe has begun to imitate and equal.

They have known, for 2,000 years, how to produce glass but less beautiful and transparent than ours.

Printing was invented by them at the same time. This printing is done by engraving wood boards, as Gutenberg[3] practiced it first in Mainz in the fifteenth century. The art of engraving characters on wood is more perfected in China. Our method of employing metal-cast, movable characters, much superior to theirs, has not yet been adopted by them: so much they are attached to their ancient methods.

Their use of large bells is of the greatest antiquity. We have had them in France only since the sixth century A.D. They have developed chemistry, and without ever having become good physicians, they have invented gunpowder. But they have only used this for festivals in the art of fireworks, in which they have surpassed other nations. It was the Portuguese who, in the most recent centuries, have taught them the

---

[1] Here referring generally to the Turkic and Mongolian peoples of central Asia.
[2] Ethnic Manchurian people who established the Qing dynasty in China in 1644.
[3] Johannes Gutenberg (early 15th century–c. 1468), German craftsman from the town of Mainz often credited with inventing movable type in printing.

use of artillery, and the Jesuits who taught them to found cannons. If the Chinese did not apply themselves to invent these destructive instruments, we are not obliged to praise their virtue for this, for this did not lead them to go to war any less.

They only developed astronomy as a science of the eyes and the fruit of patience. They observed the heavens assiduously, recording all the phenomenon and transmitting them to posterity. . . .

Why have the Chinese, so advanced in such distant eras, always remained in that state; why is Chinese astronomy so ancient and so limited; why do they still ignore half-tones in music. It seems that nature gave to this type of man, so different from us, organs designed to discover quickly everything necessary to him yet incapable of going beyond. We, in contrast, gained knowledge very slowly but have perfected it rapidly. . . .

If one searches for why so many of the arts and so many of the sciences, cultivated without interruption for such a long time in China, have made, however, so little progress, there are perhaps two reasons for this. First, the prodigious respect these people have for everything transmitted by their fathers so that they consider all ancient things perfect. The second is the nature of their language, foundation of all knowledge.

The art of making known their ideas by writing, which should be only a simple method, is the most difficult Chinese art. Each word has different characters: the savants in China are those who know the greatest number of these characters. Some have arrived at old age before knowing how to write well.

What they have best known, have best cultivated, and have most perfected are ethics and laws. The respect of children for their fathers is the foundation of Chinese government. Paternal authority is never weakened there. A son is able to plead against his father only with the consent of all the parents, friends, and magistrates. The educated officials are regarded as the fathers of the towns and provinces, and the king as the father of the empire. This idea, instilled in the heart, forms a family of this immense State. . . .

The voyagers, and especially the missionaries, believed they saw despotism everywhere [in China]. One judges everything by the exterior. One sees men prostrating themselves and then takes them to be slaves. He before whom they prostrate themselves must be absolute master of the life and fortune of 150,000,000 men. His will alone must serve as law. This is not so. . . . In the most ancient times of the monarchy, it was permitted to write on a long table, placed in the palace, whatever one found reprehensible in the government. This was practiced actively under the reign of Wendi,[4] two centuries before our common era, and in peaceful times ever since, representations of tribunals have always had the force of law. This important observation destroys the vague imputations found in *The Spirit of the Laws* against this government, the oldest in the world.

QUESTIONS FOR ANALYSIS

1. What are Voltaire's criteria for approving of certain Chinese practices and condemning others? Of what importance is technology to Voltaire's analysis of China?

2. What does Voltaire identify as China's most advanced accomplishment? How does he respond to Chinese patriarchy?

---

[4] Emperor Han Wendi (179–157 B.C.).

3. On what basis does Voltaire disagree with Montesquieu's description of China as despotic (Source 1)? What are the similarities and differences in their analyses?

4. What reasons does Voltaire give for the lack of continued progress in Chinese science, arts, and manufacturing? How might this critique be useful to Voltaire in his critique of the sources of intolerance in European society?

3

"They abhor the laws of Society . . ."

Cornelius de Pauw
Philosophical Inquiry into the Americas (1768–1769)

Although relatively obscure today, the Dutch abbé Cornelius de Pauw (1739–1799) was a leading figure in "the Dispute of the New World." The dispute, which lasted for several decades in the late eighteenth century, centered on the contention of de Pauw and others that American plants and animals were inferior in strength and variety to those in Europe, Asia, and Africa and that plants and animals (including humans) brought from the Eastern Hemisphere to the Western Hemisphere degenerated, losing vigor and becoming stunted. Reacting to the diverse images of Amerindian civilization that had appeared in the Jesuit Relations *(Chapter 3, Source 1), advocates of the "degeneracy thesis" claimed to use rigorous scientific methods to collect and analyze data and to rely only on natural causes to explain natural effects. In the excerpt below from de Pauw's work, he describes America and its inhabitants.*

The climate of America, at the moment of its discovery, was very adverse to the majority of quadruped [four-footed] animals, who occur there one-sixth smaller than the analogous animals of the old continent. . . . In the new continent, between the Tropics, no large quadruped animals have existed. Naturalists, who have long noted this point, have suspected that large seeds were not able to develop in this climate, which is disadvantageous to the primary productions of the animal kingdom and favorable only to insects and serpents. . . .

This climate was especially pernicious to humans, dulled, enervated, corrupted in an astonishing manner in every part of their organisms. . . . The Americans, although light and agile at running, had lost this lively and physical power that results from the tension and the resistance of the muscles and nerves. The least vigorous of Europeans would crush them easily in a fight: what a difference, therefore, between them and the ancient savages of Gaul and Germany who had acquired such a reputation by the power of their robust members and their massive and

Cornelius de Pauw, *Recherches philosphique sur les Americains* (Berlin, 1771), 4, 12, 34, 35, 94–95, 153–54, 206–7. (Translated by David Kammerling Smith.)

indefatigable bodies. The constitution of the Americans, little defective in appearance, fell fundamentally short of the mark by its weakness: they wore themselves out under the least burden; and in transporting the baggage of the Spaniards, one person has counted that in less than one year more than 200,000 among them died under the weight of the load, in spite of the fact that one had employed ten times more people for these transports than would have been employed in Europe. . . .

In our Hemisphere existed people reunited in society from time immemorial, who perfected their manners and morals, honored the sciences, cultivated the arts, striven at industry, raised ornated towns by the genius of beautiful architecture, uprooted the sterile trees, multiplied the fruitful vegetables, introduced all the animals useful for domestication, drained the swamps, leveled the terrain, altered the course of rivers, changed the lands in pasturage, sowed them, and by the hand of agriculture, from an immense countryside, embellished all their horizons.

In the opposite Hemisphere all of nature was savage, the air foul and unhealthy, the thick forests extending without beginning or end, where the rays of the sun had never penetrated. . . . The humans . . . were marked by their weakness and exhaustion. They lacked the genius for forging iron even though they knew of the [iron] mines, without being able to exploit the metal from it.

America contains nearly 2,140,212 square leagues, yet on this massive foundation only two nations have been discovered that are united into a type of political society. All the rest, roving and dispersed in hordes and families, only knew savage life, living passively in the shade of the forests and demonstrating barely enough intelligence to procure nourishment for themselves. . . .

To the present, we have considered the peoples of America only by their physical faculties, which being essentially corrupted, lead to the loss of their moral faculties. The degeneration having impaired their senses and their organs, their soul became depraved in proportion to their body. Nature, having deprived one hemisphere of this globe to give to the other, placed in America only the infants that have not been able to be made into men. When the Europeans arrived in the West Indies, in the fifteenth century, there was not an American who could read or write; there is now yet an American in our day who knows how to think. . . .

A stupid insensibility forms the basis of the character of all Americans: their laziness prevents them from being attentive to instructions, not having any passion sufficient to move their soul or raise themselves up. Superior to the animals, because they have use of their hands and of language, they are actually inferior to the least of the Europeans. Deprived at the same time of intelligence and perfectibility, they only obey their instinctual impulses. No motive of glory is able to penetrate their hearts. Their unpardonable cowardice keeps them in the slavery in which they are lost or in the savage life that they do not have the courage to leave. It has been nearly three centuries since America was discovered. During this time Americans have been constantly brought to Europe, and all types of culture have been tried on them, but none of them have been able to make a name in the sciences, the arts, or the skilled crafts. . . .

Is it not surprising that one finds only on one-half of this globe men without beards, without intellect, attacked by venereal disease, and so fallen from the dignity of human nature that they were not disciplined, which is the companion of stupidity. The inclination that the Americans have always had, and that they still have, for savage life proves that they abhor the laws of Society and the shackles of education, which, in taming the most intemperate passions is alone able to elevate man above the animals. It is necessary to deprive man a part of his liberty in order to ennoble his existence and cultivate his genius: and without this cultivation, he is nothing. The trees that are pruned, that are torn open for grafting, that are subdued, produce delicious fruit. The seedling that has never been touched by the hand of a gardener only grows for itself. Its produce is either harmful, useless, or worthless. Savage man thus lives only for himself. He helps no one and no one helps him. No link, no pact of fraternity unites him to his fellow man. He is alone in the world and ignores his ability to be benevolent, charitable, and generous. One could not imagine a greater debasement of our nature than this state of indolence and inertia where one does not know the virtue of doing good and where one never acts except to think of one's self or of one's masters.

QUESTIONS FOR ANALYSIS

1. How does de Pauw provide "natural" explanations for the phenomena he describes? What evidence does he provide for his explanations?
2. To what does de Pauw ascribe human progress? Why have Amerindians not achieved progress?
3. How does de Pauw establish a contrast between active Europeans and passive Americans? How does his analysis "justify" European dominance over the Amerindians?
4. How does de Pauw's evidence of European progress compare to Voltaire's evidence of European progress (Source 1)? How does each emphasize human artifice—that is, manipulation of nature?

". . . THE MAN WHO MEDITATES IS A DEPRAVED ANIMAL."

Jean-Jacques Rousseau
Discourse on the Origins of Inequality (1755)

One of the most original thinkers and powerful writers of the Enlightenment, the Genevan Jean-Jacques Rousseau (1712–1778) arrived in Paris at the age of thirty, quickly rose to prominence as a philosophe, and participated in the most public of Enlightenment projects, the Encyclopédie, *an important voice for radical and anticlerical opinion. Rousseau, however, became disenchanted with intellectual life in Parisian society and broke with most of his fellow philosophes. In a series of writings beginning in the 1750s, Rousseau critiqued the artificiality and corruption of his own society that*

Jean-Jacques Rousseau, *Discourse on the Origins of Inequality*, trans. Donald A. Cress (Indianapolis: Hackett, 1992), 18–24, 26–27, 34, 41–42.

harmed the natural goodness of humans. In 1755, the Academy of Dijon announced an essay contest on the question "What is the origin of the inequality among men, and is it justified by natural law?" Rousseau responded to that question with Discourse on the Origins of Inequality. *In the excerpt below from that text, Rousseau compares the noble savage to the domesticated man of his day.*

O man, whatever country you may be from, whatever your opinions may be, listen: here is your history, as I have thought to read it, not in the books of your fellow-men, who are liars, but in nature, who never lies. . . .

When I strip [man in his natural state], thus constituted, of all the supernatural gifts he could have received and of all the artificial faculties he could have acquired only through long progress; when I consider him, in a word, as he must have left the hands of nature, I see an animal less strong than some, less agile than others, but all in all, the most advantageously organized of all. I see him satisfying his hunger under an oak tree, quenching his thirst at the first stream, finding his bed at the foot of the same tree that supplied his meal; and thus all his needs are satisfied. . . .

Since the savage man's body is the only instrument he knows, he employs it for a variety of purposes that, for lack of practice, ours are incapable of serving. And our industry deprives us of the force and agility that necessity obliges him to acquire. If he had had an axe, would his wrists break such strong branches? If he had had a sling, would he throw a stone with so much force? If he had had a ladder, would he climb a tree so nimbly? If he had had a horse, would he run so fast? Give a civilized man time to gather all his machines around him, and undoubtedly he will easily overcome a savage man. But if you want to see an even more unequal fight, pit them against each other naked and disarmed, and you will soon realize the advantage of constantly having all of one's forces at one's disposal, of always being ready for any event, and of always carrying one's entire self, as it were, with one. . . .

Pit a bear or a wolf against a savage who is robust, agile, and courageous, as they all are, armed with stones and a hefty cudgel, and you will see that the danger will be at least equal on both sides, and that after several such experiences, ferocious beasts, which do not like to attack one another, will be quite reluctant to attack a man, having found him to be as ferocious as themselves. . . .

The extreme inequality in our lifestyle: excessive idleness among some, excessive labor among others; the ease with which we arouse and satisfy our appetites and our sensuality; the overly refined foods of the wealthy, which nourish them with irritating juices and overwhelm them with indigestion; the bad food of the poor, who most of the time do not have even that, and who, for want of food, are inclined to stuff their stomachs greedily whenever possible; staying up until all hours; excesses of all kinds, immoderate outbursts of every passion, bouts of fatigue and mental exhaustion; countless sorrows and afflictions which are felt in all levels of society and which perpetually gnaw away at souls: these are the fatal proofs that most of our ills are of our own making, and that we could have avoided nearly all of them by preserving the simple, regular and solitary lifestyle prescribed to us by nature. If nature has destined us to be healthy, I almost dare to affirm that the state of reflection is a state contrary to nature and that the man who meditates is a depraved animal. . . .

Therefore we must take care not to confuse savage man with the men we have before our eyes. Nature treats all animals left to their own devices with a predilection that seems to show how jealous she is of that right. The horse, the cat, the bull, even the ass, are usually taller, and all of them have a more robust constitution, more vigor, more strength, and more courage in the forests than in our homes. They lose half of these advantages in becoming domesticated; it might be said that all our efforts at feeding them and treating them well only end in their degeneration. It is the same for man himself. In becoming habituated to the ways of society and a slave, he becomes weak, fearful, and servile; his soft and effeminate lifestyle completes the enervation of both his strength and his courage. . . .

So far I have considered only physical man. Let us now try to look at him from a metaphysical and moral point of view. . . .

Whatever the moralists may say about it, human understanding owes much to the passions, which, by common consensus, also owe a great deal to it. It is by their activity that our reason is perfected. We seek to know only because we desire to find enjoyment; and it is impossible to conceive why someone who had neither desires nor fears would go to the bother of reasoning. The passions in turn take their origin from our needs, and their progress from our knowledge. For one can desire or fear things only by virtue of the ideas one can have of them, or from the simple impulse of nature; and savage man, deprived of every sort of enlightenment, feels only the passion of this latter sort. His desires do not go beyond his physical needs. The only goods he knows in the universe are nourishment, a woman and rest; the only evils he fears are pain and hunger. . . .

His soul, agitated by nothing, is given over to the single feeling of his own present existence, without any idea of the future, however near it may be, and his projects, as limited as his views, hardly extend to the end of the day. . . .

[I]f we understand the word *miserable* properly, it is a word which is without meaning or which signifies merely a painful privation and suffering of the body or the soul. Now I would very much like someone to explain to me what kind of misery can there be for a free being whose heart is at peace and whose body is in good health? I ask which of the two, civil or natural life, is more likely to become insufferable to those who live it? We see about us practically no people who do not complain about their existence; many even deprive themselves of it to the extent they are able, and the combination of divine and human laws is hardly enough to stop this disorder. I ask if anyone has ever heard tell of a savage who was living in liberty ever dreaming of complaining about his life and of killing himself. . . .

Let us conclude that, wandering in the forests, without industry, without speech, without dwelling, without war, without relationships, with no need for his fellow men, and correspondingly with no desire to do them harm, perhaps never even recognizing any of them individually, savage man, subject to few passions and self-sufficient, had only the sentiments and enlightenment appropriate to that state; he felt only his true needs, took notice of only what he believed he had an interest in seeing; and that his intelligence made no more progress than his vanity. If by chance he made some discovery, he was all the less able to communicate it to others because he did not even know his own children. Art perished with its inventor. There was neither education nor progress; generations were multiplied to no purpose. . . .

[I]t is easy to see that, among the differences that distinguish men, several of them pass for natural ones which are exclusively the work of habit and of the various sorts of life that men adopt in society. Thus a robust or delicate temperament, and the strength or weakness that depend on it, frequently derive more from the harsh or effeminate way in which one has been raised than from the primitive constitution of bodies. The same holds for mental powers; and not only does education make a difference between cultivated minds and those that are not, it also augments the difference among the former in proportion to their culture; for were a giant and a dwarf walking on the same road, each step they both take would give a fresh advantage to the giant. Now if one compares the prodigious diversity of educations and lifestyles in the different orders of the civil state with the simplicity and uniformity of animal and savage life, where all nourish themselves from the same foods, live in the same manner, and do exactly the same things, it will be understood how much less the difference between one man and another must be in the state of nature than in that of society, and how much natural inequality must increase in the human species through inequality occasioned by social institutions.

QUESTIONS FOR ANALYSIS

1. What advantages does Rousseau suggest that savage man has over modern man? How does he use savage man's advantages to critique modern society?
2. According to Rousseau, how is savage man appropriate for his place in the state of nature?
3. What role does Rousseau ascribe to savage woman?
4. What does Rousseau suggest are the causes of human progress? How does Rousseau's analysis compare to Voltaire's (Source 2) and de Pauw's (Source 3) emphasis on human artifice as evidence of human progress?

5

"THE MATERNAL AFFECTION IS EVERY WHERE CONSPICUOUS AMONG THEM. . . ."

Mungo Park
Travels in the Interior Districts of Africa (1797)

In 1795, the Scottish explorer Mungo Park (1771–1806) received backing from the African Association to explore the course of the Niger River, one of the first European efforts to explore the inland African continent. Park's harrowing two-year journey included terrible illness, starvation, and imprisonment by a Muslim chief. On return to Britain, Park described his adventures in Travels in the Interior Districts of Africa. *Such travel literature, written for popular consumption and with a concern for commercial*

Mungo Park, *Travels in the Interior Districts of Africa* (London, 1807), 390–95, 405–6, 408–9.

sales, became widely popular in the eighteenth century and served as many Europeans'
primary source of information on non-European peoples. In the excerpt below from
Travels, *Park describes the Mandingo (Malinke) people, who cared for him for seven*
months while he was seriously ill with fever.

The Mandingoes, in particular, are a very gentle race; cheerful in their dispositions, inquisitive, credulous, simple, and fond of flattery. Perhaps, the most prominent defect in their character, was that insurmountable propensity, which the reader must have observed to prevail in all classes of them, to steal from me the few effects I was possessed of. For this part of their conduct, no complete justification can be offered, because theft is a crime in their own estimation; and it must be observed, that they are not habitually and generally guilty of it towards each other. This, however, is an important circumstance in mitigation; and before we pronounce them a more depraved people than any other, it were well to consider whether the lower order of people in any part of Europe, would have acted, under similar circumstances, with greater honesty towards a stranger, than the Negroes acted towards me. It must not be forgotten, that the laws of the country afforded me no protection; that every one was at liberty to rob me with impunity; and finally, that some part of my effects were of as great value, in the estimation of the Negroes, as pearls and diamonds would have been in the eyes of a European. . . . Notwithstanding I was so great a sufferer by it [theft], I do not consider that their natural sense of justice was perverted or extinguished: it was overpowered only, for the moment, by the strength of a temptation which it required no common virtue to resist.

On the other hand, as some counterbalance to this depravity in their nature, allowing it to be such, it is impossible for me to forget the disinterested charity, and tender solicitude, with which many of these poor heathens (from the sovereign of Sego,[1] to the poor women who received me at different times into their cottages, when I was perishing of hunger) sympathised with me in my sufferings; relieved my distresses; and contributed to my safety. This acknowledgment, however, is perhaps more particularly due to the female part of the nation. Among the men, as the reader must have seen, my reception, though generally kind, was sometimes otherwise. It varied according to the various tempers of those to whom I made application. The hardness of avarice in some, and the blindness of bigotry in others, had closed up the avenues to compassion; but I do not recollect a single instance of hardheartedness towards me in the women. In all my wanderings and wretchedness, I found them uniformly kind and compassionate. . . .

[T]he maternal affection (neither suppressed by the restraints, nor diverted by the solicitudes of civilized life) is every where conspicuous among them; and creates a correspondent return of tenderness in the child. An illustration of this . . . "Strike me," said my attendant, "but do not curse my mother." The same sentiment I found universally to prevail, and observed in all parts of Africa, that the greatest affront which could be offered to a Negro, was to reflect on her who gave him birth.

---

[1] Sego (Ségou), influential city-state of the western Sudan on the Niger River.

It is not strange, that this sense of filial duty and affection among the Negroes, should be less ardent towards the father than the mother. The system of poligamy, while it weakens the father's attachment, by dividing it among the children of different wives, concentrates all the mother's jealous tenderness to one point, the protection of her own offspring. I perceived with great satisfaction too, that the maternal solicitude extended not only to the growth and security of the person, but also, in a certain degree, to the improvement of the mind of the infant; for one of the first lessons in which the Mandingo women instruct their children, is *the practice of truth*. The reader will probably recollect the case of the unhappy mother, whose son was murdered by the Moorish banditti,[2] at Funingkedy. . . . Her only consolation, in her uttermost distress, was the reflection that the poor boy, in the course of his blameless life, *had never told a lie*. Such testimony, from a fond mother, on such an occasion, must have operated powerfully on the youthful part of the surrounding spectators. It was at once a tribute of praise to the deceased, and a lesson to the living. . . .

The Mandingoes, and I believe the Negroes in general, have no artificial method of dividing time. They calculate the years by the number of *rainy seasons*. They portion the year into *moons,* and reckon the days by so many *suns*. The day, they divide into morning, mid-day, and evening; and further subdivide it, when necessary: by pointing to the sun's place in the Heavens. I frequently inquired of some of them what became of the sun during the night, and whether we should see the same sun, or a different one, in the morning: but I found that they considered the question as very childish. The subject appeared to them, as placed beyond the reach of human investigation; they had never indulged a conjecture, nor formed any hypothesis about the matter. . . .

Some of the religious opinions of the Negroes, though blended with the weakest credulity and superstition, are not unworthy [of] attention. I have conversed with all ranks and conditions, upon the subject of their faith, and can pronounce, without the smallest shadow of doubt, that the belief of one God, and of a future state of reward and punishment, is entire and universal among them. It is remarkable, however, that, except on the appearance of a new moon, . . . the Pagan natives do not think it necessary to offer up prayers and supplications to the Almighty. They represent the Deity, indeed, as the creator and preserver of all things; but in general they consider him as a Being so remote, and of so exalted a nature, that it is idle to imagine the feeble supplications of wretched mortals can reverse the decrees, and change the purposes of unerring Wisdom. If they are asked, for what reason then do they offer up a prayer on the appearance of the new moon; the answer is, that custom has made it necessary: they do it, because their fathers did it before them. Such is the blindness of unassisted nature!

QUESTIONS FOR ANALYSIS

1. How does Park create an ambiguous image of the Mandingo culture and society as neither ideal nor horrific? How do European standards guide his judgments of Mandingo society?

---

[2] Banditti, plural form of bandit.

2. How does Park use gender stereotypes in describing Mandingo family life?

3. Why would Park place importance on knowledge about the heavens?

4. How would Park's description of Mandingo religion be attractive to Enlightenment readers? How would Voltaire (Source 1) and Rousseau (Source 2) respond to his conclusion about "unassisted nature"?

6

"WHAT SEEMS TO MATTER IS NOT THAT THESE SERVANTS ARE AFRICAN, MUSLIM, OR INDIAN, BUT THAT THEY ARE EXOTIC. . . ."

Beth Fowkes Tobin
Picturing Imperial Power (1999)

*In her recent study, Beth Fowkes Tobin integrates art history with economic and social history to investigate the use of colonial peoples in eighteenth-century British painting. In the excerpt below, she interprets an engraving—*A Harlot's Progress *(1732) by the great English artist William Hogarth (1697–1764)—and a painting—*The Family of Sir William Young, Baronet *(1770) by the German-born British artist Johan Zoffany (1733–1810). Through these paintings she traces the "domesticization" of the products of the British Empire in the eighteenth century.*

Several eighteenth-century portraits and conversation pieces contain the figure of the black servant. Most frequently a boy or an adolescent male, the servant is dressed in livery[1] and wears either a turban or a skullcap. Both head coverings are exotic and allude to the Turkish, Moslem, and Mughal[2] cultures of the Levant,[3] northern Africa, and the Indian subcontinent. This conflation of Arabic, African, and Indian origins is typical of many eighteenth-century representations of black servants. What seems to matter is not that these servants are African, Muslim, or Indian, but that they are exotic, that they originate in tropical, fertile, and remote lands. Their status as exotics is reinforced by the frequency with which they are associated in prints and paintings with the consumption of foreign luxury goods such as sugar, tea, tobacco, and coffee, all commodities associated with the dark others of the world. . . . As attitudes toward the consumption of exotic commodities shifted

---

[1] Distinctive clothing style worn by a servant.

[2] Muslim dynasty that ruled most of northern India from the early sixteenth to the mid-eighteenth centuries.

[3] The lands of the eastern Mediterranean.

Beth Fowkes Tobin, *Picturing Imperial Power: Colonial Subjects in Eighteenth-Century British Painting* (Durham, N.C.: Duke University Press, 1999), 27–29, 32–33, 36–37, 39–42, 45–46.

over the course of the century from intense feelings of anxiety and/or excitement to a complacent acceptance of coffee, tea, and sugar as naturally belonging to the English domestic scene, so did attitudes change toward the figure of the black servant. In the early part of the century, the black page is often portrayed as naughty or disruptive and is frequently placed in scenes that contain innuendoes of sexuality or moral laxity. However, as the century progressed, the figure of the black servant was placed in closer proximity to children and mothers, signaling the incorporation of the exotic into the everydayness of the domestic scene. . . .

The processes whereby colonial wealth, products, and peoples were absorbed into British society aroused anxiety in some late eighteenth-century observers. However, in comparison with the earlier part of the century, such anxieties were mild, for overseas trade and colonialism had been a volatile issue in the first third of the century, provoking a range of responses from righteous condemnation to eager acceptance. With the expansion of colonial domains, the exploitation of colonial resources, and the global circulation of merchant capital, early eighteenth-century critics and admirers of empire focused their attention on the impact of the consumption of foreign commodities on the English character and domestic economy. . . . Some writers saw the exotic as insidious, sapping native [British] enterprise and ingenuity and spreading the seeds of moral and economic decay; others argued that the conspicuous consumption of luxury goods was not necessarily antithetical to virtuous conduct; and still others celebrated England as the center of a global system of exchange. . . .

Hogarth participated in this morally and politically charged discourse on the consumption of the exotic with his portrayal of Moll Hackabout and her decline into a life of harlotry, disease, and death [in a series of paintings]. In the second plate of *A Harlot's Progress* (1732) Hogarth places the figure of the black servant, a turbaned boy carrying a pot of hot water, at the far right side of the picture [see page 120]. His body is in motion, as if he is walking into the scene, and his face has a look of surprise, his eyebrows arched in shock and his eyes wide open. His gaze directs our gaze across the room to the monkey (a sign of exotic and deviant sexuality) and the upset tea table. This print is full of movement—the Jew's wig is falling off; Moll Hackabout's gown is sliding off, exposing her right breast; her lover is gliding out the door; the teapot and cups are falling off the table; the monkey is running away; the servant is entering the room—and the direction of all this movement is right to left. Because our gaze moves across the print from right to left, as if directed by the boy's gaze, it is almost as if his gaze initiates the movement and sets in motion all the disorder we see. The right-to-left movement mimics the movement of the eye when reading Arabic, Hebrew, and Chinese and therefore is associated with foreign practices that can be quite destabilizing for a Western viewer. This right-to-left movement associates disorder with the foreign in much the same way as the boy's turban (Arabic), the Jewish patron (Hebrew), and the china and tea (Chinese), as exotic items, are all linked to moral dissolution. The disruptive energy of the black servant's entrance into the scene and the moral disorder associated with his presence are not limited to what is depicted in this second plate but spill over into the next several plates, moving Moll through several more scenes in a downward spiral that ends in her moral and physical destruction. In detailing the corruption of a native English country girl, *A Harlot's Progress* functions

WILLIAM HOGARTH, A HARLOT'S PROGRESS

as a critique of London, the trading capital of the world, a place polluted by foreign interpenetration and made a site of moral instability. . . .

Whereas the Hogarth prints . . . stress the exoticism of the black page, Johan Zoffany's depiction of a black servant domesticates the servant's exotic origins by firmly locating him within the bosom of an English family. Zoffany's *The Family of Sir William Young, Baronet* (1770) is a portrait of a large family group of eleven members arranged in three groups [see page 121]. The center of the painting is occupied by Sir William, who was governor of the Caribbean island of Dominica and commissioner of St. Vincent, and his wife, both playing musical instruments. . . .

The arrangement of the figures lends them a lovely sense of intimacy, harmony, and family unity. Everyone in this picture is joined to someone else. Hands touch, bodies overlap, and gazes intersect. . . .

The other element that unites these figures is their dress. With the exception of the black servant, each is dressed in Van Dyck–style[4] costumes, as if for a party, a masquerade, or a family performance. . . .

The black servant participates in this domestic scene, sharing in its gay and warm family life. A gentle smile and fond look grace his face as he holds one child and looks at another. He is an integral part of the scene: his arm is criss-crossed by the arms of the two boys holding hands. But he is also a support, like the horse, and, like the dog, gazes on the standing boy's face. He is included in the family portrait,

---

[4] Anthony Van Dyck (1599–1641), prolific seventeenth-century Flemish painter, especially noted for portraits of European aristocrats.

JOHAN ZOFFANY, THE FAMILY OF SIR WILLIAM YOUNG, BARONET

like the animals, as an accoutrement or prop to help communicate this family's qualities. His pleasant face conveys the feeling that he seems to care about the family and to be particularly fond of Sir William's children. His attachment to the family speaks well of him but even more so of the family, as worthy of this loyalty. His well-being reflects well on them.

Zoffany has so skillfully woven this group together with affectionate gazes and gracefully linked arms and hands that we almost forget the material relations that undergird this family's social, economic, and political position. As [art historian] Sacheverell Sitwell coolly remarks, "Sir William was a West Indian magnate, being Governor of the islands of St. Vincent and Dominica. For this reason a negro servant occurs in the picture." The glint of gold (or brass, perhaps) that shines from beneath the black servant's neckcloth is a metal collar that slaves wore much the same way dogs wear collars. This black servant, a slave, is emblematic of more than Sir William's colonial post; he stands in for the hundreds of slaves that the Youngs owned on their several West Indian sugar plantations. . . .

In Zoffany's portrait of the Young family, the only reminder of this system that brutalized Africans for profit is the figure of the servant. His presence is eclipsed by the warmth of domestic affection and the casual intimacy that this family's musical performance generates. The family's elegance and grace rewrite the origins of their social position, locating their socially and economically privileged position in their genteel artistic and musical accomplishments. The Van Dyck costumes lend to Sir William and his family an aristocratic and cultured past, and the musical instruments and sheet music imply domestic harmony and this family's ease with their European cultural heritage. . . .

The art (in the form of Van Dyck portraiture) and music alluded to in this conversation piece declare this family's cultural superiority, a superiority reinforced by the presence of their black servant. He represents the ignorant slave and unenlightened African who has benefited by his association with this family, sharing in the warmth of its domestic harmony. . . . The warmth of the Youngs' domestic ties and their pleasure in their participation in the arts work to justify not only their black servant's servitude but slavery as well. The servant's affectionate look and gentle smile erase the material conditions of his own exploitation and the egregious abuses of power that marked Britain's colonial rule of the West Indies. The black servant's presence reminds us of Sir William's West Indian legacy but immediately transforms that brutal colonial power into an elegant, graceful, and refined celebration of English art, music, and domestic life.

QUESTIONS FOR ANALYSIS

1. How did changes in British paintings reflect changes in British attitudes to exotic commodities?
2. According to Tobin, how does the colonial figure in the Hogarth painting serve the opposite function as the colonial figure in the Zoffany painting?
3. How did some British paintings serve to justify slavery? What is the significance of the patriarchal family model to Tobin's analysis?
4. How does Tobin's interpretation of the exoticism and eventual domesticization of the colonial subjects in British paintings compare to Park's presentation of both exoticism and familiarity in African society (Source 5)?

7

". . . THE DIFFERENCE BETWEEN THESE TWO RACES OF MAN . . ."

Immanuel Kant
Observations on the Feeling of the Beautiful and the Sublime   (1764)

Born of a Prussian artisanal family of modest means, Immanuel Kant (1724–1804) became one of the most influential philosophers in European history. Kant's mature philosophy subsumed the rationalist tradition (which emphasized reason) and the empiricist tradition (which emphasized experience) into a new critical philosophy that

---

Immanuel Kant, *Observations on the Feeling of the Beautiful and the Sublime*, trans. John T. Goldthwait (Berkeley: University of California Press, 1960), 97, 99–105, 109–12.

explored the universal faculties or abilities of the mind that structure human experience. In 1764, before Kant's philosophy reached maturity, he published the essay Observations on the Feeling of the Beautiful and the Sublime *in which he used the philosophical categories of "beautiful" and "sublime" to distinguish among the peoples of the world. Kant understood both of these categories to be* finer *or superior feelings of pleasure. An individual or a society had to cultivate its talents and refine itself to experience and enjoy these pleasures. Thus, the society that created and enjoyed the beautiful and the sublime was superior to the society that did neither or did so imperfectly. To distinguish between the beautiful and the sublime, Kant analyzed the response of the beholder (the subject): the beautiful inspired joy in the beholder, while the sublime inspired awe and admiration. For example, human relationships can be beautiful, such as when joy is created by acts of politeness, or relationships can be sublime, such as when admiration is produced by acts of loyalty. By emphasizing the individual's response to an act or experience, Kant's philosophy developed a subjectivist component that recognized the individual's active and creative role in interpreting nature and experience. Kant's subjectivism become central to his mature philosophy and served as a foundation to the Romantic movement that emerged in Europe in the late eighteenth century.*

Of the peoples of our part of the world, in my opinion those who distinguish themselves among all others by the feeling for the beautiful are the Italians and the French, but by the feeling for the sublime, the Germans, English, and Spanish. . . .

The mental characters of peoples are most discernible by whatever in them is moral, on which account we will yet take under consideration their different feelings in respect to the sublime and beautiful from this point of view. . . .

The Frenchman has a predominant feeling for the morally beautiful. He is gracious, courteous, and complaisant. He becomes familiar very quickly, is jesting and free in society, and the expression "a *man* or a *lady of good tone*" has an understandable meaning only for him who has acquired the polite feeling of a Frenchman. Even his sublime sensations, of which he has not a few, are subordinated to the feeling of the beautiful and obtain their strength only through harmony with the latter. He likes very much to be witty and will without hesitation sacrifice something of the truth for a conceit. On the other hand, where one cannot be witty, he displays just as profound an insight as someone from any other country, for example in mathematics and in the other dry or profound arts and sciences. To him a *bon mot*[1] has not a fleeting worth, as elsewhere; it is eagerly spread about and preserved in books like the most momentous event. . . . The object to which the merits and national talents of this people refer most often is woman. Not as if she were loved or treasured here more than elsewhere, but because she gives the best occasion to display in her light the most favorite talents of wit, politeness, and good manners. Besides, a vain person of either sex always loves only himself; to him, the opposite sex is merely a plaything. The Frenchman does not actually lack noble qualities, but these can be brought to life only by the feeling of the beautiful; thus the fair sex here

---

[1] A witty remark.

would be able to have a mightier influence to arouse the noblest deeds of the male and to set them astir than perhaps anywhere else in the world, if one were minded to favor this bent of the national spirit a little. . . .

The Englishman is cool in the beginning of every acquaintance, and indifferent toward a stranger. He has little inclination to small complaisances;[2] on the other hand, as soon as he is a friend, he is laid under great performances of service. He takes little trouble to be witty in society, or to display a polite demeanor; but rather, he is reasonable and steady. He is a bad imitator, cares very little about what others judge, and follows solely his own taste. In relation to woman he is not of French politeness, but displays toward her far more respect, and perhaps carries this too far, as in marriage he generally grants to his wife an unlimited esteem. He is steadfast, sometimes to the point of obstinacy, bold and determined, often to audacity, and acts according to principles generally to the point of being headstrong. He easily becomes an eccentric, not out of vanity but because he concerns himself little about others, and does not easily do violence to his taste out of complaisance or imitation; on that account he is seldom as much loved as the Frenchman, but when he is well known, generally more highly esteemed.

The German has a feeling mixed from that of an Englishman and that of a Frenchman, but appears to come nearer to the first, and any greater similarity to the latter is only affected and imitated. He has a fortunate combination of feeling, both in that of the sublime and in that of the beautiful; and if in the first he does not equal an Englishman, nor in the second a Frenchman, he yet surpasses both so far as he unites them. He displays more complaisance in society than the first, and if indeed he does not bring as much pleasant liveliness and wit into the company as the Frenchman, still he expresses more moderation and understanding. In love, just as in all forms of taste, he is reasonably methodical, and because he combines the beautiful with the noble he is cool enough in each feeling to occupy his mind with reflections upon demeanor, splendor, and appearances. Therefore family, title, and rank, in civil relations as well as in love, are of great significance to him. Far more than the aforementioned nationalities, he asks *how people might judge him;* and if there is something in his character which could arouse the wish for a general improvement, it is this weakness whereby he does not venture to be original although he has all the talents needed for that, and occupies himself too much with the opinion of others. This takes away all support from his moral qualities, as it makes them fickle and falsely contrived. . . .

If we cast a fleeting glance over the other parts of the world, we find the . . . Negroes of Africa have by nature no feeling that rises above the trifling. Mr. Hume[3] challenges anyone to cite a single example in which a Negro has shown talents, and asserts that among the hundreds of thousands of blacks who are transported elsewhere from their countries, although many of them have even been set free, still not a single one was ever found who presented anything great in art or science or any other praiseworthy quality, even though among the whites some continually rise aloft from the lowest rabble, and through superior gifts earn respect in the world.

---

[2] Courtesies.
[3] David Hume (1711–1776), Scottish philosopher and essayist who made the following remarks in his essay "Of National Characters" (1748).

So fundamental is the difference between these two races of man, and it appears to be as great in regard to mental capacities as in color. The religion of fetishes so widespread among them is perhaps a sort of idolatry that sinks as deeply into the trifling as appears to be possible to human nature. A bird feather, a cow's horn, a conch shell, or any other common object, as soon as it becomes consecrated by a few words, is an object of veneration and of invocation in swearing oaths. The blacks are very vain but in the Negro's way, and so talkative that they must be driven apart from each other with thrashings.

Among all savages there is no nation that displays so sublime a mental character as those of North America. They have a strong feeling for honor, and as in quest of it they seek wild adventures hundreds of miles abroad, they are still extremely careful to avert the least injury to it when their equally harsh enemy, upon capturing them, seeks by cruel pain to extort cowardly groans from them. The Canadian savage, moreover, is truthful and honest. The friendship he establishes is just as adventurous and enthusiastic as anything of that kind reported from the most ancient and fabled times. He is extremely proud, feels the whole worth of freedom, and even in his education suffers no encounter that would let him feel a low subservience. Lycurgus[4] probably gave statutes to just such savages; and if a lawgiver arose among the Six Nations [of the Iroquois], one would see a Spartan republic rise in the New World; for the undertaking of the Argonauts[5] is little different from the war parties of these Indians, and Jason excels Attakakullakulla[6] in nothing but the honor of a Greek name. All these savages have little feeling for the beautiful in moral understanding, and the generous forgiveness of an injury, which is at once noble and beautiful, is completely unknown as a virtue among the savages, but rather is disdained as a miserable cowardice. Valor is the greatest merit of the savage and revenge his sweetest bliss. The remaining natives of this part of the world show few traces of a mental character disposed to the finer feelings, and an extraordinary apathy constitutes the mark of this type of race.

QUESTIONS FOR ANALYSIS

1. How does Kant use the categories of the beautiful and the sublime to distinguish among the various peoples he discusses?

2. In what ways does Kant relate gender and family to the beautiful and the sublime in his critique of European peoples? How does this compare to his discussion of Africans and Amerindians?

3. For Kant, how do the categories of the beautiful and the sublime promote progress in society? How do the Africans and Amerindians relate to this possibility of progress?

4. How does Kant's discussion of African society compare to Park's discussions (Source 5)? Contrast Kant's emphasis on the beautiful and the sublime as cultivated, refined qualities with Rousseau's praise of savage life (Source 4).

---

[4] Lycurgus (7th century B.C.), traditionally, lawgiver for the Greek city-state of Sparta.
[5] Legendary story of an ancient Greek band of fifty heroes who sailed with Jason to retrieve the Golden Fleece.
[6] Spelled *Attakullaculla,* an eighteenth-century Cherokee chieftain.

8

"... NATURE TOOK HIM IN HAND. ..."

Johann Gottfried von Herder
Outlines of a Philosophy of the History of Man   (1784)

A student of Immanuel Kant, Johann Gottfried von Herder (1744–1803) diverged from Kant's philosophy in important ways. Whereas Kant believed that the world existed only as an object of thought by particular human minds, Herder argued that the world existed independently of human thought. For Herder, the world was transformed by humans while at the same time humans acquired their character from their particular situations in the world. Thus, having originated from different situations, the values and goals of differing human cultures could be both mutually incompatible and equally self-validating. While one civilization may be more advanced than another, according to Herder no single, universal code of human conduct existed, for different codes developed for the particular situations of different cultures. In the excerpt below from his Outlines of a Philosophy of the History of Man, *Herder discusses the "particular situations" that produced the peoples of Africa.*

It is but just, when we proceed to the country of the blacks, that we lay aside our proud prejudices, and consider the organization of this quarter of the Globe with as much impartiality, as if there were no other. Since whiteness is a mark of degeneracy in many animals near the pole, the negro has as much right to term his savage robbers albinoes and white devils, degenerated through the weakness of nature, as we have to deem him the emblem of evil, and a descendant of Ham, branded by his father's curse.[1] I, might he say, I, the black, am the original man. I have taken the deepest draughts from the source of life, the Sun: on me, and on every thing around me, it has acted with the greatest energy and vivacity. Behold my country: how fertile in fruits, how rich in gold! Behold the height of my trees! the strength of my animals! Here each element swarms with life, and I am the centre of this vital action. Thus might the negro say; let us then enter the country appropriate to him with modesty. . . .

But I forget, that I had to speak of the form of the negroes, as of an organization of the human species; and it would be well, if natural philosophy had applied its attention to all the varieties of our species, as much as to this. The following are some of the results of its observations.

---

[1] According to the Jewish scriptures, Ham, son of Noah, was cursed with a mark after having looked on his drunken, naked father. Some Europeans identified this mark as black skin.

Johann Gottfried Herder, *Outlines of a Philosophy of the History of Man,* trans. T. Churchill (1800); (reprint, New York: Bergman, n.d.), 146, 149–52.

1. The black colour of the negro has nothing in it more wonderful than the white, brown, yellow, or reddish, of other nations. Neither the blood, the brain, nor the seminal fluid of the negro is black, but the reticular membrane beneath the cuticle, which is common to all, and even in us, at least in some parts, and under certain circumstances, is more or less coloured. Camper has demonstrated this;[2] and according to him we all have the capacity of becoming negroes. . . .

2. All depends therefore on the causes, that were capable of unfolding it here: and analogy instructs us, that sun and air must have had great share in it. For what makes us brown? What makes the difference between the two sexes in almost every country? What has rendered the descendants of the Portuguese, after residing some centuries in Africa, so similar in colour to the negroes? Nay, what so forcibly discriminates the negro races in Africa itself? The climate, considered in the most extensive signification of the word, so as to include the manner of life, and kind of food. The blackest negroes live precisely in that region, where the east wind, blowing wholly over the land, brings the most intense heat: where the heat is diminished, or cooled by the sea-breeze, the black is softened into yellow. The cool heights are inhabited by white, or whitish people: while in the close lower regions the oil, that occasions the black appearance beneath the cuticle, is rendered more adust[3] by the heat of the Sun. Now if we reflect, that these blacks have resided for ages in this quarter of the World, and completely naturalized themselves to it by their mode of life: if we consider the several causes, that now operate more feebly, but which in earlier periods, when all the elements were in their primitive rude force, must have acted with greater power: and if we take into the account, that so many thousands of years must have brought about a complete revolution as it were of the wheel of contingencies, which at one period or another turns up every thing that can take place upon this Earth: we shall not wonder at the trifling circumstance, that the skin of some nations is black. . . .

5. But the peculiar formation of the members of the human body says more than all these: and this appears to me explicable in the African organization. According to various physiological observations, the lips, breasts, and private parts, are proportionate to each other: and as Nature, agreeably to the simple principle of her plastic art, must have conferred on these people, to whom she was obliged to deny nobler gifts, an ampler measure of sensual enjoyment, this could not but have appeared to the physiologist. According to the rules of physiognomy, thick lips are held to indicate a sensual disposition; as thin lips, displaying a slender rosy line, are deemed symptoms of a chaste and delicate taste; not to mention other circumstances. What wonder then, that in a nation, for whom the sensual appetite is the height of happiness, external marks of it should appear? A negro child is born white: the skin round the nails, the nipples, and the private parts, first become coloured; and the same consent of parts in the disposition to colour is observable in other nations. A hundred children are a trifle to a negro; and an old man, who had not above seventy, lamented his fate with tears.

---

[2] Petrus Camper (1722–1789), Dutch zoologist and human anatomist.
[3] Sunburned.

6. With this oleaginous[4] organization to sensual pleasure, the profile, and the whole frame of the body, must alter. The projection of the mouth would render the nose short and small, the forehead would incline backwards, and the face would have at a distance the resemblance of that of an ape. Conformably to this would be the position of the neck, the transition to the occiput, and the elastic structure of the whole body, which is formed, even to the nose and skin, for sensual animal enjoyment. Since in this quarter of the Globe, as the native land of the solar heat, the loftiest and most succulent trees arise, herds of the largest, strongest, and most active animals are generated, and vast multitudes of apes in particular sport, so that air and water, the sea and the sands, swarm with life and fertility; organizing human nature could not fail to follow, with respect to its animal part, this general simple principle of the plastic powers. That finer intellect, which the creature, whose breast swells with boiling passions beneath this burning sun, must necessarily be refused, was countervailed by a structure altogether incompatible with it. Since then a nobler boon[5] could not be conferred on the negro in such a climate, let us pity, but not despise him; and honour that parent, who knows how to compensate, while she deprives. He spends his life void of care in a country, which yields him food with unbounded liberality. His limber body moves in the water, as if it had been formed for that element: he runs and climbs, as if each were his sport: and not less strong and healthy than light and active, his different constitution supports all the accidents and diseases of his climate, under which so many Europeans sink. What to him are the tormenting sensations of superiour joys, for which he was not formed? The materials were not wanting: but Nature took him in hand, and formed of him what was most fit for his country, and the happiness of his life. Either no Africa should have been created, or it was requisite, that negroes should be made to inhabit Africa.

QUESTIONS FOR ANALYSIS

1. What "particularities" does Herder focus on to explain African civilization? What is the importance of African sexuality to Herder's argument?

2. How does Herder integrate the physical and social components of Africans and African civilization? On what type of evidence does he base his argument?

3. How does Herder suggest both his belief in the superiority of European civilization and his respect for African civilization?

4. How does Herder's argument permit a sense of cultural relativism? How does this contrast with Kant's interpretation (Source 7)?

5. What similarities and differences exist between Herder's use of nature to explain African civilization and Montesquieu's use of nature in his discussion of China (Source 1)?

---

[4] Oil-based.
[5] Benefit.

CHAPTER QUESTIONS

1. What various ideas of progress did the Enlightenment authors promote? What standards did they use to define progress?

2. How do Enlightenment authors reach different conclusions about the progress made by Europe and by other countries? What roles are played by gender and family relations in the authors' various analyses?

3. How do Montesquieu's and Voltaire's assessments of China's political system compare to the assessment made by Matteo Ricci (Chapter 3, Source 4)? What is the basis for each writer's analysis?

4. How do the Enlightenment authors' critiques of the wider world compare to earlier Western efforts to assess non-European civilizations, such as the Renaissance debates between Sepúlveda and Las Casas (Chapter 1, Sources 7 and 8) and the critiques by Jesuit missionaries such as Ricci and Brébeuf in the seventeenth century (Chapter 3)? In what ways do the presuppositions by which Europeans judged other civilizations change between the Renaissance and the Enlightenment?

Chapter 6

SLAVERY, ABOLITIONISM, AND REVOLUTION

The enslavement and trading of human beings has a long and varied history, beginning in the ancient world and continuing to the present. The forced migration of black Africans to the Western Hemisphere from the sixteenth to nineteenth century is perhaps the most dramatic part of that history. During these nearly four hundred years, European traders from Portugal, Holland, France, Britain, and even Denmark and Prussia transported black Africans to the Americas to work on newly established plantations and farms, growing crops such as coffee, tobacco, and sugar that could produce substantial wealth. The slave trade expanded dramatically throughout the Western Hemisphere to provide needed labor. Before 1650, slave traders brought about seven thousand Africans each year to the Western Hemisphere. Between 1650 and 1675, this rate doubled and then nearly doubled again between 1675 and 1700. By the mid-nineteenth century, more than eleven million Africans had arrived in the Americas, not counting the two to three million more who had died during the passage across the Atlantic (Map 6.1).

The European slave traders could not have extracted such a mass of humanity from Africa without the participation of Africans. The institution of slavery was long practiced in Africa, where it served diverse social purposes. Individuals became slaves through warfare, tribute payment, and indebtedness and as punishment for crimes; however, they could regain their freedom through marriage or adoption into their owners' families, through purchase of their freedom by wealth they had accumulated as slaves, or as a gift from their owners in recognition of years of service. Europeans established long-term relationships with African rulers and traders, who procured slaves for the Europeans through all the traditional means as well as by kidnapping. Africans carried these slaves to the trading centers on the coast, where they were loaded on ships, were shackled, and began the horrific "middle passage." After the three-month voyage, most slaves entered into the brutal plantation economy. They worked long hours and received inadequate nourishment and shelter. Not surprisingly, their poor living conditions resulted in high rates of death. Despite these conditions, no strong movement for the abolition of the slave trade or of slavery itself appeared in Europe until the late eighteenth century. This chapter looks at the emergence of this abolitionist movement and the first experiment in the abolition of slavery, which occurred in the midst of the French Revolution.

THE RISE OF THE ABOLITIONIST MOVEMENT

Despite the horrors of the slave trade and of slavery, the abolitionist movement grew slowly in Europe. In the sixteenth, seventeenth, and early eighteenth centuries,

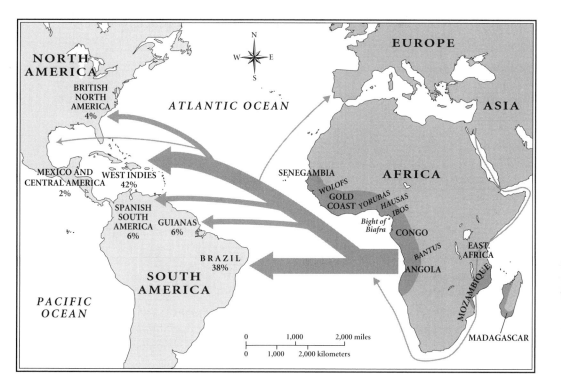

MAP 6.1 THE ATLANTIC SLAVE TRADE

The Atlantic slave trade linked the African slave system and its ability to procure large numbers of slaves through warfare and raids, with the high demand for labor in the European colonies of the Americas, especially on the sugar plantations of Brazil and the Caribbean islands. Typically, Africans carried slaves to the African coast, where they boarded European ships for passage across the Atlantic.

some individuals challenged the European practice of slavery in the Americas, but no distinct abolitionist movement emerged until the Enlightenment. Beginning in the 1750s, antislavery and antislave trade sentiment gained momentum among some liberal thinkers and Christian reformers. Particularly influential for the movement's growth in France were rationalistic Enlightenment debates on the natural, universal rights of man—rights that transcended differences of race, culture, and religion. In Great Britain, Adam Smith's *The Wealth of Nations* (Source 1), a classic work of the Enlightenment, encouraged politicians such as Edmund Burke, William Pitt the Younger, and Charles Fox to recognize economic and political disadvantages to slave labor. In the 1780s, a religious reform movement, which included Quakers, Methodists, and evangelical Anglicans, swept across England. The abolitionist movement gained broad-based support as these reformers used a language of Christian righteousness and retribution in their condemnation of slavery and the slave trade. In France, the Society for the Friends of Blacks copied the general program of the English abolitionists, but instead of drawing on the evangelicals' religious fervor to build a mass movement, the more secular French Society focused on attracting important, well-connected members. Nevertheless, as France began its own very public debates over rights and privileges in the years preceding the French Revolution, the French Society for the Friends of Blacks found growing support for recognizing the rights of all people.

1

". . . RENDERS THE SLAVE LESS CONTEMPTIBLE . . ."

Adam Smith
The Wealth of Nations   (1776)

The Scottish social philosopher and political economist Adam Smith (c. 1723–1790) brought to fruition the Enlightenment's most original contribution to the human sciences—the discipline of economics. His The Wealth of Nations *synthesized the previous one hundred years of advancements in economic analysis. Smith emphasized the factors that contributed to sustainable economic growth, most centrally the economic advantages that accrue from permitting individuals to pursue their own economic interests. In the passage preceding the text below, Smith explains that in comparison to the Spanish, Portuguese, and French governments, Great Britain had given its North American colonies greater economic and political liberties, including greater self-governance, and that as a result the British North American colonies had experienced more economic progress than the other colonies. Smith then explains an apparent exception to his analysis—the French and British Caribbean island colonies and their sugar production based on slave labor.*

The progress of the sugar colonies of France has been at least equal, perhaps superior, to that of the greater part of those of England; and yet the sugar colonies of England enjoy a free government nearly of the same kind with that which takes place in her colonies of North America. But [in] the sugar colonies of France . . . , the genius of their government naturally introduces a better management of their Negro slaves.

In all European colonies the culture of the sugar cane is carried on by Negro slaves. The constitution of those who have been born in the temperate climate of

Adam Smith, *An Inquiry into the Nature and Causes of the Wealth of Nations: Representative Selections,* ed., Bruce Mazlish (Indianapolis: Bobbs-Merrill, 1961), 212–14.

Europe could not, it is supposed, support the labor of digging the ground under the burning sun of the West Indies; and the culture of the sugar cane, as it is managed at present, is all hand labor, though, in the opinion of many, the drill plow might be introduced into it with great advantage. But, as the profit and success of the cultivation which is carried on by means of cattle depend very much upon the good management of those cattle, so the profit and success of that which is carried on by slaves must depend equally upon the good management of those slaves; and in the good management of their slaves the French planters, I think it is generally allowed, are superior to the English. The law, so far as it gives some weak protection to the slave against the violence of his master, is likely to be better executed in a colony where the government is in a great measure arbitrary, than in one where it is altogether free. In every country where the unfortunate law of slavery is established, the magistrate, when he protects the slave, intermeddles in some measure in the management of the private property of the master; and, in a free country, where the master is perhaps either a member of the colony assembly, or an elector of such a member, he dare not do this but with the greatest caution and circumspection. The respect which he is obliged to pay to the master renders it more difficult for him to protect the slave. But in a country where the government is in a great measure arbitrary, where it is usual for the magistrate to intermeddle even in the management of the private property of individuals, and to send them, perhaps, a *lettre de cachet*[1] if they do not manage it according to his liking, it is much easier for him to give some protection to the slave; and common humanity naturally disposes him to do so. The protection of the magistrate renders the slave less contemptible in the eyes of his master, who is thereby induced to consider him with more regard, and to treat him with more gentleness. Gentle usage renders the slave not only more faithful, but more intelligent, and therefore, upon a double account, more useful. He approaches more to the condition of a free servant, and may possess some degree of integrity and attachment to his master's interest, virtues which frequently belong to free servants, but which never can belong to a slave who is treated as slaves commonly are in countries where the master is perfectly free and secure.

That the condition of a slave is better under an arbitrary than under a free government is, I believe, supported by the history of all ages and nations. In the Roman history, the first time we read of the magistrate interposing to protect the slave from the violence of his master is under the emperors. When Vedius Pollio, in the presence of Augustus, ordered one of his slaves, who had committed a slight fault, to be cut into pieces and thrown into his fishpond in order to feed his fishes, the emperor commanded him, with indignation, to emancipate immediately not only that slave, but all the others that belonged to him.[2] Under the republic no magistrate could have had authority enough to protect the slave, much less to punish the master.

---

[1] Sealed royal letter that authorized the imprisonment of an individual.
[2] Smith paraphrases and alters somewhat a story related by the Roman philosopher and statesman Lucius Annaeus Seneca (c. 4 B.C.–A.D. 65) and by the Roman historian Dio Cassius (c. 150–235).

QUESTIONS FOR ANALYSIS

1. How does Smith distinguish between French and British colonial governments? Why does Smith hold that slaves are better off under French colonial rule than British?

2. What is Smith's rationale for asserting that the French held an advantage in the cultivation of sugar cane? How does Smith recognize a common humanity shared by slaves and nonslaves?

3. What assumptions does Smith make about the behavior of slaves? Of their masters?

4. Smith's argument does not call for an end to slavery, but why might it have encouraged some members of the British Parliament to question the value of slavery in the British colonies?

2

"I NOW WISHED FOR THE LAST FRIEND, DEATH, TO RELIEVE ME. . . ."

Olaudah Equiano
The Interesting Narrative of the Life of Olaudah Equiano (1789)

Born into Ibo society in what is now eastern Nigeria, Olaudah Equiano (c. 1745–1797) was captured at around age ten by local raiders searching for slaves. Over the next several months he was carried down river, passing through several different hands until he arrived at the seacoast, where he was sold to European slavers and shipped to the West Indies. Eventually purchased by sea captain Michael Pascal, Equiano traveled with Pascal and obtained some education. He continued his education and travels under another master, the Philadelphia Quaker merchant Robert King, who permitted Equiano to purchase his freedom in 1766. Equiano, who embraced Christianity, soon settled in England and became an eloquent spokesperson for the antislavery movement. He traveled across England making speeches and promoting his book, The Interesting Narrative of the Life of Olaudah Equiano, or Gustavus Vassa the African, written by Himself. *In the book, which was meant to further the antislavery cause, Equiano provided a narrative of his life. The following excerpt describes Equiano's experience during the Middle Passage, when carried from the African coast to the West Indies.*

Equiano's Travels: His Autobiography: The Interesting Narrative of the Life of Olaudah Equiano or Gustavus Vassa the African, ed. Paul Edwards (Oxford: Heinemann, 1967), 25–32.

The first object which saluted my eyes when I arrived on the coast was the sea, and a slave ship which was then riding at anchor and waiting for its cargo. These filled me with astonishment, which was soon converted into terror when I was carried on board. . . . When I looked round the ship too and saw a large furnace or copper boiling and a multitude of black people of every description chained together, every one of their countenances expressing dejection and sorrow, I no longer doubted of my fate; and quite overpowered with horror and anguish, I fell motionless on the deck and fainted. . . .

I was soon put down under the decks, and there I received such a salutation in my nostrils as I had never experienced in my life: so that with the loathsomeness of the stench and crying together, I became so sick and low that I was not able to eat, nor had I the least desire to taste anything. I now wished for the last friend, death, to relieve me; but soon, to my grief, two of the white men offered me eatables, and on my refusing to eat, one of them held me fast by the hands and laid me across I think the windlass,[1] and tied my feet while the other flogged me severely. I had never experienced anything of this kind before, and although, not being used to the water, I naturally feared that element the first time I saw it, yet nevertheless could I have got over the nettings I would have jumped over the side, but I could not; and besides, the crew used to watch us very closely who were not chained down to the decks, lest we should leap into the water: and I have seen some of these poor African prisoners most severely cut for attempting to do so, and hourly whipped for not eating. This indeed was often the case with myself. In a little time after, amongst the poor chained men I found some of my own nation, which in a small degree gave ease to my mind. I inquired of these what was to be done with us; they gave me to understand we were to be carried to these white people's country to work for them. I then was a little revived, and thought if it were no worse than working, my situation was not so desperate: but still I feared I should be put to death, the white people looked and acted, as I thought, in so savage a manner; for I had never seen among my people such instances of brutal cruelty. . . . The stench of the [ship's] hold while we were on the coast was so intolerably loathsome that it was dangerous to remain there for any time, and some of us had been permitted to stay on the deck for the fresh air; but now that the whole ship's cargo were confined together it became absolutely pestilential. The closeness of the place and the heat of the climate, added to the number in the ship, which was so crowded that each had scarcely room to turn himself, almost suffocated us. This produced copious perspirations, so that the air soon became unfit for respiration from a variety of loathsome smells, and brought on a sickness among the slaves, of which many died, thus falling victims to the improvident avarice, as I may call it, of their purchasers. This wretched situation was again aggravated by the galling of the chains, now become insupportable, and the filth of the necessary tubs, into which the children often fell and were almost suffocated. The shrieks of the women and the groans of the dying rendered the whole a scene of horror almost inconceivable. Happily perhaps for myself I was soon reduced so low here that it was thought necessary to keep me almost always on deck, and from my extreme youth I was not put in fetters. In this

---

[1] Large barrel turned by a crank around which a hoisting rope is wound.

situation I expected every hour to share the fate of my companions, some of whom were almost daily brought upon deck at the point of death, which I began to hope would soon put an end to my miseries. . . . At last we came in sight of the island of Barbados, at which the whites on board gave a great shout and made many signs of joy to us. We did not know what to think of this, but as the vessel drew nearer we plainly saw the harbour and other ships of different kinds and sizes, and we soon anchored amongst them off Bridgetown. Many merchants and planters now came on board, though it was in the evening. They put us in separate parcels and examined us attentively. They also made us jump, and pointed to the land, signifying we were to go there. We thought by this we should be eaten by these ugly men, as they appeared to us; and when soon after we were all put down under the deck again, there was much dread and trembling among us, and nothing but bitter cries to be heard all the night from these apprehensions, insomuch that at last the white people got some old slaves from the land to pacify us. They told us we were not to be eaten but to work, and were soon to go on land where we should see many of our country people. This report eased us much; and sure enough soon after we were landed there came to us Africans of all languages. We were conducted immediately to the merchant's yard, where we were all pent up together like so many sheep in a fold without regard to sex or age. . . . We were not many days in the merchant's custody before we were sold after their usual manner, which is this: On a signal given, (as the beat of a drum) the buyers rush at once into the yard where the slaves are confined, and make choice of that parcel they like best. The noise and clamour with which this is attended and the eagerness visible in the countenances of the buyers serve not a little to increase the apprehensions of the terrified Africans, who may well be supposed to consider them as the ministers of that destruction to which they think themselves devoted. In this manner, without scruple, are relations and friends separated, most of them never to see each other again. I remember in the vessel in which I was brought over, in the men's apartment there were several brothers who, in the sale, were sold in different lots; and it was very moving on this occasion to see and hear their cries at parting. O, ye nominal Christians! might not an African ask you, Learned you this from your God who says unto you, Do unto all men as you would men should do unto you? Is it not enough that we are torn from our country and friends to toil for your luxury and lust of gain? Must every tender feeling be likewise sacrificed to your avarice? Are the dearest friends and relations, now rendered more dear by their separation from their kindred, still to be parted from each other and thus prevented from cheering the gloom of slavery with the small comfort of being together and mingling their sufferings and sorrows? Why are parents to lose their children, brothers their sisters, or husbands their wives? Surely this is a new refinement in cruelty which, while it has no advantage to atone for it, thus aggravates distress and adds fresh horrors even to the wretchedness of slavery.

QUESTIONS FOR ANALYSIS

1. What literary strategies or devices does Equiano use to evoke a sense of the horror he experienced during the Middle Passage? How does Equiano's description suggest his and the other slaves' dehumanization?

2. How does Equiano establish a universal, common humanity between African slaves and Europeans? In what ways does Equiano's appeal to the common humanity of African slaves and Europeans compare to Smith's (Source 1)?
3. How does Equiano use Western ideas to critique Western practices of slavery?
4. What Christian themes are developed in Equiano's conclusion? What importance does the idea of family have in Equiano's text?

3

". . . SO IMPORTANT A MORAL AND RELIGIOUS DUTY . . ."

Plymouth Committee of the Society for the Abolition of the Slave Trade

Plan of an African Ship's Lower Deck   (1788)

During the late 1700s, numerous antislavery and antislave trade societies or committees formed in Great Britain, many of which loosely associated themselves with the Society for the Abolition of the Slave Trade. The Society collected information and evidence, which it then deployed in a public relations campaign to bring pressure against participants in the slave trade and, most important, within Parliament. The local committees, in which women actively participated, produced antislave trade tracts and images, wrote letters, collected signatures on petitions, and organized boycotts. The local committee in Plymouth, led by the banker William Elford, produced the following image and text as part of its propaganda efforts.

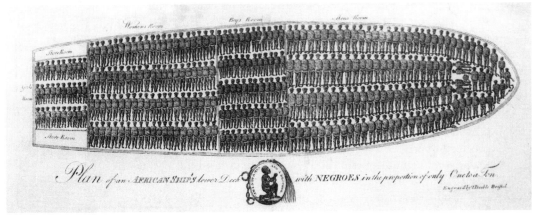

J. R. Oldfield, *Popular Politics and British Anti-Slavery: The Mobilisation of Public Opinion against the Slave Trade 1787–1807* (Manchester: Manchester University Press, 1995), 164.

The . . . Plate represents the lower deck of an African Ship of 297 tons burden, with the Slaves stowed on it, in the proportion of not quite one to a ton.

In the Men's apartment, the space allowed to each is six feet length, by sixteen inches in breadth.—The Boys are each allowed five feet by fourteen inches.—The Women, five feet ten inches, by sixteen inches: and the Girls, four feet by one foot each.—The perpendicular height between the Decks, is five feet eight inches.

The men are fastened together two and two, by handcuffs on their wrists, and by irons riveted on their legs.—They are brought up on the main deck every day, about eight o'clock, and as each pair ascend, a strong chain, fastened by ring-bolts to the deck, is passed through their Shackles; a precaution absolutely necessary to prevent insurrections.—In this state, if the weather is favorable, they are permitted to remain about one-third part of the twenty four hours, and during this interval they are fed, and their apartment below is cleaned; but when the weather is bad, even these indulgences cannot be granted them, and they are only permitted to come up in small companies, of about ten at a time, to be fed, where after remaining a quarter of an hour, each mess is obliged to give place to the next in rotation. . . .

The above mode of carrying the Slaves, however, is only one among a thousand other miseries, which those unhappy and devoured creatures suffer from this disgraceful Traffick of the Human Species; which in every part of its progress, exhibits scenes that strike us with horror and indignation.—If we regard the first stage of it on the Continent of Africa, we find that a hundred thousand Slaves are annually produced there for exportation, the greatest part of whom consists of innocent persons, torn from their dearest friends and connections, sometimes by force, and sometimes treachery. Of these, experience has shown, that five and forty thousand perish, either in the dreadful mode of conveyance before described, or within two years after their arrival at the plantations, before they are seasoned to the climate.—Those who unhappily survive these hardships, are destined like beasts of burden, to exhaust their lives in the unremitting labors of a Slavery, without recompense, and without hope.

The *Inhumanity* of this Trade, indeed, is so notorious, and so universally admitted, that even the advocates for the continuance of it, have rested all their arguments on the political inexpediency of its abolition; and in order to strengthen a weak cause, have either maliciously or ignorantly confounded together the emancipation of the negroes already in Slavery, with the abolition of the Trade; and thus many well-meaning people have become enemies to the cause, by the apprehensions that private property will be materially injured by the success of it.—To such, it becomes a necessary information, that liberating the Slaves forms no part of the present system: and so far will the prohibition of a future trade be from injuring private property, that the value of every Slave will be very considerably increased, from the moment that event takes place, and a more kind and tender treatment will immediately be insured to them by their Masters, from the necessity every Planter will then be under to keep up his stock, by natural means; a practice which some humane inhabitants of the Islands have pursued with the greatest success, and upon whose estates no new Negroes have been purchased for a number of years, the death vacancies having been supplied by young ones, born and bred in their own Plantations.—Thus then the value of private property will not only suffer no diminution, but will be very considerably enhanced by the abolition of the Trade. . . .

As then the *Cruelty* and *Inhumanity* of this Trade must be universally admitted and lamented, and as the policy or impolicy of its abolition is a question which the wisdom of the Legislature must ultimately decide upon, and which it can only be enabled to form a just estimate of, by the most thorough investigation of all its relations and dependencies, it becomes the indispensable duty of every friend to humanity, however his speculations may have led him to conclude on the political tendency of the measure, to stand forward, and to assist the [Antislavery] Committees, either by producing such facts as he may himself be acquainted with, or by subscribing [joining], to enable them to procure and transmit to the Legislature, such evidence as will tend to throw the necessary lights on the subject.— And people would do well to consider that it does not often fall to the lot of individuals, to have an opportunity of performing so important a moral and religious duty, as that of endeavouring to put an end to a practice, which may, without exaggeration, be styled one of the greatest evils at this day existing upon the earth.

QUESTIONS FOR ANALYSIS

1. What literary tools and devices does the Committee use to provoke outrage in its British audience against the slave trade? How are these similar or different from Equiano's efforts (Source 2)?

2. What image of African slaves is created by the text? How do the text and image emphasize the cruelty of the slave trade?

3. How does the Committee position itself as reasonable or moderate in its demands? Why might it do so?

4. What actions does the Committee hope to inspire with the text?

4

"LIBERTY IS THE PROPERTY OF ONE'S SELF."

Abbé Raynal
History of the East and West Indies   (1770, rev. 1780)

Educated as a Jesuit priest, Guillaume-Thomas, the abbé de Raynal (1712–1796) left religious life to work as an author and editor in Enlightenment Paris. In 1770, he published his six-volume History of the East and West Indies *in close collaboration with Denis Diderot, one of Enlightenment Paris's most influential figures. Diderot, in fact, most likely wrote several sections of the work. The popular work established an anticlerical and antiroyalist tone in its attack on European colonization and became*

Guillaume Raynal. *A Philosophical and Political History of the Settlements and Trade of the Europeans in the East and West Indies,* trans. J. O. Justamond (London, 1987) (Reprinted New York: Negro University Press, 1969), 4:102–3, 116–18.

increasingly radical as it went through subsequent editions. The Catholic church banned the work, and Raynal was ordered into exile. In the excerpt below, translated from the more radical 1780 edition of the work, Raynal considers the European practice of slavery in the Americas.

[F]ourteen or fifteen hundred thousand blacks, who are now dispersed over the European colonies of the New World, are the unfortunate remains of eight or nine millions of slaves that have been conveyed there. This dreadful destruction cannot be the effect of the climate, which is nearly the same as that of Africa, much less of the disorders, to which, in the opinion of all observers, but few fall a sacrifice. It must therefore originate from the manner in which these slaves are governed: and might not an error of this nature be corrected?

The first step necessary in this reformation would be, to attend minutely to the natural and moral state of man. Those who go to purchase blacks on the coasts of savage nations; those who convey them to America, and especially those who direct their labours, often think themselves obliged, from their situation, and frequently too for the sake of their own safety, to oppress these wretched men. The heart of those who conduct the slaves is lost to all sense of compassion, is ignorant of every motive to enforce obedience, except those of fear or severity, and these are exercised with all the ferocious spirit of a temporary authority. If the proprietors of plantations would cease to regard the care of their slaves as an occupation below them, and consider it as an office to which it is their duty to attend, they would soon discard these errors that arise from a spirit of cruelty. The history of all mankind would show them, that, in order to render slavery useful, it is at least necessary to make it easy; that force doth not prevent the rebellion of the mind; that it is the master's interest that the slave should be attached to life, and that nothing is to be expected from him the moment that he no longer fears to die.

This principle of enlightened reason, derived from the sentiments of humanity, would contribute to the reformation of several abuses. Men would acknowledge the necessity of lodging, clothing, and giving proper food to beings condemned to the most painful bondage that hath ever existed since the infamous origin of slavery. They would be sensible, that it is naturally impossible that those who reap no advantage from their own labours, can have the same understanding, the same economy, the same activity, the same strength, as the man who enjoys the produce of his industry. That political moderation would gradually take place, which consists in lessening labour, alleviating punishment, and rendering to man part of his rights, in order to reap, with greater certainty, the benefit of those duties that are imposed upon him. The preservation of a great number of slaves, whom disorders occasioned by vexation or regret deprive the colonies of, would be the natural consequence of so wise a regulation. Far from aggravating the yoke that oppresses them, every kind of attention should be given to make it easy, and to dissipate even the idea of it. . . .

Liberty is the property of one's self. Three kinds of it are distinguished: natural liberty, civil liberty, and political liberty; that is to say the liberty of the individual, the liberty of the citizen, and the liberty of a nation. Natural liberty is the right granted by nature, to every man to dispose of himself at pleasure. Civil liberty is the right which is ensured by society to every citizen, of doing every thing which is not contrary to the laws. Political liberty is the state of a people who have not alienated their sovereignty, and who either make their own laws, or who constitute a part in the system of their legislation.

The first of these liberties is, after reason, the distinguishing characteristic of man. Brutes are chained up, and kept in subjection, because they have no notion of what is just or unjust, no idea of grandeur or meanness. But in man, liberty is the principle of his vices or his virtues. None but a free man can say, *I will* or *I will not;* and consequently none but a free man can be worthy of praise, or be liable to censure.

Without liberty, or the property of one's own body, and the enjoyment of one's mind, no man can be either a husband, a father, a relation, or a friend; he hath neither a country, a fellow-citizen, nor a God. The slave, impelled by the wicked man, and who is the instrument of his wickedness, is inferior even to the dog, let loose by the Spaniard upon the American; for conscience which the dog hath not, still remains with the man. He who basely abdicates his liberty, gives himself up to remorse, and to the greatest misery which can be experienced by a thinking and sensible being. If there be not any power under the heavens, which can change my nature and reduce me to the state of brutes, there is none which can dispose of my liberty. God is my father, and not my master; I am his child and not his slave. How is it possible that I should grant to political power, what I refuse to divine omnipotence?

Will these eternal and immutable truths, the foundation of all morality, the basis of all rational government be contested? They will, and the audacious argument will be dictated by barbarous and sordid avarice. Behold that proprietor of a vessel, who leaning upon his desk, and with the pen in his hand, regulates the number of enormities he may cause to be committed on the coasts of Guinea; who considers at leisure, what number of firelocks he shall want to obtain one Negro, what fetters will be necessary to keep him chained on board his ship, what whips will be required to make him work; who calculates with coolness every drop of blood which the slave must necessarily expend in labour for him, and how much it will produce; who considers whether a Negro woman will be of more advantage to him by her feeble labours, or by going through the dangers of child-birth. You shudder!—If there existed any religion which tolerated, or which gave only a tacit sanction to such kind of horrors; if, absorbed in some idle or seditious questions, it did not incessantly exclaim against the authors or the instruments of this tyranny; if it should consider it as a crime in a slave to break his chains; if it should suffer to remain in its community, the iniquitous judge who condemns the fugitive to death; if such a religion, I say, existed, ought not the ministers of it to be suffocated under the ruins of their altars?

QUESTIONS FOR ANALYSIS

1. How does Raynal criticize the practice of slavery in the Americas on grounds of practicality or utility?

2. According to Raynal, what are the three kinds of liberty? How does slavery violate a person's natural liberty?

3. How do the practical critiques of slavery and the theoretical critiques of slavery based on liberty reinforce each other?

4. How does Raynal both use and criticize religion in his argument? Compare Raynal's argument to the arguments of Smith (Source 1), Equiano (Source 2), and the Plymouth Committee (Source 3).

SLAVERY AND REVOLUTION

During the French Revolution, debates over the ideas of rights, liberty, and citizenship swept broadly over the French-speaking world. While revolutionary assemblies in France sought to define these ideas in both word and deed, similar debates emerged in the French colonies, especially in the French Caribbean colony of Saint Domingue (modern-day Haiti, the western third of the island of Hispaniola). Sustained by the lucrative sugar trade, by 1789 Saint Domingue had a diverse population of black slaves, free former black slaves, free though discriminated-against mulattos or persons of color (people of mixed African and European ancestry, many of whom were slave owners), and French colonists, who accounted for a small minority of the population. As news of the tumultuous events in France during 1789 reached Saint Domingue, the colony's mulatto and black populations took inspiration from the attacks on legal privilege and feudal obligations in France to challenge the legal proscriptions under which they suffered. Mulattos and blacks were themselves often at odds, however, as mulattos sought to establish their political rights as French men but retain their property rights over slaves.

In August 1791, a slave revolt broke out that soon brought François Toussaint-L'Ouverture into leadership of the black population. In 1793, when France and Spain went to war, Toussaint joined forces with the Spaniards of Santo Domingo (modern-day Dominican Republic, the eastern two-thirds of Hispaniola). By 1794, French control of Haiti nearly collapsed under the combined pressure of Toussaint, mulatto rebels, and British dominance of the coast; however, after the French National Convention abolished slavery in all French colonies in February 1794, Toussaint switched allegiances, and soon both the British and Spanish forces, whose governments still supported slavery, were expelled from Haiti.

Between 1794 and 1802, Toussaint consistently outmaneuvered rivals and commissioners sent from France to oversee his leadership of the colony and established his command over the entire island of Hispaniola. A stern leader, Toussaint instituted military discipline to return the newly freed blacks to work, although under less brutal conditions than under slavery and with a share in the profits that plantations made. Saint Domingue's economy, however, did not quickly recover from the prolonged civil and foreign wars. Seeking to reestablish order and profits in the colony, Napoleon Bonaparte sent a large French force to Saint Domingue in 1802, and Toussaint was arrested, brought to France, and died after repeated interrogations in 1803. Nevertheless, when Saint Domingue's large black population learned that Napoleon's forces were reinstituting slavery in other colonies, blacks and mulattos rebelled again, successfully defeating the French military and declaring the independent republic of Haiti on December 31, 1803.

5

"MEN ARE BORN AND REMAIN FREE. . . ."

Declaration of the Rights of Man and Citizen (1789)

The Declaration of the Rights of Man and Citizen was one of the earliest and most important documents to emerge from the French Revolution. Written and debated in the six weeks following the storming of the Bastille, the Declaration sought to be a universal statement about the foundations of legitimate government and the sanctity of individual rights — two issues that the Declaration linked together. The Declaration's "universalistic" sentiment drew on Enlightenment natural law theory, which had been developed in debates among British, French, Dutch, and other Enlightenment thinkers. Influenced by the scientific revolution's assertion that laws of nature governed the physical universe, Enlightenment authors claimed that similar laws of nature governed the political, economic, and social worlds of human interaction and that as laws of nature, these laws were universally applicable to all people. Because of its universalistic framework, the Declaration of the Rights of Man and Citizen has remained an influential document to this day, establishing an idea of universal human rights—a universality not lost on the opponents of slavery during the French Revolution.

The representatives of the French people, constituted as a National Assembly, and considering that ignorance, neglect, or contempt of the rights of man are the sole causes of public misfortunes and governmental corruption, have resolved to set forth in a solemn declaration the natural, inalienable, and sacred rights of man: so that by being constantly present to all the members of the social body this declaration may always remind them of their rights and duties; so that by being liable at every moment to comparison with the aim of any and all political institutions the acts of the legislative and executive powers may be the more fully respected; and so that by being founded henceforward on simple and incontestable principles the demands of the citizens may always tend toward maintaining the constitution and the general welfare.

In consequence, the National Assembly recognizes and declares, in the presence and under the auspices of the Supreme Being, the following rights of man and the citizen:

1. Men are born and remain free and equal in rights. Social distinctions may be based only on common utility.

2. The purpose of all political association is the preservation of the natural and imprescriptible rights of man. These rights are liberty, property, security, and resistance to oppression.

Lynn Hunt, ed. and trans., *The French Revolution and Human Rights: A Brief Documentary History* (Boston: Bedford/St. Martin's, 1996), 77–79.

143

3. The principle of all sovereignty rests essentially in the nation. No body and no individual may exercise authority which does not emanate expressly from the nation.

4. Liberty consists in the ability to do whatever does not harm another; hence the exercise of the natural rights of each man has no other limits than those which assure to other members of society the enjoyment of the same rights. These limits can only be determined by the law.

5. The law only has the right to prohibit those actions which are injurious to society. No hindrance should be put in the way of anything not prohibited by the law, nor may any one be forced to do what the law does not require.

6. The law is the expression of the general will. All citizens have the right to take part, in person or by their representatives, in its formation. It must be the same for everyone whether it protects or penalizes. All citizens being equal in its eyes are equally admissible to all public dignities, offices, and employments, according to their ability, and with no other distinction than that of their virtues and talents. . . .

10. No one should be disturbed for his opinions, even in religion, provided that their manifestation does not trouble public order as established by law.

11. The free communication of thoughts and opinions is one of the most precious of the rights of man. Every citizen may therefore speak, write, and print freely, if he accepts his own responsibility for any abuse of this liberty in the cases set by the law.

12. The safeguard of the rights of man and the citizen requires public powers. These powers are therefore instituted for the advantage of all, and not for the private benefit of those to whom they are entrusted.

13. For maintenance of public authority and for expenses of administration, common taxation is indispensable. It should be apportioned equally among all the citizens according to their capacity to pay.

14. All citizens have the right, by themselves or through their representatives, to have demonstrated to them the necessity of public taxes, to consent to them freely, to follow the use made of the proceeds, and to determine the means of apportionment, assessment, and collection, and the duration of them.

15. Society has the right to hold accountable every public agent of the administration.

16. Any society in which the guarantee of rights is not assured or the separation of powers not settled has no constitution.

17. Property being an inviolable and sacred right, no one may be deprived of it except when public necessity, certified by law, obviously requires it, and on the condition of a just compensation in advance.

QUESTIONS FOR ANALYSIS

1. In its preamble, what does the Declaration establish as the basis or justification for its specific articles?

2. Which articles of the Declaration would bear on slavery and the slave trade? How?

3. How might both proslavery and antislavery forces find support in the Declaration?

4. How does the Declaration, both in the preamble and in the propositions, indicate its universal framework?

6

"... CEASE BUTCHERING THOUSANDS OF BLACKS. ..."

Society of the Friends of Blacks
Address to the National Assembly in Favor of the Abolition of the Slave Trade (1790)

With the passage of the Declaration of the Rights of Man and Citizen, the Society of the Friends of Blacks had a clear foundation on which to base arguments that addressed slavery and the slave trade in the French colonies. Nevertheless, the membership of the Society, drawn largely from the French social elite, believed that the French colonies could not survive without slavery and that French national interests must be supported. Further, the Society knew that powerful commercial interests opposed any changes in French policies with regard to slavery or the slave trade. In the "Address," excerpted below, the Society negotiates around these various concerns while also extending, at least partially, the principles stated in the Declaration of the Rights of Man and Citizen beyond the shores of France itself.

The humanity, justice, and magnanimity that have guided you in the reform of the most profoundly rooted abuses gives hope to the Society of the Friends of Blacks that you will receive with benevolence its demand in favor of that numerous portion of humankind, so cruelly oppressed for two centuries.

This Society,[1] slandered in such cowardly and unjust fashion, only derives its mission from the humanity that induced it to defend the blacks even under the past despotism. Oh! Can there be a more respectable title in the eyes of this august Assembly which has so often avenged the rights of man in its decrees?

You have declared them, these rights; you have engraved on an immortal monument[2] that all men are born and remain free and equal in rights; you have restored to the French people these rights that despotism had for so long despoiled; ... you

---

[1] Society of the Friends of Blacks.
[2] Declaration of the Rights of Man and Citizen (August 26, 1789) (Source 5).

Lynn Hunt, ed. and trans., *The French Revolution and Human Rights: A Brief Documentary History* (Boston: Bedford/St. Martin's, 1996), 107–8. Part of this document is an original translation by David Kammerling Smith from *Société des amis des noirs de Paris, Adresse à l'Assembléé Nationale, pour l'abolition de la traite des noirs* (Paris, 1790), pp. 8–10, 13.

have broken the chains of feudalism that still degraded a good number of our fellow citizens; you have announced the destruction of all the stigmatizing distinctions that religious or political prejudices introduced into the great family of humankind. . . .

We are not asking you to restore to French blacks those political rights which alone, nevertheless, attest to and maintain the dignity of man; we are not even asking for their liberty. . . .

The immediate emancipation of the blacks would not only be a fatal operation for the colonies; it would even be a deadly gift for the blacks, in the state of abjection and incompetence to which cupidity has reduced them. It would be to abandon to themselves and without assistance children in the cradle or mutilated and impotent beings.

It is therefore not yet time to demand that liberty; we ask only that one cease butchering thousands of blacks regularly every year in order to take hundreds of captives; we ask that one henceforth cease the prostitution, the profaning of the French name, used to authorize these thefts, these atrocious murders; we demand in a word the abolition of the slave trade. . . .

Some will tell you that the abolition of the Slave Trade will strike a most deadly blow to the Navy, to public tax revenues, to the Colonies, and to commerce.

We will demonstrate to you that each year this commerce carries to the tomb half of the sailors who are condemned to work there; makes the other half physically and morally gangrenous, and infects with its contagion the remaining commerce.

We will demonstrate to you that the Slave Trade is a burden weighing on the public revenues; that in order to support the slave trade, the State is obligated to maintain at great expense settlements in Africa; that it is again obliged to pay annually a subsidy of around 2,500,000 livres and that this subsidy is triply deadly: in that it feeds a bloody commerce; in that the funds to supply this subsidy are raised on the fruit of the labor of the indigenous inhabitants of our countryside; and in that this subsidy, for the most part, is poured into the hands of English ship-owners, to whom the French merchants do not blush to lend their names in order to elude the intentions of the Government. . . . Is not the French slave trade in reality only a pretext to rob the State for the profit of foreigners. . . .

In regard to the colonists, we will demonstrate to you that if they need to recruit blacks in Africa to sustain the population of the colonies at the same level, it is because they wear out the blacks with work, whippings, and starvation; that, if they treated them with kindness and as good fathers of families, these blacks would multiply and that this population, always growing, would increase cultivation and prosperity. . . .

Hey! Do not step back from the duty that humanity imposes here upon you, for fear of some interruption in the minor work that the slave trade occasions in France? Did you heed this fear when with bold hand you overturned all the abuses which hindered a free Constitution? These abuses, however, supported thousands of individuals; the commotion caused by this revolution threw all fortunes into incertitude, tightened all investment capital, suspended nearly all work. What evil citizen dares, however, complain of this necessary suspension! It is not, however, your blood that your tyrants shed; they do not violate constantly the haven of your house; they do not unjustly condemn you in order to have the right to sell you; they do not snatch you from your home to plunge you in eternal captivity in a foreign land. . . .

If some motive might on the contrary push them [the blacks] to insurrection, might it not be the indifference of the National Assembly about their lot? Might it not be the insistence on weighing them down with chains, when one consecrates everywhere this eternal axiom: *that all men are born free and equal in rights.* So then therefore there would only be fetters and gallows for the blacks while good fortune glimmers only for the whites? Have no doubt, our happy revolution must re-electrify the blacks whom vengeance and resentment have electrified for so long, and it is not with punishments that the effect of this upheaval will be repressed. From one insurrection badly pacified will twenty others be born, of which one alone can ruin the colonists forever.

It is worthy of the first free Assembly of France to consecrate the principle of philanthropy which makes of humankind only one single family, to declare that it is horrified by this annual carnage which takes place on the coasts of Africa, that it has the intention of abolishing it one day, of mitigating the slavery that is the result, of looking for and preparing, from this moment, the means.

QUESTIONS FOR ANALYSIS

1. On what grounds does the Society criticize the slave trade?
2. In its argument, how does the Society distinguish between slavery and the slave trade? How does the Society justify the distinction?
3. What varied attitudes does the text express toward African slaves? How do these attitudes leave undecided the question of slavery?
4. How does the Society use nationalistic sentiments to leave slavery in place while attacking the slave trade?

7

". . . THE SACRED INTEREST OF THE REVOLUTION . . ."

Antoine Barnave

Speech to the National Assembly   (1790)

Antoine Barnave (1761–1793) was a lawyer from southeastern France who rose to prominence in the National Assembly in the early months of the French Revolution. In 1790, he was elected to the Committee on the Colonies, which was to investigate French colonies and make a report to the full Assembly. Barnave drafted several proposals that

Lynn Hunt, ed. and trans., *The French Revolution and Human Rights: A Brief Documentary History* (Boston: Bedford/St. Martin's, 1996), 109, 111. Part of this document is an original translation by David Kammerling Smith from *Archives parlementaires* (Paris) 12 (1881): 68–70.

emphasized the importance of colonial trade to France's national interests, including the proposal excerpted below. Although attacked by more radical deputies for his continued support of slavery and the slave trade, Barnave's position was favored by the majority of deputies in 1790. In September 1791, Barnave retired to his home in Dauphiné, but he was arrested in 1792 for his royalist sympathies and tried and executed in 1793 during the Reign of Terror. Two months later, the National Convention abolished slavery throughout the French colonies.

Sirs, the commerce [the merchant community] of France has made known to you its wishes and its worries on several objects in which it is interested, and particularly on the various relations between France and her colonies.

At the same time that these petitions [from French merchants] were addressed to you, news arrived from Saint Domingue and Martinique that held all of your attention. You sensed the necessity of taking, with regard to the colonies, a wise and prompt resolution. And perceiving an intimate connection between the causes of their [the two colonies'] agitation and the requests of commerce, you named a committee to investigate these together and present to you an outcome proper to reconcile the various interests.

In discerning, Sirs, the goals of our mission, we soon recognized that all the questions that are presented reduce themselves, at the present moment, to extremely simple terms.

The interest of the French nation to support its commerce, to preserve its colonies, and to favor their prosperity by every means compatible with the interests of the metropole [homeland], appeared to us, by every point of view, as an incontestable truth.

The measures to take, in order to achieve this, appeared to us not less clearly indicated by the principles and by the circumstances.

Reassure the colonies on their most dear interests, receive from them instructions on the system of government which is convenient to their prosperity and that it is finally time to establish; invite them to present their views, concurrently with French commerce, on their reciprocal relations: such is the procedure that the circumstances, justice, and reason have appeared to prescribe to us. . . .

It is not a question, in fact, of examining if France should seek to establish a commerce or to found some colonies. These things already exist. At the moment in which we are speaking, all the aspects of our social existence are intimately linked and merged with the existence of large-scale trade with our colonies. Thus, it is only a question of knowing if the suppression, if the sudden loss of these immense resources would not produce a violent and destructive jolt, would not be a great disaster for the nation?

It is a question of knowing above all if, in our present situation, engaged in a revolution of which the completion assures forever the glory and prosperity of the French nation and of which the failure will plunge the French nation into an unfathomable evil, this violent jolt would not present the most formidable stumbling block; if the situation of our finances would not suffer from this a blow without remedy; if the force of the malcontents would not increase from this beyond all proportion; if, finally, the constitution, which alone would be able with time to repair these great calamities, would not be itself overthrown by this.

When one is willing to consider the question from these points of view, the question no longer will present any doubts; one will appreciate that it is necessary, above all, to prevent the evils that most closely menace us, and that all other speculations become foreign when it is a question of the sacred interest of the Revolution and of the destiny of the several million Frenchmen who are attached to the prosperity of our commerce, to the possession of our colonies.

It would be, in fact, the fruit of a great ignorance, or of a strange evil faith, to claim to separate the prosperity of national commerce from the possessions of our colonies.

Our colonies not only constitute the greatest portion of our maritime and exterior relations, but the value of our agricultural produce, the activity of our industries, our transports, our internal commerce, are, in large measure, the effect of our relations with the colonies. . . .

Abandon the colonies, and these sources of prosperity will disappear or diminish.

Abandon the colonies, and you will import, at great price, from foreigners what they buy today from you.

Abandon the colonies at the moment when your establishments there are based on possessing them, and listlessness will replace activity, misery abundance: the mass of workers, of useful and hardworking citizens, will pass quickly from a state of ease into the most deplorable situation; finally, agriculture and our finances will soon be struck by the same disaster experienced in commerce and manufactures.

And how easy would it be, in carrying these issues further, to establish the relationship of this branch of our commerce with all its other branches, with our maritime existence, and with the general system of European power? . . .

You should only, you can only speak here one language, that of truth, which consists in disavowing the false extension that has been given [to some of your decrees]. You have not been able to change anything in all of what concerns the colonies, for the laws that you have decreed did not have them in mind; you have not been able to change anything because public security and humanity itself would offer insurmountable obstacles to what your hearts have inspired in you [the abolition of the slave trade or of slavery itself]. Let us say it then at this moment, since doubts have been raised: you have broken no new ground. This declaration will suffice; it can leave no alarm remaining. It is only just to accompany it with an arrangement suitable for reassuring the colonies against those who, with criminal plots, would seek to bring trouble there, to excite uprisings there. These men whom some have affected to confuse with peaceful citizens occupied with seeking through reflection means for softening the destiny of the most unfortunate portion of the human race [the slaves], these men, I say, only have perverse motives and can only be considered as enemies of France and of humanity. . . .

Here then, Sirs, is the project for a decree that your committee has unanimously voted to propose to you: . . .

Declares that, considering the colonies as a part of the French empire, and desiring to enable them to enjoy the fruits of the happy regeneration that has been accomplished in the empire, it never intended to include them in the constitution that it has decreed for the kingdom or to subject them to laws which might be incompatible with their particular, local proprieties. . . .

Moreover, the National Assembly declares that it never intended to introduce innovations into any of the branches of indirect or direct commerce between France and its colonies [thus it leaves the slave trade untouched] and hereby puts the colonists and their properties under the special protection of the nation and declares criminal, toward the nation, whoever works to excite uprisings against them.

QUESTIONS FOR ANALYSIS

1. On what bases does Barnave justify the continuation of the slave trade?
2. How does Barnave account for the principles set out in the Declaration of the Rights of Man and Citizen (Source 5)?
3. How does he distinguish revolution in France from revolution in the colonies? What do this distinction and the way it is asserted indicate about his attitudes toward individuals living in the colonies?
4. How does Barnave's recognition of the humanity of the slaves compare to the Society of the Friends of Blacks' recognition of the humanity of slaves (Source 6)? How do these recognitions affect their arguments?

8

"HIS MANNER DISARMED ME. . . ."

My Odyssey (1793)

When a massive slave revolt broke out in Saint Domingue in August 1791, the island was plunged into three years of bloody warfare. The anonymous author of the following text had been born in Saint Domingue of French parents of the planter class and sent to France as a child, where he was educated. The day preceding the slave revolt, at age sixteen or seventeen, he returned to his family's plantation in Saint Domingue. In the excerpt below, from long letters written in 1793 that described his experiences, the author describes the day of his arrival and the days following.

How often, from what I have seen, have I been able to recognize the injustice of those written diatribes, that were flooding Europe, against the poor planters of Saint Domingue! What lies! What exaggerated pictures! What ignorance of the country, the customs, the habits, and the laws.

Althéa de Puech Partham, ed. and trans., *My Odyssey: Experiences of a Young Refugee from Two Revolutions* (Louisiana State University Press, 1959), 23–25, 27–28, 31–34.

During the past months, between the different revolts and insurrections, I have seen everywhere Negroes who were fat, well cared for, and happy. I have seen them many times, about a hundred of them occupied with work that twenty Europeans could achieve in much less time. Their cabins appeared sanitary, commodious, and furnished with the necessary utensils for their needs. These cabins were surrounded with land where they raised pigs and a variety of fowl; they had me observe their individual gardens, which were perfectly tended and abundantly planted with all the necessary products of our country. I noticed that the hospital was the finest edifice on each plantation. I was told that a doctor visited them each day and that women looked after the sick. Other women had the care of the children, to bathe, comb, etc. each morning. I often found idle groups, and was told that these were convalescents, nursing mothers, pregnant women, and old people, who were exempt from service. . . .

For those who question the discipline under which they live, it is certainly not more rigorous than that which is observed for soldiers and sailors; and when one realizes that thirty thousand whites are in the center of six hundred thousand semi-barbaric Africans, one should not hesitate to say that discipline is necessary.

The young adult Negroes of our plantation, informed of our return, gathered in a crowd before us, and by a thousand bizarre demonstrations testified to the joy they had in seeing us. . . .

My voyage has offered you nothing so far but about agreeable happenings to me; but, Oh, my friend, what a cruel account I must now make to you! The day after my arrival, while partaking with my family of the pleasures of an excellent lunch, a courier arrived to deliver to my step-father, commander of the district in which our property is located, a letter full of the most terrifying news. The slaves, enflamed by emissaries sent from France, had burned the habitations of our neighbors near the Cape,[1] after assassinating the proprietors without distinction of age or sex.

Already the insurrection was causing devastation on all sides, and they feared it would soon reach our place of habitation. The report of this terrific catastrophe was widely spread. The frightened families among our neighbors met together at our plantation. The men armed to face the storm; the mothers, wives, sisters were lamenting and gathering in all haste a few precious effects. Desolation and fear were painted on all faces. The sky seemed on fire. Guns could be heard from afar and the bells of the plantations were sounding the alarm. The danger increased. The flames at each moment were approaching and enclosing about us. There was no time to lose; we fled. The victims who escaped at sword's point came to swell the number of fugitives, and recounted to us the horrors which they had witnessed. They had seen unbelievable tortures to which they testified. Many women, young, beautiful, and virtuous, perished beneath the infamous caresses of the brigands, amongst the cadavers of their fathers and husbands. Bodies, still palpitating, were dragged through the roads with atrocious acclamation. Young children transfixed upon the points of bayonets were the bleeding flags which followed the troop of cannibals. . . .

---

[1] On the north central coastline of Saint Domingue.

[*The following day, the author joins a small contingent of French militia troops.*]

We were sitting down to dinner when we saw their [the rebel slaves] signal, which is always the burning of some stalks of sugar-cane. Our general, a man of appetite as well as of combat, decided we should continue with our repast, and after giving several orders for the safety of our quarters, sat down to dinner. We were eating heartily until the moment a cannonball passed through the window and carried away, right under our beards, the table and all the plates. The general, infuriated by this mishap, mounted his horse with food still in his mouth, and left camp with six hundred men and four pieces of artillery. Two hours later one could not find a living Negro within a circle of two and a half miles, and the roads were strewn with their bloody remains. . . .

I will terminate this martial chapter by a character sketch which can give you an idea of the type of people which we have to combat.

I pursued a Negro whose regalia caused me to judge him to be one of the principal chiefs. As I was about to overtake him, he turned around, took aim, but happily for me, could not make his powder fire as it was too damp. I prepared myself to cleave his head with my sword, whereupon he fell to his knees, kissed my boots, and told me, with tears in his eyes, that he was my Mother's godson, that he was present at my birth, and carried me in his arms more than once, and beseeched me not to kill him; that he was a good Negro and that he had always loved the Whites. His manner disarmed me; I dismounted from my horse before having him conducted to camp. However, a soft sound made me quickly turn my head, and I saw the miserable hypocrite, who had recharged his gun, aiming point-blank at my head; being troubled at finding himself discovered, prevented him from aiming accurately, and the bullet went past me. I fell upon him, but he was on guard for my attack; and there we were both acting as if playing Prisoner's Base. I caught my runner at the moment when he was about to slash me and threw him into some weeds. Even then he had the impudence to maintain that *I had not seen correctly,* and that he loved the son of his godmother too much to try to kill him. When he heard himself convicted by a number of soldiers who had just arrived and had witnessed the incident, he changed his tune and told me in his jargon: "Master, I know that is true. It is the Devil who gets inside of this body of mine. I am a good nigger, but against my will the Devil is too strong." His excuse made me laugh despite my anger, and had I been alone, I would certainly have saved him; but the soldiers seized him and bound him to a tree to be shot. When he saw that his fate was sealed, he began to laugh, sing, and joke. At times, however, reviling us in a furious tone, at times jeering at us in mockery. He gave the signal himself and met death without fear or complaint. We found in one of his pockets pamphlets printed in France, filled with commonplaces about the Rights of Man and the Sacred [French] Revolution; in his vest was a large packet of tinder and phosphate of lime. On his chest he had a little sack full of hair, herbs, bits of bone, which they call a fetish; with this, they expect to be sheltered from all danger; and it was, no doubt, because of this amulet, that our man had the intrepidity which the philosophers call Stoicism.[2]

---

[2] Greek philosophy often marked by an indifference to pain or pleasure.

QUESTIONS FOR ANALYSIS

1. How does the author defend Saint Domingue's slavery? What image does he create of the slaves of Saint Domingue?
2. How does the author's description of slavery compare to the descriptions of slavery by Raynal (Source 4) and by the Society of the Friends of Blacks (Source 6)? What accounts for the similarities and differences?
3. What are the similarities and differences in the author's comparison of slave atrocities and French atrocities? How do these serve to elicit sympathy for the planters?
4. What explanation does the author offer to account for the slave revolt? How does this explanation justify the continuation of slavery?

9

"... CONSTANTLY FAITHFUL TO FRANCE."

François Toussaint-L'Ouverture
Letters   (1797 and 1799)

François Toussaint-L'Ouverture (1743–1803) was born into slavery in the French colony of Saint Domingue. The son of an educated slave, he gained some education himself and moved upward in the plantation hierarchy. When freed in 1777, Toussaint lived a simple and purposely austere life until the 1791 slave revolt. During the decade-long turmoil of civil and foreign wars in the colony, Toussaint played a central role (see the section introduction). Below are two selections from Toussaint's letters to the French government. In the first letter, written to the French naval minister in 1799, Toussaint explains the complex events that took place during the first few years of rebellion in Saint Domingue when he fought for the Spanish and against the French. In the second letter, Toussaint writes to the Directory that ruled France between 1794 and 1799 to defend himself and the blacks of Saint Domingue against accusations by members of the French legislative assembly, most notably by Vienot Vaublanc, that blacks lacked the capacity for freedom.

Letter to the Minister of Marine, April 13, 1799

The first successes obtained in Europe by the partisans of liberty over the agents of despotism were not slow to ignite the sacred fire of patriotism in the souls of all Frenchmen in St. Domingue. At that time, men's hopes turned to France, whose

George F. Tyson Jr., ed., *Toussaint L'Ouverture* (Englewood Cliffs, N.J.: Prentice-Hall, 1973), 30–31, 37–38.

first steps toward her regeneration promised them a happier future; . . . they [the French colonists] wanted to escape from their arbitrary government, but they did not intend the revolution to destroy either the prejudice that debased the men of color or the slavery of the blacks, whom they held in dependency by the strongest law. In their opinion, the benefits of the French regeneration were only for them. They proved it by their obstinate refusal to allow the people of color to enjoy their political rights and the slaves to enjoy the liberty that they claimed. Thus, while the whites were erecting another form of government upon the rubble of despotism, the men of color and the blacks united themselves in order to claim their political existence; the resistance of the former having become stronger, it was necessary for the latter to rise up in order to obtain [political recognition] by force of arms. The whites, fearing that this legitimate resistance would bring general liberty to St. Domingue, sought to separate the men of color from the cause of the blacks in accordance with Machiavelli's principle of divide and rule. Renouncing their claims over the men of color, they accepted the April Decree [1792].[1] As they had anticipated, the men of color, many of whom were slaveholders, had only been using the blacks to gain their own political demands. Fearing the enfranchisement of the blacks, the men of color deserted their comrades in arms, their companions in misfortune, and aligned themselves with the whites to subdue them.

Treacherously abandoned, the blacks fought for some time against the reunited whites and the men of color; but, pressed on all sides, losing hope, they accepted the offers of the Spanish king, who, having at that time declared war on France, offered freedom to those blacks of St. Domingue who would join his armies. Indeed, the silence of pre-Republican France on the long-standing claims for their natural rights made by the most interested, the noblest, the most useful portion of the population of St. Domingue . . . extinguished all glimmer of hope in the hearts of the black slaves and forced them, in spite of themselves, to throw themselves into the arms of a protective power that offered the only benefit for which they would fight. More unfortunate than guilty, they turned their arms against their fatherland. . . .

Letter to the Directory, October 28, 1797 . . .

If, upon the arrival of the [investigating]Commission [from France], St. Domingue groaned under a military government, this power was not in the hands of the blacks; they were subordinate to it, and they only executed the orders of General Laveaux. These were the blacks who, when France was threatened with the loss of this Colony, employed their arms and their weapons to conserve it, to reconquer the greatest part of its territory that treason had handed over to the Spanish and English. . . .

Such was the conduct of those blacks in whose hands citizen Vienot Vaublanc said the military government of St. Domingue found itself, such are those negroes he accuses of being ignorant and gross; undoubtedly they are, because without

---

[1] Decree of the French Assembly that gave full rights and privileges to all people of mixed African and European ancestry.

education there can only be ignorance and grossness. But must one impute to them the crime of this educational deficiency or, more correctly, accuse those who prevented them by the most atrocious punishments from obtaining it? And are only civilized people capable of distinguishing between good and evil, of having notions of charity and justice? The men of St. Domingue have been deprived of an education; but even so, they no longer remain in a state of nature, and because they haven't arrived at the degree of perfection that education bestows, they do not merit being classed apart from the rest of mankind, being confused with animals. . . .

Undoubtedly, one can reproach the inhabitants of St. Domingue, including the blacks, for many faults, even terrible crimes. But even in France, where the limits of sociability are clearly drawn, doesn't one see its inhabitants, in the struggle between despotism and liberty, going to all the excesses for which the blacks are reproached by their enemies? The fury of the two parties has been equal in St. Domingue; and if the excesses of the blacks in these critical moments haven't exceeded those committed in Europe, must not an impartial judge pronounce in favor of the former? Since it is our enemies themselves who present us as ignorant and gross, aren't we more excusable than those who, unlike us, were not deprived of the advantages of education and civilization? Surrounded by fierce enemies, oft cruel masters; without any other support than the charitable intentions of the friends of freedom in France, of whose existence we were hardly aware; driven to excessive errors by opposing parties who were rapidly destroying each other; knowing, at first, only the laws of the Mother-Country that favored the pretensions of our enemies and, since our liberty, receiving only the semiyearly or yearly instructions of our government, and no assistance, but almost always slanders or diatribes from our old oppressors—how can we not be pardoned some moments of ill-conduct, some gross faults, of which we were the first victims? Why, above all, reflect upon unreproachable men, upon the vast majority of the blacks, the faults of the lesser part, who, in time, had been reclaimed by the attentions of the majority to order and respect for the superior authorities? . . .

If General Rochambeau[2] had reflected philosophically on the course of events, especially those of the human spirit, he would not find it so astonishing that the laws of liberty and equality were not precisely established in an American country whose connection with the Mother Country had been neglected for so long; he would have felt that at a time when Europeans daily perjured themselves by handing over their quarters to the enemies of their country, prudence dictated that Government entrust its defense to the men of color and blacks whose interests were intimately linked to the triumph of the Republic; he would have felt that the military government then ruling the colony, by giving great power to the district commanders, could have led them astray in the labyrinths of uncertainty resulting from the absence of laws; he would have recalled that Martinique, defended by Europeans, fell prey to the English, whereas, St. Domingue, defended by the blacks and men of color whom Rochambeau accuses, remained constantly faithful to France.

---

[2] General Donatien Marie Joseph de Vimeur, vicomte de Rochambeau (1755–1813), lieutenant general in command of the French Windward Islands, fought frequently to defend French interests in Saint Dominigue. A friend of the white planters of Saint Dominigue, Rochambeau had written a report extremely critical of the blacks living there.

QUESTIONS FOR ANALYSIS

1. How does Toussaint defend his and the blacks' alliance with Spanish forces? In what terms does he criticize the activities of whites and men of color?

2. What similarities and differences exist in Toussaint's description of the violence that has been committed by the blacks and the description of that violence written by the anonymous author of *My Odyssey* (Source 8)?

3. How do Toussaint and the author of *My Odyssey* (Source 8) account for the rebellion's violence? How does each writer's explanation reinforce his justification or criticism of the rebellion?

4. How does Toussaint link the interests of the blacks with French interests?

CHAPTER QUESTIONS

1. What various attitudes toward black Africans are expressed by Smith (Source 1), Raynal (Source 4), the Society of the Friends of Blacks (Source 6), Barnave (Source 7), and the author of *My Odyssey* (Source 8)? How do these attitudes compare to the attitudes expressed by the Jesuits Brébeuf and Ricci toward the Amerindians and the Chinese (Chapter 3, Sources 1 and 4) and the French officials toward the Amerindians (Chapter 4, Source 2)? What might account for similarities and differences?

2. On what foundations do the authors in this chapter ground their various arguments? How do these foundations compare with the foundations used by de Las Casas and Sepúlveda in their writings about the status of the Amerindians (Chapter 1)? How did European intellectual standards evolve between the late fifteenth century and the late eighteenth century?

3. Compare the documents in this chapter with the documents in Chapters 1 and 3 to show the changes in how Christianity was portrayed in European definitions of Europe's relationships with other civilizations.

Chapter 7

NAPOLEON IN EGYPT

During the confusion and, at times, chaos of the French Revolution, a young artillery officer named Napoleon Bonaparte rose to power. Born in Corsica of a poor noble family, Napoleon was educated at French military schools and graduated from the Paris Military Academy in 1785, where he was ranked near the bottom of his class. He gained a commission as second lieutenant in the French artillery and continued his studies at the artillery training school at La Fère. During these years, Napoleon underwent a rigorous education that connected him to the many currents of Enlightenment thought and practice. In its official training, the French artillery school emphasized mathematics and the sciences, yet this theoretical education was linked consistently to the practical application of science to warfare in a way that served the needs of the state. Privately, Napoleon read the works of such authors as Voltaire and Rousseau (Chapter 5) and became convinced of the need for political and social reforms within France.

In 1791, Napoleon was appointed to an artillery regiment and quickly rose to prominence. In March 1796, at age twenty-six, Napoleon was appointed commander-in-chief of the French Army of Italy. His military success in the Italian campaigns brought Napoleon a national reputation and public celebrations on his return to Paris in late 1797. Napoleon quickly tired of Paris and turned his attention to a new adventure—an invasion of Egypt and perhaps lands farther east. Napoleon stated, "I see that if I linger here [Paris], I shall soon lose myself. Everything wears out here; my glory has already disappeared. This little Europe does not supply enough of it. I must seek it in the East, the fountain of glory." Egypt and the East inspired Napoleon's imagination. He could be the modern Alexander the Great, marching his armies from Egypt to India. And as Napoleon recognized, capturing Egypt for France would threaten England's prize colonial possession—India. The Directory that ruled France in 1798 readily agreed to the plan, happy to have this popular general far removed from the center of political power in Paris.

The Egypt that Napoleon would invade was itself in an era of transition. The Turkish Ottoman empire based in Istanbul had declined in power throughout the eighteenth century and by the time of Napoleon's invasion held only nominal authority over Egypt. Effective political power in Egypt rested with Mamluks, a class of slave-soldiers who virtually controlled the government and the army. Ottoman authority was reduced to recognizing the autonomy of whichever Mamluk faction provided annual revenues to the Ottomans.

In early 1798, as Napoleon undertook military preparations for his invasion of Egypt with the 36,000-man Army of the East, he also organized a Commission of Arts and Sciences to participate in the expedition. Composed of 151 mathematicians, astronomers, architects, economists, musicians, sculptors, linguists, artists, botanists, mineralogists, and engineers, among other experts, the members of the

Commission sought to uncover, discover, and record the natural and human his-tory of Egypt within the spirit and ideals of the Enlightenment. The supplies Napoleon carried to Egypt for the Commissioners included a library and a collec-tion of scientific equipment. After arriving in Egypt on July 1, 1798, Napoleon orga-nized the Commission into the Institute of Egypt (also called the Institute of Cairo, where the Institute met). The Institute conducted scientific experiments and pub-lished reports on the works of its members. Other members of the Commission traveled with army units, collecting information and data on Egypt.

Despite his initial military success in Egypt, Napoleon recognized that the Army of the East was trapped in Egypt. Further, the military and political situation in France had deteriorated to a point that Napoleon believed he could take advan-tage of the situation. In August 1799, Napoleon secretly left Egypt for France and three months later established himself as First Consul in France. The Army of the East desperately held its position in Egypt until July 1801, when it was forced to ac-cept British surrender terms. Ironically, many of the artifacts that the Commission of Arts and Sciences had collected were seized by the British and still reside in the British Museum. The commissioners, however, kept the massive amount of infor-mation that they had collected, organizing and refining their material until in 1809 they published the first of the twenty-three-volume *Description of Egypt,* the last volume appearing in 1828. The *Description of Egypt* sought to fulfill the promise of its title—to describe the lands and people of Egypt in their entirety to a European audience.

1

"... THE STUDY AND PUBLICATION OF ALL FACTS ..."

Louis Antoine Fauvelet de Bourrienne
Memoirs of Napoleon Bonaparte   (1829)

Louis Antoine Fauvelet de Bourrienne (1769–1834) served as Napoleon's private sec-retary between 1797 and 1802. During these years, which included both the Egyptian campaign and Napoleon's political ascendancy in France, Bourrienne was Napoleon's closest friend and confidant, sharing the same office as the future emperor. In 1802, Bourrienne lost his favored place when he became enmeshed in a financial scandal, and he remained bitter toward Napoleon throughout the remainder of his life. In Memoirs, *published in 1829, Bourrienne describes the man Napoleon in detail, his ac-tions and his attitudes. In the following excerpt, Bourrienne recounts part of the Egyptian campaign.*

Louis Antoine Bourrienne, *Memoirs of Napoleon Bonaparte,* rev. ed., Vol. 1, ed., R. W. Phipps (New York: Scribner's, 1895), 130–31, 143–44, 166–69.

It was determined that Bonaparte should undertake an expedition of an unusual character to the East. I must confess that two things cheered me in this very painful interval; my friendship and admiration for the talents of the conqueror of Italy, and the pleasing hope of traversing those ancient regions, the historical and religious accounts of which had engaged the attention of my youth.

It was at Passeriano[1] that, seeing the approaching termination of his labours in Europe, he first began to turn serious attention to the East. During his long strolls in the evening in the magnificent park there he delighted to converse about the celebrated events of that part of the world, and the many famous empires it once possessed. He used to say, "Europe is a mole-hill. There have never been great empires and revolutions except in the East, where there are 600,000,000 men." He considered that part of the world as the cradle of all religions, of all metaphysical extravagances. This subject was no less interesting than inexhaustible, and he daily introduced it when conversing with the generals with whom he was intimate, with Monge,[2] and with me. . . .

Bonaparte . . . conceived the happy idea of joining to the expedition men distinguished in science and art, and whose labours have made known, in its present and past state, a country, the very name of which is never pronounced without exciting grand recollections. . . .

[The fleet departs for Egypt on May 19, 1798.]

One of Bonaparte's greatest pleasures during the voyage was, after dinner, to fix upon three or four persons to support a proposition and as many to oppose it. He had an object in view by this. These discussions afforded him an opportunity of studying the minds of those whom he had an interest in knowing well, in order that he might afterwards confide to each the functions for which he possessed the greatest aptitude. It will not appear singular to those who have been intimate with Bonaparte, that in these intellectual contests he gave the preference to those who had supported an absurd proposition with ability over those who had maintained the cause of reason; and it was not superiority of mind which determined his judgment, for he really preferred the man who argued well in favour of an absurdity to the man who argued equally well in support of a reasonable proposition. He always gave out the subjects which were to be discussed; and they most frequently turned upon questions of religion, the different kinds of government, and the art of war. One day he asked whether the planets were inhabited; on another, what was the age of the world; then he proposed to consider the probability of the destruction of our globe, either by water or fire; at another time, the truth or fallacy of presentiments, and the interpretation of dreams. . . .

[The French fleet lands in Egypt on July 1, 1798, and the army begins military operations.]

On the 21st of August Bonaparte established at Cairo an institute of the arts and sciences. . . .[3]

---

[1] Or Passariano, small town in northeastern Italy.
[2] Gaspard Monge (1746–1818), French mathematician and politician.
[3] Bourrienne included the following three paragraphs as a footnote.

The Institute of Egypt was composed of members of the French Institute, and of the men of science and artists of the commission who did not belong to that body. They assembled and added to their number several officers of the artillery and staff, and others who had cultivated the sciences and literature.

The Institute was established in one of the palaces of the beys.[4] A great number of machines, and physical, chemical, and astronomical instruments had been brought from France. They were distributed in the different rooms, which were also successively filled with all the curiosities of the country, whether of the animal, vegetable, or mineral kingdom.

The garden of the palace became a botanical garden. A chemical laboratory was formed at headquarters, Berthollet[5] performed experiments there several times every week, at which Napoleon and a great number of officers attended.

In founding this Institute, Bonaparte wished to afford an example of his ideas of civilisation. The minutes of the sittings of that learned body, which have been printed, bear evidence of its utility, and of Napoleon's extended views. The objects of the Institute were the advancement and propagation of information in Egypt, and the study and publication of all facts relating to the natural history, trade, and antiquities of that ancient country.

It has been alleged that Bonaparte, when in Egypt, took part in the religious ceremonies and worship of the Mussulmans [Muslims]; but it cannot be said that he *celebrated* the festivals of the overflowing of the Nile and the anniversary of the Prophet.[6] The Turks invited him to these merely as a spectator; and the presence of their new master was gratifying to the people. But he never committed the folly of ordering any solemnity. He neither learned nor repeated any prayer of the Qur'an, as many persons have asserted; neither did he advocate fatalism, polygamy, or any other doctrine of the Qur'an. . . .

Doubtless Bonaparte did, as he was bound to do, show respect for the religion of the country; and he found it necessary to act more like a Mussulman than a Catholic. A wise conqueror supports his triumphs by protecting and even elevating the religion of the conquered people. Bonaparte's principle was, as he himself has often told me, to look upon religions as the work of men, but to respect them everywhere as a powerful engine of government. However, I will not go so far as to say that he would not have changed his religion had the conquest of the East been the price of that change. All that he said about Mahomet [Muhammad], Islamism, and the Qur'an to the great men of the country he laughed at himself. He enjoyed the gratification of having all his fine sayings on the subject of religion translated into Arabic poetry, and repeated from mouth to mouth. This of course tended to conciliate the people. . . .

If Bonaparte spoke as a Mussulman, it was merely in his character of a military and political chief in a Mussulman country. To do so was essential to his success, to the safety of his army, and, consequently, to his glory.

---

[4] Provincial governors of the Ottoman empire.
[5] Claude-Louis Berthollet (1748–1822), French chemist.
[6] Muhammad (570–632), founder of Islam.

QUESTIONS FOR ANALYSIS

1. What images of Napoleon emerge from Bourrienne's description?
2. According to Bourrienne, what attitudes toward Egypt and the Egyptians and toward Islam does Napoleon express? What does Napoleon's relationship with the scientists and artists indicate about his attitudes toward them?
3. What are Napoleon's goals in founding the Institute of Egypt? How do these goals relate to his attitudes toward the Egyptians, religion, and the scientists?
4. How might Bourrienne's relationship with Napoleon—at the time when the events described occurred and at the time when he wrote *Memoirs*—influence the image he presents of Napoleon and his actions and attitudes?

2

"... WE ARE ALSO FAITHFUL MUSLIMS."

Napoleon Bonaparte
Statements and Proclamation on the Egyptian Campaign
(1798–1804)

Napoleon Bonaparte dreamed of glory on an epic scale. He also was a practical politician who used force and power to create and defend an empire. The following three texts show these two sides of Napoleon. The first two texts are brief statements by Napoleon reflecting on the Egyptian campaign. The third text is a proclamation issued by Napoleon when he arrived in Egypt.

Conversation, Early 1800s

In Egypt, I found myself freed from the obstacles of an irksome civilization. I was full of dreams, and I saw the means by which I could carry out all that I had dreamed. I saw myself founding a religion, marching into Asia, riding an elephant, a turban on my head and in my hand the new Qur'an that I would have composed to suit my needs. In my undertakings I would have combined the experiences of the two worlds, exploiting for my own profit the theater of all history, attacking the power of England in India, and, by means of that conquest, renewing contact with

J. Christopher Herold, ed. and trans., *The Mind of Napoleon: A Selection from His Written and Spoken Words* (New York: Columbia University Press, 1955), 48–49; *Pièces diverses et correspondance relatives aux operations de l'armée d'orient en Egypte* (Paris, 1801), 152–53. (Translated by David Kammerling Smith.)

the old Europe. The time I spent in Egypt was the most beautiful of my life, for it was the most ideal.

Conversation, December 3, 1804, the Day after Napoleon's Coronation as Emperor of France

I come too late, nothing great remains to be done. . . . Yes, I admit that I have had a fine career, I have gone far. But what a difference with antiquity! Look at Alexander:[1] when he had conquered Asia and presented himself to the nations as the son of Jupiter,[2] the whole Orient believed him, except for Olympias,[3] who knew better, and except for Aristotle[4] and a few Athenian pedants. Well, if I declared myself the son of the Eternal Father, if I announced that I would give my thanks to Him in that capacity, every fishwife would hoot when she saw me pass by. The masses are too enlightened these days: nothing great can be done any more.

Proclamation of Napoleon, Issued from Alexandria, Egypt, July 1, 1798

For too long, the beys[5] who govern Egypt have insulted the French nation and hurled affronts upon its merchants. The hour of their punishment has arrived. For too long this pack of slaves, purchased in the Caucasus[6] and Georgia,[7] have tyrannized the world's most beautiful homeland. But God, on whom all depends, has ordered an end to their empire.

People of Egypt, some will tell you that I come to destroy your religion. Do not believe them. Reply that I come to you to restore your rights, punish the usurpers, and that I, more than the Mamluks,[8] respect God, his prophet,[9] and the Qur'an. Tell them that all men are equal before God: wisdom, talent, and virtue alone mark the difference between them. What wisdom, what talent, what virtue distinguish the Mamluks, so that they exclusively hold everything that makes life pleasant and sweet. Is there beautiful land? It belongs to the Mamluks. Is there a beautiful slave, a beautiful horse, a beautiful house? It belongs to the Mamluks.

If Egypt is their fief, tell them to show the title-deed that God gave them for it. But God is just and merciful for the people. All the Egyptians are called to administer everywhere: Let the wisest, the most learned, and the most virtuous govern, and the people will be happy.

---

[1] Alexander the Great (356–323 B.C.).
[2] Chief Roman deity.
[3] Olympias (c. 375–316 B.C.), mother of Alexander the Great.
[4] Aristotle (384–322 B.C.), Greek philosopher and tutor of Alexander the Great.
[5] Provincial governors in the Ottoman empire.
[6] Mountainous region between the Black and Caspian Seas.
[7] Region within the Caucasus.
[8] Slave-soldiers who ruled Egypt between 1250 and 1517 and whose descendants survived in Egypt as a major political force until Napoleon's conquest.
[9] Muhammad (570–632), founder of Islam.

In days gone by, there were among you large towns, wide canals, and extensive commerce. What destroyed it all, if not the avarice, the injustice, and the tyranny of the Mamluks?

Qadis, Shaykhs, Imams, and Shurbajiyya,[10] tell the people that we are also faithful Muslims. Did we not destroy the Papal See, who always said that it is necessary to launch war against the Muslims? Did we not destroy the Knights of Malta because these madmen believed that God wanted them to attack the Muslims? Have we not at all times been the friends of the Ottoman Sultan (may God carry out his designs) and the enemy of his enemies? The Mamluks, to the contrary, have they not always revolted against the authority of the Ottoman Sultan, whom they still refuse to recognize? They only follow their own caprices.

Thrice blessed will be those [Egyptians] with us! They will prosper in their fortune and their rank. Blessed will be those who are neutral. When they have time to come to know us, they will fall in line with us.

But woe, three times woe, to those who arm themselves with the Mamluks and fight against us. There will not be any hope for them. They will perish.

---

[10] Qadis, Islamic judges; Shaykhs (or sheikhs), venerable or learned men who head religious orders, tribes, or villages; Imams, leaders of Muslim communities; Shurbajiyya, councilors of state.

QUESTIONS FOR ANALYSIS

1. What role does religion play in Napoleon's thinking about Asia?
2. How does Napoleon ascribe a mythic connotation to Asia? Why does Europe lack such a connotation?
3. In his Proclamation, how does Napoleon use religious and ethnic identity to appeal to the Egyptians? Compare his manipulation of cultural identity to Bourrienne's characterization of Napoleon's attitudes toward Islam (Source 1).
4. What carrots does Napoleon hold out to the Egyptians? What sticks does he use to threaten them?

3

". . . WITH PERFECT SKILL AND WONDROUS INVENTION . . ."

Abd al-Rahman al-Jabarti
Chronicle   (early 19th century)

The Egyptian historian and scholar Abd al-Rahman al-Jabarti (1753–1825) was stunned by the French invasion of his homeland. He strongly condemned French military activity and mocked Napoleon's claims of fraternity with Islam and the Egyptian people. Al-Jabarti, however, also deeply appreciated the European scientific and

---

Abd al-Rahman al-Jabarti, *Al-Jabarti's Chronicle of the First Seven Months of the French Occupation of Egypt,* ed. and trans. S. Moreh (Leiden: Brill, 1975), 115–17.

technical achievements that he witnessed. In the excerpt below from his Chronicle, *al-Jabarti describes the Institute of Egypt.*

To the administrators of affairs (managers), the astronomers, scholars, and scientists in mathematics, geometry, astronomy, engraving and drawing, and also to the painters, scribes, and writers they assigned al-Nāṣiriyya quarter [of Cairo] and all the houses in it. . . . The administrators, astronomers, and some of the physicians lived in this house in which they placed a great number of their books and with a keeper taking care of them and arranging them. And the students among them would gather two hours before noon every day in an open space opposite the shelves of books, sitting on chairs arranged in parallel rows before a wide long board. Whoever wishes to look up something in a book asks for whatever volumes he wants and the librarian brings them to him. Then he thumbs through the pages, looking through the book, and writes. All the while they are quiet and no one disturbs his neighbour. When some Muslims would come to look around they would not prevent them from entering. Indeed they would bring them all kinds of printed books in which there were all sorts of illustrations and maps of the countries and regions, animals, birds, plants, histories of the ancients, campaigns of the nations, tales of the prophets including pictures of them, of their miracles and wondrous deeds, the events of their respective peoples and such things which baffle the mind. I have gone to them many times and they have shown me all these various things and among the things I saw there was a large book containing the Biography of the Prophet,[1] upon whom be mercy and peace. In this volume they draw his noble picture according to the extent of their knowledge and judgement about him. He is depicted standing upon his feet looking toward Heaven as if menacing all creation. In his right hand is the sword and in his left the Book[2] and around him are his Companions, may God be pleased with them, also with swords in their hands. . . . In another picture the manner in which the Prophet's Birthday is celebrated and all the types of people who participate in it (are shown); also (there are) pictures of the Mosque of Sultan Sulaymān and the manner in which the Friday prayers are conducted in it, and the Mosque of Abū Ayyūb al-Anṣārī and the manner in which prayers for the dead are performed in it, and pictures of the countries, the coasts, the seas, the Pyramids, the ancient temples of Upper Egypt including the pictures, figures, and inscriptions which are drawn upon them. Also there are pictures of the species of animals, birds, plants and herbage which are peculiar to each land. The glorious Qur'an is translated into their language! Also many other Islamic books. . . . I saw some of them who know chapters of the Qur'an by heart. They have a great interest in the sciences, mainly in mathematics and the knowledge of languages, and make great efforts to learn the Arabic language and the colloquial. In this they strive day and night. And they have books especially devoted to all types of languages, their declensions and conjugations as well as their etymologies. They possess extraordinary astronomical instruments of perfect construction and instruments for

---

[1] Muhammad (570–632), founder of Islam.
[2] The Qur'an.

measuring altitudes of wondrous, amazing, and precious construction. And they have telescopes for looking at the stars and measuring their scopes, sizes, heights, conjunctions, and oppositions, and the clepsydras[3] and clocks with gradings and minutes and seconds, all of wondrous form and very precious, and the like.

In a similar manner they assigned [other] . . . houses to the studious and knowledgeable ones. They called this *al-Madāris* (the Schools) and provided it with funds and copious allowances and generous provisions of food and drink. They provided them with a place . . . and built in it neat and well-designed stoves and ovens, and instruments for distilling, vaporizing, and extracting liquids and ointments belonging to medicine and sublimated simple salts, the salts extracted from burnt herbs, and so forth. In this place there are wondrous retorts of copper for distillation, and vessels and long-necked bottles made of glass of various forms and shapes, by means of which acidic liquids and solvents are extracted. All this is carried out with perfect skill and wondrous invention and the like.

---

[3] A water clock that measures time by its discharge of water.

QUESTIONS FOR ANALYSIS

1. What were al-Jabarti's reactions to Napoleon's Institute of Egypt? What aspects of the Institute's operations impress al-Jabarti?
2. What aspects of French learning does he note? How does al-Jabarti present himself as learned?
3. Why might it be important to al-Jabarti that the Institute has information about Islam?
4. How does al-Jabarti's reaction to the Institute compare to Napoleon's goals for the Institute as stated by Bourrienne (Source 1)?

4

". . . AN EDIFICE SO STUPENDOUS, SO COLOSSAL . . ."

Vivant Denon
Travels in Upper and Lower Egypt   (1802)

Vivant Denon (1747–1825) was a well-respected artist when he accepted an appointment to join Napoleon's expedition to Egypt. In Egypt, Denon traveled with various military units, rapidly drawing as many images as he could under difficult and sometimes harried circumstances. On his return to France, Denon quickly published a book

---

Vivant Denon, *Travels in Upper and Lower Egypt*, Vol. 1, trans. Arthur Aikin (London, 1803) (Reprinted New York: Arno Press, 1973), ii, 263–68, 83–85.

recounting his adventures, entitled Travels in Upper and Lower Egypt, *which he dedicated to Napoleon. In 1804, Napoleon appointed Denon general director of museums in France, where he played an important role in the development of France's most prestigious art museum, the Louvre. In the excerpt below, Denon describes some of the Egyptian monuments he observed.*

Preface

My desire to meet the wishes of the Institute[1] will stimulate me to digest, without loss of time, a multitude of notes which I have made, without any other pretension than that of forgetting no part of what offered itself daily to my observation. I was engaged in travelling through a country which was known to Europe by name only: it therefore became important to describe every thing; and I was fully aware, that at my return I should be interrogated on all sides, relative to what might, according to his habitual studies or his character, the most powerfully excite the curiosity of each of my enquirers. . . .

[Denon describes the Pyramids of Giza.]

In approaching these stupendous buildings, their sloping and angular forms disguise their real height, and lessen it to the eye; and besides, as every thing regular is only great or small by comparison, and as these masses of stone eclipse in magnitude every surrounding object, and yet are much inferior to a mountain (the only thing with which our imagination can compare them) one is surprised to find the first impression given by viewing them at a distance, so much diminished on a nearer approach. However, on attempting to measure any one of these gigantic works of art by some known scale, it resumes its immensity to the mind; for as I approached to the opening, a hundred persons who were standing under it appeared so small, that I could hardly take them for men. It would be a good method for the artist to give an idea of the dimension of these edifices, by representing on the same ground-plan as the building some procession or religious ceremony analogous to the ancient customs. As it is, these monuments standing alone, and without any living scale of comparison, excepting a few detached figures in front, lose both the effect of their grand proportions, and the general impression which they would otherwise make. We have a good example of comparison in Europe in St. Peter's church at Rome, the magnitude of which is concealed by the exquisite harmony of proportion, and the crossing of the general outline, till the eye descends to a procession of the religious orders celebrating mass, and followed by a train of worshippers. . . . Another point of resemblance between these two edifices is, that nothing but the despotism of a sacerdotal government[2] could venture to undertake them, nor any thing but the stupid fanaticism of a people would submit to the labour of building. But to return to the actual state of the pyramids; let us first

---

[1] The Institute of Egypt, of which Denon was a member.
[2] Government dominated by priestly or religious class.

ascend a small heap of sand and rubbish, which is perhaps the remains of the trench of the first of these edifices which presents itself, and which now leads to the opening through which it may be reached. This opening, which is nearly sixty feet from the base, is concealed by a general stone-facing, which forms the third or inner inclosure to the solitary entrenchment around this monument. . . . Here begins the first gallery; its direction lies towards the centre and base of the edifice; but the rubbish . . . has so blocked up the passage as to render it very inconvenient to cross. At the extremity of this gallery two large blocks of granite are met with, which form a second partition to this mysterious passage.

This obstacle appears to have perplexed all those who have undertaken the research, and has led to several random attempts to surmount it. Endeavours have been made by former visitors to cut a passage through the solid stone, but this proving unsuccessful, they have returned some way, have passed round two blocks of stone, climbed over them, and thus discovered a second gallery of so steep an ascent, that it has been necessary to hew steps in the ground in order to mount it. This gallery leads to a kind of landing-place, in which is a hole usually called "the well," which is the opening to a horizontal gallery leading to a chamber known by the name of "the queen's chamber," without ornament, cornice, or any inscription whatever.

Returning to the landing-place, a perpendicular opening leads to the grand gallery, which terminates in a second landing-place, on which is the third and last partition, constructed with much more art, and which gives a striking idea of the importance which the Egyptians attached to the inviolability of their places of sepulture.

Lastly comes the royal chamber, containing the sarcophagus, . . . a narrow sanctuary, which is the sole end and object of an edifice so stupendous, so colossal, in comparison of all the other works of man.

In reflecting on the object of the construction of the pyramids, the gigantic pride which gave them birth appears more enormous even than their actual dimensions; and one hardly knows which is the most astonishing, the madness of tyrannical oppression, which dared to order the undertaking, or the stupid servility of obedience in the people who submitted to the labour. In short, the most favourable view, for the honour of human nature, in which these monuments can be considered is, that man was thereby ambitious of rivalling nature in immensity and eternity, and not without success, since the mountains contiguous to these edifices are less high, and still less exempted from the ravages of time than this work of human hands.

[Denon leaves Giza and travels to Thebes.]

[I]n making a sharp turn round the point of a projecting chain of mountains, we discovered all at once the site of the ancient Thebes in its whole extent: this celebrated city, the size of which Homer[3] has characterized by the single expression of *with a hundred gates,* a boasting and poetical phrase, that has been repeated with so much confidence for many centuries; this illustrious city . . . celebrated by the number of its kings, whose wisdom has raised them to the rank of gods, by laws which have been revered without being promulgated, by science involved in pompous and

---

[3] Homer (9th century B.C.), legendary Greek epic poet.

enigmatical inscriptions, the first monuments of ancient learning which are still spared by the hand of time; this abandoned sanctuary, surrounded with barbarism, and again restored to the desert from which it had been drawn forth, enveloped in the veil of mystery, and the obscurity of ages, whereby even its own colossal monuments are magnified to the imagination, still impressed the mind with such gigantic phantoms, that the whole army, suddenly and with one accord, stood in amazement at the sight of its scattered ruins, and clapped their hands with delight, as if the end and object of their glorious toils, and the complete conquest of Egypt, were accomplished and secured by taking possession of the splendid remains of this ancient metropolis. I took a view of this first aspect of Thebes, along with the spectacle before me; the knees of the enthusiastic soldiers served me as a table, their bodies as a shade, whilst the dazzling rays of the burning sun enlightened this magnificent spectacle, and exhibited the electric emotion of a whole army of soldiers, whose delicate sensibility made me feel proud of being their companion, and glory in calling myself a Frenchman.

QUESTIONS FOR ANALYSIS

1. What methods does Denon use to describe the monuments? What contrast is created between Denon's description and his references to "inviolability," "veil of mystery," and "obscurity"?
2. How does Denon the artist establish with words the awe he felt when viewing the Egytpian monuments?
3. What purposes do the religious references serve in Denon's description?
4. How does Denon's work reflect the secular spirit of the Enlightenment? How do his descriptions of the monuments also indicate Enlightenment perspectives?

5

". . . TODAY IS PLUNGED INTO BARBARISM. . . ."

Description of Egypt (1809–1828)

Published in twenty-three volumes between 1809 and 1828, the Description of Egypt *organized and presented to the public the massive quantity of information brought back to France by the Commission of Arts and Sciences that had participated in Napoleon's Egyptian campaign. Jean-Baptiste-Joseph Fourier (1768–1830), secretary of the Institute of Egypt, wrote a "Historical Preface" to the first volume that declared the goals of both the expeditionary force and the* Description. *On the next page is an excerpt from the "Historical Preface" followed by the* Description's *report of the Colossus of Ozymandias, the Greek name for Rameses II (1279–1213 B.C.), made by*

Description de l'Egypte . . . , 2nd ed., 2 vols. (Paris, 1821), 1:iv–v, viii–ix, lv–lvii, lix, lxxxi–lxxxiv, cxxviii–cxxxv; 2:243–44.

two of the Commission's engineers—Prosper Jollois (1776–1842) and Édouard de Villiers Du Terrage (1780–1855).

One remembers the impression made on all of Europe by the astonishing news of the French expedition to the Orient. This great project, pondered over in silence, was prepared with such activity and secrecy that even our enemies' worried vigilance was deceived. They learned almost simultaneously that it had been conceived, undertaken, and executed successfully. It was provoked by the necessity of protecting our commerce from constant injurious attacks by the beys.[1] . . .

This country [Egypt], which has transmitted its knowledge to so many nations, today is plunged into barbarism. . . . [The inability of the Ottoman Sultan to guarantee the execution of its treaties in Egypt] provoked the memorable expedition of the French; however, he [Napoleon] who directed the expedition did not limit his aims to punishing the oppressors of our commerce. He elevated the project of conquest and gave it a new grandeur, imprinting it with the character of his own genius. He appreciated the influence that this event would have on European relations with the Orient and the interior of Africa, on Mediterranean shipping and the destiny of Asia. He intended to abolish the tyranny of the Mamluks,[2] to extend irrigation and agriculture, to open constant communication between the Mediterranean and the Gulf of Arabia, to create commercial establishments, to offer to the Orient a useful example of European industry, and finally to make the lives of the inhabitants more pleasant and to procure for them all the advantages of a perfected civilization.

This goal could not be achieved without the continual application of the arts and sciences. For this project, the head of the French expedition resolved to found in Egypt an institution destined to the progress of all useful knowledge. In the French capital, he selected those who concurred in his views and, by the evidence of a protective benevolence, consolidated this unaccustomed alliance of literature and the military. . . .

Of all the enterprises that the occupation of Egypt permitted, one of the most important consisted in joining, by a navigable canal, the Gulf of Arabia [Persian Gulf] and the Mediterranean—a long-celebrated question which, today, can be fully resolved. . . . Without changing entirely the current paths of commerce, it would influence the relations of Europe with India, Arabia, and Africa. . . . Further, this country [Egypt] offers to the French the very remarkable advantages of an intermediate situation: set at the gates of Asia, they are able to menace continually the rich possessions of an enemy state[3] and carry trouble or war to the sources of its opulence.[4]

The relations that would soon be formed between Egypt and the [commercial] enterprises situated in Arabia, Persia, Indostan,[5] and Africa would procure the most

---

[1] Provincial governors of the Ottoman empire.
[2] Slave-soldiers who ruled Egypt between 1250 and 1517 and whose descendants survived in Egypt as a major political force until Napoleon's conquest.
[3] England.
[4] India.
[5] Or Hindustan, usually referring to northern India.

profitable trade to the French and to the people who navigate the Mediterranean. . . . Egypt is not only useful for what it possesses, but also for what it lacks. We would be assured of selling [in Egypt] valuable fabrics, light cloths, wines, and products from various industries. We would transport to Egypt iron, lead, and especially wood destined to the construction of buildings and ships. It is, in part, through these means of exchange that we would acquire the most esteemed merchandise of India. . . .

[*Fourier outlines the military events of the Egyptian campaign.*]

The events of this campaign opened to us the sanctuary of Egypt. We discovered then the magnificent temple of ancient Tentyris, the vestiges of Thebes[6] worthy of being sung by Homer,[7] and the truly royal residences of the Pharaohs. We penetrated beyond Elephantine,[8] in this sacred island, which seems itself to be a single monument raised by the Egyptians to the glory of the gods and the fine arts. The French soldiers, whom the war had called to the banks of the Nile, were struck with admiration at seeing these immortal works and came to a standstill so seized with astonishment and respect. . . .

The application of mechanical and chemical theories had made remarkable progress at Cairo. We had assembled, in the very walls of the grand buildings destined to the sciences, all the elements able to favor the development of industry. . . . We constructed hydraulic machines, produced steel, arms, cloth, mathematical and optical instruments. Finally, these large workshops furnished, during the course of the expedition, a multitude of objects proper to contribute to the success of the war and the delights of peace. The locals did not delay participating in the advantages that resulted from these works. We observed their manufactures; we perfected the processes that they used. They considered attentively the productions of French industry and worked to imitate them. Recognizing in the victor all the genres of superiority, they submitted themselves with confidence to the protective influence of the new government. . . . The Institute of Cairo directed all the research. . . .

The literary corps that was formed in the Egyptian capital, under the protection of the French army, had received the same regulations as the academies of Europe: its goal was to cultivate and perfect all theoretical knowledge and to multiply its applications. The combination of the sciences and the arts would consolidate and embellish the French establishments at the same time that it would influence the civil condition of the indigenous population, but we would not be able to attain this so desired goal without first acquiring a profound knowledge of Egypt. The physical and historical description of this country, in truth, was only one part of the general plan that was created for the study and progress of the sciences, but it was a necessary element of this and one of the most important transmitted to Europe. Such is the object of the collection that is published today. It contains the results of the principle research that was undertaken during the French expedition and that is able to furnish knowledge of Egypt. This work is

---

[6] Capital of ancient Egypt.
[7] Homer (9th century B.C.), legendary Greek epic poet.
[8] Elephantine, island in the Nile with several temples that marked the starting point for the Sudanese trade.

composed of text and a collection of plates. The text contains reports and descriptions . . . [which] seek to render the most complete exposition of these objects, to indicate with precision everything the art of drawing could not make known, to compare the facts, to bring together the results, and to examine the inferences that they are able to furnish.

The geographic map is composed of 50 individual maps, which provide all the details that could be desired. There is not any region of Europe that has been described more completely. . . . Added there are the individual maps of the towns and ports, maps and reports relative to ancient geography, the listing of Arab names of all inhabited places, information on the population, culture, extent of fertile land, navigation, industry, public buildings, and the vestiges of the ancient towns.

We have observed with much care the geological state of the valley of the Nile and the mountains that mark its limits. . . . Mineralogical investigations have been extended to deserted and mountainous lands. . . . We have given assiduous care to study the animals in applying ourselves to verify the results already known, to correct imperfect descriptions, and to supply information missed by naturalists in preceding voyages. . . .

With regard to the monuments that have immortalized Egypt, we had only defective knowledge of them before the French expedition, or rather they [the monuments] were entirely ignored. This work will offer exact descriptions of them. We have identified the geographic position of each monument, which is marked on the maps. . . . We have measured several times, and with the most attentive care, the dimensions of the edifices and those of the principal or secondary parts, which compose them. . . . We have applied ourselves to imitate exactly the innumerable sculptures, which decorate these edifices. . . .

[*Jollois and de Villiers describe the ruin of the Colossus of Ozymandias near Thebes.*]

[There are] so many granite fragments that one believes oneself transported to the middle of a quarry. They are scattered about in a radius of more than 20 m². These are the remains of an enormous colossus of which only the head, chest, and arms to the elbow remain intact. Another block that contains the rest of the body and the thighs is right next to this and was only detached by use of wedges, which no one can doubt in light of the notches which have been made in order to insert them. The head of the colossus retains its form. The ornaments of the headdress are easily distinguishable, but the face is completely mutilated. Among the dispersed debris is the left foot and hand. The precise measurements, taken with much care, offer the following results:

The length of the ear	1.05 m
From one ear to the other, measuring around the face	2.08 m[9]
From one shoulder to the other, measuring across the chest	7.11 m
From one shoulder to the other, measuring in a straight line	6.84 m
From the joint of the shoulder to the bend of the elbow	3.90 m
Circumference of the arm at the bend of the elbow	5.33 m
Diameter of the arm between the elbow and the shoulder	1.46 m

[9] In another section of the text, this measure is listed as 4.08 meters.

Length of the index finger	1.00 m
Length of the fingernail of the middle finger	.19 m
Width of the same	.16 m
Width of the foot from the knuckle of the big toe to that of the little toe	1.40 m

. . . The pedestal of this statue is still in place. It is decorated, on its upper half, by a line of hieroglyphs where one notes daggers, half-circles, and figures of birds and animals. It is built against the back wall. It is 11.7 meters long and a width a little less than half. The statue and its pedestal are both made entirely of beautiful pink granite of Syene.[10] The surface of the material is of a rare finish that one does not expect to find on so large of surface and so hard of rock. . . . [I]t is very likely that this seated colossus was at least 17.5 meters high from the top of the head to the sole of the feet. It weighed more than 2,000,000 *livres*.[11]

---

[10] The modern city of Aswan in southern Egypt.
[11] Approximately 1,079 tons.

QUESTIONS FOR ANALYSIS

1. What does Fourier assert were the goals of the military campaign? What were the goals of the *Description of Egypt*?
2. How does Fourier define the relationship between French culture and Egyptian culture? How does his description of Egypt seek to justify Napoleon's invasion?
3. Fourier's references to Elephantine serve what purpose? How does this purpose compare with Denon's use of religion (Source 4)?
4. What topics does Fourier indicate are included in the *Description*? What methods do Jollois and de Villiers use to describe the colossus?

6

"THE COLOSSI . . ."

Images of Egypt   (early 19th century)

Visual images of Egypt played a prominent role in the Description of Egypt *and in the other books produced by participants in the Egyptian campaign. The* Description *itself contained over three thousand illustrations. These images shaped how Europeans viewed the architectural and artistic legacies of Egypt and how Europeans understood a relationship between Egypt's legacy, the Egypt of their day, and themselves. The following illustrations from Vivant Denon's* Travels in Upper and Lower Egypt *(Source 4) and from the* Description of Egypt *(Source 5) suggest how images projected a European understanding of these three components.*

Profile of the Sphinx near the Pyramids of Giza

Tomb of Paheri[1]

---

[1] An Egyptian nobleman (16th century B.C.).

The Colossi of Memnon[2] at Thebes

QUESTIONS FOR ANALYSIS

1. What does the visual contrast between the monuments and the people in these images suggest about ancient Egypt? How does this perspective compare to Napoleon's views (Source 2)?

2. How do the Europeans in these images respond to the monuments? How do the Egyptians respond? What images of Europeans and Egyptians are produced by this comparison?

3. What do these images suggest about the contrast between ancient Egypt and the Egypt of Napoleon's era?

---

[2] An Ethiopian mythic hero who fought at Troy and was killed by Achilles. These two statues fronted the mortuary temple of Amenhotep III (14th century B.C.).

7

Edward Said
Orientalism   (1978)

In his influential work Orientalism, *the modern scholar Edward Said explores the manner in which Europeans have created and used images of "the Orient." In the passage below, Said points to Napoleon's Egyptian campaign and the intellectual works that resulted from it as the beginning point in the creation of a modern Orientalist tradition.*

[Political] dealings with the Muslims were only a part of Napoleon's project to dominate Egypt. The other part was to render it completely open, to make it totally accessible to European scrutiny. From being a land of obscurity and a part of the Orient hitherto known at second hand through the exploits of earlier travelers, scholars, and conquerors, Egypt was to become a department of French learning. . . . The Institut,[1] with its teams of chemists, historians, biologists, archaeologists, surgeons, and antiquarians, was the learned division of the army. Its job was no less aggressive: to put Egypt into modern French. . . . Almost from the first moments of the occupation Napoleon saw to it that the Institut began its meetings, its experiments—its fact-finding mission, as we would call it today. Most important, everything said, seen, and studied was to be recorded, and indeed was recorded in that great collective appropriation of one country by another, the *Description of Egypt*, published in twenty-three enormous volumes between 1809 and 1828.

The *Description's* uniqueness is not only in its size, or even in the intelligence of its contributors, but in its attitude to its subject matter. . . . The first few pages of its historical preface, written by Jean-Baptiste-Joseph Fourier,[2] the Institut's secretary, make it clear that in "doing" Egypt the scholars were also grappling directly with a kind of unadulterated cultural, geographical, and historical significance. . . .

> This country presents only great memories; it is the homeland of the arts and conserves innumerable monuments; its principal temples and the palaces inhabited by its kings still exist, even though its least ancient edifices had already been built by the time of the Trojan War.[3] Homer, Lycurgus, Solon, Pythagoras, and Plato[4] all

---

[1] The Institute of Egypt established by Napoleon at Cairo.
[2] Jean-Baptiste-Joseph Fourier (1768–1830), French mathematician.
[3] Trojan War (traditionally 12th century B.C.).
[4] Homer (9th century B.C.), legendary Greek epic poet; Lycurgus (9th century B.C.), Spartan lawgiver; Solon (638?–559? B.C.), Athenian lawgiver; Pythagoras (c. 497 B.C.), Greek philosopher and mathematician; and Plato (427?–347 B.C.), Greek philosopher.

Edward Said, *Orientalism* (New York: Vintage Books, 1978), 83–87.

went to Egypt to study the sciences, religion, and the laws. Alexander[5] founded an opulent city there, which for a long time enjoyed commercial supremacy and which witnessed Pompey, Caesar, Mark Antony, and Augustus[6] deciding between them the fate of Rome and that of the entire world. It is therefore proper for this country to attract the attention of illustrious princes who rule the destiny of nations.

No considerable power was ever amassed by any nation, whether in the West or in Asia, that did not also turn that nation toward Egypt, which was regarded in some measure as its natural lot.

Because Egypt was saturated with meaning for the arts, sciences, and government, its role was to be the stage on which actions of a world-historical importance would take place. By taking Egypt, then, a modern power would naturally demonstrate its strength and justify history; Egypt's own destiny was to be annexed, to Europe preferably. In addition, this power would also enter a history whose common element was defined by figures no less great than Homer, Alexander, Caesar, Plato, Solon, and Pythagoras, who graced the Orient with their prior presence there. The Orient, in short, existed as a set of values attached, not to its modern realities, but to a series of valorized contacts it had had with a distant European past. . . .

Fourier continues similarly for over a hundred pages (each page, incidentally, is a square meter in size, as if the project and the size of the page had been thought of as possessing comparable scale). Out of the free-floating past, however, he must justify the Napoleonic expedition as something that needed to be undertaken when it happened. . . :

> This country, which has transmitted its knowledge to so many nations, is today plunged into barbarism.

Only a hero could bring all these factors together, which is what Fourier now describes:

> . . . Napoleon wanted to offer a useful European example to the Orient, and finally also to make the inhabitants' lives more pleasant, as well as to procure for them all the advantages of a perfected civilization.
>
> None of this would be possible without a continuous application to the project of the arts and sciences.

To restore a region from its present barbarism to its former classical greatness; to instruct (for its own benefit) the Orient in the ways of the modern West; to subordinate or underplay military power in order to aggrandize the project of glorious knowledge acquired in the process of political domination of the Orient; to formulate the Orient, to give it shape, identity, definition with full recognition of its place in memory, its importance to imperial strategy, and its "natural" role as an appendage to Europe; to dignify all the knowledge collected during colonial occupation with the title "contribution to modern learning" when the natives had neither been consulted nor treated as anything except as pretexts for a text whose usefulness was not to the natives; to feel oneself as a European in command, almost at

---

[5] Alexander the Great (356–323 B.C.).
[6] Pompey (106–48 B.C.), Roman general and statesman; Julius Caesar (100–44 B.C.), Roman general and statesman; Mark Antony (83?–30 B.C.), Roman general and statesman; and Caesar Augustus (27 B.C.–A.D. 14), first Roman emperor.

will, of Oriental history, time, and geography; to institute new areas of specialization; to establish new disciplines; to divide, deploy, schematize, tabulate, index, and record everything in sight (and out of sight); to make out of every observable detail a generalization and out of every generalization an immutable law about the Oriental nature, temperament, mentality, custom, or type; and, above all, to transmute living reality into the stuff of texts, to possess (or think one possesses) actuality mainly because nothing in the Orient seems to resist one's powers: these are the features of Orientalist projection entirely realized in the *Description of Egypt,* itself enabled and reinforced by Napoleon's wholly Orientalist engulfment of Egypt by the instruments of Western knowledge and power. Thus Fourier concludes his preface by announcing that history will remember how "Egypt was the theater of his [Napoleon's] glory and saves from oblivion all the circumstances of this extraordinary event."

The *Description* thereby displaces Egyptian or Oriental history as a history possessing its own coherence, identity, and sense. Instead, history as recorded in the *Description* supplants Egyptian or Oriental history by identifying itself directly and immediately with world history, a euphemism for European history. To save an event from oblivion is in the Orientalist's mind the equivalent of turning the Orient into a theater for his representations of the Orient: this is almost exactly what Fourier says. Moreover, the sheer power of having described the Orient in modern Occidental[7] terms lifts the Orient from the realms of silent obscurity where it has lain neglected (except for the inchoate murmurings of a vast but undefined sense of its own past) into the clarity of modern European science. There this new Orient figures as—for instance, in Geoffroy Saint-Hilaire's[8] biological theses in the *Description*—the confirmation of laws of zoological specialization formulated by Buffon.[9] Or it serves as a "striking contrast with the customs of the European nations," in which the "bizarre pleasures" of Orientals serve to highlight the sobriety and rationality of Occidental habits. . . .

[T]he [French] occupation gave birth to the entire modern experience of the Orient as interpreted from within the universe of discourse founded by Napoleon in Egypt, whose agencies of domination and dissemination included the Institut and the *Description.* . . .

[T]he Orient was reconstructed, reassembled, crafted, in short, *born* out of the Orientalists' efforts. The *Description* became the master type of all further efforts to bring the Orient closer to Europe, thereafter to absorb it entirely and—centrally important—to cancel, or at least subdue and reduce, its strangeness and, in the case of Islam, its hostility. For the Islamic Orient would henceforth appear as a category denoting the Orientalists' power and not the Islamic people as humans nor their history as history.

QUESTIONS FOR ANALYSIS

1. What is "orientalism" as Said uses the term? How does the "orientalist" exercise power?

---

[7] Western.
[8] Étienne Geoffroy Saint-Hilaire (1772–1844), French zoologist.
[9] Georges Leclerc, count of Buffon (1707–1788), French naturalist.

2. According to Said, how is Egypt annexed by Europe? What is the significance of this annexation for both Europe and Egypt?

3. How do the three images in Source 6 demonstrate the "orientalist" tradition?

4. Identify examples from the textual sources, especially from Denon's *Travels in Upper and Lower Egypt* (Source 4) and from the *Description of Egypt* (Source 5), that demonstrate Said's claims. Do these documents raise issues that Said ignores?

CHAPTER QUESTIONS

1. From the sources in this chapter, what consistent images of ancient Egypt do the French produce? What images of the Egyptians of the late eighteenth century do they produce?

2. How do French characterizations of Egypt and France justify French imperialism?

3. In these sources, in what ways does religion remain an important marker of identity? In what ways is it not important? How do the use and importance of religious identity in these texts compare to its use and importance in the works of Sepúlveda and de Las Casas in the sixteenth century (Chapter 1, Source 7) and Brébeuf and Ricci in the seventeenth century (Chapter 3, Sources 1 and 4)?

4. Said argues that the "orientalism" that resulted from Napoleon's Egyptian campaign and the work of the Commission of Arts and Science marked something new in Europe's relationship with other civilizations. Do the sources discussed in previous chapters, especially Chapters 1, 3, and 4, support his contention? How?

Chapter 8

THE GREAT TRANSFORMATION: RESPONSES TO INDUSTRIALIZATION AT HOME AND AWAY

eginning in the eighteenth century and expanding in the nineteenth, areas of
western and central Europe and the United States underwent transformations across nearly every facet of economic, social, political, and cultural life. The
"era of industrialization" affected deeply rooted, traditional institutions, practices,
and ideals, including the West's understanding of itself. The technological and scientific advances associated with industrialization—spectacularly demonstrated by
the new machines and tools used in homes, industry, and warfare—would themselves become an important component of Western identity (as we explore in
Chapter 9). The social and economic changes also resulted in numerous political
battles as groups and individuals sought to define the meaning and significance of
these changes and the new industrial society being forged.

One doctrine that emerged from and shaped these battles was conservatism.
Conservatives asserted that a society's stability rested on its traditions—cultural
(Christianity), social (the patriarchal family), and political (hereditary monarchy)
—and that the Enlightenment's spirit of reform based on human reason had loos-
ened society from its moorings, leading to the French Revolution's Reign of Terror
and Napoleon's authoritarian state. As conservatives sought to preserve traditional
forms of identity, a new ideology gained strength that championed moderate reforms inspired by the Enlightenment: liberalism. Nineteenth-century liberalism
included both political components, which supported constitutional government
with some guarantees of political and religious liberty, and economic components,
which supported free trade and manufacturing and each individual's liberty to
pursue his or her own economic interests. Both political and economic liberals
couched their arguments within a nationalist message that emphasized how a particular nation would enjoy prosperity and political stability by adopting liberal
policies. In short, liberalism, which drew support from the expanding middle class
of merchants, manufacturers, and professionals, challenged the traditional authority supported by conservatives. As Western political, economic, and military power
expanded dramatically throughout the century—an expansion for which liberals
claimed credit—liberalism increasingly became defined as a central component of
Western society.

The harsh conditions of the emerging industrial society provoked the development of yet a third ideology, which sought to remake society completely—socialism. In the early nineteenth century, different strands of socialist thought
appeared, many of them highly idealistic and utopian, yet nearly all concurring that

179

the laboring classes shared common interests that should unite them in seeking to restructure social relationships (sometimes including relationships between the sexes). Liberal reformers used these socialist movements and working-class unrest—or the threat of such unrest—to coerce conservatives into implementing liberal reforms; however, after the failed revolutions of 1848, in which liberals often abandoned their socialist allies and worked with conservatives to suppress radicalism, socialist movements became more independent of liberal leadership. Increasingly influenced by the theories of Karl Marx, socialists argued that the new industrial order created a society based on confrontation between two classes—the wealthy capitalists and the working class—and that liberalism, with its defense of private property and the individual's pursuit of self-interest, merely justified the continued exploitation of working men and women. Instead, socialists argued, a stable society required the elimination of the basis of capitalists' wealth and power, private property. Socialists increasingly promoted a working-class identity based on social conflict and called for radical economic and social transformations. Thus, liberalism and socialism, each drawing on the universal, natural law tradition of the Enlightenment, offered contending definitions of the new industrial society of the West and contending frameworks for Western identity.

The lands bordering the economic powerhouses of western and central Europe and the United States observed their neighbors' transformations with awe and fear—and sought to understand this phenomenon. The Russian empire had grown dramatically in the seventeenth century; however, efforts by Peter the Great to transform Russia economically and politically based on the model of western European states (Chapter 4) had produced only mixed results, as Russia saw sorely demonstrated in the Crimean War (1854–1856). Whereas the Russian empire was a growing power seeking to respond to increasingly powerful competitors, the Ottoman empire faced a more difficult scenario. Although the Turkish Ottoman empire had been the "scourge of Europe" throughout the sixteenth century (Chapter 2), by the late seventeenth century the Ottoman empire had entered a period of decline, losing territory and prestige. Faced with the growing power of the industrializing states, Russian and Ottoman political officials and intellectuals responded with calls for national renewal. These nationalist appeals ranged from the wholesale imitation of European institutions and practices to the complete rejection of the corrupting influence of the industrializing powers. Either response required individuals on the borderlands to understand and define the substance of the West that had created these changes—whether to foster that Western substance within Russia or the Ottoman empire or to keep such substance out. In short, the West was being redefined, both by the industrializing powers themselves and by those compelled to respond to its new industrial society.

DEFINING THE INDUSTRIAL ERA

The supporters of liberalism in early nineteenth-century Britain fought battles on many sides. Politically, British liberals endorsed expanding the right to vote in parliamentary elections to include the new middle class. After the Reform Act of 1832 was passed, the wealthiest one-fifth of adult male citizens could vote; however, the laboring classes, women, and most of the lower middle class remained without voting rights, leading to continuing conflicts over the issue.

Economically, the supporters of liberalism fought to enact free-trade and manufacturing legislation and resisted efforts by conservatives and radicals to institute wage and labor laws to protect workers. The abuses of the factory system, however, provoked efforts to organize workers into labor unions and encouraged radical socialist movements. After the failed revolutions of 1848 across Europe, the socialist movements developed more substantial critiques of industrial society and sought to create a working-class identity that set itself in opposition to bourgeois society, including conservative and bourgeois definitions of the position of women in society.

"... TOO LOW A STANDARD OF POLITICAL INTELLIGENCE ..."

John Stuart Mill
Considerations on Representative Government (1861)

John Stuart Mill (1806–1873) was a leading liberal philosopher and supporter of social and political reforms. In 1861, Mill published a systematic summation of his political views entitled Considerations on Representative Government. *Mill argued that "the ideally best form of government is that in which the sovereignty . . . is vested in the entire aggregate of the community, every citizen . . . having a voice [vote] in the exercise of that ultimate sovereignty." With his support of representative government, Mill then faced one of the most contentious issues in nineteenth-century Britain—the extent of the franchise or right to vote. Liberals generally favored expanding the vote further but also worried about the consequences of expanding suffrage to the "unruly" lower classes. In the excerpt below from that text, Mill addresses these concerns.*

[I]t is a personal injustice to withhold from anyone, unless for the prevention of greater evils, the ordinary privilege of having his voice reckoned[1] in the disposal of affairs in which he has the same interest as other people. If he is compelled to pay, if he may be compelled to fight, if he is required implicitly to obey, he should be legally entitled to be told what for, to have his consent asked and his opinion counted at its worth, though not at more than its worth.... No arrangement of the suffrage, therefore, can be permanently satisfactory in which any person or class is

---

[1] Voting.

John Stuart Mill, *Considerations on Representative Government*, ed. Currin V. Shields (New York: Liberal Arts Press, 1958), 131–32, 135–38, 143–44.

peremptorily excluded, in which the electoral privilege is not open to all persons of full age who desire to obtain it.

There are, however, certain exclusions, required by positive reasons, which do not conflict with this principle, and which, though an evil in themselves, are only to be got rid of by the cessation of the state of things which requires them. I regard it as wholly inadmissible that any person should participate in the suffrage without being able to read, write, and, I will add, perform the common operations of arithmetic. Justice demands, even when the suffrage does not depend on it, that the means of attaining these elementary acquirements should be within the reach of every person, either gratuitously or at an expense not exceeding what the poorest who earn their own living can afford. If this were really the case, people would no more think of giving the suffrage to a man who could not read than of giving it to a child who could not speak; and it would not be society that would exclude him, but his own laziness. When society has not performed its duty by rendering this amount of instruction accessible to all, there is some hardship in the case, but it is a hardship that ought to be borne. If society has neglected to discharge two solemn obligations, the more important and more fundamental of the two must be fulfilled first: universal teaching must precede universal enfranchisement. . . .

[*Mill also excludes the vote from individuals too poor to pay taxes, who are on poor or parish relief, or who are bankrupt or insolvent.*]

In the long run, therefore (supposing no restrictions to exist but those of which we have now treated), we might expect that all, except that (it is to be hoped) progressively diminishing class, the recipients of parish relief, would be in possession of votes, so that the suffrage would be, with that slight abatement, universal. . . . Yet in this state of things the great majority of voters, in most countries, and emphatically in this, would be manual laborers; and the twofold danger—that of too low a standard of political intelligence, and that of class legislation—would still exist in a very perilous degree. It remains to be seen whether any means exist by which these evils can be obviated.[2] . . .

But though everyone ought to have a voice—that everyone should have an equal voice is a totally different proposition. When two persons who have a joint interest in any business differ in opinion, does justice require that both opinions should be held of exactly equal value? If, with equal virtue, one is superior to the other in knowledge and intelligence, or if, with equal intelligence, one excels the other in virtue, the opinion, the judgment of the higher moral or intellectual being is worth more than that of the inferior: and if the institutions of the country virtually assert that they are of the same value, they assert a thing which is not. . . .

[N]o one needs ever be called upon for a complete sacrifice of his own opinion. It can always be taken into the calculation and counted at a certain figure, a higher figure being assigned to the suffrages of those whose opinion is entitled to greater weight. There is not, in this arrangement, anything necessarily invidious to those to whom it assigns the lower degrees of influence. Entire exclusion from a voice in

---

[2] Prevented.

the common concerns is one thing, the concession to others of a more potential voice, on the ground of greater capacity for the management of the joint interests, is another. . . .

The only thing which can justify reckoning one person's opinion as equivalent to more than one is individual mental superiority; and what is wanted is some approximate means of ascertaining that. . . . [T]he nature of a person's occupation is some test. An employer of labor is on the average more intelligent than a laborer; for he must labor with his head, and not solely with his hands. A foreman is generally more intelligent than an ordinary laborer, and a laborer in the skilled trades than in the unskilled. A banker, merchant, or manufacturer is likely to be more intelligent than a tradesman, because he has larger and more complicated interests to manage. In all these cases it is not the having merely undertaken the superior function, but the successful performance of it, that tests the qualifications; for which reason, as well as to prevent persons from engaging nominally in an occupation for the sake of the vote, it would be proper to require that the occupation should have been persevered in for some length of time (say three years). Subject to some such condition, two or more votes might be allowed to every person who exercises any of these superior functions. . . .

In the preceding argument for universal but graduated suffrage I have taken no account of difference of sex. I consider it to be as entirely irrelevant to political rights as difference in height or in the color of the hair. All human beings have the same interest in good government; the welfare of all is alike affected by it, and they have equal need of a voice in it to secure their share of its benefits. If there be any difference, women require it more than men, since, being physically weaker, they are more dependent on law and society for protection. Mankind have long since abandoned the only premises which will support the conclusion that women ought not to have votes. No one now holds that women should be in personal servitude, that they should have no thought, wish, or occupation, but to be the domestic drudges of husbands, fathers, or brothers. It is allowed to unmarried, and wants but little of being conceded to married, women to hold property and have pecuniary and business interests in the same manner as men. It is considered suitable and proper that women should think, and write, and be teachers. As soon as these things are admitted, the political disqualification has no principle to rest on.

QUESTIONS FOR ANALYSIS

1. On what basis does Mill justify the holding of voting rights? How and why does he emphasize the importance of education?

2. How does Mill include a universal ideal of equality among all people in his approach to voting rights? How does his theory of voting rights challenge equality?

3. On what basis does Mill justify extending the vote to women? How does Mill's argument indicate that women have a new status in Western society?

4. In what ways does Mill's political liberalism identify new components to identity in Western society?

2

Andrew Ure
Philosophy of Manufactures   (1835)

Andrew Ure (1778–1857), a Scottish professor of chemistry and applied science, was a prominent spokesperson for economic liberalism and the new factory system. In the 1820s and 1830s, calls for the protection of workers against the abuses of the factory system grew. As Parliament launched investigations into working conditions, Ure published his most famous work, Philosophy of Manufactures *(1835), excerpted below. He argues that the factory system, when supported by free trade and manufacturing, fosters industrial efficiency and capacity and promotes national economic strength.*

The blessings which physico-mechanical science has bestowed on society, and the means it has still in store for ameliorating the lot of mankind, have been too little dwelt upon; while, on the other hand, it has been accused of lending itself to the rich capitalists as an instrument of harassing the poor, and of exacting from the operative an accelerated rate of work. It has been said, for example, that the steam-engine now drives the power-looms with such velocity as to urge on their attendant weavers at the same rapid pace; but that the hand-weaver, not being subjected to this restless agent, can throw his shuttle and move his treddles at his convenience. There is, however, this difference in the two cases, that in the factory, every member of the loom is so adjusted, that the driving force leaves the attendant nearly nothing at all to do, certainly no muscular fatigue to sustain, while it procures for him good, unfailing wages, besides a healthy workshop *gratis*: whereas the non-factory weaver, having everything to execute by muscular exertion, finds the labour irksome, makes in consequence innumerable short pauses, separately of little account, but great when added together; earns therefore proportionally low wages, while he loses his health by poor diet and the dampness of his hovel. . . .

The constant aim and effect of scientific improvement in manufactures are philanthropic, as they tend to relieve the workmen either from niceties of adjustment which exhaust his mind and fatigue his eyes, or from painful repetition of effort which distort or wear out his frame. At every step of each manufacturing process described in this volume, the humanity of science will be manifest. . . .

Free trade consists in the entire absence of restrictions of any kind on the export and import of merchandize. Constrained trade has, for one of its principles, to encourage the productions and manufactures of our own country, by imposing taxes

---

Andrew Ure, *Philosophy of Manufactures* (1835) (Reprinted New York: Cass, 1967), 7–8, 447–48, 451, 453–54.

or prohibitions on those of other countries; and for another principle, to prohibit the exportation of such of our native productions as might be beneficial or essential to a rival foreign manufacture. Besides removing as much as possible all competition from native industry, legislatures, on many occasions, undertook to cherish it by bounties on exportation, in order to enable the manufacturer or shipper to sell his goods at a cheap rate. This system was necessarily very complex, being entangled with number- less springs and counterchecks. . . . [For example, t]he silk weaver wishes to import thrown silk only, but he is resisted by the silk throwster, who, in his turn, claims a pro- tective duty on the importation of thrown silk, however injurious to the weaver. No arrangement of human sagacity, separately or collectively exercised, could adjust all the interests placed in collision by that false principle. Individual, as well as public jus- tice, requires that trade be left free and unembarrassed, unless special reasons can be given for putting it in bondage; just as it requires that every man should enjoy perfect liberty of person, till his liberty be proved to be dangerous to others. Every man should be allowed to buy, to sell, and to manufacture in any way, and whatsoever articles he chooses, and to transport them whithersoever he shall desire; and any law which interferes, either by prohibition or regulation, with his business, is, until shown to be necessary for some legitimate purpose of public revenue, an act of oppression. . . .

The advantage of the country which is the first to adopt free trade is not merely conditional, but absolute. Under our old system of restriction, other nations could arrange and maintain equivalent restrictions; but under a system of free inter- course, they may indeed apply shackles to trade, but they cannot bind them fast. They may strive for a time to humour the wishes of the interested producers, and their dupes in their own country, but they cannot carry on the delusion long. The ruin of their own manufactures, the impoverishment of all those not directly en- riched by the monopoly, and the remonstrances of the great mass of consumers will, ere long, compel their government to adopt a wiser and a juster course. If we wait till a foreign state grant reciprocity, we are the slaves of their prejudices; if we give free admission to their produce, we become in so much their masters. . . .

In pursuing a gradually progressive but steady approach to a liberal system, we must tamper as little as possible with manufacturing or commercial industry by leg- islative regulation. Like love, its workings must be free as air; for at sight of human ties, it will spread the light wings of capital and fly away from bondage. By loosening the bands in which the unwise tenderness of our old legislators had swaddled the trade of great Britain, by letting it run wherever it may list, by exposing it freely to the breezes of competition, we have within a few years given it fresh vigour and a new life. National industry has the same principle of vigorous growth as the mountain pine. Self-sown in the clefts of the rocks, it creates a soil for its roots, shoots up a hardy stem, is invigorated by the gale which would blast the nursery plant, eventually rears its head on high, and forms a mast for some "tall ammiral." Planted in the rich compost of a parterre,[1] having its infant shoots nursed in the close atmosphere of a forcing glass, protected from extremes of heat, moisture, and drought by a watchful gardener, it remains feeble, dwarfish, and sickly, and never can become a mass of

---

[1] An ornamental bedded garden.

timber profitable to its owner, or useful to the state. The elements of industry may be expressed in one word—competition. Never was a better advice given to a monarch too ambitious of the glory of patronage, when he asked what he could do to promote trade. "Let it take its own course," was the memorable reply. This adage ought to be engraved on the portals of every legislative assembly of the old world and the new.

QUESTIONS FOR ANALYSIS

1. On what basis does Ure defend the factory system? What links does Ure make between economic liberalism and nationalism?
2. On what basis does he criticize the regulation of trade and manufacturing? On what basis does he endorse free trade and manufacturing?
3. How does Ure imply a universal framework for the ideas that he supports? What assumptions does Ure make about role of the individual in society?
4. In what ways is Ure's economic liberalism similar to and different from Mill's political liberalism (Source 1)?

$$3$$

"THINKS THAT HIS MASTERS ARE HUMANE GOOD MEN."

Testimony for the Factory Act of 1833

In the early 1800s, mills and factories employed only a small percentage of the British population, but those laborers faced working conditions that were controlled by few government regulations and that were made more severe by mill owners seeking profits in very competitive markets. Their plight drew the attention of social reformers, and beginning in the 1830s, the British Parliament investigated the conditions in factories and mills, which led to the passage of legislation that increasingly regulated the workday, especially with regard to women and children. The excerpt below, taken from the 1833 Parliamentary Papers on the committee investigating child labor in factories, is the medical report filed by David Barry on mills that he visited near and in the Scottish town of Dundee.

1. Eden Bank mill, Mr. Andrew Smith owner. There are about forty-five hands employed here, six boys, thirty-nine females. This mill has been going thirty-two years; situation good and retired. Mr. S. boards and lodges all the hands himself. The girls sleep in rooms called bothies, in one of which, measuring about twenty-one feet by twenty, there are seven bed frames, five of which are occupied by three

British Parliamentary Papers: Factories Inquiry Commission; Second Report Together with Supplementary Report Part I: Employment of Children in Factories with Minutes of Evidence and Reports of Medical and District Commissioners, vol. 4, *Industrial Revolution: Children's Employment* (Shannon: Irish University Press, 1968), A.3.10–A.3.12.

in each bed. There is a good eating room; saw the young people at breakfast on excellent porridge and milk, which I tasted; the supply seemed abundant. Mr. Smith charges 2*s*. 10*d*.[1] a week for board and lodging. Dinner, potatoes, kale, oat cake or barley cake, eggs, and pig meat occasionally; beef only once a year.

Mill-owners who lodge their own workers are eager to meet with widows who have three or four or more daughters. Anney Williamson, for instance, a widow, has been three years here: she has four children in the mill, two of whom earn nine shillings a week. They support their mother, who states if there were no mills she must starve. This family provide their own food.

The highest wages given by Mr. S., with board and lodging, is 8£.[2] per annum. Not one sick at present; only four deaths in thirty-two years. No cholera.

2. Mr. Moon, called Russell's Mill, eighty hands. No cholera. No death since 1828. This establishment appears to be most liberally conducted, both Mr. and Mrs. Moon paying great attention to the health, comfort, and morals of their people. The situation is detached, beautiful, and healthy. The girls have a green paddock as a play-ground. Mr. Moon states that there has not been a bastard child amongst his people for the last twenty-one years. They all look healthy and contented. . . .

When Mr. Moon has a large family in his employ he allows the older children a quarter[3] annually for school, taking in the younger children as substitutes for the time. . . .

Medical Report on the Flax and Tow Dry Spinning-factory of Messrs. Chalmers and Hackney, worked by steampower, at Dundee.

The total number of persons employed in the mill is 166, of whom thirty-five are males and 131 females. The females change their gowns always on going out, and change between the frames. Work begins at half past five in the morning and ends at seven in the evening. Stoppages are made up, but paid for. Half an hour at nine in the morning, and half an hour at two P.M., are allowed for breakfast and dinner. The cleaning of the machinery takes place during meal times, and is done by a man — "an oiler." They have two holidays in the year. On Sundays they go to kirk,[4] and to a Sunday school kept at the expence of the owner. Three times a week they likewise go to school, which is open from half past seven P.M. to a quarter before nine. They have porridge for breakfast: broth for dinner, which is purchased at neighbouring shops. They sup at home. Their drink at and between meals is water. The owners and overseer of the factory state the health of the operatives to be generally good. Their appearance is dusty, unwashed, and rather heated. . . .

1. WILLIAM BROWN, aged nineteen, being solemnly sworn, declares that he has lost his arm by the carding machine, between nine and ten years ago, in Messrs. Chalmers and Hackney's old mill. That he was then sent to the infirmary, when his arm was amputated. Returned to Mr. Chalmers's works between five and six years ago, after having been at a nursery school about a year, and Mr. Boyack's mill about

---

[1] *s* = shilling, *d* = pence. British currency units.
[2] £ = pound. British currency unit.
[3] Three months.
[4] Church.

a year. That when he next saw the same carding machine, about two years ago, it was much better boxed in than when he was hurt. . . .

3. DAVID YULE.—Not now employed in this mill. His father, here present, being solemnly sworn, states that his son lost his left arm about two years ago, by the said machine in new mill. The boy was twelve years of age then. The accident took place about three o'clock P.M. The boy is now at school. The working hours were then, as now, half past five to seven. David Yule senior, the father, has six children living, of eight; had another boy at the mill when the accident happened, but took him away immediately, and has not allowed any other child of his to be so employed, from fear of accidents. Earns himself seventeen shillings per day as fireman. Through the interest of masters, his son was placed in a bursary school,[5] where he now is. Thinks that his masters are humane good men.

4. ANN MILLER.—Severe wound across the tendons of the right wrist, with fracture of the bones of fore-arm. Hand totally disabled. Was a spinner; is fifteen years of age. Had 6s. 2d. a week; receives now 3s. 6d. per week. Lives at home with her mother. Accident happened about eleven o'clock in the morning, from putting her hand into the machinery to take out some waste. Cannot write.

5. ANN WARD.—Married. No children. Very hoarse. Aged twenty-five. Employed in carding room. Began mill-work about six years ago. Has felt her chest much oppressed about nine months ago: threw up a tea-cup-full of dark blood with thick spittle this day at two o'clock. Breathing much oppressed with wheezing; is really very ill. If any other employment presented, would leave the mill. Was brought up at country service. Obliged to sit up in bed at night from difficulty of breathing. Earns 5s. per week. Cannot write.

6. JOHN DAWSON, aged fifteen.—Slightly hoarse. A rover: 4s. per week. Tongue quite clean. Eyelids slightly inflamed. Sleeps well at night. Eats his porridge well. Cannot write.

7. ANN HAXTON, aged twenty.—Two years and a half at mill-work. Feels her breathing oppressed towards morning. Sometimes pain across the chest. Wheezes, and expectorates with difficulty. Coughs at her work. Is thin and pale; thinks herself thinner of late. Was changed from feeding to roving frame, her breath being bad, and not able to continue as a feeder. Earns 5s. per week.

QUESTIONS FOR ANALYSIS

1. What types of information does Barry collect? How does the issue of gender affect the information that Barry collects about the laborers?

2. What problems might Barry have encountered while collecting this information at the mills?

3. How does the image of child labor within this source compare to the image of factory work presented by Ure (Source 2)? What does Barry's tone indicate about his attitudes toward these working conditions? Why might this be the case?

4. How does the image of the working classes presented in Barry's report reinforce or challenge Mill's concerns about voting rights (Source 1)?

---

[5] School operated for poor children who had received scholarships to attend.

Karl Marx and Friedrich Engels
The Communist Manifesto (1848)

The German Jewish socialist Karl Marx (1818–1883) undertook an intense study of philosophy, history, and economics through which he moved socialist theory away from its early utopian idealism. He argued that history developed by inalterable historical laws and that this development had led to the dominance of a class called the bourgeoisie—the group of people in an industrial society who own the means by which wealth is produced and transferred (the means of production, as Marx called it). The bourgeoisie's ownership of factories and banks permitted it to establish a new capitalist system, and from this economic foundation, Marx argued, the bourgeoisie created the theories of political and economic liberalism that justified its power. Marx claimed, however, that capitalism would collapse when the exploited working class (the proletariat*) arose against the bourgeoisie, eliminated private ownership of the means of production, and established a socialist (and eventually a communist) society. He did not reject industrialization itself, for he believed that its productive power would permit humankind to end poverty. Rather, Marx asserted that the bourgeoisie used the political, legal, social, and cultural structures of liberal society to maintain power and prevent the emergence of the socialist society that would eliminate private property and permit the benefits of industrialization to flow fairly to all members of society. In 1848, Marx and his collaborator, Friedrich Engels (1820–1895), wrote a platform for an international workers' organization called the Communist League. That platform, known as the* Communist Manifesto, *had little influence at the time of its publication but provided one of the most concise, powerful, and accessible statements of Marx and Engels's social theory as well as a call for action by the laboring class.*

The bourgeoisie, by the rapid improvement of all instruments of production, by the immensely facilitated means of communication, draws all, even the most barbarian, nations into civilisation. The cheap prices of its commodities are the heavy artillery with which it batters down all Chinese walls,[1] with which it forces the barbarians' intensely obstinate hatred of foreigners to capitulate. It compels all nations, on pain of extinction, to adopt the bourgeois mode of production; it

---

[1] With the First Opium War (1839–1842), Britain forced China to allow British manufactured goods to be imported into the Chinese empire.

The Marx-Engels Reader, ed. Robert C. Tucker (New York: Norton, 1972), 339–42.

189

compels them to introduce what it calls civilisation into their midst, i.e., to become bourgeois themselves. In one word, it creates a world after its own image. . . .

The bourgeoisie, during its rule of scarce one hundred years, has created more massive and more colossal productive forces than have all preceding generations together. Subjection of Nature's forces to man, machinery, application of chemistry to industry and agriculture, steam-navigation, railways, electric telegraphs, clearing of whole continents for cultivation, canalisation of rivers, whole populations conjured out of the ground—what earlier century had even a presentiment that such productive forces slumbered in the lap of social labour? . . .

[However, t]he productive forces at the disposal of society no longer tend to further the development of the conditions of bourgeois property; on the contrary, they have become too powerful for these conditions, by which they are fettered, and so soon as they overcome these fetters, they bring disorder into the whole of bourgeois society, endanger the existence of bourgeois property. The conditions of bourgeois society are too narrow to comprise the wealth created by them. And how does the bourgeoisie get over these crises? On the one hand by enforced destruction of a mass of productive forces; on the other, by the conquest of new markets, and by the more thorough exploitation of the old ones. That is to say, by paving the way for more extensive and more destructive crises, and by diminishing the means whereby crises are prevented. . . .

But not only has the bourgeoisie forged the weapons that bring death to itself; it has also called into existence the men who are to wield those weapons—the modern working class—the proletarians.

In proportion as the bourgeoisie, i.e., capital, is developed, in the same proportion is the proletariat, the modern working class, developed—a class of labourers, who live only so long as they find work, and who find work only so long as their labour increases capital. These labourers, who must sell themselves piece-meal, are a commodity, like every other article of commerce, and are consequently exposed to all the vicissitudes of competition, to all the fluctuations of the market.

Owing to the extensive use of machinery and to division of labour, the work of the proletarians has lost all individual character, and consequently, all charm for the workman. He becomes an appendage of the machine, and it is only the most simple, most monotonous, and most easily acquired knack, that is required of him. Hence, the cost of production of a workman is restricted, almost entirely, to the means of subsistence that he requires for his maintenance, and for the propagation of his race. But the price of a commodity, and therefore also of labour, is equal to its cost of production. In proportion, therefore, as the repulsiveness of the work increases, the wage decreases. Nay more, in proportion as the use of machinery and division of labour increases, in the same proportion the burden of toil also increases, whether by prolongation of the working hours, by increase of the work exacted in a given time or by increased speed of the machinery, etc.

Modern industry has converted the little workshop of the patriarchal master into the great factory of the industrial capitalist. Masses of labourers, crowded into the factory, are organised like soldiers. As privates of the industrial army they are placed under the command of a perfect hierarchy of officers and sergeants. Not only are they slaves of the bourgeois class, and of the bourgeois State; they are daily and hourly enslaved by the machine, by the over-looker, and, above all, by the individual bourgeois manufacturer himself. The more openly this despotism proclaims gain to be its end and aim, the more petty, the more hateful and the more embittering it is.

The less the skill and exertion of strength implied in manual labour, in other words, the more modern industry becomes developed, the more is the labour of men superseded by that of women. Differences of age and sex have no longer any distinctive social validity for the working class. All are instruments of labour, more or less expensive to use, according to their age and sex. . . .

The proletariat goes through various stages of development. With its birth begins its struggle with the bourgeoisie. At first the contest is carried on by individual labourers, then by the workpeople of a factory, then by the operatives of one trade, in one locality, against the individual bourgeois who directly exploits them. They direct their attacks not against the bourgeois conditions of production, but against the instruments of production themselves; they destroy imported wares that compete with their labour, they smash to pieces machinery, they set factories ablaze, they seek to restore by force the vanished status of the workman of the Middle Ages. . . .

But with the development of industry the proletariat not only increases in number; it becomes concentrated in greater masses, its strength grows, and it feels that strength more. The various interests and conditions of life within the ranks of the proletariat are more and more equalised, in proportion as machinery obliterates all distinctions of labour, and nearly everywhere reduces wages to the same low level. The growing competition among the bourgeois, and the resulting commercial crises, make the wages of the workers ever more fluctuating. The unceasing improvement of machinery, ever more rapidly developing, makes their livelihood more and more precarious; the collisions between individual workmen and individual bourgeois take more and more the character of collisions between two classes.

QUESTIONS FOR ANALYSIS

1. For Marx and Engels, what is the significance of industrial development? How do their arguments demonstrate their belief in the existence of universal laws for the historical development of humankind?

2. In Marx and Engels's analysis, by what means do the bourgeoisie dominate the laboring classes? How does Marx and Engels's characterization of the laboring classes compare to the descriptions of Ure (Source 2) and the "Testimony for the Factory Act of 1833" (Source 3)?

3. According to Marx and Engels, how is working-class identity transformed by industrialization? What becomes the focus of working-class identity as bourgeois society matures?

4. What role does gender serve in Marx and Engels's argument? How does their argument indicate the limits of nationalism and other divisions of people?

5

"... THE WOMAN IS EVERYTHING IN THE LIFE OF THE WORKER."

Flora Tristan
Workers' Union (1843)

With the growth of industrial labor, some workers organized themselves into labor unions to press for higher wages, shorter hours, and improved working conditions. As unionists sought to build legal and popular support for their movement, they often faced resistance from liberals, who viewed labor unions as infringements on individual freedoms, and from some socialists, who believed that labor unions undermined the movement toward more radical actions by the laboring classes. Facing this hostile environment, union supporters typically based unions on traditional social norms, particularly the economic superiority of men over women. In France, Flora Tristan (1803–1844) challenged that assumption. During several trips to England, she saw the oppressive social consequences of the industrializing process and joined movements to create working-class unions. Tristan, however, became frustrated with the male-dominated labor unions that ignored the concerns of female laborers, and she began touring France, promoting the unification of male and female workers into single unions that would protect everyone's interest and supporting the creation of educational institutions for the children of laborers. In the excerpt below from her book Workers' Union, *Tristan seeks to convince male union leaders and workers of the need to consider female labor.*

Notice that in all the trades engaged in by men and women, the woman worker gets *only half* what a man does for a day's work, or, if she does piecework, her rate is less than half. Not being able to imagine such a flagrant injustice, the first thought to strike us is this: because of his muscular strength, man doubtless does *double* the work of woman. Well, readers, just the contrary happens. In all the trades where skill and finger dexterity are necessary, women do almost *twice* as much work as men. . . . What is happening? The manufacturers, seeing the women laborers work *more quickly* and at *half price*, day by day dismiss men from their workshops and replace them with women. Consequently the man crosses his arms and dies of hunger on the pavement! That is what the heads of factories in England have done. Once started in this direction, women will be dismissed in order to replace them with *twelve-year-old children.* A saving of *half the wages!* Finally one gets to the point of using only *seven- and eight-year-old children.* Overlook one injustice and you are sure to get thousands more.

Flora Tristan: Utopian Feminist. Her Travel Diaries and Personal Crusade, trans. Doris and Paul Beik (Bloomington: Indiana University Press, 1993), 116, 118–19.

The result of this is that the husband at the very least treats his wife with much disdain. . . .

After the bitter chagrins caused by the husband, next come the pregnancies, the illnesses, the lack of work, and the poverty—poverty that is always planted at the door like the head of Medusa.[1] Add to all that the incessant irritation caused by four or five crying children, unruly, tiresome, who turn round and round the mother, and all that in a small laborer's room where there is no place to stir. Oh! One would have to be an angel descended on earth not to be irritated, not become brutal and ill-natured in such a situation. However, in such a family milieu, what becomes of the children? They see their father only evenings and Sundays. This father, always in a state of irritation or of drunkenness, speaks to them only in anger, and they get only insults and blows from him; hearing their mother's continual complaints about him, they dislike and scorn him. As for their mother, they fear her, obey her, but do not love her; for man is so made that he cannot love those who mistreat him. And what a great tragedy it is for a child not to be able to love his mother! If he is troubled, on whose breast will he go to weep? If through thoughtlessness or from being led astray he has committed some grave fault, in whom can he confide? Having no inclination to remain near his mother, the child will look for any pretext to leave the maternal home. Bad associations are easy to make, for girls as for boys. From loafing one will go on to vagrancy, and often from vagrancy to thieving.

Among the unfortunates who people the houses of prostitution, and those who lament in prison, how many there are who can say: "If we had had a mother *capable of raising us,* we certainly would not be here."

I repeat, the woman is everything in the life of the worker. As mother, she influences him during his infancy; it is from her and only from her that he draws the first notions of that science so important to acquire, the science of life, that which teaches us to live befittingly toward ourselves and toward others, according to the milieu in which fate has placed us. . . . As wife, she influences him for three-fourths of his life. Finally, as daughter she influences him in his old age. Notice that the position of the worker is quite different from that of the idle rich. If a child of the rich has a mother incapable of raising him, he is put into a pension or given a governess. If the rich young man has no mistress, he can fill his heart and imagination with study of the fine arts or science. If the rich man has no wife, he has no lack of distractions in the world. If the rich old man has no daughter, he finds some old friends or nephews who willingly consent to make up his game of Boston,[2] whereas the worker, to whom all these pleasures are forbidden, has for his only joy, his only consolation, the society of the women of his family, his companions in misfortune. It follows from this situation that it would be of the greatest importance from the point of view of the *intellectual, moral,* and *material* betterment of the working class for the women of the people to receive from their infancy a rational, solid education, suitable for developing all their good, natural bents, in order that they

---

[1] Fierce female figure from Greek mythology who had snakes for hair and whose gaze could turn people into stone.
[2] Popular card game.

might become skillful workers in their trade, good mothers of families, capable of raising and guiding their children and of being for them, as *la Presse*[3] says, *natural free-of-charge school-mistresses,* and in order, too, that they might serve as *moralizing agents* for the men over whom they have influence from birth to death.

Do you begin to understand, you man who exclaim in horror before being willing to examine the question, why I claim *rights for women?* Why I would like them to be placed in society on an *absolutely equal* footing with men, and enjoy it by virtue of the *legal right that every person has at birth?*

I demand rights for women because I am convinced that *all the ills of the world come from this forgetfulness and scorn that until now have been inflicted on the natural and imprescriptible rights of the female.* I demand rights for women because that is the *only way that their education will be attended to* and because on the education of women depends that of men in general, and *particularly of the men of the people.* I demand rights for women because it is the only means of obtaining their rehabilitation in the eyes of the church, the law, and society, and because that preliminary rehabilitation is necessary *if the workers themselves are to be rehabilitated.* All the ills of the working class are summed up by these two words: poverty and ignorance, ignorance and poverty. But to get out of this labyrinth, I see only one way: *to start by educating women, because women are entrusted with raising the children, male and female.*

QUESTIONS FOR ANALYSIS

1. According to Tristan, what injustices do workingwomen suffer? How are these injustices maintained?

2. How does Tristan integrate the issues of class and gender in her argument? How does her argument in favor of women's rights rely on gender distinctions?

3. In what ways does Tristan want to reform traditional social relationships and the status of women? What does she understand will be the result of "rehabilitating" women?

4. How does Tristan's argument favoring women's rights compare to Mill's argument about women and voting (Source 1)? How does Tristan's use of gender when analyzing the working class compare to Marx and Engels's use of gender (Source 4)?

THE BORDER LANDS

As the economic power of western and central Europe and the United States rapidly expanded in the nineteenth century, the lands bordering the industrializing powers found themselves compelled to respond to their neighbors' growing might. Individuals within Russia and the Ottoman empire sought to understand the origin of the industrializing nations' power—not simply their economic and technological advancements but also the causes of those advancements—and to understand if industrialization should be applied to their own countries and how they might do

---

[3] A French daily newspaper.

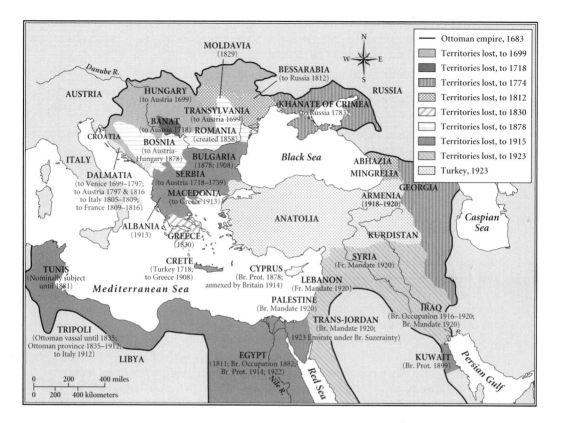

MAP 8.1 DECLINE OF THE OTTOMAN EMPIRE TO 1923

At the pinnacle of their power in the late seventeenth century, the Ottoman Turks ruled vast territories of land in Africa, Asia, and Europe. Beginning in 1699, however, Ottoman power waned, and a slow process of disintegration ensued where the Ottoman state lost territorial control over some lands and lost political control over others. The rising tide of nationalist sentiment in the nineteenth century particularly subverted Turkish authority in its distant provinces.

so. In nineteenth-century Russia, conflict developed between those who identified Russia's future with Europe (the Westernizers) and those who preferred Russia to chart a different and uniquely Slavic course (the Slavophiles, meaning "lovers of Slavic civilization").

The Ottoman empire, in contrast, had lost much of its former strength (Map 8.1). The Ottomans still held nominal authority over large portions of northern Africa, southwest Asia, and the Balkans; however, serious reforms were needed to strengthen "the sick man of Europe." Between 1839 and 1876, Ottoman bureaucrats initiated a reform movement known as the *Tanzimat* (meaning "reform" or "reorganization"). During the Tanzimat, Ottoman bureaucrats used European political and economic models to craft reforms for the Ottoman administrative structure, especially its military, legal, and educational institutions. Because these reforms challenged the power of Islamic religious institutions, Tanzimat reformers had to demonstrate that their proposed reforms corresponded with Islamic traditions. Whatever their opinion of industrial society, both reformers and their opponents in the Russian and Ottoman empires worked to identify the characteristics that created and defined the new industrial (Western) society.

6

". . . A PROFOUNDLY ATHEISTIC PEOPLE."

Vissarion Belinsky
Letter to N. V. Gogol, July 3, 1847

The son of a poor military surgeon, Vissarion Belinsky (1811–1848) became an influential literary critic who sought to reform Russian society and politics. Belinsky drew inspiration from western European liberalism and early utopian socialism but adapted these philosophies to an overwhelmingly agricultural Russia in which nobles dominated the peasantry. He called for educational and social reforms, including the emancipation of women, that would allow the Russian nation to develop into a mature society—mature according to the standards of its western European neighbors. Initially, Belinsky believed that the Russian author Nikolai Gogol (1809–1852) shared his views, and he promoted Gogol's early writings. When Gogol published Selected Passages from a Correspondence with Friends *in 1847, however, and defended the traditional Russian institutions of serfdom, autocracy, mysticism, and the Russian Orthodox church, Belinsky wrote a letter, excerpted below, that not only criticizes Gogol's book but also attacks the institutions Gogol had praised.*

Russia sees her salvation not in mysticism, nor asceticism, nor pietism, but in the successes of civilization, enlightenment and humanity. What she needs is not sermons (she has heard enough of them!) or prayers (she has repeated them too often!), but the awakening in the people of a sense of their human dignity lost for so many centuries amid the dirt and refuse; she needs rights and laws conforming not with the preaching of the church but with common sense and justice, and their strictest possible observance. Instead . . . she presents . . . a country [Russia] where there are not only no guarantees for individuality, honour and property, but even no police order, and where there is nothing but vast corporations of official thieves and robbers of various descriptions. The most vital national problems in Russia today are the abolition of serfdom and corporal punishments and the strictest possible observance of at least those laws which already exist. This is even realized by the government itself . . . , as is proven by its timid and abortive half-measures for

V. G. Belinsky, *Selected Philosophical Works* (Moscow: Foreign Languages Publishing House, 1956), 537–40, 543.

the relief of the white Negroes [Russian serfs] and the comical substitution of the single-lash knout by a cat-o'-three tails.[1]

Such are the problems which prey on the mind of Russia in her apathetic slumber! And at such a time a great writer [Gogol], whose beautifully artistic and deeply truthful works have so powerfully contributed towards Russia's awareness of herself, enabling her as they did to take a look at herself as though in a mirror—comes out with a book in which he teaches the barbarian landowner in the name of Christ and Church to make still greater profits out of the peasants and to abuse them still more. . . . And you would expect me not to become indignant? . . . Why, if you had made an attempt on my life I could not have hated you more than I do for these disgraceful lines. . . . And after this, you expect people to believe the sincerity of your book's intent! No! Had you really been inspired by the truth of Christ and not by the teaching of the Devil you would certainly have written something entirely different in your new book. You would have told the landowner that since his peasants are his brethren in Christ, and since a brother cannot be a slave to his brother, he should either give them their freedom, or, at least, allow them to enjoy the fruits of their own labour to their greatest possible benefit, realizing as he does, in the depths of his own conscience the false relationship in which he stands towards them. . . .

That you base such teaching on the Orthodox Church I can understand: it has always served as the prop of the knout and the servant of despotism; but why have you mixed Christ up in this? What in common have you found between Him and any church, least of all the Orthodox Church? He was the first to bring to people the teaching of freedom, equality and brotherhood[2] and set the seal of truth to that teaching by martyrdom. And this teaching was men's *salvation* only until it became organized in the Church and took the principle of Orthodoxy for its foundation. The Church, on the other hand, was a hierarchy, consequently a champion of inequality, a flatterer of authority, an enemy and persecutor of brotherhood among men—and so it has remained to this day. But the meaning of Christ's message has been revealed by the philosophical movement of the preceding century. And that is why a man like Voltaire[3] who stamped out the fires of fanaticism and ignorance in Europe by ridicule, is, of course, more the son of Christ, flesh of his flesh and bone of his bone, than all your priests, bishops, metropolitans and patriarchs—Eastern or Western. Do you mean to say you do not know it! It is not even a novelty now to a schoolboy. . . . [D]o you really mean to say you do not know that our clergy is held in universal contempt by Russian society and the Russian people? Of whom do the Russian people relate obscene stories? Of the priest, the priest's wife, the priest's daughter and the priest's farm hand. Does not the priest in Russia represent for all Russians the embodiment of gluttony, avarice, servility and shamelessness? Do you mean to say that you do not know all this? Strange! According to you the Russian people is the most religious in the world. That is a lie! The basis of religiousness is pietism, reverence, fear of God. Whereas the Russian man utters the name of the

---

[1] In accordance with the Russian Criminal Code of 1845, the single-lash knout was replaced with the cat-o'-three tails as an instrument of punishment.
[2] Slogan of the French Revolution associated with traditional liberalism.
[3] Voltaire, pen name of François Marie Arouet (1694–1778), French author and satirist.

Lord while scratching himself somewhere. He says of the icon: *if it isn't good for praying it's good for covering the pots.*

Take a closer look and you will see that it is by nature a profoundly atheistic people. It still retains a good deal of superstition, but not a trace of religiousness. . . .

[Y]our latest book has been an utter and disgraceful failure. And here the public is right, for it looks upon Russian writers as its only leaders, defenders and saviours against Russian autocracy, orthodoxy and nationality,[4] and therefore, while always prepared to forgive a writer a bad book, will never forgive him a pernicious book. This shows how much fresh and healthy intuition, albeit still in embryo, is latent in our society, and this likewise proves that it has a future. If you love Russia rejoice with me at the failure of your book!

---

[4] Motto used by Tsar Nicholas I in favor of traditional conservatism.

QUESTIONS FOR ANALYSIS

1. What does Belinsky criticize about Russian society? How do his issues of criticism compare to the positions supported in Western conservatism, liberalism, and socialism (see the chapter introduction)?

2. What values does Belinsky praise? How does he establish these as positive values?

3. In what different ways does Belinsky use Christianity in the text? Why does he emphasize the public reaction to Gogol's book?

4. In criticizing Russian society, how does Belinsky define a future for Russia in the tradition of Western liberalism?

7

"... EUROPEANIZATION, THE ORIGIN OF EVERY EVIL IN RUSSIA."

Nikolai Danilevsky
Russia and Europe (1869)

In his work Russia and Europe, *Nikolai Danilevsky (1822–1885) produced an influential defense of Slavophilism and a call for pan-Slavism (the unification of the Slavic peoples, usually under Russian leadership). Danilevsky believed that Latin-Germanic Europe marked a civilization distinct from and incompatible with the Slavic civilization exemplified by Russia. In Danilevsky's view, European civilization, following predetermined historical laws, had peaked in the sixteenth and seventeenth centuries and had since entered a long era of decline. Desperate to protect its power, Europe resisted decline by attacking its eventual successor, the ascending Slavic civilization. Russia, as the leader of Slavic civilization, needed to defend itself not only against Europe's mili-*

The Mind of Modern Russia: Historical and Political Thought of Russia's Great Age, ed. Hans Kohn (New York: Harper and Row, 1955), 200–204, 206–10.

tary encroachments but also against efforts to destroy Slavic civilization by importing European political, economic, and intellectual values into Russia. In the excerpt below, Danilevsky argues for the superiority of Slavic civilization.

And now let us turn to the Slav world, and chiefly to Russia, its only independent representative, in order to examine the results and the promises of this world, a world still only at the beginning of its cultural-historical life. We must examine it from the viewpoint of the . . . four foci of reference: religion, culture, politics, and socio-economic structure, in order to elucidate what we rightfully expect as well as hope from the Slav cultural-historical type.

Religion constituted the most essential element of ancient Russian life, and at the present time, the overwhelming spiritual interest of the ordinary Russian is also involved in it; in truth, one cannot but wonder at the ignorance and the impertinence of these people who could insist (to gratify their fantasies) on the religious indifference of the Russian people.

From an objective, factual viewpoint, the Russian and the majority of Slav peoples became, with the Greeks, the chief guardians of the living tradition of religious truth, Orthodoxy, and in this way they continued the high calling, which was the destiny of Israel and Byzantium:[1] to be the chosen people. . . .

If we turn to the political aspect . . . , the vast majority of the Slav tribes (at least two-thirds of them, if not more) have built a huge, continuous state, which has already had an existence of a thousand years and is all the time growing in strength and power in spite of the storms which it has had to weather during its long historical life. This one fact of the first magnitude demonstrates the political sense of the Slavs or at least of a significant majority of them. . . .

Here we may turn our attention to the special character of this political ability and show how it manifested itself during the growth of the Russian state. The Russians do not send out colonists to create new political societies, as the Greeks did in antiquity or the English in modern times. Russia does not have colonial possessions, like Rome or like England. The Russian state from early Muscovite times on has been Russia herself, gradually, irresistibly spreading on all sides, settling neighboring nonsettled territories, and assimilating into herself and into her national boundaries foreign populations. This basic character of Russian expansion was misunderstood because of the distortion of the original Russian point of view through Europeanization, the origin of every evil in Russia. . . .

But the expansion of the state, its attainment of stability, strength, and power, constitutes only one aspect of political activity. It has still another one, consisting of the establishment of equal relationships between the citizens themselves and between them and the state, i.e., in the establishment of civil and political freedom. A people not endowed with this freedom cannot be said to possess a healthy political sense. . . .

---

[1] The Jewish scriptures identify the Israelites as God's chosen people. According to the Russian Orthodox tradition, at the death of Jesus this status passed from the Jews to the Christians, particularly the Orthodox Christian tradition based in Byzantium (or Constantinople), from which the Russian Orthodox church evolved.

[T]here hardly ever has existed or exists a people so capable of enduring such a large share of freedom as the Russians and so little inclined to abuse it, due to their ability and habit to obey, their respect and trust in the authorities, their lack of love for power, and their loathing of interference in matters where they do not consider themselves competent. If we look into the causes of all political troubles, we shall find their root not in the striving after freedom, but in the love for power and the vain cravings of human beings to interfere in affairs that are beyond their comprehension. . . .

This nature of the Russian people is the true reason why Russia is the only state which never had (and in all probability never will have) a political revolution, i.e., a revolution having as its aim the limitation of the power of the ruler. . . .

Thus we may conclude that the Russian people, by their attitude towards the power of the state, by their ability to sacrifice to it their own personal interests, and by their attitude towards the use of political and civil freedom, are gifted with wonderful political sense.

In the socio-economic sphere, Russia is the only large state which has solid ground under its feet, in which there are no landless masses, and in which, consequently, the social edifice does not rest on the misery of the majority of the citizens and on the insecurity of their situation. In Russia, only, there cannot and does not exist any contradiction between political and economic ideals. This contradiction threatens disaster to European life, a life which has embarked on its historical voyage in the dangerous seas between the Charybdis of Caesarism or military despotism and the Scylla[2] of social revolution. The factors that give such superiority to the Russian social structure over the European, and give it an unshakable stability, are the peasant's land and its common ownership. On this health of Russia's socio-economic structure we found our hope for the great socio-economic significance of the Slav cultural-historical type. This type has been able for the first time to create a just and normal system of human activity, which embraces not only human relations in the moral and political sphere, but also man's mastery of nature, which is a means of satisfying human needs and requirements. Thus it establishes not only formal equality in the relations between citizens, but a real and concrete equality. . . .

The difficulty of the political task which was the lot of the Russian people was such that it is no wonder that it took one thousand years and demanded all the national energy. . . . In Russia, . . . where foreign enemies threatened on all sides, at first primarily from the East and later from the West, a lack of the governmental centralization needed to repel the enemies would inevitably have entailed the irrevocable loss of national independence.

Thus arose the need for the utmost concentration of governmental power, i.e., for an autocratic and monolithic government which would with unlimited strength drive and direct individual activity towards general goals. . . .

The requisite preliminary achievement of political independence has still another importance in the cultural as well as in all other spheres: the struggle against the Germano-Roman world (without which Slav independence is impossible) will help to eradicate the cancer of imitativeness and the servile attitude towards the West, which through unfavorable conditions has eaten its way into the Slav body and soul.

---

[2] In Greek mythology, the rock Scylla and the whirlpool-sea monster Charybdis presented sailors with two equally dangerous alternatives.

QUESTIONS FOR ANALYSIS

1. According to Danilevsky, what are the strengths of Slavic culture? In what ways does his version of Slavic identity reject western European liberalism?

2. According to Danilevsky, what threat is posed by the Germano-Roman world? Why would he predict the unlikelihood of political revolution in Russia?

3. How does Danilevsky understand the freedom of the Russian people? Compare Danilevsky's critique of Russian freedom and religion to Belinsky's critique (Source 6).

4. In discussing the "socio-economic sphere," how does Danilevsky's rejection of industrialization define industrialization as central to Western identity? On what basis does he assert the superiority of the Russian social structure?

8

". . . RESTING ON PILLARS OF JUSTICE AND CONSULTATION . . ."

Khayr al-Din al-Tunisi
The Surest Path   (1869)

Khayr al-Din al-Tunisi (1820s–1889), a Tunisian government official, implemented various political and educational reforms in Tunisia, which was an autonomous part of the Ottoman empire. Khayr al-Din was aware of the successes and failures of the early Tanzimat reforms and of the resistance raised to these reforms, especially by some Islamic religious officials who saw the reforms as challenging their dominance over many aspects of intellectual, cultural, and economic life. In 1869, Khayr al-Din published The Surest Path, *excerpted below, in which he defends the reform movement by providing Islamic theoretical and religious justifications for borrowing from European political, intellectual, and economic models.*

With God's help I have collected all possible information about European inventions related to economic and administrative policies, with reference to their situation in earlier times. . . .

The purpose in mentioning how the European kingdoms attained their present strength and worldly power is that we may choose what is suitable to our own circumstance which at the same time supports and is in accordance with our *shari'a*.[1] . . .

The first task is to spur on those statesmen and savants having zeal and resolution to seek all possible ways of improving the condition of the Islamic *umma*[2]

---

[1] Islamic holy law.
[2] Community of Muslims.

The Surest Path: The Political Testament of a Nineteenth-Century Muslim Statesman, trans. Leon Carl Brown (Cambridge: Harvard University Press, 1967), 73–74, 77–79, 81–84, 123–24, 129.

and of promoting the means of its development by such things as expanding the scope of the sciences and knowledge, smoothing the paths to wealth in agriculture and commerce, promoting all the industries and eliminating the causes of idleness. The basic requirement is good government from which is born that security, hope and proficiency in work to be seen in the European kingdoms. No further evidence is needed of this.

The second task is to warn the heedless among the Muslim masses against their persistent opposition to the behavior of others that is praiseworthy and in conformity with our Holy Law simply because they are possessed with the idea that all behavior and organizations of non-Muslims must be renounced, their books must be cast out and not mentioned, and anyone praising such things should be disavowed. This attitude is a mistake under any circumstances. . . .

[I]f we reflect on the situation of those critical Muslims and the European actions they approve of, we find them refusing to accept *tanzimat*[3] and its results while not avoiding other things which harm them. We see them vying with each other in clothing, home furnishings and such everyday needs just as in weapons and all military requirements. The truth is that all of these things are European products. There is no hiding the disgrace and the deficiencies in economic development and public policy which overtake the *umma* as a result. The disgrace is our needing outsiders for most necessities, indicating the backwardness of the *umma* in skills. . . .

As for political imperfections, the kingdom's need for others stands as an obstacle to its independence and a weakener of its vigor especially when linked to the need for military necessities which if easy to purchase in peacetime are not easy in time of war even at many times the value. There is no reason for all this except European technical progress resulting from *tanzimat* based on justice and liberty. How can a thinking man deprive himself of something which, in itself, he approves of? . . . [C]an we today attain such a level of preparation without progress in the skills and bases of growth to be seen among others? Can this progress be successful without our implementing political *tanzimat* comparable to those we see among others? These institutions are based on two pillars—justice and liberty—both of which are sources in our own Holy Law. It is well known that these two are the prerequisites for strength and soundness in all kingdoms. . . .

Europe has attained these ends and progress in the sciences and industries through *tanzimat* based on political justice, by smoothing the roads to wealth, and by extracting treasures of the earth with their knowledge of agriculture and commerce. The essential prerequisite for all of this is security and justice which have become the normal condition in their lands. It is God's custom in His world that justice, good management and an administrative system duly complied with be the causes of an increase in wealth, peoples and property, but that the contrary should cause a diminution in all of these things. This is well known from our Holy Law and from both Islamic and non-Islamic histories. . . .

Among the most important of the *shari'a* principles is the duty of consultation. . . .

---

[3] Meaning "reform" in general but also an Ottoman reform movement of the mid-nineteenth century that sought to introduce western European practices into the Ottoman empire.

Among the sayings of 'Ali,[4] may God be pleased with him, is, "There can be no right behavior when consultation has been omitted."...

[I]t is incumbent upon the '*ulama*[5] and the notables of the *umma* to resist evil. The Europeans have established councils and have given freedom to the printing presses. In the Islamic *umma* the kings fear those who resist evil just as the kings of Europe fear the councils and the opinions of the masses that proceed from them and from the freedom of the press. The aim of the two [i.e., European and Muslim] is the same—to demand an accounting from the state in order that its conduct may be upright, even if the roads leading to this end may differ....

The Islamic *umma* is bound in its religious and worldly activities by the heavenly *shar*'[6] and by the divine limits, fixed by the justest of scales, which are sufficient guarantee both for this world and the next. Now, there are certain important, or even absolutely essential activities relating to the public interest by which the *umma* secures its prosperity and proper organization. If there is no specific rule in the *shar*' either providing for or forbidding such actions, and if instead the principles of the *shari'a* require these actions in general and view them with a favorable eye, then the course to follow is whatever is required by the interests of the *umma*. Any activity for this purpose so that conditions are improved and a great victory achieved in the domain of progress is contingent upon the unity and organization of a group from within the *umma* who are in harmony—those learned in the *shari'a* and those knowledgeable in politics and the interests of the *umma* and also well-informed both in domestic and foreign affairs and in the origins both of harms and benefits. This group would cooperate to the benefit of the *umma* by furthering its interests and warding off its corruptions so that all would act as a single person.... Thus, the politicians discern the public interest and the sources of harm while the '*ulama* assure that the action taken in accordance with the public interest is in agreement with the principles of the *shari'a*....

Thus one of the most important duties imposed upon the princes of Islam, their ministers and the '*ulama* of the *shari'a* is their joining together in the establishment of *tanzimat* resting on pillars of justice and consultation, which will secure education of the subjects, improve their circumstances in a manner which will plant love of the homeland in their breasts and make them aware of the benefit accruing to them both individually and collectively. Then they will not heed the gossip of certain rash persons that these *tanzimat* are not suitable for the condition of the Islamic *umma*.

QUESTIONS FOR ANALYSIS

1. What does Khayr al-Din identify as the central components of European progress? How does Khayr al-Din situate these components within an Islamic context?

2. Why might he do so? What evidence does he use to make this argument?

3. How does Khayr al-Din's description of Islamic political-religious arrangements compare to the ideals of western European liberalism?

---

[4] Muhammad 'Ali (c. 600–661), son-in-law and cousin of Muhammad.
[5] The learned community of Islam, which produces religious teachers.
[6] Islamic holy law.

"WHAT A CHIC OUTFIT. . . ."

Ottoman Cartoons (1909 and 1911)

Throughout the Tanzimat era and continuing under the reign of Abd ül-Hamid, Otto-man officials implemented progressive reforms but carefully censored the press to stifle criticism and preclude widespread debate about growing European economic and cultural influences, especially in the cosmopolitan Ottoman capital of Istanbul. When Abd ül-Hamid's regime collapsed in 1908, hundreds of new newspapers, journals, and gazettes sprang into existence and expressed pent-up anxieties about these influences. These publications neither consistently supported nor rejected the reform movement

Man: *What a chic outfit. How much did it cost you?*
Woman: *My husband gave me five dollars, but it cost twenty.*

I can no longer bear these old iron balls. I will break the fetters that bind my legs!

but tended to endorse Turkish nationalism, often personified in cartoons as a Turkish woman. The appearance of women in public was regulated by Ottoman and Muslim law and social norms. Since the mid-nineteenth century, wealthy Ottoman women had adopted French fashions; however, in public they traditionally covered their French-styled dresses with two-piece garments that hid their hair and bodies and covered their faces with a light veil. In addition, young women did not go out alone in public or interact with strange men. Reprinted here are two cartoons that appeared during these years of press freedom. The first appeared in the gazette Kalem in 1911 and depicts two individuals who chat while passing on the street. The second appeared in the gazette Laklak in 1909 and depicts a woman in traditional Turkish garb representing Ottoman constitutionalism. The iron balls by which she is weighed down read "ignorance" and "capitulations," the latter referring to economic privileges that the Ottoman state had long granted to European powers.

QUESTIONS FOR ANALYSIS

1. How does the first cartoon express anxieties over European influences? What aspects of Ottoman society are threatened by European influences?

2. How does the second cartoon express anxieties over European influences? On what is Ottoman hopefulness based?

3. How does the second cartoon also accept European influences? Compare the inferences made by the second cartoon to Khayr al-Din's effort to integrate European practices into Islamic traditions (Source 8)?

4. How does the second cartoon present a more virtuous image of Ottoman women than the first cartoon does?

CHAPTER QUESTIONS

1. What similarities and differences exist between liberalism as expressed within western Europe (Mill and Ure) and liberalism as adopted by Belinsky and Khayr al-Din? What similarities and differences exist between reactions against liberalism within western Europe (Marx and Engels) and the reaction against liberalism by Danilevsky?

2. What similarities and differences exist between Belinsky's and Khayr al-Din's efforts to adapt western European ideals to Russian and Ottoman contexts?

3. To what aspects of political and economic liberalism are individuals in the borderland most strongly attracted and which do they react against? How do these responses compare to earlier examples of responses to European ideals and practices by the Chinese scholar-bureaucrats (Chapter 3, Source 5), by Toussaint-L'Ouverture (Chapter 6, Source 9), and by al-Jabarti (Chapter 7, Source 3)?

Chapter 9

THE FIRST OPIUM WAR

Seventeenth-century Jesuit missionaries had promoted an image of the Chinese as builders of a great civilization that warranted respect, admiration, and even emulation by Europeans (Chapter 3)—more so than any other living civilization. Beginning in the eighteenth century, however, some authors and philosophers of the Enlightenment challenged that image (Chapter 5). This rethinking of China was reinforced by trade tensions that had been growing since the 1720s between China and the European colonial powers, especially Britain. The Qing dynasty that ruled China responded to the growing number of foreign merchants visiting its shores by placing heavy restrictions on trade between China and the European powers: all trade was restricted to the port of Guangzhou (formerly Canton), foreigners could reside in that city only from October through March, and all trade (and official contact) had to be conducted through the Hong merchant guild. Despite these restrictions, when the British East India Company began to consolidate its authority over the Indian subcontinent in the 1760s, British merchants used their Indian bases to seek further trade with China. As they sent large sums of silver bullion into China to obtain growing quantities of silks, porcelains, and teas, British merchants became concerned that a serious trade deficit had developed for themselves, especially because the Qing state actively discouraged the importation of European manufactured goods. In their new Indian territories, however, the British discovered a product that would find a large market in China—opium.

The opium poppy grew luxuriantly in regions of northern India, and the British soon organized the production and sale of opium as a cash crop that brought profits to the East India Company. In 1773, the British transported to China about 1,000 chests of opium (each chest contained 130 to 160 pounds of opium), and by 1790, British merchants had increased their sales to 4,000 chests. Trade grew slowly during the wars of the French Revolution and Napoleon, reaching only around 5,000 chests in 1815, but afterward trade boomed, reaching 7,000 chests by 1823, 13,000 by 1828, 23,600 by 1832, and 40,000 by 1838. By the 1820s, enough British opium was entering China to sustain the habits of 1 million addicts, and Qing officials became increasingly alarmed. British officials also were becoming concerned with opium consumption in Britain itself, where the drug was unregulated and widely consumed as a sedative and for many ailments. By the 1830s, the Parliament launched investigations into opium use in Britain, especially among the lower classes. Nevertheless, for British merchants and the East India Company, the opium trade had become an exceptionally profitable enterprise that had to be defended. For the Qing dynasty, the opium trade had become a problem to which it had to respond (Map 9.1).

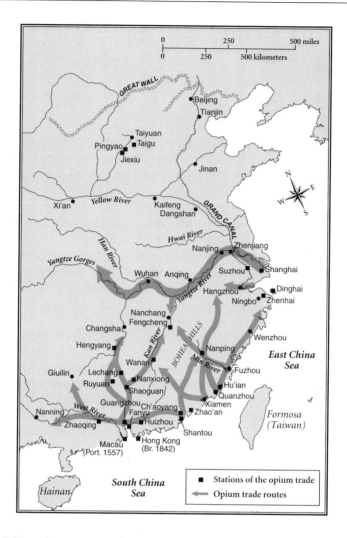

MAP 9.1 THE OPIUM TRADE IN CHINA

The opium trade followed traditional trade routes along China's waterways, moving deep into the interior of China.

THE OPIUM CRISIS

In the 1830s, the scholar-bureaucrats who governed China debated among themselves how best to respond to the growing opium crisis. Some factions believed that the opium trade should be legalized, regulated to prevent its worst abuses, and taxed to benefit a government in constant need of revenues. By the late 1830s, however, as the influx of opium continued to rise, the Emperor Daoguang sided with scholar-bureaucrats who favored stronger, and more strongly enforced, prohibitions on the trade. In 1838, Daoguang issued a new decree banning all traffic in opium and appointed Lin Zexu "special imperial commissioner" to implement his will.

When he arrived in Guangzhou in March 1839, Lin acted quickly to suppress the opium trade. He punished Chinese participants in the drug trade and issued an edict that required foreign merchants to hand over all opium on board their ships within three days. When the merchants refused, Lin issued an arrest warrant for one of the most prominent British merchants, Lancelot Dent. Supported by the merchant community and by the British superintendant, Charles Elliot, Dent refused to hand himself over to the imperial commissioner, which led Lin to blockade the foreign settlement in Guangzhou. Elliot then ordered the British merchants to deliver their 20,000 chests of opium to him, and he handed over the opium to Lin. The blockade remained for forty-seven days until all the opium was delivered. Lin destroyed the confiscated opium and further demanded that the foreign merchants sign bonds that they would never again participate in the opium trade, on pain of death.

Prior to the dramatic events of 1839, the opium trade was little known in Britain. A small anti-opium clique, led by Protestant missionary societies, had decried the trade on moral grounds but to little public notice. After the actions of Commissioner Lin, however, public debate within Britain grew with regard to the opium trade and the appropriate British response to the Chinese seizure of British property. The British merchants in Guangzhou designated William Jardine as their agent in London to lobby for government intervention to support the opium trade. They provided Jardine with $20,000—one dollar for each chest of confiscated opium— to wage a propaganda war in the London newspapers in favor of the trade and to demand financial compensation from Parliament for the 20,000 chests of opium the merchants had handed over to Elliot, an official of the British government, who had handed it over to the Chinese. These debates continued throughout the period of military conflict, which the British government decided to launch in the fall of 1839 under pressure from British mercantile interests and in favor of free trade.

1

"... WHERE IS YOUR CONSCIENCE?"

Lin Zexu

Letter to Queen Victoria (1839)

Lin Zexu (1785–1850) was a well-respected scholar and government official when appointed "special imperial commissioner" by Emperor Daoguang. In Guangzhou, Lin used legal authority, coercion, reason, and moral suasion to attack the trade and use of opium by both the Chinese and the "barbarian" British. After his seizure of British

Ssu-yu Teng and John K. Fairbank, *China's Response to the West: A Documentary Survey* (Cambridge: Harvard University Press, 1965), 24–27.

opium in 1839, Lin wrote a letter to Britain's Queen Victoria, excerpted below, that appealed to her moral responsibility to control her subjects' activities.

The kings of your honorable country by a tradition handed down from generation to generation have always been noted for their politeness and submissiveness. We have read your successive tributary memorials[1] saying, "In general our countrymen who go to trade in China have always received His Majesty the Emperor's gracious treatment and equal justice," and so on. Privately we are delighted with the way in which the honorable rulers of your country deeply understand the grand principles and are grateful for the Celestial grace. For this reason the Celestial Court[2] in soothing those from afar has redoubled its polite and kind treatment. The profit from trade has been enjoyed by them continuously for two hundred years. This is the source from which your country has become known for its wealth.

But after a long period of commercial intercourse, there appear among the crowd of barbarians[3] both good persons and bad, unevenly. Consequently there are those who smuggle opium to seduce the Chinese people and so cause the spread of the poison to all provinces. Such persons who only care to profit themselves, and disregard their harm to others, are not tolerated by the laws of heaven and are unanimously hated by human beings. His Majesty the Emperor, upon hearing of this, is in a towering rage. . . .

We find that your country is sixty or seventy thousand *li*[4] from China. Yet there are barbarian ships that strive to come here for trade for the purpose of making a great profit. The wealth of China is used to profit the barbarians. That is to say, the great profit made by barbarians is all taken from the rightful share of China. By what right do they then in return use the poisonous drug to injure the Chinese people? Even though the barbarians may not necessarily intend to do us harm, yet in coveting profit to an extreme, they have no regard for injuring others. Let us ask, where is your conscience? I have heard that the smoking of opium is very strictly forbidden by your country;[5] that is because the harm caused by opium is clearly understood. Since it is not permitted to do harm to your own country, then even less should you let it be passed on to the harm of other countries—how much less to China! Of all that China exports to foreign countries, there is not a single thing which is not beneficial to people: they are of benefit when eaten, or of benefit when used, or of benefit when resold: all are beneficial. Is there a single article from China which has done any harm to foreign countries? Take tea and rhubarb, for example; the foreign countries cannot get along for a single day without them. If China cuts off these benefits with no sympathy for those who are to suffer, then what can the barbarians rely upon to keep themselves alive? Moreover the woolens,

---

[1] Official statements from one government to another, accompanying tributary gifts.
[2] Traditional term for the Chinese imperial court.
[3] British merchants.
[4] Three *li* equal roughly one mile.
[5] Lin is incorrect in this statement. Opium was not illegal in Britain but was consumed in numerous forms and prescribed by many physicians for various ailments.

camlets, and longells[6] of foreign countries cannot be woven unless they obtain Chinese silk. If China, again, cuts off this beneficial export, what profit can the barbarians expect to make? As for other foodstuffs, beginning with candy, ginger, cinnamon, and so forth, and articles for use, beginning with silk, satin, chinaware, and so on, all the things that must be had by foreign countries are innumerable. On the other hand, articles coming from the outside to China can only be used as toys. We can take them or get along without them. Since they are not needed by China, what difficulty would there be if we closed the frontier and stopped the trade? Nevertheless our Celestial Court lets tea, silk, and other goods, be shipped without limit and circulated everywhere without begrudging it in the slightest. This is for no other reason but to share the benefit with the people of the whole world.

The goods from China carried away by your country not only supply your own consumption and use, but also can be divided up and sold to other countries, producing a triple profit. Even if you do not sell opium, you still have this threefold profit. How can you bear to go further, selling products injurious to others in order to fulfill your insatiable desire? . . .

We have further learned that in London, the capital of your honorable rule, and in Scotland, Ireland, and other places, originally no opium has been produced. Only in several places of India under your control . . . has opium been planted from hill to hill, and ponds have been opened for its manufacture. For months and years work is continued in order to accumulate the poison. The obnoxious odor ascends, irritating heaven and frightening the spirits. Indeed you, O King, can eradicate the opium plant in these places, hoe over the fields entirely, and sow in its stead the five grains.[7] Anyone who dares again attempt to plant and manufacture opium should be severely punished. This will really be a great, benevolent government policy that will increase the common weal and get rid of evil. For this, Heaven must support you and the spirits must bring you good fortune, prolonging your old age and extending your descendants. . . .

Now we have set up regulations governing the Chinese people. He who sells opium shall receive the death penalty and he who smokes it also the death penalty. Now consider this: if the barbarians do not bring opium, then how can the Chinese people resell it, and how can they smoke it? The fact is that the wicked barbarians beguile the Chinese people into a death trap. How then can we grant life only to these barbarians? He who takes the life of even one person still has to atone for it with his own life; yet is the harm done by opium limited to the taking of one life only? Therefore in the new regulations, in regard to those barbarians who bring opium to China, the penalty is fixed at decapitation or strangulation. This is what is called getting rid of a harmful thing on behalf of mankind. . . .

May you, O King, check your wicked and sift your vicious people before they come to China, in order to guarantee the peace of your nation, to show further the sincerity of your politeness and submissiveness, and to let the two countries enjoy together the blessings of peace. How fortunate, how fortunate indeed!

---

[6] Types of textiles.

[7] Wheat, barley, and so on.

QUESTIONS FOR ANALYSIS

1. What different types of arguments (e.g., ethical, religious, economic, etc.) does Lin make to convince Victoria to act against the opium trade?

2. How does Lin establish China's superiority over Great Britain? How does Lin establish the Chinese emperor as a moral example that Victoria should follow?

3. What authority does Lin assume that Victoria has as queen? Why might he make those assumptions?

2

". . . WE HOLD OUR EASTERN EMPIRE BY MORAL POWER. . . ."

Algernon Thelwell
The Iniquities of the Opium Trade with China (1839)

The Reverend Algernon Thelwell (1795–1863) was secretary to the Trinitarian Bible Society and an active figure in London's religious community. Sometime in the late 1830s, his attention was drawn to the opium trade, and he determined to rouse British public opinion to oppose it. In 1839, he published The Iniquities of the Opium Trade with China, *even though he as yet was unaware of the most recent events in China surrounding the opium trade and had no personal experience with the trade or with China. Following the practice of the age, Thelwell quoted frequently from previous authors' writings on the opium trade. Thelwell's arguments, excerpted below, brought much wider recognition to the anti-opium movement and clarified the moral argument against the opium trade.*

Remarkable, and most deeply—most intensely interesting, is the present position of our country. Ruling an empire upon which the sun never sets—possessed of an extent of dominion, such as Rome in her greatest glory never saw—and containing a population, with which no empire upon earth but that of China can compare,—Great Britain, in regard to all the elements of earthly glory,—in regard to power, dominion, and wealth,—seems indeed to be lifted up as an object of admiration and envy to the whole world. And great in proportion to the glory and exaltation of our country, must be her responsibility in the sight of Him, before whom all nations are counted as the drop on the bucket, and as the small dust of the balance. And the consideration of this responsibility becomes the more solemn, when we consider the vast multitudes of *Heathen* that are subject to the British sceptre. . . .

Algernon Thelwell, *The Iniquities of the Opium Trade with China* (London: Allen, 1839), 134–37, 141–46.

What but the special help and blessing of Almighty God can possibly uphold and preserve us? and, under this, that moral strength which is founded on the deep respect, if not the affectionate gratitude, of those with whom we have to do; and, more especially, of the nations that are subjected to our sway, and dependent on our protection?

But has our conduct been in the generations that are past, or is in *now,* such as is calculated to secure either the blessing of the Most High, or the deep respect and affectionate gratitude of the people under our dominion, or those with whom, in various ways, we are connected? . . .

Let us look at the facts of the Opium Trade with China; and *then* let each put home to his own conscience the plain question, Is this traffic calculated to bring upon us, as a nation, the blessing of the Most High? or to gain for us the respect and affection of the inhabitants of Eastern Asia, to whom those facts are known? . . .

Is it self-evident, that we hold our Eastern Empire by *moral power,* and not by *physical strength*? And do we acknowledge the vast importance of that *moral power,* which is greater than fleets and armies?

Is it, indeed, one of the foremost elements of national strength and greatness, and one of the strongest bulwarks of national security? If so, how stands our national character in the East, with reference hereunto? How *is* this affected?—How *must* this be affected—by the fact, that, while we profess and call ourselves Christians, in opposition to the poor idolatrous Heathen,—enlightened and civilized, in opposition to a dark and ignorant, and (at best) semi-barbarous people,—we are seen continually implicated in iniquities, which the natives of India and of China have discernment enough to look upon with detestation? The heathen government of China has long regarded opium smoking, and the opium trade, with such just and merited abhorence, that it utterly refuses to grow rich, and to increase its resources, by the sanction of one or the other! Shall *we,* then, consent, as Christians and as Britons, to lend ourselves to this traffic? to amass wealth by dealing in poison? to be judged in the eyes of half the population of the world—to have our national character estimated among five hundred millions of our fellow-creatures, mainly by the obvious, well-known fact, that *thus* it is that we grow rich? and that we have so little sense of the very first principles of right and justice, that we countenance and abet our countrymen in this daring, persevering, systematic violation of the laws and regulations of a country, with which we are at peace? For this we do,— so long as, unhindered and unrebuked, we permit them to go on (as they have done for more than forty years) in smuggling Opium into China. . . .

But are we concerned for something more—for something better—than mere temporal dominion? Are any of my readers interested in the success of Christian Missions, and in the progress of the Gospel among the countless inhabitants of Eastern Asia? I do not question, for one moment, the absolute omnipotence of that influence from on high, which alone can give success to the preached Gospel; but I know that the Scriptures do not warrant us to expect the blessing, when our iniquities have separated between us and our God, and our sins have hid His face from us, that He will not hear, (Isiah 49:2): nor to think that the Word of God will have free course and be glorified, when the name of God and His Anointed is blasphemed among the heathen, on account of the open, notorious vices of those who profess and call themselves Christians. What kind of attention do we give ourselves to the man, who lifts up his voice like a trumpet to preach the Gospel, but contradicts every word that he utters by the more intelligible language of his life? *Deeds, not words,* is a principle, which the poorest slave in India, or in China, can readily comprehend: and, while we connive at gross, atrocious, systematic iniquity, can we, or dare we, expect, that the cause of the Gospel should prosper in our hands? . . . And when we preach to the heathen, may *they* not fitly say, "Go, preach to your own countrymen. Persuade them to cease from that traffic in poison, by which they grow rich themselves, and murder us." But why should I enlarge upon this point? . . . It is only needful to add, that it is not in China alone, but throughout the length and breadth of Eastern Asia, wheresoever the facts are known, that this traffic brings disgrace and scandal on the Christian name, and effectually hinders the progress of the Christian Missions.

QUESTIONS FOR ANALYSIS

1. According to Thelwell, what is the foundation of Britain's power over its empire, and how must Britain act to maintain its power? What evidence does he give to verify this assertion?
2. According to Thelwell, what are the political consequences of acting sinfully?
3. What is Thelwell's view of the Chinese and Indians? How does he praise them and degrade them?
4. How do Thelwell's attitudes toward China compare to Lin Zexu's attitudes toward Britain (Source 1)? How does each express his sense of cultural superiority?

3

". . . NO PRETENCE IS TOO BARE-FACED, NO LIE TOO MONSTROUS. . . ."

Samuel Warren
The Opium Question   (1840)

A barrister and best-selling author, Samuel Warren (1807–1877) published in early 1840 The Opium Question—*a cogent and explicit statement in support of the British opium merchants. Warren most likely wrote the pamphlet with the financial support of William Jardine, a leading opium merchant who had been provided funds by the British merchants in China to finance a propaganda war in London in their favor. In* The Opium Question, *Warren took on several tasks. Most centrally, he argued that*

Samuel Warren, *The Opium Question* (London: Ridgway, 1840), 61, 64, 72–77, 114–15, 117–18.

the British government owed financial recompense to the British merchants who had turned over their opium to Charles Elliot, the British Superintendant of Trade in China, who in turn had turned over the opium to Commissioner Lin. Warren, however, moved beyond such legal arguments. As the excerpt below suggests, for Warren the commercial conflict with China was broader than simply an issue of opium.

To proceed, however, to the main question forced into this part of the case:—Is the trade in opium an *immoral* trade; and ought the country, on that ground, to refuse to recognize the claims now under consideration,[1] which have arisen out of it? On this score no inconsiderable feeling has been excited in several quarters. The vilest and most sordid motives are attributed to the opium merchants, who are represented as, for their own miserable gain, corrupting the morals and destroying the lives of the Chinese. The Emperor is presented to us in a noble, a sublime attitude . . .—disdaining to enrich his treasury with a revenue derived from so polluted a source; a Pagan, shaming the vices of Christians, and by his disinterested and virtuous conduct challenging the sympathies and admiration of all mankind. . . .

That the Emperor of China opposes, or that we are given by his representatives to understand that he opposes, and that vehemently, the introduction of opium into his dominions, is admitted; the question is, what is his REAL GROUND for doing so? Is it a paternal and virtuous regard for the morals and health of his people, or does it arise from a very different cause, a chimerical *dread of draining the silver out of his dominions,* and a desire to FORCE US TO A DIFFERENT FOOTING OF COMMERCE— FROM SALE TO BARTER? . . .

[*Warren reviews a long series of Chinese edicts that indicate that the Chinese government feared the exportation of silver to purchase opium more than the importation of opium itself.*]

Surely the above evidence is conclusive to establish the fact, whatever importance, in any view, may be attached to it, that the Emperor's apprehension of the injury inflicted by opium on the minds and health of his people, is not a genuine apprehension; but is assumed only as a device to cloke his real wishes and purposes. The true state of the case is this. The Chinese, having long felt uneasy, under a suspicion of the fact, have at length made the discovery, that the balance of trade is fairly against them. That however great the advantages they have so long derived from foreign commerce, they have not been sufficiently sagacious and sharp-sighted, to deal with their "barbarian" competitors in traffic. In spite of all their petty vexatious shifts and devices, during a long series of years, they find the scale constantly inclining towards the foreigners; and are at length making desperate efforts— the mere spasms of weakness, however—to retrieve a fancied false position. This affords a key to their whole conduct; it throws a new light on all their documents. Their dread of exhausting the silver of their country is indeed ridiculous and chimerical. . . .

---

[1] Claims by British merchants for financial reimbursement from the British government.

Had we been content ... to take the produce and manufactures of the Chinese in exchange for our opium; not only to take goods for our opium, but bring our silver for *their* goods, which shows the extent to which the Chinese were disposed to go in their demands—does any one that has read the foregoing pages believe that we should ever have heard of these their wild denunciations of the drug, or experienced the monstrous extent of fraud, insult, and outrage which they have at last presumed to inflict upon us? ...

Any one not thoroughly familiar with the character of the Chinese would be charmed by the simplicity, gentleness, and virtue breathing in all the documents which they design to come before the eyes of foreigners. The Emperor here speaks as the Patriarch—the virtuous and pious father of his people, whose best interests he cherishes with the fondest jealousy, and would promote by every act of his life. Alas! how much reason is there to believe that on a near inspection nothing is visible but fraud, hypocrisy, and falsehood! With the Chinese, no pretence is too barefaced, no lie too monstrous, to be resorted to, in order to conceal an object, or gain an end. The author of these remarks was one who was for some time deluded, by these means, into the persuasion that the Chinese, though a quaint, eccentric, and violent people, were full of simplicity and straightforwardness; but the more he read of their documents, and the better he became acquainted with the history of our intercourse with that people, the more quickly were his opinions changed to contempt and indignation at their meanness and insincerity. ...

ADDITION. 14th January, 1840 ...

Events have just taken place in China which are without a parallel in our national experience. Our countrymen, under the full protection of the British flag, and under the sanction of British authority, resident in China, in pursuit of the objects of national commerce, have—since the happening of the events commemorated in the preceding pages—been most ignominiously expelled from China; British property to a great amount has been again sacrificed; British blood has been wantonly shed, by the Chinese, under circumstances of revolting barbarity; one of our countrymen has been dreadfully mangled and mutilated; the known Representative of the Queen of Great Britain has been treated with signal and evidently premeditated indignity and violence, by the representative of the Emperor of China; attempted to be forcibly cut off from all supplies of food; and his vessel, bearing the British Flag, has been fired upon, and obliged in self-defence to return the fire. Attempts, it seems, were made to *poison the wells* supplying our countrymen with water. ...

And what now? Has enough been AT LENGTH done to rouse us from our long apathy,—to make us start indignant from our posture of cringing and ignominious humiliation? Must all this also be submitted to? Must we still kiss the rod of the Emperor of China? Or are we, at this moment, at open war with China? ...

[Commissioner Lin] is at this moment probably gloating over ... the immortal renown in China which he is earning by his present wise, vigorous, and successful proceedings against Great Britain. He may believe that he has at length effectually vindicated the dignity of the Celestial Empire; exalting it as high as he has plunged us, barbarians, into degradation and dishonour. He imagines, perhaps, that henceforth no more silver shall "ooze out from the ports of China;" and that if the "reverently submissive Tributary," the Queen of Great Britain, henceforth desire the produce of China, she must pay for them in her own silver.—These, and such like, may be the dreams of LIN, till awoke by quite a novel sound, and quite a novel sight—the military and naval force of Great Britain, suddenly disturbing all the ancient fooleries of his nation, and giving him and the Sublime Emperor a somewhat new and astounding view of the "petty barbarians," whom he has insulted, oppressed, and tyrannized over so long. He may find his Celestial master's junks blown out of the water, and his forts crumbling into dust beneath the cannonading of his puny and despised opponents; all his ports blockaded—in short, the shock may abate the fever which for centuries has inflated that strange people to such a pitch of presumption, and make them fit for intercourse with the civilized world.

QUESTIONS FOR ANALYSIS

1. According to Warren, what is the basis for the conflict between China and Britain?
2. How do Warren's argument and image of the Chinese emperor compare to Algernon Thelwell's (Source 2) and Lin Zexu's (Source 1)? How does each express his own sense of cultural superiority?
3. What evidence does Warren present to verify his claims? Of what importance is it that Warren "was for some time deluded" but that eventually "his opinions changed"?
4. How does Warren seek to shift the debate from a moral issue to an economic issue? How does he also fail to do so?

"THE VIOLENT DEATH INFLICTED UPON THE LUCRATIVE OPIUM TRAFFIC . . ."

Bombay Times
Editorial of May 23, 1839

The Bombay Times *was a British newspaper published in India that circulated widely among the large British community there, which included East India Company officials, military personnel, government administrators, merchants, and missionaries. It reported on the growing conflict between China and Great Britain in the context of issues of concern to the British community in India. The British Indian perspective had*

"Editorial," *Bombay Times*, May 23, 1839, reprinted in *Times* (London), September 27, 1839, 6.

great influence in Great Britain because newspapers in Britain had difficulty obtaining current information on events in Asia and therefore republished articles from British newspapers in India. The article below, appearing in the May 23, 1839, Bombay Times *and republished in the September 27, 1839,* Times *(London), demonstrates how Indian concerns shaped such news reports.*

There exists, we believe, but one opinion as to the character of those extraordinary events which have just occurred in China, and the vast influence which they must inevitably exercise upon the condition and prospects of India. The least attentive observer of the passing scene must have long since perceived that the opium trade carried on between this country and China had assumed far more than merely commercial interests. When we reflect that the annual revenue derived by the Indian Government[1] from this source had grown to the enormous sum of between 1,000,000*l.* and 2,000,000*l.* sterling,[2] we cannot but feel that the late events possess a political importance superior to that derived from their commercial character, and, in speculating upon their national results, we almost forget the vast individual interests which are at stake. But the general question of the opium trade must be viewed in another aspect of far deeper moment than that derived from its commercial or political importance; its direct bearings upon public health (of mind as well as body), upon social intercourse between distant countries, and, above all, upon national and individual morality and happiness, claim for it the most serious consideration. . . .

The late proceedings of the Chinese Government, viewed merely in their probable results upon the present prosperity of this country, are unquestionably discouraging to the advocates of Indian improvement.[3] The sudden vigor displayed by the newly appointed imperial delegates during the last year, in driving the trade from what they term "the inner waters,"[4] was looked upon by most persons with contempt, as the ebullition of fictitious zeal not yet bribed into connivance. Others, with a more discerning eye, perceived that the opium traffic, in all its branches, was drawing rapidly to a close, but congratulated themselves upon the fact that, owing to the notorious weakness of the Chinese Government, the extinction of that trade would necessarily be tedious and difficult, thus happily affording to our Indian statesmen the opportunity of gradually contracting the cultivation of the poppy in this country, and providing for the deficiency in its annual revenue by devising new sources of income, or, if necessary, by instituting further retrenchments. How little even the best informed among us appear to understand the genius of Chinese institutions! The [Chinese] Government, whose imbecility all had agreed in despising, suddenly puts forth its hand, and with a vigor which, perhaps, no other in the world could emulate. In one week the traffic has been utterly destroyed; not by the

---

[1] The Indian government was under the direction of the British East India Company, which shared power with a government-approved Board of Control in London.
[2] British monetary unit.
[3] British officials within India sought to implement many economic, political, and social reforms, all based on European models.
[4] Waterways leading into Guangzhou.

slow withering of its stem, but, to use their own official phrase, by cutting up its roots. An immense annual revenue is thus rudely torn from the hands of the Indian Government, at the very moment when, to meet the vast expenditure attending its present military operations, an increased income has become almost indispensable. Viewed in this light, we fear that the late occurrences in China will prove a serious obstruction in the way of those measures of improvement which the public, both here and at home, have of late been so anxiously looking for. The establishment of a national system of education upon a proper basis; the construction of roads and canals; the introduction of an improved system of police and magistracy; these, and all such schemes of public utility, necessarily demand a great pecuniary outlay. The violent death inflicted upon the lucrative opium traffic, and the military attitude which we have so suddenly been called on to assume, must, we fear, in some degree, postpone these happy changes. It is well if the people of Great Britain, and more especially those upon whom the destinies of this country immediately devolve, should learn that they must be ready to encounter great difficulties, perhaps to make great sacrifices, in executing those duties which they owe to their own real interests, no less than to the interests of the people over whom they rule.

Serious as these financial embarrassments unquestionably are, they appear to us, however, merely of a transient character. . . . But those losses, whoever may be the sufferer, cannot permanently interfere with Indian prosperity. The ground, the labor, the enterprise, and the capital, which are at present devoted to the production of opium, will, assuredly, not continue long idle. Other articles of export will no doubt soon be discovered, and we may possibly devise some which may secure to us all the advantages we have up to the present time derived from the poppy, without inflicting upon our fellows the awful evils which we have hitherto distributed amongst them. Before the origin of the opium trade, cotton-wool was the great article of export from this country to China, and would, doubtless, have increased to an amazing extent, but that the exorbitant profits derived from the former source had rendered every other article contemptible in the public eye. Judging from the proclamation of the Imperial commissioner,[5] the Chinese are willing to receive every thing at our hands, except this one prescribed commodity. "Suppose," observes his Excellency, "that you did not carry on this traffic in opium any longer, then the quantum of legal business that you did would be much increased, and so much more, consequently, would be the profit that you would reap; thus you might get riches before, and your consciences being void of offense, and no evil deeds laying in store for you against a day of retribution, how happy, how joyful might you feel; but if you are determined to carry on the trade in opium, it must cause your general intercourse with us to stop." We agree in the views of political economy thus ably propounded by his Excellency.

QUESTIONS FOR ANALYSIS

1. How does the author link the opium trade to the concerns of British India? How does the author respond to the problems raised by the conflict over opium?

---

[5] Lin Zexu (1785–1850), imperial commissioner appointed by the Chinese emperor to destroy the opium trade in China.

2. What are the author's attitudes toward the opium trade and toward China?
3. How does the author indicate a respect for the Chinese response to the opium traffic and its suppression?
4. How does the author establish a calm, reasoned tone in his article? Why might such a tone be important to the author?

5

"WE REPUDIATE THEIR CLAIM. . . ."

Leeds Mercury
Editorial of September 7, 1839

Not until the late summer and early fall of 1839 did news about the merchant crisis in China begin to filter back to Britain, due to a six-month delay in communication between China and Great Britain. The British Foreign Office, under the direction of Foreign Secretary Lord Palmerston, kept official government information closely guarded. As newspapers and magazines began to cover the story, they sought information on China wherever possible. Interested parties such as William Jardine provided information and other inducements to promote publications favorable to the opium merchants. Newspapers also turned to Christian missionaries who had knowledge or experience of China. The text below from the Leeds Mercury *represents the confluence of interests between missionaries anxious to discredit the opium trade and newspapers anxious to build readership with an exciting, somewhat scandalous story.*

A Mandarin,[1] in high office, has the following remarks on the effects of the drug, in a memorial to the Emperor on the Opium Trade:—"When any one is long habituated to inhaling it, it becomes necessary to resort to it at regular intervals, and the habit of using it being inveterate, is destructive of time, injurious to property, and yet dear to one even as life. Of those who use it to great excess, the breath becomes feeble, the body wasted, the teeth black; the individuals themselves clearly see the evil effects of it, yet cannot refrain from it. It will be found on examination that the smokers of Opium are idle, lazy vagrants, having no useful purpose before them; and though there are smokers to be found who have overstepped the threshold of age, yet they do not attain to the long life of other men." . . .

Mr. Medhurst,[2] the well-known Chinese Missionary, says the unhappy victims "may be seen hanging their heads by the doors of the Opium shops, which the

---

[1] Chinese scholar-bureaucrat.
[2] Walter H. Medhurst (1822–1885), Christian missionary who in 1838 published *China: Its State and Prospects, with Especial Reference to the Spread of the Gospel.*

"Editorial," *Leeds Mercury,* September 7, 1839, 4–6.

hard-hearted keepers, having fleeced them of their all, will not permit them to enter; and shut out of their own dwellings, either by angry relatives or ruthless creditors, *they die in the streets unpitied and despised.*" With regard to the prevalence of Opium smoking, the same writer informs us "Opium shops are as plentiful in some towns of China, as gin shops are in England. The sign of these receptacles is a bamboo screen hanging before the door, which is as certain an intimation as the checquers[3] are here, that the slave of intemperance may be gratified."

The above extracts exhibit the strong family resemblance between Opium and Alcohol, but it must be borne in mind that the progress of this destructive appetite in China, is unchecked by moral or religious principle or example. The religious systems of the Chinese are based on *atheism,* and the people are therefore an easy prey to the temptation of momentary pleasure and sensual indulgence, living under the practical influence of the maxim, "Let us eat and drink, for to-morrow we die." This consideration alone can explain the fearfully rapid increase in the consumption of Opium. . . .

Such is an imperfect survey of the effects of the British Opium Trade. It has not a redeeming feature. A *trade* it is not in any creditable sense, but a nefarious system of organized and daring contravention of the laws of China. Its elements are unlimited bribery, violence, and deceit. . . . If it be asked who are the agents, the same authorities[4] will inform him—*the English and the English only.* Yet the guilty parties unblushingly lay claim to the character of British merchants—men of respectability, and honour, and christian principle. We repudiate their claim with indignation.

We come now to the share of the East India Company in this traffic. The Opium introduced into China is, with very little exception, the produce of India. Half is grown in the province of Malwa,[5] under native Princes allied to the East India Company, and pays a duty to the Company on its transit through their territory. The remainder is cultivated in their own dominions, for the *exclusive* benefit of the East India Company, under a system of the severest monopoly, and by *compulsory* labour. The Anti-Slavery Societies will no doubt feel that this part of the case falls within their province. The frightful abuses of the whole system of Opium-growing in India, are only inferior to the evils inflicted by the trade on China.

QUESTIONS FOR ANALYSIS

1. What means does the author use to create a sensationalistic tone but also to give the arguments and evidence a sense of validity?

2. What purpose does the reference to alcohol serve? The reference to slavery?

3. How does the author use religion to consider the moral character of the Chinese and the British merchants?

4. How does the style and substance of reporting in the *Leeds Mercury* compare to the reporting in the *Bombay Times* (Source 4)? Why might there be similarities and differences?

---

[3] Chessboard hung or posted to indicate an inn.
[4] Chinese officials.
[5] In central India.

6

". . . THE SACRED DUCKS OF FANQUI HAVE BEEN TURNED LOOSE . . ."

Punch
Important News from China   (1841)

The British satirical magazine Punch *began publication in 1841 and continues to this day to poke fun at political, social, and cultural issues around the world. At its inception,* Punch *sought to establish a middle ground of publication between respectable, formal newspapers such as the* Times *(London) and the scandalous broadsheets published by various radical groups. In its early years,* Punch *had a radical and reforming focus. Humor and satire, however, were its trademarks, which* Punch *used to appeal to mass British society. During the First Opium War, as* Punch *was establishing itself, the Chinese became topics for ridicule, as was done by* Punch *in the mock Chinese newspaper article below.*

August 28, 1841.

We have received expresses from the Celestial Empire[1] by our own private electro-galvanic communication. As this rapid means of transmission carries dispatches so fast that we generally get them even before they are written, we are enabled to be considerably in advance of the common daily journals; more especially as we have obtained news up to the end of next week.

The most important paper which has come to hand is the *Macao Sunday Times*. It appears that the fortifications for surrounding Beijing are progressing rapidly, but that the government have determined upon building the ramparts of japanned canvas[2] and bamboo rods, instead of pounded rice, which was thought almost too fragile to resist the attacks of the English barbarians. Some handsome guns, of blue and white porcelain, have been placed on the walls, with a proportionate number of carved ivory balls, elaborately cut one inside the other. These, it is presumed, will split upon firing, and produce incalculable mischief and confusion. Within the gates a frightful magazine of gilt crackers, and other fireworks, has been erected; which, in the event of the savages penetrating the fortifications, will be exploded one after another, to terrify them into fits, when they will be easily captured. This precaution has been scarcely thought necessary by some of the mandarins, as our great artist, Wang, has covered the external joss-house with frantic figures that must strike terror to every barbarian. Gold paper has also been kept constantly

---

[1] China.

[2] Canvas stiffened by several layers of varnish.

"Important News from China," *Punch* (August 28, 1841).

burning, on altars of holy clay, at every practicable point of the defences, which it is hardly thought they will have the hardihood to approach, and the sacred ducks of Fanqui[3] have been turned loose in the river to retard the progress of the infidel fleet.

During the storm of last week the portcullis,[4] which had been placed in the northern gate, and was composed of solid rice paper, with cross-bars of chop-sticks, was much damaged. It is now under repair, and will be coated entirely with tea-chest lead, to render it perfectly impregnable. The whole of the household troops and body-guard of the emperor have also received new accoutrements of tin-foil and painted isinglass.[5] They have likewise been armed with varnished bladders, containing peas and date stones, which produce a terrific sound upon the least motion.

An Englishman has been gallantly captured this morning, in a small boat, by one of our armed junks. He will eat his eyes in the palace-court this afternoon; and then, being enclosed in soft porcelain, will be baked to form a statue for the new pagoda at Bo-Lung, the first stone of which was laid by the late emperor, to celebrate his victory over the rude northern islanders.

QUESTIONS FOR ANALYSIS

1. What aspects of Chinese civilization and practices does *Punch* satirize? What aspects are satirized most frequently?

2. By what rhetorical means does *Punch* produce its satirical or comical effect?

3. Through its satire, what assumptions about Chinese civilization does *Punch* promote?

4. How does *Punch*'s satire compare to the criticisms of Chinese civilization by Warren (Source 3)?

RESPONSES TO THE OPIUM WARS

During the Opium Wars, British naval superiority permitted the British to roam the Chinese coast, blockading Chinese ports and exerting military power wherever it seemed convenient. Britain employed new naval technology, particularly the steam-driven, paddle-wheel vessel *Nemesis*, which could operate in shallow coastal waters. Qing officials responded to Britain's new military technology by building five new Chinese paddle-wheel boats armed with cast brass guns and a nearly completed double-decker man-of-war with thirty guns. But British military advantages proved too strong, and in late 1842, as the British prepared to capture Nanjing, a former capital of China and a city of symbolic political importance, the Qing sued for peace and accepted the harsh terms of the Treaty of Nanjing—payment of

---

[3] In 1838, the English surgeon C. Toogood Downing published *The Fan-qui in China in 1836–7* in which he described Chinese duck boats that released large numbers of ducks into harvested rice paddies to scavenge the remaining grains of rice.

[4] Iron grate that is hung over the gateway of a fortified building and that can be lowered to prevent passage.

[5] Thin sheets of fragile mica.

$6 million for the confiscated opium, a further $12 million for British expenses during the war, surrender of the island of Hong Kong to Britain in perpetuity, opening of Guangzhou and four other cities to trade by British merchants, abolishment of the Hong merchant guild, and use of mutually respectful and egalitarian terms of address between British and Chinese officials. The Opium Wars marked the first decisive political reversal for the Qing and provoked self-reflection and discussion within China about how China should respond to the military power of the European "barbarians." Within Europe, the Opium Wars brought to fruition the reevaluation of Chinese civilization that had begun during the Enlightenment.

7

". . . THEY THEREFORE STUCK RIGIDLY TO THE PATTERN. . . ."

Arthur Cunynghame
The Opium War: Being Recollections of Service in China   (1845)

Arthur Cunynghame (1812–1884) had a long and distinguished career in the British military, serving across Asia and southern Africa. Early in his career, during the First Opium War, Cunynghame served as aide-de-camp to Major-General Lord Saltoun and saw military action throughout the conflict. As he would do throughout his career, on his return to Britain Cunynghame published his "recollections" of the events he had experienced. Meant for a popular audience, such military memoirs emphasized new images of the defeated China.

[*Cunynghame arrives in Zhoushan.*]

On our way towards the landing-place we visited a gigantic junk.[1] . . . She was laden with silks and copper, and was supposed to be from Japan. . . .

This huge box (I cannot bring myself to call it by any other name) was far the most extraordinary thing of the kind I had ever seen, although, after being constantly accustomed to see them, the novelty soon wears off; yet the first impression cannot fail to be one of wonder, how any people could dream of navigating the trackless ocean in this huge coffin. She must have far exceeded 500 tons burden, according to a rough calculation, which by eyesight alone we made of her. The upper part of her poop[2] was at least as high as that of a seventy-four,[3] with curious stair-

---

[1] Large Chinese ship.
[2] Stern or rear of a ship.
[3] Large British ship.

Arthur Cunynghame, *The Opium War: Being Recollections of Service in China* (Philadelphia: Zieber, 1845) (Reprinted Wilmington, Del.: Scholarly Resources, 1972), 49–53.

cases and passages communicating to the different portions of the ship, more after the fashion of a house; her mast was a magnificent spar, eleven feet in circumference, and of prodigious height; her cables, composed of coir, made from the outer covering of the cocoanut, for durability and lightness unequalled, and her wooden anchors, although primitive in their construction, would, I doubt not, have answered perfectly well in any but a rocky bottom, which is scarcely ever to be met with on the coasts or harbours they are accustomed to anchor in. Her sides were painted with a rude imitation of ports,[4] and what with her numberless flags and streamers, her huge, unwieldy mat sails, her gigantic rudder, and antediluvian-looking[5] crew, she presented a novel and striking sight; but certainly she could in no way merit the terms of "walking the waters like a thing of life."

Her captain, a fine old fellow, had previously made ten successful voyages in her from Shanghai to Japan, and when first captured he was requested to act as pilot up the Yangzi River; with the intricate navigation among the sands and shoals of which river he did not profess to be unacquainted. He stated that nothing should induce him to undertake this office; that, on the contrary, if forced upon him, he would speedily put an end to his existence, by throwing himself in the river, as death, he was certain, would soon be his fate, were he to comply with our wishes, as no one could escape detection and the consequent punishment attending it, were they to offend in any way the Imperial Government. He greatly magnified the dangers of the mighty stream, declaring it was utterly impossible for our gigantic ships to ascend; that we should speedily be encompassed with sand-banks and other difficulties, from which we could never extricate ourselves; and, moreover, were we partially to succeed, the vengeance of the gods would speedily overtake us, for our rashness, and we should all be totally destroyed. A few short weeks were sufficient to show him how ridiculous were all his prognostications. . . .

[*Cunynghame walks to the summit of the city.*]

Mounted on a carriage, beside some of our own guns, was a Chinese brass nine-pounder carronade.[6] This had been cast the year previous at Zhenhai, in imitation of one which they had procured from the unfortunate brig Kite, which vessel was lost upon their coast during our previous occupation of the island. . . . This gun was almost a fac-simile of our own; but the tangent screw for elevation and depression, in the original, had no doubt become corroded by the action of the salt water, it having lain some short time at the bottom of the sea. Adhering closely to the model, they had cast their screw and gun all in one piece; with all their ingenuity being totally at a loss to divine its use or meaning, but being determined to act steadily up to the old maxim, of fighting the barbarians with their own weapons; they therefore stuck rigidly to the pattern they had received.

We had also a capital view of the laborious defences which they erected, between the first time of our evacuating Zhoushan and that of its being retaken by the army

---

[4] Openings through which canons or guns may be fired.
[5] Appearing so primitive that they seemed as if they lived before the story of Noah and the flood in the Jewish scriptures.
[6] Short, light cannon.

under Sir Hugh Gough. It was astonishing to observe the long walls of mud which they had industriously thrown up, fancying that because we took possession of the town by a front attack in the former instance, we should proceed precisely the same way to attack it a second time, solely devoting all their energies to the erection of defences on the sea-side, to the neglect of those faces of the city towards the land. Such is their detestation to change and novelty, that they fancy nothing whatever can be accomplished in a way the least deviating from that in which it had formerly been executed.

QUESTIONS FOR ANALYSIS

1. What does Cunynghame praise and criticize among the things that he sees in China?
2. What is Cunynghame's attitude toward Chinese technology and toward the Chinese sea captain?
3. How do Cunynghame's descriptions of Chinese military technology and practices compare to the satirical descriptions in *Punch* (Source 6)?
4. What characteristics is Cunynghame implicitly praising that Chinese technology, military practices, and even the sea captain fail to demonstrate? Why might these characteristics be important to Cunynghame?

8

"... THEY HAD NOT ADVANCED BEYOND FIRECRACKERS. ..."

Michael Adas
Machines as the Measure of Men (1989)

Michael Adas is a modern historian who has investigated the shifting standards by which Europeans have judged and evaluated other civilizations. In the passage below, Adas discusses the changing image of China in Europe in the decades before and during the Opium Wars.

As the French essayist and novelist Pierre Mille observed in the early 1900s, when merchants, scientists, and technicians replaced missionaries and philosophers as arbiters of European opinion, beginning in the late eighteenth century, European awe of and desire to emulate China shifted to hostility, contempt, and an urge to remake the country in accord with Western designs. Mille mused, not without sar-

---

Michael Adas, *Machines as the Measure of Men: Science, Technology, and Ideologies of Western Dominance* (Ithaca, N.Y.: Cornell University Press, 1989), 177, 186–93.

casm, that because China lacked railroads, spinning jennies,[1] and leaders like the German General Helmuth von Moltke,[2] it could no longer hide its scientific and technological shortcomings and general backwardness from the progressive and aggressive Western powers. . . .

With the Opium War of 1839–42, the full meaning of China's military backwardness was brutally revealed. In a series of engagements on land and sea—rather modest confrontations by European standards—British ships and British-led Indian infantry routed the numerically superior Chinese forces. . . . In what proved to be the most memorable clash of the war, [the iron-clad paddle-steamer *Nemesis*] singlehandedly engaged a fleet of fifteen Chinese war junks. The British ship took the initiative by reducing the lead junk to a roaring ball of smoke and fire with a Congreve missile. As the remaining junks fled or were hastily abandoned by their demoralized crews, the *Nemesis* continued up the coast, forced the panic-stricken inhabitants of a small town to evacuate their homes, sank a second war junk and captured another.

The contrast between the *Nemesis* and the Chinese junks—which with their mat sails and painted eyes struck one British officer as "apparitions from the Middle Ages"—cast further doubt on the already much-contested image of China as a powerful and advanced civilization. These and later military setbacks convinced virtually all European observers that China was no match for Europe. . . . In order to imagine that China was Europe's equal, John Crawfurd[3] mused nearly a decade later, "we must fancy a Chinese fleet and army capturing Paris and London, and dictating peace to the French and English."

Chinese ineptness at using up-to-date military technology provided the material for most of the anecdotes of bumbling "natives" which European commanders and travelers, like their counterparts in Africa, included in their memoirs to illustrate the great distance that separated the scientifically minded, industrializing Western peoples from all others. During the Opium War, J. Elliot Bingham, a lieutenant aboard the British corvette *Modeste,* mocked the ignorance and credulity of the Chinese, who had attempted to block the passage of the English fleet up the Pearl River to Guangzhou by lining up large earthen jars in the hope that the Europeans would believe them to be batteries of cannon. Bingham assured his readers that such "childlish" ruses were commonly employed by the Chinese against the British invaders. Later authors cited similar attempts at deception— lighting fires in huge iron tubes to frighten the English with smoke; wearing huge and hideous masks to make the Europeans think they were "fighting monsters"— to demonstrate the "tricks worthy of children" to which the Chinese were forced to resort because of their technological inferiority. Frederic Farrar[4] sneered at the "asinine ignorance of the Chinese gunners who held lights near their cannon to allow

---

[1] Multiple-spindle machine for spinning wool or cotton that was an important technological development in England's industrial revolution.
[2] Helmuth von Moltke (1800–1891), Prussian and German military chief of staff and architect of the Prussian victories over Denmark (1864), Austria (1866), and France (1871).
[3] John Crawfurd (1783–1868), British diplomat, employee of British East India Company, and scholar of Asian languages and culture.
[4] Frederic Farrar (1831–1903), Anglican religious official, popular religious author, and philologist who was born in India.

them to fire at night." The English journalist Henry Norman noted that the Chinese were so foolish that they dried percussion caps and dynamite on steam boilers. Lord Curzon[5] claimed that when Chinese soldiers were given modern weapons, they tended to jam them because they regarded all rifle cartridges as identical and thus did not bother to make sure they had the right gauge for the weapon they were using. . . . He claimed that it was widely believed in China that Christian missionaries used parts of the human body to concoct medicines and to mix chemicals such as those used in photography. . . .

Two basic positions developed in the nineteenth century regarding China's failure to match European achievements in technology and the sciences. Elements of the first approach, which stressed early advance and then stagnation, had been suggested by eighteenth-century writers. Their stress on stagnation was supplemented in the nineteenth century by a sense of overall decline, which appeared to be confirmed by the breakdown of the Qing empire. In 1855 an anonymous reviewer of E. R. Huc's account[6] acknowledged that China had been responsible for the three inventions—the compass, printing, and gunpowder—which had been the "principal material agents of the progress of the modern world." . . . But the reviewer, writing when England's industrial supremacy was at its height, merely used this praise for China's past accomplishments to set up an extended critique of its present backwardness and its failure to develop the full potential of these important inventions. He noted that the Chinese had not used the compass to explore the globe or expand trade, that they had not advanced beyond firecrackers after their initial discovery of gunpowder, and that their invention of printing had not led to a distinguished literary tradition. The reviewer went on to argue that though the Chinese knew about the circulation of the blood, their general knowledge of human anatomy was on a par with that of the rudest savages. He asserted that even in areas of manufacture in which they had displayed the greatest skill, such as the production of silk textiles and porcelain, Chinese tools and techniques had not improved for centuries. . . .

Numerous authors commented on the stultification of Chinese creativity and a related reluctance to import innovations from other civilizations, but none matched Frederick Farrar's utter disdain for things Chinese. Having established that the "Aryan" race had excelled over all others in all fields, Farrar singled out the "semi-civilized" Chinese as a perfect example of "arrested development" and "mummified intelligence." He contended that their early inventions had "stopped short" at the "lowest point" in contrast to the constantly modified and improved devices of the Europeans. . . . Even their language, which, he said, had not developed beyond "hieroglyphics," exuded a sense of rigidity and stagnation; it was, he concluded, little more than a "petrified fragment of primeval periods."

The explanations for Chinese inertia offered by the proponents of the early invention–long term stagnation approach varied considerably, from Farrar's insistence on innate racial deficiencies to a focus . . . on Chinese despotism and veneration for tradition. John Barrow[7] touched on the latter but emphasized the absence

---

[5] George Curzon (1859–1925), British statesman, viceroy of India, and foreign secretary.
[6] Evariste Huc (1813–1860), French missionary who published *The Chinese Empire* in 1855.
[7] John Barrow (1764–1848), British naval official and travel author.

of theory in Chinese thought as a whole. He expressed his displeasure at several mandarins' lack of curiosity regarding the reasons why alum caused mud particles to sink to the bottom of a vessel filled with water. He commented that though they were adept at dyeing and tinting "all manner of objects," the Chinese had no theory of colors. He pronounced them "totally ignorant" of the "basic principles" of astronomy, which, he snidely added, they professed to "value so much" but in fact "understood so little." It was this lack of interest in underlying principles, Barrow concluded, that had prevented the cumulative increase of scientific knowledge in China ... [and] had stunted technological development throughout their history. . . .

[E. R. Huc] claimed that the natural sciences had no place in formal education in China, that the preservation of scientific knowledge and technical knowhow was left to "ignorant workmen." Consequently, the Chinese had actually lost scientific ideas and had forgotten techniques they had once mastered. . . .

The second and minority position regarding China's technological and scientific backwardness, despite its promising beginnings, was even less flattering to the Chinese than the early creativity-stagnation thesis. As early as 1819 William Lawrence[8] suggested that Caucasians from Persia had been the source of the artistic and scientific accomplishments of "the East" (by which he appears to have meant China, Japan, and India). Similar theories were proposed by several authors later in the century. The most influential of these, the Count de Gobineau,[9] substituted Aryan invaders for Caucasian migrants.

In the writings of such extreme Anglo-Saxon supremacists as Robert Knox,[10] China's backwardness and stagnation were seen as proofs that its past achievements had been highly overrated. Knox insisted that the Chinese had neither "invented nor discovered" anything, and that what they had borrowed they had not understood and thus could not improve upon. Unable to generate their own scientific and technological breakthroughs, the hapless Chinese had waited passively since the time of Alexander the Great for their destruction at the hands of more creative and dynamic peoples. . . . The refusal to acknowledge China's great contributions to technological innovation and scientific discovery facilitated the efforts of the more extreme advocates of white supremacy to denigrate the one civilization that had clearly rivaled and, in many categories of material achievement, surpassed Europe in the preindustrial era.

QUESTIONS FOR ANALYSIS

1. According to Adas, how did attitudes toward China shift beginning in the late eighteenth century?
2. What two "positions" about the development of Chinese civilization does Adas identify? What do these positions have in common, and how do they differ?

---

[8] William Lawrence (1783–1867), British anatomist and naturalist.
[9] Joseph Arthur, Count de Gobineau (1816–1882), French diplomat and ethnologist whose influential work on racial purity influenced later nineteenth- and twentieth-century racial theorists.
[10] Robert Knox (1791–1862), British anatomist and influential racial theorist.

3. What types of evidence do the various authors that Adas cites offer as proof of their assessments? Why might this evidence and these arguments be attractive in mid-nineteenth-century Europe?

4. How do the British sources in this chapter compare to Adas's argument about shifting attitudes toward China and shifting standards of judgment?

9

"WHY ARE THEY SMALL AND YET STRONG?"

Feng Guifen
Theory of Self-Strengthening   (1860)

The First Opium War (1839–1842) dramatically initiated three decades of strife in China that shook the Qing dynasty to its foundations. In the wake of the Treaty of Nanjing (1842), the governments of the United States and France pressured the Qing into treaties that granted even further commercial and political benefits to foreign merchants. Efforts by Britain, in concert with the United States and France, to open the interior of China to trade led to the Second Opium War (1857–1860). The Treaty of Tianjin, signed during the course of this war, opened large sections of China to further trade and protected the work of Christian missionaries. The Qing's defeat in the First Opium War had created even more dramatic civil conflict. Between the late 1840s and late 1860s, revolts sprang up across China resulting in millions of deaths. In the midst of this confusion, a few scholar-bureaucrats called for fundamental reforms within China. Feng Guifen (1809–1874) held many scholarly and administrative positions within the Qing state. In 1860, he wrote a series of essays arguing that China must "strengthen itself." In the excerpts below from those essays, Feng sets out the basic principles and strategies for what became known as the "Self-Strengthening Movement"— principles that he believed China must adopt to compete with the European powers.

On the Adoption of Western Knowledge

The world today is not to be compared with that of the Three Dynasties (of ancient China). . . . Now the globe is ninety-thousand *li*[1] around, and every spot may be reached by ships or wheeled vehicles. . . . According to what is listed on the maps by the Westerners, there are not less than one hundred countries. From these one hundred countries, only the books of Italy, at the end of the Ming dynasty,[2] and

---

[1] Three *li* equal roughly one mile.
[2] The Ming dynasty ruled China from 1369 to 1644.

Ssu-yu Teng and John K. Fairbank, *China's Response to the West: A Documentary Survey* (Cambridge: Harvard University Press, 1965), 51–54.

now those of England have been translated into Chinese, altogether several tens of books. Those which expound the doctrine of Jesus are generally vulgar, not worth mentioning. Apart from these, Western books on mathematics, mechanics, optics, light, chemistry, and other subjects contain the best principles of the natural sciences. In the books on geography, the mountains, rivers, strategic points, customs, and native products of the hundred countries are fully listed. Most of this information is beyond the reach of our people. . . .

If today we wish to select and use Western knowledge, we should establish official translation offices at Guangzhou and Shanghai. Brilliant students up to fifteen years of age should be selected from those areas to live and study in these schools on double rations. Westerners should be invited to teach them the spoken and written languages of the various nations, and famous Chinese teachers should also be engaged to teach them classics, history, and other subjects. At the same time they should learn mathematics. (Note: All Western knowledge is derived from mathematics. Every Westerner of ten years of age or more studies mathematics. If we now wish to adopt Western knowledge, naturally we cannot but learn mathematics . . .). . . .

After three years all students who can recite with ease the books of the various nations should be permitted to become licentiates;[3] and if there are some precocious ones who are able to make changes or improvements which can be put into practice, they should be recommended by the superintendent of trade to be imperially granted a *juren* degree as a reward. As we have said before, there are many brilliant people in China; there must be some who can learn from the barbarians and surpass them. . . .

If we let Chinese ethics and famous [Confucian] teachings serve as an original foundation, and let them be supplemented by the methods used by the various nations for the attainment of prosperity and strength, would it not be the best of all procedures? . . .

On the Manufacture of Foreign Weapons

The most unparalleled anger which has ever existed since the creation of heaven and earth is exciting all who are conscious in their minds and have spirit in their blood; their hats are raised by their hair standing on end. This is because the largest country on the globe today, with a vast area of 10,000 *li*, is yet controlled by small barbarians. . . . According to a general geography by an Englishman, the territory of our China is eight times larger than that of Russia, ten times that of America, one hundred times that of France, and two hundred times that of England. . . . Yet now we are shamefully humiliated by those four nations in the recent treaties—not because our climate, soil, or resources are inferior to theirs, but because our people are really inferior. . . . Why are they small and yet strong? Why are we large and yet

---

[3] Entrance into the Chinese bureaucracy was regulated by an examination system that tested knowledge of classical Chinese literature and arts. The examination system had three levels of exams—the *shengyuan* (local), the *juren* (provincial), and the *jinshi* (national). Feng suggests that these prestigious titles should be given to those who obtain Western knowledge.

weak? We must try to discover some means to become their equal, and that also depends upon human effort. Regarding the present situation there are several major points: in making use of the ability of our manpower, with no one neglected, we are inferior to the barbarians; in securing the benefit of the soil, with nothing wasted, we are inferior to the barbarians; in maintaining a close relationship between the ruler and the people, with no barrier between them, we are inferior to the barbarians; and in the necessary accord of word with deed, we are also inferior to the barbarians. The way to correct these four points lies with ourselves, for they can be changed at once if only our Emperor would set the general policy right. There is no need for outside help in these matters. . . .

What we then have to learn from the barbarians is only the one thing, solid ships and effective guns. When Wei Yuan[4] discussed the control of the barbarians, he said that we should use barbarians to attack barbarians, and use barbarians to negotiate with barbarians. . . . In my opinion, if we cannot make ourselves strong but merely presume on cunning and deceit, it will be just enough to incur failure. Only one sentence of Wei Yuan is correct: "Learn the strong techniques of the barbarians in order to control them. . . ."

Funds should be assigned to establish a shipyard and arsenal in each trading port. Several barbarians should be invited and Chinese who are good in using their minds should be summoned to receive their instructions so that they may in turn teach many artisans. When a piece of work is finished and is indistinguishable from that made by the barbarians, the makers should be given a *juren* degree as a reward, and be permitted to participate in the metropolitan examination on an equal footing with other scholars. Those whose products are superior to the barbarian manufacture should be granted a *jinshi* degree as a reward, and be permitted to participate in the palace examinations on the same basis as others. The workers should be double-paid so as to prevent them from quitting.

Our nation has emphasized the civil service examinations, which have preoccupied people's minds for a long time. Wise and intelligent scholars have exhausted their time and energy in such useless things as the eight-legged essays,[5] examination papers, and formal calligraphy. . . . Now let us order one-half of them to apply themselves to the pursuit of manufacturing weapons and instruments and imitating foreign crafts. . . . The intelligence and wisdom of the Chinese are necessarily superior to those of the various barbarians, only formerly we have not made use of them. When the Emperor above likes something, those below him will pursue it even further, like the moving of grass in the wind or the response of an echo. There ought to be some people of extraordinary intelligence who can have new ideas and improve on Western methods. At first they may learn and pattern after the foreigners; then they may compare and try to be their equal; and finally they may go ahead and surpass them—the way to make ourselves strong actually lies in this.

---

[4] Wei Yuan (1794–1856), a Chinese scholar who composed several books on geography, history, and economics.
[5] Highly stylized essays divided into eight paragraphs.

QUESTIONS FOR ANALYSIS

1. What does Feng identify as the basis of "Western knowledge" and the value within that knowledge? Why might he emphasize these issues?

2. What is Feng's attitude toward the "barbarians"? How does Feng project a tone of anger throughout the two essays?

3. How does Feng integrate his desire for new "Western knowledge" into traditional Chinese practices?

4. How do Feng's attitudes and tone compare to Lin Zexu's (Source 1)? How does Feng's argument compare to Adas's argument about the changing Western perception of China (Source 8)?

CHAPTER QUESTIONS

1. What roles do the ethnic, economic, and religious interests of the authors presented in this chapter play in how the authors approach the conflict between China and Britain? How do the various authors seek to build public sentiment for their positions?

2. Adas contends that European judgments about other civilizations shifted away from moral and philosophical considerations and toward technological or scientific considerations in the nineteenth century. In considering Adas's argument, how do the standards of European judgments of people from other countries expressed in Chapters 1 and 3 compare to the standards expressed in Chapter 7 and this chapter? Where would the standards of the Enlightenment expressed in Chapter 5 fit into Adas's argument?

3. How does the response of Feng Guifen to Western industrial and military power compare to the responses of Russians and Ottoman Turks in the borderland nations (Chapter 8, Sources 6–9)? What similarities and differences exist in their understanding of the foundation of Western industrial power, and why might this be the case?

Chapter 10

THE IMPERIALIST IMPULSE ABROAD AND AT HOME

In the last third of the nineteenth century, the political ambitions and resentments of many Western nations focused again on foreign territories and imperial conquest. Statesmen such as Chancellor Otto von Bismarck of Germany recognized (or hoped) that imperial conquest could be used to resolve tensions among the European powers, tensions exacerbated by the unification of Germany in 1871. European statesmen also sought to achieve national glory by establishing and expanding imperial power. Further, as Germany, the United States, and France followed Great Britain through the process of industrialization, many statesmen feared that the overproduction of goods would cause economic decline and widespread unemployment. Colonial markets seemed a necessary outlet for surplus European manufacturing products, although it was unclear whether colonized peoples would provide an effective market for Europe's manufactured and agricultural products. These varied hopes and ambitions expressed themselves most forcefully in the early 1880s as England, France, Belgium, Portugal, Italy, and Germany began rapidly seizing direct control of African territories in the "scramble for Africa." As tensions escalated, Bismarck hosted the Berlin Conference in 1884 and 1885 in which European diplomats divided Africa into territorial colonies. These dramatic and well-publicized events encouraged public discussion of imperialism, in which its supporters justified and its detractors criticized the imperialist venture.

Imperialism was not only a matter of foreign territories, however. Consumer goods produced in the colonies or manufactured in Europe from colonial materials became increasingly common in European stores. European artists, especially the Impressionists, integrated Asian and African motifs and styles into their works. A colonial literature emerged that included both Western authors, such as Rudyard Kipling and Joseph Conrad, and non-Western authors, such as Thomas Mofolo and Lal Behari Day. The large volume of newspapers, journals, and books that were available at low cost permitted a broad European and American audience to read about the exploits of Henry Stanley as he searched Africa for the missing missionary Dr. David Livingstone and to follow the political controversies surrounding the scramble for Africa, the Boer War, and other colonial events. In short, imperialism became an integral and influential part of Western culture.

IMPERIALISM AWAY

As Western nations turned their ambitions to imperial conquest, the goals, purposes, and even value of imperialism were vigorously debated. While Western mis-

234

sionaries continued to promote a "Christianizing mission" (Chapters 3 and 9), national and economic motivations (Chapters 4 and 9) also continued to find strong advocates, as did the idea of a Western duty to support a "civilizing mission" that brought the benefits of Western civilization to "primitive peoples." The debates of the late nineteenth century were influenced strongly by two additional considerations, however. First, Western governments had become distinctly concerned about whether the costs of their imperial endeavors could be justified by the benefits gained. The economic benefits of imperialism occurred unevenly in a national economy: they were central to some industries and insignificant to others. As individual industries pressured national legislatures and administrators to support the colonial trade necessary to their industries, governments were left to determine the value and costs—political and economic—of such support. Second, nationalism had become a potent political force within Western political culture. Advocates of imperialism often linked their arguments to nationalist sentiments that would appeal to the broad voting public. Through these arguments, authors established imperialism as a central component of Western identity.

1

"... Divisions"

Maps of Africa

Maps can identify many different things, such as political boundaries, ethnic territories, linguistic regions, economic systems, and environmental zones. Comparing maps can reveal many important issues. Prior to 1870, Europeans and European settlers had established political authority in Africa along the Nile River in Egypt, on the southern tip of the continent, and on some coastlines. The vast African interior remained unexplored and unknown to Europeans. Nevertheless, the Berlin Conference of 1884–1885 politically divided Africa into regions of European colonial control. The following three maps of Africa identify the colonial division of Africa as of 1914, locate ethnic groups within Africa, and mark the ecological divisions within Africa.

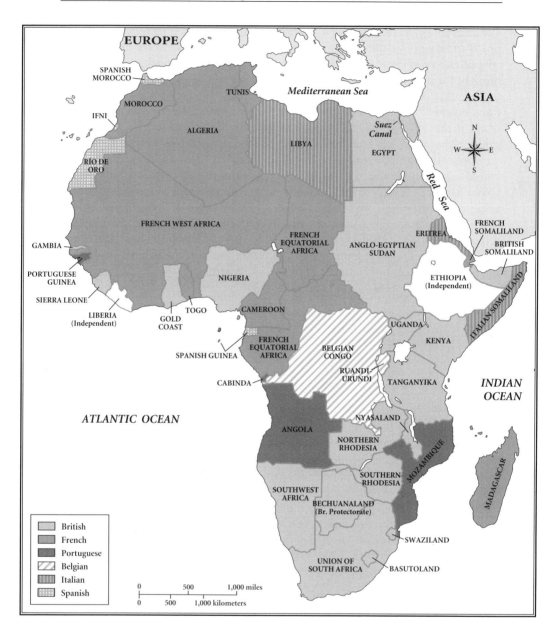

MAP 10.1 POLITICAL DIVISIONS IN AFRICA, 1914

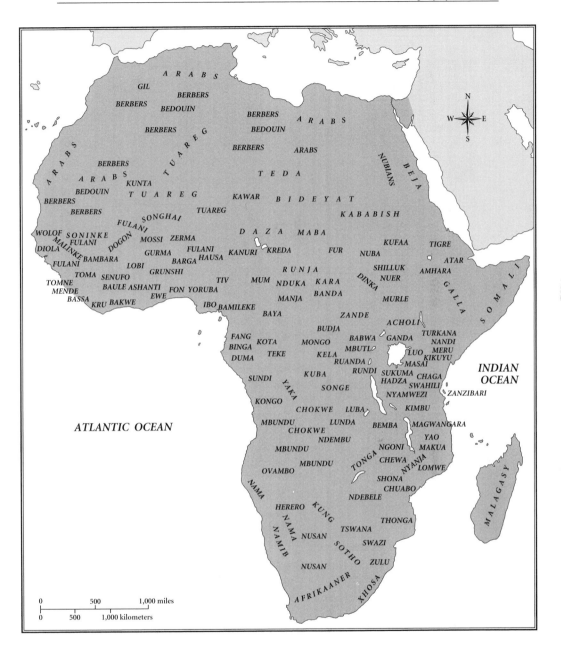

MAP 10.2 ETHNIC GROUPS IN AFRICA

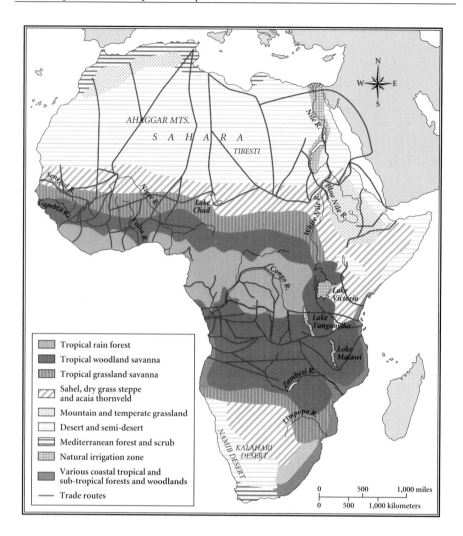

MAP 10.3   ENVIRONMENTAL ZONES AND TRADE ROUTES IN AFRICA

QUESTIONS FOR ANALYSIS

1. How does a comparison of these three maps indicate that the participants in Bismarck's Berlin Conference failed to consider ethnicity and environment in drawing political boundaries in Africa? Identify specific examples.

2. What are some consequences of dividing ethnic groups among two or more colonial authorities? What are some consequences of placing several ethnic groups within a single colonial territory?

3. What might be some consequences of dividing environmental systems among two or more colonial authorities? Why might the participants at the Berlin Conference have ignored environmental and ethnic considerations?

2

"Natural Selection Acts Only Tentatively."

Charles Darwin
The Descent of Man (1871)

The English naturalist Charles Darwin (1809–1882) stunned mid-Victorian England with his work On the Origin of Species *(1859). In this work, Darwin documented the process of evolution and provided a theory for its operation in the idea of "natural selection." Whereas previous naturalists had focused on the battle for survival among species, Darwin focused on the contest for survival within a single species. He argued that each individual creature within a single species differs. Creatures with advantageous traits—such as longer claws, stronger beaks, or brighter plumage—that permit them to survive and reproduce most effectively will, in the aggregate, bring about an evolution of the species (or perhaps permit the emergence of a new species) by passing on the advantageous traits to succeeding generations. In* On the Origin of Species, *Darwin only alluded to the application of his ideas to humankind. He tackled that question directly in his following work,* The Descent of Man, *excerpted below, in which he expanded the range of evolution to include moral and intellectual traits as well as physical ones, while still recognizing all evolution as originating from biological and natural factors.*

Mr. Wallace[1] . . . argues that man, after he had partially acquired those intellectual and moral faculties which distinguish him from the lower animals, would have been but little liable to bodily modifications through natural selection or any other means. For man is enabled through his mental faculties "to keep with an unchanged body in harmony with the changing universe." He has great power of adapting his habits to new conditions of life. He invents weapons, tools, and various stratagems to procure food and to defend himself. When he migrates into a colder climate he uses clothes, builds sheds, and makes fires; and by the aid of fire cooks food otherwise indigestible. He aids his fellow-men in many ways, and anticipates future events. Even at a remote period he practised some division of labour. . . .

[T]he intellectual and moral faculties of man . . . are variable; and we have every reason to believe that the variations tend to be inherited. Therefore, if they were formerly of high importance to primeval man and to his ape-like progenitors, they would have been perfected or advanced through natural selection. Of the high importance of the intellectual faculties there can be no doubt, for man mainly owes

---

[1]Alfred Russel Wallace (1823–1913), influential British naturalist. He and Darwin came to many of the same ideas independently of one another.

Charles Darwin, *The Descent of Man* (New York: Modern Library), 496–97, 501–4, 507–8.

to them his predominant position in the world. We can see, that in the rudest state of society, the individuals who were the most sagacious, who invented and used the best weapons or traps, and who were best able to defend themselves, would rear the greatest number of offspring. The tribes, which included the largest number of men thus endowed, would increase in number and supplant other tribes. . . .

At the present day civilised nations are everywhere supplanting barbarous nations, excepting where the climate opposes a deadly barrier; and they succeed mainly, though not exclusively, through their arts, which are the products of the intellect. It is, therefore, highly probable that with mankind the intellectual faculties have been mainly and gradually perfected through natural selection. . . .

With savages, the weak in body or mind are soon eliminated; and those that survive commonly exhibit a vigorous state of health. We civilised men, on the other hand, do our utmost to check the process of elimination; we build asylums for the imbecile, the maimed, and the sick; we institute poor-laws; and our medical men exert their utmost skill to save the life of every one to the last moment. There is reason to believe that vaccination has preserved thousands, who from a weak constitution would formerly have succumbed to small-pox. Thus the weak members of civilised societies propagate their kind. No one who has attended to the breeding of domestic animals will doubt that this must be highly injurious to the race of man. It is surprising how soon a want of care, or care wrongly directed, leads to the degeneration of a domestic race; but excepting in the case of man himself, hardly any one is so ignorant as to allow his worst animals to breed.

The aid which we feel impelled to give to the helpless is mainly an incidental result of the instinct of sympathy, which was originally acquired as part of the social instincts, but subsequently rendered, in the manner previously indicated, more tender and more widely diffused. Nor could we check our sympathy, even at the urging of hard reason, without deterioration in the noblest part of our nature. The surgeon may harden himself whilst performing an operation, for he knows that he is acting for the good of his patient; but if we were intentionally to neglect the weak and helpless, it could only be for a contingent benefit, with an overwhelming present evil. We must therefore bear the undoubtedly bad effects of the weak surviving and propagating their kind. . . .

We will now look to the intellectual faculties. If in each grade of society the members were divided into two equal bodies, the one including the intellectually superior and the other the inferior, there can be little doubt that the former would succeed best in all occupations, and rear a greater number of children. Even in the lowest walks of life, skill and ability must be of some advantage; though in many occupations, owing to the great division of labour, a very small one. Hence in civilised nations there will be some tendency to an increase both in the number and in the standard of the intellectually able. . . .

In regard to the moral qualities, some elimination of the worst dispositions is always in progress even in the most civilised nations. Malefactors are executed, or imprisoned for long periods, so that they cannot freely transmit their bad qualities. Melancholic and insane persons are confined, or commit suicide. Violent and quarrelsome men often come to a bloody end. The restless who will not follow any steady occupation—and this relic of barbarism is a great check to civilisation— emigrate to newly-settled countries, where they prove useful pioneers. . . .

It has been urged by several writers that as high intellectual powers are advantageous to a nation, the old Greeks, who stood some grades higher in intellect than any race that has ever existed, ought, if the power of natural selection were real, to have risen still higher in the scale, increased in number, and stocked the whole of Europe. Here we have the tacit assumption, so often made with respect to corporeal structures, that there is some innate tendency towards continued development in mind and body. But development of all kinds depends on many concurrent favourable circumstances. Natural selection acts only tentatively. Individuals and races may have acquired certain indisputable advantages, and yet have perished from failing in other characters. The Greeks may have retrograded from a want of coherence between the many small states, from the small size of their whole country, from the practice of slavery, or from extreme sensuality; for they did not succumb until "they were enervated and corrupt to the very core." The western nations of Europe, who now so immeasurably surpass their former savage progenitors, and stand at the summit of civilisation, owe little or none of their superiority to direct inheritance from the old Greeks, though they owe much to the written works of that wonderful people. . . .

Obscure as is the problem of the advance of civilisation, we can at least see that a nation which produced during a lengthened period the greatest number of highly intellectual, energetic, brave, patriotic, and benevolent men, would generally prevail over less favoured nations.

QUESTIONS FOR ANALYSIS

1. According to Darwin, how does natural selection function on the intellectual and moral faculties of humans?
2. In what ways, according to Darwin, is the process of natural selection limited, and how can it be limited? Of what significance is "sympathy" in Darwin's argument?
3. How does Darwin's argument suggest that natural selection is a process of both nature and society? How might this be comforting or discomforting to European imperialists?

3

"... THE STRUGGLE OF RACE WITH RACE ..."

Karl Pearson
National Life from the Standpoint of Science (1901)

Following the publication of Charles Darwin's major works, numerous authors vulgarized Darwin's ideas into a theory known as Social Darwinism. Social Darwinists argued that the fittest peoples (defined sometimes as races, nations, or cultures) would (or should) dominate the less fit. One prominent Social Darwinist was the English

Karl Pearson, *National Life from the Standpoint of Science* (London: Adam and Charles Black, 1901), 13–15, 17–25.

mathematician Karl Pearson (1857–1936), a founder of modern statistics. Unlike many authors who simply added a Darwinist vocabulary to racial arguments, Pearson sought to apply statistics to the biological issues of heredity and evolution, in part to demonstrate that racism derived from nature itself as guided by natural selection. In the text that follows, excerpted from Pearson's address to the Literary and Philosophical Society of Newcastle, Pearson sets out his central ideas.

What, from the scientific standpoint, is the function of a nation? What part from the natural history aspect does the national organization play in the universal struggle for existence? . . .

I want you to look with me for awhile on mankind as a product of Nature, and subject to the natural influences which form its environment. I will, first, notice a point which bears upon man as upon all forms of animal life. The characters of both parents—their virtues, their vices, their capabilities, their tempers, their diseases—all devolve in due proportion upon their children. . . .

Now, if we once realize that this law of inheritance is as inevitable as the law of gravity, we shall cease to struggle against it. This does not mean a fatal resignation to the presence of bad stock, but a conscious attempt to modify the percentage of it in our own community and in the world at large. Let me illustrate what I mean. A showman takes a wolf and, by aid of training and nurture, a more or less judicious administration of food and whip, makes it apparently docile and friendly as a dog. But one day, when the whip is not there, it is quite possible that the wolf will turn upon its keeper, or upon somebody else. Even if it does not, its offspring will not benefit by the parental education. I don't believe that the showman's way can be a *permanent* success; I believe, however, that you might completely domesticate the wolf, as the dog has been domesticated, by steadily selecting the more docile members of the community through several generations, and breeding only from these, rejecting the remainder. Now, if you have once realized the force of heredity, you will see in natural selection—that choice of the physically and mentally fitter to be the parents of the next generation—a most munificent provision for the progress of all forms of life. Nurture and education may immensely aid the social machine, but they must be repeated generation by generation; they will not in themselves reduce the tendency to the production of bad stock. Conscious or unconscious selection can alone bring that about.

What I have said about bad stock seems to me to hold for the lower races of man. How many centuries, how many thousands of years, have the Kaffir[1] and the Negro held large districts in Africa undisturbed by the white man? Yet their intertribal struggles have not yet produced a civilization in the least comparable with the Aryan. Educate and nurture them as you will, I do not believe that you will succeed in modifying the stock. History shows me one way, and one way only, in which a high state of civilization has been produced, namely, the struggle of race with race, and the survival of the physically and mentally fitter race. If you want to know whether the lower races of man can evolve a higher type, I fear the only course is to

---

[1] Southern African Bantu-speaking people.

leave them to fight it out among themselves, and even then the struggle for existence between individual and individual, between tribe and tribe, may not be supported by that physical selection due to a particular climate on which probably so much of the Aryan's success depended.

If you bring the white man into contact with the black, you too often suspend the very process of natural selection on which the evolution of a higher type depends. You get superior and inferior races living on the same soil, and that co-existence is demoralizing for both. They naturally sink into the position of master and servant, if not admittedly or covertly into that of slave-owner and slave. Frequently they intercross, and if the bad stock be raised the good is lowered. . . .

You may possibly think that I am straying from my subject, but I want to justify natural selection to you. I want you to see selection as something which renders the inexorable law of heredity a source of progress, which produces the good through suffering, an infinitely greater good which far outbalances the very obvious pain and evil. Let us suppose the alternative were possible. Let us suppose we could prevent the white man, if we liked, from going to lands of which the agricultural and mineral resources are not worked to the full; then I should say a thousand times better for him that he should not go than that he should settle down and live alongside the inferior race. The only healthy alternative is that he should go, and completely drive out the inferior race. That is practically what the white man has done in North America. . . .

I venture to assert, then, that the struggle for existence between white and red man, painful and even terrible as it was in its details, has given us a good far outbalancing its immediate evil. In place of the red man, contributing practically nothing to the work and thought of the world, we have a great nation, mistress of many arts, and able, with its youthful imagination and fresh, untrammelled impulses, to contribute much to the common stock of civilized man. . . .

Further back in history you find the same tale with almost every European nation. Sometimes when the conquering race is not too diverse in civilization and in type of energy there is an amalgamation of races, as when Norman and Anglo-Saxon ultimately blended; at other times the inferior race is driven out before the superior, as the Celt drove out the Iberian. The struggle means suffering, intense suffering, while it is in progress; but that struggle and that suffering have been the stages by which the white man has reached his present stage of development, and they account for the fact that he no longer lives in caves and feeds on roots and nuts. This dependence of progress on the survival of the fitter race, terribly black as it may seem to some of you, gives the struggle for existence its redeeming features; it is the fiery crucible out of which comes the finer metal. You may hope for a time when the sword shall be turned into the ploughshare, when American and German and English traders shall no longer compete in the markets of the world for their raw material and for their food supply, when the white man and the dark shall share the soil between them, and each till it as he lists. But, believe me, when that day comes, mankind will no longer progress; there will be nothing to check the fertility of inferior stock; the relentless law of heredity will not be controlled and guided by natural selection. Man will stagnate; and unless he ceases to multiply, the catastrophe will come again.

QUESTIONS FOR ANALYSIS

1. What similarities and differences exist between Darwin's ideas (Source 2) and Pearson's adaptation of them?

2. Compare Pearson's emphasis on "the inexorable law of heredity" to Darwin's emphasis on the social context of natural selection. What is the significance of these two different ideas?

3. What are the implications of Pearson's wolf analogy? On what basis does Pearson justify his definition of the "white man" as superior to the Amerindians of North America?

4. According to Pearson, how does progress occur, and how is it inhibited? How does this justify permanent Western dominance?

4

"... TO RESUME ITS COLONISING VOCATION ..."

Friedrich Fabri
Does Germany Need Colonies?   (1879)

The Lutheran pastor Friedrich Fabri (1824–1891), born to a family of German schol-ars, became director of the Barmen Rhine Missionary Society in 1857. Fabri himself, however, had no experience as a missionary and never traveled overseas. Fabri be-lieved that missionary activity should be united with economic activities to provide fi-nancial support for religious work; however, his efforts in this direction led to fiscal disaster and his resignation from the Society in 1884. In his influential pamphlet Does Germany Need Colonies?, *Fabri avoided moralistic or religious arguments in favor of colonization. Instead, he focused on the development of colonies as beneficial to German economic and political power and to the German working class, both of which were suffering from a severe downturn in the economy in the late 1870s. In the selec-tion below, Fabri links colonization to national political and economic interests.*

A German colonial policy can of course only develop gradually. If today Britain or Holland, in a spirit of the most sublime disinterest and in defiance of the old, yet ever new politico-diplomatic principle of *do, ut des,*[1] should propose to cede one of their trading colonies to us, such munificence would, initially at least, place us in

---

[1] "Give that you may receive" (Latin).

Friedrich Fabri, *Bedarf Deutschland des Colonien?/Does Germany Need Colonies?*, ed. and trans. E. C. M. Breuning and M. E. Chamberlain, in *Studies in German Thought and History* (Lewiston: Edwin Mellen Press, 1998), 2:177, 179, 181.

an embarrassing position. For what do we, as yet, know of colonies and colonial policy? . . . [I]n regard to colonies, we are in the earliest preliminary stage. It is, above all, important to promote awareness of the importance and necessity of colonial possessions, and, on this basis, strongly to encourage the nation's resolve to focus upon this object. If, from this point of departure, and having overcome all difficulties and obstacles, we arrive at the start of real action, then these first attempts will justify the effort and difficulty inseparable from all new beginnings. But cannot the German nation, traditionally bred to the sea, well equipped for industry and trade, more suited than most for agrarian colonisation, and endowed with a more abundant and more freely available labour force than that of any other modern civilised people, make a successful start upon this new course too? We doubt this the less, the more confident we are that the colonial question has already today become a matter of vital importance for Germany's development. Were it to be tackled judiciously yet firmly, this would produce the most fruitful results for our economic situation, indeed for our whole national development. The very fact that we have here a new question, whose many implications offer the German people what is in truth an untrodden and virgin field of action, may have a wholesome effect in many ways. There is in the new Reich already much that has been so envenomed, so soured and poisoned by futile party bickering, that the opening up of a new and promising path of national development might well have, as it were, a widely liberating effect, in that it would powerfully stimulate the national spirit in new directions. This too would be gratifying, and an advantage. More important, it is true, is the consideration that a people which has been led to the pinnacle of political power, can succeed in maintaining its historic position only for as long as it recognises and asserts itself as the *bearer of a cultural mission.* This is at the same time the only way of ensuring the continuance and growth of the national prosperity, the necessary basis for the continued exercise of power. The days are past when Germany's share in carrying out the tasks of our century consisted almost exclusively in intellectual and literary activity. We have become political, and powerful as well. But political power, when it forces itself into the foreground as an end in itself among a nation's aspirations, leads to cruelty, indeed barbarism, if it is not ready and willing to fulfil the cultural tasks of its age, ethical, moral and economic. The French political economist Leroy Beaulieu concludes his works on colonisation with the words: "That nation is the world's greatest which colonises most; if it is not the greatest today, it will be tomorrow."[2] No-one can deny that in this direction Britain far surpasses all other States. There has admittedly often been talk during the past decade, particularly in Germany, of "the declining power of Britain." Those who can only estimate the power of a State in terms of the size of its standing army (as has indeed become almost the custom in our iron age), may well regard this opinion as justified. But those who let their gaze wander over the globe and survey Great Britain's mighty and ever-increasing colonial empire, those who consider what strength she derives from that empire, with what skill she administers it, those who observe how commanding a position the Anglo-Saxon race enjoys in all countries overseas, to them this talk will seem the reasoning of an ignoramus. That Britain,

---

[2] Paul Leroy-Beaulieu (1843–1916) in *De la colonisation chez les peuples modernes.*

moreover, maintains her world-wide possessions, her position of predominance over the seas of the world, with the aid of troops whose numbers scarce equal one quarter of the armies of one of the military States of our continent, constitutes not only a great economic advantage, but also the most striking testimony to the solid power and the cultural strength of Britain. True, Great Britain today will remain as much as possible aloof from continental mass wars, or at most will only engage in action jointly with allies, which, however, will not harm the island kingdom's power position. It would, in any case, be advisable for us Germans to learn from the colonial skill of our Anglo-Saxon cousins and begin to emulate them in peaceful competition. When, centuries ago, the German Reich stood at the head of the States of Europe, it was the foremost trading and seagoing Power. If the new German Reich wishes to entrench and preserve its regained power for long years to come, then it must regard that power as a cultural mission and must no longer hesitate to resume its *colonising vocation* also.

QUESTIONS FOR ANALYSIS

1. How does Fabri use Great Britain in his justification for German colonization?

2. What aspects of British colonization does Fabri praise? Which economic and political concerns does Fabri call on in his argument?

3. What does Fabri mean by a "colonising vocation"? How does the idea of a "bearer of a cultural mission" compare to the idea of the "Christianizing mission" as a justification for European imperialism?

4. What is the "mission" of imperialism in Fabri's argument? How does Fabri's appeal to German nationalism compare to Pearson's emphasis on the strength of Western nations (Source 3)?

5

". . . THE TORCH OF IMPERIAL PATRIOTISM . . ."

Joseph Chamberlain
The True Conception of Empire (1897)

The British politician Joseph Chamberlain (1836–1914) was a successful businessman, liberal social reformer, and dedicated imperialist. Chamberlain championed the "mandate system," which held that Britain had a duty to spread the fruits of civilization to the "backward peoples," educating and preparing them for eventual self-government.

Joseph Chamberlain, "The True Conception of Empire," in *Mr. Chamberlain's Speeches,* ed. Charles Ward (Boston: Houghton Mifflin, 1914), 2:2–6.

Chamberlain believed that as these peoples advanced under British tutelage and assumed the responsibilities of self-rule, they would remain grateful to and politically allied with Britain within an imperial system. In the speech below, which Chamberlain gave at the Annual Colonial Institute Dinner, he summarizes his idea of the British national mission.

[W]e have now reached the third stage in our history, and the true conception of our Empire.

What is that conception? As regards the self-governing colonies[1] we no longer talk of them as dependencies. The sense of possession has given place to the sentiment of kinship. We think and speak of them as part of ourselves, as part of the British Empire, united to us, although they may be dispersed throughout the world, by ties of kindred, of religion, of history, and of language, and joined to us by the seas that formerly seemed to divide us.

But the British Empire is not confined to the self-governing colonies and the United Kingdom. It includes a much greater area, a much more numerous population in tropical climes, where no considerable European settlement is possible, and where the native population must always vastly outnumber the white inhabitants; and in these cases also the same change has come over the Imperial idea. Here also the sense of possession has given place to a different sentiment—the sense of obligation. We feel now that our rule over these territories can only be justified if we can show that it adds to the happiness and prosperity of the people, and I maintain that our rule does, and has, brought security and peace and comparative prosperity to countries that never knew these blessings before.

In carrying out this work of civilisation we are fulfilling what I believe to be our national mission, and we are finding scope for the exercise of those faculties and qualities which have made of us a great governing race. I do not say that our success has been perfect in every case, I do not say that all our methods have been beyond reproach; but I do say that in almost every instance in which the rule of the Queen has been established and the great *Pax Britannica*[2] has been enforced, there has come with it greater security to life and property, and a material improvement in the condition of the bulk of the population. No doubt, in the first instance, when these conquests have been made, there has been bloodshed, there has been loss of life among the native populations, loss of still more precious lives among those who have been sent out to bring these countries into some kind of disciplined order, but it must be remembered that that is the condition of the mission we have to fulfil. There are, of course, among us—there always are among us, I think—a very small minority of men who are ready to be the advocates of the most detestable tyrants,

---

[1] Colonies in which domestic governance was controlled by colonial legislatures dominated by ethnic European populations. Britain's self-governing colonies included Canada, Australia, and New Zealand.

[2] Literally, "British Peace," meaning that peace descends wherever British authority is secured (from *Pax Romana*, a two-hundred-year period of peace and prosperity begun by Augustus in 27 B.C.).

provided their skin is black—men . . . who denounce as murderers those of their countrymen who have gone forth at the command of the Queen, and who have redeemed districts as large as Europe from the barbarism and the superstition in which they had been steeped for centuries. . . .

You cannot have omelettes without breaking eggs; you cannot destroy the practices of barbarism, of slavery, of superstition, which for centuries have desolated the interior of Africa, without the use of force; but if you will fairly contrast the gain to humanity with the price which we are bound to pay for it, I think you may well rejoice in the result of such expeditions as those which have been recently conducted with such signal success in Nyassaland, Ashanti, Benin, and Nupé[3]—expeditions which may have, and indeed have, cost valuable lives, but as to which we may rest assured that for one life lost a hundred will be gained, and the cause of civilisation and the prosperity of the people will in the long run be eminently advanced. But no doubt such a state of things, such a mission as I have described, involves heavy responsibility. In the wide dominions of the Queen the doors of the temple of Janus[4] are never closed, and it is a gigantic task that we have undertaken when we have determined to wield the sceptre of empire. Great is the task, great is the responsibility, but great is the honour; and I am convinced that the conscience and the spirit of the country will rise to the height of its obligations, and that we shall have the strength to fulfil the mission which our history and our national character have imposed upon us. . . .

[L]et it be our endeavour, let it be our task, to keep alight the torch of Imperial patriotism, to hold fast the affection and the confidence of our kinsmen across the seas, that so in every vicissitude of fortune the British Empire may present an unbroken front to all her foes, and may carry on even to distant ages the glorious traditions of the British flag.

QUESTIONS FOR ANALYSIS

1. What organizational structure does Chamberlain envision for the future British empire? What will the empire require to remain unified?

2. How does Chamberlain link imperialism and nationalism? How does he define Britain's national mission?

3. Compare Chamberlain's ideas of the national mission with his description of the conditions in Africa. How do these two create a British identity that justifies imperialism?

4. How does Chamberlain's idea of Britain's national mission compare to Friedrich Fabri's idea of Germany's national mission (Source 4)? How are the two similar and different?

---

[3] African peoples and empires brought under British control in the late nineteenth century.
[4] Roman god of doorways (comings and goings), typically depicted with two faces.

6

"THE 'NEGATION OF GOD' . . ."

Edmund D. Morel
King Leopold's Rule in Africa   (1904)

Working at a shipping firm in Liverpool, England, Edmund D. Morel (1873–1924) heard horrible stories and rumors about the activities of British and other European merchants working in Africa. He began working as a part-time journalist to investigate the stories and focused his investigations on the rubber trade in the Congo Free State. In the treaties of the Berlin Conference in 1885, King Leopold II of Belgium had gained private authority over the Congo as his personal fiefdom. Leopold established a series of trusts to manage the Congo, which soon implemented a viciously coercive system of forced labor. The Congolese had to fulfill work quotas, especially to supply rubber, which grew wild in the region. In 1904, Morel founded the Congo Reform Association to pressure European governments to act against those guilty of human rights abuses and to persuade the Belgian government to overthrow Leopold's private rule of the Congo by annexing the territory and reforming its administration. In the same year, he published King Leopold's Rule in Africa, *excerpted below, to make the public case against unrestrained imperialism as practiced in the Congo.*

[E]verywhere [in the Congo] we see the same policy [of forced labor] at work, with the same results. What are the chief symptoms of the effects of that policy upon native life?

Outwardly the most striking effect is depopulation: slaughter, mutilation; emigration; sickness, largely aggravated by cruel and systematic oppression; poverty, and even positive starvation, induced by unlimited taxation in food-stuffs and live stock; a hopeless despair, and mental depression engendered by years of grinding tyranny; neglect of children by the general maltreatment of women, one of the most odious and disgraceful features of the system—these are some of the many recorded causes of depopulation which, in certain districts, has assumed gigantic proportions. . . .

What a sum total of human wretchedness does not lie behind that bald word "depopulation"! To my mind, the horror of this curse which has come upon the Congo peoples reaches its maximum of intensity when we force ourselves to consider its everyday concomitants; the crushing weight of perpetual, remorseless oppression; the gradual elimination of everything in the daily life of the natives which makes that life worth living. Under the prevailing system, every village is a penal settlement. Armed soldiers are quartered in every hamlet; the men pass nearly the

Edmund D. Morel, *King Leopold's Rule in Africa* (1904) (Reprinted Westport, Conn.: Negro University Press, 1970), 236, 242, 247–49, 253, 255–56.

whole of their lives in satisfying the ceaseless demands of the "Administration," or its affiliates the Trusts. . . .

The cumulative effects of depopulation and infantile mortality by dragging women away from their homes for forced labour requisitions—seizing them as "hostages," and "tying them up," whether virgins, wives, mothers, or those about to become mothers, in order to bring pressure to bear upon brothers, husbands, and fathers for the adequate supply of rubber or food taxes; flinging them into "prison," together with their children, often to die of starvation and neglect; flogging them, sometimes even unto death; leaving them at the mercy of the soldiers; distributing them after punitive raids among hangers-on—must be enormous. There we have depopulation through the infamous torture of women—often enough shot outright or mutilated—and the neglect and the mutilation of young children and boys; most of whom, it may be presumed, when so mutilated do not survive the operation, in order to have "the bad taste to show their stumps to the missionaries,"[1] as one of the Belgian deputies said in the course of the Congo debate in the Belgian House last year.

What has come over the civilised people of the globe that they can allow their Governments to remain inactive and apathetic in the face of incidents which recall in aggravated form the worst horrors of the over-sea slave trade, which surpass the exploits of Arab slave catchers? What could be worse than scenes such as these, which can be culled by the dozen. . . .

The Congo Government boasts that, in stopping intertribal warfare, it has stopped the selling of tribal prisoners of war into domestic slavery. The condition of the domestic slave under the African system is blissful beyond words, if you compare his lot with that of the degraded serf under the Leopoldian system. . . .

Enough has been said to show that under this system of "moral and material regeneration," constituting a monstrous invasion of primitive rights which has no parallel in the whole world, the family life and social ties of the people are utterly destroyed. . . .

If Gladstone[2] had been alive he would perhaps have found a phrase adequate to describe the revival of the slave trade under the ægis of a European Sovereign in Equatorial Africa, and the forms which that revival takes. But I doubt if even he could have found one more fittingly characterising it than that he so truly applied to other quarters. The "Negation of God" erected with a system—yes, indeed!

Why are these people allowed to suffer thus cruelly? What crime have they collectively committed in past ages that they should undergo to-day so terrible an expiation? Are they "groaning and dying" under this murderous system as a great object-lesson to Europe? What price, then, will Europe later on have to pay for the teaching? Inscrutable are the decrees of Providence. One wonders whether the deepening horror of this colossal crime will end by a reaction so violent that an era of justice will, for the first time in the history of Caucasian relationship with the Dark Continent, arise, never to be eradicated, for the peoples of Africa. Or that some day tropical Africa may breed brains as she breeds muscles, and then . . . ? But

---

[1] Amputation of a hand was a common form of punishment in the Belgian Congo.
[2] William Gladstone (1809–1898), four-time British prime minister, who spoke eloquently against Turkish atrocities in the Balkans in the 1870s and in Armenia in the 1890s.

it bodes little to dwell among the mists of conjecture. The future is closed to us. We grope in the dark, puzzled, incensed, impatient. The future is with God. To the past man may look and gather consolation in the knowledge that evils such as these bring their own Nemesis upon the nation whose moral guilt is primarily involved. Belgium, technically unconcerned, is morally responsible, and Belgium will suffer. . . .

If the policy of the Congo State were a national policy; if the Congo tribes were being systematically bled to death either through distorted zeal . . . or through lust of conquest; if the Congo Basin were capable of being colonised by the Caucasian race, the policy we condemn and reprobate would still be a crime against humanity, an outrage upon civilisation. But the Congo territories can never be a white man's country; the "Congo State" is naught but a collection of individuals—with one supreme above them all—working for their own selfish ends, caring nothing for posterity, callous of the present, indifferent of the future, as of the past, animated by no fanaticism other than the fanaticism of dividends—and so upon the wickedness of this thing is grafted the fatuous stupidity and inhumanity of the Powers in allowing the extermination of the Congo races to go on unchecked, barely, if at all, reproved.

QUESTIONS FOR ANALYSIS

1. What rhetorical tools does Morel use to describe the evil of Leopold's rule in the Congo? What "standards" does Morel call on in defining various actions in the Congo as evil?
2. How does Morel use the word *civilization* in his argument? How does his use of the word compare to Fabri's (Source 4) and to Chamberlain's (Source 5)?
3. How does Morel use religion in his argument? Does Morel's use of religion create a sense of a "civilizing mission"?
4. In what sense does Morel's argument transcend nationalist sentiment?

7

". . . THE REDIVISION OF THE WORLD."

Vladimir Lenin
Imperialism: The Highest Stage of Capitalism (1917)

Following in the tradition of Karl Marx, the radical left in Europe opposed European imperialism as an expansion of the capitalist system. The Russian Vladimir Lenin (1870–1924) studied Marx's writings and became a committed Marxist, eventually founding the Russian Communist Party. In addition, Lenin was a revolutionary theorist whose

Vladimir Lenin, *Imperialism, The Highest State of Capitalism,* in *V. I. Lenin: Selected Works* (New York: International Publishers, 1967), 1:744–47, 750–51, 773–74.

writings expanded and developed Marxist theory. In 1917, Lenin published Imperialism, The Highest Stage of Capitalism, *in which he argued that capitalism had changed in the late nineteenth century as competitive capitalism was replaced by monopoly capitalism. In monopoly capitalism, as Lenin explains in the excerpt below, a small number of banks and large industrial firms dominate economic life and promote imperialism to gain monopolistic control over markets and raw materials.*

Imperialism emerged as the development and direct continuation of the fundamental characteristics of capitalism in general. But capitalism only became capitalist imperialism at a definite and very high stage of its development, when certain of its fundamental characteristics began to change into their opposites, when the features of the epoch of transition from capitalism to a higher social and economic system had taken shape and revealed themselves in all spheres. Economically, the main thing in this process is the displacement of capitalist free competition by capitalist monopoly. Free competition is the basic feature of capitalism, and of commodity production generally; monopoly is the exact opposite of free competition, but we have seen the latter being transformed into monopoly before our eyes, creating large-scale industry and forcing out small industry, replacing large-scale by still larger-scale industry, and carrying concentration of production and capital to the point where out of it has grown and is growing monopoly: cartels, syndicates and trusts, and merging with them, the capital of a dozen or so banks, which manipulate thousands of millions. At the same time the monopolies, which have grown out of free competition, do not eliminate the latter, but exist above it and alongside it, and thereby give rise to a number of very acute, intense antagonisms, frictions and conflicts. Monopoly is the transition from capitalism to a higher system. . . .

[W]ithout forgetting the conditional and relative value of all definitions in general, which can never embrace all the concatenations of a phenomenon in its full development, we must give a definition of imperialism that will include the following five of its basic features:

(1) the concentration of production and capital has developed to such a high stage that it has created monopolies which play a decisive role in economic life; (2) the merging of bank capital with industrial capital, and the creation, on the basis of this "finance capital," of a financial oligarchy; (3) the export of capital as distinguished from the export of commodities acquires exceptional importance; (4) the formation of international monopolist capitalist associations which share the world among themselves, and (5) the territorial division of the whole world among the biggest capitalist powers is completed. Imperialism is capitalism at that stage of development at which the dominance of monopolies and finance capital is established; in which the export of capital has acquired pronounced importance; in which the division of the world among the international trusts has begun, in which the division of all territories of the globe among the biggest capitalist powers has been completed. . . .

The characteristic feature of imperialism is *not* industrial *but* finance capital. It is not an accident that in France it was precisely the extraordinarily rapid development of *finance* capital, and the weakening of industrial capital, that from the . . . [1880s] onwards, gave rise to the extreme intensification of annexationist (colonial) policy. The characteristic feature of imperialism is precisely that it strives to annex *not only* agrarian territories, but even most highly industrialised regions (German appetite for Belgium; French appetite for Lorraine), because (1) the fact that the world is already partitioned obliges those contemplating a *redivision* to reach out for *every kind* of territory, and (2) an essential feature of imperialism is the rivalry between several great powers in the striving for hegemony, i.e., for the conquest of territory, not so much directly for themselves as to weaken the adversary and undermine *his* hegemony. (Belgium is particularly important for Germany as a base for operations against Britain; Britain needs Baghdad as a base for operations against Germany, etc.) . . .

We see three areas of highly developed capitalism (high development of means of transport, of trade and of industry): the Central European, the British and the American areas. Among these are three states which dominate the world: Germany, Great Britain, and the United States. Imperialist rivalry and the struggle between these countries have become extremely keen because Germany has only an insignificant area and few colonies; the creation of "Central Europe" is still a matter for the future, it is being born in the midst of a desperate struggle. For the moment the distinctive feature of the whole of Europe is political disunity. In the British and American areas, on the other hand, political concentration is very highly developed, but there is a vast disparity between the immense colonies of the one and the insignificant colonies of the other. In the colonies, however, capitalism is only beginning to develop. The struggle for South America is becoming more and more acute.

There are two areas where capitalism is little developed: Russia and Eastern Asia. In the former, the population is extremely sparse, in the latter it is extremely dense; in the former political concentration is high, in the latter it does not exist. The partitioning of China is only just beginning, and the struggle for it between Japan, the U.S., etc., is continually gaining in intensity. . . .

[M]onopoly has grown out of colonial policy. To the numerous "old" motives of colonial policy, finance capital has added the struggle for the sources of raw materials, for the export of capital, for spheres of influence, i.e., for spheres for profitable deals, concessions, monopoly profits and so on, economic territory in general. When the colonies of the European powers, for instance, comprised only one-tenth of the territory of Africa (as was the case in 1876), colonial policy was able to develop by methods other than those of monopoly—by the "free grabbing" of territories, so to speak. But when nine-tenths of Africa had been seized (by 1900), when the whole world had been divided up, there was inevitably ushered in the era of monopoly possession of colonies and, consequently, of particularly intense struggle for the division and the redivision of the world.

QUESTIONS FOR ANALYSIS

1. According to Lenin, what are the principal features of finance capitalism? How does finance capitalism reinforce monopoly capitalism?

2. What role do colonies play in monopoly capitalism, according to Lenin? How does imperialism serve as a tool of monopoly capitalism?

3. How does imperialism transcend national boarders? How does it expand national conflict?

IMPERIALISM AT HOME

While statesmen and others debated the value and meaning of Europe's colonial possessions in the late nineteenth and early twentieth centuries, the colonies themselves came to have a significant presence in European social, political, and cultural life. Increasingly, colonized peoples traveled to Europe for economic, political, and educational purposes, and a growing number immigrated permanently. Similarly, many Europeans immigrated to North and South America, Australia, and New Zealand, creating family connections across the oceans that could be maintained through improved transportation and postal systems. Further, the practices and language of imperialism found use in European domestic political and social contexts as individuals linked European domestic controversies, political affairs, and intellectual concerns to the issues of imperialism.

8

"... TO PERFORM CULTURES THAT WERE NOT THEIR OWN."

Andrew Zimmerman
Anthropology and Antihumanism in Imperial Germany (2001)

Europeans had long read with fascination the descriptions of non-European cultures written by missionaries, colonial officials, travelers, and others. By the nineteenth century, Europeans had the opportunity to view these cultures more directly as colonial authorities, anthropologists, and the producers of zoos and popular entertainments cooperated to bring non-Europeans to Europe to perform and demonstrate their "authentic cultures." Historian Andrew Zimmerman has investigated these popular colonial shows and the context of their production in Germany, and he suggests in the excerpt below how these shows reinforced the legitimacy of German colonial power.

[I]ndividuals [from German colonial territories] were enlisted to perform in German zoos and variety shows. ...

Andrew Zimmerman, *Anthropology and Antihumanism in Imperial Germany* (Chicago: University of Chicago Press, 2001), 16, 18–20, 24–26, 28–30.

[Z]oological gardens and other arenas of popular amusement were ready markets for non-European performers, who could draw large crowds to ethnographic displays, or *Völkerschauen,* in which they presented what were supposed to be their native customs, dances, and other entertaining practices. . . .

[Promoters of these events] worked in close contact with Berlin anthropologists in staging and promoting these shows. This was not merely because of their own scientific interests but also because they needed anthropologists to attest to the authenticity of their performers and to legitimate them to the police. These shows brought non-Europeans into Germany, sometimes violated child labor laws, often included more sexualized nudity than the law generally tolerated, and seemed generally weird and suspicious to the Prussian police. There was even the suggestion that the exotic performances were a cover for "a bordello of the worst sort." The appearance of what was often referred to as "a certain scientific interest" behind these shows helped allay official suspicions and get the required police approval. . . .

Performers were thus expected to conform to a certain anthropological understanding of the non-European. . . . [A]nthropologists expected Africans, indigenous Americans, Pacific Islanders, and marginalized societies in Europe and Asia to be "natural peoples" (*Naturvölker*). Natural peoples supposedly lacked writing, culture, and history and thus contrasted sharply with "cultural peoples" (*Kulturvölker*), such as Europeans. Anthropologists believed that in natural peoples they would be able to glimpse human nature directly, unmasked by the complications of history or culture. . . . [T]hese anthropological expectations shaped the interactions and mutual misunderstandings that occurred between the natives of Germany and the travelers who came from abroad. . . .

One of the greatest, and certainly the best documented, ethnographic performances took place as part of the 1896 Berlin Colonial Exhibition, when the Colonial Section of the German Imperial Foreign Office, in cooperation with a group of private financial backers, brought more than one hundred people from German colonies in Africa and the Pacific to live and perform next to a carp pond in Treptow Park.[1] The Foreign Office requested that each colonial government organize a group of indigenous people for the exhibition. The German state tried to recruit indigenous elites as performers, hoping to bolster colonial domination by impressing them with German museums, theaters, zoos, and military parades during their stay in Berlin. The German state thus conceived of the colonial exhibition as a kind of two-way *Völkerschau,* performing foreign lands for the Germans and Germany for the colonial performers. . . .

[A] German commercial agent working in the region assembled a group of eight inhabitants of New Britain, an island in the Bismarck Archipelago,[2] to represent Germany's Pacific colonies at the colonial exhibition. Because the organizers assumed that Pacific Islanders would have particular difficulty adjusting to the European climate, they sent only strong men who had already had extensive contact with Germans. This group knew so little about the societies that it was to represent that the commercial agent had to purchase "traditional" objects to send with the performers,

---

[1] Park south of Berlin.
[2] Island group in the southwest Pacific Ocean.

acquire the material for their "traditional" dwellings, and explain to the natives how to set up an "ancestor house." He even had to clarify what an ancestor house was. . . .

The German government in the [African] coastal capital Dar es Salaam[3] . . . organized performers like a labor gang for railroad building or plantation work, recruited, managed, and accompanied by a German commercial agent. . . . The East African government decided to supplement this rather paltry selection of East African societies by hiring Swahili workers to dress like Wamakonde.[4] The group of forty East Africans brought along a large number of local products and the material to build the supposedly traditional houses in which they would live and be displayed. As with the Pacific Island performers, the East African group's manager thought it necessary to enlist a European expert . . . to help set up their dwellings. During their stay in Berlin, the East Africans enacted lifestyles and staged dances and songs presumed to be characteristic of societies from their home country. In the evenings, after the visitors had gone home and they no longer had to perform, the East Africans amused themselves with German folk songs and even sang "Deutschland über Alles,"[5] accompanied on the violin by a member of the group.

The managers of the exhibition made a point of strictly regulating the lives of the performers. A volume commemorating the exhibition described this discipline in detail. Performers had to rise each morning at six to wash themselves, which must have been miserable in the unusually cold summer of 1896. They were then required to clean their living spaces, after which they carried out supposedly traditional tasks, such as grinding meal or weaving. They were given a midday break until three o'clock, when their performances began. Except for the Herero,[6] most performed dances, although the Duala[7] also rowed boats around the carp pond. At ten in the evening (which would have been just after nightfall in Berlin summers), the performers were required to retire to their huts, where they were allowed to socialize among themselves. Such discipline did not constitute merely a means of control; it was also an argument about both colonialism and anthropology. Colonialism, this well-ordered exhibition suggested, imposed a European form on a non-European content. Despite the enormous amount of power exercised by exhibition promoters as well as by the colonial state generally, the colonized, this exhibition suggested, neither shaped nor were shaped by European colonists. Such a spectacle of disciplined colonial subjects implied German control without suggesting any kind of cultural hybridity between colonizer and colonized. Such hybridity might have undermined the legitimacy given to German imperialism by describing Europeans as cultural peoples and those they ruled in Africa and the Pacific as natural peoples. . . .

Of course the exhibition organizers could not help but be aware that the Africans and Pacific Islanders present in Berlin had been coached by anthropologists and other European experts to perform cultures that were not their own.

---

[3] Large port town on the east African coast.
[4] East African coastal people.
[5] "Germany over all." Song that became the German national anthem in 1922.
[6] Bantu-speaking people from southwest Africa.
[7] Bantu-speaking people from west central Africa.

However, it seems to have been the general view that the authenticity of the performances was secured—not undermined—by knowledgeable European directors.... Indeed, the fact that a European expert had instructed the performers from the Bismarck Archipelago on the meaning and construction of an ancestral hut was cited as evidence for its authenticity, against the criticism that it was a mere *"curiosity shop."* The show's promoters evidently assumed that the European directors helped the colonial subjects represent more authentic cultures than they otherwise could have. In the very content of the show, as well as in the disciplined regime forced on the performers, European direction proved fundamental to the construction of primitive cultures but at the same time effaced itself as formal direction separate from authentic content.

QUESTIONS FOR ANALYSIS

1. According to Zimmerman, on what basis did anthropologists distinguish between "natural peoples" and "cultural peoples"? How did the regulation of the performers' lives while in Germany reinforce this distinction?

2. How do the difficulties that the shows' producers had in obtaining performers demonstrate the weaknesses of the anthropologists' categories of "natural peoples" and "cultural peoples"? How did this structuring of identity reinforce German colonialism?

3. Compare the image of colonized peoples described by Pearson (Source 3) to the image presented in the ethnographic displays described by Zimmerman. Explain both similarities and differences.

9

". . . THE STRONGEST AND BEST . . ."

British Imperial Advertisements   (1885 and 1891)

In the late nineteenth century, cheap newspapers and magazines and the new department store facilitated the growth of consumer culture and the practice of mass advertising. As corporations and retail merchants induced consumers to purchase their products, they drew on popular themes that both reflected and shaped popular culture. Imperialism—especially when paired with nationalist sentiment and pride—was a frequent theme as advertisers linked their products to imperial adventures and successes. Following are two British advertisements within that tradition. The first advertisement, promoting Liebig Company's Extract of Meat and published in the magazine Lady's Pictorial *in 1891, quoted a reference to that product from Henry Stanley's widely popular account of his voyages in Africa,* In Darkest Africa. *The second, a showcard from 1885, promotes Fry's Cocoa.*

IN DARKEST AFRICA

Effect of the Liebig Company's Extract of Meat on a Madi Carrier.—"On the 22nd, soon *after the advance had reached camp, a cold and heavy shower of rain fell, which demoralised many in the column: their failing energies and their impoverished systems were not proof against cold. Madis and Zanzibaris dropped their loads in the road, and rushed helter-skelter for the camp. One Madi managed to crawl near my tent, wherein a candle was lit, for in a rainstorm the forest, even in daylight, is as dark as on an ordinary night in the grassland. Hearing him groan, I issued out with the candle, and found the naked body rigid in the mud, unable to move. As he saw the candle-flame his eyes dilated widely, and he attempted to grasp it with his hands. He was at once borne to a fire, and laid within a few inches of it, and with the addition of a pint of hot broth made from the* **Liebig Company's Extract of Meat,** *we restored him to his senses. On the road in front of the rear guard two Madis died, and also one Zanzibari of the rear column, stricken instantaneously to death by the intensely cold rain."* —Stanley's "In Darkest Africa."

SHOWCARD FOR FRY'S COCOA, 1885

Accompanying Text:

The World's Verdict.—My Lord, this International Jury has come to the unanimous conclusion that **Fry's Pure Concentrated Cocoa** *is the "strongest and best which can possibly be produced."*

QUESTIONS FOR ANALYSIS

1. What relationships are suggested between the British subjects and the colonial subjects in the two advertisements? In what different ways are British superiority and leadership clearly marked?

2. How does each advertisement indicate the salutary effect of British rule over colonial peoples? How does this salutary component compare with the ideas projected by the ethnographic displays discussed by Zimmerman (Source 8)?

3. In the Liebig Company image, how does the image of the candle support British imperial power? In the Fry's Cocoa advertisement, how does the "World's Verdict" also do so?

4. How do the ideas projected in these advertisements compare to the arguments made by Chamberlain (Source 5)? How do they link imperialism and nationalism?

10

William Booth
In Darkest England (1890)

The revivalist British minister William Booth (1829–1912) dedicated himself to preaching salvation and social reform. In 1878, he founded the Salvation Army, which he modeled on the British army with himself as its first general. Although harassed vigorously during the early years, Booth and the Salvation Army came to be respected for their efforts to aid the outcasts of society. In 1890, Booth published In Darkest England, *in which he proposes a series of remedies for poverty and vice that gained wide public support and received considerable financial backing. In the excerpt below, Booth begins the work justifying the need for aid to the British poor by comparison to the peoples of Africa.*

This summer the attention of the civilised world has been arrested by the story which Mr. Stanley[1] has told of "Darkest Africa" and his journeyings across the heart of the Lost Continent. In all that spirited narrative of heroic endeavour, nothing has so much impressed the imagination, as his description of the immense forest, which offered an almost impenetrable barrier to his advance. The intrepid explorer, in his own phrase, "marched, tore, ploughed, and cut his way for one hundred and sixty days through this inner womb of the true tropical forest." The mind of man with difficulty endeavours to realise this immensity of wooded wilderness, covering a territory half as large again as the whole of France, where the rays of the sun never penetrate, where in the dark, dank air, filled with the steam of the heated morass, human beings dwarfed into pygmies and brutalised into cannibals lurk and live and die. . . .

It is a terrible picture, and one that has engraved itself deep on the heart of civilisation. But while brooding over the awful presentation of life as it exists in the vast African forest, it seemed to me only too vivid a picture of many parts of our own land. As there is a darkest Africa is there not also a darkest England? Civilisation, which can breed its own barbarians, does it not also breed its own pygmies? May we not find a parallel at our own doors, and discover within a stone's throw of our cathedrals and palaces similar horrors to those which Stanley has found existing in the great Equatorial forest? . . .

The Equatorial Forest traversed by Stanley resembles that Darkest England of which I have to speak, alike in its vast extent . . . ; its monotonous darkness, its

---

[1] Henry Stanley (1841–1904), British American explorer whose successful effort to locate Dr. David Livingstone in Africa captivated European imaginations in the early 1870s.

William Booth, *In Darkest England and The Way Out* (London: Salvation Army, 1890) (Reprinted New York: Garrett Press, 1970), 9, 11–15.

malaria and its gloom, its dwarfish de-humanized inhabitants, the slavery to which they are subjected, their privations and their misery. That which sickens the stoutest heart, and causes many of our bravest and best to fold their hands in despair. . . . It is the great Slough of Despond[2] of our time.

And what a slough it is no man can gauge who has not waded therein, as some of us have done, up to the very neck for long years. Talk about Danté's Hell, and all the horrors and cruelties of the torture-chamber of the lost! The man who walks with open eyes and with bleeding heart through the shambles of our civilisation needs no such fantastic images of the poet to teach him horror. Often and often, when I have seen the young and the poor and the helpless go down before my eyes into the morass, trampled underfoot by beasts of prey in human shape that haunt these regions, it seemed as if God were no longer in His world, but that in His stead reigned a fiend, merciless as Hell, ruthless as the grave. Hard it is, no doubt, to read in Stanley's pages of the slave-traders coldly arranging for the surprise of a village, the capture of the inhabitants, the massacre of those who resist, and the violation of all the women; but the stony streets of London, if they could but speak, would tell of tragedies as awful, of ruin as complete, of ravishments as horrible, as if we were in Central Africa; only the ghastly devastation is covered, corpse-like, with the artificialities and hypocrisies of modern civilisation.

The lot of a negress in the Equatorial Forest is not, perhaps, a very happy one, but is it so very much worse than that of many a pretty orphan girl in our Christian capital? We talk about the brutalities of the dark ages, and we profess to shudder as we read in books of the shameful exaction of the rights of feudal superior.[3] And yet here, beneath our very eyes, in our theatres, in our restaurants, and in many other places, unspeakable though it be but to name it, the same hideous abuse flourishes unchecked. A young penniless girl, if she be pretty, is often hunted from pillar to post by her employers, confronted always by the alternative—Starve or Sin. And when once the poor girl has consented to buy the right to earn her living by the sacrifice of her virtue, then she is treated as a slave and an outcast by the very men who have ruined her. Her word becomes unbelievable, her life an ignominy, and she is swept downward ever downward, into the bottomless perdition of prostitution. . . .

The blood boils with impotent rage at the sight of these enormities, callously inflicted, and silently borne by these miserable victims. Nor is it only women who are the victims, although their fate is the most tragic. Those firms which reduce sweating to a fine art, who systematically and deliberately defraud the workman of his pay, who grind the faces of the poor, and who rob the widow and the orphan, and who for a pretence make great professions of public-spirit and philanthropy, these men nowadays are sent to Parliament to make laws for the people. The old prophets sent them to Hell—but we have changed all that. . . .

Darkest England, like Darkest Africa, reeks with malaria. The foul and fetid breath of our slums is almost as poisonous as that of the African swamp. Fever is almost as chronic there as on the Equator. Every year thousands of children are killed off

---

[2] Quoted from John Bunyan's *Pilgrim's Progress* (1678), referring to a deep bog that is so difficult to cross that it causes one to lose hope.
[3] Legendary European feudal right of lords to sleep with any vassal's bride on her wedding night.

by what is called defects of our sanitary system. They are in reality starved and poisoned, and all that can be said is that, in many cases, it is better for them that they were taken away from the trouble to come.

Just as in Darkest Africa it is only a part of the evil and misery that comes from the superior race who invade the forest to enslave and massacre its miserable inhabitants, so with us, much of the misery of those whose lot we are considering arises from their own habits. Drunkenness and all manner of uncleanness, moral and physical, abound. Have you ever watched by the bedside of a man in delirium tremens? Multiply the sufferings of that one drunkard by the hundred thousand, and you have some idea of what scenes are being witnessed in all our great cities at this moment. As in Africa streams intersect the forest in every direction, so the gin-shop stands at every corner with its River of the Water of Death flowing seventeen hours out of the twenty-four for the destruction of the people. A population sodden with drink, steeped in vice, eaten up by every social and physical malady, these are the denizens of Darkest England amidst whom my life has been spent, and to whose rescue I would now summon all that is best in the manhood and womanhood of our land.

QUESTIONS FOR ANALYSIS

1. What comparisons does Booth draw between "darkest Africa" and "darkest England"? Of what significance is the metaphor of darkness?

2. How does Booth assess blame for problems in England and in Africa?

3. How does Booth emphasize the way oppressive conditions in the lives of Africans and in the lives of the poor in Britain affect the human body? What role does gender play in his text?

4. How does Booth's descriptions of Africa compare to the images of Africans that Europeans encountered at the ethnographic displays described by Zimmerman (Source 8)?

11

". . . TO SHARE IN THIS NATIONAL AND IMPERIAL POWER . . ."

Antoinette M. Burton
The White Woman's Burden (1992)

Historian Antoinette Burton has written numerous books and articles on the impact of imperialism on British culture in the nineteenth and twentieth centuries. In the following reading, Burton has just noted the frequent references to Asian women in the British feminist press of the late nineteenth and early twentieth centuries. She then

---

Antoinette M. Burton, "The White Woman's Burden: British Feminists and 'The Indian Woman,' 1865–1915," in *Western Women and Imperialism: Complicity and Resistance,* ed. Nupuir Chaudhuri and Margaret Strobel (Bloomington: Indiana University Press, 1992), 147–51.

*suggests the significance of imperialism to one of the most important domestic politi-
cal issues of that time—the right of women to vote.*

What all this attention to Indian women represents is an objectification of "the
Oriental woman" by English feminist interpreters. Largely as a result of the journal-
istic exposure given to the topic, by the 1890s discussion of "the position of Indian
women" had become so formulaic that one writer feared, "There is perhaps some danger of . . . [the public] becoming wearied by a too frequent repetition of the story."
The recital of woes usually began with a description of the inside of the *zenana*,[1]
followed by observations of the relationship between an Indian husband and his
wives, then commentary on the practice of child-marriage, culminating in what
was perceived as the final condemnation of Indian life: the treatment of widows
as outcasts. . . .

[T]here was an assumption on the part of many British feminists that their "fe-
maleness" gave them an understanding of Indian women that transcended national
and racial boundaries. The common bond of motherhood was also considered a
transcendent link. This may appear to be a spontaneous reaction between women
of different cultures; indeed, it became a tenet of "international sisterhood." But in
this instance it must be located in its specifically British feminist-imperial context.
British feminists of the period *posited* "woman" the world over as one class, one
race, one nation—a static type that, in "less civilized" societies than Britain, was
corrupted by heathen cultures and religions. In light of this construct, the attention
lavished on India and its women in periodicals like the *Women's Penny Paper* had
the effect of stripping Indian women of their foreignness, their exoticism, thereby
domesticating them for a British audience. . . . [F]eminists writing for periodicals
were concerned with defusing the eroticism often attributed to women of the East
by Western male commentators. But since Indian women rarely spoke for themselves in these controlled textual spaces, British feminists robbed them of their
power to name themselves, effectively silencing them in the name of feminist "sis-
terly" protectiveness. In the process, they underscored their own moral purity and
legitimized themselves as the imperial authorities on "Indian womanhood." . . .

The militants proclaimed that the cause of woman was one throughout the
world, and by the twentieth century they were noting with pride the progress made
by their Eastern "sisters," many of whom were quitting the harem, becoming educated, and leaving the life of *purdah* (seclusion) for good. The editors of *Votes for
Women* were greatly intrigued by the upheavals in Turkey and observed with ap-
probation that Turkish women were being included in the new reform councils.
Their enthusiasm, however, was tempered. In an editorial in September 1908
Christabel Pankhurst[2] warned that Eastern women should not expect to be given
political equality when their Western sisters were still denied this fundamental
right. British women, she wrote,

---

[1] Harem.
[2] Christabel Pankhurst (1880–1958), militant suffragist leader and political strategist.

have nothing to say against the enfranchisement of their fellow creatures in any part of the world, but they feel it hard, that being the rightful heirs to the constitutional liberty built up by their foremothers and forefathers, they should have that inheritance withheld, while men of other races are suddenly and almost without preparation leaping into possession of constitutional power.

Both moderates and militants advocated the vote for white women over black men but rarely were their priorities (or their resentments) so baldly spelled out. Pankhurst went on to claim that the British had created the very idea of sex equality, and therefore to British women emancipation would and should come first.

Pankhurst voiced a sentiment that was expressed by many suffrage workers, both militant and nonmilitant, during the first decade of the twentieth century—namely, that England was the "storm-centre" of the international women's movement and that British feminists should fight their own sex equality battles first, so that they could then aid women of other nations in doing the same. It seemed fitting to this generation of feminists that, since England was the Mother of Parliaments *and* the mother country of the empire, it should be acknowledged as the "Mother of the new world-wide movement" as well. They saw it not only as the role of women of other nations, both West and East, to fall in behind, but also as part of the natural order of things in a world where Britain was the imperial leader. Feminists' preoccupation with the condition of women in India and the East not only expresses their imperial assumptions but also underscores a militant national and racial pride which characterized the diverse campaigns for female emancipation in Britain.

This pride is immediately apparent in suffrage literature, where feminists, in claiming their right to citizenship, also claimed their right to be part of the political nation and empire. At times suffragists conflated the idea of nation with the idea of empire. In other words, they believed that the nation into which they sought admission did not just extend to empire, but that citizenship in the nation meant citizenship in the empire as well. Winning the vote "for the women of the empire," bringing female emancipation to "England and her Dependencies"—these were standard feminist cries. It went without saying that the "women" who were to receive the grant of citizenship hoped for by suffragists were the white women of England and the colonies. For late nineteenth- and early twentieth-century middle-class feminists, as for many of their contemporaries, whether they sympathized with votes for women or not, pride in empire was as "natural" and as "right" as pride in nation, since empire and nation could be taken as one and the same. . . . What feminists wanted above all was to share in this national and imperial power, to participate in what one suffragist called "the moral government of the world."

It bears emphasizing here that feminists believed in the idea of racial progress, and that for them as for many Victorians empire itself was an outward and visible sign of Britain's racial supremacy. Even if the idea of conquering native peoples offended some sensibilities, the promotion of enlightened government through moral example appealed enormously to feminists who believed that the redemptive power of their sex lay in its superior moral qualities. Progress . . . did not, could not exist in a vacuum. It had necessarily to function in comparison to something else, something less well developed and, ultimately, something less "civilized." For

British feminists of the period that point of comparison was the woman of the East. She was a pivotal reference in arguments for female emancipation and she became the embodiment of personal, social, and political subjection in a decaying civilization—the very symbol, in short, of what British feminists were struggling to progress away *from* in their own struggle for liberation. . . .

Although Indian women of the period were active in social reform and feminist causes of their own making, many British feminists insisted on creating them as passive colonial subjects partly in order to imagine and to realize their own feminist objectives within the context of the imperial nation into which they sought admission.

QUESTIONS FOR ANALYSIS

1. According to Burton, what role did Indian women play in British feminism? What role did imperialism play?

2. How does Burton distinguish between Indian women and the "Indian women" of British feminism?

3. What attitudes did British feminists hold toward the British empire? How does Burton's description of the imperial attitudes of British feminists compare with the imperial attitudes of Fabri (Source 4) and Chamberlain (Source 5)?

4. Given Burton's analysis, what irony arises in the British feminists' assertion of an "international sisterhood"?

CHAPTER QUESTIONS

1. How do the themes used by the authors to justify imperialism compare to the imperialistic themes integrated into European domestic affairs? What themes occur most strongly in both contexts?

2. How do the themes used by late nineteenth-century authors to justify imperialism compare to the justifications for colonialism written in the sixteenth century (Chapter 1) and the seventeenth century (Chapters 3 and 4)? What continuities exist between their arguments? What new issues were raised?

3. How do Europeans' attitudes toward their imperial territories compare to the argument of Michael Adas (Chapter 9, Source 8) about the shifting attitudes of Europeans toward non-Western peoples?

Chapter 11

EUROPE SHAKEN

The supreme self-confidence that the Western world enjoyed at the beginning of the twentieth century soon would be severely shaken. Challenges to Western culture, science, and knowledge arose in many forms—in the abstract art of Pablo Picasso and Wassily Kandinsky, in the modernist music of Igor Stravinsky and Arnold Schönberg, in the physical science of Albert Einstein and Max Planck, in the analytical philosophy of Ludwig Wittgenstein, and in the psychotherapy of Sigmund Freud. However, the most dramatic blow to Western self-assurance came from the First World War, which confronted the West with the destructive power that a technologically sophisticated society could produce when it marshaled its economic capabilities for warfare. The war had begun with much nationalistic fervor and fanfare; however, the massive loss of life and areas of devastated landscape led many to question the benefits of Europe's industrial transformation and the meaning of its allegedly superior civilization. Further, toward the end of the war, in 1917, a small group of communists led by Vladimir Lenin seized political power in Russia. For some, the creation of the Soviet Union marked the beginning of a hopeful new era that would lead to a more just society. For others, the existence of the Soviet Union threatened the economic and political values that had established European supremacy worldwide—a threat reinforced by Lenin's criticism of imperialism (Chapter 10).

European supremacy itself was under question in the decades around the turn of the century. The rapid transformation of Japanese economic and political life during the Meiji era (1868–1912) demonstrated that industrialization, democratic politics, and nationalist sentiment were not limited to Western societies. Furthermore, Japan's pursuit of its own imperial ambitions in Asia suggested that non-Western societies could turn the tools of Western economic and military expansion against Western colonial powers. Nationalist challenges also threatened the most formidable of the colonial systems—the British empire. In India, nationalists began to question aggressively the benefits of British rule. These years marked a transition from the years of triumphant Western colonialism to a period of uncertainty and retrenchment.

CHALLENGES IN EUROPE

The First World War disrupted early twentieth-century Europe as thoroughly as Napoleon had a century earlier. The staggering loss of life during the war stood as horrible testimony to the "productive capabilities" of the newly industrialized societies. As the first fully industrialized conflict, the war was fought not only on the battlefield but also on the home front. As governments organized their nations for war, the extensive participation and sacrifices required of civilians ensured that the war and its consequences were experienced throughout the belligerent societies. As the war came to a conclusion, the revolution in Russia and the establishment of the Soviet Union cast a continuing shadow over the postwar West. The new Soviet government presented itself as the vanguard of an international socialist movement whose aim was to foment working-class revolutions throughout the industrialized world and champion the liberation of colonized peoples. In 1919, Lenin founded an affiliation of international communist parties and organizations called the Comintern (the Communist International or the Third International) to promote this agenda—an act that fueled distrust of the new Soviet government among the governments of the industrialized states.

1

"THEY SOBBED WITH RAGE."

Ernst Jünger
The Storm of Steel (1921)

As a nineteen-year-old student from Hanover, Ernst Jünger eagerly enlisted in the German army in the first year of World War I. He soon rose to the rank of platoon lieutenant, commanding a small group of men in the German trenches of northeastern France and receiving over twenty wounds. Although Jünger himself remained an enthusiastic warrior to the end, his description of his wartime experiences in the book The Storm of Steel *portrays the dreadful conditions faced by soldiers on all sides of the conflict—a far cry from the romantic notions of war many held at the war's beginning. In the excerpt below, Jünger recounts his experiences of trench warfare in late 1915.*

7.10 [7 October], 1915. Standing at dawn near my section's post on the fire-step opposite our dugout when a rifle bullet tore one of the men's caps from front to back without hurting him. Just at this time two pioneers were wounded on our wire. One shot through both legs. The other shot through the ear.

During the morning the left-flank post was shot through both cheek-bones. The blood spurted in thick streams from the wound. To finish the bad luck, Lieutenant Ewald came to our sector to-day to photograph sap[1] N, which is only 50 metres from the trench. As he turned to get down off the fire-step a shot shattered the back of his head. He died instantly. . . .

---

[1] Extension of a trench.

Ernst Jünger, *The Storm of Steel* (London: Chatto and Windus, 1929) (Reprinted New York: Fertig, 1975), 47–49, 51–54.

30.10. Owing to heavy rain in the night the trench fell in in many places, and the soil mixing with the rain to a sticky soup turned the trench into an almost impassable swamp. The only comfort was that the English were no better off, for they could be seen busily scooping the water out of their trench. As we were on higher ground, they had the benefit of the superfluous water we pumped out as well. The collapse of the trench walls brought to light a number of those who fell [died] in the last autumn's fighting. . . .

21.11. I took an entrenching party from the Altenburg Redoubt to C sector. One of them, Landsturmsman Diener, climbed on to a ledge in the side of the trench to shovel earth over the top. He was scarce up when a shot fired from the sap got him in the skull and laid him dead on the floor of the trench. He was married and had four children. His comrades lay in wait a long while behind the parapet to take vengeance. They sobbed with rage. It is remarkable how little they grasp the war as an objective thing. They seem to regard the Englishman who fired the fatal shot as a personal enemy. I can understand it. . . .

11.12. One morning, when, thoroughly wet through, I went up out of the dugout into the trench, I could scarcely believe my eyes. The field of battle that hitherto had been marked by the desolation of death itself had taken on the appearance of a fair. The occupants of the trenches on both sides had been driven to take to the top, and now there was a lively traffic and exchange going on in schnaps, cigarettes, uniform buttons, etc., in front of the wire. The crowds of khaki-coloured figures that streamed from the hitherto so deserted English trenches had a most bewildering effect.

Suddenly there was a shot that dropped one of our fellows dead in the mud. . . . Whereupon both sides disappeared like moles into their trenches. I went to the part of the trench opposite the English sap and shouted across that I wished to speak to an officer. Some of the English did in fact go back, and presently returned from their main trench with a young man who was distinguished from them, as I could see through my glasses, by a smarter cap. At first we conversed in English and then rather more fluently in French, while the men stood round listening. I put it to him that one of our men had been killed by a treacherous shot. He replied that this was the doing of the company on his flank and not of his men. "There are some swine also on your side," he remarked when some shots from the sector next to ours passed close to his head; and thereupon I made ready to take cover forthwith. We said a good deal to each other in the course of the interview in a fashion that can only be described as sportsmanlike, and would gladly at the end have made some exchange of presents in memory of the occasion.

It has always been my ideal in war to eliminate all feelings of hatred and to treat my enemy as an enemy only in battle and to honour him as a man according to his courage. It is exactly in this that I have found many kindred souls among British officers. It depends, of course, on not letting oneself be blinded by an excessive national feeling, as the case generally is between the French and the Germans. The consciousness of the importance of one's own nation ought to reside as a matter of course and unobtrusively in everybody, just as an unconditional sense of honour does in the gentleman. Without this it is impossible to give others their due.

In order to be on a clear footing again we made a solemn declaration of war within three minutes of breaking off our parley. . . .

We spent Christmas Eve in the line. The men stood in the mud and sang Christmas carols that were drowned by the enemy machine-guns. On Christmas Day we lost a man in No. 3 platoon by a flanking shot through the head. Immediately after, the English attempted a friendly overture and put up a Christmas tree on their parapet. But our fellows were so embittered that they fired and knocked it over. And this in turn was answered with rifle grenades. In this miserable fashion we celebrated Christmas Day.

QUESTIONS FOR ANALYSIS

1. How does Jünger bring to life for the reader the experience of trench warfare?
2. Of what importance are Jünger's sense of honor and duty to his life within the trenches?
3. How does Jünger both link himself with and distinguish himself from the men under his command? How does Jünger connect himself with his British opponents?
4. What role does nationalism play in Jünger's response to the war? How does Jünger sustain a sense of identity based both on nation and on class?

2

". . . TO GUARD AND PROTECT THE LIFE OF MY FAMILY. . . ."

Anna Eisenmenger
Blockade (1918)

World War I was fought not only on the battlefield but also in the factories and with the sacrifices that national populations made at home. Similar to many others, Anna Eisenmenger, the middle-class wife of a Viennese physician, suffered the deprivations and losses of war. In 1914, the Eisenmenger family consisted of Anna and her husband; three sons, Otto, Karl, and Erni; a daughter, Liesbeth; Liesbeth's husband, Rudi; and Liesbeth's newborn son, Wolfi. By 1918, Eisenmenger's husband had died from overwork and poor nutrition, Otto had been missing for several years on the Russian front, and Karl and Rudi both had been wounded but had returned to the front, where they were joined by Erni in 1917. Liesbeth and Wolfi lived with Eisenmenger, and they were aided by a former servant named Kathi. Eisenmenger kept a diary during the war, which was published shortly afterward. In the following excerpt she describes the closing weeks of the war and the immediate aftermath.

Anna Eisenmenger, *Blockade: The Diary of an Austrian Middle-Class Woman 1914–1924* (New York: Long and Smith, 1932), 16–21, 39, 44–45.

October 25th, 1918

At last a letter from Karl, delivered to us by one of his comrades on the journey to the Western Front. This man told me that Karl had been transferred to the trenches as the result of a dispute with his superior officer. . . .

[The letter reads:] "The life here is unworthy of any human being. I ask myself again and again how the motley collection of older men and young boys in these front positions endure this life. Insufficient food, tattered shoes and uniforms. No possibility of keeping one's self clean. Are our human sensibilities already utterly stupefied? . . .

I feel convinced that we can't go on like this. The War will end soon, one way or another. See that you get in food supplies, for Vienna will be eaten out of house and home by the soldiers when they come back. I too suffer from chronic hunger."

I talked it over with Liesbeth. She thinks that Karl's letter is exaggerated. But Liesbeth's catarrh[1] is worse, and Wolfi is begging for milk; it is now a week since we had the ¼-pint of milk due to us on our ration cards. I resolve to "*hamster*."[2] During my husband's lifetime, I dared not do this. When he was seriously ill, I did it without his knowledge. I did not feel that I was becoming demoralised—on the contrary, I might almost say: Have I not the right to guard and protect the life of my family? For all its rigorous organisation, the State could not feed its citizens, and it cannot do so to-day. . . . If the War is to end soon, as Karl declares and as I pray to God it may, I shall have to provide for another three hungry stomachs in addition to Wolfi and his ailing mother. Although I had now and then had recourse to one of the much abused "*Schleichhändler*"[3] in order to procure the necessary foodstuffs for our household, such as milk, eggs, butter or fat, I was far from having accumulated any surplus stores. The foodstuffs distributed by the Government were very dear, but the prices charged by the Schleichhändler were often five or six times as high. . . .

Already in the year 1914 we housewives began to suffer from measures of economy, which were not improved when the military authorities took over the control of supplies. We submitted uncomplainingly, because we received news of victories both on the Western and the Eastern Fronts and of hundreds of thousands of prisoners. And each of these victories must be bringing blessed peace nearer to us. Now, at the end of the fourth year of war, when the Central Powers and their whole civilian population are like a besieged fortress cut off from all external supplies and without any hope of breaking through the hunger blockade, I am no longer disposed to sacrifice any more members of my family to the Moloch[4] of war. . . .

[*Eisenmenger's youngest son, Erni, returns from the war blind. A few days later, Karl returns home.*]

Karl looked very ill. He had no underlinen or socks. His uniform was dirty and in rags. "Mother, I am famished!" he said, and walking straight into the kitchen

---

[1] Inflammation of a mucous membrane, especially of the air passages of the head and throat.
[2] Hoard food.
[3] Smugglers.
[4] Malevolent deity of the Moabites that was mentioned in the Jewish scriptures and that required human sacrifice and self-mutilation of its worshipers.

without waiting for me to bring him something he began to devour our rations of bread and jam. "Forgive me, Mother, but we have got into the habit of taking what we can find." He only greeted us very casually and did not notice until much later that Erni, who had come in to welcome him on Liesbeth's arm, was wounded. "Hullo! So it's caught you too!" and then, still hurriedly chewing and swallowing: "Well, just wait! We'll pay them out yet, the war profiteers and parasites. We've grown wiser out there in the trenches, far wiser than we were. Everything must be changed, utterly changed." . . .

November 6th, 1918

[*Anna persuades a reluctant Karl to accompany her on a "hamstering" expedition.*]

When we left the house, we found the streets filled with excited crowds. There were some desperate-looking types among them.

Several times we saw officers being mishandled in the streets in order to force them to take the imperial eagle[5] from their caps. I was indignant, but Karl seemed delighted: "The imperial eagle is at the point of death. Quite a different phoenix will arise from its ashes."

An elderly higher-grade officer was being jostled by some hooligans, because he refused to strip off his former distinctions. "Karl, go and help him. . . ." "I shouldn't dream of doing such a thing. It's these great men who have grown fat on the War and looked after their own safety. I wouldn't raise a finger to help one of them." Karl's conduct appalled me. But just then the officer helped himself. He gave the most aggressive of his assailants a vigorous box on the ear, whereupon all five heroes retreated in confusion. It was clear that they were not used to encountering resistance. I had just made up my mind to go to the help of the old gentleman and I shouted to him a loud "Bravo!" And turning to Karl I said: "What right have these young hooligans to rob our officers of distinctions which it is only their duty to wear?"

"Oh, Mother," said Karl, "the difference between officers and soldiers has vanished with the War, just as in future there will be no privileged social class. No emperor, no princes, no counts, no barons."

"Tell me, Karl," I said, "where did you get hold of these anarchistic or nihilistic ideas? You always used to be a good, patriotic Austrian."

"My ideas are neither anarchistic nor nihilistic. I am a communist."

"Good heavens, Karl! You are not speaking seriously?"

"Quite seriously, Mother. How is it possible to be anything else, when one sees the injustice suffered by those who are not born into the privileged classes of society?"

My face must have worn an expression of horror, for Karl cast a sidelong glance at me and said laughing:

"Come, come! That doesn't mean that I'm a criminal!"

---

[5] Symbol of the Habsburg dynasty that had ruled Austria since the thirteenth century. Five days after the events described here, the last Habsburg emperor abdicated.

QUESTIONS FOR ANALYSIS

1. On what types of issues (e.g., political, social, economic, personal) does Eisenmenger focus? Provide examples. How do her interests compare to Karl's interests?

2. What changes in Eisenmenger's attitude toward the war occurred between 1914 and 1918? How does she account for these changes?

3. What changes does Eisenmenger suggest occurred in Karl's attitudes, and how does she account for these changes?

4. How does Karl challenge national identity? How do Karl's reactions to the war compare to Ernst Jünger's reactions (Source 1)?

3

". . . THE WORKERS OF EUROPE ARE SLAUGHTERING EACH OTHER. . . ."

Vladimir Lenin and Georgy Chicherin
Are You a Trade Unionist? An Appeal to British Workers (1920)

With the communists' seizure of power in Russia in 1917, a period of political and military struggle began in Russia that resulted in civil war between 1918 and 1920. The anti-Soviet White forces were led by former tsarist military officers and well supplied by the British and French governments, and their defeat by the communists surprised and disturbed Western observers. The communists' greatest asset was Lenin's brilliant political leadership, for he secured support for the revolution (or at least neutrality toward it) from various social and ethnic factions by promises of land and political self-determination. In the midst of the civil war, Lenin, with the Soviet diplomat Georgy Chicherin (1872–1936), wrote and published the pamphlet below in which they appeal to British workers to oppose British support of the anti-Soviet forces.

If you are a trade unionist, do you thoroughly understand the reason of your membership of a trade union? You know that the employer does not employ you for love, you know that, if he can, he will press your wages down to the lowest level, you know that when you are organised you are better able to get your demands accepted than when your employer has to deal with each man separately. Even so, your employers have resisted your demands, and you have been compelled to come out on strike.

Vladimir Lenin and Georgy Chicherin, *Are You a Trade Unionist? An Appeal to British Workers* (London: People's Russian Information Bureau, 1920), 2–7.

You have learnt that masters are no friends of workers.

You have learnt the need for working class discipline, and working class loyalty: for you will agree that there is no more contemptible creature than a blackleg.[1] But being a trade unionist means much more than this. Have you ever asked yourself why it is that in spite of your organisation, in spite of your strikes, even successful strikes, your position as a worker has not improved? . . .

You see then merely to be a trade unionist is not enough. You are not merely up against the particular employer you work for, but against all employers as a class.

Your interests are not merely identical with the workers in your particular trade or industry, but with all workmen.

The Class War

In fact you are up against the whole capitalist system. What is capitalism? Capitalism is the system under which the land, the railways, factories, and the means of obtaining a livelihood are owned by private individuals, who use them for their own benefit.

Who owns England? Do you? Can you point to any part of England and say: "This is mine"? If you can, you are one of the lucky ones. There are not many working men in England who can say that. The England that you call "your country" is not your country, but the landlords'. In England women whose husbands are fighting "for their country" are being evicted from their houses. If you do not pay rent to the landlord you cannot live in "your country."

The tremendous industry of England is not run for the purpose of providing you and your family with food and clothing. It is run for the purpose of providing profit and interest for the capitalists, financiers, and for rich shirkers generally to lead idle and luxurious lives while you slave and toil to create it.

All wealth comes from labour. Does labour get it? If it did there would be no poor people in England. The worker is robbed of the product of his labour. He is robbed by those who take the rent profit and interest, i.e., the landlords and the capitalists. Between you and them there is an irreconcilable antagonism. As long as there are capitalists, workmen will be robbed, and continue to remain poor. Your aim as a trade unionist, desiring to improve your conditions in life, should be to abolish capitalism and landlordism, and take possession of your country. You would be doing more good for yourself, if you conquered England for the English people.

The War and the Class War

The productivity of labour has increased to such an extent that the capitalists have to find new markets to dispose of the surplus wealth and profits you have created. This is what this war is about. The German capitalists and the Allied capitalists are competing with each other as to who shall control the undeveloped parts of the world for the purpose of investing the profits they wrung out of the labour of their

---

[1] Worker who opposes trade unions and crosses union picket lines; scab.

respective workers. This is why you have been brought to Russia. Your capitalists see in our country a rich field for investment. And so you have been brought here to overthrow our workers' government, and bring back the rule of the landlords, capitalists, and the Tzar. It is indeed a grim jest, that the workers of Europe are slaughtering each other by the thousand for the purpose of deciding where the wealth they have been plundered of, shall go. Even during the war the class war has gone on. At the outbreak of the war the capitalists said to you: "We must not quarrel now. We are of the same race, we must all unite and show a solid front to the enemy." The workers believed them, and gave up everything in defence of their country. But the capitalists continued in their old business of bleeding the workers. With them it was "business as usual," only more so. For the people the war has been the cause of ruin, sorrow, grief, and disaster. For the capitalists it has been an El-Dorado.[2] They have made such profits as they have never in their lives dreamed of. Immense fortunes have been made out of the blood and tears of the working people.

It has been the same in every country. In every country the capitalists have used the workers as cannon-fodder on the battlefields, and as material for exploitation at home. The capitalist class worships no other god but profit, and owns allegiance to any country where profit can be obtained.

Does not this show that the peoples are not divided according to nationality, but according to class?

The workers of each country are not enemies to each other. Their real enemies are at home, the capitalists, who are robbing and exploiting the people, and who have set the workers against each other, in order that they may be able to fleece them the more.

The workers can only put an end to this exploitation, and mutual slaughter by overthrowing the capitalists and taking control into their own hands.

This is the logical outcome of being a trade unionist.

Our Revolution

We, the workers of Russia, in our fights with the capitalist have always taken this view. In October last we swept the capitalists out of power, and declared that Russia belongs to the whole of the Russian people. . . .

The Russian capitalists do not stand an earthly chance against us by themselves. But your capitalists know that their interests are the same as those of the Russian capitalists, and have come to their assistance.

Why do you not recognise your class interest in the same way? You as trade unionists are fighting your capitalists, we have settled our account with ours.

What are you going to do? Are you going to undo the work we have commenced? Are you going to do the dirty work of your enemies, the capitalist class? Or will you remain loyal to your own class—the working class—and support our effort to secure the world for labour!

---

[2] Legendary city of gold.

QUESTIONS FOR ANALYSIS

1. How do Lenin and Chicherin challenge nationalism as a framework for identity? What abuses of national sentiment do they identify?
2. What do these authors promote as a new source of identity, and how do they justify this source?
3. How does this depiction of class conflict compare to Anna Eisenmenger's description of her son Karl's attraction to communism (see Source 2)?
4. Why would the Western industrialized powers believe themselves threatened by the new Soviet Union under Lenin's leadership? How does Lenin's message as communicated in this pamphlet challenge many components of Western thought (for example, liberalism, imperialism, and nationalism)?

4

"... THE MOST GRISLY OF ALL WEAPONS."

Winston Churchill
The World Crisis   (1929)

Winston Churchill (1874–1965), the son of a British aristocratic politician and an American mother, had a tumultuous political career. He rose to early prominence but often became involved in public controversies that led him to lose governmental positions. During World War I, he served in several offices in the war ministries, and in 1919, after the war had ended, he was appointed Secretary of War. By prolonging British intervention in the Russian Civil War, he hoped to overthrow the new communist government, the Soviet Union. Again out of office by 1922, Churchill began an autobiographical history of the war entitled The World Crisis. *In the fifth volume of this work, published in 1929 and excerpted below, Churchill, a passionate anticommunist, discusses Vladimir Lenin and the Bolshevik Revolution in Russia.*

In the middle of April [1917] the Germans took a sombre decision. . . . Upon the Western front they had from the beginning used the most terrible means of offence at their disposal. They had employed poison gas on the largest scale and had invented the "Flammenwerfer."[1] Nevertheless it was with a sense of awe that they turned upon Russia the most grisly of all weapons. They transported Lenin in a

---

[1] Flamethrower.

Winston Churchill, *The World Crisis* (New York: Scribner's, 1929), 5:63–66.

sealed truck[2] like a plague bacillus[3] from Switzerland into Russia. Lenin arrived at Petrograd on April 16. Who was this being in whom there resided these dire potentialities? Lenin was to Karl Marx what Omar was to Muhammad.[4] He translated faith into acts. He devised the practical methods by which the Marxian theories could be applied in his own time. He invented the Communist plan of campaign. He issued the orders, he prescribed the watchwords, he gave the signal and he led the attack.

Lenin was also Vengeance. Child of the bureaucracy, by birth a petty noble, reared by a locally much respected Government School Inspector, his early ideas turned by not unusual contradictions through pity to revolt extinguishing pity. Lenin had an unimpeachable father and a rebellious elder brother. This dearly loved companion meddled in assassination. He was hanged in 1894.[5] Lenin was then sixteen. He was at the age to feel. His mind was a remarkable instrument. When its light shone it revealed the whole world, its history, its sorrows, its stupidities, its shams, and above all, its wrongs. It revealed all facts in its focus—the most unwelcome, the most inspiring—with an equal ray. The intellect was capacious and in some phases superb. It was capable of universal comprehension in a degree rarely reached among men. The execution of the elder brother deflected this broad white light through a prism: and the prism was red. . . .

Implacable vengeance, rising from a frozen pity in a tranquil, sensible, matter-of-fact, good-humoured integument![6] His weapon logic; his mood opportunist. His sympathies cold and wide as the Arctic Ocean; his hatreds tight as the hangman's noose. His purpose to save the world: his method to blow it up. Absolute principles, but readiness to change them. Apt at once to kill or learn: dooms and afterthoughts: ruffianism and philanthropy: but a good husband; a gentle guest; happy, his biographers assure us, to wash up the dishes or dandle[7] the baby; as mildly amused to stalk a capercailzie[8] as to butcher an Emperor. The quality of Lenin's revenge was impersonal. Confronted with the need of killing any particular person he showed reluctance—even distress. But to blot out a million, to proscribe entire classes, to light the flames of intestine war in every land with the inevitable destruction of the well-being of whole nations—these were sublime abstractions. . . .

Lenin was the Grand Repudiator. He repudiated everything. He repudiated God, King, Country, morals, treaties, debts, rents, interest, the laws and customs of centuries, all contracts written or implied, the whole structure—such as it is—of human society. In the end he repudiated himself. He repudiated the Communist system. He confessed its failure in an all important sphere. He proclaimed the New

---

[2] Railroad car.
[3] Plague-producing bacteria.
[4] Umar Ibn Al-Khattab (586–644), the second Muslim caliph, conquered lands adjacent to the Arabian peninsula, transforming the Islamic state from an Arabian territory to a world power.
[5] Lenin's eldest brother was hanged in 1887 for conspiring to assassinate Tsar Alexander III.
[6] Enveloping layer, such as skin.
[7] Affectionately bounce.
[8] Ground-dwelling bird.

Economic Policy and recognised private trade.[9] He repudiated what he had slaughtered so many for not believing. They were right it seemed after all. They were unlucky that he did not find it out before. But these things happen sometimes: and how great is the man who acknowledges his mistake! ...

Lenin's intellect failed at the moment when its destructive force was exhausted, and when sovereign remedial functions were its quest.[10] He alone could have led Russia into the enchanted quagmire; he alone could have found the way back to the causeway. He saw; he turned; he perished. The strong illuminant that guided him was cut off at the moment when he had turned resolutely for home. The Russian people were left floundering in the bog. Their worst misfortune was his birth: their next worst—his death.

QUESTIONS FOR ANALYSIS

1. In what terms does Churchill express admiration for Lenin? Condemnation?
2. What paradoxes does Churchill note in Lenin's character? How does his description account for these paradoxes?
3. What is the purpose of Churchill's reference to imperialism? Why does Churchill regret Lenin's death?
4. How does Churchill's description of Lenin and his political skill find reinforcement or contradiction in Lenin and Chicherin's appeal to British workers (Source 3)?

IMPERIALISM CHALLENGED

European nations that were confidently expressing their political, economic, and military strength around the globe in the late nineteenth century soon found their power challenged on many fronts. As Asian and African territories of the British empire matured in the nineteenth century, local populations called for greater political autonomy. In the most important British colony, India, a home-rule movement emerged that, in its moderate form, sought Indian control over Indian affairs. In its radical form, home rule rejected not simply British rule but much of Western civilization. In Japan, which had not been colonized, an equally powerful challenge emerged to Western colonial ambitions in Asia—the Japanese adoption of Western economic and technical prowess and some Western political ideals and practices. Japan's rapid industrial transformation and military defeat of Russia in the Russo-Japanese War of 1904 to 1905—fought largely over political influence in China—stunned the Western powers, and its own imperial ambitions threatened European imperialism in Asia.

---

[9] After the Bolshevik economic policies of War Communism (1918–1921) led the economy to near collapse, Lenin had the Communist Party adopt the New Economic Policy as a strategic retreat, which temporarily permitted the return of some private ownership in land, manufacture, and trade.

[10] Lenin died following a stroke in January 1924.

5

". . . TO CLING TO THE OLD INDIAN CIVILISATION . . ."

Mohandas Gandhi
Indian Home Rule   (1909)

Born to a political family in India, Mohandas Gandhi (1869–1948) prepared to enter the Indian administrative elite by studying law in London, where he became acquainted with British humanitarians and radicals who criticized industrial society and valued moral good over material goods. Gandhi took on the mantle of political leadership when working as a lawyer in southern Africa between 1893 and 1914. He resisted efforts by local leaders of European descent and by British colonial officials to restrict the political and civil rights of the Indian population living there. In 1909, in connection with this work, Gandhi visited London and held discussions with Indian students about the desire for Indian "home rule." These students rejected the British colonial rule of India but wished to retain British political, economic, and social norms. That same year, Gandhi published Indian Home Rule, *written in the form of a dialogue between himself and a reader who represented the typical Indian student in London, to set out his own vision of what home rule should mean to India.*

Reader: . . . Now will you tell me something of what you have read and thought of this [modern European] civilisation?

Editor: Let us first consider what state of things is described by the word "civilisation." Its true test lies in the fact that people living in it make bodily welfare the object of life. We will take some examples. The people of Europe to-day live in better-built houses than they did a hundred years ago. This is considered an emblem of civilisation, and this is also a matter to promote bodily happiness. Formerly, they wore skins, and used as their weapons spears. Now, they wear long trousers, and, for embellishing their bodies, they wear a variety of clothing, and, instead of spears, they carry with them revolvers containing five or more chambers. If people of a certain country, who have hitherto not been in the habit of wearing much clothing, boots, etc., adopt European clothing, they are supposed to have become civilised out of savagery. Formerly, in Europe, people ploughed their lands mainly by manual labour. Now, one man can plough a vast tract by means of steam-engines, and can thus amass great wealth. This is called a sign of civilisation. Formerly, the fewest men wrote books, that were most valuable. Now, anybody writes and prints anything he likes and poisons people's minds. Formerly, men travelled in waggons; now they fly through the air in trains at the rate of four hundred and more miles

Mohandas Gandhi, *Indian Home Rule* (1909) (Madras: Ganesh, 1919), 26–28, 30, 65–69, 71.

per day. This is considered the height of civilisation. . . . Formerly, when people wanted to fight with one another, they measured between them their bodily strength; now it is possible to take away thousands of lives by one man working behind a gun from a hill. This is civilisation. Formerly, men worked in the open air only so much as they liked. Now, thousands of workmen meet together and for the sake of maintenance work in factories or mines. Their condition is worse than that of beasts. They are obliged to work, at the risk of their lives, at most dangerous occupations, for the sake of millionaires. Formerly, men were made slaves under physical compulsion, now they are enslaved by temptation of money and of the luxuries that money can buy. . . .

This civilisation is such that one has only to be patient and it will be self destroyed. According to the teaching of Mahomed[1] this would be considered a Satanic civilisation. Hinduism calls it the Black Age. I cannot give you an adequate conception of it. It is eating into the vitals of the English nation. It must be shunned. . . .

Reader: You have denounced railways, lawyers and doctors. I can see that you will discard all machinery. What, then, is civilisation?

Editor: The answer to that question is not difficult. I believe that the civilisation India has evolved is not to be beaten in the world. . . .

Civilisation is that mode of conduct which points out to man the path of duty. Performance of duty and observance of morality are convertible terms. To observe morality is to attain mastery over our mind and our passions. So doing, we know ourselves. The Gujarati[2] equivalent for civilisation means "good conduct."

If this definition be correct, then India, as so many writers have shown, has nothing to learn from anybody else, and this is as it should be. We notice that mind is a restless bird; the more it gets the more it wants, and still remains unsatisfied. The more we indulge our passions, the more unbridled they become. Our ancestors, therefore, set a limit to our indulgences. They saw that happiness was largely a mental condition. A man is not necessarily happy because he is rich, or unhappy because he is poor. The rich are often seen to be unhappy, the poor to be happy. Millions will always remain poor. Observing all this, our ancestors dissuaded us from luxuries and pleasures. We have managed with the same kind of plough as it existed thousands of years ago. We have retained the same kind of cottages that we had in former times, and our indigenous education remains the same as before. We have had no system of life-corroding competition. Each followed his own occupation or trade, and charged a regulation wage. It was not that we did not know how to invent machinery, but our forefathers knew that, if we set our hearts after such things, we would become slaves and lose our moral fibre. They therefore, after due deliberation, decided that we should only do what we could with our hands and feet. They saw that our real happiness and health consisted in a proper use of our hands and feet. They further reasoned that large cities were a snare and a useless encumbrance, and that people would not be happy in them, that there would be gangs of thieves and

---

[1] Muhammad (570–632), founder of Islam.
[2] One of the two official languages of modern India, and the language in which Gandhi typically wrote.

robbers, prostitution and vice flourishing in them, and that poor men would be robbed by rich men. They were, therefore, satisfied with small villages. They saw that kings and their swords were inferior to the sword of ethics, and they, therefore, held the sovereigns of the earth to be inferior to the Rishis[3] and the Fakirs.[4] A nation with a constitution like this is fitter to teach others than to learn from others. . . .

The tendency of Indian civilisation is to elevate the moral being, that of the western civilisation is to propagate immorality. The latter is godless, the former is based on a belief in God. So understanding and so believing, it behoves every lover of India to cling to the old Indian civilisation even as a child clings to its mother's breast.

---

[3] Religious sages.
[4] Holy men who possess miraculous powers.

QUESTIONS FOR ANALYSIS

1. What does Gandhi criticize about early twentieth-century European civilization? What does he praise about Indian civilization?
2. What principles shape Gandhi's assessments of these civilizations?
3. What does Gandhi imply would constitute Indian home rule?
4. What similarities and differences exist between Gandhi's rejection of industrial society and Lenin and Chicherin's appeal to the British working classes (Source 3)? What might account for these similarities and differences?

6

". . . TO GIVE INDIANS SOMETHING . . ."

Gilbert Elliot-Murray-Kynynmound, the Earl of Minto
Despatch to John Morley, March 21, 1907

Gilbert Elliot-Murray-Kynynmound, the fourth earl of Minto (1845–1914), served in several prominent positions in Great Britain's colonial administration, rising to the position of viceroy of India between 1905 and 1910. Minto believed that moderate political reforms in India would quell radical Indian nationalist demands and earn the loyalty of the Indian landowning and commercial classes, yet he also resorted to harsh measures against those who encouraged armed resistance to British rule. Excerpted here is a dispatch from Minto to John Morley, Secretary of State for India, in which he explains the need for and goals of political reform in India.

"Despatch from Viceroy The Earl of Minto-in-Council to John Morley, 21 March 1907," in *The Dominions and India since 1900: Select Documents on the Constitutional History of the British Empire and Commonwealth,* ed. Frederick Madden and John Darwin (Westport, Conn.: Greenwood Press, 1993), 662–63.

We have to deal with a . . . force—a force that has not yet begun to agitate, but which is quietly and surely establishing its base for future operations. We are confronted with the growth of an educated class, as yet but little connected with Congress[1] machinery, and composed of many moderate, thoughtful, and loyal men. The spread of education which British rule has done so much to encourage is bearing fruit. Important classes of the population are learning to realise their own position; to estimate for themselves their own intellectual capacities; and to compare their claims for an equality of citizenship with those of the ruling race. . . .

The question we have to face is not how to deal with a local and transient agitation, it is rather what attitude are we to assume towards the results of the education we have ourselves imparted, how are we to receive the awakening of the Eastern world; are we to recognise the natural aspirations of educated men to share in the government of their country; are we to entrust them with a fraction of our power and responsibility; or are we to continue to govern as conquerors and aliens regardless of the natural ambitions of the people we rule over, regardless of the future consequences of our refusal to recognise their claims? . . .

[The government of India was not advocating representative government along western lines. . . . "As trustees of British principles and traditions we are equally bound to consult the wishes of the people." It was necessary to provide machinery through which their views could be expressed.]

To say this, is not to advocate the introduction of popular representation. The Government of India must remain autocratic and the supreme power must be vested in British hands, and cannot be delegated to any kind of representative assembly. No such assembly could claim to speak on behalf of the Indian people so long as the uneducated masses, forming nearly 90 per cent of the adult male population, are absolutely incapable of understanding what representative government means and of taking an effective part in any system of election. . . .

[Was it possible to fuse the Indian principle of autocracy and the British principle of constitutionalism into a "constitutional autocracy—and thus give to our administration a definite and permanent shape?"]

[The proposals] which we recommend in principle for your provisional acceptance represent an advance in the direction of associating the people of India with ourselves in the work of legislation and administration. They may fairly be described as an attempt to give to India something that may be called a constitution framed on sufficiently liberal lines to satisfy the legitimate aspirations of all but the most advanced Indians, whilst at the same time enlisting the support of the conservative elements of native society—a constitution based upon the traditions and practice of both Indian and English rulers,—not an experimental makeshift, but a working machine representing all interests that are capable of being represented and providing for an adequate expression of the sentiments and requirements of the masses of the people, and in particular of the great agricultural class forming two-thirds of the entire population. All experience goes to show that when a given set of political institutions

---

[1] Founded in 1885, the Congress Party dominated Indian national politics and the movement for independence from British rule, although prior to 1917 the Congress Party proposed primarily moderate reforms.

has once been called into existence, those institutions tend, if they are only moderately well adapted to the practical needs of the people, to attract to themselves the conservative instinct, the distaste for change as such, which is everywhere strong and nowhere stronger than in India. We are not without hope that in the course of a few years the constitution which we propose to establish will come to be regarded as a precious possession round which conservative sentiment will crystalise and will offer substantial opposition to any further change. We anticipate that the aristocractic elements in society and the moderate men, for whom at present there is no place in Indian politics, will range themselves on the side of the Government and will oppose any further shifting of the balance of power and any attempt to democratise Indian institutions. However this may be, we should be on firm ground in refusing to make any further concessions until the constitution had had a fair trial, and in assuming this attitude we believe that we should have the support of the best opinion both in India and in England.

QUESTIONS FOR ANALYSIS

1. How does Minto explain the increased political agitation in India? How does Minto's explanation reinforce the idea of the superiority of British rule over Indian rule?
2. What type of political arrangement does Minto envision evolving between Britain and India? How does he hope to secure the continuation of this arrangement?
3. What can be inferred from Minto's letter about his expectations for the future of imperialism?
4. How does Minto's discussion of Indians and their political ambitions demonstrate a European perspective on these issues? How does his perspective compare to Gandhi's perspective (Source 5)?

"... TO WORK IN CONCERT WITH JAPAN ..."

Baron Albert d'Anethan
Dispatches from Japan (1894 and 1904)

Baron Albert d'Anethan (1849–1910) enjoyed a long career as a Belgium diplomat, serving from 1873 to 1875 as secretary to the Belgian legation in Tokyo and from 1893 to his death in 1910 as the Belgian government's chief representative in Japan. A sympathetic student of Japanese history, d'Anethan wrote numerous dispatches to Belgian

---

The D'Anethan Dispatches from Japan, 1894–1910: The Observations of Baron Albert d'Anethan Belgian Minister Plenipotentiary and Dean of the Diplomatic Corps, ed. and trans. George Alexander Lensen (Tallahassee: Diplomatic Press and Tokyo: Sophia University, 1967), 7–8, 187–90.

officials, providing information and advice, especially as Japan pressed territorial and political conflicts with Russia that eventually led to Japan's stunning victory in the Russo-Japanese War. In the excerpt below from his dispatches, d'Anethan reflects on the changes he had seen Japan undergo and on Japan at the commencement of the Russo-Japanese War.

Dispatch of March 12, 1894

What was Japan like when he [Emperor Meiji][1] succeeded to the throne? A country less known and less important than Siam[2] and Korea in our own day. And now he sees about him the Representatives of all the Sovereigns of Europe, the most powerful of whom will soon vie for his alliance.

The few junks[3] which hugged the coast as they sailed to fish, have now been replaced by hundreds of steamers [steam ships] that are engaged in large-scale trade in the Inland Sea[4] and with China and Korea. Japanese lines transport native products as far as Bombay[5] and are getting ready to compete with European companies in the ports of America and England.

The railway allows the Sovereign to scour all parts of his Empire in thirty-six hours. . . . In the palace, from where he can communicate by telephone, electricity has been installed.

Material progress is matched by moral advances of even greater significance. Public spirit has developed. Instruction at all levels has spread everywhere. In the remotest villages children find schools, and in Tokyo superb buildings of universities and colleges of higher education rise proudly. . . .

If the most complete peace reigns in the interior, Japan possesses also the means of making herself respected by the foreign countries. Her Army, constantly drilled and commanded by trained officers, can match European troops. . . .

In his determined pursuit of Western progress and civilization, the Emperor has bestowed on his people a liberal Constitution, and Japan alone in Asia has respect for individual rights, religious tolerance for all creeds, equal justice for all, and the abolition of torture.

The few difficulties which the institution of a parliamentary regime has created for the Government are no greater than in countries long accustomed to liberty. They do not diminish in any way the grandeur of the conception [of the Constitution] of 1889, which more than any of the reforms of the past quarter of a century has contributed to placing Japan on a footing of equality with the civilized nations. . . .

---

[1] Meiji (1852–1912), emperor of Japan during whose reign Japan was dramatically transformed from a feudal country into one of the great powers of the modern world.
[2] Thailand.
[3] Ships.
[4] Body of water and major sea transportation route lying between three Japanese islands.
[5] India's principal port city on the Arabian Sea and its chief financial and commercial center.

Dispatch of May 7, 1904

As far as Japan is concerned, I am convinced—and if Your Excellency will be so good as to reread my correspondence, you will see that I get my information from reliable sources—that the Imperial Government will not demand after the war or at a moment favorable for peaceful intervention from Europe or from Washington more complete assurances than those formulated for Russia during the negotiations. It wants neither "one stone of the fortresses of Port Arthur[6] nor one inch of Chinese territory." It will not demand any concessions or any privilege that would not be accorded to all the nations interested in China, and will even recognize the economic interests acquired by Russia through the construction of railroads.

Japan . . . does not want to attempt the revival of China single-handedly. She wants to work with the European nations and America. It has been her ambition—consistent with her interests—to join the Concert of the Great Powers. She has succeeded partly by her attitude at the time of the siege of Beijing and by her alliance with England. Today she wants that no difference be made in the orchestra between her and the musicians of the white race.

In . . . 1901 . . . Marquis Ito[7] told me, that "Japan would commit national suicide if she refused to cooperate loyally [with the Powers] toward a better administration of the Chinese Empire" and also that, "in Europe one is inclined too much to believe that we strive primarily for a political influence which would be detrimental to the Western Nations. One says the Japanese and Chinese are of another race and the yellow race will always have the tendency to draw together and unite against the white race. Nothing is farther from the truth or more absurd." . . .

Dispatch of May 28, 1904

A dispatch from our Legation in Washington, kindly sent to me by Your Excellency, says that there are misgivings in certain circles that Japan one day will want to head a movement of "Asia for the Asians," a slogan coined a few years ago by Count Okuma.[8] Considering the policy followed by Japan for the past half a century and trusting the words of the statesmen who under the direction of the Emperor have presided over the extraordinary destinies of this country, which has astonished the world with her progress as much as she has now made it shudder with the exploits of her armies and fleets, we do not hesitate to say that these fears are absolutely fanciful. Strong in her insular position and secured by her protectorate over Korea, Japan will only ask to develop her resources, expand her industries, and share with the other commercial Powers the great market of China. If her rights are respected, Japan will not threaten either England or the United States, or France, or even

---

[6] Lüshun, formerly called Port Arthur, city and strategic naval port in China.
[7] Ito Hirobumi (1841–1909), Japanese elder statesman and premier.
[8] Okuma Shigenobu (1838–1922), Japanese elder statesman and twice prime minister.

Russia, which (except for China where they have occupied only certain points) have divided the richest part of the Asian continent among themselves.

As for our country, which has only economic interests, it will be to our advantage to work in concert with Japan ... in the development of our commerce and the expansion of our industrial enterprises.

I am aware that there is a fairly general feeling in Europe that Russia will emerge from the war victorious, that Japan, in view of the numerical force of the Russians, will soon be drained of men and money. One thought the same in Europe when Japan attacked China. The delusions under which one labors today regarding the relative strength of the Powers facing each other are due to the fact, that one ignores in Europe the enormous preparations made in Japan for years to fight and sustain the war until the desired objective has been attained.

QUESTIONS FOR ANALYSIS

1. What does d'Anethan point to as evidence of the progress made by Japan as a nation? How do his choices indicate his own Western origins?

2. How does d'Anethan respond to the issue of race raised by Europeans with regard to Japan? Why does he discount the issue?

3. Why does d'Anethan anticipate a Japanese victory over Russia? How does d'Anethan's dispatch of 1894 reinforce his arguments in 1904?

4. How does d'Anethan's explanation for Japan's transformation compare to Minto's understanding of the sources of change in India (Source 6)?

8

"REMARKABLE SYSTEM!"

Punch
Three Cartoons   (1904 and 1905)

By the early twentieth century, the British satirical magazine Punch *(first described in Chapter 9, Source 6) had established itself as a mainstay of popular entertainment. Continuing to rely on humor and satire to poke fun at political, social, and cultural affairs,* Punch *both reflected and shaped popular attitudes about public issues. During the First Opium War,* Punch *had encouraged the popular perception of China as a weak, backward land. With the Russo-Japanese War,* Punch *continued to poke irreverent fun at war and its participants, yet a distinctly new image emerged of Japan and the relationship between Japan and the Western powers.*

A LESSON IN PATRIOTISM.

JOHN BULL. "*YOUR* ARMY SYSTEM SEEMS TO WORK SPLENDIDLY. HOW DO YOU MANAGE IT?"
JAPAN. "PERFECTLY SIMPLE. WITH US EVERY MAN IS READY TO SACRIFICE HIMSELF FOR HIS COUNTRY —*AND DOES IT!*"
JOHN BULL. "REMARKABLE SYSTEM! I MUST TRY AND INTRODUCE THAT AT HOME!"

Note: John Bull *is a traditional personification of Great Britain.*

AN EMERGENCY EXIT.

Russian Bear. "I'M CUTTING RATHER A POOR FIGURE IN THIS COMPETITION. I THINK I SHALL GET OUTSIDE ON TO THE DANGEROUS PART, AND THEN THEY'LL HAVE TO RESCUE ME. . . . I SHOULD RATHER LIKE TO BE RESCUED."

ALLIES.

" *Oh, East is East, and West is West* . . . . . .
But there is neither East nor West, Border, nor Breed, nor Birth,
When two strong men stand face to face, tho' they come from the ends of the earth!"—RUDYARD KIPLING.

Note: With Japan's success in the Russo-Japanese War, Britain formed an alliance with Japan in 1905. Rudyard Kipling (1865–1936) was an English poet and short-story writer whose works celebrated British imperialism.

QUESTIONS FOR ANALYSIS

1. What images of Japanese power does each cartoon project? How do the images characterize the relationship between Japan and the Western powers?

2. How do the images of power in the cartoons compare to d'Anethan's description of the changes in Japan (Source 7)?

3. How do the cartoons use "comparisons" to establish Japanese power? How do these comparisons identify Japan as a great power?

4. How does the Rudyard Kipling quotation reinforce Japan's new status?

9

"... A BASIS FOR NATIONAL REORGANIZATION ..."

Kita Ikki
Plan for the Reorganization of Japan (1919)

As Japan gained international prominence in the early twentieth century, numerous variants of Japanese ultranationalism flourished. Some ultranationalists rejected all Western influences in Japan, but most wished to integrate Western technologies and practices with Japanese ideas and institutions. Kita Ikki (1884–1937) became the chief spokesperson for ultranationalist revolutionaries in Japan in the 1910s, 1920s, and 1930s. In 1919, he published Plan for the Reorganization of Japan, *excerpted below, which calls for radical reforms in Japan. By curbing the power of financial and industrial interests, elected politicians, and bureaucrats, revolutionaries hoped to produce a powerful Japanese society that was under direct leadership of the emperor and able to fulfill Japan's declared mission of leading and protecting Asia from Western imperialism. After an attempted coup in 1936 by some of Ikki's supporters in the military, Kita was arrested and executed.*

At present the Japanese empire is faced with a national crisis unparalleled in its history; it faces dilemmas at home and abroad. The vast majority of the people feel insecure in their livelihood and they are on the point of taking a lesson from the collapse of European societies, while those who monopolize political, military, and economic power simply hide themselves and, quaking with fear, try to maintain their unjust position. Abroad, neither England, America, Germany, nor Russia has kept its word, and even our neighbor China, which long benefited from the protection we provided through the Russo-Japanese War, not only has failed to repay us but instead despises us. Truly we are a small island, completely isolated in the Eastern Sea. One false step and our nation will again fall into the desperate state of crisis—dilemmas at home and abroad—that marked the period before and after the Meiji Restoration.

Ryusaku Tsunoda, William Theodore de Bary, and Donald Keene, eds., *Sources of the Japanese Tradition* (New York: Columbia University Press, 1958), 775–80.

The only thing that brightens the picture is the sixty million fellow country-men with whom we are blessed. The Japanese people must develop a profound awareness of the great cause of national existence and of the people's equal rights, and they need an unerring, discriminating grasp of the complexities of domestic and foreign thought. The Great War in Europe was, like Noah's flood, Heaven's punishment on them for arrogant and rebellious ways. It is of course natural that we cannot look to the Europeans, who are out of their minds because of the great destruction, for a completely detailed set of plans. But in contrast Japan, during those five years of destruction, was blessed with five years of fulfillment. Europe needs to talk about reconstruction, while Japan must move on to reorganization. The entire Japanese people, thinking calmly from this perspective which is the re-sult of Heaven's rewards and punishments, should, in planning how the great Japanese empire should be reorganized, petition for a manifestation of the impe-rial prerogative establishing "a national opinion in which no dissenting voice is heard, by the organization of a great union of the Japanese people." Thus, by hom-age to the emperor, a basis for national reorganization can be set up.

Truly, our seven hundred million brothers in China and India have no path to independence other than that offered by our guidance and protection. And for our Japan, whose population has doubled within the past fifty years, great areas ade-quate to support a population of at least two hundred and forty or fifty millions will be absolutely necessary a hundred years from now. . . . [T]he noble Greece of Asian culture must complete her national reorganization on the basis of her own national polity. At the same time, let her lift the virtuous banner of an Asian league and take the leadership in a world federation which must come. In so doing let her proclaim to the world the Way of Heaven in which all are children of Buddha, and let her set the example which the world must follow. So the ideas of people like those who oppose arming the nation are after all simply childish.

Section One: The People's Emperor

Suspension of the Constitution

In order for the emperor and the entire Japanese people to establish a secure base for the national reorganization, the emperor will, by a show of his imperial pre-rogative, suspend the Constitution for a period of three years, dissolve both houses of the Diet,[1] and place the entire nation under martial law. . . .

The True Significance of the Emperor

The fundamental doctrine of the emperor as representative of the people and as pillar of the nation must be made clear. . . .

There is no scientific basis whatever for the belief of the democracies that a state which is governed by representatives voted in by the electorate is superior to a state which has a system of government by a particular person. Every nation has its own na-tional spirit and history. It cannot be maintained, as advocates of this theory would

---

[1] Japanese legislature.

have it, that China during the first eight years of the republic[2] was more rational than Belgium, which retained rule by a single person.[3] The "democracy" of the Americans derives from the very unsophisticated theory of the time which held that society came into being through a voluntary contract based upon the free will of individuals; these people, emigrating from each European country as individuals, established communities and built a country. But their theory of the divine right of voters is a half-witted philosophy which arose in opposition to the theory of the divine right of kings at that time. Now Japan certainly was not founded in this way, and there has never been a period in which Japan was dominated by a half-witted philosophy. Suffice it to say that the system whereby the head of state has to struggle for election by a long-winded self-advertisement and by exposing himself to ridicule like a low-class actor seems a very strange custom to the Japanese people, who have been brought up in the belief that silence is golden and that modesty is a virtue.

---

[2] The Chinese republic was established when the Qing dynasty was overthrown in 1911.
[3] Belgium had a constitutional monarchy with an elected legislature as the primary governing authority.

QUESTIONS FOR ANALYSIS

1. What religious language does Ikki use to justify Japan's need for reorganization? What nationalistic language does he use?
2. What similarities and differences can be identified between Ikki's characterization of Japan and the images of Japan in *Punch* (Source 8).
3. How does d'Anethan's discussion of changes in Japanese politics (Source 7) compare to Ikki's methods of reform? How might Ikki's reform methods reinforce political authoritarianism?
4. What similarities and differences occur between Ikki's call for reform and Gandhi's (Source 5)? How does each use religious language to arrive at different ends?

10

"THE YELLOW PERIL . . ."

William Inge
The White Man and His Rivals   (1922)

A professor of divinity and dean of St. Paul's Cathedral in London, William Inge (1860–1954) became a nationally known religious author in Britain. Also known for his pessimism, in 1919 and 1922 Inge published a two-volume collection of his lectures, many of which commented on the current state of world affairs. In "The White Man

---

William Inge, *Outspoken Essays,* 2nd ser. (Longmans Green, 1922) (Reprinted New York: Greenwood Press, 1969), 214–19, 224–25.

and His Rivals," excerpted below, Inge outlines a feared shifting balance of world power toward Asia.

[Until] a few years ago it was assumed as probable that the remaining Asiatic Empires would follow the same path as India, and fall under one or other of the European powers. . . .

The shock came in 1904, when Russia, who with the help of France and Germany had robbed Japan of the fruits of her victory over China, extended covetous hands over Manchuria and threatened Korea. The military prestige of Russia at that time stood very high, and Europe was startled when an Asiatic people, poor and relatively small in numbers, threw down the gauntlet to the Colossus of the North. Kuroki's victory on the Yalu,[1] though due to the blunder of a subordinate general, will perhaps rank as one of the turning-points of history. It was followed by a series of successes, both by land and sea, which amazed Europe, and sent waves of excitement and hope through the entire continent of Asia. A Frenchman has described the arrival of the first batch of tall Russian prisoners at a Japanese port. The white men present consisted of French, Germans, English, and Americans; but at the sight of Europeans in the custody of Asiatics they forgot their rivalries; a feeling of horror went through them all, and they huddled together as if they realised that something uncanny was happening which threatened them all alike. There was in reality nothing mysterious in the Japanese victories. A few European officers had seen their army before the war, and a distinguished Anglo-Indian had reported that they were "quite as good as Gurkhas."[2] Russia was honeycombed with disaffection and corruption, and was never able to bring her whole force to bear in the Manchurian battlefields. But the decisive factor was the German training of the Japanese army, which had learnt all that the best instructors could teach, with wonderful thoroughness and ability. This was the momentous lesson of the war. An Asiatic army, with equally good weapons and training, is a match for the same number of Europeans; and there is no part of European military or naval science which the Asiatic cannot readily master. . . .

More interesting [than military issues] is the growing consciousness of Pan-Asiatic sympathy, which finds vent in the cry "Asia for the Asiatics." . . . An Indo-Japanese association has existed for some years; its object is certainly not to maintain the British Raj.[3] "Let us go to India, where the people are looking for our help!" exclaims Count Okuma[4] in 1907.

Many Anglo-Indian writers, and among them Mr. Townsend,[5] have commented on the extreme slenderness of the threads by which we hold India. "Above

---

[1] Tamesada Kuroki (1844–1911), Japanese general whose victory at Yalu marked the turning point in the Russo-Japanese War.
[2] Well-respected Nepalese soldiers of ethnically diverse backgrounds who were heavily recruited by the British military.
[3] British rule of India.
[4] Okuma Shigenobu (1838–1922), Japanese elder statesman and twice prime minister.
[5] Meredith Townsend (1831–1911), British author of several works on Asia.

this inconceivable mass of humanity, governing all, protecting all, taxing all, rises what we call the Empire, a corporation of less than 1500 men, who protect themselves by finding pay for a minute white garrison of 65,000 men, one-fifth of the Roman legions. There is nothing else. To support the official world and its garrison there is, except Indian opinion, absolutely nothing. . . ." It is not surprising that the growth of nationalism in India seems to many to portend the approaching end of our rule. . . .

[Today, however, t]he yellow peril, so far as it exists, is the peril of economic competition. . . .

The introduction of Western industrialism into these countries has had the effect of increasing the population, and of creating a class of native capitalists, some of whom, like the merchants of Singapore and the mill-owners of Osaka, are immensely rich. It has also brought the East into direct economic competition with the West. The Japanese, in their haste to make money, have tolerated a system of labour in their factories no better than that of England a hundred years ago, and discontent is already manifest among the wage-earners; but it is certain that the ratio of wages to output all over the East gives native manufacturers a great advantage over the European and American, and that this advantage is not likely to disappear. . . .

If the conditions in the white countries become unfavourable to enterprise, we may be sure that both capital and business ability will be transferred to the economically strong countries. Asia will be industrialised; India and China and Japan will be full of factories, equipped with all the latest improvements, and under skilled management, which at first will be frequently white. Wealth will be so abundant in Asia that the Governments will be able without difficulty to maintain fleets and armies large enough to protect their own interests, and to exact reparation for any transgressions of international law by the whites. Only a wealthy country can be powerful by sea; and a nation which has lost most of its foreign trade will not think it worth while to bid for naval supremacy. The policy of exclusion will, therefore, be powerless to prevent those races which possess economic superiority from increasing in wealth and then in military power.

The suicidal war which devastated the world of the white man for four years[6] will probably be found to have produced its chief results, not in altering the balance of power in Europe, but in precipitating certain changes which were coming about slowly during the peace. The period which these changes would naturally have occupied was shortened by perhaps fifty years. The first of these is the change in the relation of wages to output, which has been suddenly and enormously altered to the detriment of the consumer. The second change is the transference of political and financial supremacy from Europe to the United States, a change which was no doubt bound to occur within half a century, since America has a decisive advantage in her geographical position, equally adapted for the Pacific and the Atlantic trade. . . . The third change is that to which this article is directed. The peril from the coloured races, which before the war loomed in the distance, is now of immediate urgency. The white peoples, exhausted and crippled by debt, will be less able to compete with Asia.

---

[6] World War I.

QUESTIONS FOR ANALYSIS

1. How does Inge describe the threat to European power in India as well as the threat posed by Japan? What reactions to Japanese military power by Europeans does Inge note?

2. How does Inge explain the rise of Japanese power? How do these explanations indicate a European perspective on Asia?

3. What significance does Inge note for national and pan-Asiatic consciousness?

4. How does Inge's characterization of Indian and Japanese power compare to d'Anethan's (Source 7) and Minto's (Source 6) characterizations?

CHAPTER QUESTIONS

1. How does the language of imperialism expressed in the age of confidence (Chapter 10) compare to the language of imperialism expressed in this chapter's age of confusion? How do the documents by Minto, d'Anethan, and Inge and the cartoons in *Punch* redefine the developing relationship between the Western powers and other parts of the world?

2. Compare the challenges that European political leaders faced internally during the First World War and during the Russian Revolution with the external challenges posed by the rise of Japan and colonial discontent. What similarities and differences existed in these challenges? Why might these challenges bring into question the Western world's understanding of itself?

3. What similarities and differences can be found between the critiques of industrial society by Lenin and Chicherin and by Gandhi and the support for industrial society by Inge, d'Anethan, and Ikki? How do the Japanese and Indian responses to Western industrial society compare to the responses made by writers in Russia (Chapter 8) and in China (Chapter 9)?

4. How did the First World War challenge technology's role as a basis for imperialistic ideas, as suggested by Michael Adas (Chapter 9, Source 8)?

Chapter 12

ETHNICITY AND NATIONALISM IN STALIN'S SOVIET UNION AND HITLER'S THIRD REICH

The treaties ending World War I could not end the crisis of confidence that was suffered by Western society in the early twentieth century (Chapter 11). Economic dislocation, calls for greater social welfare programs, discontent with the treaties ending the war, continued unrest in colonies, Japanese aggression in Asia, and the specter of communism in the new Soviet Union were only some of the factors sustaining the sense of anxiety that pervaded Western society. Even Marxists could not leisurely enjoy their victory in the Soviet Union, for the new leaders there believed themselves besieged on all sides by capitalist forces seeking their overthrow.

Politicians, opinion makers, and demagogues struggled to give voice to and manipulate these varied anxieties. And to achieve their diverse ends, many public figures promoted the powerful sentiments of nationalism, ethnicity, and class. Nationalist sentiment emphasized devotion to the nation, usually defined by political state boundaries. Ethnic sentiment emphasized loyalty to a group defined by culture, language, and common history. Class sentiment emphasized loyalty among people of similar economic circumstances. These sentiments, carefully managed by political parties through the new techniques of mass advertising and propaganda, could inspire hope, rally support for a cause, and also justify the cruelest ends. In the Soviet Union, class and nationalism became central issues as the new Soviet state used the ideology and language of Marxism to strengthen the Soviet state against opposition from the capitalist states and to implement communist ideals in Soviet society—measures increasingly enforced through Joseph Stalin's system of political terror. In Germany, Adolph Hitler and the leadership of the Nazi Party called on nationalism and ethnicity to assert a "proper" place for the Aryan race and its personification in the German state, to explain the alleged ills within Germany society, and to justify the Nazi's "final solution" to those ills. Both the communists and the Nazis defined anew the requirements for membership in civil society. Individuals who were defined as outside the bounds of civil society—whether Ukrainian nationalists, entrepreneurial peasants, Jews, Gypsies, or homosexuals—faced regimes determined to eliminate these "threats" to their idealized societies. Both regimes killed millions; however, why they killed and whom they killed also mark significant differences between them.

NATIONALITY AND AGRICULTURE IN THE SOVIET UKRAINE

In 1921, the Bolshevik Party, victorious in civil war, secured its claim of authority over the new Soviet Union. Establishing governmental control over the vast array of differing ethnic groups who lived in the territories of the former Russian empire, however, provided new challenges. Some ethnic groups, such as the Ukrainians, held distinctly nationalist aspirations. The Ukrainian peasants, some 80 percent of the Ukrainian population, had participated in the civil war as a struggle for national liberation from Russian control. When the civil war concluded in 1921, Ukrainian guerrilla bands, some as large as eight hundred members, continued to fight against Soviet forces for several more years. The Soviet leadership recognized that to solidify its power the Ukrainian peasants, along with other ethnic groups, had to be induced to accept the Soviet government as their own. The leadership therefore introduced the New Economic Program (NEP) and halted unpopular agricultural collectivization. Russian Soviet authorities introduced a policy known as "indigenization," which instructed non-Russian Soviet regimes to establish themselves within the local ethnic setting by using local languages and recruiting local inhabitants into the Communist Party. In the Ukraine, intellectual and political leaders embraced indigenization, and "Ukrainization" strengthened the Soviet Ukrainian state under the leadership of Ukrainian communists.

By 1928, however, the Bolshevik Party had secured its authority within the Soviet states, and Joseph Stalin had won the power struggle among the Bolshevik leaders following Lenin's death. Seeking to reestablish central authority, Stalin overturned the NEP, forced state-directed industrialization on the economy, and recommenced the collectivization of agriculture. In the collectivization process, the Soviet government identified three classes of peasants. Poor peasants were assumed to be the rural allies of the urban proletariat (or industrial laborers) and were targeted for rapid movement to collective farms. Kulaks ("rich" or entreprenurial peasants) were marked as the evil defenders of capitalist agriculture and the main enemies of socialism. Kulaks were stripped of their property and often killed or sent to prisons or labor camps. The middle peasants were identified as potential allies of either the poor peasants or the kulaks. Further, Stalin repudiated the "indigenization" campaign he had previously supported, for he believed that the indigenization campaign had encouraged nationalist sentiment among non-Russian ethnic groups and that local communist leaders used the indigenization campaign to resist control by the Soviet state.

The Ukraine, which had embraced fully the "indigenization campaign" and which had a large and powerful kulak class, faced the full fury of Stalin's efforts to eliminate any rivals to his authority. He purged the ruling Ukrainian communist leadership and pursued the collectivization of agriculture more forcefully and rapidly in the Ukraine than in any other Soviet territory. Rather than permit the state to seize their assets, Ukrainian peasants responded by committing terrorist acts, destroying farm equipment, and slaughtering livestock. Even when Stalin slowed collectivization in 1930, resistance to the Soviet regime and its control over agricultural production continued among Ukrainian peasants. Stalin blamed that resistance on those "defenders of capitalist agriculture" and Ukrainian nationalism—the kulaks. When the Ukrainian grain harvest of 1932 produced only two-thirds of the grain harvested in 1930, Stalin determined to stomp out continued defiance by the Ukrainian peasants—or, as Stalin understood it, by the kulaks and their henchmen—and imposed higher procurement quotas on Ukrainian grain. Soviet authorities ruthlessly seized all grain supplies and created a famine in 1932 and 1933 that resulted in some five to ten million deaths in the Ukraine. Although Stalin committed similar atrocities on other peoples, including Russian kulaks, he never achieved the same concentrated loss of life.

1

". . . ELIMINATING THE KULAKS AS A CLASS."

Joseph Stalin
Problems of Agrarian Policy in the USSR (1929)

Born Josef Dzhugashvili (1879–1953), the son of a poor cobbler, Joseph Stalin joined Russia's leftist political underground in his early twenties and slowly advanced in the Bolshevik Party organization. As Lenin's health failed between 1922 and 1924, several Bolshevik officials began jockeying for power. Stalin slowly isolated and discredited his competitors and achieved unrivaled power by 1928. During the late 1920s and 1930s, Stalin secured his power through a system of state terror that crushed any perceived threat to his authority. For Stalin, these threats arrived not only from the educated classes but also from the peasantry, which he believed would provide the armed force for any national movement that resisted the Soviet state. As Stalin stated, "The national question is, in essence, a peasant question." In the excerpt below from Stalin's 1929 speech on Soviet agriculture, he outlines his effort to destroy the peasantry as a political force by destroying the anticommunist leaders of the peasantry—the kulaks.

The main fact of our social-economic life at the present time, a fact which is attracting general attention, is the enormous growth of the collective farm movement.

The characteristic feature of the present collective farm movement is that not only are separate groups of poor peasants joining the collective farms, as has been the case hitherto, but that the mass of the middle peasants are also joining the collective farms. This means that the collective farm movement has been transformed from a movement of separate groups and sections of the laboring peasants into a movement of millions and millions, of the bulk of the peasantry. This, by the way, explains the tremendously important fact that the collective farm movement, which has assumed the character of a mighty and growing *anti-kulak* avalanche, is sweeping the resistance of the kulak from its path, is breaking kulakdom and clearing the road for extensive socialist construction in the rural districts. . . .

Joseph Stalin, *Problems in Agrarian Policy in the USSR,* in *Selected Writings* (New York: International, 1942), 145, 155–58, 160.

The October Revolution[1] abolished the private ownership of land, abolished the sale and purchase of land, established the nationalization of the land. What does this mean? It means that the peasant has no need to buy land in order to produce grain. Formerly he was compelled to save up for years in order to buy land; he got into debt, went into bondage, only to acquire a piece of land. The expenses which the purchase of land involved naturally entered into the cost of production of grain. Now, the peasant does not have to spend money on the purchase of land. He can produce grain now without buying land. Does this ameliorate the condition of the peasants or not? Obviously it does.

Further. Until recently, the peasant was compelled to dig the soil with the aid of obsolete implements by individual labor. Everyone knows that individual labor, equipped with obsolete, now unsuitable, means of production, does not produce the results required to enable one to lead a tolerable existence, systematically to improve one's material position, to develop one's culture and to get out onto the high-road of socialist construction. Today, after the accelerated development of the collective farm movement, the peasants are able to combine their labor with the labor of their neighbors, to unite in collective farms, to break up virgin soil, to cultivate waste land, to obtain machines and tractors and thereby double or even treble the productivity of their labor. And what does this mean? It means that today the peasant, by joining the collective farms, is able to produce much more than formerly with the same expenditure of labor. It means, therefore, that grain will be produced much more cheaply than was the case until quite recently. It means, finally, that, with stable prices, the peasant can obtain much more for his grain than he has obtained up to now. . . .

Of course, there are contradictions in the collective farms. Of course, there are individualistic and even kulak survivals in the collective farms, which have not yet disappeared, but which are bound to disappear in the course of time as the collective farms become stronger, as they are provided with more machines. But can it be denied that the collective farms as a whole, with all their contradictions and shortcomings, the collective farms as an *economic* fact, represent, in the main, a new path of development of the countryside, the *socialist* path of development of the countryside as *opposed* to the kulak, *capitalist* path of development? Can it be denied that the collective farms (I am speaking of real collective farms and not of sham collective farms) represent, under our conditions, a base and a nucleus of socialist construction in the countryside—a base and a nucleus which have grown up in desperate fights against the capitalist elements? . . .

The characteristic feature of our work during the past year is: (a) that we, the party and the Soviet government, have developed an offensive on the whole front against the capitalist elements in the countryside; and (b) that this offensive, as you know, has brought about and is bringing about very palpable, *positive* results.

What does this mean? It means that we have passed from the policy of *restricting* the exploiting proclivities of the kulaks to the policy of *eliminating* the kulaks

---

[1] Bolshevik seizure of power in Russia in 1917.

as a class. This means that we have made, and are still making, one of the most de-cisive turns in our whole policy.

QUESTIONS FOR ANALYSIS

1. According to Stalin, how has the elimination of private property affected peasant farming?
2. On what basis does Stalin justify the policy of eliminating the kulaks as a class?
3. What is the importance of a kulak identity to Stalin's argument? How does this kulak class identity relate to Stalin's fears of national movements?
4. As the economic and political leaders of the Ukrainian peasants, how do the Ukrainian kulaks pose a double threat to the Soviet Union within Stalin's worldview?

2

"... A CAMPAIGN TO DESTROY THE UKRAINIAN NATION ..."

James E. Mace
Communism and the Dilemmas of National Liberation   (1983)

The historian James E. Mace has worked to unravel the threads of communist ideology and Russian nationalism that Stalin and the Soviet leadership brought together to justify the Ukrainian famine. In the excerpt below, Mace begins by considering the Bolsheviks' use of ethnic sentiment in the form of the "indigenization" policies of the 1920s.

The question of what became of Ukraine's quest for its own national road to socialism is inseparable from the larger question of the nature of the transformation that the Soviet Union underwent [between 1928 and 1938]. . . .

[*One part of this transformation was replacing civil society with state agencies so that the state controlled all important aspects of life.*]

This process [the development of Ukrainian National Socialism] could have taken place on the basis of the "indigenized" national republics of the twenties. However, had this option been chosen, Stalin would have been only the first among equals,

---

James E. Mace, *Communism and the Dilemmas of National Liberation: National Communism in Soviet Ukraine, 1918–1933* (Cambridge: Harvard University Press, 1983), 264–65, 280–83.

presiding over a collection of national totalitarian states to a greater or lesser extent dominated by his Russia, but nevertheless distinct from it. By the mid-1930s, however, he was clearly creating a unitary Russocentric totalitarian state in which all inhabitants would be equally and directly subject to his personal despotism, without the mediating levels of strong and nationally conscious republican governments. To achieve this goal, he had to crush the republics as relatively autonomous entities, usually by purging their elites of "national deviationists"[1] and ending the indigenization programs. . . . In Soviet Ukraine the Ukrainization policy had gone farther and deeper than elsewhere; consequently, the destruction of society necessary to obliterate what was euphemistically referred to as "bourgeois nationalism," had to go much further, to the point of an undeclared but nevertheless real war against the Ukrainian nation as such. As a result of these transformations, from a heterogeneous assemblage of Soviet republics, the USSR became an administratively centralized entity and adopted a distinctly Russian national character, relegating non-Russian nations to the status of the "little brothers" of the Great Russian "elder brother." In other words, the Soviet Russian Empire was born. . . .

The Collectivization of Agriculture and Ukrainian Famine of 1933

The Ukrainians were basically a nation consisting of a peasantry and a national intelligentsia. Although Ukrainization encouraged many Ukrainians to move into other social roles and to retain their Ukrainian identity, the vast majority of Ukrainians still worked the land in 1933. For Ukrainians, NEP [National Economic Program] and Ukrainization were but two sides of the same coin: both were concessions designed to placate social forces on which the Bolsheviks had been unable to inflict a decisive defeat. During the 1920s official statements in the Soviet Ukrainian press defined the Party's main task as winning over the "rural masses" in general and the rural intelligentsia in particular. . . .

Yet, if the regime had failed to win the hearts and minds of the Ukrainian peasantry, its representatives at least succeeded in penetrating the countryside they had confronted as something completely alien during the revolution. In addition to the newly-created *selkor* movement,[2] the old *komnezamy*[3] were retained, albeit in somewhat different form. . . . In addition, the secret police established a system of residents on the *raion* (district) level who, as one account explains it,

> disguised as instructors, statisticians, insurance agents, agronomists, and so on, worked ceaselessly to create a dense network of secret collaborators known as *seksoty*. The fact that the *seksoty* were not acquainted with one another greatly assisted the activities of the OGPU,[4] especially in their control of the *seksoty* themselves. Soon no one knew who could be trusted and mutual confidence disap-

---

[1] Those who supported nationalist aspirations.
[2] Village correspondents who contributed stories about village life to the Soviet press.
[3] Committees of nonwealthy peasants who were the main organ of communist rule in the Ukrainian countryside in the 1920s.
[4] Acronym for the Soviet secret police from 1923 to 1934.

peared. Sons denounced fathers and brothers denounced brothers. This was one of the most frightful measures of terrorism under the Soviet regime.

The district OGPU residents and their secret collaborators enabled the regime to identify not only those who were openly hostile, but also potential enemies. In contrast to the situation existing at the time it was established, the Soviet Ukrainian regime now had a substantial network in the village, greatly increasing its strength. Whenever the Party should decide the time was right for the final reckoning of accounts, the regime would be ready.

The regime always identified the kulaks as its main enemy in the countryside, an omnipresent foe whose role in the Bolshevik world view was comparable to that of the Jews in Nazi ideology: evil incarnate. Since the kulaks were also perceived to be the basis of Ukrainian nationalism, the regime seemed even more hostile to Ukrainian kulaks than to their Russian counterparts. The retention of the *komnezamy* illustrates this hostility, as does the fact that these organizations were charged with carrying out a program of dekulakization (that is, confiscation and redistribution of "surplus" kulak land and property, not complete expropriation) until the end of 1923. Even after the program officially ended, Ukrainian head of state Hryhorii Petrovskyi[5] praised it, saying: "Our revolution solved the land question, and with dekulakization we only cut off the tail of what was left over from the revolution." The final elimination of the kulaks as a class was, in fact, an ideological imperative with which no communist could disagree in principle. . . .

The kulaks were estimated as constituting between four and five percent of the rural population and, in some places, as low as one or two percent. The trouble arose from the flexibility of the allied category of "kulak henchmen," . . . , a category which could be applied to any peasant who resisted official policies, and which during dekulakization was used to extend the repression of the kulaks to anyone considered suspect. During dekulakization, even poor peasants were often labeled kulak henchmen and deported—or worse. The category of kulak henchmen rested on attitude rather than the material standing of the person to whom it was applied. The poorest individual in the village could be labeled a kulak henchman. . . . In addition, Bolshevik ideology identified the peasantry as the basic reservoir of nationality. As Stalin wrote, "The nationality problem is, *according to the essence of the matter,* a problem of the peasantry." Thus, the mixing of the notions of class and nation made it possible for the ideology of class struggle to serve as justification for what was in essence a campaign to destroy the Ukrainian nation as a social organism and political factor.

QUESTIONS FOR ANALYSIS

1. According to Mace, why was the Soviet policy of indigenization brought to an end? Why did the Ukraine suffer particularly severe repression?

2. Through what means did the Soviet regime penetrate the countryside and identify its enemies?

---

[5] Hryhorii Petrovskyi (1878–1958), chair of the All-Ukrainian Central Executive Committee of Soviets from 1920 to 1938.

3. How does Mace assert that *kulak* represented more than simply an economic category?

4. According to Mace, how did the notions of both class and nation work to justify the Ukrainian famine? How does Mace's argument compare to the ideas expressed by Stalin (Source 1)?

3

"THIS IS YOUR TASK."

Antonina Solovieva
Sent by the Komsomol   (1964)

As a young woman in the 1920s living in the city of Sverdlovsk, Antonina Solovieva joined the local branch of the communist youth organization, the Komsomol. In 1930, the Communist Party began assigning some Komsomol members to work in the countryside under the direction of party officials. Komsomol members were usually urban youths, and they recruited reluctant peasants to join collective farms and gathered information on the activities of those resisting collectivization or grain seizures. In the 1960s, former participants in events such as the Collectivization Campaigns joined a popular trend to collect and publish their stories. In the excerpt below published in 1964, Solovieva remembers her participation in the "heroic" campaign to collectivize the countryside around the Russian city of Votkinsk.

[*After spending a few weeks working in a regional Komsomol office, Solovieva is called to a meeting.*]

The Communist Ermakov stood up, revealing his giant frame, and said softly:

"Comrade Komsomol members, we have assembled you here today because you, along with us Communists, will be going out to the countryside to help the collective farms and village soviets get ready for the spring sowing season. The situation in the villages is alarming. As you know, the country is counting on kolkhoz[1] grain, while kulak scoundrels are hiding and spoiling the seeds and disorganizing the peasants. Your task is to engage in mass agitational work among the village youth from the unaffiliated middle stratum[2] and to find out where the kulaks are hiding the grain and who is wrecking the agricultural machinery. On top of every-

---

[1] Collective farm.
[2] The middle peasants, whose support the communists often sought in opposing the kulaks.

Antonina Solovieva, "Sent by the Komsomol," in *In the Shadow of Revolution: Life Stories of Russian Women from 1917 to the Second World War,* ed. Sheila Fitzpatrick and Yuri Slezkine, trans. Yuri Slezkine (Princeton, N.J.: Princeton University Press, 2000), 236–39.

thing else, owing to the intimidation on the part of the kulaks and their henchmen, many of the poor households have not yet joined the collective farms. This means that you will need to talk to these people and explain party policies and collectivization to them. This is your task."

This was a huge task; were we up to it? . . .

[*Solovieva and the other Komsomol workers leave for the villages.*]

After presenting their papers at the village soviet, the arriving Komsomol members would be sent to some collective farm or individual household—to the hardest possible spot. The objective was to talk individual peasants into joining the collective farm; to make sure that the collective farm was ready to begin sowing; and, most important, to find out where and by whom state grain was being hidden. Usually, our first task was to organize a group of activists (preferably from among the village youth), gain their trust, and start a frank conversation. . . .

One of our Komsomol activists, Kostia Lutkov, was particularly good at this. He acted completely natural, joking around, laughing a lot, and improvising funny rhymes. The men respected him, and the girls admired him. Sooner or later the subject of the kolkhoz would come up. Some of those who came to the get-togethers were under the kulaks' influence, but Kostia would listen patiently until everyone had spoken and then join the conversation as if he were one of them. Once a local field hand, Mitia Varlamov, asked Kostia for some tobacco. Kostia offered him some and said: "Just look at yourself, kid: your coat is all torn; you're wearing bast shoes;[3] and your pants are made of sackcloth. Now, in the collective farm you could make some money, receive your grain ration, and even buy cologne for your evening get-togethers."

Mitia Varlamov, who was eighteen years old, looked at Kostia and asked shyly: "I can't really make that much in the kolkhoz, can I?"

"Just think about it," said Kostia, "All the land will be collectivized, so the kolkhoz will have plenty of it; all the horses will be in the same stable in the large collective farm yard; and all the machines—harvesting, sowing, and threshing—will stand next to each other in the same collective farm yard. With all that land and all those horses and machines—if you just work hard, you will be well-fed and well-dressed."

Mitia still did not get it. "But if you take all the machines away from the rich people, what are the field hands going to work on?" he asked.

"They aren't going to work for the rich people anymore," said Kostia. "In any case, most of them are already in the collective farm. The point is for you to work for yourself, not for the rich."

"And not just any old way, but on a machine," dark-eyed Nastia joined in. "Have you seen the red threshing machine they took away from Stepan last week?"

"I sure have," Mitia drawled. "Two years ago I spent the better part of the fall season threshing on that machine. Got paid peanuts for it, too." The kid looked hurt and turned away.

---

[3] Shoes made of flexible wood bark.

"That's what we're talking about," said Nastia, with a sly glance in Kostia's direction. "Just sign up, and nobody will cheat you anymore. You'll get what you earn."

The young people would leave the get-together feeling transformed, and Kostia would add new names to his list of youngsters who wished to build a new collective farm future.

It was through these young collective farm members that we were able to find out who was hiding grain and wrecking collective farm property. This information would be transmitted secretly, "through the grapevine." We would not know where the information had originated but would always check it out and, sure enough, often it would turn out to be correct. . . .

But things did not always go so smoothly. The enemy tried to retaliate whenever opportunity afforded.

Once we were taking inventory of the confiscated property of a kulak. . . .

Suddenly we heard the sound of the window breaking, and then the lamp burst into little pieces and went out. A heavy object fell onto the table. Cherepanov[4] ordered us to sit on the floor between the windows, and then he lit a match. On the table lay a half-pint bottle filled with river sand—another kulak weapon used not infrequently to kill people.

Two days later I learned from Liza who had thrown the bottle and who the intended victim had been. It turned out that the Kosachevo kulaks were out to get Sasha.[5] I decided to go to Kosachevo immediately—to conduct an on-the-spot investigation and to inform the appropriate authorities of the attack. Unfortunately, the chairman of the village soviet would not let me go. Then later, in 1932, I discovered that the Kosachevo kulaks had been planning to drown me in the Kama River.

QUESTIONS FOR ANALYSIS

1. How does Solovieva express her identity as a supporter of the Communist Party? How does she create a clear sense of good and evil operating in the process of collectivization?

2. In what ways does Solovieva suggest that she and the other Komsomol members assisted in the process of collectivization?

3. To gain Mitia Varlamov's support for collectivization, what appeals does Kostia Lutkov use?

4. How do Solovieva's activities compare to Mace's description of the Soviet state's activities in rural Ukraine (Source 2)? How might the context in which the document was composed affect the document's heroic tone?

---

[4] Representative of the Communist Party district committee.
[5] Communist Party worker.

4

"... TO ANNIHILATE US ..."

Miron Dolot
Execution by Hunger   (1985)

As a young lad growing up in a Ukrainian village, Miron Dolot lived through the famine of 1932 and 1933. After World War II, in which he was captured by the Germans, he immigrated to the United States, where in the early 1950s he recorded his memories of the famine years. In 1985, he published his complete recollections. Below is an excerpt in which Dolot describes himself coming to understand these terrible events as Soviet officials seized all food supplies from his home region.

Sometime by the end of August [1932], the Grain Collection Campaign reopened with even greater intensity. Day and night we were reminded that we were still lagging behind in the fulfillment of the grain delivery quota. Endlessly long meetings were again conducted daily. All this was beyond our comprehension. We had been members of the collective farm for more than two years. This meant that we had no land of our own and therefore, logically, we could not have any grain of our own. Since collectivization had been started, the state Bread Procurement Commission had crisscrossed our village several times and requisitioned all of our grain reserves. As a result, our villagers were slowly starving to death. . . .

[T]he collecting of foodstuffs did not advance as quickly as the officials desired. Something drastic had to be done, so in time, the official line of reasoning acquired a new tone: the farmers were now considered too ignorant to understand such a highly patriotic deed as collecting and delivering food to the state. The Party and the government meant well for the farmers, and if they did not appreciate what the Party meant for them—well, that was the farmers' fault. The farmers were to be treated like children, and that put the Party and the government in the position of parents. The farmers had to follow the Party and the government without asking questions. There was no alternative. And, as unruly children are punished by parents, so would the unruly farmers be punished by the Party and the government.

In accordance with this philosophy, the commission no longer tried to enlighten us in the matter of food collection. There was another way. To put it in official terms, this was "direct contact of officials with the masses of people." In plain language, it meant that the Bread Procurement Commission was ordered to visit the farmers individually at their homes.

Miron Dolot, *Execution by Hunger: The Hidden Holocaust* (New York: Norton, 1985), 162, 165, 175, 207–8.

The commission members would go to a certain house and inform the house-holder about the amount and kind of food he should deliver. If he didn't have any grain, the commission would proceed with a thorough search for "hidden bread." Of course, anything found would be confiscated.

The Thousanders and their lieutenants could now do whatever they wanted without regard to the formalities of the law. They could use all their tricks or threats to lure or force the farmers into their traps. Going from house to house, searching, and carrying off everything they wanted satisfied their greed and criminal urges while allowing them successfully to serve the Party and the government. . . .

It was precisely at this time, the end of December 1932, that the government introduced a single passport system for the entire country in order to prevent the starving farmers from leaving their villages for the cities. . . .

The passportization was supposedly directed against the kulaks as Soviet prop-aganda proclaimed: "Passportization is a mortal blow against the kulaks!" This murderous slogan revived the old question: *"Who is a kulak?"* All villagers had been collectivized by this time. There was not a single independent farmer left in our vil-lage by the end of 1932. Could the members of a collective farm be kulaks? It was difficult for us to understand such logic. But, at this point, such faulty reasoning didn't matter to us anymore.

Now it began to dawn on everyone why there wasn't any food left in the village; why there weren't any prospects of getting any more; why our expectation that the government would surely help us to avert starvation was naive and futile; why the Bread Procurement Commission still searched for "hidden" grain; and why the government strictly forbade us to look for means of existence elsewhere. It finally became clear to us that there was a conspiracy against us; that somebody wanted to annihilate us, not only as farmers but as people—as Ukrainians.

At this realization, our initial bewilderment was succeeded by panic. Neverthe-less, our instinct for survival was stronger than any of the prohibitions. It dictated to those who were still physically able that they must do everything to save them-selves and their families. . . .

I saw many tragic events in which children were the innocent victims, but one episode in particular emerges from my memories of that spring as a symbol of hu-manity gone completely mad. It was sometime at the onset of April. One early morning while we still lay in our beds, we heard a child's cry and a weak knocking on the door. I was the first to jump out of bed. As I opened the door, I saw a small girl of about four. She stood trembling from the cold and exhaustion with streams of tears flowing down her famished little cheeks. We knew her! It was Maria, the daughter of our neighbor Hana, who also had a seven-year-old son and lived about half a mile from us. Hana's husband, a young and industrious farmer, had been ar-rested like many others, for no apparent reason, and exiled somewhere to a con-centration camp about two years before. Hana was left alone with her two children to struggle for food, like all the rest of us. However, as winter came and starvation struck us, we lost track of her.

I let the child into the house.

"My mommy won't wake up!" the child announced, wiping away the tears with the sleeve of her dirty coat.

Mother and I glanced at each other. A short while later, my brother Mykola and I were on our way to Hana's home. When we entered the house, our fears were confirmed. Hana was dead, lying on her back on the sleeping bench. Her bulging glassy eyes seemed to be looking at us. Her widely opened mouth still seemed to be gasping for air. We could see that she had met her death not too long before Maria had knocked on our front door. On Hana's cheek we could still see the traces of her tears; we could also see the lice still moving back and forth like ants, in search of a warm spot. Next to her, wrapped in some cloth, lay her dead son. The one-room house was empty and dirty. There was no furniture except for two benches, and no trace of food. The mud floor had been dug up all over, and there were holes in the walls. The chimneys of the cooking and heating stoves were totally ruined. We recognized immediately the work of the Bread Procurement Commission. There was no doubt that they had been there recently, searching for "hidden" foodstuffs.

Mykola and I stood there aghast. I felt the impulse to either run away screaming, or to sit down next to their dead bodies and hold their cold hand in mine in sorrow and sympathy, but I did neither. I just stood there petrified, and looking at the dead mother and her young son, I asked the question:

"Why? Why did they have to die?"

QUESTIONS FOR ANALYSIS

1. What are the several different frameworks that Dolot uses to explain the actions of the Communist Party? How does he come to understand the famine in ethnic terms?

2. How would Stalin disagree with Dolot's explanation for the famine? Is Dolot correct in his assertion that Stalin was seeking to destroy the Ukrainians as a people? Why or why not?

3. What are the multiple layers of blame that the story of Hana places on the Communist Party? How does Dolot create a tone that critically mocks the Communist Party?

4. How does Dolot's tone compare to Solovieva's heroic tone (Source 3)? How might the context in which each document was composed affect its tone?

ETHNICITY AND CITIZENSHIP IN NAZI GERMANY

The Nazi Party emerged from the political and economic confusion of Germany's immediate postwar years. After a failed effort to seize political power in Munich in 1923, the party's leader, Adolf Hitler, determined that the Nazis should seek power through electoral politics and developed a propaganda campaign to broaden the party's base of support. At the center of their propaganda was a highly nationalistic message that glorified the image of a powerful Germany that would soon reclaim its "rightful place" in the world as the most highly developed civilization. Included within this message was the idea that Germany's resurrection could not be achieved until the elements that were polluting and destroying German culture and society were eliminated.

As the Nazis achieved political power in the 1930s, Hitler sought to demonstrate the vigor of Nazism by overturning the Versailles Treaty and expanding public works projects. To support his programs, he established an authoritarian police state dominated by Nazi Party organizations such as the SS (*Schutzstaffel*, or Protection Squad) and the Gestapo (acronym for *Geheime Staatspolizei*, or Secret State Police). In addition, the Nazi Party acted on its stated goal of reclaiming Germany from alleged pollution and domination by "foreign" forces. Between 1933 and 1935, the Nazi Party passed new laws that denied citizenship and civil rights to Jews, gypsies, and others defined as foreigners or deviants. As they secured their control within Germany and became increasingly unresponsive to international pressure, especially after World War II commenced in 1939, the Nazis pursued the "purification" of Germany to a horrific end.

5

"HE IS AND REMAINS A TYPICAL PARASITE. . . ."

Adolf Hitler
Mein Kampf (1925)

During his youth in Austria, Adolf Hitler (1889–1945) had a lonely, unstable life as an unsuccessful artist, fueling a hatred for established society. With the outbreak of World War I, Hitler joined the German army and found direction in the camaraderie, discipline, heroism, and authoritarianism of military life. After Germany's defeat in 1918, Hitler joined a few other veterans in an obscure political party that would become the Nazi Party. Hitler and the Nazis adopted a fiercely nationalistic message that attracted several thousand followers. Arrested after a failed attempt to seize power in the German province of Bavaria in 1923, Hitler recognized that the party would need to obtain power by the legal means of electoral politics. He turned the trial into an indictment of Germany's first republic—the Weimar government—showcasing his ideas and bringing wide attention to the party. Seeking to build on this publicity, Hitler spent his short imprisonment preparing the first volume of Mein Kampf, *which served as the foundation of Nazi doctrine and policy. In the excerpt below from* Mein Kampf, *Hitler explains his basic vision of world civilizations.*

If we were to divide mankind into three groups, the founders of culture, the bearers of culture, the destroyers of culture, only the Aryan could be considered as the representative of the first group. From him originate the foundations and walls of all human creation, and only the outward form and color are determined by the changing traits of character of the various peoples. He provides the mightiest building stones and plans for all human progress and only the execution corresponds to

Adolf Hitler, *Mein Kampf*, trans. Ralph Hanheim (Boston: Houghton Mifflin, 1943), 290–91, 296–97, 300, 302–3, 305.

the nature of the varying men and races. In a few decades, for example, the entire east of Asia will possess a culture whose ultimate foundation will be Hellenic spirit and Germanic technology, just as much as in Europe. Only the *outward* form—in part at least—will bear the features of Asiatic character. It is not true, as some people think, that Japan adds European technology to its culture; no, European science and technology are trimmed with Japanese characteristics. . . .

If beginning today all further Aryan influence on Japan should stop, assuming that Europe and America should perish, Japan's present rise in science and technology might continue for a short time; but even in a few years the well would dry up, the Japanese special character would gain, but the present culture would freeze and sink back into the slumber from which it was awakened seven decades ago by the wave of Aryan culture. . . . [I]f it is established that a people receives the most essential basic materials of its culture from foreign races, that it assimilates and adapts them, and that then, if further external influence is lacking, it rigidifies again and again, such a race may be designated as *"culture-bearing,"* but never as *"culture-creating."* . . .

The question of the inner causes of the Aryan's importance can be answered to the effect that they are to be sought less in a natural instinct of self-preservation than in the special type of its expression. The will to live, subjectively viewed, is everywhere equal and different only in the form of its actual expression. In the most primitive living creatures the instinct of self-preservation does not go beyond concern for their own ego. Egoism, as we designate this urge, goes so far that it even embraces time; the moment itself claims everything, granting nothing to the coming hours. In this condition the animal lives only for himself, seeks food only for his present hunger, and fights only for his own life. As long as the instinct of self-preservation expresses itself in this way, every basis is lacking for the formation of a group, even the most primitive form of family. Even a community between male and female beyond pure mating, demands an extension of the instinct of self-preservation, since concern and struggle for the ego are now directed toward the second party; the male sometimes seeks food for the female, too, but for the most part both seek nourishment for the young. Nearly always one comes to the defense of the other, and thus the first, though infinitely simple, forms of a sense of sacrifice result. As soon as this sense extends beyond the narrow limits of the family, the basis for the formation of larger organisms and finally formal states is created.

In the lowest peoples of the earth this quality is present only to a very slight extent, so that often they do not go beyond the formation of the family. The greater the readiness to subordinate purely personal interests, the higher rises the ability to establish comprehensive communities.

This self-sacrificing will to give one's personal labor and if necessary one's own life for others is most strongly developed in the Aryan. The Aryan is not greatest in his mental qualities as such, but in the extent of his willingness to put all his abilities in the service of the community. . . .

The mightiest counterpart to the Aryan is represented by the Jew. In hardly any people in the world is the instinct of self-preservation developed more strongly than in the so-called "chosen."[1] . . .

[T]he Jew is led by nothing but the naked egoism of the individual.

---

[1] In Jewish scriptures, Jews are identified as God's chosen people.

That is why the Jewish state—which should be the living organism for pre-serving and increasing a race—is completely unlimited as to territory. For a state formation to have a definite spatial setting always presupposes an idealistic attitude on the part of the state-race, and especially a correct interpretation of the concept of work. In the exact measure in which this attitude is lacking, any attempt at form-ing, even of preserving, a spatially delimited state fails. And thus the basis on which alone culture can arise is lacking.

Hence the Jewish people, despite all apparent intellectual qualities, is without any true culture, and especially without any culture of its own. For what sham cul-ture the Jew today possesses is the property of other peoples, and for the most part it is ruined in his hands. . . .

To what an extent the Jew takes over foreign culture, imitating or rather ruin-ing it, can be seen from the fact that he is mostly found in the art which seems to require least original invention, the art of acting. But even here, in reality, he is only a "juggler," or rather an ape; for even here he lacks the last touch that is required for real greatness; even here he is not the creative genius, but a superficial imitator, and all the twists and tricks that he uses are powerless to conceal the inner lifelessness of his creative gift. Here the Jewish press most lovingly helps him along by raising such a roar of hosannahs about even the most mediocre bungler, just so long as he is a Jew, that the rest of the world actually ends up by thinking that they have an artist before them, while in truth it is only a pitiful comedian.

No, the Jew possesses no culture-creating force of any sort, since the idealism, without which there is no true higher development of man, is not present in him and never was present. Hence his intellect will never have a constructive effect, but will be destructive. . . .

[A] Jew never thinks of leaving a territory that he has occupied, but remains where he is, and he sits so fast that even by force it is very hard to drive him out. His extension to ever-new countries occurs only in the moment in which certain con-ditions for his existence are there present, without which . . . he would not change his residence. He is and remains the typical parasite, a sponger who like a noxious bacillus[2] keeps spreading as soon as a favorable medium invites him. And the effect of his existence is also like that of spongers: wherever he appears, the host people dies out after a shorter or longer period.

Thus, the Jew of all times has lived in the states of other peoples, and there formed his own state, which, to be sure, habitually sailed under the disguise of "re-ligious community" as long as outward circumstances made a complete revelation of his nature seem inadvisable. But as soon as he felt strong enough to do without the protective cloak, he always dropped the veil and suddenly became what so many of the others previously did not want to believe and see: the Jew.

QUESTIONS FOR ANALYSIS

1. Explain Hitler's three categories of people. What evidence does he provide to justify these categories?

---

[2] Microscopic organism, such as the one that caused the bubonic plague.

2. For Hitler, what is the central productive force of history? What is the ultimate product of this force?
3. Which biological metaphors does Hitler frequently use in his arguments? What does this biological language imply about the status of the individual?
4. Compare Hitler's theorizing to Stalin's social analysis (Source 1). What similarities and differences can be found in the means they use to make their arguments convincing?

6

"... ON AN INTENSIFIED AND METHODOLOGICAL SCALE."

Nazi Jewish Policies (1935, 1939, 1942)

When Adolf Hitler became chancellor of Germany in January 1933, the Nazi Party, working through both the official organs of government and the unofficial organs of the Nazi Party, began to persecute Germany's Jewish population, other ethnic minorities, and those defined as social deviants. The documents that follow mark the development of Nazi Jewish policies and suggest a logic to this development.

Reich Citizenship Law (September 15, 1935)

The Reichstag has adopted unanimously, the following law, which is herewith promulgated.

Article 1

1. A subject of the State is a person, who belongs to the protective union of the German Reich, and who, therefore, has particular obligations towards the Reich.
2. The status of the subject is acquired in accordance with the provisions of the Reich and State Law of Citizenship.

Article 2

1. A citizen of the Reich is only that subject, who is of German or kindred blood and who, through his conduct, shows that he is both desirous and fit to serve faithfully the German people and Reich.
2. The right to citizenship is acquired by the granting of Reich citizenship papers.

Office of the United States Chief of Counsel for Prosecution of Axis Criminality, *Nazi Conspiracy and Aggression* (Washington, D.C.: U.S. Government Printing Office, 1946), 4:7–8, 636–37, 8–9, 97–99; *Trials of the War Crimes before the Nuernberg Military Tribunals under Control Council Law No. 10* (Washington, D.C.: U.S. Government Printing Office, 1952), 13:211–12.

3. Only the citizen of the Reich enjoys full political rights in accordance with the provision of the laws.

Law for the Protection of German Blood and German Honor (September 15, 1935)

Thoroughly convinced by the knowledge that the purity of German blood is essential for the further existence of the German people and animated by the inflexible will to safe-guard the German nation for the entire future, the Reichstag has resolved upon the following law unanimously, which is promulgated herewith:

Section 1

1. Marriages between Jews and nationals of German or kindred blood are forbidden. Marriages concluded in defiance of this law are void, even if, for the purpose of evading this law, they are concluded abroad. . . .

Section 2

Relation outside marriage between Jews and nationals of German or kindred blood are forbidden.

First Regulation to the Reich Citizenship Law (November 14, 1935)

Article 1

1. Until further issue of regulations regarding citizenship papers, all subjects of German or kindred blood, who possessed the right to vote in the Reichstag elections, at the time the Citizenship Law came into effect, shall, for the time being, possess the rights of Reich citizens. . . .

Article 2

1. The regulations in Article 1 are also valid for Reichs subjects of mixed, Jewish blood. . . .

Article 3

Only the Reich citizen, as bearer of full political rights, exercises the right to vote in political affairs, and can hold a public office. . . .

Article 4

1. A Jew cannot be a citizen of the Reich. He has no right to vote in political affairs, he cannot occupy a public office.

2. Jewish officials will retire as of 31 December 1935.

Letter from Reinhard Heydrich[1] to Chiefs of Einsatzgruppen[2]
(September 21, 1939)

Concerning: The Jewish problem in the occupied zone.

I refer to the conference held in Berlin today, and again point out that the *planned joint measures* (i.e. the ultimate goal) are to be kept *strictly secret*.

Distinction must be made between

(1) the ultimate goal (which requires a prolonged period of time) and

(2) the sectors leading to fulfillment of the ultimate goal, (each of which will be carried out in a short term). . . .

I. The First Prerequisite for the Ultimate Goal Is First of All, the Concentration of the Jews from the Country to the Larger Cities.

This is to be carried out speedily. . . .

[T]here shall be established as few concentration points as possible so that future measures may be accomplished more easily. One must keep in mind that only such cities are chosen as concentration points which are located either at railroad junctions or at least along a railroad. . . .

II. Councils of Jewish Elders

(1) In each Jewish community, a Council of Jewish Elders is to be set up which, as far as possible, is to be composed of the remaining influential personalities and rabbis. The Council is to be composed of 24 male Jews (depending on the size of the Jewish community).

It is to be made *fully responsible* (in the literal sense of the word) for the exact execution according to terms of all instructions released or yet to be released. . . .

(4) The Councils of Elders are to be made acquainted with the time and date of the evacuation, the evacuation possibilities and finally the evacuation routes. They are, then, to be made personally responsible for the evacuation of the Jews from the country. . . .

III . . .

In the execution of this plan, care must be taken that economic security suffer no harm in the occupied zones.

(1) The needs of the army, should particularly be kept in mind e.g. it will not be possible to avoid leaving behind here and there some Jews engaged in trade who absolutely must be left behind for the maintenance of the troops, for lack of any other way out. In such cases, the immediate aryanization of these plants is to be planned for and the emigration of the Jews is to be completed later in agreement with the competent local German administrative authorities.

---

[1] Reinhard Heydrich (1904–1942), Nazi official originally responsible for organizing and implementing the Holocaust.

[2] Four paramilitary units assigned to kill ethnic minorities and social deviants.

Extracts of the Minutes of the Wannsee Conference[3] (January 20, 1942) [Stamped "Top Secret"]

At the beginning of the meeting the Chief of the Security Police and the SD, SS Lieutenant General Heydrich, reported his appointment by the Reich Marshal[4] to serve as Commissioner for the Preparation of the Final Solution of the European Jewish Problem, and pointed out that the officials had been invited to this conference in order to clear up the fundamental problems. The Reich Marshal's request to have a draft submitted to him on the organizational, factual, and material requirements with respect to the Final Solution of the European Jewish Problem, necessitated this previous general consultation by all the central offices directly concerned, in order that there should be coordination in the policy.

The primary responsibility for the administrative handling of the Final Solution of the Jewish Problem will rest centrally with the Reich Leader SS[5] and the Chief of the German Police (Chief of the Security Police and the SD)—regardless of geographic boundaries.

The Chief of the Security Police and the SD thereafter gave a brief review of the battle conducted up to now against these enemies. The most important aspects are—

a. Forcing the Jews out of the various fields of the community life of the German people.

b. Forcing the Jews out of the living space of the German people.

In execution of these efforts there was undertaken—as the only possible provisional solution—the acceleration of the emigration of the Jews from Reich territory on an intensified and methodical scale. . . .

The emigration program has now been replaced by the evacuation of the Jews to the East as a further solution possibility, in accordance with previous authorization by the Fuehrer.

These actions are of course to be regarded only as a temporary substitute; nonetheless, here already, the coming Final Solution of the Jewish Question is of great importance.

In the course of this Final Solution of the European Jewish Problem, approximately 11 million Jews are involved.

QUESTIONS FOR ANALYSIS

1. Describe the development of the Nazis' Jewish policies as put forth in these documents. How does this policy progression compare with Heydrich's synopsis?

2. What similarities can be found between Hitler's ideas about the individual and the state (Source 5) and the ideas of citizenship legislated by the Nazis in 1935?

---

[3] Meeting of fifteen top Nazi officials to finalize their plan to kill all of Europe's Jews.

[4] Hermann Göring (1893–1946), leading Nazi Party official who held many of the highest offices in Nazi Germany.

[5] Heinrich Himmler (1900–1945), head of the Gestapo and the SS.

3. How do the documents from the early period of Nazi rule (1935) redefine the status of Jews living within Germany? How does the status of Jews in Nazi Germany compare with the status of kulaks in Stalin's Soviet Union?

4. What limitations to Nazi control over the Jewish populations are suggested by these documents?

7

". . . TURN TO YOUR LOCAL PARTY ORGANIZATION."

Nazi Art (1930s)

As the Nazi Party identified and persecuted the "evil" forces destroying German society, its members also developed and promulgated an ideal image of that society. Beginning in the mid-1930s, Nazi control over the production of art, literature, cinema, and other artistic forms allowed the party to promote its vision of German society—a vision in which the social role of women played an important part. Hitler explained, "However

NAZI CALENDAR, 1939

Future Mothers, ground which lies fallow is not joyful, just as the woman who has grown beautiful but remains childless for a long time.

NAZI POSTER, 1930S

Countrymen, if you need advice or aid, turn to your local [Nazi] Party organization.

broadly we may define woman's field of activity, the raising of a family will always be the central goal of her organic and logical development. The family is the smallest but the most precious unit in the entire structure of the state." As this quotation suggests, Nazi thought emphasized the naturalness (organicity) of women, defined a woman's life goal by reference to that naturalness, and glorified that goal—production of a family—as a fundamental building block of the state. Shown here are two Nazi propaganda images that draw on these themes. The first is a photo from a 1939 Nazi pictorial calendar. The second is a Nazi wall poster.

QUESTIONS FOR ANALYSIS

1. What qualities of German women are depicted in these images? How do these images correspond to Hitler's statement in the introduction to this source?

2. How does Hitler's argument about the origins of "culture-creating" societies (Source 5) emphasize the importance of women and families to German society?

3. How do the captions tie the two visual images to Nazi ideas?

8

"... THE BOGEY-MAN, 'THE JEW.'"

Melita Maschmann
Account Rendered   (1963)

As a young woman, Melita Maschmann (b. 1918) joined the female branch of the Hitler Youth organization and rose to become head of its Department for Press and Propaganda. Held in a detainment camp for a few years following the war, Maschmann over the next decade confronted the crimes of the Nazi regime. In 1963, she published Account Rendered, *written in the form of a long letter to her closest friend from her youth, who was Jewish. In the work, Maschmann explains her involvement in the Nazi regime and, in the excerpt below, her accommodations to the Nazis' violent anti-Semitism.*

My parents certainly grumbled about the Jews, but this did not stop them having a genuine liking for the Lewys[1] and having social relations with my father's Jewish colleagues.

For as long as we could remember, the adults had lived in this contradictory way with complete unconcern. One was friendly with individual Jews whom one liked, just as one was friendly as a Protestant with individual Catholics. But while it occurred to nobody to be ideologically hostile to *the* Catholics, one was, utterly, to *the* Jews. In all this no one seemed to worry about the fact that they had no clear idea of who "*the* Jews" were. They included the baptized[2] and the orthodox, yiddish speaking second hand dealers and professors of German literature, Communist agents and First World War officers decorated with high orders, enthusiasts for Zionism[3] and chauvinistic German nationalists. ...

---

[1] Jewish family friends.
[2] Christian Jews.
[3] Movement to establish a Jewish state in Palestine.

Melita Maschmann, *Account Rendered: A Dossier on My Former Self,* trans. Geoffrey Strachan (New York: Abelard-Shuman, 1964), 40–41, 55–57.

When you came into my class at Easter 1933 from another Berlin school I made friends with you, although I knew you were Jewish and despite the fact that I had joined the Hitler Youth at almost the same time.

I had learned from my parents' example that one could have anti-semitic opinions without this interfering in one's personal relations with individual Jews. There may appear to be a vestige of tolerance in this attitude, but it is really just this confusion which I blame for the fact that I later contrived to dedicate body and soul to an inhuman political system, without this giving me doubts about my own individual decency. In preaching that all the misery of the nations was due to the Jews or that the Jewish spirit was seditious and Jewish blood was corrupting, I was not compelled to think of you or old Herr Lewy or Rosel Cohn:[4] I thought only of the bogey-man, "*the* Jew." And when I heard that the Jews were being driven from their professions and homes and imprisoned in ghettos, the points switched automatically in my mind to steer me round the thought that such a fate could also overtake you or old Lewy. It was only *the* Jew who was being persecuted and "made harmless." . . .

On the evening of November 9 1938[5] I took part in a demonstration in front of the old gothic town hall in Frankfurt. I cannot remember now the details of this event. It was one of the routine occasions which I generally allowed to pass over my head in boredom and indeed regarded as a waste of time for people like myself, who had no further need of "orientation." I only remember that the Frankfurt S.S.-Führer[6] asked my friends and me after the demonstration if we felt like coming with him as something else was planned for that night.

Perhaps he took some of us into his confidence. I myself did not hear what was proposed. I only know that everyone said, "We're not coming. We're too tired."

Next morning—I had slept well and heard no disturbance—I went into Berlin very early to go to the Reich Youth Leadership office.[7] I noticed nothing unusual on the way. I alighted at the Alexanderplatz.[8] In order to get to the Lothringerstrasse[9] I had to go down a rather gloomy alley containing many small shops and inns. To my surprise almost all the shop windows here were smashed in. The pavement was covered with pieces of glass and fragments of broken furniture.

I asked a patrolling policeman what on earth had been going on there. He replied: "In this street they're almost all Jews."

"Well?"

"You don't read the papers. Last night the National Soul boiled over."

I can only remember the sense but not the actual wording of this remark, which had an undertone of hidden anger. I went on my way shaking my head. For the space of a second I was clearly aware that something terrible had happened there. Something frighteningly brutal. But almost at once I switched over to accepting what had happened as over and done with and avoiding critical reflection. I said

---

[4] Jewish classmate.

[5] Kristallnacht or the Night of Broken Glass, when Nazis destroyed nearly every synagogue and Jewish institutional building in Germany.

[6] Head of the SS in Frankfurt.

[7] Offices of the Hitler Youth.

[8] Alexander Square.

[9] Lothringer Street.

to myself: The Jews are the enemies of the new Germany. Last night they had a taste of what this means. Let us hope that World Jewry, which has resolved to hinder Germany's "new steps towards greatness," will take the events of last night as a warning. If the Jews sow hatred against us all over the world, they must learn that we have hostages for them in our hands.

With these or similar thoughts I constructed for myself a justification of the pogrom. But in any case I forced the memory of it out of my consciousness as quickly as possible. As the years went by I grew better and better at switching off quickly in this manner on similar occasions. It was the only way, whatever the circumstances, to prevent the onset of doubts about the rightness of what had happened. I probably knew, beneath the level of daily consciousness, that serious doubts would have torn away the basis of my existence from under me. Not in the economic but in the existential sense. I had totally identified myself with National Socialism.

QUESTIONS FOR ANALYSIS

1. What explanation does Maschmann offer for her attitude toward Jews in the early Nazi era? How does she explain her acceptance of Nazi anti-Jewish violence?
2. How do Maschmann's views on Jews compare to Hitler's vision of Jewish culture in *Mein Kampf* (Source 5)?
3. Compare Maschmann's identification with the Nazi Party to Hitler's statements about the ideal role of the individual within society. How are they similar or different?
4. In what ways should the context in which this piece is written—long after the events described and in the form of a letter to a Jewish childhood friend—raise questions about how we might interpret this text?

9

". . . HE WILL BE A HOLLOW MAN. . . ."

Primo Levi
Survival in Auschwitz (1947)

When World War II began in 1939, the Nazis and their sympathizers isolated and brutalized Jewish populations, especially in eastern and southern Europe, where large Jewish populations lived. Jews responded to German atrocities in many different ways—by fleeing and emigrating, by accepting Gestapo-ordered Jewish control over ghettoized

---

Primo Levi, *Survival in Auschwitz: The Nazi Assault on Humanity,* trans. Stuart Woolf (New York: Simon and Schuster, 1995), 22–27.

Jewish populations, by joining underground resistance movements, and sometimes simply by seeking to survive. The excerpt below is from the Italian Jewish writer and chemist Primo Levi's Survival in Auschwitz—*a powerful account of his experiences in a concentration camp. It describes his arrival at Auschwitz and his understanding of the Nazi attack on his identity.*

... Then the lorry stopped, and we saw a large door, and above it a sign, brightly illuminated (its memory still strikes me in my dreams): *Arbeit Macht Frei,* work gives freedom.

We climb down, they make us enter an enormous empty room that is poorly heated. We have a terrible thirst. The weak gurgle of the water in the radiators makes us ferocious; we have had nothing to drink for four days. But there is also a tap—and above it a card which says that it is forbidden to drink as the water is dirty. Nonsense. It seems obvious that the card is a joke, "they" know that we are dying of thirst and they put us in a room, and there is a tap, and *Wassertrinken Verboten.* I drink and I incite my companions to do likewise, but I have to spit it out, the water is tepid and sweetish, with the smell of a swamp.

This is hell. Today, in our times, hell must be like this. A huge, empty room: we are tired, standing on our feet, with a tap which drips while we cannot drink the water, and we wait for something which will certainly be terrible, and nothing happens and nothing continues to happen. What can one think about? One cannot think any more, it is like being already dead. Someone sits down on the ground. The time passes drop by drop.

We are not dead. The door is opened and an SS man enters, smoking. He looks at us slowly and asks, *"Wer kann Deutsch?"* [Who knows German?] One of us whom I have never seen, named Flesch, moves forward; he will be our interpreter. The SS man makes a long calm speech; the interpreter translates. We have to form rows of five, with intervals of two yards between man and man; then we have to undress and make a bundle of the clothes in a special manner, the woollen garments on one side, all the rest on the other; we must take off our shoes but pay great attention that they are not stolen.

Stolen by whom? Why should our shoes be stolen? And what about our documents, the few things we have in our pockets, our watches? We all look at the interpreter, and the interpreter asks the German, and the German smokes and looks him through and through as if he were transparent, as if no one had spoken.

I had never seen old men naked. Mr. Bergmann wore a truss[1] and asked the interpreter if he should take it off, and the interpreter hesitated. But the German understood and spoke seriously to the interpreter pointing to someone. We saw the interpreter swallow and then he said: "The officer says, take off the truss, and you will be given that of Mr. Coen." One could see the words coming bitterly out of Flesch's mouth; this was the German manner of laughing.

---

[1] Supportive device, usually a pad with a belt, worn to prevent enlargement of a hernia.

Now another German comes and tells us to put the shoes in a certain corner, and we put them there, because now it is all over and we feel outside this world and the only thing is to obey. Someone comes with a broom and sweeps away all the shoes, outside the door in a heap. He is crazy, he is mixing them all together, ninety-six pairs, they will be all unmatched. The outside door opens, a freezing wind enters and we are naked and cover ourselves up with our arms. The wind blows and slams the door; the German reopens it and stands watching with interest how we writhe to hide from the wind, one behind the other. Then he leaves and closes it.

Now the second act begins. Four men with razors, soapbrushes and clippers burst in; they have trousers and jackets with stripes, with a number sewn on the front; perhaps they are the same sort as those others of this evening (this evening or yesterday evening?); but these are robust and flourishing. We ask many questions but they catch hold of us and in a moment we find ourselves shaved and sheared. What comic faces we have without hair! The four speak a language which does not seem of this world. It is certainly not German, for I understand a little German.

Finally another door is opened: here we are, locked in, naked, sheared and standing, with our feet in water—it is a shower-room. We are alone. Slowly the astonishment dissolves, and we speak, and everyone asks questions and no one answers. If we are naked in a shower-room, it means that we will have a shower. If we have a shower it is because they are not going to kill us yet. But why then do they keep us standing, and give us nothing to drink, while nobody explains anything, and we have no shoes or clothes, but we are all naked with our feet in the water, and we have been travelling five days and cannot even sit down.

And our women?

Mr. Levi asks me if I think that our women are like us at this moment, and where they are, and if we will be able to see them again. I say yes, because he is married and has a daughter; certainly we will see them again. But by now my belief is that all this is a game to mock and sneer at us. Clearly they will kill us, whoever thinks he is going to live is mad, it means that he has swallowed the bait, but I have not; I have understood that it will soon all be over, perhaps in this same room, when they get bored of seeing us naked, dancing from foot to foot and trying every now and again to sit down on the floor. But there are two inches of cold water and we cannot sit down.

We walk up and down without sense, and we talk, everybody talks to everybody else, we make a great noise. The door opens, and a German enters; it is the officer of before. He speaks briefly, the interpreter translates. "The officer says you must be quiet, because this is not a rabbinical school." One sees the words which are not his, the bad words, twist his mouth as they come out, as if he was spitting out a foul taste. We beg him to ask what we are waiting for, how long we will stay here, about our women, everything; but he says no, that he does not want to ask. This Flesch, who is most unwilling to translate into Italian the hard cold German phrases and refuses to turn into German our questions because he knows that it is useless, is a German Jew of about fifty, who has a large scar on his face from a wound received fighting the Italians on the Piave [in northern Italy]. He is a closed, taciturn man, for whom I feel an instinctive respect as I feel that he has begun to suffer before us.

The German goes and we remain silent, although we are a little ashamed of our silence. It is still night and we wonder if the day will ever come. The door opens again, and someone else dressed in stripes comes in. He is different from the others, older, with glasses, a more civilized face, and much less robust. He speaks to us in Italian.

By now we are tired of being amazed. We seem to be watching some mad play, one of those plays in which the witches, the Holy Spirit and the devil appear. He speaks Italian badly, with a strong foreign accent. He makes a long speech, is very polite, and tries to reply to all our questions.

We are at Monowitz, near Auschwitz, in Upper Silesia, a region inhabited by both Poles and Germans. This camp is a work-camp, in German one says *Arbeitslager;* all the prisoners (there are about ten thousand) work in a factory which produces a type of rubber called Buna, so that the camp itself is called Buna.

We will be given shoes and clothes—no, not our own—other shoes, other clothes, like his. We are naked now because we are waiting for the shower and the disinfection, which will take place immediately after the reveille, because one cannot enter the camp without being disinfected.

Certainly there will be work to do, everyone must work here. But there is work and work: he, for example, acts as doctor. He is a Hungarian doctor who studied in Italy and he is the dentist of the Lager [camp]. He has been in the Lager for four and a half years (not in this one: Buna has only been open for a year and a half), but we can see that he is still quite well, not very thin. Why is he in the Lager? Is he Jewish like us? "No," he says simply, "I am a criminal."

We ask him many questions. He laughs, replies to some and not to others, and it is clear that he avoids certain subjects. He does not speak of the women: he says they are well, that we will see them again soon, but he does not say how or where. Instead he tells us other things, strange and crazy things, perhaps he too is playing with us. Perhaps he is mad—one goes mad in the Lager. He says that every Sunday there are concerts and football matches. He says that whoever boxes well can become cook. He says that whoever works well receives prize-coupons with which to buy tobacco and soap. He says that the water is really not drinkable, and that instead a coffee substitute is distributed every day, but generally nobody drinks it as the soup itself is sufficiently watery to quench thirst. We beg him to find us something to drink, but he says he cannot, that he has come to see us secretly, against SS orders, as we still have to be disinfected, and that he must leave at once; he has come because he has a liking for Italians, and because, he says, he "has a little heart." We ask him if there are other Italians in the camp and he says there are some, a few, he does not know how many; and he at once changes the subject. Meanwhile a bell rang and he immediately hurried off and left us stunned and disconcerted. Some feel refreshed but I do not. I still think that even this dentist, this incomprehensible person, wanted to amuse himself at our expense, and I do not want to believe a word of what he said.

At the sound of the bell, we can hear the still dark camp waking up. Unexpectedly the water gushes out boiling from the showers—five minutes of bliss; but immediately after, four men (perhaps they are the barbers) burst in yelling and shoving and drive us out, wet and steaming, into the adjoining room which is freezing; here other shouting people throw at us unrecognizable rags and thrust into our hand a pair of broken-down boots with wooden soles; we have no time to understand and we already find ourselves in the open, in the blue and icy snow of dawn, barefoot and naked, with all our clothing in our hands, with a hundred yards to run to the next hut. There we are finally allowed to get dressed.

When we finish, everyone remains in his own corner and we do not dare lift our eyes to look at one another. There is nowhere to look in a mirror, but our appearance stands in front of us, reflected in a hundred livid faces, in a hundred miserable and sordid puppets. We are transformed into the phantoms glimpsed yesterday evening.

Then for the first time we became aware that our language lacks words to express this offence, the demolition of a man. In a moment, with almost prophetic intuition, the reality was revealed to us: we had reached the bottom. It is not possible to sink lower than this; no human condition is more miserable than this, nor could it conceivably be so. Nothing belongs to us any more; they have taken away our clothes, our shoes, even our hair; if we speak, they will not listen to us, and if they listen, they will not understand. They will even take away our name: and if we want to keep it, we will have to find ourselves the strength to do so, to manage somehow so that behind the name something of us, of us as we were, still remains.

We know that we will have difficulty in being understood, and this is as it should be. But consider what value, what meaning is enclosed even in the smallest of our daily habits, in the hundred possessions which even the poorest beggar owns: a handkerchief, an old letter, the photo of a cherished person. These things are part of us, almost like limbs of our body; nor is it conceivable that we can be deprived of them in our world, for we immediately find others to substitute the old ones, other objects which are ours in their personification and evocation of our memories.

Imagine now a man who is deprived of everyone he loves, and at the same time of his house, his habits, his clothes, in short, of everything he possesses: he will be a hollow man, reduced to suffering and needs, forgetful of dignity and restraint, for he who loses all often easily loses himself. He will be a man whose life or death can be lightly decided with no sense of human affinity, in the most fortunate of cases, on the basis of a pure judgement of utility. It is in this way that one can understand the double sense of the term "extermination camp," and it is now clear what we seek to express with the phrase: "to lie on the bottom."

QUESTIONS FOR ANALYSIS

1. How does Levi express a sense of terror? What significance does information have in creating the sense of terror?

2. How is the issue of identity central to Levi? How does he demonstrate the stripping away of identity? What identity does he ultimately lose?

3. How does Levi's understanding of the Nazi attack on his identity compare to Maschmann's description of the Nazis' creation of identity (Source 8)?

CHAPTER QUESTIONS

1. Compare Soviet and Nazi expressions of nationalism and respondes to ethnicity in the 1920s and 1930s? How did each regime use these issues?

2. To what extent do the Soviet justifications for policies that resulted in the deaths of millions resemble the Nazi justifications for policies that resulted in the Holocaust? In what ways are they different?

3. How did Soviet and Nazi thought and practices challenge the ideas of liberalism (Chapter 8, Sources 1 and 2)?

4. How do the nationalism and ethnic superiority expressed in Nazi Germany and the Soviet Union in the 1920s and 1930s compare to the variants of racism expressed in western Europe during the height of imperialism in the 1880s and 1890s (Chapter 10, Sources 3 and 5)?

Chapter 13

THE CALL FOR LIBERATION IN THE ERA OF THE COLD WAR

The military victory of the Allied powers over Nazi Germany and its allies in 1945 gave way to celebration and to anxiety. Beyond the parades that marked the end of hostilities, many celebrated the Allied victory over the fascist armies as a triumph of Western civilization and its values of freedom, individual rights, and constitutional government. Anxieties quickly arose, however, as rivalries emerged between the war's two dominant victors—the United States and the Soviet Union. A "cold war" developed as each power saw itself threatened by the other and sought strategic advantages internationally in a postwar world that was adapting to peace. While the Soviet Union secured its hold on the eastern European nations, the United States aggressively pursued aid policies to the central and western European nations, whose economies had been shattered by the war. Western European statesmen soon faced an additional problem as they realized that their countries no longer had the economic resources and the political strength to sustain their vast colonial empires.

Colonial peoples had provided crucial resources—in the form of both war materiel and troops—to the Allies in pursuit of victory. Western officials had promised colonial peoples greater political rights and autonomy in return for their support. When the war ended, people in Asia, Africa, and the Middle East began to demand full autonomy as independent nations. The era of decolonization had begun. In some cases, Western nations offered little resistance to the demands and sought to build ties that allowed their economic and political interests to continue to flourish in the newly independent states. In other cases, Western efforts to stifle movements of national liberation merged with colonial conflicts over the leadership of those independence movements.

As decolonization gained momentum in the late 1950s and early 1960s, new nations emerged across the globe, and many suffered considerable domestic turmoil (Map 13.1). The leaders of colonial liberation movements, who often had received Western educations, used Western political ideals of universal personal and political rights to justify their rebellions to a world audience—and to attack their own domestic political rivals. The new cold war rivalry provided an overarching structure to the international turmoil. The United States and the Soviet Union each sought to manipulate decolonization for its own strategic advantage; however, as the cold war rivals sought to use proxies to compete for influence in the young nations, so the contending factions in individual nations sought to use and manipulate the cold war rivals for their own purposes. The resulting political confusion left deep scars and unsavory regimes supported by the United States and the Soviet Union.

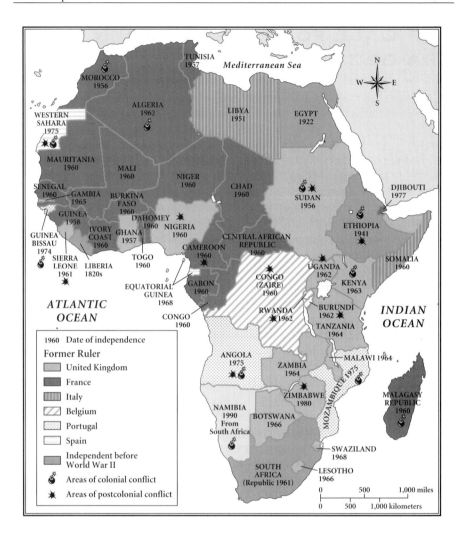

MAP 13.1 THE DECOLONIZATION OF AFRICA, 1951 TO 1990

The liberation of Africa from European rule was an uneven process, sometimes occurring peacefully and at other times requiring armed struggle. The difficult process of nation building following liberation involved establishing state institutions, including educational and other services. By assisting their former colonies in the state-building process, European states often continued to influence their former colonies.

The international policies pursued in response to colonial movements soon became important domestic political issues in Western nations, where politicians and opinion makers saw Western civilization and national power threatened either by their loss of colonies or by their support for colonial regimes that denied Western values of political rights. The colonial liberation movement's language of liberty, justice, human rights, national decline, and economic disaster inflamed domestic politics and brought the colonial conflicts home. Further, this language of rights and liberty found resonance among groups within Western society who themselves had long been subject to discrimination and who began to call for liberation at home.

INDEPENDENCE IN THE CONGO: 1960

A large, sparsely populated land with vast natural resources, the Congo sits at the center of Africa, bordering nine other nations. When the Congo gained independence from Belgium in 1960, both its geographic centrality and its vast natural resources made many individuals and governments interested in the new nation's fate. Unfortunately, Belgian colonial officials had done little to prepare the Congolese people for self-government. Congolese political aspirations had appeared suddenly in the mid 1950s, as numerous political parties emerged. Most of these parties, however, were tied to one of the Congo's two hundred tribes. Tribal identity provided the central organizing principle for Congolese politics. Little sense of national or Congolese identity existed, for the Congo as a territory had been created by European governments and did not result from African political arrangements.

When anti-European violence erupted in 1959, the Belgian government quickly embraced the goal of Congolese independence. At a January 1960 conference of Congolese political organizations convened by the Belgian government, Belgian officials agreed to almost immediate decolonization, and on June 30, 1960, the Republic of Congo was born. Elections held just prior to independence determined that the new president would be Joseph Kasavubu, a leader of the Bakongo, one of the largest tribal groups in the Congo and the basis of his political power. Kasavubu and his allies, however, had been outpolled in Parliamentary elections by the Congolese National Movement, led by Patrice Lumumba, who became the new prime minister. A member of the small Batetela tribe, Lumumba, more than any other politician, had adopted a message of Congolese nationalism militantly opposed to Belgian rule and in favor of a unified Congo led by a strong central state. For Lumumba, a stable, prosperous Congo could emerge only as Congolese national identity replaced tribalism and tribal rivalries as the central framework for Congolese politics.

Five days following independence, the "Congo crisis" was triggered by an army mutiny in the capital of Leopoldville (now Kinshasa) over resentment against Belgian military commanders who had continued in their military posts. Rivalry between Kasavubu and Lumumba paralyzed the new government's ability to respond. As sporadic violence spread and Belgian citizens were attacked, on July 9 the Belgian government asserted a right to protect Belgian citizens and property and, against the wishes of Kasavubu and Lumumba, deployed paratroops in the Congo. On July 11, Katanga province declared its independence from Congo and accepted covert military and technical assistance from Belgium. Moise Tshombe was president of Katanga Province, leader of the large and powerful Lunda tribe, and head of the Conakat Party, which was backed by the Lunda tribe and by the Belgian mining monopoly that controlled the province's rich copper mines. Lumumba demanded the immediate withdrawal of Belgian troops from the Congo and accused the Belgian government of seeking to reinstitute colonial authority. Further, to reestablish control over all of the Congo by the central government, Lumumba, with Kasa-vubu, on July 12 appealed to the United Nations for military assistance.

With the entrance of the United Nations, the Congo crisis encountered the cold war conflict. The United States and its Western allies distrusted Lumumba, who was a charismatic but erratic spokesperson. In addition to his militant nationalism and support of state centralism, Lumumba had allied himself with the pan-African movement, which called for colonial liberation across Africa and many of whose leaders had socialist and communist associations. The United States feared that Lumumba's personal charisma would overshadow the more moderate Kasavubu and that he would lead the Congo away from Western-style democratic and capitalist policies, allying the Congo with the Soviet Union. The Soviet Union and its satellite nations saw the Belgian military intervention and the Katanga province secession as an opportunity to embarrass the Western imperial powers, especially before the developing nations of Africa and Asia—many of them only recently freed or soon to be freed from imperial burdens. These international perspectives became integrated into the Congo's domestic conflicts.

1

"... THE INSTALLATION OF A REIGN OF TERROR ..."

Proclamation of Independence of Katanga   (1960)

Prior to independence, Moise Tshombe (1919–1969) had promoted the idea of a Congo in which individual provinces would hold the weight of political authority (and thereby tribal considerations would hold prominence). Tshombe's idea lost to the strong central state proposal of Patrice Lumumba, and Tshombe's Conakat Party showed poorly in the national elections preceding independence; however, the Conakat won a majority in Katanga province, and Tshombe became the province's president. On July 11, 1960, Tshombe declared the independence of Katanga province from Congo, and the Katanga Council of Ministers issued the Declaration of Independence excerpted below.

Belgium has granted independence to the Congo.

It has done so according to its promise of January 13, 1959.

This promise and the royal message which accompanied it were intended to endow us with democratic institutions, and, in keeping with the stipulations of the Charter of the United Nations, which pledges to respect the right of all peoples to self-determination, it was intended to endow us, not with a slavish copy of Western

---

"Text of the Proclamation of Independence of Katanga," in Jules Gérard-Libois, *Katanga Secession*, trans. Rebecca Young (Madison: University of Wisconsin Press, 1966), 328–29.

democratic institutions, but with a regime which the various regions composing the Congo would choose according to their own conceptions and the traditions which they hold dear.

The independence of the Congo is an established fact since June 30, 1960.

What do we behold at present?

Throughout the Congo and particularly in Katanga and in Leopoldville province, we see a tactic of disorganization and terror at work, a tactic which we have seen applied in numerous instances and in how many countries now under Communist dictatorship.

After improper elections in certain provinces, which gave the majority to a single party, a number of electors being unable to cast their votes, a central government with an extremist majority was constituted.

Hardly was it constituted, before this government, setting at naught the stipulations of the *Loi Fondamentale*,[1] attempted to meddle in affairs which properly belonged solely within the competent jurisdiction of the provincial governments. . . .

The tactic of disruption and subversion of authority is the very same that was ever employed by the propagandists and sectaries[2] of the Communist Party.

The result was not long in coming.

Since July 5, soldiers knowing no discipline have given themselves over to acts of insubordination, of threats, to brutalities aimed principally against the European population, to searches and illegal arrests, to pillages, and finally, to murders.

The goal of these maneuvers and their premeditation were amply proven by the repeated protests of the Prime Minister[3] of the Congo against the dispatch of Belgian troops from Belgium to protect property and human lives.

We declare that what the current central Congolese government wants is nothing less than the disintegration of the whole military and administrative apparatus, the installation of a regime of terror which ousts our Belgian colleagues.

It desires, by this method, to replace the destroyed cadres as rapidly as possible by an administration which it seems already to have recruited amongst nationals of countries under Communist rule.

Katanga cannot bow to such proceedings. The Katangan government was elected by a provincial assembly, itself elected on the basis of a program for order and peace.

Under these circumstances, and before the dangers we would bring down upon us by prolonging our submission to the arbitrary will and Communistic intentions of the central government, the Katangan government has decided to proclaim the independence of Katanga.

This INDEPENDENCE is TOTAL. However, aware of the imperative necessity for economic cooperation with Belgium, the Katangan government, to which Belgium has just granted the assistance of its own troops to protect human life, calls upon Belgium to join with Katanga in close economic community.

---

[1] "Fundamental Law" Charter passed by the Belgian parliament to serve as a temporary constitution for the Congo during its first year of independence.
[2] Members of a sect or party.
[3] Prime Minister Patrice Lumumba.

Katanga calls upon Belgium to continue its technical, financial, and military support.

It calls upon her to assist in re-establishing order and public safety.

If Belgium refuses to fulfill this imperative duty and if she refuses to recognize Katanga as a country free and independent and its government as the only legal government, Katanga appeals to the ENTIRE FREE WORLD and calls upon ALL to recognize its right, which is that of all its people, to self-determination.

QUESTIONS FOR ANALYSIS

1. How does the Proclamation justify Katanga province's declaration of independence? What and whom does the Proclamation blame for Katanga's need for independence?

2. How does the Proclamation link the Katangese cause with the political traditions of the Western democracies? How does the Proclamation seek to use and to limit the application of those traditions in the Congo, thus allowing for Congolese political frameworks?

3. How does the Proclamation associate the national government, and Lumumba himself, with communism? What types of political practices are identified as communist?

4. What does the argument of the Proclamation suggest about its intended audience?

2

"... SEEKING TO BRING THE COLD WAR TO THE HEART OF AFRICA."

United Nations Security Council Official Record

Statements of Ambassadors from the Soviet Union and the United States   (July 20, 1960)

The United Nations' entrance into the Congo crisis, by request of the Congolese government, provided a stage—the U.N. Security Council—on which the international community could respond to the crisis. Most prominently, the cold war rivalry between the United States and the Soviet Union provided a script for the Security Council debates on the crisis—a script encouraged by the secessionist forces in Katanga (Source 1). On July 14, 1960, the Security Council approved a resolution calling on Belgium to withdraw its troops and authorizing the U.N. Secretary General to provide the

United Nations, *Security Council Official Records* (New York: United Nations, July 20–21, 1960), 877:31–38.

Congolese government with military assistance. Below are excerpted statements on the Congo crisis made in the Security Council on July 20—five days after the initial deployment of U.N. forces in the Congo—by the Soviet Union's First Deputy Minister of Foreign Affairs, Vasily Kuznetsov, and by the United States' representative to the United Nations, Henry Cabot Lodge.

Comments of Vasily Kuznetsov

[T]he Government of Belgium is stubbornly and brazenly ignoring the Council's decision of 14 July. In doing so, that Government continues to make use of the favourite excuse of the colonialists—the alleged need to protect the interests of Belgian nationals.

As may be seen from the Secretary-General's report, the Belgian Government has stated that the Belgian authorities will continue to take "the necessary security measures" in the case of grave and imminent danger. But the question whether or not an imminent danger exists is one which the Belgian authorities themselves intend to settle at their own discretion. What this actually means is that the colonialists have no intention of abiding by the Council's decision, but that they want to continue their armed intervention against the Congo until they have attained their basic objective, which is to strangle and dismember the young Republic.

We now know that the expansion of military intervention in the Congo is being accompanied by efforts to dismember the young State. As so often in the past, the colonialists are here trying to apply the principle of "divide and rule." They have succeeded in finding a stooge to be used to that end in the person of one Tshombe who, only a few days after the proclamation of the Republic's independence, came out with the idea of separating from the new-born African State one of its most important provinces, namely Katanga.

It is hardly surprising that the activities of Tshombe should have caused the financial and industrial moguls to exult. Behind these attempts to dismember the Congo can easily be discerned the desire of the Western Powers to reserve for themselves the economically valuable areas of the former Belgian colonies, which are among the chief sources of enrichment for the capitalist monopolies. . . .

Moved by feelings of friendship for the heroic people of the Congo and firmly resolved to do what it can to bring about the triumph of the just cause for which the Republic of the Congo, in upholding its independence, is fighting, the Soviet Government has decided to furnish that Republic with food and other assistance and to inform the Secretary-General of the United Nations accordingly. . . .

The example of the Congo shows how tenaciously the advocates of the colonialist system cling to the past and employ any means to preserve their rule so that they may continue to plunder the very rich natural resources of the Congo and keep the industrious Congolese people in colonial bondage. They do not want to recognize that the era of the shameful colonialist system is gone for ever. Everything must be done to ensure that that colonialist system shall finally be liquidated within the shortest possible time. The struggle of the peoples against that disgrace of the twentieth century cannot be halted. Nevertheless, there are still some in the West who think that if they make a few concessions here and there they can keep the old system fundamentally intact. That was what the foreign monopolists thought when they posed as being "zealous" for the Congolese people's welfare. The statement made today by the Belgian Minister for Foreign Affairs is a case in point. If the interpretation was correct, he said, speaking of the people of the Congo, that they were a people "entrusted to our care." Were they, then, so entrusted by God in order that they might the more easily be exploited?

The representative of Belgium is surprised that the Congolese delegate here should have dared to speak aloud of the Belgian Government's perfidy, that he should have dared to speak out in protest against the fact that Belgian troops had unlawfully occupied the country in disregard of the relevant agreement, had violated the treaty and had adopted a course clearly aimed at strangling the young Republic. Does the Belgian Government expect the people of the Congo and the Congolese representatives here to thank it for such acts?

The people of the Congo thought otherwise. They decided once and for all to throw off the colonial yoke, to take their fate into their own hands and to build a new life, using the rich natural resources in which the soil of the Congo abounds, and the fruit of their own labour for the benefit of the country with its 13 million inhabitants, and not for the enrichment of a clique of international monopolists.

That alarmed the foreign enslavers. They dropped their hypocritical mask of humanity and began trying to subdue the people by fire and sword. . . .

It should be noted that in the oral report which the Secretary-General made to the Council on 13 July it was particularly indicated that military personnel belonging to the armies of the great Powers would not be sent to the Congo. In this connexion we deem it essential to draw the attention of the Security Council to a press report to the effect that a detachment of the United States Army which had previously been stationed in West Germany arrived at Leopoldville[1] airport on 17 July under the pretext of co-operating in the evacuation of refugees and assisting the operations of the United Nations Force in the Republic of the Congo.

On instructions from the Government of the USSR, the Soviet delegation registers its objection to the introduction of United States troops into the Republic of the Congo on any pretext, and insists on the immediate withdrawal of all United States military personnel from Congolese territory.

Comments of Henry Cabot Lodge

Here . . . are some basic facts.

First, the United Nations has moved quickly and effectively and, I might say, decisively. Many nations and countless individuals have contributed to the success of this operation. In the forefront of the United Nations effort is the quick and ready response of African States whose armed contingents are already in the Congo helping to restore public order there. These men, far from their native countries and climates, are in the Congo on behalf of all of us—the entire United Nations. Three thousand, five hundred United Nations troops are already in the Congo; 460

---

[1] Capital of the Congo.

troops from Ethiopia, 770 from Ghana, 1,250 from Morocco and 1,020 from Tunisia. An additional 500 Ghanaian troops were air-lifted today, as were approximately 635 men of the Swedish battalion in the United Nations Emergency Force. About 700 men from Guinea will be air-lifted starting on Friday. Commitments have been made to air-lift other battalions of African troops to Leopoldville over the next few days. These include an additional 1,250 Moroccans, 1,000 Tunisians and 600 Ghanaians. Soon these men will be joined by other troops and police units from other States, African and non-African. We hope that in a few days the United Nations force will reach a strength close to 10,000 men.

The United Nations has also moved rapidly on the food front. Contributions have been pledged by a number of countries. Hundreds of tons of flour and other foodstuffs have already arrived in the Congo to help alleviate the threatened food shortage. Other United Nations Members are expected to provide needed assistance in other ways. Clearly, this is a collective effort on the part of the United Nations.

The United States has been happy to help in the field of transport and communications. We have responded quickly to the request of the Secretary-General. The United States Air Force has flown many thousands of miles. It has air-lifted most of the troops which are now in the Congo. It has carried great quantities— many tons—of good and equipment. We are providing at the request of the Secretary-General needed equipment and other logistic support to the United Nations. We will continue to respond to the requests of the Secretary-General since our objective is to do everything we can to make the United Nations effort a success. . . .

In the light of this rapid and impressive international effort, we believe the Government of the Republic of the Congo should feel protected and reassured. Problems remain for this young Government, but surely the desire of the United Nations to assist and its ability to do so effectively has been made abundantly clear. The United Nations will not permit the Congo to founder and we know perfectly well that once fear has been conquered, it is possible to tackle the outstanding problems realistically and effectively.

There is a second important fact to mention. It relates to the question of withdrawal of the Belgian forces. We think we can understand the feelings of everyone concerned with this problem. We can understand the fears of the Congolese leaders when troops of the former administering Power returned to the Congo. We can understand equally well the anxieties of the people and Government of Belgium and their feeling that they had to send urgent contingents to protect their nationals. The atrocities committed are certainly deplorable.

In my statement of 13 July I made clear that the United States interpreted the provisions of the Security Council resolution of that date calling upon the Government of Belgium to withdraw its troops as being contingent upon the successful carrying out of the entire resolution by the United Nations.[2]

The Belgian representative stated in the Security Council early last Thursday morning that Belgian troops would be withdrawn when security had been reestablished and properly assured by a responsible authority. . . .

---

[2] Reestablishment of security.

It is regrettable to note tonight that the Soviet Union is evidently seeking to bring the cold war to the heart of Africa. Its demand tonight that the United States withdraw the few American technicians who are at present in Leopoldville with the approval of the United Nations is clearly another effort by the Soviet Union to obstruct the United Nations effort to restore order in Leopoldville. All the world knows, except apparently the Soviet Union and others who are like-minded, that the small group of American service personnel in Leopoldville are there in connexion with the specific request of the United Nations to provide transport, communications and food. They will stay there only as long as they are needed to support the United Nations efforts in the Congo. In the sense in which the word is customarily used here in the United Nations, they are not troops at all. . . .

There have been reports that the Soviet Union might intervene in the Congo directly with troops, and before I yield the floor I would just like to say a word about that. The position of the United States Government on this point is unequivocally clear, both for itself and for others. For . . . despite an official request from the Government of the Congo some days ago for United States troops we insisted that all American help should be sent through the United Nations. The United Nations effort, we think, offers the best way of restoring order and making possible the speedy withdrawal by stages, of Belgian forces. Obviously, no troops should be introduced into the Congo other than those requested by the Secretary-General pursuant to the Security Council's resolution of 14 July. The United States can, accordingly, be counted on to continue its vigorous support of the United Nations in the Congo. With other United Nations Members we will do whatever may be necessary to prevent the intrusion of any military forces not requested by the United Nations. Such forces, if they were introduced, not only would be in defiance of the United Nations but would seriously jeopardize any effort to bring stability and order to the Congo.

QUESTIONS FOR ANALYSIS

1. How does Kuznetsov define the actions of the United Nations and the United States in the Congo crisis within the cold war context and within a Marxist-Leninist framework of imperialism? How does he defend Soviet aid for the Congo government?

2. What defenses of U.N. and U.S. actions in the Congo crisis does Lodge make? What allowances for Belgian activity in the Congo does he make?

3. In what ways is Lodge's response to reports of Soviet activity in the Congo similar to and different from the claims of the Katanga Proclamation of Independence (Source 1)? How do the arguments of Kuznetsov and Lodge call on traditional Western political ideals in terms of the role and responsibility of government?

4. How do Lodge's references to the Western powers working with and through the United Nations imply a new framework for interactions between the Western powers and the rest of the world?

3

Patrice Lumumba
Radio Address   (1960)

Patrice Lumumba (1925–1961) achieved political prominence in the Congo in the late 1950s as the leader of the Congo's militant nationalists. When Lumumba became the Congo's first prime minister, most Western nations viewed him as a dangerous, potentially communist presence in the new republic. Lumumba, however, was frustrated with the limited mandate given to the United Nations military forces, which were barred from interfering in the "domestic conflict" of Katangese secession. On July 22, 1960, shortly before leaving for New York to press for further assistance from the United Nations to suppress disorder and especially the Katangese revolt, Lumumba gave the radio address excerpted below to the Congolese people.

We [Kasavubu and Lumumba] want all territorial administrators throughout the country to be Congolese; we want all district commissioners to be Congolese. A plot has been hatched with the fascists of Katanga to ensure that it will be Belgians who continue to hold these posts. They are trying to set up an economic dictatorship in Katanga, contrary to the interests of the popular masses. Our brother Tshombe will regret this. Katanga will never be independent; Katanga remains a Congolese province, a province of our republic. Those who have hatched plots against our republic, those who have launched this attack against the external safety of our state, will be brought before the bar of justice of our republic. The chief of state [Kasavubu] and I have pledged our solemn word to the entire nation that we will safeguard the unity and the integrity of this country. It is this unity, this strength, which will make the Congo a great power, a great nation, in the heart of Black Africa. People have tried to cause dissension between the chief of state and me. For to divide is to rule. We realized this. Therefore there is perfect accord between the chief of state, Mr. Kasavubu, and myself; we have exactly the same opinions and think exactly alike. . . . It is this unity which has led us to protest to the United Nations day after day, demanding the immediate departure of the Belgian troops, of the enemy troops, of the occupation troops; and the United Nations has listened to us today, and we have said that if there was no way of obtaining immediate satisfaction, we would ask for Soviet and Afro-Asiatic troops. We are not now communists and we never will be, despite the campaign of destruction and obstruction that enemies of our independence

---

Jean Van Lierde, ed., *Lumumba Speaks: The Speeches and Writings of Patrice Lumumba, 1958–1961*, trans. Helen R. Lane (Boston: Little Brown, 1972), 282–85.

have waged throughout the country. We are simply Africans. We do not want to subject ourselves to any foreign influence, we want nothing to do with any imported doctrines, whether from the West, from Russia, or from America. The Congo remains the Congo. We are Africans. We want to make the Congo a great free nation. We do not want to escape one dictatorship[1] only to fall beneath another. We are not what people think we are, because we are a decent people.

We are honest; if we had wanted to sell our country out, to get money from imperialists, as they have offered, there would be no change, there would be no problems today. Because we want to serve the interests of our people, of our nation, nothing matters to us except defending our country and serving the nation. Those who want to make deals with the capitalists can do so; that is their business; those who want to make millions can do so; that is their business, and they are the ones who will have a guilty conscience. Dear brothers, you can now see the benefits of unity. We ask our deputies, our senators, all the people to unite, to follow our example, so that as children of this united country, workers and intellectuals, rich and poor, adults and children, boys and girls, all of us together may build a great Congo, a strong Congo, so as to liberate the rest of Africa, to liberate our brothers who are still under foreign domination; dear brothers, the work that we are pursuing, the work of national liberation, of building the country, is a work that I might rightly call a divine work; we must forgive those who are attacking us today. We must live with the Europeans who remain among us as brothers. We must welcome them to our country; our enemies will depart.

We are going to expel all undesirable elements, those who still want to mistreat you, who still want to oppress you. We will allow only friends to stay here with us, Belgians and Europeans of good will, of good faith, those who realize that the Congo has changed, that the Congo belongs to the Congolese, that the Congolese must run their own country. These people must stay, and we will also call on other nations, on other Belgians in Belgium, who obviously do not approve of what the members of the government in power are doing in their attempt to see to it that the Congo remains a conquered country—isn't that right?

I am going to the United States today with a delegation of your leaders. We are going to establish contact with many groups with regard to problems concerning industrialization and the development of our country. Many technicians[2] have left. Our courts have no magistrates today. There has been blackmail. People have tried to sabotage our independence; but we are still on our feet. We are going to tighten our belts and prove that, like the United States, our country will be built by the labor of its sons and not by holding out our hands and begging here and there. . . . [W]hen I come back with technicians, with teachers, with engineers for all the necessary cadres, we will then send the best of our sons abroad to learn, so that in five years the Congo may have its own technicians in every field. The enemies who are sabotaging us today will knock on the Congo's doors tomorrow to ask for hospitality and we will tell them: the Congolese people are a proud people who feel no bitterness. You can come back here, dear brothers. I urge you to follow this watchword and rejoice, and not treat the Europeans cruelly or raise a hue and cry against them, but rather make them feel at home in our country.

---

[1] Belgian colonial rule.
[2] Individuals with technical training in science, law, engineering, and other fields.

QUESTIONS FOR ANALYSIS

1. How does Lumumba express both Congolese nationalism and pan-African unity in his address? How does he allow for a continued Belgian presence in the Congo?

2. How does Lumumba use the language of political liberty to reject the cold war frameworks expressed in the United Nation's Security Council (Source 2)? How does he also try to manipulate cold war tensions?

3. What common purposes exist between Lumumba's attitudes toward economic development and his Congolese nationalism? How do these purposes also serve him in his effort to manipulate cold war tensions?

4. What similarities and differences exist between Lumumba's description of his goals and the accusations made against him in the Katanga Proclamation of Independence (Source 1)?

POSTSCRIPT

Lumumba followed through on his threat to seek military assistance from the Soviet Union. As Soviet supplies and advisors arrived in the Congo, Western governments pressured other Congolese leaders to stop Lumumba's actions, and the United States' Central Intelligence Agency sought Lumumba's assassination. A complete rupture soon occurred between President Kasavubu and Prime Minister Lumumba. As the political system broke down, the head of the army, Joseph Mobutu, took over the reins of government in September 1960 and ordered all Soviet bloc advisors and technicians to leave immediately. Supported by the CIA and other Western governments, Mobutu placed Lumumba under detention in December and in January 1961 handed him to troops of Katanga province president Tshombe, who quickly executed him. Mobutu remained head of the army until 1965, when he overthrew the government of Kasavubu, renamed the country Zaire, and claimed the country's presidency until forced from power in 1997.

ALGERIAN INDEPENDENCE IN FRANCE: 1957 TO 1959

French Algeria held an anomalous place within the French political world. Since 1848, the French government had defined Algeria not as a colony but as part of France itself, with representatives from French Algeria seated in the French National Assembly. These representatives were elected by the *colons*—the large European population of Spanish, French, Italian, and Maltese descent that constituted some 10 percent of the population of French Algeria. The *colons* dominated the region's political and economic life, successfully resisting efforts in the National Assembly to moderate the legal restrictions on the Algerian population. Frustrations grew among non-European Algerians, which exploded in 1954 into open rebellion led by the National Liberation Front (Front de Libération Nationale, or FLN).

The FLN advocated political equality for all who lived in Algeria and asserted that this equality could be achieved only by open conflict—guerrilla warfare, raids, and sabotage—that would make French rule in Algeria unbearable to the French government. France responded by sending 500,000 troops to Algeria to suppress the rebellion. In 1957, the FLN countered with terrorism meant to paralyze the French administration in Algeria. French paratroopers replied with the use of torture to extract information from captured FLN prisoners.

The growing conflict in French Algeria proved disastrous to France's postwar government, the Fourth Republic. In the wake of World War II, the leaders of the Fourth Republic had hoped to restore France's greatness and self-respect; however, the Republic's weak political structure, in which short-lived coalition governments succeeded one after the other, prevented French leaders from effectively addressing the most difficult issue facing the Republic and one that directly challenged France's "greatness"—that of colonial independence. Between 1946 and 1954, France fought a bloody and failed war in Vietnam to reclaim control over its colony of Indochina. Six months after warfare ended in Vietnam, the revolt in Algeria began. Still stinging from having just lost Vietnam, receiving determined support from the *colons,* and aware of recently discovered oil reserves in southern Algeria, the leaders of the Fourth Republic held on to Algeria even as they granted independence to Algeria's neighbors, Tunisia and Morocco. As the actions of the French military and the FLN became increasingly brutal, serious debate emerged at home over the role that France should play in Algeria, the legitimacy of the Algerian revolt, and the appropriateness of the actions taken by the French military. These debates helped to undermine the political legitimacy of the Fourth Republic itself, which collapsed in May 1958 when confronted by the seizure of Algiers, the Algerian capital, by anti-independence *colon* activists seeking to influence a vote in the National Assembly. Following two weeks of negotiations, the National Assembly granted full power to Charles de Gaulle, hero of World War II. The military, the *colons,* and the conservative nationalists in France anticipated that de Gaulle would establish a tough regime prepared to crush the FLN and the Algerian uprising.

4

". . . THE ENTREPRENEURS OF NATIONAL DESTRUCTION."

Jean-Paul Sartre
You Are Super   (1957)

Philosopher, novelist, and playwright Jean-Paul Sartre (1905–1980) was one of France's most influential public intellectuals for over thirty years. Sartre was one of the writers known as existentialists, a group that included Albert Camus (Source 7) and Sartre's lifelong companion, Simone de Beauvoir (Source 9). Sartre's account of existentialist philosophy asserted that life had no inherent meaning and the individual

---

Jean-Paul Sartre, "Vous êtes formidables," *Les Temps Modernes* 135 (May 1957), 1642–45, 1647. (Translated by David Kammerling Smith.)

was not defined by any predetermined status or fate. Rather, the individual was free to define his or her existence—the meaning of his or her life—by his or her conscious acts. Sartre particularly examined the social responsibility implied within the individual's freedom. In 1945, Sartre and Beauvoir founded the journal Les Temps Modernes. *Dedicated to "engaged literature,"* Les Temps Modernes *considered how freely made choices should be adapted to socially useful ends. In the May 1957 issue Sartre's essay "You Are Super," excerpted below, considered the French collective guilt in the Algerian conflict, especially in response to recent reports that French soldiers were torturing captured Algerian rebels.*

For the last eighteen months, our country has been a victim of what the Code[1] has named an "enterprise of demoralization." A nation is not demoralized by first sabotaging its morals; it is done by lowering its morality. As to the method, everyone knows it: in rushing us into a wretched adventure, a social culpability has been placed within us from the outside. But we vote, we give the mandates, and in a certain fashion we are able to revoke them. The swirl of public opinion makes governments fall. The crimes that are committed in our name we must be personally complicit in, since it remains in our power to stop them. We must reclaim responsibility for this culpability that has rested in us, inert, foreign, and we must debase ourselves for having supported it.

Yet we have not fallen so low that we cannot hear the cries of a tortured child without horror. How simple everything would be, how quickly everything would be resolved if one time, a single time, these cries struck our ears. But our ears have been stuffed. It is not cynicism, it is not hatred that demoralizes us. No, it is only the false ignorance in which we have been made to live, and we ourselves contribute to its continuation. To ensure our peace and quiet, the care of our governing class goes as far as to undermine secretly the freedom of expression. The truth is hidden or filtered. When the Fellagha[2] massacre a European family, the national press spares us nothing, not even the photos of mutilated corpses. But when a Muslim lawyer, against his French tormentors, finds no other recourse than suicide, the fact is reported in three lines to spare our sensibilities. Hide, deceive, lie: this is a duty for the informants of the mother country. . . .

If only we were able to sleep, ignoring everything. If we were separated from Algeria by a wall of silence! If we could be truly fooled. Foreigners would be able to question our intelligence but not our candor.

We are not candid; we are dirty. Our consciences have not been troubled; however, they are troubled. Our governing class knows it well; this is how they like us. This is what they want to achieve by their attentive cares and their proclaimed concerns. This is, under the cover of a faked ignorance, our complicity. Everyone has heard about the tortures—something has filtered through of the tortures in spite of the mainstream press. The honest but least circulated newspapers have published

---

[1] The French legal code.
[2] Algerian resistance forces.

some of the eyewitness reports; some pamphlets circulate; the soldiers return and speak. But this merely serves the demoralizers. . . . Most Frenchmen have not read these newspapers or pamphlets, are not able to read them;[3] they know of men who read them. Many of us have never heard the testimony of a recalled soldier; we have reported to us what certain soldiers have said. . . . It is here that we look for "the enterprise" [of demoralization]; alas, it is here that we look out for ourselves. Why should we believe in these gossips? Where are the documents? Where are the witnesses? Those who declare themselves convinced were so beforehand. Certainly, the possibility can no longer be rejected a priori[4] . . . but it is necessary to wait, not to judge before being truly informed. Thus, one does not judge. But one does not even investigate. . . . He who works all day and who suffers in his office the thousand small aggressions of daily life cannot be asked to spend the evening collecting information on the Arabs.

And this is the first of our lies. The demoralizers have only to cross their arms; we will accomplish the work ourselves. . . . If we refuse to make an investigation of the French truth ourselves . . . it is because we are afraid. Afraid of seeing naked our own true image. This is the lie—and the excuse of the lie: yes, we lack proofs; thus we are able to believe nothing. But we do not look for the proofs because in spite of ourselves, we know. . . .

Our second lie has already been prepared. The snare—this is the safeguard commission. If only we could have confidence in it! . . . The government has made a gesture [in creating the commission]; Mollet[5] has declared himself "upset." He says that he wants enlightenment. We believe this, and we are excusable: the human word is made to be believed. We do not believe this, and we are yet more excusable: the word of Mollet is made to be questioned. We know that the commission will be composed of irreproachable men; we know also that it will be able to do nothing. Their honesty serves to mask from us their impotence. Thus, we refuse to give our confidence to the government, and yet we count on it to dispel our mistrust.

Culpable. Twice culpable. Already we feel like the victim of a confused malaise. This is not yet the horror but the foreboding that the horror exists, very near, the more menacing because we are not able nor do we want to look at it straight in the face. . . .

There is yet time to thwart the entrepreneurs of national destruction. It is yet possible to break the infernal circle of this irresponsible responsibility, of this culpable innocence, of this ignorance that yearns to know. Look at the truth. It will force each of us either to condemn publicly the crimes committed or to endorse them in full knowledge of the cause.

QUESTIONS FOR ANALYSIS

1. What does Sartre mean by the "enterprise of demoralization"? How does this enterprise create public culpability in the activities of the French state in Algeria?

---

[3] Due to the limited circulation of these publications.

[4] Prior to examination.

[5] Guy Mollet (1905–1975), socialist politician who served as premier of France from January 1956 to May 1957.

2. According to Sartre, how does the safeguard commission both encourage mistrust and dispel it? How are the French culpable in accepting the lies given to them?

3. How does Sartre's analysis of this public culpability undermine nationalist sentiment?

4. How does Sartre's analysis of public culpability compare to his existentialist emphasis on individual freedom? What significance would nationalism retain in Sartre's existentialism?

5

". . . EVERYTHING DEPENDS ON THIS CHOICE. . . ."

Jacques Soustelle
The Algerian Drama and French Decadence (1957)

A scholar of pre-Columbian America, Jacques Soustelle (1912–1990) served in several administrative positions during and after the Second World War. Appointed governor-general of Algeria in 1955, Soustelle promoted the economic and political integration of Algeria with France. Recalled from this position a year later by a new government, Soustelle became a vocal advocate for a French-controlled Algeria. In 1957, amid growing criticism of French policies in Algeria, Soustelle published The Algerian Drama and French Decadence, *excerpted below, in which he warned, often in a harshly satirical tone, of the decline of France.*

We are told that on condition of abandoning Algeria, relieving us of this too weighty burden, we will recover an equilibrium and that, in the absence of something better, our "thought" will be "disseminated" throughout the world.

The dissemination of thought—this is the consolation that is promised to us in exchange for renouncing the rights and duties of power: the impalpable realm that would reward our resignation. What a delusion!

Look, thus, at the world today, where the language of one of the two empires advances with the dollar and that of the other with the armored division.[1] Behind both are power, numbers, the nuclear weapon. For some years, the solemn experts of the Quai d'Orsay[2] have shown us that France has had to suffer all the affronts of

---

[1] The United States and the Soviet Union, respectively.
[2] French foreign affairs headquarters.

Jacques Soustelle, *Le Drame Algérien et la decadence française: response à Raymond Aron* (Paris: Librarie Plon, 1957), 64–69. (Translated by David Kammerling Smith.)

the Arab League without responding in order to protect the cultural patrimony implanted in the Near East: the gesture of an Egyptian Führer[3] sufficed to sweep away without profit all this and all the humiliations that had been consented to.

The truth is that if some countries profoundly impregnated with our civilization—for example, those of Latin America—cling still to our language and to our culture, it is because they hope that France will remain in the future an independent power. They would break away, the heart in mourning, from a poor, small state that has disavowed itself.

The dissemination of a country is indivisible: it is at once that of its universities, its literature, its art, its diplomacy, its army, its industry. . . . I do not claim that we must excel in everything, but I assert (and whoever knows a bit about the problem of French influence in a foreign country will be of my opinion) that this influence is of a single piece—that it must proceed, to be effective, at once from the theater and from commerce, from medicine and from metallurgy. It exerts itself through the scientific researcher, the traveling lecturer, the military envoy, the technical exposition. Above all, it nourishes itself on the prestige of France: suppress this prestige and everything vanishes.

Certainly, it is possible for a country in the pangs of death to dispense yet for a time some cultural riches. It diffuses the light of a waning star; soon come the dusk and the night.

After the withdrawal to the hexagon,[4] the withdrawal to the immaterial. Africa will be abandoned for the mother country; the mother country for Sirius. Ah! How beautiful France will be when there are no longer any French.

Everyone understands well—even those who do not admit it—that in reality the drama is not even that of Algeria; it is that of decadence. This is the question . . . that is posed to each and every one of us: "Do you accept the decadence of France?"

This is, in effect, the question, and there are not twenty responses: two and two alone—yes or no.

Yes: this is to give in, sometimes, as Raymond Aron,[5] in painting resignation in the colors of courage, in invoking obscure myths agreeable to the spirit of the times and to historic fatality.

No: this is to resist. This is to believe that the will and sacrifice of humans weigh in the balance. . . . This is to remember that the Afrika Corps rushed toward Egypt but there was an El-Alamein, that the Wehrmacht trampled the shores of the Volga but there was a Stalingrad.[6] This is to realize that every historical trend knows its flux and reflux, that the occasion always arrives where the invading cavalry turns back, that one has seen one hundred times stubborn, besieged defenders break the

---

[3] Gamal Abdel Nasser (1918–1970), president of Egypt (1956–1970), who in 1956 nationalized the Suez Canal, which had been controlled by British and French interests.

[4] France.

[5] Raymond Aron (1905–1983), French sociologist who wrote in favor of Algerian independence.

[6] During the Second World War, the defeat of the German Afrika Corps at El Alamein turned the war in northern Africa in favor of the Allied forces, and the German Wehrmacht army stormed across the western Soviet Union only to have its advance halted at Stalingrad.

momentum of the conquerors who batter the walls, and that finally one always has an opportunity to win a battle, on condition of giving battle.

With a gloomy dejection, France has witnessed the submersion of its sinking territories in the Far East and the Maghrib.[7] A certain formal logic exhorts us to let Algeria disappear—and tomorrow black Africa: "Since you have lost Indochina,[8] Tunisia, and Morocco, why do you maintain Algeria?" Thus reason certain "friends" of France in the shadow of the skyscrapers. As for Aron, he marvels, becomes angry, even, from seeing that "self-respect clinches up over the possession of Algeria."

Self-respect? No. This is a profound logic; this is the vital sentiment of a nation that knows that its existence is menaced. This logic expresses itself as follows: "It is precisely *because* we have lost Indochina, Tunisia, and Morocco that it is necessary at any price, under any form, and under any pretext not to lose Algeria." Losses have a cumulative effect like certain poisons. Beyond a certain dosage, there is a danger of death. . . .

France is alerted and alarmed. She recognizes more or less clearly . . . that in abandoning Algeria she would commit the act of suicide, that she would demolish the last levee that still contains the flood waters, that she would subscribe herself to her downfall.

To abandon Algeria is to condemn France to decadence; to save Algeria is to give a counterblow to the dreadful march of decline, to restore to our country, to its people, to its youth their fortune and their future.

Such is the choice. . . . And everything depends on this choice, since the true danger is not in the strength of the enemy but in our weakness: it is in ourselves.

QUESTIONS FOR ANALYSIS

1. What arguments does Soustelle present in favor of sustaining French control over Algeria? How does he mock arguments in favor of abandoning French claims on Algeria?

2. How does Soustelle both reject and use arguments focused on French culture? How would Soustelle characterize the relationship between French culture and French power?

3. On what basis does Soustelle implicitly justify ignoring the political liberty and rights of Algerians?

4. How does Soustelle's concern with decadence compare to Sartre's analysis of the "enterprise of demoralization" (Source 4)? What assumptions about the condition of France and about its status in the world of the 1950s do they have in common?

---

[7] Regions of northern Africa bordering the Mediterranean Sea.
[8] French colonial lands in southeast Asia.

6

"THE BETRAYAL OF LEGALITY BY THE STATE . . ."

Paul Ricoeur
The Etienne Mathiot Case (1958)

In December 1957, the French Lutheran pastor and peace activist Etienne Mathiot was arrested on the charge of having helped the Algerian National Liberation Front political leader Si Ali to hide in France and escape to Switzerland. In part to protect his brother-in-law, also a Lutheran pastor, Mathiot confessed his guilt when confronted by French police officers and was brought to trial in March 1958. The French protestant philosopher Paul Ricoeur (b. 1913) served as a witness for the defense in the trial and as the trial began published an influential essay defending Mathiot's actions in Esprit, *a left-leaning magazine influential among French Catholic intellectuals. In that essay, excerpted below, Ricoeur sought to justify Mathiot's actions.*

There is a Mathiot case; I would like to make the case understood. . . .

It is easy to get rid of Mathiot; it is sufficient to let his deed fall in the balance on the side of acts either useful or harmful to the conduct of the Algerian war. In adopting this elementary principle of calculation and its short view, the public prosecutor will attempt to reduce this act to an indirect, but real, contribution to the Algerian rebellion. Decent people will be persuaded of this and will carry on with their lives. Mathiot, they will say, at best is foolhardy and naive, at worst a traitor; there is no Mathiot case—convict him.

Yes, there is a Mathiot case!! And this case rises before the conscience of those same individuals who do not believe that we ought to participate in the Algerian insurrection as a military or terrorist undertaking. The case originated from the motive that Mathiot continually alleges. Pastor Mathiot declared, "I agreed to take him under my protection only because I knew that he was a political leader. My conduct would have been otherwise if he had been a killer. My acts do not signify that I approve of all of the FLN's policies. I am opposed to all atrocities, all tortures. With all my might I want to defend men against suffering. This is why I shielded Si Ali from the police investigations. I knew that he was sought by the Algerian public prosecutor's office. I wanted to save him from torture."

The act of Mathiot is entirely defined by this motive. It is a question neither of arms nor of a network; there is nothing else to "confess." It is entirely alone and by itself that this act speaks to us. What does it tell us?

Paul Ricoeur, "Le 'Cas' Etienne Mathiot," *Esprit* 259 (March 1958), 450–52. (Translated by David Kammerling Smith.)

When a country plunges into illegal violence —illegal even in the eyes of its exceptional legislation—when the recourse to torture threatens to become an integral part of its system of war, an act such as Mathiot's becomes, for its part, possible, comprehensible, justifiable. The betrayal of legality by the state drives the citizen to bear witness by illegality. Mathiot's act is one of the paths—the path of scandal—by which justice, exiled by official policy, collects its thoughts and protests. Mathiot's act is that of an ethic of distress. It is the product of the demoralization of the nation by the state and the citizen's rejection of this demoralization. It is the act of a man who, in a concrete situation, found nothing to do other than to carry aid to someone who through circumstances has been made his enemy, in order to protest against the illegal violence to which he believed, with complete conviction, that this man was subjected. . . .

But this is a sterile act of protest, you say!—There are acts of protest that are also acts of reaffirmation.

In offering a hand to an Arab, Etienne Mathiot called on the foundations of laws on which our country rests and the values that create her honor and her brilliance. It is here that his act offers another significance. . . . It secretly registered to the benefit of French-Muslim friendship. One day—perhaps, if Mathiot's prosecutors have not destroyed everything—people will remember his act as a gesture, lost in its context, an act outside of the law, but one that will have contributed, in its fashion, to enlighten in a future conflict.

And then Etienne Mathiot is a pastor. This is not a superfluous detail. His act troubles his parish, leaves some colleagues hesitant or prudent. His "offense" has a profound sense, since he is a pastor. It registers, in an account more hidden than all military and political history, as a statement of contradiction. Such a statement of distress has been rendered inevitable and desirable as much by the history of the church as by the failure of the state.

So much compromising by Christians and by the leaders of churches, in the past and in the present, so many unjust wars and so much pillaging, covered over by the silence of Christians! Then come some men who twist against the grain of a bent conscience; the evidence of the contradiction is *he who remains* when all the weight of a community takes to the same side—that of active or tacit complicity with the established illegality.

QUESTIONS FOR ANALYSIS

1. How does Ricoeur use Mathiot's statement of his motivation to justify Mathiot's action? What role does Ricoeur's distinction between the nation and the state play in this justification?
2. What does Ricoeur mean by the idea of distress? How does Ricoeur find hope in Mathiot's statement of distress?
3. How does Mathiot's focus on demoralization compare to Sartre's use of this idea (Source 4)?
4. How does Ricoeur's use of Christianity compare to Sartre's focus on the individual? What similarities and differences exist in how each writer understands individual identity in the context of the state or nation?

7

"THERE HAS NEVER YET BEEN AN ALGERIAN NATION."

Albert Camus
Algeria (1958)

Born into poverty among the French Algerian population, the novelist, essayist, and moralist Albert Camus (1913–1960) explored in his writings the problems of the alienation of the individual and the way that values such as truth, moderation, and justice can be preserved. In post–World War II Europe, Camus gained fame for his writings, earning the 1957 Nobel Prize for literature. Critical of the injustices that were institutionalized by French policies in Algeria, Camus also believed that a French Algeria was not simply a colonial fiction. In the excerpt from Algeria *below, Camus defends the idea of French Algeria by responding to the claims of Algerian nationalists.*

If the Arab claim, such as it is expressed today, was entirely legitimate, Algeria probably would be autonomous now, with the consent of French opinion. However, . . . the Arab claim remains equivocal. This ambiguity, and the confused reactions that it arouses in our governments and in the country, explains the ambiguity of the French reaction, the omissions and the incertitudes with which it protects itself. The first thing to do is to clarify this claim to try to define clearly an agreeable response.

A. What is legitimate in the Arab claim?

It is right, and all the French know it, to denounce and refuse

1. Colonialism and its abuses, which are already established.
2. The repeated lie of assimilation, always proposed but never realized. . . .
3. The evident injustice of the distribution of agricultural lands and of the distributions of revenues. . . .
4. The psychological suffering: an attitude often scornful or detached among many French, which produces among the Arabs (by a series of stupid measures) a humiliation complex that is at the center of the present drama. . . .

B. What is illegitimate in the Arab claim?

The desire to rediscover a dignified and free life, the total loss of confidence in any political solution guaranteed by France, and also the romanticism characteristic of very young rebels who lack a political culture have led certain combatants and their military leaders to reclaim national independence. No matter how well disposed to the Arab claim, one must recognize nevertheless that with regard to

Albert Camus, *Actuelles III: Chroniques algériennes, 1939–1958* (Paris: Gallimard, 1958), 199–206. (Translated by David Kammerling Smith.)

Algeria, national independence is a formula of pure passion. There has never yet been an Algerian nation. Jews, Turks, Greeks, Italians, and Berbers would have as much right to reclaim the direction of this virtual nation. Actually, the Arabs themselves do not form Algeria alone. The importance and the antiquity of the French settlement [in Algeria], in particular, suffice to create a problem that is incomparable with anything else in history. The French of Algeria also are, in the strong sense of the term, indigenous. It must be added that a purely Arab Algeria would not be able to accede to the economic independence without which political independence is only an alluring illusion. . . .

The Arabs, at least, are able to call on their sentiment of attachment not to a nation but to a sort of Muslim empire, spiritual or temporal. Spiritually this empire exists, its cement and its doctrine being Islam. But a Christian empire also exists, at least as important, but no one intends to introduce it into temporal history. For the moment, the Arab empire does not exist historically but only in the writings of Colonel Nasser,[1] and it could materialize only by the worldwide upheavals that would signify the soon-to-come third world war. It is necessary to consider the claim of Algerian national independence in part as one of the manifestations of this new Arab imperialism, which Egypt, overestimating its strength, asserts to lead and which, for the moment, Russia uses for some goals of its anti-Western strategy. That this claim is unreal does not hinder its strategic use—well to the contrary. The Russian strategy, which can be read on all the maps of the globe, consists of calling for the status quo in Europe—this is to say the recognition of Russia's own colonial system—and stirring up the Middle East and Africa to encircle Europe by the south. The happiness and liberty of the Arab people have little to do with this affair. . . . Russia simply makes use of these dreams of empire to serve its own designs. In any case one must attribute to this nationalist and imperialist claim, in the precise sense of the word, the unacceptable aspects of the Arab rebellion and principally the systematic murder of French and Arab civilians, killed without discrimination solely for being French or friends of the French.

We thus find ourselves before an ambiguous claim that we can approve in its source and some of its formulations but that we cannot accept in any manner in certain of its developments. The error of the French government since the beginning of these events was of never distinguishing anything and consequently of never speaking clearly. This permitted all the skepticism and overbidding among the Arab masses. The result was to reinforce on both sides the extremist and nationalist factions.

The only chance of making progress on this problem is, thus, today as yesterday, choosing clear language. . . .

Then the French government must make known clearly

1. That it is prepared to render all justice to the Arab people of Algeria and to liberate them from the colonial system.
2. That it will cede nothing on the rights of the French of Algeria.

---

[1] Gamal Abdel Nasser (1918–1970), president of Egypt (1956–1970), who called for pan-Arab unity.

3. That it cannot accept that this justice, which it will consent to render, signifies for the French nation the prelude to a sort of historic death and, for the West, the risk of an encirclement that would lead to the Kadarization[2] of Europe and the isolation of America.... [T]hat she refuses, in particular, to serve the dream of an Arab empire at the expense of herself, of the European people of Algeria, and, finally, of world peace.

---

[2] János Kádár (1912–1989), Hungarian communist who led the Hungarian government under Soviet auspices after the Soviet Union invaded Hungary in 1956 and suppressed a popular revolt.

QUESTIONS FOR ANALYSIS

1. On what basis does Camus deny Algerian nationhood? How does Camus sever the link between nationhood and political liberties and forms of injustice?
2. What criticisms of French policies in Algeria does Camus make? How does his proposed declaration for the French government address those abuses?
3. How does Camus's argument against Algerian independence compare to Soustelle's argument (Source 5)?
4. How does Camus's use of cold war tensions in his argument compare to Soustelle's concerns about the Soviet Union and the United States? How does it compare to Lumumba's efforts to manipulate cold war tensions (Source 3)?

8

". . . THE ESTABLISHMENT OF A HAPPY AND DEMOCRATIC ALGERIA."

Ahmed Taleb-Ibrahimi
Letter to Albert Camus (1959)

Born into a politically prominent Muslim family in French Algeria, Ahmed Taleb-Ibrahimi (b. 1932) obtained a medical degree in Paris, where he became active in student organizations promoting Algerian nationalism. In 1956, he became head of the FLN branch in France, which led to his arrest and imprisonment from 1957 to 1961. While in prison, Taleb-Ibrahimi wrote numerous letters, including one to Albert Camus, excerpted below. In this letter, Taleb-Ibrahimi responds to Camus's rejection of Algerian nationalism.

[W]hat you have never wished to admit was the existence of the Algerian Nation fighting to build its own future independently. Faithful to an obsolete point of view

---

Ahmed Taleb-Ibrahimi, "Open Letter to Albert Camus," in Ahmed Teleb-Ibrahimi, *Letters from Prison, 1957–1961* (1966) (New Delhi: Allied, 1988), 35–39.

you have continued to distinguish between the "Arabs" and the "French," to speak of an "Arab revolt" whereas the facts tell you that it was an Algerian revolution where Jews and Christians fought shoulder to shoulder with their Muslim brothers, be it in the forests or in the camps, in the prisons or in cities. They all laboured for the independence of their country, fully aware that this independence was only one step towards the establishment of a happy and democratic Algeria. . . .

[Y]ou only talk of French Algeria threatened by a strange coalition which is uniting Madrid, Cairo and Budapest[1] against us? From an impassioned spokesman of the European minority you have become a sneering critic of the Arab movement that dreams of pan-Islamism without a second thought for the growing material needs of the masses—a pan-Islamism which is better off in the imaginations of Cairo than when faced with the realities of history.

It is indeed regrettable that a man of your calibre should take recourse to such absurd arguments, you who know deep inside you that the Algerian revolution is the incarnation of the deepest aspirations of its people, the work of its sons. How else could one explain such a heroic resistance for five years to a powerful modern army of more that half a million men?

Besides, it is strange to note that on the one hand, you claim to love your Arab "Brothers," but on the other you show supreme contempt for all that is Arab, Muslim and Oriental. You who claim that Algeria is your "real homeland" are unaware of its heritage to the extent that you dare to talk of Algerian cities being "without any history." Even a superficial knowledge of Maghrebin[2] history would have been enough to indicate to you that the Algerian nation is not a subsidiary phenomenon and though it may be Mediterranean, it is equally African and Arab in identity. . . .

Indeed, when . . . [in 1958], you took up your pen again to define your stand, it was a veritable accusation that you levelled at the Algerian Revolution. In two articles[3] which breathe insincerity with every word, there is no mention of the wounded and admirable Algeria, where heroism increases with suffering. After four years of war, you deliberately ignored the valiant deeds of a tortured people, of those intrepid men, those serene unflinching women who withstood arms, fire and famine without batting an eyelid. For you, the Algerian revolution is summed up as terrorism and all its fighters, enemy, resistance only massacre of the innocents, an act of cutthroats and mutilators.

Why talk only of terrorism why not of armed combat that the resistance carried on for a whole year before that? Why emphasise terrorism and talk in passing only of "pacification," that oppressive peace similar to the one that reigned in Warsaw,[4] that euphemism which scarcely disguised the policy of extermination which was so barbaric that it led to the birth of terrorism?

You who condemned terrorism for fear that your beloved ones will be its victims, who often speak of your mother in such touching terms, do you know that some of us have lost entire families following search operations by the French army,

---

[1] Three cities representing fascist, Islamic nationalist, and communist forces.
[2] North African.
[3] "Algeria (1958)" (Source 7) and "Avant-Propos," both published in *Actuelles III*.
[4] After a failed uprising against Nazi rule in 1944 in Warsaw, Hitler ordered the population of Warsaw deported and the city destroyed.

and that others saw their mothers (yes Camus, their mothers) humiliated by French soldiers in the most ignoble manner.

But you do not wish to see and you do not wish to know. You do not seem to realise that you yourself are victim of this hoax that you had denounced in *L'homme Revolte*,[5] the crime being "parading the remains of innocence." You seem to have adjusted very well to this nightmare world, this Orwellian universe[6] where war is baptised as "pacification," rape and plunder as "protection of the population," concentration camps as "transit camps," assassinations as "suicides" etc. . . .

Besides, you allege that Algeria's independence does not constitute a legitimate cause as it has not received the consent of the French public opinion. Let us suppose then, that if this be necessary (of course, this needs to be verified) it is, to say the least, surprising that Camus the great democrat should be so contemptuous of the Algerian public opinion itself.

According to you, this independence would signify the eviction of 1,200,000 Europeans. Why do you never quote the other view, you who claim to base all arguments on "intellectual independence"? Had you but cared to read the FLN's manifesto you would have found that "the objective of the Revolution is not to throw Algerians of European origin into the sea, but to get rid of the inhuman colonial yoke; that the Revolution is neither a civil war nor a religious war; that it wants to win national independence in order to install a democratic, socialist republic that would guarantee real equality to all citizens of the country, without discrimination." In short, our Revolution, to use an expression of *L'homme revolte* (The Rebel), denies all rights to Europeans in Algeria "as masters, but not as human beings."

QUESTIONS FOR ANALYSIS

1. What does Taleb-Ibrahimi establish as the basis of Algerian nationalism? How does his argument counter Camus's argument against Algerian nationalism (Source 7)?

2. How does Taleb-Ibrahimi draw on traditional Western ideas of democratic politics?

3. For what reasons does Taleb-Ibrahimi criticize Camus's description of the Algerian revolution?

4. How does Taleb-Ibrahimi turn Camus's writings against him? How does Taleb-Ibrahimi try to establish a position that is morally superior to that of Camus?

POSTSCRIPT

After assuming the presidency in the new Fifth Republic, Charles de Gaulle soon indicated his willingness to compromise on Algerian independence. Conservative Algerian *colons* and members of the French army saw de Gaulle's actions as a betrayal,

---

[5] *The Rebel*, published by Camus in 1951.
[6] George Orwell, pen name of Eric Blair (1903–1950), whose novel *Nineteen Eighty-Four* was a warning against repressive totalitarian governments that hide their abuse of power by controlling language.

and by 1961 a group of army officers entered into open sedition, staged a coup in Algiers, and, on its failure, resorted to terrorism and even assassination attempts on de Gaulle. Convinced that Algerian independence was unavoidable, de Gaulle negotiated an agreement with the Algerian provisional government to recognize Algerian independence with guarantees for the safety and property of French Algerians. French voters approved the agreement overwhelmingly in April 1962, which caused 750,000 French Algerians to flee from Algeria to France. In place of colonial rule, de Gaulle's government established a program of economic, military, educational, and cultural support for former French colonies that helped to maintain political and economic ties and enhance French power in international affairs.

LIBERATION AT HOME

The idea of liberation that infused international political environments from the late 1940s through the 1960s also showed its influence within Western culture. Populations defined by sex—long discriminated against within the Western world—began to make stronger claims for their own liberation. Women had gained the right to vote in most Western nations and now explored more deeply the nature of subjugation, challenging the many factors—political, social, economic, and cultural—that repressed women and restricted their positions within society. Similarly, homosexuals also began to call for gay liberation. Supporters of women's and gay liberation often faced hostile resistance as they sought to expand the Western ideas of rights and freedom to issues associated with sexuality.

9

". . . TO LIVE FOREVER ON HER KNEES."

Simone de Beauvoir
The Second Sex (1949)

In 1949, the French existentialist author and intellectual Simone de Beauvoir (1908–1986) published The Second Sex, *a landmark in modern feminism. Drawing on the existentialist idea that the individual creates his or her authentic existence by conscious acts, Beauvoir argued that women had denied their authentic selves and had embraced definitions of themselves as passive "others," living the lives that male authorities deemed appropriate for them.* The Second Sex *called on women to assert themselves and their freedom from such definitions, culturally and psychologically as well as legally and politically. In the following excerpt from* The Second Sex, *Beauvoir considers the conflict between men and women.*

Simone de Beauvoir, *The Second Sex,* trans. and ed. H. M. Parshley (New York: Knopf, 1952), 717–19, 727–29.

[S]exuality has never seemed to us to define a destiny, to furnish in itself the key to human behavior, but to express the totality of a situation that it only helps to define. The battle of the sexes is not immediately implied in the anatomy of man and woman. The truth is that when one evokes it, one takes for granted that in the timeless realm of Ideas a battle is being waged between those vague essences the Eternal Feminine and the Eternal Masculine; and one neglects the fact that this titanic combat assumes on earth two totally different forms, corresponding with two different moments of history.

The woman who is shut up in immanence[1] endeavors to hold man in that prison also; thus the prison will be confused with the world, and woman will no longer suffer from being confined there: mother, wife, sweetheart are the jailers. . . .

Today the combat takes a different shape; instead of wishing to put man in a prison, woman endeavors to escape from one; she no longer seeks to drag him into the realms of immanence but to emerge, herself, into the light of transcendence. Now the attitude of the males creates a new conflict: it is with a bad grace that the man lets her go. He is very well pleased to remain the sovereign subject, the absolute superior, the essential being; he refuses to accept his companion as an equal in any concrete way. She replies to his lack of confidence in her by assuming an aggressive attitude. It is no longer a question of a war between individuals each shut up in his or her sphere: a caste claiming its rights goes over the top and it is resisted by the privileged caste. Here two transcendences are face to face; instead of displaying mutual recognition, each free being wishes to dominate the other. . . .

The quarrel will go on as long as men and women fail to recognize each other as peers; that is to say, as long as femininity is perpetuated as such. Which sex is the more eager to maintain it? Woman, who is being emancipated from it, wishes none the less to retain its privileges; and man, in that case, wants her to assume its limitations. . . . It is vain to apportion praise and blame. The truth is that if the vicious circle is so hard to break, it is because the two sexes are each the victim at once of the other and of itself. Between two adversaries confronting each other in their pure liberty, an agreement could be easily reached: the more so as the war profits neither. But the complexity of the whole affair derives from the fact that each camp is giving aid and comfort to the enemy; woman is pursuing a dream of submission, man a dream of identification. Want of authenticity does not pay: each blames the other for the unhappiness he or she has incurred in yielding to the temptations of the easy way; what man and woman loathe in each other is the shattering frustration of each one's own bad faith and baseness. . . .

Woman is the victim of no mysterious fatality; the peculiarities that identify her as specifically a woman get their importance from the significance placed upon them. They can be surmounted, in the future, when they are regarded in new perspectives. Thus, . . . through her erotic experience woman feels—and often detests—the domination of the male; but this is no reason to conclude that her ovaries condemn her to live forever on her knees. Virile aggressiveness seems like a lordly privilege only within a system that in its entirety conspires to affirm masculine sovereignty; and woman *feels* herself profoundly passive in the sexual act only because she already

---

[1] Indwelling.

thinks of herself as such. Many modern women who lay claim to their dignity as human beings still envisage their erotic life from the standpoint of a tradition of slavery: since it seems to them humiliating to lie beneath the man, to be penetrated by him, they grow tense in frigidity. But if the reality were different, the meaning expressed symbolically in amorous gestures and postures would be different, too: a woman who pays and dominates her lover can, for example, take pride in her superb idleness and consider that she is enslaving the male who is actively exerting himself. And here and now there are many sexually well-balanced couples whose notions of victory and defeat are giving place to the idea of an exchange.

As a matter of fact, man, like woman, is flesh, therefore passive, the plaything of his hormones and of the species, the restless prey of his desires. And she, like him, in the midst of the carnal fever, is a consenting, a voluntary gift, an activity; they live out in their several fashions the strange ambiguity of existence made body. In those combats where they think they confront one another, it is really against the self that each one struggles, projecting into the partner that part of the self which is repudiated; instead of living out the ambiguities of their situation, each tries to make the other bear the abjection and tries to reserve the honor for the self. If, however, both should assume the ambiguity with a clear-sighted modesty, correlative of an authentic pride, they would see each other as equals and would live out their erotic drama in amity. The fact that we are human beings is infinitely more important than all the peculiarities that distinguish human beings from one another. . . .

I shall be told that all this is utopian fancy, because woman cannot be "made over" unless society has first made her really the equal of man. Conservatives have never failed in such circumstances to refer to that vicious circle; history, however, does not revolve. If a caste is kept in a state of inferiority, no doubt it remains inferior; but liberty can break the circle. Let the Negroes vote and they become worthy of having the vote; let woman be given responsibilities and she is able to assume them. The fact is that oppressors cannot be expected to make a move of gratuitous generosity; but at one time the revolt of the oppressed, at another time even the very evolution of the privileged caste itself, creates new situations; thus men have been led, in their own interest, to give partial emancipation to women: it remains only for women to continue their ascent, and the successes they are obtaining are an encouragement for them to do so. It seems almost certain that sooner or later they will arrive at complete economic and social equality, which will bring about an inner metamorphosis.

QUESTIONS FOR ANALYSIS

1. How does Beauvoir characterize the conflict between men and women? What importance does she give to the biological differences between men and women?

2. What does Beauvoir mean by the "vicious circle" of male-female conflict? What are its consequences?

3. How does she indicate that the conflict between men and women can be overcome? What role do cultural-psychological factors and economic-political factors play in overcoming the conflict?

4. How does Beauvoir draw on the idea of liberation in her argument? How does her understanding of liberation compare to the colonial liberation called for by Lumumba (Source 3), Sartre (Source 4), and Taleb-Ibrahimi (Source 8)?

10

"... THE LIBERTY FOR EVERYONE TO MAKE LOVE AS HE PLEASES ..."

Daniel Guérin
Shakespeare and Gide in Prison (1959)

During the 1950s, the French journalist and social activist Daniel Guérin (1904–1988), a committed anticolonialist, supported the Algerian independence movement. He also published his first defense of homosexuality, a collection of essays entitled Shakespeare and Gide in Prison. *In the excerpt below from that work, Guérin, sometimes called the grandfather of the French homosexual movement, integrates the themes of political and sexual liberation.*

There does not exist, in actual fact—or more exactly, there ought not to exist—a problem specific to homosexuality. The love against which is held so strong a prejudice that it dares not speak its name is only a special case—a variant of love. And if the author felt the need to consecrate the essays assembled in the present volume to this special case, the fault for this rests with those who misjudge it, parody it, vilify it, and hunt it down more tenaciously than other forms of eroticism.

But the true problem is not that of homosexuality. The problem goes beyond and broadens it to that of sexual liberty—even more, of liberty and nothing else.

Eroticism is one of the instruments of liberty. It contains, as Simone de Beauvoir has said, a *principle hostile to society* or, more exactly, to the society of oppression of men by men, to authoritarian society.

In *Carmen*[1] is sung

Love is a Bohemian child.
It has never, never known any laws.

The French [law] Code, however so bourgeois, so anachronistic, and so vexatious, all the same came under the libertarian influence, in a certain measure, of the Great

---

[1] Opera by the French composer Georges Bizet (1838–1875).

Daniel Guérin, *Shakespeare et Gide en Correctionnelle?* (Paris: Les Editions du Scorpion, 1959), 9–11. (Translated by David Kammerling Smith.)

French Revolution. The Code has shown itself relatively tolerant with regard to eroticism. It does not entirely penalize prostitution, and, at least until the ordinances of occupation promulgated arbitrarily by Philippe Pétain,[2] then confirmed a little too hastily by the provisional government of the Republic, *it did not say a word about homosexuality.* For the generations raised with a respect for the rights of man (so limited and so fallacious had been the famous rights), the individual was master of his body, and no collectivity had the right to stipulate what he could or could not do with it.

But today one witnesses this cruel and ridiculous paradox that, by the terms of the recent antisexual laws, Shakespeare[3] and Gide,[4] if they were still of this world, would be sent to prison!

Today, the extremes agree to deny man the liberty to make use of his epidermis. On one side, hard-pressed Puritanism braces itself to try to stem a rising tide of liberty that it knows is irresistible and irreversible. On the other side, the purists of the Social Revolution,[5] justly disgusted by the pollution of eroticism by Money, believe that they have to include in the same reprobation capitalism and eroticism. However, if one wants to make free men, it is necessary to *unchain,* and not repress, the Flesh. It is necessary to teach the young, inexperienced generations to make better use of this liberty that has been so recently won and that certainly is too often used clumsily and foolishly. It is necessary to teach them to cultivate healthily and joyously this *art* of eroticism.

Moreover, modern life—dominated by the machinery of the police (the growing influence of totalitarian state control) and of the race to atomic weapons—leads to a progressive annihilation of the individual by the community. We see taking shape little by little this gigantic, centralized termitary;[6] this tyranny more and more intolerant and intolerable; this existence of a factory, a barracks, or a prison; this universe of concentration camps; this fanatical conformism that would see coming with horror a Maurice Maeterlinck.[7]

To this dreadful menace of subjugation, a measured individualism, fraternal and altruistic, offers the indispensable antidote. And free eroticism is (at least for the physically robust) one of the most efficacious ways and, at the same time, but yes, the most inoffensive ways of safeguarding their Self.

In a society too organized, too blueprinted, too mechanized, too regimented, the liberty for everyone to make love as he pleases, including in the manner of Shakespeare and Gide, is one of the last rights, one of the last fantasies that remain to us. It must remain . . . one of the methods of defending Man.

---

[2] (Henri-)Philippe Pétain (1856–1951), French general and World War I hero who served as chief of state of the Nazi-allied Vichy government during World War II.

[3] William Shakespeare (c. 1564–1616), British poet and dramatist, who referred to homosexuality in his writings. Some scholars interpret his writings as indicating that Shakespeare had homosexual experiences.

[4] Andre Gide (1869–1951), French writer, humanist, and moralist, who wrote of his homosexual experiences.

[5] Marxists.

[6] Termite nest.

[7] Maurice Maeterlinck (1862–1949), Belgian symbolist poet and playwright.

QUESTIONS FOR ANALYSIS

1. How does Guérin reject criticisms of sexual liberation by both conservative and radical forces? What does Guérin imply are the forces of sexual and political repression?

2. What are the historical components to his argument?

3. How does Guérin link sexual liberation and political liberation? For Guérin, what is the broader political importance of sexual liberation?

4. How do Guérin's and Beauvoir's (Source 9) arguments broaden the idea of liberation beyond political questions? In doing so, how do they both retain a political significance to their arguments?

CHAPTER QUESTIONS

1. How do the authors in this chapter shape ideas of political liberation to draw different conclusions? How do these documents extend Western ideas of political liberation to non-Western settings?

2. How do the arguments supporting and criticizing decolonization compare to the arguments promoting and attacking imperialism (Chapter 10)? What do the documents indicate about the primacy of Western concerns to the decolonization process?

3. What similarities and differences occur between the arguments of politicians faced with directing policies in the face of decolonization and the French intellectuals reflecting on the political situations of their era?

4. How do Beauvoir's and Guérin's calls for sexual liberation compare to the use of sexuality in political argumentation by women seeking the vote described by Antoinette Burton (Chapter 10, Source 11)?

Chapter 14

THE NEW EUROPE?

The rise of the cold war and the decolonization movement shaped the political landscape in Europe in the 1950s and early 1960s. International political leadership of the West passed to the United States, a fact that made many Europeans uneasy. Under Charles de Gaulle's leadership, France withdrew from the United States–led North Atlantic Treaty Organization (NATO), an act that encouraged many western European leaders to chart political courses that were more independent of the United States. Eastern European leaders who sought greater independence from the Soviet Union suffered direct repercussions, as the Soviet Union crushed reform movements in Hungary (1956) and Czechoslovakia (1968). Yet for most Europeans, the political tensions of the cold war were largely offset by general prosperity as Europe recovered from the economic devastation of the Second World War. In western Europe, this prosperity was aided by the creation in 1957 of the European Economic Community (EEC), or Common Market, which worked to remove trade barriers and establish a common commercial policy among member states. The prosperity that ensued allowed European nations to absorb immigrant and foreign populations, especially from former colonies, as laborers.

By the late 1960s, however, economic and political changes were occurring. First, economic growth slowed. When Arab nations quadrupled the price of oil in 1973 in protest against the United States' continued support of the state of Israel, unemployment soared in most Western nations to between 10 and 15 percent. The era of "stagflation"—high unemployment and high inflation—had begun. At the same time, the Japanese economy, also dependent on oil imports, sustained tremendous economic growth and emerged as a formidable economic competitor of the United States and western Europe. By the late 1970s, these economic threats led the leaders of western Europe to try to enhance their ability to compete economically. Among the broader population, resentment grew toward immigrants and foreign populations, accused by some opportunistic politicians of driving up unemployment. Xenophobia and racism reclaimed a prominent presence in Western politics and popular culture, raising questions as to who did or could belong within "the West."

The second change that occurred in the late 1960s was the policy of détente pursued by the United States and the Soviet Union as they sought to recast their relationship away from the conflicts of the cold war. As the cold war alignments became less important in both international and domestic politics, European leaders and the broader public found that they had greater room to pursue their own interests. Among the Soviet bloc nations, Poland took the lead in the 1980s as the Solidarity labor movement pressed for reforms. Western European leaders in the late 1970s and beyond expanded the Common Market, establishing the European Community (EC) (later called the European Union, EU) to secure and promote European political and economic interests worldwide. With the collapse of the Soviet Union and its empire between 1989 and 1991, which left the United States as the sole remaining superpower, the EC leaders worked vigorously to create an integrated Europe able to pursue economic, political, and military interests independently of the leadership of the United States. The pursuit of this vision raised questions as to what this new Europe was to be in contrast to the nations that made it up and in comparison with "the West."

THE NEW EUROPEANS

Migration and immigration have long been practiced among European populations, usually as people follow labor demands and economic vitality. These factors also have long drawn non-European peoples to Europe; however, unlike the United States, which declares itself a nation of immigrants, many European nations assert nearly the opposite. Citizenship remains stringently limited, and families who have lived in some nations for two or three generations find they are still legally classified as aliens and guests. In several nations in the late 1970s and 1980s, anti-immigrant and racist movements began to call for the expulsion of "foreign" populations. These movements have appealed most strongly to working-class youth, who tend to suffer from high unemployment and reduced social benefits. In nearly every European nation, political parties have organized and built on this resentment and in some cases have significantly affected national politics. Yet even beyond disaffected skinheads and racist political parties, mainstream politicians and intellectuals have struggled with understanding how these immigrant and foreign populations should situate themselves within the dominant populations. Should immigrants assimilate to the dominant national culture? Integrate socially? Or can a European nation be multicultural?

1

". . . FOREIGN RESIDENTS . . ."

Measuring the New Europe   (1950–1997)

Foreign residents have long lived in European nations, and their presence within these nations has elicited varying responses at different times. Following are two maps and a set of statistics that bear on the foreign populations in selected European nations and the rise of antiforeigner violence.

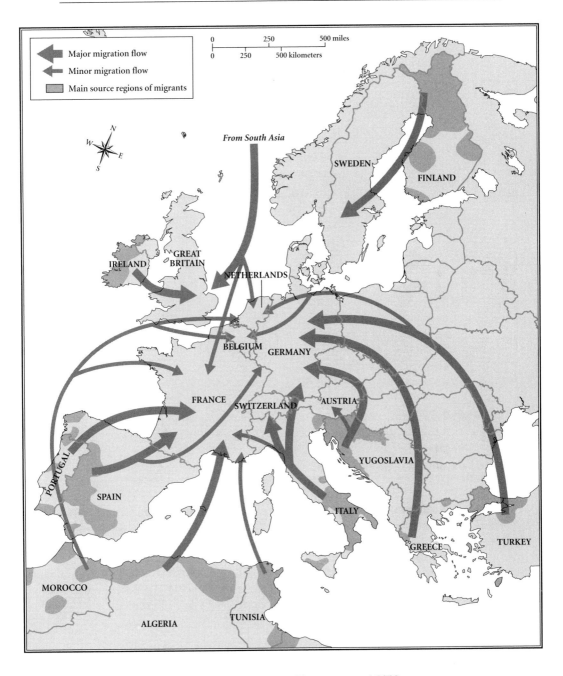

MAP 14.1 EUROPEAN MIGRATION FLOWS, C. 1970

NOTE: F=Fertility rate; U=Unemployment rate

MAP 14.2 STATISTICS ON SELECTED EUROPEAN NATIONS, C. 1993
The fertility rate needed to replace a current population is around 2.1. A rate below that figure indicates that national population is declining, not counting immigration into that nation.

TABLE 14 .1 PERCENTAGE OF TOTAL POPULATION WHO ARE FOREIGN RESIDENTS IN SELECTED EUROPEAN COUNTRIES

	1950	1982	1997
Austria	4.7	4.0	9.1
Belgium	4.3	9.0	8.9
France	4.1	6.8	6.3
Germany:			
West	1.1	7.6	—
Unified	—	—	9.0
Netherlands	1.1	3.9	4.4
Switzerland	6.1	14.7	19.0
United Kingdom	—	3.9	3.6

QUESTIONS FOR ANALYSIS

1. How do the various factors indicated in the data—percentage of foreign population, place of origin of immigrants, fertility rate, and unemployment rate—play a role in anti-immigrant sentiment? Which factors do you expect would be the most significant in anti-immigrant sentiments? Why?

2. Comparing the various nations, which nation seems most susceptible to anti-immigrant sentiment? Which seems the least susceptible? Why?

3. What influences on anti-immigrant sentiment are not included in these statistics? What are the limitations of these statistics on explaining anti-immigrant sentiment?

2

". . . HEED THE WHITE CALL."

Skrewdriver
Song Lyrics   (1982–1984)

In the early 1980s, the British band Skrewdriver became an important force in the development of the skinhead and neo-Nazi movements. Led by Ian Stuart (Donaldson) (1958–1993), Skrewdriver emerged from the Punk rock scene of the mid-1970s and combined driving, pounding music with lyrics that included a strong component of "racial nationalism" and working-class economic frustrations. The music found initial support with British skinheads, a diverse group of fiercely nationalistic and usually working-class individuals, some of whom also were associated with neo-Nazi gangs and clubs. The right-wing British National Front Party promoted Skrewdriver, recognizing that the group's music was a primary recruitment tool for new members. In the early to mid-1980s, Skrewdriver's music gained popularity and imitators, facilitating the growth of the neo-Nazi and skinhead movements across Europe and North America. Below are the lyrics from three of Skrewdriver's songs, written by Stuart, who in 1986 was convicted of assaulting a black person and sentenced to twelve months in prison. He died in an automobile accident in 1993.

"White Power" (1982)

I stand and watch my country, going down the drain.
We are all at fault now, we are all to blame.
We are letting them come over, we just let them come.
Once we had an empire, but now we've got a slum.

Skrewdriver, *Boots and Braces/Voice of Britain* (White Noise Recordings, n.d.); Skrewdriver, *Hail the New Dawn* (Bruhl, Germany: Rock-o-Rama Records, 1984).

Chorus:
White power, for England
White power, today
White power, for Britain
Before it gets too late.

We've seen a lot of riots, we just sit and scoff.
We've seen a lot of muggings, but the judges let them off.
(Chorus)

We've got to do something, to try to stop the rot.
The traitors that have used us, they should all be shot.
(Chorus)

Are we going to sit and let them come?
Have they got the white man on the run?
The multiracial society is a mess.
We aren't going to take much more of this.
What do we need?
(Chorus)

If we don't win our battle, and all does not go well,
It's apocalypse for Britain, and we'll see you all in Hell.
(Chorus)

"Power from Profit" (1984)

We've got to face the music, we've let our country down.
Upon the face of our nation, there seems to be a frown.
Once we were all proud men of this cool and pleasant land,
But we've lost a lot of tears over you.

Very soon our time will come, our nation's doom will toll.
They've bought up all our industries, and they've tried to buy our souls.
And then our nation's working men, will be the rich man's slaves.
Yes, we've lost a lot of tears over you.

Chorus:
It's power from profit, they're buying our souls.
It's power from profit, puts you on the dole.[1]
It's power from profit, a good job's hard to find.
It's power from profit, they'll soon own our minds.

I think it's time our people stood together all as one
And took back all our nation's wealth when the profiteers have gone.
Our working men would be fairly paid, for all their sweat and toil.
Yes, we've lost a lot of tears over you.
(Chorus)

---

[1] Government welfare support.

It's power from profit, the capitalist's a thief.
If he stands against us, he better stay out of our reach.
We will fight against them with a hammer and a gun,
And when our people start to rise, the traitor's time will come.
(Chorus)

And when our time has finally come, and we've gained our brave new world,
The people stand and hail the dawn, the banners are unfurled.
We've got to be on guard to see they don't come again
Because we've lost a lot of tears over you.

"Before the Night Falls" (1984)

They come here to this country from the jungles and from the trees.
The traitors in the parliament give them a better deal
Spend the nation's money, to cater to their needs.
They all accept our charity, then bite the hand that feeds.

Chorus:
Before the night falls, heed the White call.
Before the night falls, when the reaper calls you.

Our forefathers fought in two world wars, they thought to keep us free.
But I'm not sure that in those wars, who was our enemy.
The Zionists own the media, and they're known for telling lies.
And I could see, that it could be, we fought on the wrong side.
(Chorus)

European unity, the North teutonic[2] dream
To scoop to save humanity, leave Europe with the cream.
But now our once proud Europe, looks like a melting pot.
But melting pots boil over, and it's getting pretty hot.
(Chorus)

QUESTIONS FOR ANALYSIS

1. What themes appear in Skrewdriver's lyrics? Who and what are criticized or attacked?
2. How do Skrewdriver's lyrics justify racial and economic fears? How do these fears compare with the demographic and economic statistics cited in Source 1?
3. How are Skrewdriver's lyrics a call to action?
4. What markers of national power do Skrewdriver's lyrics use? In what ways do they imply a diversity of nationalism?

---

[2] People of the Germanic languages.

3

"AUSTRIA IS NOT AN IMMIGRATION COUNTRY."

Austrian Freedom Party
"Austria First" Petition   (1992)

The small, marginal Austrian Freedom Party grew in size and political significance in the 1980s under the leadership of Jörg Haider (b. 1950). A lawyer from rural Austria whose parents had been members of the Nazi Party in Austria, Haider placed a fiercely anti-immigrant theme at the center of the Freedom Party's message. In late 1992, the Freedom Party drafted the "Austria First" petition and attempted to collect 100,000 signatures, which would have required the Austrian parliament to discuss and vote on whether to adopt the petition into law. The petition, which is reprinted below with notes from a Freedom Party explanatory brochure justifying individual points in the petition, was defeated in the Austrian parliament, but most of its propositions have since been adopted into law. In 2000, after receiving 27 percent of the vote in parliamentary elections, the Freedom Party formed a coalition with another conservative party and gained control of the Austrian parliament.

Austria First

Through the creation of legal measures which permanently secure the right to a fatherland for all Austrian citizens and, from this standpoint, ensure a restrained immigration policy in Austria

1. The adoption of a national law to anchor the national regulatory goal "Austria is not an immigration country" into the federal constitutional law of 1920.

2. Legal standardisation of a halt to immigration until the question of illegal immigration is satisfactorily resolved, until the housing shortage is eliminated, until unemployment is reduced to 5 per cent, as well as the creation of legal measures which ensure that subsidised housing is granted in future solely to Austrian citizens, to the extent that this is not prohibited by international agreements and norms.

3. The adoption of a federal law to institute a general identification requirement for foreign workers at their place of employment, whereby the work permit and application for health insurance are prerequisites for this identity card.

Martin Reisigl and Ruth Wodak, *Discourse and Discrimination: Rhetorics of Racism and Anti-Semitism* (New York: Routledge, 2001), 152–54, 158–59.

4. An increase in executive powers (in particular for foreign and criminal police), including their improved remuneration, and equipment for the apprehension of illegal immigrants and for greater effectiveness in the fight against crime, in particular organised crime.

5. The adoption of a federal law for the immediate creation of permanent border troops (customs, gendarmerie) instead of federal army troops.

6. The adoption of a federal law to change the law governing the organisation of schools so that the proportion of pupils in compulsory and vocational school classes whose native language is not German is limited to 30 per cent; where the percentage of children whose native language is not German is higher than 30 per cent, regular classes for foreigners are to be established.

7. Easing the tension in the school situation by having children whose native language is not German participate in regular classes only if they possess sufficient knowledge of German (preparatory classes).

8. Creation of a regulation in party law that ensures that only Austrian citizens participate in party-internal primary proceedings, where lists are created for the general elections to general representational bodies.

9. The adoption of a federal law to restrict the practice of premature conferring of citizenship.

10. The adoption of a federal law to end illegal business activities (as, for example, in foreigner associations and clubs), as well as to establish rigorous measures against the abuse of social benefits.

11. Creation of the legal basis for the possibility of immediate deportation and imposition of residence prohibitions for foreign criminals.

12. The adoption of a federal law to establish an Eastern Europe Foundation to prevent migrational movement. . . .

Explanation of Point 2

A state under the rule of law and order cannot accept these sorts of conditions. The existing problems in the area of the shadow economy and growing criminality are being further exacerbated through the permanent increase of "illegals." Moreover, in Austria the housing shortage is rapidly increasing. . . .

Explanation of Point 6

For a number of Socialists, . . . who, as always, promote the idea of a multicultural society, our cultural identity is practically worthless, indeed politically suspect. This can be read in the official writings of the Minister of Education. In order to preserve our cultural identity, to achieve the successful integration of children whose mother tongue is not German, to be able to continue to finance education, but also to guarantee a solid education for our children, the percentage of children whose native language is not German must be limited to about 30. . . .

Explanation of Point 10

Specifically in population centres, especially in the federal capital, Vienna, foreigners are increasingly gathering together in associations and clubs. In this area, however, there is a degree of abuse going on that reaches far beyond the legal basis of Austrian association regulations. With increasing frequency, many [such] associations and clubs take the form of eating establishments which fall considerably short of meeting the [relevant] business, sanitary or building codes (lack of sanitary facilities, no closing hours, no noise protection, prohibited gambling, secret prostitution, black market, etc.). Consequently, irritation and justified displeasure are created among indigenous residents and businesses. Only a revised legal code and its strengthened enforcement would be able to re-establish order in this area. In the last few years, there has been an increase in the abuse of social welfare by foreigners, which makes counter-measures necessary. In this context examples include new birth certificates, which allow for the premature drawing on pension benefits; children who exist only on paper, and who make [foreigners] eligible for family assistance; the feigning of a domestic place of residence so that considerable compensatory benefits—which cannot be financed through contribution payments—are added to minimal pensions.

QUESTIONS FOR ANALYSIS

1. How do the petition and brochure define the "Austrian citizens" mentioned in the petition's introduction? What groups of people are identified in the petition and brochure?

2. How do these documents use the issues of crime and criminality? How are immigrants linked to crime?

3. In rejecting the idea of a multicultural society, what idea of social culture do the documents promote? What immigrant practices violate this social culture?

4. What are the similarities and differences in the ideas and the tone of the "Austria First" documents as compared to the Skrewdriver lyrics (Source 2)? What similar types of grievances do they both make (e.g., political, economic, religious, social)?

4

"... THEY ARE BEWILDERED. ..."

The Affair of the Headscarf   (1989)

On September 18, 1989, in Creil, France, three secondary school students of North African origin were suspended from school for wearing headscarves in class. The school's director asserted that the headscarves were religious garments that violated the secular principles of state educational establishments. The controversy quickly gained national attention and cut across traditional political divisions. Central to the debate were disagreements over the nature of French society and the role of the secular school in sus-

taining that society. Is France, with its large foreign population, a multicultural society whose schools play a central role in integrating diverse peoples, or is French society based upon a largely unified, secular French culture taught through the public schools that turn the sons and daughters of foreigners into Frenchmen and women? Two sides of this debate appear in the two documents below. The first is an October 1989 interview with the weekly news magazine Le Nouvel Observateur (The New Observer) in which Lionel Jospin (b. 1937), a member of the French Socialist Party and Minister of National Education during the controversy, defends his decision to order the admittance of the Muslim girls even if they continue to wear headscarves. The second, appearing the following week in Le Nouvel Observateur, is an open letter to Jospin challenging his decision written by five prominent intellectuals: Elisabeth Badinter, Régis Debray, Alain Finkielkraut, Elisabeth de Fontenay, and Catherine Kintzler.

Le Nouvel Observateur Interview with Lionel Jospin

Le Nouvel Observateur: Mr. Minister of National Education, Yes or no? Is it necessary to let young Muslim women wear a headscarf in secondary schools?

Lionel Jospin: The secular school is a place of confessional neutrality. Thus, religious symbols must not be worn there. I ask parents and the young to respect these rules. But the wearing of a headscarf or some other sign of attachment to a religious community cannot constitute grounds for excluding a student. On a first occurrence, the directors of the establishment must begin a dialogue with the parents and the children involved to convince them to renounce these manifestations and explain to them the principles of secularism. . . . But when this cannot be resolved, and especially when the debate takes a national importance, I believe that the responsibility of resolution cannot weigh solely on the shoulders of the educational community. It is my duty to indicate to them some practical steps to adopt. I say to them, thus, if, at the end of these discussions, some families still do not agree to renounce all religious symbols, the child—for which school attendance is the priority—must be welcomed in the public establishment, this is to say in the classroom as in the playground. The French school is made to educate, to integrate, not to reject.

On the other hand, the school must strictly forbid all proselytizing. . . . Finally, the students must accept without exception the rules of the organization, notably the required class materials and the safety regulations (for example, in the workshops) of academic establishments. I mean by this that no one can avoid classes in physical education, music, art, or biology by claiming that the contents of these classes would be in contradiction with the Qur'an. If a family or a child objects to elements of the public, secular school—in its organization or the contents of its lessons—then the parents of the child must make another choice for him.[1] This occurs elsewhere for some of them.

---

[1] Send the child to a religious school.

"Un entretien avec le ministre de l'éducation nationale," *Le Nouvel Observateur* (October 26, 1989), 38–39 (translated by David Kammerling Smith); Elisabeth Badinter, Régis Debray, Alain Finkielkraut, Elisabeth de Fontenay, and Catherine Kintzler, "Profs, ne capitulons pas!" *Le Nouvel Observateur* (November 2, 1989), 30–31. (Translated by David Kammerling Smith.)

N.O.: To establish secular education, it was necessary to fight against the Catholic church. To maintain it, is it not necessary to battle against Islam?

L.J.: In France, secularism was founded, at the beginning of the twentieth century, against the Catholic church, which itself was opposed to the Republic. The separation of the church and state was one of the foundational elements of the modern Republic. Today, it is a completely different question. I would say [it is a question] of reflecting on secularism itself. This affair of the headscarves that occupies us today is a formidable homage rendered to the public school. . . . The public school . . . welcomes all children. Thus, it is normal that these new problems arise in it and that it gropes to find the means to resolve them. But it will do it. Society has shifted; it is plural. Secularism no longer needs to be a secularism of combat. To the contrary, it must be a benevolent secularism made precisely to avoid wars—including wars of religion!

N.O.: The secular school, free and obligatory for everyone, rests on the equality of men and women. In other respects, French society fought to win an equality of rights in all spheres. To the contrary, in Islam the wearing of a headscarf, veil, or chador[2] sanctions inequality between people. Will you have to accept this promotion of a retrograde status for women in academic establishments?

L.J.: Obviously, I support equality between men and women, and the school must contribute to its promotion. It seems though in several cases the young girls who wear a headscarf also had an all-powerful father at their side. But I do not believe that this model dominates in the French Muslim community. It would be a serious mistake, in adopting a rigid attitude, to overgeneralize and confuse a few isolated elements with the vast majority of this community. I worry about the abusive generalization that descends on Islam. It is not by provoking disobedience, in practicing exclusion, that we will promote the evolution of Islam in the Western world. Of course, the public school, which is moreover a school of integration and no longer of assimilation, is not going to begin to proclaim the model of the veiled woman! But in accepting the child or the young girl, in offering her an education—an opening to the world—the public school gets her out of familial isolation; it proposes elements of reflection to her. Who says to you that in ten years these young Muslims who today are in the news will still wear the headscarf, that they will not be emancipated? The young are not outraged by the headscarf. But they are bewildered by it. Listen to them a little.

Open Letter to Lionel Jospin

Mr. Minister,

The future will tell if the year of the Bicentennial[3] will be the Munich[4] of the republican school.

---

[2] The headscarf lightly covers the head, the veil lightly covers the face, and the chador heavily covers the entire head and body.
[3] 1989, the two hundredth anniversary of the French Revolution.
[4] The Munich conference, at which the Western powers conceded to Hitler's demands to seize territory from Czechoslovakia based on his promise that he would seek no additional territory, symbolizes the failed policy of appeasement.

It is good, you say, to appease the intellect without playing the game of the fanatics. You would have saved the academic and social peace at the cost of some minor concessions. And you would be, of course, uncompromising on the essential. . . .

You say, Mr. Minister, that it is excluded to exclude. Although touched by your kindness, we respond to you . . . that *it is permitted to forbid.* An exclusion is discriminatory only when it aims at those who have abided by the rules in force in an establishment. When it touches the student who broke the rules in force, it is *disciplinary.* The present confusion between discipline and discrimination ruins discipline. And if discipline is no longer possible, how do you teach the [academic] disciplines? If the law is applied only to those who want to submit to it, how is a professor able to exercise his craft?

To negotiate, as you do, announcing that you are going to cede, carries a name: capitulation. One such "diplomatic act" only emboldens those who it intends to soften—and if they ask tomorrow that the study of Rushdie[5] (Spinoza, Voltaire, Baudelaire, Rimbaud[6]. . .) who congest our lessons be spared to *their* children, how will we refuse this to them? By exclusion?

Have you not repudiated the authority of professors and directors of establishments in giving the impression that you automatically identify the exclusion as racism?

Students must have the leisure of forgetting their community of origin and think of other things than what they are in order to be able to think by themselves. If one wants the professors to be able to assist them here, and the school to remain what it is—*a place of emancipation*—the sentiment of attachment [to a specific community] must not rule in the school.

In departing from this foundational principle, you do not improve, as you pride yourself in doing, the teaching condition. You render more impossible the already difficult life of those who are no longer called instructors and professors, and you betray the mission of the school.

The "right to be different" that is so dear to you is a liberty only if it is paired with the right to be different from this difference. The opposite case is a snare, even a slavery.

Mr. Minister, a secular school is not constructed by bringing together in the same place a little Catholic and a little Muslim and a little Jew. The school strives to establish a space where authority bases itself on reason and experience—accessible to everyone. Therefore, and because it is meant for everyone, the school does not permit to those that it welcomes any distinctive sign that marks deliberately and a priori a sentiment of attachment. The school cannot admit either a single exception to its programs or to its schedule. The respect of traditions does not concern the school: only the traditions and the differences that contradict neither the rights of men nor the principle of free inquiry are to be respected. However, in affirming

---

[5]Salman Rushdie (b. 1947), Indian novelist whose book *Satanic Verses* led Iranian Muslim clerics in 1989 to call for his death.
[6]All standard authors studied in French schools whose works challenge religion: Benedict de Spinoza (1632–1677), Dutch-Jewish philosopher; Voltaire, pen name of François-Marie Arouet (1694–1778), French author and satirist; Charles Baudelaire (1821–1867), French poet; and Arthur Rimbaud (1854–1891), French poet.

a belief as being above all else, in affirming a distinction of nature between human beings, the Islamic headscarf contradicts these two principles.

"Welcome all children," you say. Yes. But this has never signified having the religion of their parents as such enter with them. Tolerating the Islamic headscarf is not to welcome a free being (in this instance, a young girl); it is to open the door to those who have decided one time for all and without discussion to constrain her. In place of offering to this young girl a place of liberty, you indicate to her that there is no difference between the school and the house of her father.

In authorizing de facto the Islamic headscarf, the symbol of feminine submission, you give a blank check to the fathers and brothers—this is to say, to the harshest patriarchy on the planet. Without appeal, this is no longer to respect the equality of the sexes and free will, which rules [now] in France.

With a single phrase you have disarmed these thousands of young Muslim girls who fight here and there for their dignity and their liberty. The best ally against the authoritarianism of the fathers was the secular, republican school. Today, they have lost it. You have made a fool's bargain, Mr. Minister, in exchanging the liberation and integration, certain and tangible, of young Muslim girls for the hypothetical hope of a return to the tolerance of religious traditionalists, by definition enemies of tolerance.

The partisans of the "new secularism," in the ranks of which you place yourself, advocate an indistinct tolerance. They want a school open to community, religious, and economic pressures, a school where each professor is held to submit to the social environment, a school where each student is constantly returned to his parents, recalled to his condition, bound to his "roots." This is a school of *social predestination*. With this same movement [new secularism], the school offers itself to the world of business and religious dignitaries. This is a school that sells itself, a school enslaved by the rule of idiosyncrasies and foreign interests. In our society, the school is the only institution that is vested in the universal. This is why free men and women are not ready to compromise on its independence in principle, perpetually menaced by economic, ideological, or religious factors and by reality. . . .

Dedicated to free examination, linked to the progress of knowledge, and confident in the sole natural light of men, the School is the foundation of the Republic. This is why the destruction of the School would precipitate that of the Republic.

QUESTIONS FOR ANALYSIS

1. What is Jospin's basis for defending his decision to permit headscarves in public schools? Of what significance is Jospin's assertion that society is plural?

2. On what basis do the intellectuals criticize Jospin's decision? What is the significance of free inquiry to their argument?

3. Comparing Jospin and the intellectuals, what does each assert is the function served by the public schools for French society and for the Muslim girls?

4. What similarities and differences exist in Jospin's and the intellectuals' understanding of how immigrants and foreign peoples must fit themselves into French society?

THE EUROPEAN EXPERIMENT

The idea of European economic and political integration extends back into the Middle Ages and has been dreamed of, and occasionally pursued, by visionaries and conquerors alike. The idea again gained force in the 1950s as Europe recovered from its second devastating war of the century and as western European nations found their international stature diminished in the wake of decolonization and the cold war. As western and central European governments increasingly pursued integration from the 1950s into the 1980s, their goals focused on economic development that could help European nations to compete with the United States and rising Asian economic powers, especially Japan, in an increasingly global marketplace. By the 1990s, however, with the United States remaining as the sole superpower, the proponents of European integration turned increasingly toward political integration, especially to offer a political counterweight to the United States' international dominance. Further, the collapse of Yugoslavia and the ensuing vicious ethnic wars in the Balkans left the European Union embarrassed by its inability to act effectively in an international setting in its own backyard. In 1997, the members of the European Union signed the Treaty of Amsterdam, which committed the Union to establishing common foreign and security policies. As European integration has matured—though it is far from complete—Europeans have argued over the significance of this new political form. Is it merely a pragmatic agreement among friendly nations? Is it something to which one gives allegiance? What are the purposes and goals of this European unification? And how does this European Union relate to the idea of the West?

5

". . . OUR GREATEST INHERITANCE AND OUR GREATEST STRENGTH."

Margaret Thatcher
Speech at the College of Europe (1988)

The first woman to serve as prime minister of a European nation, Margaret Thatcher (b. 1925) rose to prominence in the British Conservative Party. During her years as prime minister (1979–1990), the "Iron Lady," as she was dubbed, reduced social benefits in health care, education, and housing, privatized state industries, and promoted British interests internationally. Thatcher closely allied British foreign policy with that of the United States, both in opposition to the Soviet Union and in support of the United States–led NATO alliance. Thatcher became a persistent critic of European unification, distrusting the centralization of authority in the European Community's

A. G. Harryvan and J. van der Harst, eds., *Documents on European Union* (New York: St. Martin's Press, 1997), 242–47.

bureaucracy. In 1988, Thatcher gave a speech at the College of Europe in Bruges, Belgium, excerpted below, in which she set out her views on European integration.

I want to start by disposing of some myths about my country, Britain, and its relationship with Europe. And to do that I must say something about the identity of Europe itself.

Europe is not the creation of the Treaty of Rome.[1] Nor is the European idea the property of any group or institution. We British are as much heirs to the legacy of European culture as any other nation. Our links to the rest of Europe, the continent of Europe, have been the dominant factor in our history. . . .

Nor should we forget that European values have helped to make the United States of America into the dynastic defender of freedom which she has become.

The European Community belongs to *all* its members, and must reflect the traditions and aspirations of *all* of them in full measure.

And let me be quite clear. Britain does not dream of an alternative to the European Community, of some cosy, isolated existence on its fringes. Our destiny is in Europe, as part of the Community. That is not to say that it lies *only* in Europe. But nor does that of France or Spain or indeed any other members.

The Community is not an end in itself. It is not an institutional device to be constantly modified according to the dictates of some abstract theory. Nor must it be ossified by endless regulation. It is the practical means by which Europe can ensure its future prosperity and the security of its people in a world in which there are many other powerful nations and groups.

We Europeans cannot afford to waste our energies on internal disputes or arcane institutional debates. They are no substitute for effective action.

I want this evening to set out some guiding principles for the future which I believe will ensure that Europe *does* succeed, not just in economic and defence terms but in the quality of life and the influence of its people.

My first guideline is this: willing and active cooperation between independent sovereign states is the best way to build a successful European Community.

To try to suppress nationhood and concentrate power at the centre of a European conglomerate would be highly damaging and would jeopardise the objectives we seek to achieve.

Europe will be stronger precisely because it has France as France, Spain as Spain, Britain as Britain, each with its own customs, traditions and identity. It would be folly to try to fit them into some sort of identikit European personality. . . .

I am the first to say that on many great issues the countries of Europe should try to speak with a single voice. I want to see them work more closely on the things we can do better together than alone. Europe is stronger when we do so, whether it be in trade, defence or in our relations with the rest of the world. But working more closely together does not require power to be centralised in Brussels[2] or decisions to be taken by an appointed bureaucracy.

---

[1] The 1957 treaty establishing the European Economic Community.
[2] Belgian city that is the headquarters for the European Union.

Indeed, it is ironic that just when those countries such as the Soviet Union, which have tried to run everything from the centre, are learning that success depends on dispersing power and decisions *away* from the centre, some in the Community seem to want to move in the opposite direction.

We have not successfully rolled back the frontiers of the state in Britain, only to see them reimposed at a European level, with a European super-state exercising a new dominance from Brussels.

My second guiding principle is this. The Community policies must tackle present problems in a practical way, however difficult that may be. If we cannot reform those Community policies which are patently wrong or ineffective and which are rightly causing public disquiet, then we shall not get the public's support for the Community's future development. . . .

My third guiding principle is the need for Community policies which encourage enterprise if Europe is to flourish and create the jobs of the future.

The basic framework is there: the Treaty of Rome itself was intended as a Charter for Economic Liberty. But that is not how it has always been read, still less applied.

The lesson of the economic history of Europe in the 70s and 80s is that central planning and detailed control *don't* work, and that personal endeavour and initiative *do.* That a State-controlled economy is a recipe for low growth; and that free enterprise within a framework of law brings better results.

The aim of a Europe open for enterprise is the moving force behind the creation of the Single European Market[3] by 1992. By getting rid of barriers, by making it possible for companies to operate on a Europe-wide scale, we can best compete with the United States, Japan and the other new economic powers emerging in Asia and elsewhere.

It means action to *free* markets, to *widen* choice and to produce greater economic convergence through *reduced* government intervention. . . .

My fourth guiding principle is that Europe should not be protectionist. The expansion of the world economy requires us to continue the process of removing barriers to trade, and to do so in . . . multilateral negotiations. . . .

My last guiding principle concerns the most fundamental issue, the European countries' role in defence. Europe must continue to maintain a sure defence through NATO. There can be no question of relaxing our efforts even if it means taking difficult decisions and meeting heavy costs. We are thankful for the peace that NATO has maintained over 40 years. The fact is things *are* going our way: the democratic model of a free enterprise society *has* proved itself superior; freedom *is* on the offensive, a peaceful offensive, the world over for the first time in my life-time.

We must strive to maintain the US commitment to Europe's defence. . . .

What we need now is to take decisions on the next steps forward rather than let ourselves be distracted by Utopian goals.

However far we may all want to go, the truth is that you can only get there one step at a time.

Let us concentrate on making sure that we get those steps right. Let Europe be a family of nations, understanding each other better, appreciating each other more,

---

[3] Unified, free-trade market of most western, central, and northern European nations.

doing more together but relishing our national identity no less than our common European endeavour.

Let us have a Europe which plays its full part in the wider world, which looks outward not inward, and which preserves that Atlantic Community—that Europe on both sides of the Atlantic—which is our greatest inheritance and our greatest strength.

QUESTIONS FOR ANALYSIS

1. In Thatcher's guiding principles, how does her discussion of political issues seek to limit the power of the European Community government? How is her discussion of economic issues ambivalent with regard to the power of the European Community?
2. For Thatcher, what seems to be the main reason for the European Community?
3. Of what significance is the United States in Thatcher's speech? How does her emphasis on the United States act as a counterweight to the idea of European unification?
4. How does Thatcher seek to maintain an idea of "the West"?

6

". . . NATIONALISM MEANS WAR!"

François Mitterand
Speech to the European Parliament (1995)

Prominent in French politics for nearly fifty years, François Mitterand (1916–1996) served as president of France from 1981 to 1995. In 1983, Mitterand turned his energies toward European integration, discovering a willing partner in that process in Helmut Kohl, chancellor of Germany from 1982 to 1998. Mitterand and Kohl's alliance provided the political bases for the Single Europe Act of 1987 and the creation of the European Union in 1991—acts that began to transfer significant portions of political authority to new institutions of the European Union. With his political career coming to a conclusion, in 1995 Mitterand addressed the European Parliament to set out his vision of the continuing development of European integration.

Besides the essential coordination of our policies, . . . we must also, in the longer term, build the foundations of a Europe in which renewed—and, I hope, strong,

A. G. Harryvan and J. van der Harst, eds., *Documents on European Union* (New York: St. Martin's Press, 1997), 294–97, 299–300.

sound and lasting—economic growth can take place. This will be possible, if we prove capable of using three of our major assets to the full. What is the first of those assets? It is the size of our internal market. So far, we have essentially succeeded in removing the administrative, customs and regulatory barriers which partitioned this vast economic area. That is the task that was accomplished by means of the Single European Act. We now have to eliminate or reduce the remaining barriers—which are far from insignificant—including the physical barriers which still restrict the free movement of people, goods and ideas. . . .

Our second major asset is, of course, economic and monetary union, which is the natural and essential complement, in my view, to the single market, and without which the single market—which I and, of course, others were so anxious to achieve, and which was the object of so much hard work—would be a recipe for anarchy and the worst forms of unfair competition. . . .

Our third major asset in the European Union's technological excellence. Our research scientists have been responsible for countless innovations. Such capital cannot fail to yield a profit if we prove capable of utilising it properly, and on a European scale. . . .

Since the very beginnings of the European Community, I, like many of you in the House today, have defended the idea that we must build a social Europe. . . .

Let us make no mistake: markets are no more than instruments, no more than mechanisms which are all too often governed by the law of the strongest, mechanisms which can lead to injustice, exclusion and dependence, unless the necessary counterweight is provided by those who can assert their democratic legitimacy. Alongside the markets, there is room for economic and social activities based on the concepts of solidarity, cooperation, partnership, reciprocity and the common interest—in short, public services. So far, we have drawn the outline of a social Europe, but it has no content. And will it not be an exciting, exhilarating venture to provide that content? Will it not be the task of the coming months and years? At that point, I shall be observing the social progress made from the outside and I shall rejoice whenever I see all Europe's leaders coming together—leaving behind their natural divisions and differences of opinion—to ensure that the Europe which is being built does not simply resemble a mechanical or Meccano toy,[1] but is the potent work of men and women who are capable of shaping their own destiny. At present, there are some difficulties, but I hope that in collaboration with the social partners, we shall succeed in taking initiatives in the areas of training, education, the organisation of labour, and the campaign against all forms of exclusion. Indeed, nothing will be possible unless the social partners take their rightful place in the process of European integration. . . .

Such a Europe, our Europe, must be embodied in something more than simply balance sheets and freight tonnages. I would go as far as to say, while not wishing to become too rhetorical, that it needs a soul, so that it can give expression—and let us use more modest language here—to its culture, its ways of thinking, the intellectual make-up of its peoples, the fruits of the centuries of civilisation of which

---

[1] Toy metal construction set.

we are the heirs. The expressions of Europe's many forms of genius are rich and diverse; and, as in the past, we must share with the whole world—while not seeking to impose them, somewhat differently from in the past—our ideas, our dreams and, to the extent that they are of the right kind, our passions.

In the GATT[2] negotiations, a year ago, the principle of cultural exception was upheld. This is the idea that works of the intellect are not simply goods like any others. It stems from the belief that the cultural identity of our nations, the right of each people to develop its own culture, is in jeopardy. It embodies the will to defend freedom and diversity for all countries, to refuse to cede the means of representation—in other words, the means of asserting one's identity—to others.

Since then, scarcely any progress has been made and there is a growing need, I can assure you, to give to the cultural dimension of the process of European integration the importance it deserves. I am among those who are firmly in favour of doing so. I represent France, a country which is conscious of the threats surrounding it in this context and which is well acquainted with the rivalry of languages. When I think of other peoples, however, which are equally deserving of respect, but whose languages are not as geographically widespread as French, which in turn is not as geographically widespread as some other languages, I wonder what will become of the soul, the means of expression of, for instance, Gaelic, Flemish or Dutch? . . .

To strengthen our approach, let us rediscover those places and objects which represent our common past. I should like to see the devising and implementation of a vast project to develop the sites of our European heritage. At the same time, let us teach about Europe. Let us educate our children on the subject. Let our schools prepare them for citizenship. Let them develop the teaching of history, geography and culture. Let us encourage the twinning of schools and universities, exchanges of schoolchildren and students. Let us stress the importance of multilingualism. . . .

I did not acquire my own convictions in this way by chance. . . . When I was an escaped prisoner of war—or rather, when I was in the process of escaping—I met some Germans, then I spent some time in a prison in Baden-Württemberg, and I used to talk to the people, Germans, there and I came to realise that the Germans liked the French more than the French liked the Germans.

I say this without wishing to denigrate my country, which is no more nationalistic than any other, far from it. I say this to make it clear that, at that time, everyone saw the world from his or her own viewpoint, and that those viewpoints were generally distorting. We must overcome such prejudices. What I am asking you to do is almost impossible, because it means overcoming our past. And yet, if we fail to overcome our past, let there be no mistake about what will follow: ladies and gentlemen, nationalism means war!

War is not only our past, it could also be our future! And it is us, it is you, ladies and gentlemen, the Members of the European Parliament, who will henceforth be the guardians of our peace, our security and our future!

---

[2] General Agreement on Trade and Tariffs, a series of trade agreements initially established in 1947 whose goal was to reduce trade restrictions among its signatories. In 1995, GATT was replaced by the World Trade Organization (WTO).

QUESTIONS FOR ANALYSIS

1. What does Mitterand identify as the three major assets of European growth? What does he identify as the limitations of these assets?

2. What does Mitterand mean by the term "social Europe" and by saying that Europe needs a "soul"? How would Margaret Thatcher (Source 5) respond to these claims?

3. How does Mitterand's discussion of culture and heritage reinforce the idea of European unification? What place remains for "the West" in Mitterand's framework?

7

"... THE BEST MEANS TO AVOID NATIONALISTIC WARFARE IS PRECISELY TO RESPECT THE LIBERTY OF NATIONS."

The National Front
The Patriot's Talking-Points   (2001)

Established in 1972 by former French paratrooper Jean-Marie Le Pen (b. 1928), the National Front established itself as Europe's most prominent party of right-wing, anti-immigrant nationalism throughout the 1980s and 1990s. Generally winning around 15 percent of the popular vote in France, the National Front won seats in local governments, the French National Assembly, and the European Parliament. In addition to promoting various plans to expel both legal and illegal immigrants from France, Le Pen has harshly critiqued European integration as a violation of France's sovereignty and a diminution of its power. In his run for the presidency of France in the elections of 2002, Le Pen published on his campaign Web page "talking points" designed for use by his supporters in convincing their friends and neighbors to vote for National Front candidates. Following are excerpts from the "talking points" on the topic of "Euro-federalism," written in a style meant to teach National Front supporters how to respond to their friends' statements and questions. In April 2002, Pen stunned the French political establishment by placing second in the first round of the presidential election with 17 percent of the vote (the first-place candidate, the conservative Jacques Chirac, had received 20 percent of the vote in a field that included sixteen candidates). Two weeks of protests and demonstrations followed in France as millions sought to distance themselves, and France, from Le Pen's positions. Students especially led the demonstrations protesting Le Pen's policies toward immigrants, and business leaders warned of economic disaster if France sought to pull out of the European Union. In the runoff election, Chirac easily defeated Le Pen, receiving 82 percent of the vote to Le Pen's 18 percent.

"Argumentaire du Patriote," was published at www.front-national.com/programme/ argumentaire/eurofeder/1.htm. (Translated by David Kammerling Smith.)

They say: "But Europe is on the march. It can no longer be stopped."

Response: Well, yes [it can be stopped]! For in a democracy, the nation is the depositary of sovereignty and is therefore free to choose its destiny. The popular will thus expresses itself beyond the signature of a treaty[1] because (1) the political has priority over the judicial, and an international accord is not able to supersede the Fundamental Laws of France, ratified by 2000 years of history and (2) it is sufficient to denounce the treaty. . . .

They say: "But we retain the possibility of controlling what occurs at the European level."

Response: (1) But we no longer control anything! Previously, to impose a European law it was necessary to have unanimous consent of the states. If a single state refused, this law was not adopted. Today, if a majority appears at the center of the states, it is possible to impose on a people something that they do not want. By this, our production of unpasteurized cheese soon will be forbidden, and we will be obliged to accept night shifts for women.[2]

(2) In numerous areas, power belongs even to nonelected technocrats. The French law court becomes simply a chamber to register Brussels'[3] laws. Democracy— that is to say, the power that people possess to make their own laws—disappears to the advantage of the power of the "experts."

They say: "It is necessary to make a federal Europe because the European economies are more and more interdependent."

Response: (1) But the economic does not control the political, except in the view of Marxists and the ultraliberal supporters of the new world order. In democracy and the Republic, the primacy of politics is simply the possibility for people to choose the economic, foreign, and social policies that they wish. The people remain the people, interdependent or not.

(2) This interdependence is, moreover, very relative. Since the beginning of the century, Japan and the United States have not ceased to protect their domestic market. On the other hand, France and Germany have opened themselves more and more to commercial exchanges and immigration. "The imbrication[4] of economies" concerns only the Europeans and resembles less interdependence than a veritable dependence on the United States and Japan. . . .

They say: "Sovereignty, at the moment of economic globalization, is no longer worth speaking about. We must conform ourselves to this evolution."

Response: (1) Globalization is the alibi for all of our renouncements. Since the fall of the Berlin Wall [1989], many people think that everything is radically new. But international commercial and financial relations are very ancient, as is, moreover, travel to foreign lands. And this never prevented nations from being sovereign— this is to say, from choosing freely their destiny. Recent economic studies have demonstrated that at the beginning of the century, the economies were even rather

---

[1] Any of the treaties of unification.
[2] Two French traditions that have been altered by European Union regulations.
[3] Belgian city that is the headquarters for the European Union.
[4] Overlapping.

more open than those of today. And this did not prevent the First World War, a conflict between sovereign nations. It is the globalist ideology that wants to make globalization a radical novelty that would render the sovereignty of nations obsolete. . . .

They say: "It is necessary to create federal Europe because there is a European civilization."

Response: The existence of a community of civilization that unites the different Europe peoples is not contestable. This civilization is based on a specific genius (organizational genius, creative and constructive genius, technical genius); common values (Christianity, individualism, liberty . . .); a similar mode of life (food and clothing customs . . .).

(1) But a civilization does not create a nation; the existence of a common civilization does not signify that a European nation exists, which itself will justify a European state. The Islamic civilization exists, but there is no universal Islamic state—because the sentiment of attachment to the national community, the place of expression for deeply profound emotional and cultural solidarities, has priority over all other sentiments of attachment.

(2) The European Union in any case forgets the foundational values of the civilization of our continent. The European civilization is precisely that of a free and equal people—this is to say, the civilization of the diversity of national cultures. A federal Europe would deny this diversity. This standardization, contrary to the European tradition, moreover denies the carefully considered interest of Europe itself. Today, federal Europe is a flag of convenience that disguises the progression of American civilization, a simple mode of materialist life resting on the benevolent virtues of mass consumption.

They say: "Nationalism is old-fashioned, past its prime."

Response: But what has been proposed to us? A large federal structure with a very important bureaucratic apparatus in the hands of specialists in economic and legal questions. This administrative dinosaur corresponds to the organizational schemes of the 1950s, strongly marked by the Soviet system. Our era, where the rapid flux of communication is essential, calls for the opposite—for structures less rigid and thus able to react rapidly. The hour is past for centralized decision making but for cooperation, participation, and the association of small organizations on timely projects. This is why the nation is now better than all the federal models.

They say: "It is necessary to create federal Europe so that there will never again be war in Europe. Europe is peace."

Response: . . . (3) The best means to avoid nationalistic warfare is precisely to respect the liberty of nations. In effect, when the liberty of the people is misunderstood, it always ends by breaking their chains. The destinies of the last empires in Europe show this clearly. The former USSR and the former Yugoslavia crumbled under the violent attacks of the people, giving rise to terrible wars. It is, thus, precisely the negation of national identities that leads to war.

QUESTIONS FOR ANALYSIS

1. According to Le Pen, where does sovereignty originate? Where does it reside?

2. How does Le Pen criticize bureaucratic experts? How do his ideas compare to Thatcher's (Source 5)?

3. How does Le Pen understand the idea of European civilization? On what basis does he assert the importance of national identity?

4. What is Le Pen's attitude toward the United States? Of what significance would "Western civilization" be to Le Pen?

8

"WHAT IS THE ULTIMATE GOAL . . .?"

Philippe de Schoutheete
The Case for Europe   (2000)

Philippe de Schoutheete (b. 1932) served in Belgium's Foreign Ministry from 1956 to 1997, including ten years as Belgium's permanent representative to the European Union, where he participated in many of the negotiations leading to greater European integration. Yet despite his own efforts in support of integration, Schoutheete recognizes, as indicated in the excerpt below from his book The Case for Europe, *that the argument in favor of European integration has not yet been made effectively.*

For more than thirty years, the participating countries [of European integration] have abstained from raising among themselves the fundamental questions of the purposes of European integration. What is the ultimate goal of the exercise? What model are we heading toward? How far do our ambitions extend? . . .

"Having no shared vision, nor even any clear and consensual individual perspective of the future of the European venture, the States have preferred to regard it as a pragmatic process with an undetermined and perpetually deferred end-point."[1]

There is no doubt that this approach involving small steps, no long-term visions, and no great leaps has had considerable merits. . . . It has enabled successive enlargements to be negotiated without too much quarreling. It has allowed time, which has changed mentalities to such an extent that in the eyes of a new generation, Europe seems self-evident. It has rendered the integration process if not irreversible, then at least difficult to turn back.

However, . . . [b]y obscuring objectives so as to focus on instruments, Europe has denied itself a justification and hence an element of legitimacy. To adapt the means to the ends that one is pursuing is the very essence of the art of politics. And,

---

[1] Quotation from Laurent Cohen-Tanugi, *Le choix de l'Europe* (1995).

Philippe de Schoutheete, *The Case for Europe: Unity, Diversity, and Democracy in the European Union,* trans. Andrew Butler (Boulder, Colo.: Rienner, 2000), 97, 99–103, 105.

in a democracy, those ends must be known and publicly accepted. How can they be accepted if they are not discussed?

Under those circumstances, public opinion is divided between incomprehension and indifference. The Europe of visionaries, general ideas, grand designs, and great ambitions certainly exists in the minds of some people, but it is left to one side, passed over without comment, or put away in the utopia box. All that we see today is the Europe of regulations, directives, and complex procedures—in other words, the Europe of technocrats and administrators. We see the *how* but not the *why*. No explicit political justification, no mobilizing myth, no symbols, and thus no emotion, little enthusiasm, and scarcely any passion.

That may suffice if one wishes to consider European integration as having no other aim than the management of interdependencies. . . .

European integration has focused on markets: first the common market, then the internal market. It has attached considerable importance to setting up policies—agriculture, industry, trade, regional development. It also extends to research, the environment, fishing, and finally currency. It has developed intergovernmental cooperation on foreign policy and internal security, and has endeavored to incorporate or at least connect that cooperation into the Community's institutional machinery. All that is fundamental for the future; but the markets, the policies, and the various forms of cooperation will only ever be instruments, even in the case of foreign policy or currency. What aims are they to serve? The absence of a reply to that question and the confusion that is maintained between the end and the means, the objectives and the instruments, constitute a great weakness. They make Europe "a soulless body with an obscure destiny."[2]

Without a vision of the future there can be no strategy. . . . Is the Community still fueled by a shared tangible vision? How can that vision be defined?

The actual history of the Community can of course serve as a guide. The trodden path reveals a direction. A structure of such complexity is not created by chance. It reflects a shared intention: the will to face up to the challenges of the moment and to the lessons of history. It implies an ambition, and therefore a goal, even though the meaning and scope of the venture have, to some extent, been dimmed by the passage of time and the lack of debate. . . .

The idea is to manage certain resources and policies together while respecting the identity of nations and without excessive intervention, and maintaining the cohesion and solidarity of the Union, its openness to the rest of the world, its competitiveness, and hence its prosperity. It is to exercise a collective power in world affairs, jointly and peacefully. Peace, prosperity, and power!

Taking the reasoning a step further, one might say that the aim of the joint venture pursued in Western Europe for almost half a century has been to develop a model of society. "The sense of a shared destiny, based on one same vision of mankind, represents both the cause and the condition of common policy and common legislation."[3]

Models of society are distinguished from one another primarily through the different relations that they establish between the individual and the collective, or

---

[2] Quotation from Maurice Duverger, *L'Europe des hommes* (1994).
[3] Quotation from Chantal Millon-Delsol, *Le principe de subsidiarité* (1993).

between individual interests and the general interest. From that point of view, the European model is entirely different from its Asian, Islamic, or African counterparts. As a result of its historic consanguinity, it is close to the U.S. model, but it differs from that model through its emphasis on solidarity and social protection, and through the diversity of its constituent parts.

Diversity is clearly one of the keys to European society. It is already very prominent, and sometimes a source of conflict inside many of the member states. Within the Union it is structural, and it gives the Union its singular nature. The bonds created by history and the upholding of shared values coexist with cultural diversity and national identities. That is reflected in multiple attachments, a plurality of allegiances, and diverse sources of legitimacy.

To ensure that this coexistence would be peaceful and respectful, which it had not always been in the past, was one of the primary goals of the European integration process. To defend diversity against the standardizing pressures of globalization, computerization, and technology is undoubtedly another, more recent goal. Like other states before them, the European states are discovering that their diversity can only be defended through a joint effort.

Pursuing that reasoning to its conclusion, one could say that the gradual development of the European structure does in fact reveal an ultimate goal, even though that goal remains largely unformulated. It is to establish a political and legal structure responsible for maintaining, developing, and defending a model of society that is specific to the participating countries. They base that model on a number of political considerations, such as diversity, and on certain ethical values, such as solidarity, which they essentially share. "Societies gain their cohesion from shared values. Those values are rooted in culture, religion, history and tradition."[4]

Although those aims are implicit in the historic development of the Community, they are not expressly stated anywhere. The validity of the reasoning through which they are identified is far from being universally accepted. Even some of those who recognize its validity differ as to the conclusions to be drawn from it, the implementation of these conclusions, and the institutional machinery required for that purpose. All discussion on that subject turns to discord. To conceal those differences and to prevent discord, the debate is avoided. And without a debate, one loses the support of public opinion, which is needed if the objectives are to be attained. How can one escape that contradiction?

The most obvious solution lies in organizing difference. Because the member states have conflicting views on the future of Europe, let us organize different Europes to address them! . . .

The idea of structuring the Union as a group of differentiated zones[5] is not new, for it underpins the provisions of the Maastricht Treaty concerning economic and monetary union. The European structure has always been more flexible than it is said to be. But to make that approach systematic, no longer a last resort but normal practice, by taking steps yet to be defined (and that vary considerably from

---

[4] Quotation from George Soros, "The Capitalist Threat," *Atlantic Monthly* (February 1997).
[5] A plan that only some EU member nations would join certain EU organizations, creating overlapping zones of authority.

one opinion to the next), is neither simple nor without danger for the cohesion of the Union. All discussions on this matter are full of unspoken reservations. Nevertheless, it is no doubt the only way to reconcile, across the entire continent, the diversity of the states' respective situations and ambitions with coherent pursuit of the European idea....

A diversified Europe will no doubt be more complex. Will it be more obscure, more distant, and even less legible? That need not be the case. Provided that we seize the opportunity to enter into a real debate, to discuss our different views, to define political objectives, and group together those who share them, it should be possible to give a meaning and thus a soul to an enterprise that currently seems to have none. Enlargement carries a risk of dilution. Conversely, it may also provide the opportunity to gather together, from both East and West, those who share a political ambition and accept its constraints.

QUESTIONS FOR ANALYSIS

1. According to Schoutheete, how and why has European integration progressed without any specific goal? How has this lack of goals affected the legitimacy of the European Union?

2. What relationship between national and European concerns does Schoutheete establish? What emerges as the goal of European integration?

3. What does Schoutheete mean by "differentiated zones"?

4. How does Schoutheete's understanding of the goals of European integration compare to Mitterand's emphasis on Europe's need to have a soul (Source 6)? How does it compare to Thatcher's argument about the purpose of integration (Source 5)?

CHAPTER QUESTIONS

1. How is the nationalism discussed in the sources for European integration similar and different to the nationalism discussed in the sources on European immigration? What similar issues are identified as markers of national identity?

2. In the sources on European integration, what relationships between European and national identity do the authors' propose?

3. How is the idea of "the West" used in the controversies over immigration and unification? To what extent is the "Europe" that is being proposed something that might require a redefinition of "the West"?

4. How does the nationalism expressed in the debates over immigration and unification compare to the nationalism referred to in the debates over decolonization by both Europeans and non-Europeans (Chapter 13)?

Conclusion

WHITHER THE WEST?

What challenges face the West today? As we have discovered in the sources in this book, since the Renaissance the West developed as a set of ideas, largely in the lands of western and central Europe.[1] These ideas were defined and redefined over time as the people in these lands shaped their understanding of themselves. This Western identity also spread to some of the lands that Europeans colonized around the globe. This twin framework for Western identity—the West as a set of ideas and the West as a group of institutions and nations that define themselves as deriving from a common history—forms an important context for understanding the West in the wider world today.

We have now seen how a new idea of the West emerged as the medieval concept of a unified Christendom dissolved. In the sixteenth through nineteenth centuries, Europeans established their political and economic power across the globe, industrial societies emerged, and the authority of Christian religious institutions waned while that of central governments expanded. As Europeans responded to these changes, a new Western identity emerged that was defined by scientific and technological prowess, a broadly secular society, and political and economic liberalism. In place of a distinctly religious justification for these ideals, Western authors, profoundly shaped by the secularism of the Enlightenment, drew on the "universalist" tradition in Christianity and Greco-Roman philosophy and encoded these values in documents such as the French Declaration of the Rights of Man and Citizen (1789). Western universalism, in its most influential formulation, asserted that natural, universal laws guide human behavior and that if human laws and customs reflect these universal laws, then human happiness and goodness will be promoted. Western universalism also asserted that these universal laws transcend all civilizations and that their appropriate application to human society can best be discovered through self-criticism and unfettered public debate, practices that also became central components of Western identity. Western society's identification with these ideals justified to Westerners a mission to bring the benefits of their "superior civilization" to all peoples, whether they wanted it or not. By the end of the nineteenth century, "Western triumphalism" stood supreme: most Europeans and Americans believed that the progress of Western political and economic power unequivocally demonstrated the superiority of Western civilization and its values.

The Western governments, however, often honored the ideals of Western identity in theory more than they implemented them in practice, especially within col-

---

[1] Interestingly, in creating a history of Western civilization, historians have established the origins of the West outside of western and central Europe, emphasizing instead the Middle East (Mesopotamia), the Near East (Israel, Palestine, and Asia Minor), Northern Africa (Egypt and Carthage), and southeast Europe (Greece).

384

onized lands. When Western imperial authority weakened in the wake of two devastating wars in the twentieth century, the West itself provided those who wished to challenge Western imperialism with two ways to critique it. First, the West's universal tenets offered moral authority to any people, Western or otherwise, who mastered modern science and technology, who adopted political and economic liberalism, or who challenged Western practices that violated universal human rights. Second, the Marxist-Leninist critique of industrial Western society, particularly of political and economic liberalism, provided many colonized peoples with an explicit justification for resisting imperial authority. These two critiques—the West's own scientific, political, economic, and moral tenets and Marxist-Leninist economic and social theories—shared many features, including a claim to universalism, an acknowledged secularism, and a strong endorsement of modern science and technology. Nevertheless, they became established as distinct opponents in the cold war conflict, expressed most significantly in the efforts by the Soviet Union and the United States to shape to their own advantage the decolonization movement of the 1950s and 1960s. Some radical critiques of Western imperialism arose outside of the Western world and rejected not only imperialism but also the Western model of society and its claims of universality. Most prominently, Mohandas Gandhi asserted that modern Western society itself was deeply flawed and should not be universally imposed on other cultures and civilizations.

In the late 1980s, the collapse of the Soviet empire undermined international support for the Marxist-Leninist critique of Western political and economic liberalism, and the idea of Western civilization reclaimed its triumphal status. In 1989, the political scientist Francis Fukuyama went so far as to publish an article entitled "The End of History," in which he argued that liberal democracy—the product of Western political liberalism—had gained consensus as a legitimate system of government, free from any fundamental internal contradictions, and marked the final form of human political evolution. However, the broader critique—and rejection—of Western society found within the work of Gandhi continues to find its disciples, and the idea of the West and its values can be understood in many, even contradictory, ways.

Despite Fukuyama's excessive optimism, many challenges remain today to the ideals of the West and thus to the West's understanding of itself. These challenges arise in a variety of forms and from all sides of the political spectrum. Identifying some of them will help us understand how the idea of the West, as historically shaped by people for diverse ends, expresses itself in and continues to shape our world today.

The idea of multiculturalism challenges the idea of the West. In the United States, which long has defined itself as "a nation of immigrants," studies that emphasize the nation's multicultural foundations—Hispanic, Amerindian, African, and Asian as well as European—call into question the distinctly European (and Western) origins of American society. Perhaps the nation that has come to lead the Western world is not as singularly Western as it has imagined. In western and central Europe, the immigration of large groups of foreign nationals, whether of African, Asian, Middle Eastern, or eastern European origin, has led to debate about how France, Germany, Austria, and Great Britain should understand themselves. Are they to take up a multicultural identity alongside or in replacement of national, European, or Western conceptions of themselves? Can the idea of the West sustain itself if the lands in which Western civilization developed abandon a sense of their distinct Western-ness in favor of a multicultural pluralism? The American politician Patrick Buchanan has argued that foreign immigration will lead to the "death of the West" as these individuals bring non-Western traditions and values into Western society. Conversely, if the West is understood as a set of universal ideals, then could not those ideals overlay and help organize the diverse elements that live in a pluralistic, multicultural society?

These universal ideals, however, have come under criticism from multicultural and feminist scholars, who have argued that Western political and cultural values derive from sexist, racist, and homophobic assumptions. Historically, those who have not had the proper qualities—maleness, whiteness, and heterosexuality—were excluded from the "universal" framework and suffered restrictions on their political and economic rights and on their participation in public life. These scholars have disagreed among themselves about whether Western values are unalterably sexist, racist, and homophobic—and therefore must be rejected or overthrown—or whether they may be purged of these flaws and thereby fulfill their universal promise. Whatever position is held, the debates over multicultural and feminist scholarship have resulted in serious consideration of the nature of Western identity and its claims of universality.

The end of the cold war also has raised challenges to the idea of the West. In the 1950s through 1980s, the cold war conflict between the Soviet Union and the West promoted a sense of cohesion among Western nations. They established a series of institutions that coordinated their governmental policies—for example, the North Atlantic Treaty Organization (NATO) and the Group of Seven (G-7) economic summits (which included the Western powers' most important Asian ally, Japan). However, with the cold war over and the pressure for coordination to resist the Soviet threat abated, will conflicts grow among the traditional Western powers? For example, will European unification promote a European identity that is apart from American identity and that undermines the universal idea of the West? Will the United States' status as the sole superpower, with techno-military capabilities far advanced of its allies, lead it increasingly to pursue unilateral policies that do not reflect the wishes of its Western allies? And more broadly, can the universal ideals of the West sustain themselves if sharp divisions grow among the Western powers themselves?

Globalization, in its twenty-first-century manifestation, also presents challenges to the idea of the West. The role played by multinational corporations, many of which are based in Western nations, in organizing the world economy has expanded the economic and political power of Western nations. This integration often is justified in the name of the "universal laws" of economic liberalism. Yet economic exploitation and political corruption frequently have accompanied economic development, and resentment has arisen among large populations whose corrupt local leaders gain vast wealth while cooperating with corporate business interests. Such forces often foster a hatred of the West among local peoples, who observe Western ideals justifying poverty and brutish regimes. Yet here the universal aspect of Western political liberalism can become an important weapon of the weak and disenfranchised. A central component of Western political liberalism—the idea of universal human rights—is a powerful tool that may be pressed into service by critics of unsavory political regimes.

The ideal of "universal human rights" would seem to promote the idea and values of Western civilization, and yet this concept also challenges the West. First, and perhaps most paradoxically, the "universal" component of these rights undermines the idea of a distinct, identifiable West. If the end product of the West is something universal—something that transcends all civilizations—then the West itself dissolves into the universal. We are left to ponder whether the consequence of the West's "success" is the destruction of its own distinctiveness. Will the West—as a distinct entity—wither away or at least become insignificant?

Second, the content or definition of these universal rights is not fully agreed upon. The United Nations' Universal Declaration of Human Rights, proclaimed in 1948, includes political, social, and economic rights within its provisions, such as the right to life, liberty, security, property, marriage, family, work, adequate standard of living, leisure, education, and participation in the cultural life of a community. The breadth and ambiguity of these rights have weakened their potency as political ideals and left Western and other governments room to manipulate, ignore, or promote these ideals opportunistically and partially as they pursue their own interests. When Western governments support regimes such as those of Saudi Arabia, Sierra Leone, and Peru, where human rights have been widely abused by the ruling governments, local populations can turn their resentments against both their own governments and also Western governments and the ideals they publicly espouse. When Western governments do not support in practice the ideals they proclaim in theory, they undermine the credibility of their own governments and help to create the contexts in which Western values themselves are rejected.

Third, following within the Western tradition, the United Nations' Universal Declaration of Human Rights promotes a Western concept of political life that establishes the individual, as opposed to the community or nation, as the central political figure—as the holder of rights and the source of political legitimacy. In the 1990s, a number of Asian political leaders challenged this individualist notion of human rights and adopted a position known as Asian Values, which asserts that human rights are not "universal" but "contextual" or particular, defined by local cultures, value systems, and levels of economic development. Singapore's former prime minister Lee Kuan Yew has argued that East Asian culture upholds the primacy of group interests over individual interests and that developing nations and economies are justified in requiring individuals to sacrifice political rights to aid the economic development of all of society. Further, Lee has argued that as these economies develop, a distinctly Asian version of human rights will evolve that places less emphasis on the "extreme individualism" of the Western model and more on the relationships between groups within society. Eventually, Lee has asserted, Western culture will draw back from its destructive forms of extreme individualism, recognize the value of greater concern for the community, and benefit as truly universal values emerge that reflect the highest aspirations of all civilizations. Many

Asian political activists, however, have decried the Asian Values position as a desperate ploy by corrupt regimes to justify their suppression of political dissent and to sustain their authoritarian governments. These activists have called on the United Nations and Western governments to press harder for individual human rights as an antidote to corrupt governments. By pursuing the debate over the Western notion of human rights, both the supporters and detractors of the Asian Values position highlight and help sustain the idea of the West and Western values.

Globalization also provokes challenges to the ideals of the West among those who oppose the economic dislocation and environmental damage caused by economic development. An often surprising collection of forces—labor unions, environmental movements, and human rights organizations—at times have worked in concert to challenge and disrupt the activities of organizations such as the World Trade Organization and the World Bank that promote free trade and economic development on the principles of economic liberalism. Many opponents of economic integration see the principles of economic liberalism as a convenient justification for the expanding exploitation of workers around the globe by multinational corporations. Economic liberalism, they argue, does not produce economic fairness. Rather, they assert, political rights become subjugated to the workings of market capitalism as governments and corporations restrict people in labor unions or civic organizations from opposing certain economic practices. Some environmental activists go further, challenging the moral validity of the scientific and technological practices of modern economies. The claim of "economic progress," they assert, cannot justify deforesting lands, polluting watersheds and aquifers, and driving animals and plants into extinction—actions that harm all the members of the community. Some radical environmental activists reject the very principles of modern (Western) science, while others seek to extend the principles of political liberalism to include the rights of animals, plants, and nature itself. Universal rights, they argue, are not limited to humans.

Globalization includes not only political and economic relationships but also the absorption of Western—and especially American—culture by societies around the globe. Whether expressed in music, cinema, or television, over the Internet, or through the presence of a fast-food restaurant, Western cultural values—especially the value placed on individualism—transform local cultures. On the one hand, local peoples may embrace the consumer products of Western science and technology (and sometimes the science and technology itself) as an indicator of "progress." On the other hand, the pervasiveness of this Western cultural presence, and the resentment felt toward the political and military activities of Western nations, have encouraged the growth of local movements to resist "foreign influences," often in defense of national, cultural, or religious identity.

In some instances, resistance has been relatively mild, as when activists try to protect local languages from an infusion of English or to defend national film industries from being overwhelmed with imports from Hollywood. In other cases, local movements that gain national power aggressively have sought to protect their societies by censoring Western cultural products, especially in film, television, and publishing, and by restricting the activities of Western guests, such as missionaries, aid workers, and journalists. Perhaps the fiercest controls have occurred in regimes led by radical Islamic organizations in nations such as Iran, Sudan, and, until recently, Afghanistan. Here regimes have instituted harsh censorship, limited foreign travel, destroyed art and other products of their country's cultural heritage that violate their current religious dogmas, and forced individuals—especially women—to accept severely proscribed roles within society. These movements, along with others acting to defend nationalist interests, have sponsored terrorist activities and organizations seeking to destroy a Western world identified as the expression of evil. The tragic events of September 11, 2001—when Islamic terrorists hijacked airplanes and crashed them into the World Trade Center towers in New York City and the Pentagon in Washington, D.C., buildings symbolizing American economic and political power—horrifically demonstrate the anger that the Western nations are able to provoke. After the attacks, which killed nearly three thousand people, Osama bin Laden, leader of the al-Qaeda terrorist organization that carried out these attacks, clearly stated his vision of the West's future: "I tell you, freedom and human rights in America are doomed. . . . The U.S. government will lead the American people—and the West in general—into an unbearable hell and a choking life." Ironically, in their efforts to expose, reject, and destroy the West—a West they define as secular, materialistic, yet still carrying a Christian prejudice against Islam—these groups dramatically reinforce the idea of and support for the West. Similarly, the idea of the West is reinforced when Western leaders place in relief an "enemy" who rejects the West's universal values.

Terroristic sentiments are not limited to "foreign terrorists," however. In many Western nations, individuals and local groups have committed acts of terror against their own national governments, which they believe threaten their existence and identity. Basque separatists in Spain and the Irish Republican Army in Northern Ireland long have used terror as a political weapon against national governments that they believe threaten their ethnic identity and nationalist aspirations. In Germany and Austria, right-wing nationalists have expressed their anger at national governments that they believe are permitting "foreigners" to overwhelm their countries by attacking government buildings used to provide refuge for foreign asylum seekers and even by attacking the asylum seekers themselves. And in the United States, groups and individuals associated with survivalist, militia, and white supremacist movements openly prepare to resist the agencies of a federal government that they believe is destroying American liberty and is being turned over to the United Nations and other such representatives of a malevolent world government. With their emphasis on specific, local, and particular frameworks for identity—ethnic, political, and cultural—these groups challenge the idea that any significant "universal" framework exists for Western identity.

As we have seen throughout these readings, civilizations, including Western civilization, do not "exist" but are created and re-created, defined and redefined by myriad factors and individuals for many and diverse purposes. This process of creating and defining a civilization is not simply an internal process. We have seen that the people and the ideas that the West has encountered in the wider world have transformed Western societies and the idea of the West itself and continue to do so. We cannot predict the future of the West or of its relationship to other civilizations—or even know if such divisions between civilizations will be meaningful in the future.

Future generations will create their own distinctive identities, dividing the world into groups according to geography, religion, economic status, political beliefs, and the like as is appropriate to their needs. Rather, we can look at the process by which the idea of the West has been created and re-created in the past. We can investigate the forces that seem to have been most significant in shaping that idea, the foundations for those forces, and their ultimate ends. And we can use that knowledge to seek to understand the conflicting efforts to create, define, and interact with the West—by Westerners and non-Westerners alike, in our own age and in ages to come.

Acknowledgments

Chapter 1: Two Worlds Collide
The European Arrival
1. Christopher Columbus, "Log of the First Voyage (1492)." Excerpts from *The Diario of Christopher Columbus's First Voyage to America, 1492–1493* translated and edited by Oliver C. Dunn and James E. Kelley Jr. Copyright © 1989 University of Oklahoma Press. Reprinted by permission of the publisher.
2. "Codex Florentino (1555)." Excerpts from *The Broken Spears: The Aztec Account of the Conquest of Mexico,* edited by Miguel Leon-Portilla. Copyright © 1962, 1990 by Miguel Leon-Portilla. Expanded and Updated Edition © 1992 by Miguel Leon-Portilla. Reprinted by permission of Beacon Press, Boston.
3. Hernando Cortés, "Second Dispatch to Charles V (1520)." Excerpts from *Conquest: Dispatches of Cortés from the New World,* edited by Harry M. Rosen. Published by Grosset and Dunlap, 1952.
4. Bernal Díaz, "Chronicles (c. 1560)." Excerpts from *The Bernal Díaz Chronicles: The True Story of the Conquest of Mexico,* edited and translated by Albert Idell. Copyright © 1957 by Albert Idell. Used by permission of Doubleday, a division of Random House, Inc.
Image: German woodcut of 1505. New World scene. Spencer Collection. Courtesy of The New York Public Library, Astor, Lenox, and Tilden Foundations
Image: Woodcut from "The First New Chronicle and Good Government." From Guaman Poma de Ayala, *El Primer nueva coronica y buen Gobierno.* Siglo XXI Editores, 1st edition 1980, Volume II, p. 343. Courtesy General Research Division, The New York Public Library, Astor, Lenox and Tilden Foundations. Original manuscript in which this illustration appears is archived in the Royal Library of Copenhagen.
The Americas in Europe
5. Roger Schlesinger. "In the Wake of Columbus (1996)." Excerpts from *In the Wake of Columbus: The Impact of the New World on Europe, 1492–1650* by Roger Schlesinger. Copyright © 1996 by Roger Schlesinger. Reprinted with permission of Harlan Davidson, 1996.
6. Juan Ginés de Sepúlveda, "Democrates Secundus (1544)." Excerpts from *The Spanish Tradition in America* edited by Charles Gibson. Copyright © 1968 by the University of South Carolina Press. Reprinted by permission of the University of South Carolina Press.
7. Bartolomé de Las Casas. "In Defense of the Indians (1551)." Excerpts from *In Defense of the Indians* edited and translated by Stafford Poole. Copyright © 1974 by Northern Illinois University Press. Used by permission of the publisher.
8. Michel de Montaigne. "Of Cannibals (1580s)." Excerpts from *Selected Essays of Montaigne* by Michel Montaigne, translated by C. Cotton, and W. C. Hazlit, edited by Blanchard Bates. Copyright © 1949 by Random House, Inc. Used by permission of Random House, Inc.

Chapter 2: Challenges to Christendom in Reformation Europe
Christendom and Reformation
1. Ogier Ghiselin de Busbecq. "Travels into Turkey (c. 1561)." Excerpts from *Travels into Turkey,* Third Edition.
2. Martin Luther. "'On Christian Liberty' and 'Address to the Christian Nobility of the German Nation' (1520)." "On Christian Liberty" excerpts from "The Freedom of a Christian" from *Luther's Works,* vol. 31, *Career of the Reformer: I,* edited by Harold Grimm and translated by W. A. Lambert. Gen. ed. Helmut Lehmann. Copyright © 1957 Fortress Press. Used by permission of Augsburg Fortress. "Address to the Nobility of the German Nation" from *Luther's Works,* vol. 44, *The Christian in Society: I,* translated by Charles M. Jacobs. Edited by James Atkinson. Copyright © 1966 Fortress Press. Used by permission of Augsburg Fortress.
3. Thomas More. "A Dialogue Concerning Heresies (1529)." Excerpts from *The Complete Works of Thomas More,* Volume 6, Part I, edited by Thomas M. C. Lawler, Germain Marc'hadour, and Richard C. Marius. Copyright © 1981 Yale University Press. Reprinted by permission. Orthography modernized and language clarified by David Kammerling Smith.
4. Johannes Brenz. "Booklet on the Turk (1531)." Excerpts from *The Infidel Scourge of God: The Turkish Menace as Seen by German Pamphleteers of the Reformation Era* in *Transactions of the American Philosophical Society,* Volume 58, Part 9, by John W. Bohnstedt. Copyright © 1968 The American Philosophical Society. Reprinted with permission.
5. Andreas Osiander. "Whether It is True and Believable That Jews Secretly Kill Christian Children and Use Their Blood (c. 1529)." Excerpts from *Gesamtausgabe,* Volume 7, *Schriften Und Briefe 1539 Bis Marz 1543,* edited by Gerhard Muller and Gottfried Seebass. © Gutersloher Verlagshaus Mohn 1988. Original translation from the German by Joy M. Kammerling.
6. Images: "The Ottomon Seige of Vienna" Woodcut (1830) from *The German Single-Leaf Woodcut, 1500–1550,* Volume IV, p. 1194. Hacker Books, 1974. Courtesy David Tunick, Inc. "The Ritual Murder of Simon of Trent." Engraving from *Early Italian Engraving: A Critical Catalogue with Complete Reproduction of All the Prints Described.* Part I: *Florentine Engravings and Anonymous Prints of Other Schools* by Arthur M. Hind. Plate 74, A.I. 78). Published for M. Knoedler & Company, New York by Bernard Quartich Ltd., 1938. Kraus reprint 1970. Courtesy David Tunick, Inc., New York.

Religion and the Natural World

7. Heinrich Kramer and Jakob Sprenger. "The Hammer of Witches (1486)." Excerpts from *The Malleus Maleficarum of Heinrich Kramer and James Sprenger,* translated by Montague Summers. Dover Publications, 1971. Originally published by John Rodker (London, 1928).

8. Nicolaus Copernicus. "On the Revolutions of the Heavenly Orbs (1543)." Excerpts from *Epitome of Copernican Astronomy IV and V. The Harmonies of the World, V* by Johannes Kepler. University of Chicago Great Book Collection.

9. Galileo Galilei. "Letter to the Grand Duchess Christina (1615)." Excerpts from *Discoveries and Opinions of Galileo* by Galileo Galilei, translated by Stillman Drake. Copyright © 1957 by Stillman Drake. Used by permission of Doubleday, a division of Random House, Inc.

Chapter 3: The Christianizing Mission

1. Jean de Brébeuf. "Jesuit Relations of 1636." Excerpts from *The Jesuit Relations: Natives and Missionaries in Seventeenth Century North America* edited by Allan Greer. Copyright © 2000 by Allan Greer. Reprinted by permission of Bedford/St. Martin's.

2. Venerable Marie de l'Incarnation. "Relation of 1654." Excerpts from *The Autobiography of Venerable Marie of the Incarnation, O.S.U. Mystic and Missionary,* translated by John J. Sullivan. Copyright © 1964 Loyola University Press. Reprinted by permission of Loyola University Press.

3. A Micmac Leader, reported by Chrestien LeClerq. "New Relation of Gaspesia (1691)." Excerpts from *New Relation of Gaspesia: With the Customs and Religion of the Gaspesian Indians,* translated by William F. Ganong. Originally published by The Champlain Society, 1910. Greenwood Press, 1968.

4. Matteo Ricci. "Journals (1615)." Excerpts from *China in the Sixteenth Century: The Journals of Matthew Ricci: 1583–1610,* translated by Louis J. Gallagher S.J. Copyright © 1942, 1953 and renewed 1970 by Louis J. Gallagher S.J. Used by permission of Random House, Inc.

5. "History of the Ming (18th century)." Excerpts from *China in Transition, 1517–1911,* 1st edition, edited by J. Dun Li. Copyright © 1969. Reprinted with permission of Wadsworth, an imprint of the Wadsworth Group, a division of Thomson Learning.

Chapter 4: European Colonization and the Early Modern State

Colonizing Abroad

1. "The Tsars' Correspondence in the Conquest of Siberia (17th century)." Excerpts from *Russia's Conquest of Siberia, 1558–1700: A Documentary Record* edited and translated by Basil Dmytryshyn, EAP Crownhart-Vaughn, and Thomas Vaughn. Copyright © 1985 Western Imprints, The Press of the Oregon Historical Society, Portland, Oregon. Reprinted with permission.

2. "French Administrative Correspondence with Its American Colonies (17th century)." Excerpts from *Lettres, Instructions, et Mémoires de Colbert,* Vol. III, Part II. *Instructions au Marquis de Seignlay Colonies,* edited by Pierre Clement (1865). Translated from the French by David Kammerling Smith.

3. Otreouti. "Speech to the Governor of New France (1684)." From *The History of the Five Indian Nations: Depending on the Province of New York in America* (1727). Reprinted by Cornell Univeristy Press (1958).

4. Anthony Pagden. "Lords of All the World (1995)." Excerpts from *Lords of All the World* by Anthony Pagden. Copyright 1995 Yale University Press. Reprinted by permission.

Colonizing at Home

5. Cardinal Richelieu. "Political Testament (c.1630s)." Excerpts from *The Political Testament of Cardinal Richelieu,* edited and translated by Henry Bertram Hill. Copyright © 1961. Reprinted by permission of the University of Wisconsin Press.

6. "Administrative Correspondence within France (17th century)." Excerpts from *Historie du Systeme Protecteur en France* and *Lettres, Instructions, et Mémoires de Colbert,* Vol. II, Part II. *Industrie, Commerce,* edited by Pierre Clement. Translated by David Kammerling Smith. Excerpts from *Louis XIV and Absolutiusm: A Brief Study with Documents* by William Biek Copyright © 2000 by William Biek. Reprinted by Permission of Bedford/St. Martin's.

7. "Decrees of Peter the Great (early 18th century)." Excerpts from *Imperial Russia: A Source Book, 1700–1917,* edited by Basil Dmytryshyn. Copyright © 1967 Holt, Rinehart and Winston. Excerpts from *A Source Book for Russian History from Early Times to 1917,* Vol. II, *Peter the Great to Nicholas I,* edited by George Vernadsky. Copyright © 1972 Yale University Press. Excerpts from *Peter the Great, Emperor of Russia,* edited by Eugene Schuyler. Published by Charles Scribner's Sons, 1884.

Chapter 5: Rethinking the World

1. Baron de Montesquieu. "The Spirit of the Laws (1748)." Excerpts from *The Spirit of the Laws,* by Charles de Montesquieu. Translated and edited by Anne M. Cohler. Carolyn Miller and Harold Samuel Stone. Copyright © 1989 Cambridge University Press. Reprinted with the permission of Cambridge University Press.

2. Voltaire. "Essay on the Customs and Spirit of Nations (1756)." Excerpts from *Essai sur les moeurs et l'esprit des nations,* Volume 1, by Voltaire. Editions Garnier Frères. Reprinted with the permission of Infomedia, Paris. Original translation from the French by David Kammerling Smith.

3. Cornelius de Pauw. "Philosophical Inquiry into the Americas (1768–1769)." Excerpts from *Recherches philosophiques sur les Americains* by Cornelius de Pauw (1771). Original translation from the French by David Kammerling Smith.

4. Jean-Jacques Rousseau. "Discourse on the Origins of Inequality (1755)." Excerpts from *Discourse on the Origin of Inequality* by Jean-Jacques Rousseau. Translated by Donald A. Cress. Copyright © 1992 by Hackett Publishing Company, Inc. Reprinted by permission of Hackett Publishing Company, Inc. All rights reserved.

5. Mungo Park. "Travels in the Interior Districts of Africa (1797)." Excerpts from *Travels in the Interior of Districts of Africa* (London, 1807).

6. Beth Fowkes Tobin. "Picturing Imperial Power (1999)." Excerpts from *Picturing Imperial Power: Colonial Subjects in Eighteenth-Century British Painting,* by Beth Fowkes Tobin. Copyright © 1999 Duke University Press. Reprinted with permission. All rights reserved.

Images: From *The Harlot's Progress,* Plate 2, by William Hogarth. Engraving, 1732. Courtesy of the Print Collection, Lewis Walpole Library, Yale University. "The Family of Sir William Young" by Johann Zoffany. Oil on canvas, c. 1766. Walker Art Gallery, Liverpool, Merseyside, UK/Trustees of National Museums & Galleries on Merseyside/Bridgmen Art Library.

7. Immanuel Kant. "Observations on the Feeling of the Beautiful and the Sublime (1764)." Excerpts from *Observations on the Feeling of the Beautiful and the Sublime* by Immanuel Kant. Translated by John T. Goldthwait. Copyright © 1960. Reprinted by permission of the Regents of the University of California and the University of California Press.

8. Johann Gottfried von Herder. "Outlines of a Philosophy of the History of Man (1784)." Excerpts from *Outlines of a Philosophy of the History of Man* by Johann Gottfried von Herder. Translated by T. Churchill. Originally published in 1800 and republished in the United States by Peter Bergman Publishers. Reprinted by permission of Annie Bergman.

Chapter 6: Slavery, Absolutism, and Revolution

The Rise of the Abolitionist Movement

1. Adam Smith. "The Wealth of Nations (1776)." Excerpts from *An Inquiry into the Nature and Causes of The Wealth of Nations: Representative Selections* edited by Bruce Mazlish. Copyright © 1961 Published by Bobbs-Merrill Company. Reprinted by permission of Pearson Education, Inc., Upper Saddle River, NJ.

2. Olaudah Equiano. "The Interesting Narrative of the Life of Olaudah Equiano (1789)." Excerpts from *Equiano's Travels: His Autobiography: The Interesting Narrative of the Life of Olaudah Equiano or Gustavius Vassa the African* edited by Paul Edwards. Copyright © 1967 Heinemann International. Reprinted by permission of Heinemann Educational Publishers.

3. Plymouth Committee of the Society for the Abolition of the Slave Trade. "Plan of an African Ship's Lower Deck (1788)." Courtesy Bristol Record Office, Bristol, UK.

4. Abbé Raynal. "History of the East and West Indies (1780)." Excerpts from *A Philosophical and Political History of the Settlements and Trade of the Europeans in the East and West Indies,* Volume IV, by Guillaume Raynal. Translated by J. O. Justamond (1798). Reprinted by Negro University Press, A Division of Greenwood Publishing Corp. (1969).

Slavery and Revolution

5. "Declaration of the Rights of Man and Citizen (1789)." Excerpts from *The French Revolution and Human Rights: A Brief Documentary History* edited and translated by Lynn Hunt. Copyright © 1996 by Lynn Hunt. Reprinted by permission.

6. Society of the Friends of Blacks. "Address to the National Assembly in Favor of the Abolition of the Slave Trade (1790)." Excerpts from *The French Revolution and Human Rights: A Brief Documentary History* edited and translated by Lynn Hunt. Copyright © 1996 by Lynn Hunt. Reprinted by permission. Additional excerpts from *Adresse à l'Assemblée nationale* (1790). Translation from the French by David Kammerling Smith.

7. Antoine Barnave. "Speech to the National Assembly (1790)." Excerpts from *The French Revolution and Human Rights: A Brief Documentary History* edited and translated by Lynn Hunt. Copyright © 1996 by Lynn Hunt. Reprinted by permission. Additional excerpts from *Archives parlementaires* 12 (1881). Translation from the French by David Kammerling Smith.

8. "My Odyssey (1793)." Excerpts from *My Odyssey: Experiences of a Young Refugee from Two Revolutions* translated and edited by Althea de Puech Parham. Copyright © 1959 Louisiana State University Press. Reprinted by permission of the publisher.

9. François Toussaint-L'Ouverture. "Letters (1797 and 1799)." Excerpts from *Toussaint L'Ouverture,* edited by George F. Tyson Jr. Copyright © 1973 by Prentice-Hall, Inc. Reprinted with the permission of Simon & Schuster Adult Publishing Group.

Chapter 7: Napoleon in Egypt

1. Louis Antoine Fauvelet de Bourrienne. "Memoirs of Napoleon Bonaparte (1829)." Excerpts from *Memoirs of Napoleon Bonaparte* by Louis Antoine Bourrienne, Volume 1, edited by R. W. Phipps. Charles Scribner's Sons, 1895.

2. Napoleon Bonaparte. "Statements and Proclamation on the Egyptian Campaign (1798–1804)." Conversations excerpts from *The Mind of Napoleon: A Selection from His Written and Spoken Words* edited and translated by J. Christopher Herold. Published by Columbia University Press, 1955. Proclamation from *Pièces diverses et correspondance aux operations de l'armée d'orient en Égypte* (Paris, 1801). Original translation from the French by David Kammerling Smith.

3. Abd al-Rahman al-Jabarti. "Chronicle (early 19th century)." Excerpts from *Chronicle,* edited and translated by S. Moreh. Published by E. J. Brill, 1975.

4. Vivant Denon. "Travels in Upper and Lower Egypt (1802)." Excerpts from *Travels in Upper and Lower Egypt,* Volume 1, translated by Arthur Aikin. Originally published in the UK, 1803. Published in the United States by Arno Press, 1973.

5. "Description of Egypt (1809–1828)." Excerpts from *Description de l'Égypte,* 2nd edition, 1821. Translated from the French by David Kammerling Smith.

6. Images: "Profile of the Sphinx near the Pyramids of Giza" from *Travels in Upper and Lower Egypt* by Vivant Denon, translated by Arthur Alkin . Volume I, Plate IX. Courtesy Special Collections and Archives, W. E. DuBois Library, University of Massachusetts, Amherst. "Tomb of Paheri", Volume I, Plate 67 (bottom); "The Colossi of Memnon at Thebes", Volume II, Plate 20. From *Commission des monuments d'Égypte, Description d'Égypte, 1809–1828* (Imprimerie impériale imprint, Paris, France). *Antiquities: Description, 1809–1818.* Courtesy Asian and Middle Eastern Division, The New York Public Library, Astor, Lenox and Tilden Foundations.

7. Edward Said. "Orientalism (1978)." Excerpts from *Orientalism* by Edward Said. Copyright © 1978 by Edward Said. Reprinted with permission of Pantheon Books, a division of Random House, Inc.

Chapter 8: The Great Transformation
Defining the Industrial Era

1. John Stuart Mill. "Considerations on Representative Government (1861)." Excerpts from *Considerations on Representative Government* edited by Currin V. Shields. Published by The Liberal Arts Press, 1958.

2. Andrew Ure. "Philosophy of Manufactures (1835)." Excerpts from *Philosophy of Manufactures* by Andrew Ure. Copyright © 1967 Frank Cass and Company.

3. "Testimony for the Factory Act of 1833." Excerpts from *British Parliamentary Papers.* Irish Industrial Press, 1968.

4. Karl Marx and Friedrich Engels. "The Communist Manifesto (1848)." Excerpts from *The Marx-Engels Reader,* 2nd ed., edited by Robert C. Tucker. Copyright © 1978, 1972 by W. W. Norton & Company, Inc. Used by permission of W. W. Norton & Company, Inc.

5. Flora Tristan. "Workers' Union (1843)." Excerpts from *Flora Tristan: Utopian Feminist: Her Travel Diaries and Personal Crusade.* Copyright © 1994 Indiana University Press. Reprinted by permission.

The Border Lands

6. Vissarion Belinsky. "Letter to N. V. Gogol, July 3, 1847." Excerpts from *Selected Philosophical Works* by V. G. Belinsky. Foreign Language Publishing House, 1956.

7. Nikolai Danilevsky. "Russia and Europe (1869)." Excerpts *The Mind of Modern Russia: Historical and Political Thought of Russia's Great Age* edited by Hans Kohn. Copyright © 1955 by The Trustees of Rutgers College in New Jersey. Reprinted with the permission of Rutgers University Press.

8. Khayr al-Din al-Tunisi. "The Surest Path (1869)." Excerpts from *The Surest Path: The Political Testament of a Nineteenth-Century Muslim Statesman,* translated by Leon Carl Brown. By permission

9. Ottoman Cartoons (1909 and 1911). "Conspicuous Consumption" and "Breaking Her Chains" from "*Kalem,*" March 2, 1911, p. 6, and "*Laklak,*" October 7, 1909, p. 1. Courtesy of Hoover Institution Library, Stanford University. Caption: Reprinted by permission from *Image and Imperialism in the Ottoman Revolutionary Press, 1908–1911* by Palmira Brummett. Copyright © 2000, State University of New York Press. All rights reserved.

Chapter 9: The First Opium War
The Opium Crisis

1. Lin Zexu. "Letter to Queen Victoria (1839)." Excerpts from *China's Response to the West: A Documentary Survey, 1839–1923* by Ssu-yu Teng and John King Fairbank. Copyright © 1954, 1979 by the President and Fellows of Harvard College. Copyright renewed 1982 by Ssu-yu and John King Fairbank. Reprinted by permission of the publisher, Harvard University Press.

2. Algernon Thelwell. "The Iniquities of the Opium Trade with China (1839)." Excerpts from *The Iniquities of the Opium Trade with China* by Algernon Thelwell. Published 1839 by Allen & Company, London. From the Kress Collection of Business and Economics, Baker Library, Harvard Business School.

3. Samuel Warren. "The Opium Question (1840)." Excerpts from *The Opium Question* by Samuel Warren. Published 1849 by James Ridgway, London. From the Kress Collection of Business and Economics, Baker Library, Harvard Business School.

4. Bombay Times. "Editorial of May 23, 1839." Excerpts from the *Bombay Times.* Copyright © Bombay Times. Reprinted in the *Times* (London), May 23, 1939. Reprinted by permission.

5. Leeds Mercury. "Editorial of September 7, 1839." Excerpts from *Leeds Mercury,* September 7, 1839. From Kress Collection of Business and Economics, Baker Library, Harvard Business School. Originally archived at Goldsmiths' Library, University of London.

6. Punch. "Important News from China (1841)." From the First issue of *Punch,* 1841. Courtesy Punch, Ltd., London.

Responses to the Opium Wars

7. Arthur Cunynghame. "The Opium War: Being Recollections of Service in China (1845)." Excerpts from *The Opium War: Being Recollections of Service in China* by Arthur Cynynghame. Published by G. B. Zieber, 1845. Reprinted by Scholarly Resources.

8. Michael Adas. "Machines as the Measure of Men (1989)." *Machines as the Measure of Men: Science, Technology, and Ideologies of Western Dominance* by Michael Adas. Copyright © 1990 by Cornell University. Used by permission of the publisher, Cornell University Press.

9. Feng Guifen. "Theory of Self-Strengthening (1860)." Excerpts from *China's Response to the West: A documentary survey* by Ssu-yu Teng and John K. Fairbank. Copyright © 1954, 1979 by the President and Fellows of Harvard College. Copyright renewed 1982 by Ssu-yu Teng and John King Fairbank. Reprinted by permission of the publisher, Harvard University Press.

Chapter 10: The Imperialist Impulse Abroad and at Home
Imerialism Away

1. "Maps of Africa" created by Bedford/St. Martins

2. Charles Darwin. "The Descent of Men (1871)." Excerpts from *The Descent of Man* by Charles Darwin. Published by The Modern Library, now a division of Random House, Inc.

3. Karl Pearson. "National Life from the Standpoint of Science (1901)." Excerpts from *National Life from the Standpoint of Science* by Adam and Charles Black. Copyright © 1901 Karl Pearson. Reprinted with permission of A and C Black Publishers Limited.

4. Friedrich Fabri. "Does Germany Need Colonies? (1879)" Excerpts from *Bedarf Deutschland des Colonien?/Does Germany Need Colonies?* Translated and edited by E. C. M. Breuning and M. E. Chamberlain. Studies in German Thought and History, Volume II. Copyright © 1998 The Edwin Mellen Press. Reprinted by permission.

5. Joseph Chamberlain. "The True Conception of Empire (1897)." Excerpt from *Mr. Chamberlain's Speeches*, Volume II edited by Charles W. Boyd. Published by Houghton Mifflin, 1914.

6. Edmund D. Morel. "King Leopold's Rule in Africa (1904)." Excerpts from *King Leopold's Rule in Africa* by Edmund D. Morel. Originally published by William Heinemann, London, 1904. Reprinted by Negro University Press, 1970, a division of Greenwood Press, Inc.

7. Vladimir Lenin. "Imperialism: The Highest Stage of Capitalism (1917)." Excerpts from *Imperialism, the Highest Stage of Capitalism, Selected Works*, Volume I, by Vladimir Lenin. Copyright © 1967 International Publishers, Inc.

Imperialism at Home

8. Andrew Zimmerman. "Anthropology and Antihumanism in Imperial Germany (2001)." Excerpts from *Anthropology and Antihumanism in Imperial Germany*, by Andrew Zimmerman. Copyright © 2001. Reprinted by permission of the author.

9. "British Imperial Advertisements (1885 and 1891)." "Liebig Extract of Meat" advertisement. Illustration and caption from *Lady's Pictorial*, March 14, 1891. Published in *Consuming Angels: Advertising and Victorian Women* by Lori Anne Loeb. Copyright © 1994 by Lori Anne Loeb. Oxford University Press, Inc. Photo credit: British Library. "Fry's Cocoa" advertisement. Image *Rule Britannia: Trading on the British Image* by Robert Opie. Copyright © 1985 Viking Penguin Books. Reprinted by permission.

10. William Booth. "In Darkest England, (1890)." Excerpts from *In Darkest England and the Way Out* by William Booth. The Salvation Army, London, 1890. Reprinted by Garrett Press, 1970. © The Salvation Army, a Georgia Corporation. Reprinted by permission of The Salvation Army Board of Trustees.

11. Antoinette M. Burton. "The White Woman's Burden (1992)." Excerpts from "The White Woman's Burden: British Feminists and 'The Indian Woman,' 1865–1915" in *Western Women and Imperialism: Complicity and Resistence* edited by Nupuir Chanuhuri and Margaret Strobel. Copyright © Indiana University Press. Reprinted by permission of the publisher.

Chapter 11: Europe Shaken
Challenges in Europe

1. Ernst Jünger. "The Storm of Steel (1921)." Excerpts from *The Storm of Steel* by Ernst Jünger. Originally published by Chatto and Windus, 1929. Reprinted by Howard Fertig, 1975; paper edition 1996.

2. Anna Eisenmenger. "Blockage (1918)." Excerpts from *Blockade: The Diary of an Austrian Middle-Class Woman, 1914–1924* by Anna Eisenmenger. Copyright © 1932 Ray Long and Richard R. Smith, Inc.

3. Vladimir Lenin and Georgy Chicherin. "Are You a Trade Unionist? An Appeal to British Workers (1920)." Excerpts from *Are You a Trade Unionist? An Appeal to British Workers*. Published by The People's Russian Information Bureau, London, 1920.

4. Winston Churchill. "The World Crisis (1929)." Excerpts from *The World Crisis*, Volume V, by Winston Churchill. Copyright © 1929 Charles Scribner's Sons. Renewal copyright © 1957 Winston S. Churchill. Copyright renewed Curtis Brown Ltd. Reprinted by permission.

Imperialism Challenged

5. Mohandas Gandhi. "Indian Home Rule (1909)." Excerpts from *Indian Home Rule* by Mohandas Gandhi. Originally published 1909. Reprinted by permission of Ganesh & Company Publishers.

6. Gilbert Elliot-Murray-Kynynmound, the Earl of Minto. "Despatch to John Morley, March 21, 1907." Excerpts from *The Dominions and India Since 1900: Select Documents on the Constitutional History of British Empire and Commonwealth.* Volume 6, edited by Frederick Madden and John Darwin. Copyright © 1993 by Frederick Madden and John Darwin. Reproduced with permission of Greenwood Publishing Group, Westport, CT.

7. Baron Albert d'Anethan. "Dispatches from Japan (1894 and 1904)." Excerpts from *The d'anethan Dispatches from Japan, 1894-1910: The Observations of Baron Albert d'Anethan, Belgian Minister Plenipotentiary and Dean of the Diplomatic Corps,* edited and translated by George Alexander Lensen. Copyright © Japan 1967, by Sophia University. All rights reserved. Published by Sophia University in cooperation with The Diplomatic Press, Tallahassee, Florida.

8. Punch cartoons. "A Lesson in Patriotism" from *Punch,* December 28, 1904, p. 3, Volume 127. "An Emergency Exit" from *Punch,* June 28, 1905, p. 65, Volume 128. "Allies" from *Punch,* December 27, 1905, p. 245, Volume 129. Courtesy Punch Cartoon Library & Archive, Punch Ltd., London.

9. Kita Ikki. "Plan for the Reorganization of Japan (1919)." Excerpts from *Sources of Japanese Tradition* edited by Tsunoda Ryusaku, William de Bary, and Donald Keene. Copyright © 1958 by Columbia University Press. Reprinted by permission of the publisher.

10. William Inge. "The White Man and His Rivals (1922)." Excerpts from *The White Man and His Rivals* by William Inge. Outspoken Essays, 2nd Series Published by Greenwood Press, 1969.

Chapter 12: Ethnicity and Nationalism in Stalin's Soviet Union and Hitler's Third Reich
Nationality and Agriculture in the Soviet Ukraine

1. Joseph Stalin. "Problems of Agrarian Policy in the USSR (1929)." Excerpts from *Joseph Stalin: Selected Writings.* Copyright © 1942 International Publishers Company, Inc. Reprinted by permission.

2. James E. Mace. "Communism and the Dilemmas of National Liberation (1983)." Excerpts from *Communism and the Dilemmas of National Liberation: National Communism in the Soviet Ukraine, 1918–1933* by James E. Mace. Copyright © 1983 by the President and Fellows of Harvard College. Reprinted by permission of the publisher, Harvard University Press.

3. Antonina Solovieva. "Sent by the Komsomol (1964)." Excerpts from *In the Shadow of the Revolution: Life Stories of Russian Women from 1917 to the Second World War* edited by Sheila Fitzpatrick and Yuri Slezkine. Translated by Yuri Slezkine. Copyright © 2000 Princeton University Press. Reprinted by permission of Princeton University Press.

4. Miron Dolot. "Execution by Hunger (1985)." Excerpts from *Execution by Hunger: The Hidden Holocaust* by Miron Dolot. Copyright © 1985 by Miron Dolot. Used by permission of W. W. Norton & Company, Inc.

Ethnicity and Citizenship in Nazi Germany

5. Adolf Hitler. "Mein Kampf (1925)." Excerpts from *Mein Kampf* by Aldof Hitler, translated by Ralph Manheim. Copyright © 1943, renewed 1971 by Houghton Mifflin Company. Reprinted by permission of Houghton Mifflin Company. All rights reserved.

6. "Nazi Jewish Policies (1935, 1939, 1942)." Excerpts from *Nazi Conspiracy and Aggression,* Volume IV. Office of the United States Chief of Counsel for Prosecution of Axis Criminality.

7. "Nazi Art (1930s)" "Future Mothers" Photo courtesy Brandon Taylor. Weiner Library Archives, London. Published in *The Nazification of Art: Art, Design, Music, Architecture, and Film in the Third Reich* edited by Brandon Taylor. Copyright © 1990 The Winchester Press. Reprinted by permission. Nazi poster. Courtesy of the Poster Collection, Hoover Institution Archives, Stanford University.

8. Melita Maschmann. "Account Rendered (1963)." Excerpts from *Account Rendered: A Dossier on My Former Self.* Copyright © Melita Maschmann. English translation copyright © Abelard-Schuman 1964. Published by Abelard-Schuman Limited, New York, 1965.

9. Primo Levi. "Survival in Auschwitz (1947)." From *If This Is a Man (Survival in Auschwitz)* by Primo Levi, translated by Stuart Woolf. Copyright © 1959 by Orion Press, Inc., © 1958 by Giulio Einaudi editore S.P.A. Used by permission of Viking Penguin, a division of Penguin Putnam, Inc.

Chapter 13: The Call for Liberation in the Era of the Cold War
Independence in the Congo: 1960

1. "Proclamation of Independence of Katanga (1960)." Excerpts from "Text of the Proclamation of Independence of Katanga" in *Katanga Secession* by Jules Gerard-Libois. Translated by Rebecca Young. Copyright © 1966. Reprinted by permission of The University of Wisconsin Press.

2. United Nations Security Council Official Record. "Statements of Ambassadors from the Soviet Union and the United States (July 20, 1060)." Both excerpts from *Security Council Official Records,* Volume 877, July 20–21, 1960. Published by the United Nations.

3. Patrice Lumumba. "Radio Address (1960)." Excerpts from *Lumumba Speaks: The Speeches and Writings of Patrice Lumumba* by Patrice Lumumba. Copyright © 1963 by Éditions Presence Africaine. Copyright © 1972 by Little, Brown and Company, Inc. (Translation). Reprinted by permission of Little, Brown and Company, Inc.

Algerian Independence in France: 1957 to 1959

4. Jean-Paul Sartre. "You Are Super (1957)." Excerpts from "Vous êtes formidable" in *Les Temps Modernes,* Volume 135, May 1957. Original translation by David Kammerling Smith.

5. Jacques Soustelle. "The Algerian Drama and French Decadence (1957)." Réponse a Raymond Aron, Copyright © 1957 Pion. Reprinted by permission. Translated from the French by David Kammerling Smith.

6. Paul Ricoeur. "The Etienne Mathiot Case (1958)." Excerpts from "Le 'Cas' Etienne Mathiot" in *Esprit,* Volume 259, March 1958. With permission from Revue Esprit, Paris. Translated from the French by David Kammerling Smith.

7. Albert Camus. "Algeria (1958)." Excerpts from *Actuelles*, Volume III. *Chroniques algériennes, 1939–1958*. Published by Editions Gallimard, Paris. Original translation from the French by David Kammerling Smith.

8. Ahmed Taleb-Ibrahimi. "Letter to Albert Camus (1959)." Excerpts from "Open Letter to Albert Camus" in *Letters from Prison, 1957–1961* by Ahmed Taleb-Ibrahimi. Originally published by S.N.E.D. (Algiers), 1966. © SNED. Algiers. Published 1988 by Allied Publishers.

Liberation at Home

9. Simone De Beauvoir. "The Second Sex (1949)." Excerpts from *The Second Sex* by Simone De Beauvoir, translated by H. M. Parshley. Copyright © 1952 and renewed 1980 by Alfred A. Knopf, a division of Random House, Inc. Used by permission of Alfred A. Knopf, a division of Random House, Inc.

10. Daniel Guérin. "Shakespeare and Gide in Prison (1959)." Excerpts from *Shakespeare et Gide en Correctionnelle?* Edited by Jean d'Halluin. Copyright © Éditions du Scorpion 1959. All rights reserved. Original translation from the French by David Kammerling Smith.

Chapter 14: The New Europe?

The New Europeans

1. "Measuring the New Europe (1950–1997)." Maps prepared by Bedford/St. Martin's

2. Skrewdriver. "Song Lyrics (1982–1984)." Lyrics from *Power for Profit* and *Before Night Falls* from the album *Hail the New Dawn*. Released by Rock-O-Rama Records, 1984. Lyrics from *White Power* from the album *Boots and Braces/Voice of Britain* by White Noise Recordings.

3. Austrian Freedom Party. "Austria First Petition (1992)." Excerpts from *Discourse and Discrimination: Rhetorics of Racism and anti-Semitism* by Martin Reisigl and Ruth Wodak. Copyright © 2001 Martin Reisigl and Ruth Wodak. Reprinted by permission of Taylor & Francis Books Ltd.

4. "The Affair of the Headscarf (1989)." "An interview with Lionel Jospin" and "Open letter to Lional Jospin." Excerpts from *Le Nouvel Observateur*, Volume 1303, October 26, 1989 and Volume 1304, November 2, 1989. © Le Nouvel Observateur. Reprinted by permission. Translated from the French by David Kammerling Smith.

The European Experiment

5/6. Margaret Thatcher, "Speech at the College of Europe (1988)" and François Mitterand, "Speech to the European Parliament (1995)" from *Documents on European Union* edited and translated by A. G. Harryvan and J. van der Harst. Copyright © 1997 by A. G. Harryvan and J. van der Harst. Margaret Thatcher, Britain in the EC (London: Conservative Political Centre, 1988). F. Mitterand, Debates of the European Parliament, (1994/95, 4-45/45-51). Published by St. Martin's Press, Scholarly and Reference Division. Reprinted by permission of Palgrave UK.

7. The National Front. "The Patriot's Talking-Points (2001)." Excerpt from www.front-national.com/programme/argumentaire/eurofeder. Reprinted by permission of The National Front. Original translation from the French by David Kammerling Smith.

8. Philippe de Schoutheete. "The Case for Europe (2000)." Reprinted by *The Case for Europe: Unity, Diversity, and Democracy in the European Union* by Phillipe de Schoutheete. Copyright © 2000 for the English-language translation by Lynne Rienner Publishers. Reprinted with permission of Lynne Rienner Publishers, Inc.

Maps

1.1: European Voyages to the Americas

Adapted from pp. 334 and 435 in *Civilization Past and Present*, 9th edition, edited by Palmira Brummett et al. Copyright © 2000 by Addison-Wesley Educational Publishers, Inc. Reprinted by permission of Pearson Education, Inc.; p. 516 from *The Making of the West*, 1st edition, edited by Lynn Hunt et al. Copyright © 2001 by Bedford/St. Martin's. Reprinted by permission; p. 69 from *A History of Latin America*, 3rd edition. Copyright © 1988 by Houghton Mifflin Company. Used with permission.

2.1: Reformation Europe, c. 1550

Adapted from pp. 549, 558 in *The Making of the West*, 1st edition, edited by Lynn Hunt et al. Copyright © 2001 by Bedford/St. Martin's. Reprinted by permission; map in *European Jewry in the Age of Mercantilism, 1550–1750*, Second Edition, by Jonathan I. Israel. © Jonathan I. Israel, 1889. Reprinted by permission of Oxford University Press.

3.1: Native Nations and European Settlements in the Great Lake Region

Adapted from p. 8 in *The Jesuit Relations: Natives and Missionaries in Seventeenth-Century North America*, edited by Allan Greer. Copyright © 2000 by Bedford/St. Martin's.

4.1. Russian Conquest of Siberia

Adapted from p. 661 in *The Global Past*, Comprehensive Volume, 1st edition, by Lanny B. Fields et al. Copyright © 1998 by Bedford Books, a division of St. Martin's Press; *Russia's Conquest of Siberia, 1558–1700: A Documentary Record* edited and translated by Basil Dmytryshyn, E. A. P. Crownhart-Vaughn, and Thomas Vaughan. © 1985 Western Imprints, The Press of the Oregon Historical Society. Reprinted with permission.

6.1. The Atlantic Slave Trade

Adapted from p. 119 in *The American Promise: A History of the United States*, 2nd edition, by James Roark. © 2002 by Bedford/St. Martin's; p. 435 in *Civilization Past and Present*, 9th edition, by Palmira Brummett. Copyright © 2000 by Addison-Wesley Educational Publishers, Inc. Reprinted by permission of Pearson Education, Inc.

8.1. Decline of the Ottoman Empire to 1923

Adapted from *The Global Past*, Comprehensive Volume, 1st edition, by Lanny B. Fields et al. Copyright © 1998 by Bedford Books, a division of St. Martin's Press.

9.1. The Opium Trade in China

Adapted from p. 170 in *The Rise of Modern China*, 4th edition by Immanuel C. Y. Hsu. Copyright © 1995 Oxford University Press. Used by permission of Oxford University Press, Inc.

10.1. Political Divisions in Africa, 1914

Adapted from p. 849 in *The Global Past*, Comprehensive Volume, 1st edition, by Lanny B. Fields et al. © 1998 by Bedford Books, a division of St. Martin's Press, Inc.

10.2. Ethnic Groups in Africa

Adapted from *Africa on File* by Mapping Specialists Ltd. Copyright © 1995 by Facts On File, Inc. Reprinted by permission of Facts On File, Inc.

10.3. Environmental Zones in Africa

Adapted from Fig.1.1 in *History of Africa* by Kevin Shillington. Copyright © 1995 St. Martin's Press, Inc. Reprinted by permission of Macmillan Education, Ltd.; A–G from *Historical Atlas of Africa* edited by J. F. Ade Ajayi et al. Copyright © 1985 Longman/Pearsons UK. Reprinted by permission.

13.1. The Decolonization of Africa, 1951–1990

Adapted from p. 1095 in *The Making of the West: Peoples and Cultures*, Volume II: *Since 1560*. By Lynn Hunt et al.

14.1. European Migration Flows, c. 1970

Adapted from p. 24 in *Mass Migration in Europe: The Legacy and the Future* edited by Russell King. Copyright © John Wiley & Sons Limited. Reproduced with permission.